Ecuador, Peru and Bolivia

THE BACKPACKER'S MANUAL

Kathy Jarvis

Spectacled bear

Bradt Publications, UK
The Globe Pequot Press Inc, USA

First published in 2000 by Bradt Publications,
19 High Street, Chalfont St Peter, Bucks SL9 9QE, England
web: bradt-travelguides.com
Published in the USA by The Globe Pequot Press Inc, 246 Goose Lane,
PO Box 480, Guilford, Connecticut 06475-0480

British Library Cataloguing in Publication Data
A catalogue record for this book is available from the British Library
ISBN 1 898323 95 X

Library of Congress Cataloging-in-Publication Data
Jarvis, Kathy.
Ecuador, Peru & Bolivia : the backpacker's manual / Kathy Jarvis.
p. cm.
Includes index.
ISBN 1-898323-95-X
1. Backpacking—Ecuador—Guidebooks. 2. Backpacking—Peru—Guidebooks. 3. Backpacking—Bolivia—Guidebooks I. Title: Ecuador, Peru, and Bolivia. II. Title.

GV199.44.E22 J37 1999 99-048354

Photographs *Front cover* Peruvian child and llama (Hilary Bradt)
Illustrations Oliver Whalley
Maps Alan Whitaker

Typeset from the author's disc by Wakewing
Printed and bound in Italy by LegoPrint SpA, Trento

Author/Acknowledgements

AUTHOR

Kathy Jarvis was introduced to the joys of travel at an early age, being born into a family that thought nothing of working and travelling in the far corners of the world. She's been travelling throughout South America since the early 90s, initially working for various British adventure travel companies leading trekking tours in Chile and Peru. She is now a partner in her own trekking and mountain biking company, Andean Trails, organising tours to Peru, Bolivia and Patagonia. Her time is divided between keeping the office under control in Scotland, leading tours and in a quest for new routes, continuing to explore the Andes.

ACKNOWLEDGEMENTS

I would like to thank the many people who have helped me in one way or another to write this book. Thanks firstly to Hilary Bradt for asking me to write it, and to Tricia Hayne for guiding me through the process. Special thanks to my family in Scotland, especially Margaret and Paul Jarvis who have always generously provided a home to work from, encouragement and good advice. Thanks to all the people who have helped with information for the book, to those people I met along the way whose brains were picked for travelling tips, and to those who contributed directly by writing small sections. I would particularly like to thank Saoirse at the SAEC, Sandra Araujo, Barry Walker, Craig Downer, John Biggar, Lisa Crampin, Marianne van Vlaardingen, Meike Scheidat and Luis Arturo, the tourist boards in Ecuador, Peru and Bolivia, Raúl Lezama and Mark Atkinson at Base Camp, Tullio Sanchez in Lima, Raúl Yépez in Quito, Wily Gordillo in Huaraz, and others too numerous to mention. Finally I would like to thank Barry, Felippe and the Medina Figueroa family who have always welcomed me into their homes in Peru.

Contents

LIST OF MAPS

Introduction

During the five years I had spent working and travelling in South America prior to researching and writing this book it always seemed to me that there was a lack of accessible information about many aspects of the countries I was in. Fortunately, many of these gaps are now being plugged by a recent profusion of both locally produced and international books of one sort or another, and the innovation of the Internet, which has made extensive information readily available worldwide.

Although the major attractions of the central Andean countries are now generally quite well documented, this is the only book published in English to group together the three countries of Ecuador, Peru and Bolivia in an all-encompassing Backpacker's Manual. Each of the three countries included has its own unique attractions but they also have many features in common and hence form a reasonably cohesive group. Geographically, the immense 9,000km-long Andes range is central to each country, supporting a large part of the population and the majority of important cities of Ecuador, Peru and Bolivia. The presence of the Andes influences the climate, resources and conditions, making for a harshness of life and struggle for survival throughout the central Andean countries almost beyond our comprehension. Transportation and communication are the ubiquitous problems caused by the gigantic obstacle of the Andean chain. However, throughout the Andes, people have coexisted with the environment for thousands of years, creating and developing their own unique social, agricultural and technological systems to live in harmony with their surroundings.

This book is written for the first-time backpacker to the central Andean countries, with the aim of providing comprehensive information on Ecuador, Peru and Bolivia in a compact one-volume guidebook. It gives background information on each country, a brief history, geographical and climatic information, and the practical details about getting there, travelling around by public transport, health and safety, food and drink, accommodation, local festivals and suggested highlights to include in a visit. The guide then breaks down each country into geographical area and gives more in-depth information on the principal cities towns and attractions in each of these areas. It doesn't contain endless lists of hotels and restaurants, but an essential few places affordable to backpackers on a budget. For each area the guide points you in the right direction for exploring the sights and discovering something of the fascination and idiosyncrasies of where you are.

The Bradt Story

The first Bradt travel guide was written by Hilary and George Bradt in 1974 on a river barge floating down a tributary of the Amazon in Bolivia. From their base in Boston, Massachusetts they went on to write and publish four other backpacking guides to the Americas and one to Africa.

In the 1980s Hilary continued to develop the Bradt list in England, and also established herself as a travel writer and tour leader. The company's publishing emphasis evolved towards broader-based guides to new destinations – usually the first to be published on those countries – complemented by hiking, rail and wildlife guides.

Since winning *The Sunday Times* Small Publisher of the Year Award in 1997, we have continued to fill the demand for detailed, well-written guides to unusual destinations, while maintaining the company's original ethos: that adventurous travel is more enjoyable if the wishes of the local people are taken into consideration.

Travel guides are by their nature continuously evolving. If you experience anything which you would like to share with us, or if you have any amendments to make to this guide, please write; all your letters are read and passed on to the author. Most importantly, do remember to travel with an open mind and to respect the customs of your hosts – it will add immeasurably to your enjoyment.

Happy travelling!

Hilary Bradt

Hilary Bradt

19 High Street, Chalfont St Peter, Bucks SL9 9QE, England
Tel: 01753 893444 Fax: 01753 892333
Email: info@bradt-travelguides.com
web: www.bradt-travelguides.com

Part One

General Information

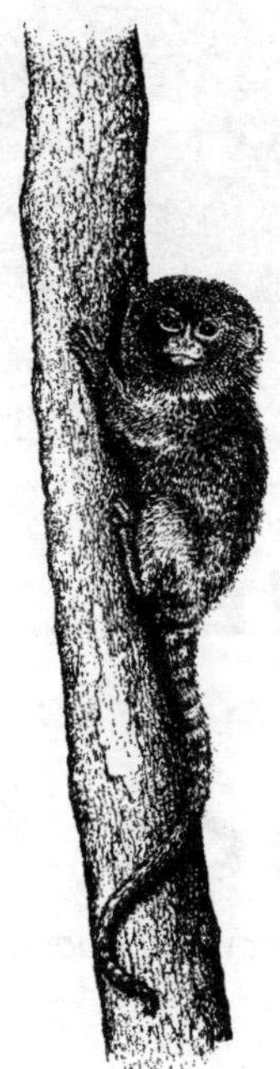

Pygmy marmoset

1 Planning and Preparation

WHEN TO GO

Deciding when to visit the central Andes is often not a matter of choice but more of personal circumstances, such as when you can get the time off and have the money available. There is nothing to stop you travelling through Peru, Bolivia or Ecuador at any time of year, but if you want to get the most out of it, especially if you are interested in trekking, it is worth avoiding the worst of the wet highland weather. If you can't choose when you travel it's not worth worrying about the weather conditions: go prepared for everything. If, however, you are lucky enough to be able to choose the time you travel, you have the luxury of being able to decide where you want to go, and then choose the best time to visit each place, taking weather conditions into account.

The central Andean countries cover a hugely diverse geographic area and consequently experience a great range of climatic conditions. These depend primarily on where you are geographically. Ecuador, Peru and Bolivia all have oscillating wet and dry seasons and not the four seasons known throughout the temperate world, although sometimes the terms summer and winter are confusingly applied to wet and dry respectively.

Ecuador

Although Ecuador lies on the Equator and theoretically has a tropical climate, conditions are influenced by the Andes, by the cold Humboldt current flowing up the coast from the South Pacific, and by the warm equatorial counter-current from the central Pacific. Ecuador is renowned for the unpredictability of its weather. On the coast temperatures average between 25°C and 30°C and vary little throughout the year. The rainy season in northern coastal areas is from January to June, when there are frequent torrential downpours. In the south the rainfall is less and falls between January and April. Inland, in the mountainous areas, the temperature varies with altitude. From 900m to 2,000m the average temperature is 20–26°C. From 2,000m to 3,000m the temperature is cooler, 12–20°C, and above 3,000m 0–12° C, whereas above the 4,500m snowline temperatures are almost always below freezing, though insolation is high. Wet and dry seasons vary according to the mountain area. In Ecuador's western mountains the dry season is late June to early September, and the wettest months are February to May, but then it doesn't rain every day, more like every other day. Low night temperatures and high winds may be a problem in the dry season, particularly in August. In the eastern mountains the climate is influenced by the Amazon lowlands and the rainy season lasts from June to August, the reverse of the western mountains. October to February are the best months for climbing and trekking in this part of the Andes. In Ecuador's Amazon area, known as Oriente, it rains most of the time, with April to July even wetter than the rest of the year.

Peru

The climate in Peru follows a simpler pattern than that of Ecuador. The influence of the cold Humboldt current means that the Peruvian coast receives very little rainfall, but most of the year, from April to December, it sits under a damp, grey sea mist known as *garúa*. This is particularly unpleasant in Lima, where day temperatures average around 20°C (10°C at night), but it's easy to feel chilled because of the 98% humidity. January, February and March can be hot and sunny, and this is the time local people flock to the beach. The water temperature is never high because of the influence of the Humboldt current, which maintains a cool water temperature supporting a very varied marine and bird life along the Peruvian and Ecuadorian coast. Moving inland, the *garúa* soon disappears and temperatures anywhere between the coast and the Andes are very pleasant all year round. As you gain altitude you move into the typical Peruvian mountain climate: the wet season lasts from October to April with January and February the wettest months; the dry season is from May to September. Temperatures do not vary much from wet to dry season, but the diurnal temperature range is large. The average is 20°C in the day and 2°C at night in Cusco, with much more extreme lows at higher altitudes. The Puno area, and islands in Lake Titicaca can be bitterly cold when the sun goes down, particularly in July and August, and it's worth remembering that hostels and restaurants very rarely have any form of heating. In the Amazon lowlands from May to October it is usually hot and humid with occasional afternoon downpours. The average day/night temperatures in Puerto Maldonado are 33°C and 18°C. Much as in the mountains, October to April is the rainy season, which may mean transport into the lowlands is impossible as roads are washed away.

Bolivia

The Bolivian highlands experience a similar climate to the Peruvian highlands, with a marked rainy season from the end of October to April. July and August are the best months for climbing and May to October for trekking. The south of Bolivia is considerably drier than the northern part, and in the Amazon basin rain falls all year round; temperatures and humidity are high. Up to 80% of Bolivia's roads can be out of action in the rainy season.

El Niño

The now well-known phenomenon of El Niño has recently severely affected the weather patterns in Peru, Ecuador and Bolivia, the El Niño of 1997–8 being the biggest, most widespread and longest lasting on record. Early in January 1998 the coming of El Niño was predicted and April saw a rise in sea temperatures in some parts of the Pacific of up to 5°C. In July conditions intensified, and by September there had been many catastrophic consequences worldwide, particularly flash floods throughout the west Andean valleys in Peru and Ecuador. El Niño is caused by a reversal of the normal pattern of trade winds and movement of water masses in the Pacific Ocean. Under normal conditions trade winds blow from east to west across the Pacific taking with them the surface water of the ocean and allowing the cooler waters from deeper down to well up along the South American Pacific coast, thus creating a cool ocean and dry air conditions. The water taken west is heated up 2°–3°C by the sun. The warm air above it picks up moisture from the water, so that when it hits the landmass of Southeast Asia it produces heavy rainfall. El Niño occurs when the warm air and water masses heading west are forced to turn back, reversing the weather patterns, causing floods on the South American coast, and drought on the western side of the Pacific.

PAPERWORK

Citizens of most of Europe, North and South America, Australia and New Zealand visiting Ecuador, Peru and Bolivia require only a valid **passport** with at least six months left to run before the expiry date. However, it is best to check with the relevant consulates or embassies before travelling as political instabilities can affect entry regulations. On arriving in each country you will be given a **tourist card** valid for between 30 and 90 days. Do not lose this tourist card, as doing so could incur a lot of hassle and expense in replacing it, and also it is important that both your passport and tourist card are stamped on entry or exit between countries.

It is possible to extend your time in any of the three countries, but do not let your tourist card expire before you do so. To extend your tourist card in Ecuador you need to go to one of the offices of the Department of Immigration (see page 65). There you can extend your stay by 30 days for a fee of US$12, and this can be done three times. You can't be in Ecuador for more than 90 days in any 12-month period. If you wish to stay longer in Peru or Bolivia you can simply cross any international border and re-enter the country, thereby obtaining a further 90 days. Alternatively you can visit the immigration office in Lima (see page 181) or Cusco (see page 236) and go through a rather complicated procedure, paying a few dollars and gaining a 30-day extension. You can do this three times. If you cross the border from Peru into Bolivia you must stay at least two days before returning to Peru, as Bolivian regulations stipulate this.

It is always a good idea to have a photocopy of your important documents, such as your passport and the tourist card, and to keep a note of the numbers of your travellers' cheques, credit card account numbers, emergency phone numbers, serial numbers and makes of any valuable items you have with you, insurance details, 24-hour emergency phone number and so on. You could also leave a list of these numbers at home in case of emergency. If you plan to spend several months in any Andean country then it is also worth registering at the embassy.

Remember to bring your **yellow fever vaccination certificate** if you plan to travel into the Amazon basin, and if you are considering hiring a vehicle bring an **international driver's licence**.

Embassies and consulates

Ecuador

Flat 3B, 3 Hans Crescent, London SW1X 0LS. Tel: 020 7584 1367
2535 15th St NW, Washington DC 20009. Tel: 202 234 7200

Peru

52 Sloane St, London SW1. Tel: 020 7235 1917
215 Lexington Ave, 21st floor, New York, NY 10016. Tel: 212 481 7410
1700 Massachusetts Ave NW, Washington DC 20036. Tel: 202 833 9860

Bolivia

106 Eaton Square, London, SW1 9AD. Tel: 020 7235 4255
211 East 43 St, Suite 702, New York. Tel: 6870530/4997401

GETTING THERE

By air

You will probably wish to fly into Quito, Lima or La Paz to start your travels, via Europe or the United States. To Lima or Quito you can fly with European airlines Iberia (via Madrid), KLM (via Amsterdam), British Airways via London connecting with Avianca in Bogotá, and Lufthansa (overnight in Frankfurt); through the States you can fly with American Airlines (via Miami), Continental (via Houston or Newark) and United Airlines. Avianca (via Bogotá) and Cubana (via Habana) also fly from Europe. It is considerably more expensive to fly into La Paz: Aerolíneas Argentinas fly to La Paz via Buenos Aires; Varig fly via Brazil; American Airlines also go but are expensive.

It is well worth shopping around the main flight sellers to get the best deal and the sort of ticket you want: standard return, open return, student ticket or open-jaw (arriving at one destination and leaving from another). Iberia currently offer the best prices from Europe. From London expect to pay £450 plus tax in the low season, and considerably more in July and August, or December just before Christmas – approximately £800 plus tax. Specialist operators can arrange internal flight passes for you, though for these you have to decide on your itinerary and dates in advance, as they are not available in the country itself. Aero Sur in Bolivia have a four-sector, 30-day, flight pass costing US$230. Specialist UK flight agents include:

Campus Travel (tel: 020 7730 3402)
Journey Latin America (tel: 020 8747 3108)
Passage to South America (tel: 020 7602 9889)
South American Experience (tel: 020 7976 5511)
STA Travel for students and those under 26 (tel: 0870 6074700)
Trailfinders (tel: 020 7938 3939)

It is not a good idea to get a one-way ticket: flights out of South America are much more expensive if you buy them there and you may have problems should immigration officials decide to check your ticket.

By road

There are regular bus connections with Argentina, Chile, and Colombia for those backpackers coming overland from other parts of South America.

Tour operators

There are dozens of companies that you can contact for flight only arrangements to Peru, Bolivia and Ecuador, or for fully organised trips.

UK

Andean Trails 47 Eskbank Rd, Dalkeith, Midlothian, Scotland EH22 3BH; tel: 0131 663 4063; fax: 0131 663 8676; email: andeantrails@belmont.abel.co.uk Trekking and mountain-biking tours in the Andes.

Andes 93 Queen St, Castle Douglas, Dumfries and Galloway, Scotland DG7 1EH; tel/fax: 01556 503929; email: john@andes.com Climbing in the Andes.

Bukima Expeditions 15 Bedford Rd, Great Barford, Beds MK44 3JD; tel: 01234 871329; fax: 01234 871886; email: bukima@compuserve.com

Caledonia Language Courses The Clockhouse, Bonnington Mill, 72 Newhaven Rd, Edinburgh EH3 6QG; tel: 0131 621 7721; fax: 0131 621 7723; email: info@caledonialanguages.co.uk Language courses.

Galápagos Adventure Tours 37–39 Great Guildford St, London SE1 0ES; tel: 020 7261 9890; email: pinzon@compuserve.com

Gane & Marshall 98 Crescent Rd, New Barnet, Herts EN4 9RJ, UK; tel: 020 8441 9592; fax: 020 8441 7376; email: holidays@ganeandmarshall.co.uk

High Places Globe Works, Penistone Rd, Sheffield S6 3AE; tel: 0114 275 7500; fax: 0114 275 3870; email: highpl@globalnet.co.uk

Journey Latin America 12 Heathfield Terrace, Chiswick, London W4 4JE; tel: 020 8747 3108; fax: 020 8742 1312; email: tours@journeylatinamerica.co.uk
Magic of Bolivia 182 Westbourne Grove, London W11 2RH; tel: 020 7221 7310; fax 020 7727 8746; web: www.bolivia.co.uk
Oasis Overland 5 Nicholson Cottages, Hinton St Mary, Dorset DT10 1NF; tel: 01258 471155; fax: 01258 471166; email: overland@travellersway.demon.co.uk
Overland Latin America 13 Dormer Place, Leamington Spa, Warks. CV32 5AA; tel: 01926 311332; fax: 01926 435567; email: worldlspa@aol.com
Sherpa Expeditions 131a Heston Rd, Middlesex TW5 ORD; tel: 020 8577 2717; fax: 020 8572 9788; email: sherpa.sales@dial.pipex.com
South American Experience 47 Causton St, Pimlico, London SW1P 4AT; tel: 020 7976 5511; fax: 020 7976 6908.
Tribes The Business Centre, Earl Soham, Bristol BS8 1JT; tel: 01728 685971; email: wl@tribes.couk; web: www.tribes.co.uk
Wildlife Worldwide 170 Selsdon Rd, South Croydon, Surrey CR2 6PJ; tel: 020 8667158; fax: 020 8667 1960; email: sales@wildlife-ww.co.uk
World Expeditions Ltd 4 Northfields Prospect, Putney Bridge Rd, London SW18 1PE; tel: 020 8870 2600; fax: 020 8870 2615; email: enquiries@worldexpeditions.co.uk

Overland companies

Dragoman Camp Green Farm, Kenton Rd, Debenham, Suffolk IP14 6LA; tel: 01728 861133; web: www.dragoman.co.uk
Encounter Overland Tel: 020 7370 6845; web: www.encounter-overland.com
Kumuka 40 Earls Court Rd, London W8 6EJ; tel: 020 7937 8855; email: sales@kumuka.co.uk; web: www.kumuka.co
Overland Latin America 13 Dormer Place, Leamington Spa, Warks CV32 5AA; tel: 01926 332222; email: worldspa@aol.com

USA

AmeriSpan PO Box 40007, Philadelphia, PA 19106–0007, USA; tel: 800 8796640; email: info@amerispan.com Language courses.
eXito 5699 Miles Av, Oakland, CA 94618; tel: 800 6554053; fax: 510 6554566; email: exito@wonderlink.com
Wildland Adventures 3516 NE 155 St, Seattle, WA98155, USA; tel: 206 3650686; fax: 206 3636615; email: sam@wildland.com

WHAT TO TAKE

In choosing what to take with you, remember that almost all necessities are available in South American cities, and most clothes are cheaper than in Europe. It is more comfortable to travel light and restock with anything you need as you go along.

Clothes

The key is to pack for a variety of conditions while trying to keep the weight to a minimum. Give some thought to your equipment selection, without splashing out on expensive, state-of-the-art items. Most things that wear out can easily be replaced in South America. It's better to take more money and less luggage.

If you are planning on spending time above 3,000m in the Andes, in a single day you may experience a wide range of temperatures, with cold, sharp nights and early mornings followed by springlike days with sometimes hot afternoons and very strong sun and chilly evenings. As the region is well within the tropics, day and night are about equal in length and the sun rises and sets very quickly, so

MAKING THE BEST OF YOUR TRAVEL PHOTOGRAPHS

Subject, composition and lighting

If it doesn't look good through the viewfinder, it will never look good as a picture. Don't take photographs for the sake of taking them; film is far too expensive. Be patient and wait until the image looks right.

People

There's nothing like a wonderful face to stimulate interest. Travelling to remote corners of the world provides the opportunity for exotic photographs of colourful people and intriguing lifestyles which capture the very essence of a culture. A superb photograph should be capable of saying more than a thousand words.

Photographing people is never easy and more often than not it requires a fair share of luck plus sharp instinct, a conditioned photographic eye and the ability to handle light both aesthetically and technically.

- If you want to take a portrait shot, always ask first. Often the offer to send a copy of the photograph to the subject will break the ice – but do remember to send it!
- Focus on the eyes of your subject.
- The best portraits are obtained in early morning and late evening light. In harsh light, photograph without flash in the shadows.
- Respect people's wishes and customs. Remember that, in some countries, infringement can lead to serious trouble.
- Never photograph military subjects unless you have definite permission.
- Be prepared for the unexpected.

Wildlife

There is no mystique to good wildlife photography. The secret is getting into the right place at the right time and then knowing what to do when you are there. Look for striking poses, aspects of behaviour and distinctive features. Try to illustrate the species within the context of its environment. Alternatively, focus in close on a characteristic which can be emphasised.

- The eyes are all-important. Make sure they are sharp and try to ensure they contain a highlight.
- Get the surroundings right – there is nothing worse than a distracting twig or highlighted leaf lurking in the background.
- A powerful flashgun can transform a dreary picture by lifting the subject out of its surroundings and putting the all-important highlights into the eyes. Artificial light is no substitute for natural light, so use judiciously.
- Getting close to the subject correspondingly reduces the depth of field; for distances of less than a metre, apertures between f16 and f32 are necessary. This means using flash to provide enough light – build your own bracket and use one or two small flashguns to illuminate the subject from the side.

Landscapes

Landscapes are forever changing; good landscape photography is all about light and mood. Generally the first and last two hours of daylight are best, or when peculiar climatic conditions add drama or emphasise distinctive features.

- Never place the horizon in the centre – in your mind's eye divide the frame into thirds and exaggerate either the land or the sky.

Cameras

Keep things simple: light, reliable and simple cameras will reduce hassle. High humidity in tropical places can play havoc with electronics.

- For keen photographers, a single-lens reflex (SLR) camera should be at the heart of your outfit. Look for a model with the option of a range of different lenses and other accessories.
- Totally mechanical cameras which do not rely on batteries work even under extreme conditions. Combined with an exposure meter which doesn't require batteries, you have the perfect match. One of the best and most indestructible cameras available is the FM2 Nikon.

- Compact cameras are generally excellent, but because of restricted focal ranges they have severe limitations for wildlife.
- Automatic cameras are often noisy when winding on, and loading film.
- Flashy camera bags can draw unwelcome attention to your kit.

Lenses

The lens is the most important part of the camera, with the greatest influence on the final result. Choose the best you can afford – the type will be dictated by the subject and type of photograph you wish to take.

For people

- The lens should ideally should have a focal length of 90 or 105mm.
- If you are not intimidated by getting in close, buy one with a macro facility which will allow close focusing. For candid photographs, a 70–210 zoom lens is ideal.
- A fast lens (with a maximum aperture of around f2.8) will allow faster shutter speeds which will mean sharper photographs. Distracting backgrounds will be thrown out of focus, improving the images' aesthetic appeal.

For wildlife

- Choose a lens of at least 300mm for a reasonable image size.
- For birds, lenses of 400mm or 500mm may be needed. They should be held on a tripod, or a beanbag if shooting from a vehicle.
- Macro lenses of 55mm and 105mm cover most subjects, creating images up to half life size. To enlarge further, extension tubes are required.
- In low light, lenses with very fast apertures help.

For landscapes

- Wide-angle lenses (35mm or less) are ideal for tight habitat shots (eg: forests) and are an excellent alternative for close ups, as you can shoot the subject within the context of its environment.
- For other landscapes, use a medium telephoto lens (100–300mm) to pick out interesting aspects of a vista and compress the perspective.

Film

Two types of film are available: prints (negatives) and transparencies (colour reversal). Prints are instantly accessible, ideal for showing to friends and putting into albums. However, if you want to share your experiences with a wider audience, through lectures or in publication, then the extra quality offered by transparency film is necessary.

Film speed (ISO number) indicates the sensitivity of the film to light. The lower the number, the less sensitive the film, but the better quality the final image. For general print film and if you are using transparencies just for lectures, ISO 100 or 200 are ideal. However, if you want to get your work published, the superior quality of ISO 25 to 100 film is best.

- Film bought in developing countries may be outdated or badly stored.
- Try to keep your film cool. Never leave it in direct sunlight.
- Do not allow fast film (ISO 800 or more) to pass through X-ray machines.
- Under weak light conditions use a faster film (ISO 200 or 400).
- For accurate people shots use Kodachrome 64 for its warmth, mellowness and gentle gradation of contrast. Reliable skin tones can also be recorded with Fuji Astia 100.
- To jazz up your portraits, use Fuji Velvia (50 ISO) or Provia (100 ISO).
- If cost is your priority, use process-paid Fuji films such as Sensia 11.
- For black-and-white people shots take Kodax T Max or Fuji Neopan.
- For natural subjects, where greens are a feature, use Fujicolour Reala (prints) and Fujichrome Velvia and Provia (transparencies).

Nick Garbutt is a professional photographer, writer, artist and expedition leader, specialising in natural history. He is co-author of 'Madagascar Wildlife' (Bradt Publications), and a winner in the BBC Wildlife Photographer of the Year Competition. John R Jones is a professional travel photographer specialising in minority people, and author of the Bradt guides to 'Vietnam' and 'Laos and Cambodia'.

temperatures can drop rapidly. At altitude, temperatures vary sharply between sun and shade, with rises and drops in altitude depending on whether you're sheltered or on an exposed, windy ridge. Bear in mind that mountain weather is notoriously changeable and often very localised, so when planning for the highlands, layering is the best system. Several layers of thin clothing are more practical and versatile than one or two heavy layers. It is worth remembering that it can rain at any time of year, not only in the rainy season. Thermal underwear is highly recommended, being light and warm, and it also makes good nightwear on cold nights. Lightweight trekking trousers are good for wearing anywhere as they are easy to wash, quick-drying and have plenty of pockets. Jeans, although very popular, are not suitable for travelling as they weigh a lot and do not dry quickly. Waterproof jackets and trousers are essential if you are thinking of doing any trekking, whatever time of year. Army trousers, or any other combat-type gear, are not a good idea because of the connotations of being associated with the military. Shorts are not always appropriate in towns and villages, and should be worn sparingly in early stages at altitude where the sun can burn skin in minutes. Long-sleeved, collared shirts are very handy, giving good protection against sun and insects, and they can be bought locally very cheaply, as can all woollens and T-shirts. A fleece jacket is very useful and lightweight for trekking as is a waterproof poncho that covers your backpack. It's probably best to bring trainers for city wear and travelling, and rubber sandals are useful. Bring enough socks and underwear for several days, though washing things out is not a problem and drying times are fast. It's also pretty easy to get washing done for a small fee in any town or city. A sunhat, sun-protection cream and glasses are essential, and don't forget a towel and swimming costume.

Carrying luggage and camping equipment

For carrying your belongings it is best to use a backpack, which should be comfortable to carry, sturdy and spacious. You may decide to go trekking and in any case you might have to carry your bag long distances from hotels to bus stations. It is also useful to have a daypack for carrying essential items when you go out for the day, or if you choose to join an organised trek. Also essential if you are going to do any walking are boots, which should be tough, have good ankle support and, ideally, be waterproof. If you might be camping a good warm sleeping bag will be necessary. Down bags are lighter and longer-lasting but more expensive than synthetic ones, which are bulkier and heavier yet equally warm. A sheet sleeping bag is useful for hostels and also insulates further if you are camping at high altitudes. A sleeping mat is also necessary if you are going to be camping, both for insulation and comfort. For cooking you will need a stove. White gas (*benzina*) can be found in a few camping shops in Peru, Bolivia and Ecuador. Kerosene is much more widely available and is for sale at petrol stations even in small towns, so it is probably best to take a multi-fuel stove like the MSR. This will burn petrol, diesel, *aguardiente*, kerosene, and white gas and also works well at altitude. Methylated spirits is available from some chemists and ironmongers and is known as *alcohol industrial*.

Reasonable camping gear can be rented or bought at a good price in the cities of Quito (see page 68), Huaraz (page 209), Cusco (page 236) and La Paz (page 312), so it's not worth taking all the camping equipment if you intend only to trek the Inca Trail in Peru.

Photographic equipment

If you are a keen photographer you will probably already know what photographic equipment you want to take with you. Good equipment is not cheap to buy in

Ecuador, Peru or Bolivia, so select with care and take everything you may need. It is worth the extra weight of a telephoto lens, especially for the Galápagos and the jungle, for wildlife photography, and for discreet shots of people, from afar, without imposing upon them. People are not happy to be photographed without permission being asked, and very often a small payment made. To my mind this is a fair exchange. If you can carry a cheap Polaroid camera and give people a photo of themselves they will generally be very happy, and allow you to take more shots. Print film is widely available locally, but it is worth taking slide film with you; although it is available in larger cities, it is expensive and may not be the speed you want, nor the make. For the mountains, film speeds of 64, 100 and 200 ISO are most suitable and a UV filter is essential to reduce haziness. For the jungle a film speed of 400 ISO is best to cope with poor light. Processing is expensive and generally poor quality, so it's better to keep your films in a cool place and take them home.

Other useful items

Other miscellaneous things worth bringing are:

- money belt to wear under clothes
- strong water bottle for trekking
- suncream, sunglasses and lipsalve
- travel alarm clock
- sewing kit
- ziploc plastic bags
- universal sink plug
- laundry soap, a washing line and a couple of pegs
- waterproofing for boots
- compass
- earplugs
- insect repellent
- loo paper
- tampons (women should note that sanitary towels are widely available, but not tampons)
- binoculars (very handy for animal viewing, especially in the jungle, and a wide variety of sizes and weights are available, so you can choose whatever suits you)
- phrasebook
- pen, address book, notebook
- a few postcards and photos of your family and home, great for showing to the local people you meet
- padlock, or combination lock for locking hotel rooms
- good first aid kit (see page 28)

MONEY

Local currency

Ecuador, Peru and Bolivia all have their own local currencies, the sucre, nuevo sol and boliviano respectively. In all three countries most things are sold in local currency, but you are likely to see some prices in cities quoted in US dollars, especially hotel prices, and expensive items such as gold. Check you know what currency is being quoted, especially in Peru where the symbols for the dollar and sol are quite similar. In major cities the dollar and local currency are virtually interchangeable, but elsewhere only local currency can be used. Exchange rates in 1999 were around 5 bolivianos to the dollar, 3.4 nuevo soles to the dollar, and between 7,000 and 10,000 sucres to the dollar. The US dollar is the most widely accepted foreign currency for exchanging, whether as travellers' cheques or cash.

Organising your finances

Travellers' cheques are the safest way to carry money around. Make sure you have a separate written record of the numbers of the cheques, and make a note of the ones you exchange as you go along. This will help in replacing them should they be lost or stolen. American Express are probably the most convenient to take. They are commission-free to exchange if you do so at one of their own offices, and should you need to replace them, a police report, a list of the numbers, a receipt of purchase and your passport should have you efficiently resupplied in 48 hours. It is best to ask for your cheques in a variety of denominations: US$50 and US$100 are most suitable. I recommend that you also take some cash in US dollars, up to the maximum amount covered by your travel insurance. Only undamaged, unwritten on, good-quality bank notes are acceptable; notes of US$10 and US$50 are probably the best as there have been a lot of forgeries of larger notes, and they can be difficult to exchange. It is not unknown for banks to give forged notes, so always check them carefully. Other currencies are much more difficult to exchange. You can exchange travellers' cheques and cash in official *casas de cambio* (money changing offices) and in Peru and Bolivia there are official *cambistas* (money changers) on street corners in the cities who will change cash for you. Always shop around a bit to get the daily rate before changing anything. In Peru especially there is always a problem with small change – nobody ever seems to have any – so it's a good idea to try to keep hold of small notes, and plenty of coins. Otherwise you may have to wait for up to half an hour while someone runs off to find you change.

You can have money wired to you fairly easily: choose a bank that is willing to cooperate, inform the person paying it in at the other end, wait 72 hours, and pick it up.

Carrying your money

Keep all your money and cheques wrapped in plastic so they are water- and sweat-proof, in a money belt worn under clothing, not in a bumbag, which can easily be pickpocketed or cut off your waist. It's a good idea to sew a couple of secret pockets into your clothes so that you can distribute your money around your body and not carry it all in one place. Where possible leave your valuables in a hotel safe, against a receipt, rather than carry them around with you. You do legally have to carry identification on you at all times, so keep your passport with you.

Credit and bank cards

Major credit cards such as Visa and Mastercard can be used in large, touristy hotels and restaurants in the cities, and for getting cash advances in the bank. If you have an American Express card you can use it to buy Amex travellers' cheques in one of their offices. Bank cards can be used to get money from automatic cash dispensers, which are in all large cities. Cirrus and Plus systems are widely used.

Costs and budgeting

Generally speaking travel in the central Andes is still very cheap, though less so than in recent years. Costs obviously vary enormously, depending on how much you are willing to rough it in hotels and hostels, how you decide to travel, what extra tours or treks you sign up for, how much and where you eat, and how many *pisco* sours or beers you drink. Accommodation, food, drink and transport will form your basic expenses on a daily basis, and Ecuador, Peru and Bolivia can be very cheap on this score. Peru is a little less cheap than neighbouring Ecuador and Bolivia, Ecuador being the cheapest. In all three countries there can be quite a big difference between prices in rural and urban areas. In the cities of Quito, Lima, Cusco and La Paz the absolute minimum you are likely to need is US$12 to US$15 a day, including around US$6 for a bed. Out in rural areas expect to reduce this by a third. However, your overall enjoyment will be considerably more if you can afford at least the luxury of a private bathroom every now and then, a good night out, some decent coffee, and the odd flight instead of a killer bus journey.

Organised activities through a local travel agent tend to be relatively expensive. Usual prices are: whitewater rafting US$30 per day; 30 minute overflights of the Nazca Lines US$30; expeditions into the jungle US$30 per day minimum depending on location and numbers, or across the salt plains US$25 per day, and along the Inca Trail from US$60. Other organised treks or mountain ascents range from US$30 to US$50 per day.

National park entry fees are now at least US$10 in Ecuador; many are US$20 and the Galápagos is $100. In Peru also expect to pay entrance fees of between US$10 and US$20 at national parks. Archaeological sites have an entry fee which varies from as little as US$1 to the US$20 it costs to see Machu Picchu. In Bolivia there are very few national parks or reserves that have tourist infrastructure, and there are no entry fees.

CULTURAL CONSIDERATIONS

Travelling through Peru, Bolivia and Ecuador you will come across backpackers who never leave the tourist trail, talk to few local people and learn very little about the local culture. It's perfectly possible to travel that way if you want to, but you'll undoubtedly get a lot more from your trip by making the effort to get away from all the other tourists and finding new places off the beaten track for yourself. The people are polite and, though not always initially friendly, they will be happy to talk to you if you speak Spanish and make an attempt to communicate. You'll learn a lot more through talking to the local people than you ever can from a book or the archetypal tourist experiences.

Local people

Whichever country you are travelling through it is important that you are conscious of the people whose country you are in and are sensitive to their culture and way of life. Learn enough Spanish to be able to talk to the people as you travel through their countries, to gain an understanding of them and their beliefs. This will enrich your trip and give the local people a greater understanding of your life too. It puts things in perspective if you can talk about the problems of your home country and the relative costs of things, and dispels the myth that life is so much better for us.

Dress

Do wear appropriate clothing, respecting the culture of the country you are travelling in. Don't wear tight revealing clothes in the mountains; save it for the big lowland cities and the coastal resorts where revealing clothing is more acceptable.

Money

Think about where the money you spend is going. Try to spread out your money wherever you are, so that as many people as possible benefit from tourist income. Buy local produce where possible and don't always eat at the same restaurants as everyone else. When you book a tour check to see who will benefit, who is running the tour and what impact it is going to have on the environment and local people. Check to see that local communities benefit, and are not being exploited.

Tribal visits

Visiting indigenous tribes is becoming an increasingly popular part of a tour into the Amazon, particularly in Ecuador. Whether this is hastening the destruction of traditional lifestyles and cultures, or is constructive because change is inevitable and tourist money provides well needed cash and employment, is a very controversial issue. Whatever you believe, respect the wishes of the people you are visiting; you are their guests. If you are going to tribal areas, check that your guide has a permit to be there and your presence is wanted by the local people. Don't assume you can walk anywhere you choose and take pictures of anything you feel like. Remember that the land you are walking on belongs to someone and you may not be welcome there. Always ask before taking any photographs of people. Most people in the Andes do not like to have their photo taken. If they offer to let you take their photo in exchange for money, respect their wishes.

Begging

Don't encourage begging by children. It only undermines the economy and allows the kids to think gringos are good for free handouts. Many of the children don't have access to dentists, who are too distant or too expensive, so it's best to ignore their pleas for sweets. I have seen children screaming with toothache on the islands on Lake Titicaca, possibly caused by years of too many tourist sweets. If you want to give something, give things to schools, and spend time talking to the children, drawing or singing or showing them some tricks. This will be much more beneficial for them.

ITINERARY AND ROUTE PLANNING

The route you take will obviously be determined by what you want to see and do and how much time and money you have. To do justice to each country I would recommend a minimum of a month in each, and more if possible in Peru and Bolivia if you want to get off the beaten track and particularly into the remoter areas.

The most popular route usually sees backpackers starting off in Bolivia, arriving at La Paz and going south to visit the southern Altiplano with the salt lakes and volcanoes, then heading for Potosí and a trip down the mines. From there most people go to Sucre and perhaps visit the market at Tarabuco, then head for La Paz. La Paz deserves a few days of your time. From there some go to Coroico to relax in the subtropical Yungas, and on to Rurrenabaque for jungle tours, returning to La Paz to travel overland to Peru through Copacabana, stopping there on the shores of Lake Titicaca to visit the Isla del Sol.

From Bolivia the usual route is to Puno on the Peruvian shore of Lake Titicaca, perhaps a visit to the floating Uros islands and the islands of Taquile and Amantani and then across the altiplano by train to Cusco. Those with enough time go to Arequipa and Nazca to see this beautiful colonial city, the nearby deep and dramatic Colca Canyon and then the enigmatic Nazca Lines. Just north from Nazca, and a few hours south of Lima, you can visit the Paracas Nature Reserve at Pisco, where sealions and flocks of seabirds, flamingoes and the Paracas textiles are the attraction. From Cusco it's hard to resist the trek along the Inca Trail though some choose to take the train to Machu Picchu, before flying direct to Lima or north overland to Ayacucho. People then tend to visit Huancayo in the central highlands or Huaraz in the Cordillera Blanca or head right through northern Peru direct to Ecuador. Some fly to the jungle town of Iquitos for jungle tours based there, or go to Manú or Tambopata from Puerto Maldonado, a short flight from Cusco.

The highlights most people try to get to see in Ecuador are Vilcabamba in the south, the colonial city of Cuenca, the train ride at Riobamba, Baños with its thermal baths, Cotopaxi National Park and then the great highland city of Quito. From Quito everybody visits Otavalo market and then some go east to the jungle, while others head for the coast. Those that can afford it also make that once in a lifetime trip to the Galápagos Islands.

Many people do a similar itinerary in reverse, starting in Ecuador or Peru, but generally visiting the same places. You will encounter a fair number of backpackers following this sort of route, and they tend to congregate in the same hostels and restaurants. However, there are numerous possibilities for varying the route and getting off the beaten track. There are some lovely places that few people get to, so given a bit of time and flexibility you can find yourself well away from other tourists.

Some highlights

The following list of highlights doesn't cover everything there is to see in Peru, Bolivia and Ecuador by a long way. However, it includes many places that are readily accessible to backpackers on a budget, and that are well worth visiting. It also includes some more remote and less accessible places that may interest anyone especially interested in climbing or wildlife. The list of highlights can be used as a basic guide when planning an itinerary. Remember that travelling in South America can be arduous, that the distances particularly in Peru and Bolivia are enormous and the roads are not too good. Avoid the rainy season if possible and try not to spend too many hours in succession sitting on buses. Internal flights are relatively cheap, and the trains, although slow, make a nice change.

Ecuador

Baños Small, lively town, centre for rafting, climbing, trekking, hot springs.
Coca Starting point for many tours into Ecuador's Amazon basin.
Cotopaxi National Park One of the highest active volcanoes in the world.
Cuenca Beautiful colonial city.
Galápagos Islands The best wildlife viewing in the world.
Ingapirca Inca site, the most important in Ecuador.
Misahuallí Gateway to the jungle of the Oriente.
Machalilla National Park Coastal park with lovely beaches and tropical dry forest, and abundant seabird life. Whale watching too.
Otavalo Home to the market of Otavalo and textile and weaving centre of Ecuador.
Quito Lively, colonial city, language schools, museums, and culture. Surrounded by volcanoes.
Riobamba Starting point for the rooftop train ride down the Devil Nose.
Vilcabamba Subtropical lush valley, gateway to Podocarpus National Park.

Peru

Arequipa Beautiful colonial city at the foot of volcanoes, and gateway to the Colca Canyon.
Ayacucho Highland city, of architectural interest for its churches.
Cajamarca Quiet, graceful northern colonial city where Atahualpa met his downfall. Beautiful countryside, good for walking, hot springs, ancient sites.
Chachapoyas A remote, beautiful area, featuring the Kuélap ruins.
Chavín de Huántar Remarkable archaeological site of the Chavín culture.
Chiclayo Home to the Temple of Sipán.
Colca Canyon Reputedly one of the world's deepest canyons, good for Andean condor viewing.

Cordillera Blanca Superb, accessible area for trekking and mountaineering amongst Peru's highest peaks.
Cusco Lively, fascinating city, with museums, Inca sites, live music, cafés, trekking and rafting centre.
Huancayo In the Mantaro Valley, a traditional craft centre, renowned for weaving, silver and carved gourds.
Inca Trail World-famous fabulous trek to Machu Picchu.
Lake Titicaca Home to many Aymara and Quechua tribes, and the Uros, dramatic *puna* landscapes and endless skies.
Machu Picchu World-renowned Lost City of the Incas, not to be missed.
Manu Biosphere Reserve Protected rainforest park, a must for wildlife lovers. Accessible from Cusco on organised tours only.
Nazca Lines Mysterious giant etchings in the desert, worth flying over for the best view.
Paracas Nature Reserve Coastal wildlife sanctuary, good for seabirds and sealions.
Sacred Valley Urubamba river valley, amazing Inca ruins at Pisac, Ollantaytambo and more.
Tambopata National Reserve Rainforest area accessible by boat from Puerto Maldonado, great for wildlife.
Taquile Island Magical island on Lake Titicaca, for traditional weavings, peace and tranquillity.
Trujillo Lively cosmopolitan city, close to the ancient Chimu city of Chan Chan, and the Huacas del Sol and La Luna, large adobe temples. Not to be missed.

Bolivia

Amboró National Park One of the world's last untouched wilderness areas.
Cochabamba Beautiful colonial city, with good climate, market and museums.
Cordillera Apolobamba Very remote mountain range north of the Cordillera Real, for climbing and treks.
Cordillera Real Spectacular mountain range that runs along the eastern shores of Lake Titicaca and provides trekking and climbing opportunities.
Coroico and the Yungas Fruit- and coca-growing warm subtropical valleys.
Island of the Sun Culturally interesting, beautifully located sacred island.
La Paz Dramatically located city, with plenty to see and do. Centre for treks and tours into outlying areas.
Noell Kempff Mercado National Park Remote and fabulous park with a diverse range of plant and animal life. Very expensive to visit.
Oruro The best place to be for carnival in February.
Pantanal A haven for wildlife lovers.
Potosí Majestic, colonial city, centre of the silver mining industry. Mine visits.
Reserva Eduardo Avaroa, Laguna Colorada and Laguna Verde Weirdly dramatic altiplano scenery, plentiful birdlife.
Rurrenabaque Remote and beautiful gateway to the Amazon. Great wildlife viewing opportunities.
Sajama National Park Climbing centre for Bolivia's highest peak, Sajama, at 6,530m.
Salar de Uyuni Unmissable, the highest and largest salt lake in the world.
Santa Cruz A booming modern city, with access to Amboró, the mission towns and Noel Kempff Mercado National Park.
Sorata Small, attractive subtropical town, a great base for relaxing and trekking.
Sucre Official capital city with interesting colonial architecture, and weaving centre.
Tarija Centre of Bolivia's wine and *singani* production.
Tiahuanaco Extensive and impressive pre-Inca archaeological site.

On the Road

GETTING AROUND

Public transport is plentiful in all but the most remote parts of Ecuador, Peru and Bolivia. However, if you are travelling overland I warn you to be prepared, for journeys can be interminably long, roads in abominable condition, and vehicles old, disintegrating, cramped and overcrowded. Having said that, if you take a relaxed approach, and a few essential supplies, the travelling itself can be the most interesting and dramatic part of your trip.

By air

Internal flights

Internal flights in Ecuador, Peru and Bolivia are frequent and relatively cheap, currently US$40 to US$80 per flight (except for the Galápagos, which are more like $380), and it's worth splashing out to save time every now and again. Air passes are available for Peru and Bolivia, but you can only purchase them outside South America, in conjunction with international flight tickets. Aero Sur in Bolivia do a 30 day pass costing US$230 for four flights. Prices change considerably from season to season, so check before you go. Always reconfirm any flight several times and make sure your reconfirmation is entered on a computer, or you could be bumped off a flight. See country chapters for further details.

By road

Very few Ecuadorians, Peruvians, or Bolivians can afford to own vehicles yet they travel a great deal, to markets, to visit relatives, visit doctors and so on, so an extensive public transport network has developed over the years to suit their needs. This means you can get just about anywhere you could want to go on public transport, except possibly into remote jungle areas or within national parks, where no people live. Road quality and bus services vary hugely throughout the central Andean countries, and depend very much on geographical and climatic factors. In the dry season there will be little problem in getting to wherever you may want to go, although it may not be quick or comfortable. In the rainy season many roads are closed for up to several months, as they periodically get washed away. The roads are without doubt better on the coast, where they are at least surfaced. Express coaches operate on the Pan American highway, which runs the length of South America, and here you may even have a choice about the type of service you take (direct or indirect), the quality and the price you pay. From La Paz, in particular, you can find special buses for tourists operating to certain locations, but generally speaking you will find the only way to travel is on the ordinary public bus, or truck.

Buses

International bus services throughout the Andean countries, and with connections to Chile and Argentina, are run by companies like Ormeño, Cruz del Sur, and

Caracol. The prices are reasonable and the buses are usually of a high standard. Check you know what is included (toilets, snacks, videos, air conditioning, meals) and always book in advance if you can. There is often a choice of express or not and prices vary accordingly. For international and local bus journeys you will have to go to a specific terminal. In Ecuador most towns have a *terminal terrestre*, a bus station, from which most buses leave. In Peru, Arequipa and Cusco have a *terminal terrestre*, but in most other towns buses leave from different parts of town, depending on the company and destination. In Bolivia, La Paz has a central bus station, but some buses leave from other places. See details in relevant chapters.

Most companies that do have their own terminals often seem to be based in seedy, dangerous parts of town, so it is wise to take a taxi both to get there and to get away. Also, bus stations are notorious for thieves, bag slashers and pickpockets, so always keep hold of your belongings, and stay alert. Your main piece of luggage will travel either in luggage compartments under the vehicle or on the roof, sometimes under tarpaulin, sometimes not. You should always try to make sure you are given some sort of ticket in exchange for your bag, although this may be impossible other than on long distance routes with the main carriers. You can take your luggage on board with you if it is small enough to go on your lap; then if you sleep, make sure it is strapped to you, and not stealable. I have never had any problems with luggage being stolen on buses, but it always pays to be cautious and make friends with the driver and his assistant. It is also worthwhile protecting your bag from rain and dirt by putting it inside a sack, available cheaply in local markets. Generally speaking the long distance buses stop every few hours at a roadside restaurant, from ten minutes to half an hour. Ask the driver personally how long the stop is and keep an eye on him, so you don't get left behind. I have seen buses pull away with empty seats and abandoned passengers left behind. These roadside restaurants are not necessarily hygienic or clean, so it may be that you will want to bring your own food and water. Whenever the bus passes through a town or village there will be local people selling food and drinks, what these are depending on the area: there may be fruit, *tamales*, a sort of maize pastie, biscuits, bread, ice-cream, or sweetcorn (*choclo*).

Be prepared for extreme temperatures on the buses, both freezing cold as you go over high mountain passes without central heating, and steaming heat as you plunge into tropical lowlands, without air conditioning.

Trucks

In more remote areas, usually because of poor road conditions, trucks are used instead of buses. They vary in size, but are invariably uncomfortable. They usually charge about the same as buses, though there are no seats and you are either exposed to the elements, or tucked under a large tarpaulin along with whatever cargo happens to be in the truck.

Hitchhiking

Hitchhiking is probably a waste of time as nobody is likely to give you a lift without expecting to be paid the going rate. Most vehicles going anywhere with any spare space are likely to be picking up paying customers along the way anyway to help with petrol costs. Whenever you stop a vehicle by the roadside always check you know the cost of the journey before getting in; it's best to ask the other people travelling how much they are paying and then agree with the driver.

Car hire

The major cities have car and jeep hire offices. Check with the tourist office in each place for details of recommended agencies.

By rail

Ecuador, Peru and Bolivia all have some train services.

Ecuador used to have a wide network of trains used mostly for cargo, but this has been considerably reduced since severe damage by the El Niño of the early 1980s. The El Niño of the late 1990s further damaged train lines, so the service is reduced to a bare minimum. Justifiably the most well known, and not to be missed, is the spectacular train ride from Alausi to Guayaquil, which forms part of the Quito to Riobamba, Alausi and Duran line. There is also a weekend tourist service from Quito to Cotopaxi and Riobamba. In the north there is an *autoferro*, a sort of bus cum train, from Ibarra to Lorenzo. Its service is severely unreliable because of landslides. In 1999 it wasn't running at all.

In **Peru** the Southern Railway from Arequipa to Puno, connecting with the line from Puno to Cusco, operates several times a week all year round. All train journeys are incredibly slow, trains reaching little more than 30km per hour. From Cusco the train line runs down the Sacred Valley of the Urubamba River, a spectacular journey, passing Machu Picchu (the only way to get there, other than along the Inca Trail on foot), and on into the jungle town of Quillabamba. In 1999 the Machu Picchu to Quillabamba section was not open because of a devastating landslide in 1998 on that section of the line. It seems doubtful that it will ever be cleared. At the time of writing the Central Railway from Lima to Huancayo is again operational, though on a somewhat irregular basis. The section from Huancayo on to Huancavelica is also still operating and well worth doing if you are in that part of the country. ENAFER, the national train company, was privatised in 1999, and is now Peru Rail. In 2000 services and prices are likely to change dramatically.

Bolivia has over 4,000km of railway linking the country with Chile, Argentina, and Brazil. The lines are possibly in an even worse state than in Peru, so if you do use the trains, be prepared for long slow journeys. There are usually people selling food and drinks on the trains and in the stations, usually some sort of meat like *chicharrones* (deep-fried pork), pasties (*salteñas*), bread, maize and fizzy drinks.

By river

Boats are of major importance in Ecuador, Peru and Bolivia for getting around in the Amazon lowlands. These are generally dugout canoes with outboard motors, seating 12–24 people, or large cargo boats. The dugouts operate as river buses in many parts of the Amazon, and cost a bit more because of greater fuel consumption. They have wooden bench seats, so it's worth bringing something to pad them with, and have in your hand luggage insect repellent, suncream, food, water, and an umbrella or rain poncho. Wear long sleeved clothes to protect you from the burning sun, bring a good book, and make sure all your luggage is waterproof.

On the larger cargo boats, you need to bring a hammock and food and water, as, although food is usually included in the price, what is served may not be clean or hygienic. Food tends to be rice and fish, meat, bananas or beans. Asking around in the ports will find you a captain and give you an idea of the price, and then you just have to hang around until departure. Take your own hammock and mosquito net and try to find a spot for your hammock away from the engine room, and from lights. There is usually some sort of toilet and pump shower, though these will be pretty basic. River trips can be great fun, and a good way to meet local people, relax and enjoy the scenery. Remember to be vigilant with your luggage.

Urban transport

Buses, especially in the larger cities, are frequent, very cheap and easy to use. Usually the destination is written on the front, and they stop to pick you up whenever you wave one down and drop you off whenever you say *baja*, meaning down. **Taxis** are also plentiful and cheap. Anyone can set themselves up as a taxi driver, there is no regulation. Especially in Lima, and also in Quito and Guayaquil, there are plenty of rumours of people being robbed in taxis, driven to strange locations, ripped off, and even worse, so be cautious. There are official taxis at airports and outside the big hotels, which usually cost considerably more than the generally beaten-up old vehicles that will pick you up on the street, but whatever type of taxi you take always set the price before even opening the door.

ORGANISED TREKS AND JUNGLE EXPEDITIONS

There are certain parts of the Amazon that you cannot easily get to if you are travelling alone, and you may have to join an organised tour. Expect to pay from US$30 to US$150 per day, depending on where you are and the level of service required. You may wish to join an organised trekking or climbing tour if you don't have the right equipment or experience, or if the maps aren't good enough, or you would enjoy some company. Costs vary, but start at around US$30 per day.

ACCOMMODATION

Affordable accommodation is easy to find in Ecuador, Peru and Bolivia. In the cities there is a wide range of prices and quality from which to choose, whereas in remote rural areas you could be restricted to the most basic of hostels, and in the Amazon you may find there are only expensive Jungle Lodges in the areas you wish to go to. During major festivals and holidays it is a good idea to book ahead or you may be stuck, but at other times there are usually more than enough places for everyone. This guidebook gives detailed listings of hostels, but there are many more, and things change, so always have a look around before accepting a room.

Hostels

For a hostel at the cheaper end of the market you will pay from as little as US$3 to US$4 per person per night for a clean, reasonable room with a shared bathroom. If you prefer to have a private bathroom, you will pay at least US$5 per person. *Hospedajes*, *residenciales*, *pensiones* and *casas familiares* are cheaper options and are usually found in the centre of towns near the stations, and markets. Most hostels will have a safe where you can leave money; always get a receipt. Room prices are displayed, but can vary with seasons, and there is often a lock-up time. The first room you are shown is usually the least attractive, so ask for a larger, lighter, quieter room, and you will probably be shown something better. Be wary of dodgy electrics in the showers, and try not to touch anything electric while you have wet hands. Plumbing is not too good either – often there is no water at all for several hours, and hot water is limited to certain times of day. Always put toilet paper in the bins provided and not in the pan, as this can block toilets.

Camping

Official campsites are few and far between, and I wouldn't recommend camping near any sizeable town, unless you stay with your things at all times and remain out of sight. The risk of theft is high. Camping in national parks is of course accepted, and you will find some official camping areas, but little in the way of facilities. If you are camping it is a good idea to arrive in daylight and ask permission if you are in a village or if there is anyone around. Often you can camp in school grounds or on the football pitch. In the more popular areas, and along hiking routes like the Inca Trail to Machu Picchu, you will unfortunately find a large amount of debris left by irresponsible hikers. Well over 20,000 people walk that trail each year, and very few carry away their rubbish or take care where they defecate. You should aim for minimum impact wherever you are: take away all your litter; take a small trowel for digging a hole well away from water courses when nature calls; do not burn firewood; bring a stove, and do not offer gifts to local people. Such gifts undermine the nature of the local culture and lead local people to view *gringos* as a free source of handouts. Offer your gifts to the local school or in exchange for something.

EATING AND DRINKING

Food

In Ecuador, Peru and Bolivia, food is everywhere. You will find most sizeable towns have a market with a food section serving good value, if somewhat carbohydrate-loaded meals, local specialities such as stuffed potatoes and stuffed peppers, and a large variety of freshly made fruit juices. Then there are always a number of restaurants to choose from. The main meal of the day is lunch, *almuerzo*, usually served from midday until about 4 o'clock in the afternoon. You can get a wide range of dishes, and there is often a *menu*, a set price, usually very cheap, two or three course lunch. The set meal tends to be soup followed by a pasta, rice or potato laden second course with a drink and sometimes a dessert. *Desayuno*, or breakfast, is very different from the breakfast we know. Other than in the large cities, where things have changed and become more Westernised, breakfast consists of a bowl of something hot often left over from the previous day, and often resembling chicken soup with all the bits of the chicken, including the feet. In hotels used to catering for tourists you will be served bread, *pan*, with jam and butter and coffee, usually made from concentrate. *Desayuno Americano* is commonly served too in hotels, this being a cooked breakfast, with eggs, *huevos* and bacon or ham, *jamon*. If you have eaten local style and had a large lunch, you will probably not want a huge dinner. However, most restaurants will also serve a fixed price *cena*, dinner, for just a few dollars. In the bigger cities and towns used to catering for tourists you will find a huge range of restaurants, the ubiquitous pizzeria, hamburger places, and a variety of quality restaurants. In remote rural areas there is less choice but food tends to be of a reasonable price and quality.

To avoid stomach problems it is best not to eat unpeeled fruit and salads. If you can wash the ingredients yourself in purified water, then that's OK, but most salad vegetables harbour bacteria from irrigation using unclean water. Street stalls often sell very appealing, cheap food, which is safe enough to eat if you can see that it has been cooked at a high temperature, and then has not come into contact with dirty hands, plates, utensils or whatever. Eat it off the grill. In all three countries there are *chifas*, Chinese restaurants, which usually produce good, cheap and varied food. Other than in *chifas* vegetarians will have a problem finding good food as there are very few vegetarian restaurants, although the Hare Krishna sect do have a chain of vegetarian restaurants in the larger cities. Seafood is great all down the coast, and most restaurants are careful about clean preparation and conditions after the cholera outbreaks of recent years. *Ceviche*, seafood marinated in lemon and served with onions and chilli peppers, is absolutely delicious, and widely eaten along the coast. In the mountains restaurants serving *pollo a la brasa*, grilled chicken with chips, are common and good. Supermarkets in the larger cities sell pretty well everything you can purchase in Europe or North America, so you can always stock up and prepare your own food from time to time.

CLIMBING IN THE ANDES

John Biggar

Many people trekking and backpacking in the Andes may be tempted to climb one of the mountains they see towering above them. The Andes are one of the world's great mountain ranges, second only to the Himalayas in terms of height, and longer than any other range in the world. They have over 600 major 5,000m peaks, over half of which are in Ecuador, Peru and Bolivia. A great variety of climbing conditions can be found in the Andes, with some of the easiest and most accessible high peaks in the world but also some of the most remote and technically difficult.

A quick guide to climbing in Ecuador, Peru and Bolivia

Ecuador's big peaks form the famous avenue of the volcanoes. Peaks such as Cotopaxi (5,897m) and Chimborazo (6,310m) have long had a reputation as ideal beginners' peaks, but with poor weather, high avalanche risk and big crevasses they are not the most suitable peaks to learn on. Bolivia or the Cordillera Occidental are far safer destinations for those without much experience. However, in Ecuador there is at least very easy access and huts high on the mountains.

Peru has many ranges and nearly half of the 6,000m peaks in the Andes. Many of these are very difficult or downright dangerous ascents. There are some easier summits in the Cordillera Blanca, including the highest peak in Peru, Huascarán Sur (6,746m) and Pisco (5,752m). Some of the easiest peaks in the Andes are the volcanoes of the Cordillera Occidental around Arequipa, eg: Misti (5,842m), Coropuna (6,425m) and Ampato (6,288m). The numerous ranges south and east of Cusco are still very remote and an ideal destination if you want to get away from the crowds. However, there are few really easy peaks in this area.

Bolivia has four major ranges, by far the most important being the spectacular Cordillera Real. Access to these mountains is very quick and in July and August the weather is incredibly stable, making the country increasingly popular with climbers. The most popular peak in the Cordillera Real is Huayna Potosí (6,088m) and there are also several good 5,000m plus peaks in the range. The highest peak in Bolivia is the extinct volcano Sajama (6,542m), located near the border with Chile.

Climate and weather

For climbing any of these big peaks it is particularly important to travel when the weather is best. In Ecuador you can climb all year except March to May but December and July–August seem to be best. For Peru and Bolivia the dry season runs from May to September, though in the Cordillera Occidental around Arequipa you can climb all year.

The climb

It is a bit difficult to generalise, but in most parts of the Andes it will take from three to seven days to climb a major summit. In Ecuador and parts of Bolivia you can climb some of the 6,000m peaks in one long day, and for the remote parts of southern Peru it may take a week or more to complete an ascent. You will need to be well acclimatised to the altitude at 3,000m or higher before attempting to climb to 6,000m. For success on an easy 6,000m peak the three most important factors are a high level of fitness, good general expedition skills and the ability to be patient with the weather and your acclimatisation.

To climb a peak you'll usually need to hire a vehicle to get you to the end of the road, then for most peaks organise pack animals to get you to the base of your mountain. You'll then often need to carry all your equipment yourself to a high camp before making an attempt on the summit. If climbing over 6,000m you'll need extra days above 4,000m for acclimatisation and it's always wise to allow time for a second attempt at the summit if the route is difficult to find or the weather is poor. Only on the busiest peaks will a route be marked across the glaciers and finding one on your own can be very time-consuming. On all peaks the conditions on the climb can change dramatically from one year to the next, so be prepared for the climb to be a grade harder than you expect!

Guides and agencies

Many beginners may want to climb with a guide or agency. In South America many of the local guides are very good, but some of them are dangerous or unreliable. A good mountaineer can soon tell the difference, but a beginner may be left not knowing any better. Only the guides in Peru are affiliated to the UIAGM, though Ecuador and Bolivia have local guide organisations. If you are worried about your safety it's much better to pay more money and use a reliable European or North American tour operator. Remember it is extremely dangerous to venture onto a glacier without the right equipment and someone experienced in glacier travel techniques.

Throughout the Andes local agencies can help with planning and organising the logistics of an ascent. There are many such agencies in the busy mountaineering centres of Quito, Huaraz and La Paz. In other towns there are always trekking or adventure travel agencies, though their experience of organising mountaineering expeditions may be limited. Agencies can organise as much or as little as you need – from a short 4x4 ride to the bottom of your mountain to a complete two week expedition with pack animals, porters, cooks and guides.

Pack animals are available almost everywhere in the Andes, but porters to carry your equipment higher on the mountains are available only on the busiest peaks in Peru and Bolivia.

Guidebooks

There are now quite a few good guidebooks available to climbing in the Andes. John Biggar's *The Andes – A Guide for Climbers* (BigR Publishing, 1999) covers the whole of the Andes and is the only available guidebook for the mountains in most of Peru. John Biggar runs the climbing agency Andes: tel: 01556 503929; email: John@andes.com.

For Bolivia, there is Yossi Brain's *Bolivia – a Climbers Guide* (The Mountaineers, 1999); for the Cordillera Blanca of Peru, try David Sharman's *Climbs of the Cordillera Blanca* (Whizzo Climbs, 1995); and for Ecuador there is *Climbing and Hiking in Ecuador* by Rob Rachowiecki, Mark Thurber and Betsy Wagenhauser (Bradt, 1997).

Drink

It is not recommended that you drink the tap water in Ecuador, Peru or Bolivia. It is much safer to buy it in a sealed bottle or sterilise it yourself. The tap water in the cities is treated, so it is probably safe, but take no chances – even local people boil it before drinking. Tea and coffee is readily available, though the coffee isn't too good. Beware of *te con leche*, milky tea made from a teabag dunked in a glass of hot milk. Coffee is usually concentrate with water added, and may have been sitting around for a long time. In the cities now you will be able to get a decent cup in one of the cafés. *Gaseosas*, soft fizzy drinks, are widely available and cheap, especially if you buy the locally produced ones. You can get all the usual as well as some strange local drinks such as Inca Cola, a yellow, chewing gum flavoured concoction. Try it. Fresh fruit juices are delicious, cheap, nutritious and safe if made without water or ice added. Ask for it *sin hielo*, no ice and *sin agua*, no water. Of course there is plenty of alcohol to choose from, some very good spirits such as *Pisco*, made into the Peruvian *pisco sour*, a great cocktail. Other drinks include *aguardiente*, distilled sugarcane alcohol, and rum. There are several kinds of beer, mostly lagers, wine of varying quality, and the local highland drink of *chicha*, a sort of fermented maize beer.

COMMUNICATIONS

Communications are not a problem in **Peru**, where telephones are easy to find (except in remote villages) and easy to use. The Spanish phone company Telefónica has recently expanded rapidly throughout Peru and their system is very similar to that of the UK. You can use coins or purchase phonecards to call from the phone boxes, and calls are cheaper after 9pm or on Sundays. In addition to phone boxes most towns boast at least one Telefónica office, from which you can phone and usually fax out. Internet and email are also becoming increasingly common in Telefónica offices, and other locations in larger towns and cities. In **Ecuador** telephones are less commonly found and you will probably have to go to the office of IETEL to make a call – there is usually one in each town. Email is widely available in Quito, Guayaquil, Cuenca and the other cities of Ecuador. In **Bolivia** ENTEL is the national phone company, and most towns have at least one ENTEL office, from which you can fax or phone out. La Paz now has several cyber cafés where you can send and receive email. Other cities in Bolivia such as Oruro, Potosí, Sucre and Santa Cruz also have Internet cafés. Some hotels also offer fax and email services to tourists.

Post

The postal service is reasonably reliable, and letters usually get to Europe within a couple of weeks. You can have mail sent to you at most towns of a reasonable size. Letters should be addressed to Lista de Correos, town name, country. Your own name should be in capitals with your surname underlined. Always check for letters under the first letter of your first name and surname anyway, and if your name begins with W check under V as there is no W in Spanish. Letters take from a week to three weeks to arrive and are kept for a minimum of a month in Poste Restante. Receiving parcels is more hassle than it's worth: you will have to pay tax and it can take all day.

TOURIST INFORMATION

Peru, Bolivia and Ecuador have tourist information offices in most towns, open to the public. They are not necessarily well resourced, but usually the staff are friendly and helpful.

Maps and guidebooks

The South American Explorers Club in Lima, Cusco and Quito is good for guidebooks, but otherwise it is best to buy them at home. Maps of the more popular treks are available from the South American Explorers Club. There is a secondhand market for guidebooks amongst travellers, but you can't guarantee you'll get what you want, when you want it. Country maps and street plans are available from bookshops in the larger cities, and detailed walking maps are available from the Instituto Geográfico offices (see listings for Quito, Lima and La Paz). I wouldn't attempt any trek without the relevant 1:50,000 or 1:100,000 walking map. Always take your passport and cash in dollars with you when you go to buy maps.

The South American Explorers Club

The South American Explorers Club is a non-profit organisation. With clubhouses in Quito, Ecuador, and Lima and Cusco, Peru, and US headquarters in Ithaca, New York, the SAEC collects and makes available to its members up-to-date, reliable information about Central and South America. Membership is US$40 ($60 couple) per year and is tax-deductible in the US. Residents outside the US (including Canada and Mexico) add US$7 for postage. Those wishing to sign up in the United Kingdom can join through Bradt Travel Guides, 19 High Street, Chalfont St Peter, Bucks SL9 9QE; tel: 01753 893444; fax: 01753 892333.

General member services

Staff and volunteers provide advice and practical information to members. The club is also a place to meet others and exchange information. Members looking for travel companions for a trip/expedition, or seeking to contact experts in a particular field, can pin up notices on club bulletin boards in Lima, Cusco and Quito, post them on the website, or put a classified ad in the *South American Explorer*. Trip reports written by members provide specialised information on just about everything: climbing, volunteering, learning Spanish, lining up a local tour operator, whitewater rafting, hiking, visiting the Galápagos, etc. For members only, trip reports are available at each of the clubhouses or by mail from Ithaca for a photocopying charge plus postage. At each of the clubhouses you will find: message boards, files of information, maps, a lending library, bookshop and exchange, magazines, equipment storage, mail, phone, email and fax. Members may receive mail at the SAEC postal addresses. The staff will take phone messages during office hours and fax messages for members.

Clubhouse addresses

Quito Clubhouse Calle Jorge Washington 311 and Leonidas Plaza, Mariscal Sucre, Quito. Postal address: Apartado 17-21-431, Eloy Alfaro, Quito, Ecuador; tel/fax: 593 2 225228; member email: member@saec.org.ec; administrative email: explorer@saec.org.ec Open 09.30–17.00 weekdays.

Lima Clubhouse Av República de Portugal 146, Breña, Lima. Postal address: Casilla 3714, Lima 100, Peru; tel/fax: 51-1 4250142; member email: memberlima@amauta.rcp.net.pe; administrative email: montague@amauta.rcp.net.pe Open 09.30–17.00 weekdays.

Cusco Clubhouse Av del Sol 930. Cusco.
Postal address Apartado 500, Cusco, Peru; tel: 084 223102; email: saec@wayna.rcp.net.pe Open 09.30–17.00 weekdays.

US Headquarters 126 Indian Creek Rd, Ithaca, NY 14850 USA; telephone 607 2770488; fax: 607 2776122; email: explorer@samexplo.org ; web: www.samexplo.org Open 09.00–17.00 weekdays.

All mail for members should be sent to the postal address (not the street address) except when using Federal Express, DHL or other express mail services. For both regular and express mail, be sure to write the member's name.

Bolivia

The *Bolivian Times* will receive mail for members in Bolivia. Address mail to: Your Name, Member SAEC, c/o Bolivian TIMES, PO Box 1696, La Paz, Bolivia. You can pick up mail at the *Bolivian Times* office: Pasaje Jauregui 2248, La Paz; tel: 591 2 390700.

HEALTH

with Dr Jane Wilson-Howarth and Dr Felicity Nicholson

Immunisations

Preparations to ensure a healthy trip to the Americas require checks on your immunisation status; you'll also need to pack lotions and long clothes to protect you from insect bites and the sun. It is wise to go – if you can – to a travel clinic a couple of months before departure to arrange your immunisations. **Tetanus** immunity needs to be boosted every ten years, as does **diphtheria**. Polio has been eradicated from the Americas (1999) and is therefore no longer necessary for these countries. For many regions immunisations against **yellow fever**, **rabies**, typhoid and hepatitis A are also needed.

The majority of travellers are advised to have immunisation against **hepatitis A** with hepatitis A vaccine (eg: Havrix Monodose, Avaxim). One dose of vaccine lasts for one year and can be boosted to give protection for up to ten years. The course of two injections costs about £100. It is now felt that the vaccine can be used even closer to the time of departure and is nearly always preferable to gamma globulin which gives immediate but partial protection for a couple of months. There is a theoretical risk of CJD (human form of mad cow disease) with this blood-derived product.

The newer **typhoid** vaccines are about 85% effective and should be encouraged unless the traveller is leaving within a few days for a trip of a week or less when the vaccine would not be effective in time. It needs boosting every three years. Immunisation against **cholera** is currently ineffective but a cholera exemption certificate is required when crossing land borders in many South American countries.

Hepatitis B vaccination should be considered for longer trips or for those working in situations where contact with blood is increased. Three injections are ideal which can be given at 0, 4 and 8 weeks prior to travel.

Travel clinics

As well as providing an immunisation service, travel clinics usually sell a good range of nets, treatment kits, repellents and malaria medicines.

UK

Berkeley Travel Clinic 32 Berkeley St, London WIX 5FA. Tel: 0171 629 6233.

British Airways Travel Clinic and Immunisation Service 156 Regent St W1, tel: 020 7439 9584. This place also sells travellers' supplies and has a branch of Stanford's travel book and map shop. There are now BA clinics all around Britain and three in South Africa. To find your nearest one, phone 01276 685040.

MASTA (Medical Advisory Service for Travellers Abroad) Keppel St, London WC1 7HT; tel: 09068 224100. This is a premium-line number, charged at 50p per minute.

Readers on the internet may prefer to check their large website: http://dspace.dial.pipex.com/masta/index

Nomad Travel Pharmacy and Vaccination Centre 3–4, Wellington Terrace, Turnpike Lane, London N8 0PX; tel: 020 8889 7014.

Thames Medical 157 Waterloo Rd, London SE1 8US; tel: 020 7902 9000. Competitively priced, one-stop travel health service. All profits go to their affiliated company InterHealth which provides health care for overseas workers on Christian projects.

Trailfinders Immunisation Centre 194 Kensington High St, London W8 7RG; tel: 020 7938 3999. Also 254–284 Sauchiehall St, Glasgow G2 3EH; tel: 0141 353 0066.

Tropical Medicine Bureau This Irish-run organisation has a useful website specific to tropical destinations: http://www.tmb.le

USA

Centers for Disease Control The Atlanta-based organisation is the central source of travel information in the USA with a touch-tone phone line and fax service: Traveler's Hot Line, (404) 332 4559. Each summer they publish the invaluable Health Information for International Travel which is available from Center for Prevention Services, Division of Quarantine, Atlanta, GA 30333.

Connaught Laboratories PO Box 187, Swiftwater, PA 18370; tel: 800 822 2463. They will send a free list of specialist tropical-medicine physicians in your state.

IAMAT (International Association for Medical Assistance to Travelers) 736 Center St, Lewiston, NY 14092. A non-profit organisation which provides lists of English-speaking doctors abroad.

Australia

TMVC Tel: 1300 65 88 44; website: www.tmvc.com.au. TMVC has 20 clinics in Australia, New Zealand and Thailand, including:

Brisbane Dr Deborah Mills, Qantas Domestic Building, 6th floor, 247 Adelaide St, Brisbane, QLD 4000; tel: 7 3221 9066; fax: 7 3321 7076

Melbourne Dr Sonny Lau, 393 Little Bourke St, 2nd floor, Melbourne, VIC 3000; tel: 3 9602 5788; fax: 3 9670 8394.

Sydney Dr Mandy Hu, Dymocks Building, 7th floor, 428 George St, Sydney, NSW 2000; tel: 2 221 7133; fax: 2 221 8401.

South Africa

There are four **British Airways travel clinics** in South Africa: *Johannesburg*, tel: (011) 807 3132; *Cape Town*, tel: (021) 419 3172; *Knysna*, tel: (044) 382 6366; *East London*, tel: (0431) 43 2359.

Medical kit

Your medical kit should include: insect repellent, after-bite ointment, iodine or water purifying tablets, antiseptic cream, Elastoplast, wound dressings, sutures, crepe and triangular bandages, safety pins, elasticated knee and ankle supports, tweezers, a blister kit, wintergreen cream or arnica ointment, Imodium, Lomotil, rehydration powders, general antibiotics, aspirin or paracetamol, painkillers, antihistamine, calamine cream, travel sickness pills, scissors, and a survival bag.

Malaria

Parts of lowland tropical South America carry a risk of malaria and some other insect-borne diseases. Only two (*Plasmodium vivax* and *P. falciparum*) of the possible four malarial strains are found in South America; the risk is less the higher you go and malaria is absent above about 2,500m (8,250ft). Seek expert advice on the best antimalarial tablets to take. For recorded information in the UK on malaria risk and prophylaxis phone 0891 600350. If mefloquine (Lariam) is suggested, start this two and a half weeks before departure to check that it suits you; stop it immediately if it seems to cause mood swings or other changes in the way you feel,visual or hearing disturbances, fits, severe headaches or changes in heart rhythm. Anyone who is pregnant, who has suffered fits in the past, has been treated for depression or psychiatric problems or who is epileptic or who has a close blood relative who is epileptic should avoid mefloquine. The usual alternative is chloroquine (Nivaquine) two weekly and proguanil (Paludrine) two daily. A newer alternative, the antibiotic doxycycline (100mg daily), is considered by many to be more effective than chloroquine and Paludrine and has the advantage that it need only be started one day before arrival in a malarial region. It may also be used by travellers with epilepsy, unlike the other regimes. Users must be warned about the possibility of allergic skin reactions developing in sunlight which can occur in approximately 5% of people. Stopping the drug is advised. Women using the oral contraceptive should use an additional method of protection for the first four weeks when taking this antimalarial prophylactic agent. All prophylactic agents should be continued for four weeks after leaving the last malarial area.

Travellers to remote parts may wish to consider carrying a course of treatment to cure malaria. Presently quinine and Fansidar is the favoured regime, but it would be best to take up-to-date advice on the current recommended treatment. Self treatment is not without risks and generally people over-treat themselves. If at all possible consult a doctor if you are taken ill since diagnosing malaria is difficult without laboratory facilities.

Whether or not you are taking malaria tablets, or carrying a cure, it is important to protect yourself from mosquito bites. Pack long, loose, 100% cotton clothes (for protection from insect bites and the sun), DEET-based repellent stick or roll-on (eg: Repel, Cutters, Off!, Autan or Jungle Jell) and either a permethrin-impregnated bednet or a permethrin spray so that you can 'treat' bednets in hotels. Permethrin treatment stops mosquitoes biting through the net if you roll against it and makes even very tatty nets protective. Putting on long clothes at dusk means you can reduce the amount of repellent needed but be aware that, since malaria mosquitoes hunt at ankle level and will bite through socks, you need to apply repellent under socks too. Keep your repellent stick or roll-on to hand at all times.

Be aware that no prophylactic is 100% protective, although those on prophylactics who are unlucky enough to catch malaria are less likely to get into serious trouble rapidly. The symptoms of malaria appear from one week to a year after exposure and may initially be no worse than a dose of flu; often however there is high fever, shivering, chills, profuse sweating, nausea and even diarrhoea and vomiting. In *falciparum* malaria there may be all this plus hallucinations, headache, numbness of the extremities and eventually fits or coma. Given prompt treatment, most people (99%) recover. A number of effective drugs treat malaria. Indeed quinine, derived from the Amazonian cinchona tree, was widely used from 1700, before the disease was understood.

Avoiding insect bites

Night biters It is crucial to avoid bites. Mosquitoes and sandflies may transmit malaria and leishmania (respectively) between dusk and dawn, so as the sun is going down, turn out the lights, don long clothes and apply repellent on any exposed flesh. Malaria mosquitoes are voracious and hunt at ankle level, biting through socks, and so it is worth applying repellent under the socks too. Sleep under a permethrin-treated bednet or in an air-conditioned room.

Day biters During days out in the forest, it is wise to wear long loose clothes with trousers/pants tucked into socks; this will help keep off ticks and chiggers as well as day-biting *Aedes* mosquitoes which may spread dengue and yellow fevers. Minute, pestilential biting day-active **blackflies** spread river blindness in some parts of tropical South America. The disease is caught close to fast flowing rivers where the flies breed. Eucalyptus-based natural repellents do not work against them.

Sandflies These are very small biters which are most active at twilight but bite throughout the night. They transmit leishmania, a protozoan disease causing painless tropical sores which, in extreme cases, grow to look like leprosy. Sandflies are able to penetrate mosquito netting but treating the net with insecticide keeps them out. Ceiling fans – if available – will help keep them off. Sandflies are more of a problem in rainforests. Leishmania is reasonably common and is difficult to treat, so precautions against being bitten must be taken seriously. The severe and untreatable form of the lowland disease is called *espundia*. In the western Andes of Peru, sandflies behave differently and stay close to villages where they bite dogs, people and anything else that seems tasty. The ulcers caused by Andean leishmania or *uta* heal by themselves.

Kissing bugs and Chagas' disease (trypanosomiasis) Chagas' disease is a very rare disease among travellers. It is a problem in lowland tropical America and affects the rural poor and those sleeping on floors in wattle and daub type village houses. A hammock will help protect you, particularly if it has a built-in mosquito net; these are marketed in South America.

Flesh maggots The Macaw or warble-fly lays her eggs on mosquitoes so that, when the mosquito feeds, the warble infants can burrow into the victim's skin. Here they grow, feasting happily until they mature to cause a boil-like inflammation that will need surgical removal. Now there's another reason to avoid mosquito bites!

Jiggers or sandfleas (*niguas*) These are minute flesh-feasters, not to be confused with chiggers (see below). They latch on if you walk bare-foot in contaminated places (locals will know where), and set up home under the skin of the foot, usually at the

QUICK TICK REMOVAL

Ticks (*garrapatas*) transmit a variety of unpleasant infections in the Americas including Rocky Mountain spotted fever, but if you remove the tick promptly and whole the chances of disease transmission are much reduced. Manoeuvre your finger and thumb so that you can pinch the tick's mouthparts as close to your skin as possible, and slowly and steadily pull away at right angles to your skin. This often hurts. Jerking or twisting will increase the chances of damaging the tick which in turn increases the chances of disease transmission. Once the tick is off, douse the little wound with alcohol (local spirit, *pisco* etc, is excellent) or iodine. If an area of spreading redness around the bite site develops, or a rash or fever emerges a few days or more after the bite occurred, take a trip to a doctor.

side of a toenail where they cause a painful boil-like swelling. These need picking out by a local expert. If the distended flea bursts during eviction, the wound should be doused in spirit, alcohol or kerosene – otherwise more jiggers will infest you.

Chiggers, *chivacoa* or itch mites Both ticks and these pestilential little mites can be kept off by applying repellent (even on your boots) and tucking pants/trousers into socks. Chiggers are related to little red harvest mites that run around in the summer in Europe. However, the American version is incredibly irritating and the itching stays with you long after the mite has gone. Eurax cream (*crotamiton*) or calamine lotion is most likely to help, plus exposing the itchy part and cool sponging.

Scorpions Most scorpion stings will be painful for a few hours, but there are some really nasty species in the Americas and a few in Central America cause some deaths, mostly in children. Scorpions come out at night and during the day snooze under stones and in rotting logs; beware of putting a hand in a crevice and, if you need to roll a stone over, roll it away from you. If the sting makes you feel very unwell with profuse sweating and the shakes you would benefit from antivenom and should seek medical help if you can.

Travellers' diarrhoea

Probably about half of those travelling to South America will suffer from a bout of travellers' diarrhoea during their trip, and the newer you are to exotic travel, the more likely you will be to suffer. Some parts of South America are very high risk, yet there are simple precautions which will protect you against travellers' diarrhoea as well as from typhoid, cholera, hepatitis, dysentery, polio, worms, etc. Travellers' diarrhoea and the other faecal-oral diseases come from getting other peoples' faeces in your mouth. This most often happens from cooks not washing their hands after a trip to the toilet, yet if your food has been thoroughly cooked and arrives piping hot, you will be safe no matter what filthy habits the cook has. The maxim to remind you what you can safely eat is:

PEEL IT, BOIL IT, COOK IT OR FORGET IT!

This means that fruit you have washed and peeled yourself and hot foods should be safe. Raw foods, cold cooked foods and salads are risky, as are foods kept lukewarm in hotel buffets. It is much more unusual to get sick from drinking contaminated water but it happens, so try to drink from safe sources. Water should have been brought to the boil (even at altitude it only needs to be brought to the boil), passed through a good bacteriological filter or purified with iodine (add four drops of tincture of iodine and allow to stand for 20–30 minutes). Chlorine (eg: Puritabs) is also adequate although theoretically less effective, and it tastes nastier. Mineral water has been found to be contaminated in many developing countries and may be no safer than tap water. If diarrhoea strikes, see box overleaf for treatment.

Safe sex

Travel is a time when we may enjoy sexual adventures, especially when alcohol reduces inhibitions. Remember that the risks of sexually transmitted infection are high, whether you sleep with fellow travellers or locals. About half of HIV infections in British heterosexuals are acquired abroad. Use condoms or femidoms. If you notice any genital ulcers or discharge get treatment promptly: sexually transmitted infections increase the risk of acquiring HIV. AIDS is known as SIDA in Spanish. HIV is not uncommon in the Americas and it is most prevalent in areas visited by tourists.

TREATING TRAVELLERS' DIARRHOEA

It is dehydration that makes you feel awful during a bout of diarrhoea, so the most important part of treatment is to drink lots of clear fluids. Sachets of oral rehydration salts give the perfect biochemical mix to replace all that is being lost but they do not taste nice. Any dilute mixture of sugar and salt in water will do you good, so if you like Coke or orange squash, drink that with a three-finger pinch of salt added to each glass. If safe water is available, make a solution of a four-finger scoop of sugar with a three-finger pinch of salt in a glass of water. Alternatively, add eight level teaspoons of sugar (18g) and one level teaspoon of salt (3g) to one litre (five cups) of safe water. A squeeze of lemon or orange juice improves the taste and adds potassium, which also needs to be replaced. Drink two large glasses after every bowel action, and more if you are thirsty. If you are not eating you need to drink three litres a day *plus* the equivalent of whatever is leaving you in sweat and down the toilet. If you feel like eating, stick to bland, high carbohydrate, foods. Heavy greasy foods will give you cramps.

If the diarrhoea is bad, if you are passing blood or slime, or if you have a fever, you will probably need antibiotics in addition to fluid replacement. A three-day course of one of the antibiotics ciprofloxacin, norfloxacin or nalidixic acid is good for dysentery and bad diarrhoea. These are far better treatment than the 'blockers' like Imodium, Lomotil or Kaopectate. Be careful about what you accept from local pharmacies: drugs like chloramphenicol (sold as Chloromycetin, Catilan or Enteromycetin) and the sulpha antibiotics (eg: streptomagma) have too many serious side effects to be worth the risk in treating simple diarrhoea. Do not take them!

Skin infections

Skin infections set in remarkably easily in warm climates and any mosquito bite or small skin nick is a potential entry point for bacteria. It is essential, therefore, to clean and cover even the slightest wound. Creams are not as effective as a good drying antiseptic such as dilute iodine, potassium permanganate (a few crystals in half a cup of water) or crystal (gentian) violet. One of these should be available in most towns. If the wound starts to throb, or becomes red and the redness starts to spread or the wound oozes, and especially if you develop a fever, five days of antibiotics will probably be needed: flucloxacillin (250mg four times a day) or cloxacillin (500mg four times a day). For those allergic to penicillin, erythromycin (500mg twice a day) should help. See a doctor if it does not start to improve within 36–48 hours of starting treatment.

Fungal infections also get a hold easily in hot moist climates so wear 100% cotton socks and underwear and shower frequently. An itchy rash in the groin or flaking or soreness between the toes is likely to be a fungal infection. This needs treatment with an antifungal cream such as Canesten (clotrimazole), or if this is not available try Whitfield's ointment (compound benzoic acid ointment) or crystal violet (although this will turn you purple!).

Sun and heat

Prickly heat

A fine pimply rash on the trunk is likely to be heat rash. Cool showers, dabbing (not rubbing) dry and talc will help; if it's bad you may need to check into an air-conditioned hotel room for a while. Slowing down to a relaxed schedule, wearing only loose baggy 100% cotton clothes and sleeping naked under a fan will reduce the problem.

Protection from the sun

The incidence of skin cancer is rocketing as Caucasians travel more and spend more time exposing themselves to the sun. Sun exposure also ages the skin, making people prematurely wrinkly; so cover up with long loose clothes, put on plenty of suncream and wear a hat when you can. Keep out of the sun during the middle of the day and, if you must expose yourself, build up gradually from 20 minutes per day. Be especially careful of sun reflected off water and wear a T-shirt and plenty of waterproof SPF15 suncream when swimming. Snorkelling often leads to scorched backs and thighs, so protect yourself with a T-shirt and a pair of bermuda shorts.

Heatstroke

This is most likely within the first week or ten days of arriving in a hotter, more humid climate. It is important to slow down, drink plenty and avoid hard physical exercise in the middle of the day, particularly at first. Treatment for heat exhaustion is rest in the shade and sponging, plus lots to drink.

Sea and freshwater problems

Foot protection

If you wear old plimsolls, sneakers or jellies on the beach or riverside, you will avoid injury and you are less likely to get venomous fish spines (together with jiggers and geography worms) in the feet. If you tread on a venomous fish, soak the foot in hot (but not scalding) water until some time after the pain subsides; this may take 20–30 minutes submersion in all. Take the foot out of the water when you top up otherwise you may scald it. If the pain returns re-immerse the foot. Once the venom has been heat-inactivated, get a doctor to check and remove any bits of fish spines in the wound.

Stingrays

There are plenty of venomous creatures in the sea but be aware that South America also boasts freshwater stingrays whose barbed tails inflict damage as well as dispensing venom. Piranhas and candiru fish are the subject of many fine travellers' tales, designed to scare the uninitiated. Don't worry about them: stories are exaggerated to the level of fiction.

Animal attacks

If you are venturing into the rainforest ask around about dangerous wildlife. If you are sleeping out, a net will keep off vampires as well as smaller biters.

Rabies

Any mammal can carry rabies. The disease is common in bats (especially vampires); village dogs must also be assumed to be rabid. Any suspect bites should be scrubbed under running water for five minutes and then flooded with local spirit or dilute iodine. Failing this washing with ordinary soap is also effective. Contact with saliva in an open cut should also be considered as a risk. At least two post-bite rabies injections are needed even in immunised people. Those who have not been immunised will need a course of injections. Rabies immunoglobulin (RIG) is also used, but this product is expensive (around US$800) and may be hard to come by. This is another reason why pre-exposure vaccination should be encouraged in travellers who are planning to visit more remote areas. Treatment should be given as soon as possible, but it is never too late to seek help as the incubation period for rabies can be very long. Bites closer to the brain are always more serious. Death from rabies is probably one of the worst ways to go!

Snakes

Snakes rarely attack unless provoked, and it is unusual for travellers to be bitten. You are less likely to get bitten if you wear stout shoes and long trousers when in the forest. Most snakes are harmless and many of the highly venomous and brightly coloured coral snakes have such small mouths they are unlikely to be able to bite you unless you offer them an earlobe to nibble. Even those larger venomous species capable of harm will only dispense venom in about half of their bites. If bitten, then, you are unlikely to have received venom; keeping this fact in mind may help you to stay calm.

In the event of a bite most first-aid techniques do more harm than good. Cutting into the wound is harmful, tourniquets are dangerous, and suction and electrical inactivation devices do not work. The only effective treatment is antivenom. In case of a bite that you fear may have been from a venomous snake:

- Try to keep calm - it is likely that no venom has been dispensed.
- Stop movement of the bitten limb by applying a splint.
- Keep the bitten limb BELOW heart height to slow down the spread of any venom.
- If you have a crepe bandage, bind up as much of the bitten limb as you can, but completely release the bandage every half hour.
- Evacuate to a hospital that has antivenom.
- NEVER give aspirin; you may offer paracetamol, which is safe.
- NEVER cut or suck the wound.
- DO NOT apply ice packs.
- DO NOT apply potassium permanganate.

If the offending snake can be captured without risk of someone else being bitten, take it to show the doctor, but beware: even a decapitated head is able to dispense venom in a reflex bite.

Local snake antivemon (*suero antiofidico*) is effective against both the rattlesnake (*cascabel*) and the fer-de-lance (*mapanare*); it should be administered by medical experts, preferably in hospital.

Mountains

Mountain sickness

Mountain or altitude sickness is caused by a lack of oxygen at altitude and an overly rapid ascent. There are three degrees of sickness: acute mountain sickness, known locally in the Andes as *soroche*, pulmonary oedema and cerebral oedema. Most people ascending from sea level to the Andean cities of Quito, Cusco, Huaraz, Puno or La Paz will experience some symptoms of mountain sickness, usually mild headaches and a shortness of breath. Sometimes these symptoms are more extreme and coupled with nausea, vomiting, loss of appetite, insomnia and a rapid pulse. To relieve the symptoms, which normally last only a day or two, take it easy, rest, and drink plenty of water to ensure you don't get dehydrated. It is important to acclimatise fully for several days or a week before making any attempts to trek or climb to higher altitudes. Plenty of time for acclimatisation must also be allowed as you climb. An ascent rate of 300–500m per day is recommended, although not always practical. If symptoms persist, descending as little as 500m is recommended.

Acetazolamide (Diamox) can be used prior to arrival at altitude to minimise the risk of developing acute mountain sickness. This may be particularly useful if there is little time for acclimatisation. Ideally it should be tried out at sea level about two weeks before arriving at 3,500m. The drug is only available on prescription and expert advice should be sought as to its suitability. Travellers with pre-existing heart and lung conditions should always see a physician before undertaking trips to altitude.

Pulmonary oedema and cerebral oedema are extremely serious conditions and are responsible for the deaths of climbers every year. They are caused by a fluid accumulation in the lungs or brain. Someone with pulmonary oedema will suffer increasing shortness of breath and a rattling cough producing blood-stained sputum. He or she will turn blue coloured and must be immediately evacuated to lower altitudes and medical care. The symptoms of cerebral oedema are extreme headaches, dizziness, confusion, aggressive behaviour and hallucinations. Again the sufferer must be taken down to lower altitudes immediately.

Hypothermia

As anywhere in adverse weather conditions, hypothermia is a real danger to the unprepared. Even on a trek such as the Inca Trail, treated lightly by many, you should remember that you are in the high Andes and can be exposed to severe weather conditions. Hypothermia is the overcooling of the core of the body which, if it isn't stopped, leads to unconsciousness, respiratory and cardiac failure and then death. This can all happen in as little as two hours. Inadequate clothing in cold, wet and windy conditions, dehydration, lack of physical fitness and illness or injury can all provoke the onset of hypothermia. The first symptoms to watch for are extreme cold and tiredness, a feeling of numbness and uncontrolled shivering, followed by a combination of other symptoms such as odd behaviour, lethargy, slurring of speech, violent outbursts, lack of muscular coordination and failure of vision.

If you recognise the onset of hypothermia in someone who is with you it is vital to get them warm again. Look for shelter, get the person warm and dry into a sleeping bag, tent or whatever is available, and give them a hot sweet drink if possible. Huddle together to rewarm the person and allow complete recovery before moving on.

The best way to deal with hypothermia is by avoiding it. Always take adequate clothing into the mountains, even for day walks. Ensure you have full waterproof covering over several base layers, and a hat and gloves.

Further reading

Self-prescribing has its hazards so if you are going anywhere very remote consider taking a health book. For adults there is *Bugs Bites & Bowels: the Cadogan Guide to Healthy Travel* by Jane Wilson-Howarth (1999). If you are travelling with children look at *Your Child's Health Abroad: a manual for travelling parents* by Jane Wilson-Howarth and Matthew Ellis, published by Bradt in 1998.

CRIME

The situation in Peru and Bolivia is much better than it was in the 1980s and early 1990s, when crime was rife and it seemed that no one could escape being robbed. However, there are still plenty of opportunistic petty criminals waiting to catch you out, so be aware at all times of who is around you and always keep a hold on your luggage. Take some simple precautions: leave all the valuables you won't need such as jewellery and expensive watches at home; carry the minimum amount of money on you when you go out on a daily basis, leaving the rest in your hotel safe where possible; take a padlock with you for locking things in cupboards in hotel rooms; use lockable bags; put your camera on a chain, rather than a strap, so it can't be slashed; try not to arrive or leave anywhere at night and if you do, take taxis rather than walking around with your luggage. Never show any money to anyone on the street, even if they claim to be police. The real police won't ask to see your money and if they ask you to hand over your identification go to a police station or large hotel.

Relative political stability in the last few years has meant a reduction in crime in Peru and Bolivia especially. In Ecuador this isn't the case and crime seems to be on the increase.

Securing your money

When you have to carry all your money with you, keep it in a hidden money belt under your clothing. You could use a leg or arm pouch, and an elastic bandage is useful to tuck money inside above your knee or elbow; alternatively sew extra hidden pockets into the inside of your clothing to put money in. Only keep the money you will need access to during the day in an accessible pocket.

Mugging and armed theft

Fortunately muggings and armed theft are rare occurrences, although in several years of working and travelling in South America I have come across many incidents, such as the friend who had her jacket stolen off her back while she was wandering around Quito, another who was knocked over and had her purse stolen in Arequipa, and three others who were held up at gunpoint in Cusco. The best way to avoid this happening to you is to take taxis at night and avoid wandering through quiet, dimly lit streets on your own.

On public transport

City stations and transport terminals are particularly risky places for theft. There tend to be a lot of people bustling and jostling around, you have all your luggage with you and you are easily distracted. Be extra cautious with your bags: keep a hold on them and only put them in or on buses when you get a receipt or see them being tied down on a roofrack. Use taxis to get to and from the stations and try not to arrive or leave towns or cities at night.

Other travellers

There is some danger of being robbed by other backpackers, so don't leave things lying unattended in dormitory rooms. Lock them up.

Bandits

There are certain bus routes which are notorious for bandits, particularly the roads from the Central Highlands in Peru to Pucallpa. Check with the local South American Explorers Club for the latest information on safety. Try to avoid travelling these routes, especially at night, if at all possible. Keep your money spread around you in various safe places, so if you are stopped you can get away with handing over only a part of it.

Pickpocketing and casual theft

Pickpockets only target people who have something easy to steal, so keep all valuables stashed away in a money belt and nothing in any pocket that you wouldn't mind losing. Be especially vigilant in crowded places, bus and train stations and markets. Watch out for people approaching you to ask questions, pointing out objects on your clothes, and generally trying to distract you. Don't fall asleep on a beach with your boots beside you, or you will wake up as I did with no shoes. I have heard of money being stolen from a restaurant table, cameras or bags taken from the floor in restaurants, necklaces snatched and watches grabbed through bus windows. If this sounds like an endless list, all the above situations were probably avoidable, but a few seconds of dropping your guard could provide the opportunity for a quick snatch.

Women travellers

Generally speaking travelling in Ecuador, Peru and Bolivia presents few more hazards to women travellers than to men. The dangers of being robbed face all travellers alike and are very real. Women face the additional hassle of unwanted male attention. This is usually harmless and can be avoided to some extent by behaving discreetly and wearing non revealing clothing, by staying in well lit busy public areas and not admitting to being single. There are enough backpackers travelling around to join up with if you get tired of being alone or feel over hassled. Women should take the usual precautions they would at home with regard to their safety and in addition check locally for any specific recommendations about places which are unsafe. The local embassy or consulate should be able to advise you of any danger spots and also will help in the case of emergencies.

Information

Both the British and US governments operate websites advising on security overseas:

UK www.fco.gov.uk/travel
USA //travel.state.gov/travel_warnings.html

Spectacled bear

Experience Argentina before you arrive.

Part Two

Ecuador

Harpy eagle

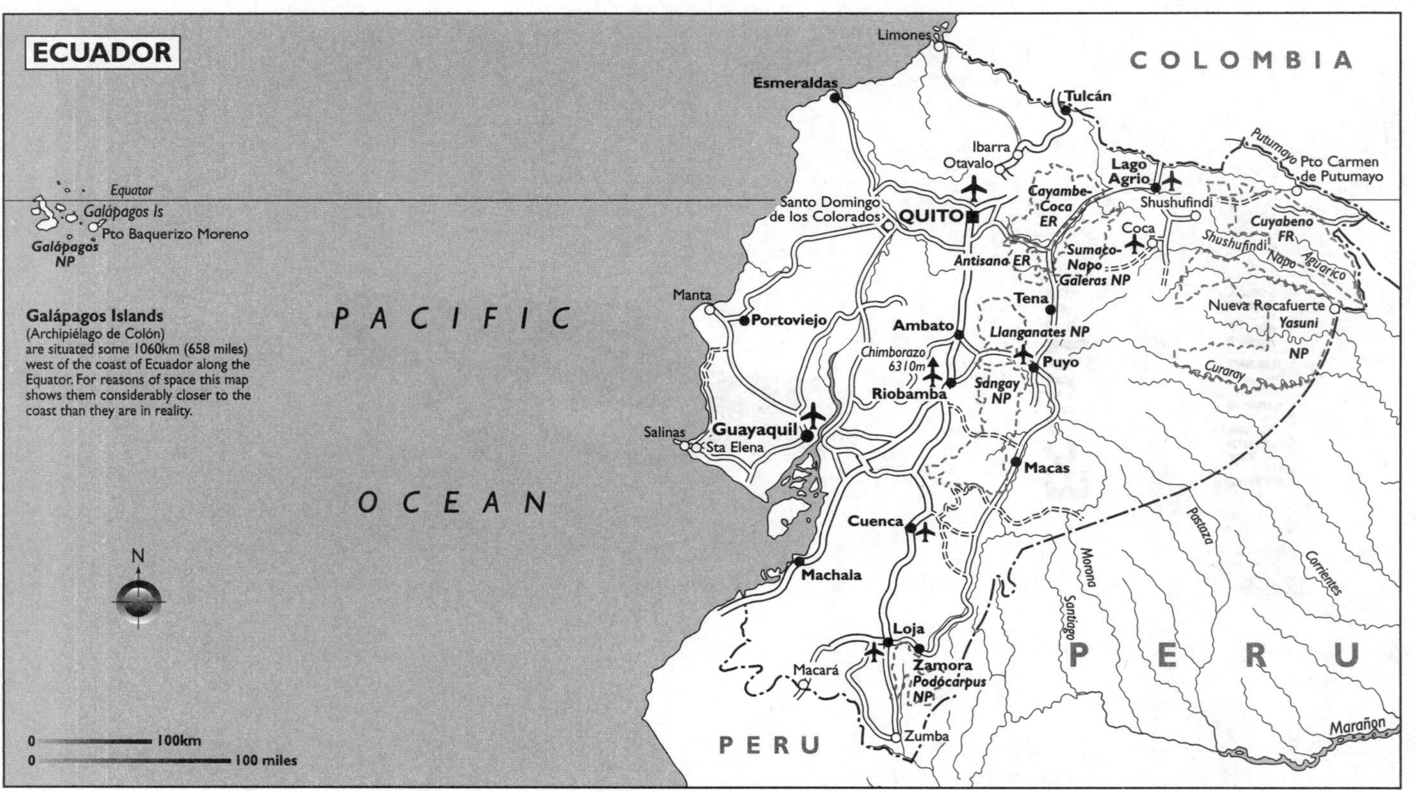
ECUADOR
COLOMBIA
PACIFIC
OCEAN
PERU
PERU
Equator
Galápagos Is
Pto Baquerizo Moreno
Galápagos NP
Galápagos Islands
(Archipiélago de Colón)
are situated some 1060km (658 miles) west of the coast of Ecuador along the Equator. For reasons of space this map shows them considerably closer to the coast than they are in reality.
N
0
100km
0
100 miles
Limones
Esmeraldas
Tulcán
Ibarra
Otavalo
Santo Domingo de los Colorados
QUITO
Cayambe-Coca ER
Lago Agrio
Shushufindi
Coca
Sumaco-Napo Galeras NP
Antisana ER
Putumayo
Pto Carmen de Putumayo
Cuyabeno FR
Shushufindi
Napo
Aguarico
Nueva Rocafuerte
Yasuni NP
Curaray
Manta
Portoviejo
Tena
Ambato
Llanganates NP
Chimborazo 6310m
Puyo
Riobamba
Sangay NP
Salinas
Guayaquil
Sta Elena
Macas
Cuenca
Machala
Pastaza
Morona
Santiago
Corrientes
Loja
Zamora
Podocarpus NP
Macará
Zumba
Marañon

The Country

4

Ecuador is a fascinating country to travel through, with amazing scenic landscapes of snow-capped towering volcanoes, deep Andean valleys, and lush tropical forests. There are fine examples of Spanish colonial architecture and a thriving indigenous culture. Ecuador rarely features prominently in the European press, and other than the world renowned Galápagos Islands, little is heard about it and still relatively few tourists visit. For the backpacker it is generally safe, cheap, and welcoming. Being a small country, it is quick and easy to get around compared with the considerably larger Andean countries of Peru and Bolivia. Unfortunately Ecuador is beset by many seemingly insuperable problems: political instability, economic insecurity and unrest, frequent earthquakes and impending volcanic eruptions, and unpredictable climatic phenomena such as El Niño which can destroy lives, and seriously damage livelihoods and transport infrastructures. All this makes everyday life for Ecuadorians far from easy, and you should be sensitive to the daily problems faced by the people here as you travel around. Fortunately for tourists backpacking isn't often seriously hampered by these problems, and so long as you travel with a bit of extra time and flexibility you should be able fully to appreciate at least a part of the great variety of landscapes, culture and wildlife that Ecuador has to offer.

GEOGRAPHY AND CLIMATE

Ecuador is the smallest of the Andean countries, with only 12 million inhabitants and an area of less than 280,000km². It sits on the Equator, at 0°, and at a longitude of between 77° and 79° west. Ecuador obviously lies within the tropics, but the

FACTS AND FIGURES

Area 270,670km²
Population 12 million
Capital Quito (1.3 million)
Borders To the north Colombia, to the south and east Peru, to the west the Pacific Ocean
Largest city Guayaquil (1.5 million)
Official time GMT –5 hours
Languages Spanish and Quichua; Cofán, Siona, Huaorani, Shuar, Tsáchila are also spoken
Currency Sucre
Head of state Dr Jamil Mahuad

climate of the country is heavily influenced by the presence of the high Andes, which reach over 6,000m in altitude. It can be hard to believe you are in the tropics when you need to wear several layers of warm clothes just to walk around the mountain towns, especially in the evenings.

This is a country of contrasts, the extreme range of climate and relief producing a diversity in animal, plant and human life which is truly amazing. It is one of the most biodiverse countries in South America, and probably in the world. The land area of Ecuador may be small, but there are three very distinct topographical areas: the Pacific coast, the high mountain peaks of the Andes and, on the eastern side of the Andes, the vast lowland area which forms part of the Amazon basin. You could conceivably travel in a day from mangrove forests on the Pacific coast, through tropical lowland dry forest, lowland rainforest, cloudforest, high mountain forest and páramo (high mountain grassland) then down the east side of the Andes through cloudforest to reach the lowland rainforest of the Amazon basin. Being on the Equator means that in Ecuador the days and nights are of equal length, and this is unchanging throughout the year. There are no seasons as such, though there are wetter and drier months. The climate is influenced in each area by the presence of the Andes mountains, the massive Amazon basin or the Pacific Ocean.

Mainland Ecuador is divided into 21 provinces. Esmeraldas, Manabí, Guayas,

Los Ríos and El Oro are in the lowland coastal strip; El Carchi, Imbabura, Pichincha, Cotopaxi, Bolívar, Tungurahua, Chimborazo, Cañar, Azuay and Loja are the Andean provinces; and Sucumbíos, Napo, Pastaza, Morona–Santiago and Zamora–Chinchipe are the lowland Amazon provinces. The other province is the Galápagos Islands.

The coast

The width of the coastal strip varies from 20km in parts of the south, south of Guayaquil, to 180km at its widest in the central area in Guayas and Manabí provinces. It covers 25% of the total land area of Ecuador, and rises from sea-level to a height of around 900m. Much of the coastal area is sedimentary and alluvial and is drained by the River Guayas. This coastal strip is far from flat but is broken up by small ranges of hills running from Esmeraldas southwards. The rivers that make up the Guayas drainage area, which covers 30,000km^2, run southwards flowing into the Pacific in the delta area of Puná Island, off Guayaquil. The northern rivers, which flow off the western slope of the Andes, flow east to west into the Pacific and are mostly tributaries of the River Esmeraldas with its mouth at Esmeraldas or the River Cayapas, which has its mouth at San Lorenzo.

The climate in this coastal area varies, with a hot humid climate in the northern mangrove areas, and a drier hot climate in the south. The average temperature is 25–30°C. On the Santa Elena Peninsula, which has some of the best beaches, the temperatures can be quite fresh, but further inland it gets pretty hot and sticky. January to April is the rainy season on the coast, and in those months it can rain heavily on a daily basis. Travelling can be made impossible by bridges and roads being washed away at this time of year too, particularly in the aftermath of the 1998 El Niño, which has left many roads weakened and bridges replaced with temporary structures.

The Andes

The Andes mountain range runs right through Ecuador from north to south, covering around 24% of the land area. In the north the Andes are characterised by high snow-capped mountains and volcanoes. The range is divided in two, the Cordillera Occidental on the west side and the Cordillera Real on the east, with a high tableland in between. There are some cross ridges between the two cordilleras, which divide the tableland into several broad inter-Andean valleys. Some of these valleys drain west and some east, forming deep gorges in the cordilleras. The high mountain areas, or páramos, between the gorges are El Angel; Imbabura; Cayambe–Antisana–Cotapaxi; Pichincha–Chimborazo; and Tungurahua–Sangay.

The higher peaks from north to south in the Cordillera Occidental are Cotacachi (4,939m), Pichincha (4,794m), which looms over Quito threatening eruption, Illinizas (5,266m), Carihuairazo (5,020m), and Chimborazo (6,310m), Ecuador's highest mountain. In the Cordillera Real from north to south, the peaks are Cayambe (5,790m), Antisana (5,705m), Cotopaxi (5,897m), Tungurahua (5,016m), El Altar (5,320m), and Sangay (5,230m). There are several active volcanoes in Ecuador, the most well known of which is Cotapaxi, one of the highest active volcanoes in the world. In the south there are fewer high peaks, but rather a mass of fragmented lower groups of volcanic hills interspersed by valleys.

Daily temperature fluctuations in the high Andean valleys can be large and frosts are common in August and September. In the north it tends to rain more in January and February than at other times, but the Ecuadorian highland climate is notoriously unpredictable.

The jungle
Below 2,000m on the eastern spurs of the Cordillera Real the tropical rainforest begins. This type of forest extends eastwards covering the foothills and the whole Amazon lowland area of Ecuador. This part of Ecuador is known as the Oriente and covers 40% of the land area of the country. The mini-mountain ranges that descend to the flatter lands of the Amazon basin to the east of the Cordillera Real are Cordillera Galeras in the north; Sierra de Cutucú in the centre; and the Cordillera del Cóndor in the south. The average temperature in the Amazon is 25°C and there is heavy rainfall throughout the year (2,000–6,000mm of annual rainfall), with April to July the wettest months.

The Galápagos
The Galápagos Islands are located almost 1,000km off mainland Ecuador. They consist of 13 islands all of volcanic origin. The islands are on the Equator but experience changing weather throughout the year; the best time to visit is between January and June. The average temperature is around 30°C. Lowland areas tend to be quite dry, whereas the highlands, above 600m are wetter.

HISTORY
Ecuador was first settled in 12,000BC, by people who came from Asia across the Bering Straits. Ecuador may have been one of the last countries to be populated because of the height of the mountains, the danger from volcanic eruptions, and the inhospitable nature of the forests along the coast – both mangrove areas and dry forests. The first inhabitants of Ecuador were hunter-gatherers, who moved around, returning to their settlements on a regular basis for certain seasons of the year.

Formative period
The first permanent and organised settlements were established around 6,000 years ago at the beginning of the formative period (4,000–600BC). Evidence of these settlements has been found by archaeologists, consisting of oval houses encircling extensive squares, together with ceremonial buildings. This is known as the **Valdivia culture**. There is pottery dating from this time, and indications that maize, beans, cotton and cassava were grown for food crops. On the coastal strip the **Machalilla culture** developed. The people survived from hunting, fishing and gathering plants to eat. At this time the coast of Ecuador began to be the nucleus for a network of tribal groups involved in trading all along the Pacific coast, including Peru and Colombia. Communication between different tribal groups became more frequent. Brilliant tropical seashells were traded and became highly prized and valuable items, sought after for their colour and symbolism and used in the manufacture of personal jewels and ceremonial objects. The red-coloured *Spondylus princeps*, widely seen in Inca and pre-Inca artefacts, was the most important shell, and was a symbol of water, fertility and reproduction. In the highlands there were other cultures, the **Chaullabamba**, who farmed alpaca and llamas, and the **Chorrera**, a hierarchical society that produced detailed ceramics. In the Quito area the **Cotocollao** flourished, living in mud thatched huts and farming maize, beans, potatoes, quinua and lupins.

Period of regional development
From 300BC to AD600 there was a time of regional development, in which a marked social structure began to emerge in most tribal groups. Ceremonial centres were built and tribal groups were ruled by a highly prestigious specialised caste.

Some of the early *tolas* (earth pyramids) found throughout Ecuadorian coastal areas, which were used as religious ceremonial centres, date from this time. Ceramics became more complex and artistic and metal was worked into items for personal decoration. The most well-known culture from this time is **La Tolita**. This was a coastal culture, but obviously of influence in the highlands, as pottery and other relics from La Tolita have been found in highland locations. The Tolita culture had a huge ceremonial centre in the island of Tolita, near Esmeraldas, to which people flocked to worship their gods, sharing in religious ceremonies. Gold, silver, stone and ceramic objects originating from this culture show a high degree of skill in workmanship and creativity.

Period of integration

The next period of cultural development has been called the period of integration, from AD600 to AD1534. During this time tribal populations grew, large-scale building and engineering works were carried out, agricultural production increased and there was a corresponding growth in inter-tribal trade. Societies became even more stratified, each social group having just one leader known as a *curaca*. This *curaca* totally controlled his subjects, taking a share of their profits, and organising festivals and meetings at the ceremonial centres. The remains of many ceremonial centres have been found in the northern sierra, the inland coast and on the northwest Andean slopes. Different tribes began to specialise in the production of certain goods. For example, cotton and seashells were exported from Manta and spindle whorls from Manabí. The coastal tribes continued their trade up and down the Pacific coast. They built and used log rafts for trading with other settlements along the coast and other traders from neighbouring countries.

One of the most influential tribes was in the Manabí area. **Salangome** was the lord of the tribe and Agua Blanca the central city. The remains of this city can be seen in Machalilla national park. This tribe exported the valuable spondylus shell, cotton weavings, gold, silver and copper objects and obsidian. In the Guayas area the **Chonos** culture developed, known for its earth pyramids and platforms (*tolas*). Archaeologists have found that the dead were placed in ceramic urns inside the tolas, and many zoomorphically decorated ceramics, and beautifully made gold and silver objects, were placed nearby. Large bamboo rafts are attributed to the Chonos, who used them for extensive travelling to exchange raw materials for luxurious and exotic items. In the highlands the Carchi, Cañari, and Puruhá settled, each culture with its own characteristic way of life. Archaeologists can only guess at the details of their cultures, traditions and beliefs from representations in their ceramics and other objects which have been found.

The Incas

Under the Inca emperor Tupac Yupanqui, who arrived in Ecuador in 1460, many Ecuadorian tribes were conquered and incorporated into the Inca Empire. This conquest took many years because of the fierce resistance from the dominant tribal groups in Ecuador. The Incas built a number of cities to maintain control, including Ingapirca near Cuenca, which is worth a visit, and Tomebamba, which lies under modern day Quito. Tupac Yupanqui had a son while he was in Ecuador, Huayna Capac, who went on to father Huáscar and Atahualpa, the two warring Inca emperors at the time of the Spanish invasion by Pizarro in 1532.

The Spanish Conquest

The Spaniard Sebastián de Benalcázar and his men marched northwards from Peru into Ecuador in 1534 with the intention of conquering Quito. When news reached Quito of the imminent arrival of the conquistadors, Rumiñahui, Atahualpa's general who lived in Quito, decided to destroy the city before the Spaniards could get there. An intense battle won Quito for Benalcázar. This was the first of many bloody battles which followed during the 15 years it took to conquer the territory known now as Ecuador. Thousands of Indians lost their lives and those who lived were forced to submit to the injustices of Spanish rule. As in Peru the *encomienda* and then the *hacienda* systems of farming were introduced. Indians were taken off their own land and in effect given as slaves to a Spanish landlord, for whom they had to work. They, in return, were supposedly given protection, religious education and a tiny plot of land in which to build a home and farm for their own needs. In fact many died from introduced diseases and forced labour. The church played a major role in the subjugation of the indigenous people and the furtherance of colonial power. Jesuit and Franciscan missionaries set off to conquer the Amazon. It wasn't until 1964 that land reforms made some difference to ownership and allowed the indigenous people to reclaim their right to the land. In the early 18th century slaves were imported from Africa to help work the plantations of cocoa on the coastal plains.

Independence

Independence was first proclaimed in Ecuador in 1820. The *criollos*, locally born descendants of the Spanish conquistadors, had had enough of being commanded from Spain, and resented the instant authority given to newly arrived Spaniards in their country. Following Napoleon's invasion of Spain in 1808, in the wake of which Spain tried to tighten its hold on Ecuador, there was a series of uprisings throughout Ecuador. Quito was seized by independence-seeking frustrated *criollos* and royalist troops had to be sent in to restore order and authority amid widespread repression. This only served to further the anger of the *criollos* who instigated more uprisings which culminated in their declaration of independence and a decisive battle, led by José de Sucre on May 24 1882 against the royalist army on the slopes of Pichincha.

The **19th century** was not a peaceful time for newly independent Ecuador as conflicting interests in the three main provinces of the country sparked many a civil war. Quito was in the hands of the Catholic church and conservative landowners. Cuenca was a city of artists, intellectuals and small farmers, of little consequence for the nation's economy and politically not influential. Guayaquil was economically and therefore politically important as the port from which cocoa was exported, and was more in touch with Europe through everyday contact with traders. Many European ideas were adopted and liberal policies sought, such as a change in the *encomienda* system to provide free labour movement and hence more workers on the cocoa plantations. The liberals wanted to remove trade restrictions. The conservatives in Quito felt threatened by any change to the status quo and didn't want imported products undermining their production.

Ecuador was led from 1861 until 1875 by Gabriel García Moreno, an extreme conservative and devout Catholic, who imposed strict religious control and persecuted nonconformists. He was eventually assassinated and, after his party lost power, was replaced by the radical liberal Eloy Alfaro in 1895. A period of economic growth in the 1880s had extended the power of the liberals. Alfaro introduced some far-reaching reforms. He allowed investment from the USA which saw the construction of the Guayaquil to Quito railway. Land owned by the church and not used was expropriated and the power of the church was diminished. Internal fighting amongst the liberals put an end to Alfaro's rule and he was imprisoned and later assassinated by pro-Catholics.

The **20th century** has seen a continuation of political instability with dozens of short-lived presidencies and military juntas. One man, the charismatic Velasco Ibarra, managed to be president no fewer than five times between the 1930s and 1972. In 1904 Ecuador accepted Spanish mediation in its seemingly endless border disputes, resulting in a large tract of Ecuadorian territory being given to Brazil. In 1916 Colombia was given an area of the Amazon, which it promptly traded with Peru for access to the Amazon River. This spelt disaster for Ecuador, giving Peru extensive access to Ecuadorian borders, which it exploited in 1941 in a massive invasion and occupation of Ecuadorian territory. In 1942 the infamous Río de Janeiro Protocol determined that Ecuador lose more than half of its territory to Peru. All maps of Ecuador clearly mark the original and post-Protocol boundary. 1995 saw heavy fighting along the border, and it wasn't until 1998 that a settlement was finally reached between Alberto Fujimori and Jamil Mahuad.

ECONOMY

Until oil became Ecuador's main export in the 1970s the economy was almost entirely based on agriculture. Before the 1950s cocoa was a major export. From the 1950s bananas achieved greater export status, and later, in the 1980s, seafood, particularly shrimps. The export market is small, most products going to the United States. Oil production began in Ecuador in 1925 in the Santa Elena Peninsula on a small scale, originally for national consumption. In 1967 oil reserves were found in the Amazon area and in 1972 the export of oil began, soon becoming Ecuador's greatest export. A pipeline over 500km long takes up to 250,000 barrels a day from the Lago Agrio area of the northern Oriente to the port of Balao, from where it is exported, crude or refined. The health of the Ecuadorian economy is as volatile as international oil prices: fluctuations are frequent and can be disastrous. Large areas of the Oriente have been seriously damaged by the oil industry's lust for money, and successive governments have done little to control or regulate the industry. Widespread misgivings about the environmental damage from oil exploration have seemingly fallen on deaf ears, as little has been done to improve the situation.

In the 1970s Ecuador experienced an annual average growth in GDP of 9.5%, but this dropped to just 2% during the 1980s. The Gulf War in the early 1990s boosted growth temporarily but it soon levelled off to an average of only 3% between 1993 and 1996, and overall an annual fall of 0.3% between 1980 and 1992.

More than half of Ecuador's foreign currency earnings still come from agriculture and fishing. Less than 30% of the workforce is employed in this sector compared with over 60% up until the 1960s. Land ownership, considerably reformed early in the 20th century and further reformed in 1964, still works against the indigenous farmer. From 1964 onwards the theory was that peasant families would have the right to their own plots of land. This did happen to some extent, the *latifundia haciendas* being divided up and distributed amongst *campesinos* (peasant farmers). However, there are still some large landowners who have managed to keep the best estates, and who employ peasant labour, and land distribution remains skewed with a small number of very large farms and a large number of plots almost too small to survive on.

Bananas are Ecuador's second biggest source of export revenue, with most of them handled by a few transnational companies. Shrimp exports are currently third in terms of export revenue, and although there are significant price swings, the general trend is upwards. Coffee is the fourth most important export, but neither the yield nor the quality is high, despite a fifth of all agricultural land being planted with the crop. Cut flowers and *tagua*, from vegetable ivory palms

(*Phytelephas spp*) are also exported and their importance in the share of export earnings is increasing. Tagua used to be used for making buttons, but is now widely used for tourist ornaments and knick-knacks. Chimborazo Province and Manta are the main production centres.

During the 1980s, high interest rates and low oil and agricultural export income forced Ecuador to borrow huge amounts of money from the IMF, much of which was just to meet interest and debt repayments. This has meant drastically low investment in health and education, an employment crisis, and one of the highest per person debts in the world. In 1996 the debt was over US$16 billion, which averages out at over US$1,400 per Ecuadorian. As a result of the economic situation there is an extremely high incidence of poverty in Ecuador. Eight out of every ten Ecuadorians have no access to what are considered to be basic necessities such as food, a house, education, healthcare and other basic services, primarily due to the fact that salaries are incredibly low.

THE PEOPLE

One of the most interesting and surprising facets of modern Ecuador is the cultural diversity of the people. The present population of Ecuador is about half *mestizo*, of Spanish and Indian blood. Around 10% of the population is black, descended from African slaves brought here in the 19th century to work on lowland plantations. The Afroecuadorians, as they have become known, mostly live in the coastal areas of Manabí and Esmeraldas. There has been virtually no intermarriage and they have maintained many of their own cultural roots, particularly in music and dance, and religious beliefs. There is a second concentration of Afroecuadorians in the northern highlands at El Chota.

There are several distinct indigenous groups in Ecuador today. Despite the odds stacked against their survival they have managed to a certain extent, some more than others, to maintain their own cultural identity. There are highland, coastal and jungle indigenous groups. The principal groups in the highlands are the Otavaleños, the Saraguros from the south, and the Cañari from Azuay. In the Oriente the predominant groups are the Cofan and Siona-Secoya from the northern Oriente, the Huaorani from the central part of the Oriente and the Shuar from the southern Oriente. On the coast, there are the Chachi or Cayapas in the north, the Awa, and further south the Tsachilas or Colorados.

NATURAL HISTORY

The coast

The north coast around San Lorenzo and part of the Gulf of Guayaquil are characterised by mangrove forests. Mangroves are evergreen trees with thick leathery leaves, that have adapted to live in salt water. The trees tend to have prop and aerial roots to enable them to breathe in anaerobic mud. The mangrove estuaries are rich in wildlife, home to over 45 bird species, 15 species of reptile, 17 of crustacean and hundreds of species of fish. Typical fish are catfish (*Arius multiradiatus*), sea-bass (*Centropomus robalito*), grouper (*Epinephelus labiformis*), pargo (*Lutjanus spp*), palometa (*Diapterus peruvianus*) and vieja (*Haliochoerres dispilus*). Typical reptiles include the green iguana (*Iguana iguana*), caiman (*Caiman crocodylus*), boa (*Boa constrictor*), and turtle (*Chelydra serpentina*). The following seabirds are commonly seen in coastal mangrove areas: pelicans (*Pelecanus occidentalis*), snowy egret (*Egretta thula*), little blue heron (*Florida caerulea*), anhinga (*Anhinga anhinga*), white-necked heron (*Ardea cocoi*), macaw (*Ara severa*), and parrot (*Amazona farinosa*). Mammals found here include the anteater (*Tamandua mexicana*), the capuchin monkey (*Cebus capucinus*), kinkajou (*Potos flavus*), tayra (*Eira barbara*), ocelot (*Felis *pardalis*), paca (*Agouti paca*) and rabbit (*Sylvilagus brasiliensis*). Above and behind the mangrove forest in the north there are less salty forests, made up of mulberry (*Mora megistosperma*), ferns (*Acrostichum aureum*) and palms (*Euterpe chaunostachys*). The mangrove forests, and local livelihoods, are at risk from large companies clearing the forest to make way for shrimp-farming ponds.

Kinkajou

The central coastal area is influenced by the convergence of the Humboldt current and the warm Panamá current. There are two distinct seasons, wet from January to May and dry from June to December. The only dry tropical forest of South America is found along the coast here with trees that are well adapted to dry conditions and salty soils, such as the carrob, ceibo (*Ceiba trichistandra*) and barbasco, muyuyo, palo santo and several species of cactus. Characteristic of the animal life along this part of the coast are the large scavenging frigate birds, comic blue-footed boobies (*Sula nebouxii*), masked boobies (*Sula dactylatra*) and the huge albatross, and occasional deer and monkeys. The sealife is also plentiful in this area with corals, beautiful fish, sea cucumbers, rays and shellfish, and mammals such as sealions and migrating humpback whales, best seen between June and September. Slightly inland the forest type changes to a more typical rainforest with a rich fauna. The national park of Machalilla including the Isla de la Plata protects this coastal area.

The southern coastal area from the Peruvian border to Guayaquil is very dry and the vegetation is lowland scrub type.

The Andes

Altitude has a major impact on the vegetation of highland Ecuador, which is anything but tropical. The permanent snowline is about 4,700m, above which virtually nothing grows and few birds or insects are seen. Between 3,000m and the snowline, is the zone known as páramo, usually a steppe-type grassland. The typical vegetation is of bunch grass (*Stipa ichu*) and other plants which have learned to adapt to the harsh highland conditions. They are generally xerophytic, similar to the plants found on the Bolivian and Peruvian altiplano, small and compact, close to the ground and with thick waxy leaves. The most notable exception to this is the frailejón (*Espeletia pycnophylla*). Typical of the northern páramo this plant can grow up to 7m tall. The best place to see it is at the Reserva Ecológica El Angel. The *Puya raimondii* is another impressive and unusual looking plant found growing in the páramo. A member of the pineapple family (*Bromeliaceae*), it grows up to 12m tall, with pineapple like spiky leaves on a thick stem with a tall flowerhead. There are few trees at this altitude

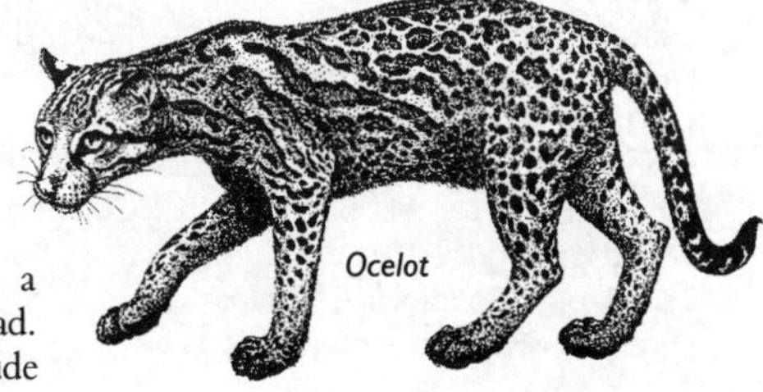
Ocelot

THE MOUNTAIN TAPIR

Craig C Downer

Many trekkers in the northern Andes are unaware that their paths have crossed those of one of the Earth's most ancient and mysterious, as well as currently endangered, animals. Yet the presence of these animals is crucial to the northern Andean cloudforest and páramo. In fact, the mountain tapir may be considered a living fossil, since tapir-like animals date back to the Cenozoic period, some 60 million years ago. Indeed, palaeontologists consider the mountain tapir to be the least changed of earth's four extant species of tapir (but a tiny remnant of this once cosmopolitan family). In whatever natural habitat, tapirs act as important seed dispersers; and the mountain tapir is no exception. My field observations and faecal germination experiments during the past decade have amply proven this point, a logical one due to the eons during which tapirs and the plants they eat and seed have co-evolved.

Common ancestors of the mountain tapir, as well as the Brazilian tapir (*Tapirus terrestris*), are believed to have first entered South America about 3 million years ago, when the isthmus of Panama again united central with South America. Since this time, the mountain tapir and the Brazilian tapir probably parted ways to form two separate species within the same genus, according to a recent genetic analysis by Dr Mary Ashley at the University of Chicago.

Typically mountain tapirs have been reported between 1,400 and 4,700 metres elevation; from lower, mid-elevation cloudforests through dwarf, or elfin forests to the treeless, tundra forest like páramo and even in to the alpine meadow zones atop páramo. Individuals have been documented ascending snowbanks on Sangay volcano, lending further mystery as to why. As with many other tropical species, tapirs supplement their mineral intake by visiting salt licks and seeps and this may provide one reason for the tapir's ascent of Sangay, whose volcanic oozings are full of minerals.

In addition to being an excellent climber, the mountain tapir loves water and is an excellent swimmer. During the past decade, I have observed it swim up rapidly flowing rivers and into the middle of large, cold Andean lakes, even at elevations of 4,000m. A mountain tapir may use water to bathe and play, squirting water with its prehensile proboscis, either at another tapir or to clean itself. When attacked, it also squirts water at its natural predators, the puma and spectacled bear, as well as at the hunting dogs that are usually employed to kill it. Its versatile trunk is proportionally shorter than that of an elephant, but equally important for its survival. This is used to sniff, reach out and grab leaves and fruit, in courtship, in rearing of young, and counts among the primary reasons for the tapir's evolutionary success. Using powerful mandibles and sharp teeth, including upper incisors and canines, an adult tapir (160kg on average, around 1m tall and 2m long and with dark brown to coal-black, dense and woolly fur) can inflict mortal wounds upon its attackers. Generally it is a peaceful mountaineer, solitary in its habits, that distributes its grazing pressure judiciously over a large home range.

The three adults I tracked in Sangay National Park for three years showed an average home range of 880 hectares. From this I conservatively calculated that for a minimally viable population of 1,000 adults, an area of 293,500 hectares would be required. The mountain tapir's home range is composed mostly of contiguous cloudforest, vital as shelter, but also includes extensive, open páramos, which are more occupied during the warmer, dry seasons, when biting insects pester the tapirs at lower elevations. It is only by preserving the mountain tapir in adequately sized areas that inbreeding will be prevented and an exuberant population again come to grace the land.

The large areas mountain tapirs require make them a 'flagship species' of the first order for the mid to high elevation northern Andes. If viable populations of this species can be preserved, so can a host of associated plants and animals, from the dwarf pudu deer to the giant Quindean wax palm which is seeded through the faeces of the mountain tapir. In my study area of Culebrillas to the west of Sangay volcano I found mountain tapirs to consume 205 of the 264 vascular species present, of which nearly a third of those present were observed (either in experiments or in the field) to successfully germinate from the faeces. These data clearly establish the mountain tapirs as a major seed disperser in the northern Andes, and, according to my statistical analyses, substantiate the symbiotic relationship existing between the mountain tapir and the Andean cloudforests and páramo it calls home. In this highland paradise the mountain tapir has co-evolved along with the geological recent rise of the Andes themselves during these past 2–3 million years.

It is estimated that less than 2,500 mountain tapirs remain as sparsely scattered individuals in cloudforest and páramo habitats that are being increasingly fragmented by roads, slash and burn agriculture, overhunting, livestock and rampant human colonisation of all remaining wilderness. As a consequence, individual tapirs are having a hard time forming reproductively viable populations, and there is only one species on earth, it appears, that can help them: us. Paradoxically, by helping them, we shall also be helping ourselves.

The highland cloudforests and páramos, home to mountain tapirs, constitute 'living sponges' of vital importance to all organisms living below them. This abundantly proven fact makes mountain tapir survival a vital concern for all co-evolving species, including humanity. When the intact, highland aquifers are destroyed by human activity, catastrophic floods and droughts result, precious soil is eroded and regional climates are destabilised. This trend has reached its tragic culmination in vast desertified stretches along the Andean cordilleras, as well as in similar abused mountains the world over.

Places where Andean trekkers can view the mountain tapir, following their distinctive three-hoofed tracks and looking for black, furry shadows with white lip and ear fringes and distinctive Roman profile: In **Ecuador**: The Reserva Ecológica El Angel, Reserva Ecológica Cotacachi–Cayapas, Reserva Ecológica Cayambe–Coca, Parque Nacional Sumaco–Napo, Parque Nacional Antisana, Parque Nacional Llangantes, Parque Nacional Sangay, Parque Nacional Podocarpus: In **Peru**: Reserva Ecológica Tabaconas–Namballe, Cordillera Las Lagunillas, Cordillera del Condor.

Should your path cross that of the mountain tapir (legally protected in or out of parks in Peru, Ecuador and Colombia), please relay any information concerning geographical location and numbers, behaviour, illegal killings, trade in hooves and snout as folklore medicine, or in pelts or meat, or consumption, as well as mountain tapir habitat destruction, especially within protected areas, to: Craig C Downer, President, Andean Tapir Fund, PO Box 456, Minden, NV 89423, email: ccdowner@olemail.com Further information on tapirs will gladly be provided and donations (tax deductible) are much needed to implement an action plan Downer has written for the IUCN Species Survival Commission for saving the admirable mountain tapir and its beautiful and ecologically vital habitats.

Red brocket deer

but you will find scattered woods of the red barked quinual (*Polylepis spp*). Animal life is sparse at these altitudes and what little there was, has been further reduced by hunting. You are most likely to see birds such as the Andean condor (*Vultur gryphus*), and other birds of prey such as the great horned owl (*Bubo virginianus*), puna hawk (*Buteo poecilochrus*), short-eared owl (*Asio flammeus*) barn owl (*Tyto alba*), caracara (*Phalcoboenus carunculatus*), aplomado falcon (*Falco femoralis*), and American kestrel (*Falco sparverius*). Other birds typical of the *páramo* are the brown-bellied swallow (*Notiochelidon murina*), Andean lapwing (*Vanellus resplendens*), Chimborazo hillstar (*Oreotrochillus estella*), buff-necked ibis (*Theristicus caudatus*) and speckled teal (*Anas flavirostris*). There are some resident mammals, but it is unlikely that you will see them unless you spend considerable time and have endless patience. The mammals there are include the white-tailed deer (*Odocoileus virginianus*), the rare red brocket deer (*Mazama americana*) and dwarf pudu (*Pudu mephistophiles*), the elusive puma (*Felis concolor*) the fox known as Andean wolf (*Dusicyon culpaeus*), the rare mountain tapir (*Tapirus pinchaque*), and the wide-ranging spectacled bear (*Tremarctos ornatus*).

BIRDWATCHING

Millions of years of evolution have created an ornithological paradise in Ecuador. There is immense variety of microclimates and vegetation types found in the river valleys, mountain and coastal areas of Ecuador, which are home to over 1,600 bird species.

The **coast** of Ecuador is relatively easily accessible from Quito, though you may need to hire a canoe to get to the most interesting areas. The best places for birds are Puerto Bolívar, 6km from Machala and easily accessible by dugout canoe from the port; Manglares Churute Ecological Reserve near Guayaquil, best visited on a day trip from the city through a travel agent; Punta Carnero and Ecuasal Lagoons, 20km from Santa Elena, west of Guayaquil; Machalilla National Park and Isla de la Plata, which are easily accessible from the coastal town of Machalilla; and the Mache-Chindul Reserve, which is not easy to visit except by boat on a day trip from San Lorenzo.

The **dry tropical forests** of the lowland coastal strip in southern Ecuador are rich in birdlife and easily accessible. Some of the better places are the Puyango petrified forest, 120km from Machala; Catacocha, 100km from Macará; Cerro Blanco, very near to Guayaquil; and Machalilla National Park.

Little remains of the **lowland rainforest**, which once covered large tracts of the western slopes of the Andes, as this usually rich soil has made it ideal for farming cattle and for banana, African palm or cocoa plantations. There are a few reserves that protect the remaining areas of lowland rainforest, including the Reserva Río Palenque, between Santo Domingo de los Colorados and Quevedo. You can stay in accommodation on the reserve. At the Reserva La Perla near La Concordia camping is possible, or you can stay in La Concordia. Reserva Jatun Sacha Bilsa near Quinindé has accommodation on the reserve.

The **cloudforests** of Ecuador are mostly intact and provide excellent opportunities for birding. Several of Ecuador's national parks have extensive areas of protected cloudforest, and there are also several private reserves. Try

The Oriente

The wet lowlands of the eastern part of Ecuador, known as the Oriente, are covered with tropical rainforest. On the eastern slopes of the Andean foothills there is upland forest known as *Tierra firme*, which has the most plant species per area of any of the world's forests. There are 1,600 species of bird in Ecuador, of which many are found in this sort of forest, where the upper edge of the Amazon basin and the foothills of the Andes meet. At higher altitudes the forests are dense, rich in lichens, mosses, orchids and bromeliads. In the lowland Amazon basin itself much of the forest is flooded for large parts of the year. Periodically inundated forest is known as *Varzea*. Flooding can be caused by silt-laden rivers, which originate in the highlands, overflowing their banks and depositing nutrient rich sediments. This enhances vegetation. Alternatively flooding can be by nutrient poor waters originating in the lowlands, often known as black water because of its dark colour caused by fallen leaves. Not many species can cope with long term flooding of this type, so these areas are less species rich. Permanently flooded forest is known as *Igapó*. In the most severely flooded forest one tree species dominates, the Morete palm (*Mauritia flexuoso*). The variety of bird and animal life in the Oriente is tremendous. Typical animals of this terrain include the dwarf deer (*Pudu mephistophiles*) and the spectacled bear (*Tremarctos ornatus*) in the higher forests, and jaguar (*Panthera onca*), puma (*Felis concolor*), ocelot (*Felis pardalis*), tapir (*Tapirus*

the following: Bosque Protector Mindo-Nambillo, 80km from Quito, with lodges in the forest or basic accommodation in the town. There is a reserve office in Mindo, run by Amigos de la Naturaleza. Reserva Cotacachi-Cayapas is accessible from San Miguel on the western side; Parque Nacional Sangay is accessible from Macas or Baños, with mountain huts or camping. Reserva Cayambe-Coca has difficult access from most areas; there are some cabins or camping is possible. Parque Nacional Podocarpus is accessible from Vilcabamba or Loja by day trip or you can camp in the park. Reserva Pasochoa, close to Quito, is easily accessible and has accommodation.

At high altitude you find the **páramos**, consisting of grasses and some shrubs and low lying plants. Most of the birds are found in small gullies, which are sheltered from the harsh climate and offer some vegetation. The best places to visit are Cotopaxi National Park, accessible from Quito, with camping possible; Antisana Reserve, also accessible from Quito with camping possible; Cayambe-Coca Reserve, access from Cayambe, camping possible; Sangay National Park; the Ilinizas area, 60km south of Quito and accessible from Machachi – you need to camp; El Cajas National Park, easily accessible from Cuenca, for a day trip or longer – refuge or camping possible; and Papallacta Pass, easily accessible from Quito (60km) and where camping is possible. There are hot springs and hostels in the village of Papallacta.

The Amazon **rainforests** are a must for anyone interested in birding in Ecuador. There are several parks, which although not readily accessible, are well worthwhile visiting for the amazing variety of wildlife. In most cases you will need to join a tour. The Cuyabeno Reserve has lodges or camping is possible – join a tour. The area of the Napo River including the Jatun Sacha Reserve, La Selva lodge, Sacha lodge and Yuturi, which are all privately owned reserves, again requires a tour, except for Jatun Sacha, which is accessible by road from Tena. There is also the Pastaza River area including Macas and the Kapawi lodge – from Macas take a tour.

terrestris), agouti (*Dasyprocta spp*), and several species of monkey in the lower forests. Despite the wealth of fauna most animals are shy and frightened of humans, so they are almost impossible to spot, even on a specialised tour with expert local guides.

Protected areas

Ecuador has a total of 25 officially protected areas including nine national parks, listed below, and biological, ecological, geo-botanical and fauna reserve areas. They are administered by INEFAN (Instituto Ecuatoriano Forestal de Areas Naturales y Vida Silvestre). INEFAN is a department of the Ministry of Agriculture, whose central office is in Quito, 8th floor, Calle Amazonas and Eloy Alfaro; tel 02 548 924. It has extensive information on all the protected areas, a comprehensive bookshop and library open to the public, and also sells entry permits to the parks (US$10–20).

Protected area	*Date established*	*Province*
Parque Nacional Cajas	1996	Azuay
Parque Nacional Cotopaxi	1975	Cotopaxi
Parque Nacional Galápagos	1936	Galápagos
Parque Nacional Llanganantes	1996	Tungurahua, Cotapaxi and Napo
Parque Nacional Machalilla	1979	Manabí
Parque Nacional Podocarpus	1982	Loja and Zamora Chinchipe
Parque Nacional Sangay	1979	Tungurahua, Chimborazo, Morona, Santiago and Cañar
Parque Nacional Sumaco Napo-Galeras	1994	Napo
Parque Nacional Yasuní	1979	Napo

PRACTICAL INFORMATION

Accommodation

Finding accommodation in Ecuador is not a problem. The cities all have a range of accommodation to choose from, generally at a very reasonable price. Popular tourist destinations like Quito, Cuenca, Riobamba, Vilcabamba and Otavalo in the mountains, Guayaquil, Atacames, Manta and Salinas on the coast and Lago Agrio and Tena in the jungle all have good backpackers' hostels for just a few dollars a night. Even in small non-touristy places there is usually a choice of places to stay, even though they may be pretty basic. The prices are cheap, even cheaper than in Peru or Bolivia, and the standard tends to be good. A hotel will cost you around US$8 a night with private bathroom, and a *residencial*, *hostal*, *pensión*, *hospedaje* or *casa familiar* will be from as little as US$3 a night. These tend to be better value for money than in Peru and Bolivia and cleaner, with fewer water problems. Most of Ecuador's cities, other than Quito and Guayaquil, are small, so it's easy to wander around and check out a few places. It is a good idea to have a lockable bag for your valuables and not to leave valuables lying around the room – at least pack them at the bottom of a rucksack out of sight. Generally speaking you don't have to book accommodation in advance, but if you are travelling during carnival it is wise to book ahead.

Books, newspapers and maps

There are several daily papers including *Hoy*, *El Comercio* and *El Tiempo* in Spanish. International papers are difficult to get hold of outside Quito. Quito has a couple of good bookshops, some of which sell books in English: Libri Mundi and Libri Express (see page 69).

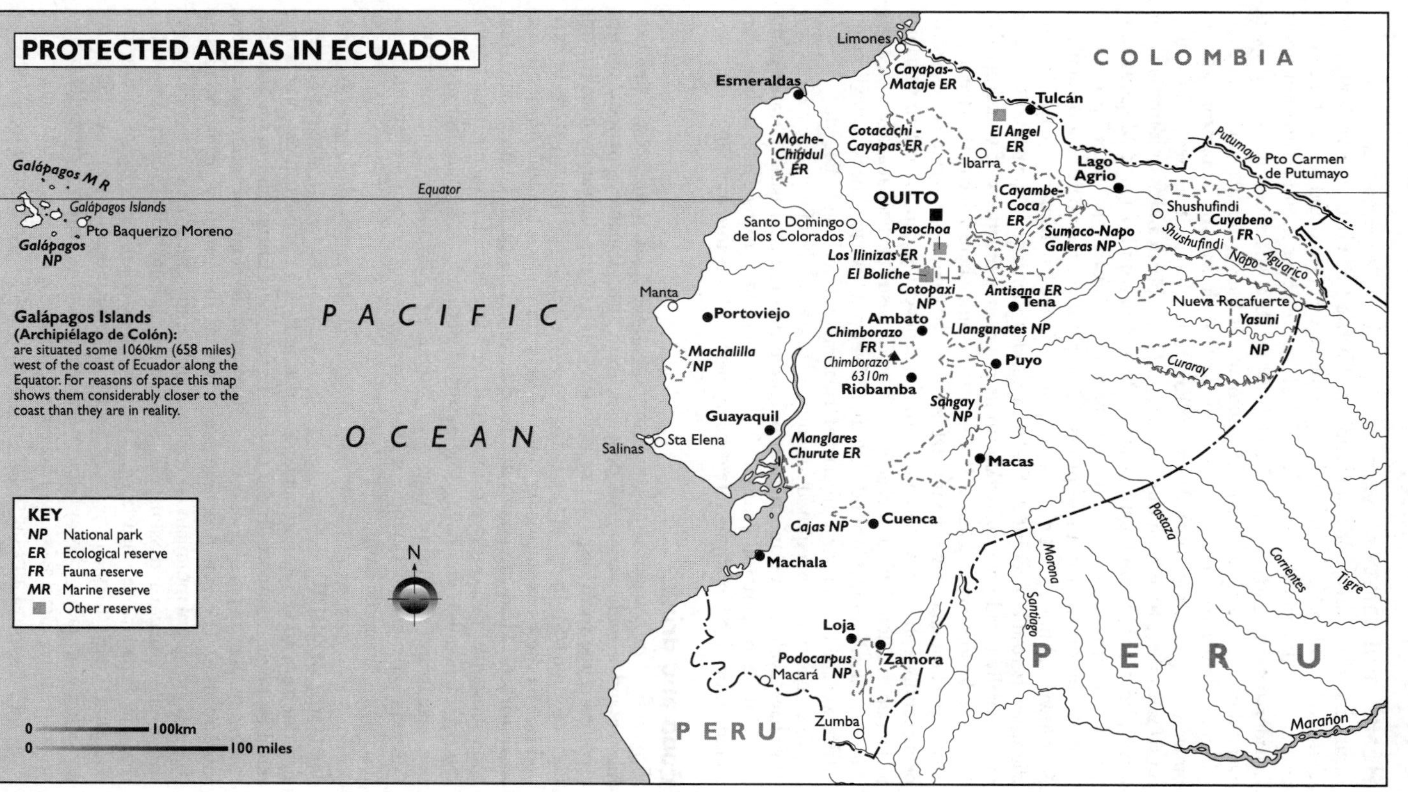
PROTECTED AREAS IN ECUADOR
Galápagos M R
Equator
Galápagos Islands
Pto Baquerizo Moreno
Galápagos NP
Galápagos Islands (Archipiélago de Colón):
are situated some 1060km (658 miles) west of the coast of Ecuador along the Equator. For reasons of space this map shows them considerably closer to the coast than they are in reality.
KEY
NP National park
ER Ecological reserve
FR Fauna reserve
MR Marine reserve
Other reserves
0 100km
0 100 miles
N
PACIFIC
OCEAN
COLOMBIA
PERU
PERU
Limones
Esmeraldas
Cayapas-Mataje ER
Tulcán
El Angel ER
Ibarra
Moche-Chindul ER
Cotacachi - Cayapas ER
Putumayo
Pto Carmen de Putumayo
Lago Agrio
Cayambe-Coca ER
QUITO
Pasochoa
Santo Domingo de los Colorados
Sumaco-Napo Galeras NP
Shushufindi
Cuyabeno FR
Shushufindi
Napo
Aguarico
Los Ilinizas ER
El Boliche
Cotopaxi NP
Antisana ER
Tena
Manta
Portoviejo
Ambato
Chimborazo FR
Chimborazo 6310m
Riobamba
Llanganates NP
Nueva Rocafuerte
Yasuní NP
Curaray
Puyo
Machalilla NP
Sangay NP
Guayaquil
Salinas
Sta Elena
Manglares Churute ER
Macas
Cajas NP
Cuenca
Machala
Pastaza
Morona
Santiago
Corrientes
Tigre
Loja
Podocarpus NP
Zamora
Macará
Zumba
Marañon

Health and safety

In my experience Ecuador is a friendly and hassle free place to travel, but crime seems to be bad in Guayaquil and on the increase in Quito and some of the other cities. This is probably a reflection of the dire economic situation most Ecuadorians have to live in. Watch out for bag snatchers and pickpockets everywhere but particularly in old Quito and at bus terminals. The other most common theft I have come across is theft of whole bags or items from bags in buses. Check with the South American Explorers Club for the latest information on safety as there have been numerous reports of robbery and assault from two or three places, for example particular streets of Guayaquil, Laguna Mojanda near Otavalo and the slopes of Pichincha near Quito. Attempts are being made to improve the situation in these places. Esmeraldas, on the coast, is a particularly poor town and not a good place to hang around in, even during the day. I had my bag stolen here at knifepoint at 15.00 on a Sunday afternoon in the main Plaza. You can generally avoid potentially dangerous places and situations. If you don't feel comfortable somewhere, leave. If you arrive somewhere after dark, take a taxi. Taxis are cheap and you are vulnerable when carrying all you own, so it's worth being cautious and only costs a little extra. Whenever you can, leave your valuables locked up in a hotel safe or lockable bag. You can usually check luggage in at a bus station, so don't wander around with more than you have to. Check at the Foreign Office website for the latest official information on travelling to Ecuador.

No vaccinations are required for entry into Ecuador, but for jungle regions you must have a yellow fever inoculation and protection against malaria. Because of the high altitude of parts of Ecuador, it is recommended that people with a heart condition or high blood pressure consult their doctor before travelling.

Food and drink

Typical food in Ecuador is based on seafood on the coast, shrimp, crab, shellfish, lobster and a wide variety of delicious fresh fish. Bananas, potatoes, or rice accompany the main dish. Maize is widely eaten in the highlands, usually with meat of some sort. In the jungle meals are often fish or chicken based. As in Peru and Bolivia there is a surprising range of fresh fruit juices, available most often at local markets. There are good value fixed menus at lunch and dinner, when you get a substantial two or three course meal for a few thousand sucres. Don't drink the tap water unless you have some means of sterilising it, and sterilise any water you take from streams or lakes while trekking. The main towns of Quito, Guayaquil, Baños and Cuenca, at least, have good coffee bars and international restaurants to choose from.

Getting around

Ecuador has a good transport network, and as in Peru and Bolivia most local people travel by public transport. In the eastern region, the Oriente, and in the southern mountains, the topography and lack of economic development mean there is less infrastructure. The Pan American highway runs the length of Ecuador, passing through the central mountainous regions. Other important roads connect Guayaquil with Quito, Cuenca and Salinas. These roads are asphalted, while most of the other roads in Ecuador are unsurfaced. There is an extensive network of private bus companies with frequent services to most destinations. There are still some periodically operating railways, the most well known of which is from Riobamba down past the Devil's Nose. These lines, primarily kept open for tourism, are frequently closed as a result of landslides on the lines. Guayaquil and Quito have international airports, and there are many small airfields, and landing strips in the jungle towns. The principal port is Guayaquil. Other important ports are at Esmeraldas, Manta, and Puerto Bolivár. In the Amazon region, Napo, Coca and Pastaza are important for river traffic. La Libertad and Balao are the main ports for oil.

By road

Public buses are the most popular form of transport except in remote jungle areas where there are no roads and boats are used. There are frequent bus services to most destinations, and the distances are not nearly so great as in Peru or Bolivia, so it takes a relatively short time to get from the coast to the mountains, and from there to the jungle. However, the roads are not in good condition, and especially during the rainy season landslides can cause road closures, which may not be cleared for several days. In the aftermath of the El Niño of 1998 many roads are still weak and have only been temporarily repaired. In the 1999 rainy season this meant many more bridges and roads washed away than normal. Don't be surprised if you have to scramble over landslides, wade through rivers or climb out of a bus window to continue your journey.

Buses generally leave on time, from the bus terminals, usually at the edge of most towns and cities. It is rarely necessary to buy your ticket more than an hour or so in advance. Bus stations, particularly at night, are not safe, especially in the larger cities, so be extra vigilant with your bags. Even once you are on the bus make sure you keep a tight hold of your bag. For short distances, there are smaller buses, which leave from the bus terminals or the main streets in the town.

Taxis in Ecuador are very cheap. They are usually metered, but make sure the meter is turned on or negotiate a price with the driver before getting into the car.

By rail

For the first 50 years of the 20th century trains were widely used, both for cargo and passengers. Now, the only train lines that operate in Ecuador are primarily for tourists. There is a train from Ibarra to San Lorenzo on the coast, which is often not running because of landslides. There is also a train between Riobamba and Guayaquil, and between Quito and Riobamba.

By boat

Both along the coast and in the Oriente boats are used to get around. See page 103.

By air

SAETA (tel: 593 2 542148) operate international flights from and to Ecuador and also some domestic flights. SAN and TAME operate domestic flights (see page 68). SAN and SAETA fly between Quito, Guayaquil, Cuenca, and San Cristobal in the Galápagos. TAME fly from Quito to Guayaquil, Cuenca, Esmeraldas, Manta, Portoviejo, Tulcan, Loja, Baltra island in the Galápagos, Lago Agrio, Coca, Macas, and Tarapoa. They also fly from Guayaquil to Quito, Cuenca, Machala, Loja and Baltra island.

There is no domestic airport tax, but international departure tax is US$25 per person.

Money

The currency in Ecuador is the sucre. Tourists often have to pay more for hotels, train journeys etc than the local people. Dollars are not widely accepted. The exchange rate fluctuates, and inflation is high enough to make it worth not changing too much cash into local currency at one time. Credit cards are becoming increasingly popular and can be used in the cities at some hotels and restaurants.

Post, telephone and email

The international code for Ecuador is 593. Quito is 02, Guayaquil 04 and Cuenca 07. Other codes are included in the relevant chapters. There are telephone offices in all the towns, which are usually open daily until 22.00. Post is not always reliable in Ecuador. Email is becoming increasingly common, and many larger companies can be accessed through it. There are Internet cafés in most larger towns, and dozens of them in Quito.

Business hours

Business hours are Mon–Fri 09.00–13.00 and 14.00–18.30. Sat 08.30–14.00. Banks are open Mon–Fri 09.00–13.30.

Public holidays

1 January	New Year's Day
End of February	Carnival
April	Holy Thursday , Good Friday and Easter Sunday
1 May	Labour Day
24 May	Anniversary of the Battle of Pichincha
Last Friday in June	Bank Holiday
24 July	Simon Bolívar Day
10 August	Independence Day
9 October	Independence of Guayaquil Day (Guayaquil only)
12 October	Dia de la Raza
2 November	Memorial Day/All Souls Day
3 November	Independence of Cuenca Day
6 December	Independence of Quito Day
25 December	Christmas Day
31 December	New Year's Eve

Tourist information offices

There are tourist information offices in most towns, which tend to be friendly and helpful, but which generally have very little in the way of resources. Their addresses are given in the relevant chapters.

GIVING SOMETHING BACK

Volunteer work

If you are interested in voluntary work in Ecuador, there are many possibilities. However, the minimum time and special skills required vary, so finding something to suit you is not necessarily quick or easy. The best way to find out about suitable organisations is to contact the South American Explorers Club. Some contacts are included below.

With people

Centro de Hospedería Campesina La Tola Valparaiso 887 and Don Bosco, Quito; tel: 581312. The director is Padre Pio Baschirotto, and the centres throughout Ecuador offer shelter and education to children.

Centro del Muchacho Trabajador (CMT) Av Pichincha and Pedro Fermin Cevallos, Quito; tel: 519044; fax: 493462. Two centres in Quito that offer technical education to children and teenagers. Minimum stay one year.

Defensa de Niños Internacional Inglaterra 1351, Quito; tel: 244729; fax: 598375/435294; email: dni@accessinter.net

Morning Star Foundation work with street children; tel: 232039 or 223328.

Movimiento de Educación Popular e Integral Fe y Algeria Av Mariana de Jesus 2307 and Marten de Utters, Quito; tel: 255015; fax: 255482; email: falegria@uio.satnet.net Many centres throughout Ecuador that have education programmes for children.

Plan Internacional Calle Mosque 378 and Av Republic de El Salvador, Quito; tel: 4426971/441496; fax: 435355; email: cecuado@plan.geis.com Work on social programmes with children.

Project Salesman Chikusa de la Calle Torque 305 and 12 de Octubre; tel: 223605; fax: 228330. All sorts of work with children.

Confederación de Nacionalidades Indigenas de Ecuador Av de Los Granados 2553 and Av 6 de Diciembre; tel: 248930; fax: 442271; email: conaie@ecuanex.net.ec Legal advice, health and education work.

Fundación Ecuatoriana del Habitat Pedro de Texelra 273; tel: 213334; fax: 471394; email: funhabit@hotmail.com Work skills, small businesses support and recycling programmes.

Fundación Niñez y Vida (Fundación Tierra de Hombres) Contact Mikhaelde Souza; tel: 550499; email: futierra@pi.pro.ec or futierra@ecnet.ec Medical, educational, social and legal programmes with children.

Fundación Pedro Vicente Maldonado Malecón 412 and Tomas Martinez, 3rd floor, Guayaquil; tel: 04 303123; fax: 307360; email: fpvm2@fpvm.org.ec Education and work skills programmes.

Iglesia Don Bosco Calle Valparaiso and Don Bosco, Guardería Maria Auxiliadora; tel: 510349. School for poor children up to 8 years old.

Environmental

Acción Ecológica Calle La Gasca, Casilla 17-15-246-C; tel: 547516; email: verde@hoy.net Involved in the collection and maintenance of information on ecology and the environment.

Centro Investigaciones Bosques Tropicales Tel: 540346; fax: 221324. Work on environmental projects, and need biologists, botanists and natural scientists.

Cerro Golondrinas Cloudforest Conservation Project Isabel La Católica 1559; tel: 226602 (Casa Eliza); email: manteca@uio.satnet.net; web: www.ecuadorexplorer.com/golondrinas. (See box on page 68.)

Fundación Antisana Mariana de Jesús and Martin de Utreras, Quito; tel/fax: 433851; email: Funan@ecuanex.net.ec They work on conservation of Antisana Park.

Fundación Jatun Sacha Tel/fax 441592; email: jatsacha@jsacha.ecuanex.net.ec or info@jatunsacha.org Opportunities to volunteer at one of three centres, research, education, community service, station maintenance, agroforestry etc.

Fundación Maquipucuña Baquerizo 238 and Tamayo, Quito; tel: 507200/507202; fax: 507201; email: fjusticia@aurora.net Volunteers needed on this reserve north of Quito for reforestation, organic gardening, trail building, teaching English, environmental education.

Fundación Natura Río Guayas 105 and Av Amazonas; tel: 242758/457253; fax: 434449. Promotes environmental awareness and education, working with a range of organisations.

Fundación pare el Desarollo Alternativo (FUNDEAL) Reina Victoria 1227 and Calama, Quito; tel: 507284/507208; fax: 507245; email: fundeal@pi.pro.ec Foundation that works with indigenous communities to support alternative development, and is concerned with research and conservation of nature. Requires volunteers with experience. Also organises 5 day nature and culture tours to the Choco Lodge.

Fundación Pro-Bosque KM 17 Via a La Costa, Guayaquil; tel: 04 871900/873100; fax: 04 873236. Works to protect the dry tropical forest of the Cerro Blanco Reserve.

Fundación Pro-Pueblo KM 17 Via la Costa, Guayaquil; tel: 04 901195/901208.; fax: 04 901195. Operates an education programme around Manglaralto.

Fundación Yawa Jee Calle Oriente and Eloy Alfaro, Baños; tel/fax: 03 740757; email:

yawajee@gye.satnet.net An indigenous foundation managed by Shuar Indians to conserve the culture and ecology of the Yawa Jee Reserve. Needs experienced volunteers.
Nature Conservancy 12 de Octubre 394; tel/fax: 565171; email: utr@q.tnc.org.ec They work in the Antisana Reserve and Cayambe-Coca to conserve biodiversity.
Río Muchacho Environmental school and farm near Bahía de Caraquez; tel: 05 691412/690597/398255; email: ecopapel@ecuadorexplorer.com Teaching, construction, tree planting, gardening and farming.
Sociedad de la Defensa de la Naturaleza Pasaje San Luis; tel: 447922/342813. Promotes the protection of nature.

Quito

Quito is a large, lively city of 1,350,000 inhabitants, at 2,850m above sea-level. It's popular with tourists, who are well catered for, particularly in the newer end of town where there are dozens of hostels and hotels of all standards, cafés and bars, Internet cafés, restaurants, museums and cinemas, shopping centres and all the other amenities of a modern city. The streets of the new town really come alive in the evenings, with pavement cafés and street sellers offering all sorts of clothing, art and typical crafts. Many come to Quito to study Spanish at one of the numerous language schools. There is a thriving nightlife and around the city there are great opportunities for all sorts of outdoor activities, from birdwatching to mountain biking. The old nucleus of Quito is historically interesting with a high concentration of colonial buildings and some particularly amazing churches. It is beautiful to wander around, and during the day is a busy commercial centre, while at night it is very quiet. Be careful of your belongings in this part of town particularly, as pickpockets are rife. Quito in general has become less safe in recent years, and it is particularly advisable to stay away from parks and take taxis after dark.

Quito is set in the province of Pichincha amidst the spectacular mountains that make up the Valley of the Volcanoes. The city has grown in an elongated form, 30km from north to south and just 3–5km across from east to west. Its width is restricted by the steep slopes of the volcano of Pichincha (4,747m) to the west and the deep river valley of the Machángara to the east. The temperature in Quito, which is just 13km south of the Equator, is quite comfortable, usually around 13°C, with warm days and cooler evenings. It tends to rain daily between December and March but the rest of the year is generally sunny.

HISTORY

Quito was founded on December 6 1534 by Sebastián de Benalcázar. Before Spanish occupation Quito was the seat of Atahualpa, one of the last of the Inca lords, who was murdered by the Spanish conquistadors as he marched south to Cusco. When the Spanish reached the city they found that the Incas had destroyed it, leaving only heaps of stones in place of magnificent temples. The land was divided amongst the conquistadors, who proceeded to construct some very fine houses around central plazas. The layout of the city today dates from the end of the 16th century. The historical centre of Quito was declared a cultural heritage site in 1978 by UNESCO, in recognition of its great archaeological and artistic merit.

GETTING THERE AND AWAY

By bus

Quito has a large, rather dingy central bus station (Terminal Terrestre de Cumandá), which can be a real hassle to get to. All the city buses seem to head for

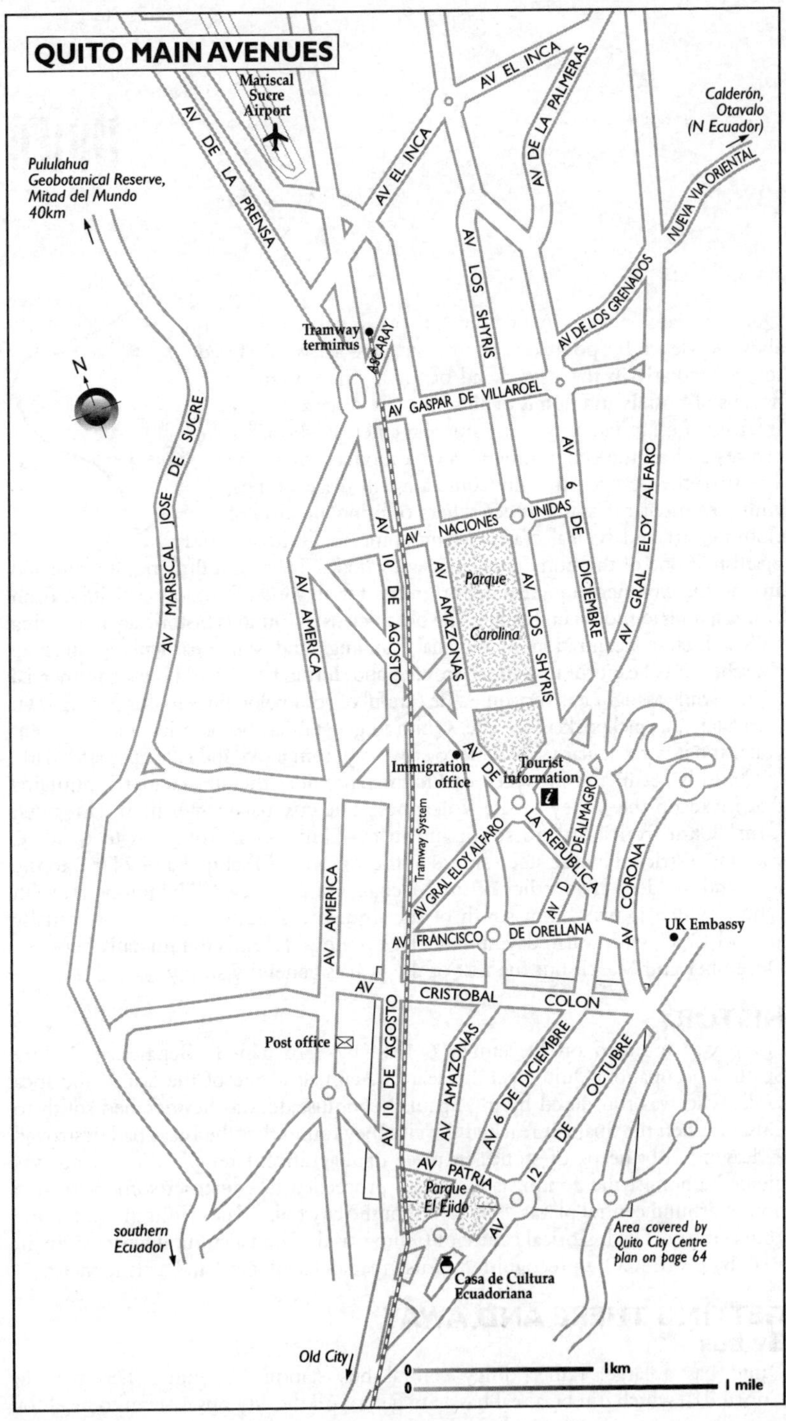
QUITO MAIN AVENUES
Mariscal Sucre Airport
Calderón, Otavalo (N Ecuador)
Pululahua Geobotanical Reserve, Mitad del Mundo 40km
AV EL INCA
AV DE LA PALMERAS
AV DE LA PRENSA
NUEVA VIA ORIENTAL
AV LOS SHYRIS
AV DE LOS GRENADOS
Tramway terminus
ASCARAY
N
AV GASPAR DE VILLAROEL
AV MARISCAL JOSE DE SUCRE
AV 6 DE DICIEMBRE
AV GRAL ELOY ALFARO
AV NACIONES UNIDAS
AV AMERICA
AV 10 DE AGOSTO
AV AMAZONAS
Parque Carolina
Immigration office
AV DE LA REPUBLICA
Tourist information
DE ALMAGRO
Tramway System
AV GRAL ELOY ALFARO
AV D
AV CORONA
AV FRANCISCO DE ORELLANA
UK Embassy
AV CRISTOBAL COLON
Post office
AV 6 DE DICIEMBRE
AV 12 DE OCTUBRE
AV PATRIA
Parque El Ejido
southern Ecuador
Area covered by Quito City Centre plan on page 64
Casa de Cultura Ecuadoriana
Old City
0 1km
0 1 mile

the terminal, so they will get you there, but the traffic jams in the streets around it can be interminable. The best way to get to the terminal is on the tram to Cumandá stop, or by taxi which will take an alternative route. There are dozens of bus companies in the bus station, and for each destination there is usually plenty of choice of company, departure times and even prices. Buses to Baños take 4 hours, Cuenca 8 hours, Lago Agrio 8 hours, on to Coca a further 3 hours, Guayaquil 8 hours, Portoviejo 8 hours, Riobamba 4 hours, Tulcán 5 hours.

There are three categories of city buses (Ejecutivo, Selectivo and Popular), and three marginally different prices. There are taxis everywhere: some are metered but it's a good idea to negotiate the price before you get in.

By train

There is a Saturday tourist train to Riobamba (6 hours, US$19 each way) and a Sunday service to Cotopaxi (7 hours, US$10 each way).

By air

The airport is 5km to the north of the new town. Take a taxi or a bus from Amazonas; allow 20–30 minutes.

WHERE TO STAY

Telephone code 02

Quito has dozens of hostels and hotels of all standards. They tend to be central, the majority within a couple of blocks of Calle Amazonas. The new town is more popular and safer than the old town, though it isn't as historically interesting.

Hostal Bask Lizardo García 537; tel: 541527. US$2 in dorm rooms of 7–8 beds. Kitchen, with TV, hot water, clean.

Hostal L'Auberge Av Colombia 1138 and Yaguachi; tel: 569886. US$4–6 per person. Located between the Old and New Towns. Use of kitchen, garden, fireplace, hot water.

Ecohostal 9 de Octubre 599 and Carrión; tel: 224483; email: ecotours@uio.satnet.net. US$8 per person with breakfast, shared rooms. Lovely old building, good beds, café, email, laundry. They also organise birdwatching tours from 1–15 days. Tours to Cuyabeno and Pañacocha from US$300.

Rincon de Castilla Versalles 1127; tel: 548097; fax 224312. US$4 per person in shared room, US$8 per person in double room. Use of kitchen until 22.00. Laundry facilities. Also has Spanish school with discount for hotel guests. English, French and German also spoken.

Hostal La Herradura Pinto 570 and Amazonas; tel: 226340. US$4.50 per person in shared room, US$5 per person in shared room with bath. SAEC member discount 10%. Centrally located, kitchen and laundry facilities.

Hostal Eva Luna Pasaje Roca 630; tel: 234799; fax 220426; email: admin@safari.ac.ecuanex.net.ec. US$5 per person in shared room, US$4.50 if staying longer than 10 nights. Women's hostel. Use of kitchen for breakfast.

Casa Eliza Isabel la Catolica 1559; tel: 226602. US$6 per person. Double and shared rooms with bath. Helpful and friendly. Kitchen facilities and laundry service.

La Casona de Mario Andalucia 213 and Galicia (1 block from Madrid); tel: 230129/544036, fax 230129. US$6 per person with shared rooms and shared bath. Discount for long-term stay. SAEC member discount 10%. Beautiful house with garden, very comfortable, kitchen and laundry facilities.

El Cafecito Luís Cordero 1124 and Reina Victoria; tel: 234862. US$6 per person. Mediterranean-style hostel with a vegetarian restaurant. Great meeting place, shared rooms. English also spoken.

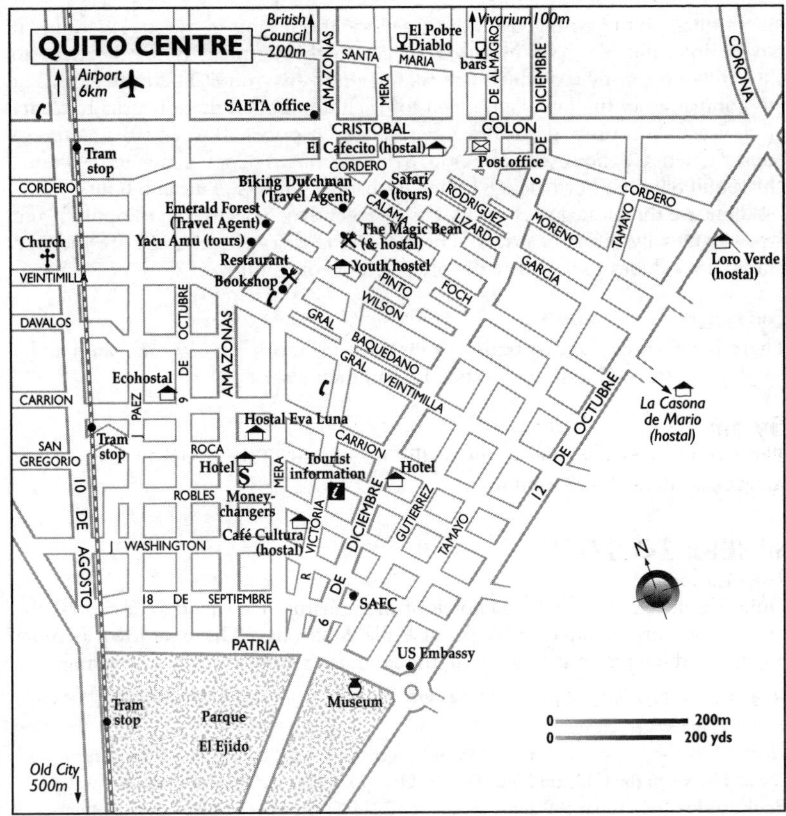

El Cipres Lerida 381 and Pontevedra; tel: 549561; fax 549558. US$7 per person with breakfast. Shared rooms. Lots of yard space, large sitting room. Continental breakfast included. French also spoken.

Hostal Posada Maple Juan Rodriguez 148 and 6 de Diciembre; tel: 544507/237375. US$7 per person in shared room (6 beds), US$12 single without bath. SAEC member discount, 10%. Small hotel with warm, family atmosphere, sun porch, TV room. English also spoken.

Pensión Parque Italia Narvaez 802 and Carvajal; tel/fax: 224393; email: parque.italia@ibm.net US$8 per night, including breakfast. Discount for long-term stays. Recommended hostel with excellent café. English and German spoken.

Hostelling International Pinto 3-25 and Reina Victoria; tel: 543995; fax 508221. US$9 private bath and breakfast, US$8 shared bath and breakfast, US$1 discount with IYH card.

Loro Verde Rodriguez 241 and Almagro; tel: 226173. US$12–20 with bath. SAEC member discount: 10%. Great location, clean, safe, friendly, kitchen in every room.

Alston Inn Hotel Juan León Mera 741 and Baquedano; tel: 229955; email: alston@uio.satnet.net US$15/22. English spoken.

Café Cultura Reina Victoria and Robles; tel: 224271; email: cafecult@pi.pro.ec US$38/$50 with bath. SAEC member discount 9%. Lovely converted mansion, good location. Excellent Danish breakfast and very comfortable beds. English, French, and German also spoken.

Residencial Casa Oriente Yaguachi 824 and Llona; tel: 546157. US$100 per month, apt for one with private kitchen, US$125 per month, apt for two with private kitchen, US$5 per day, apt for one with private kitchen. Good location, friendly, communal area with hammocks. English and French also spoken.

Old Town (Colonial Quito)

Hotel Farget Pasaje Farget 109 and Santa Prisca; tel: 570066; fax 570557. US$13–20 with bath. Good location, near Parque Alameda, between old town and new town.

Residencial Marsella Calle Los Rios 2035 and Julio Castro; tel/fax: 515884. US$6–9 shared bath, US$12 with bath. Near Parque Alameda. Two rooftop terraces and restaurant with cheap breakfast.

La Posada Colonial Paredes 188 and Rocafuerte; tel: 212859; fax 505240. US$5–9 private bath. Attractive and clean. In beautiful old building, renovated.

WHERE TO EAT

The new town has restaurants on every corner to suit all tastes, offering local food, Italian, Chifa, Mexican, fast food and international style, vegetarian and Swiss.

Magic Bean Calle Foch 681 and Juan León Mera; tel: 566181. A very popular tourist café with excellent food and coffee, and some nice rooms upstairs. Main dishes from US$4, bed and breakfast from US$8.

Super Papa Juan León Mera 741. Good for baked potatoes, popular gringo meeting place, loads of notices around the walls for flats to rent, volunteer work etc.

Vegetarian food is available at **Manantial**, Calle 9 de Octubre 591 and Carrión, and also at **El Maple**, Calle Páez and Roca.

The **Centro Cultural Tianguez** (Fundación Sinchi Sacha) sells typical art from around the country and has a café serving Ecuadorian food overlooking the Plaza San Francisco in the old town.

ENTERTAINMENT

Quito has a thriving nightlife. If you get the opportunity, try to see the dance group **Humanizarte**. They do a weekly show of beautifully choreographed, traditional Andean dance at the Bolívar Theatre in the old town. Check the local press for details. Email: humaniza@uio.satnet.net

In the new town there are some salsa clubs and bars with live music – check locally for the latest places. A great bar with a slightly Bohemian atmosphere is **Pobre Diablo** on Santa María and Mera. Within a few blocks there are dozens of popular and generally very busy, very loud pubs.

TOURIST INFORMATION

Tourist office CETUR, the government tourism department, has its main office at Calle Eloy Alfaro 1214 and Carlos Tobar; tel: 507560; fax: 507564; email: ecuainfo@interactive.net.ec; web: www.cetur.org They are helpful and can give you information and maps.

INEFAN is the government agency responsible for administration of national parks and reserves. It produces books and leaflets, and can give information on all the protected areas. Ministerio de Agricultura y Ganaderia, Instituto Ecuatoriano Forestal y de Areas Naturales y Vida Silvestre, Calle Eloy Alfaro and Amazonas, Quito; tel: 548924/563816; fax: 564037.

South American Explorers Club (SAEC) Calle Jorge Washington 311 and Leonidas Plaza; email: explorer@saec.org.ec; web: www.samexplo.org Open Mon–Fri 09.30–17.00. Free email access for SAEC members. See page 25.

Tourist police Calle Mera office for problems within Quito.

Immigration office at Calle Isla Seymour 1152. Open Mon–Fri from 08.00.

Travel agencies

The following list of travel agents does not include all the many dozens of agencies offering tours. Many of the tours offered are similar to each other, and usually the price reflects the level of quality you will be getting. Whenever you book a tour make sure you know what is included, and you are getting exactly what you want. You should also sign a contract with the agency. May, June and September to December are low season on the Galápagos and should be considerably less expensive. Remember you will have to pay US$300–400 for a flight and US$100 Galápagos tax on arrival.

Andando Tours Av Amazonas 229 and Carrión; tel: 548780; fax: 228519; email: andando2@ecnet.ec or andando1@ecnet.ec is a family operated and owned business with 25 years experience in the Galápagos. They have a sailing yacht, *Andando,* and a motor boat, *Samba*, each having a capacity of 12 passengers, and a yacht, *Sagitta,* with a capacity of 16. All have air-conditioned cabins with bath. They leave on Wed, for a 7-day programme. The price per person for the 7 day *Andando* tour is US$2,060, the *Samba* US$1,430, and the *Sagitta* US$1,580 low season. (April 15–June 30 and Sept 1–Dec 15).

Biking Dutchman Foch 714 and Juan León Mera; tel: 542806; fax: 567008; email: dutchman@uio.satnet.net, organise 1–15 day mountain biking tours. Great fun, good-quality equipment. One-day tours from US$40.

Cabañas Aliñahui Río Coca N43–78 and Isla Fernandina; tel: 253267; fax: 253266; email: alinahui@jsacha.ecuanex.net.ec. The cabins are run by two non-profit organisations, Jatun Sacha Foundation and Health and Habitat, both dedicated to research, education, and rainforest preservation. The cabins are across from Misahuallí on the Napo River near the Jatun Sacha Biological Station. Organised excursions available. Cost is US$50 + 20% tax per day with lodging and 3 meals, 10% discount for SAEC members; 15% discount for students.

Emerald Forest Amazonas 1023 and Joaquín Pinto; tel: 526403; fax: 541543; email: emerald@ecuanex.net.ec Luís Garcia at Emerald Forest guides tours out of Misahuallí and Coca to the Pañacocha area. US$280 for 5 days; US$230 for four days.

Etnotur/Etnocruises Cordero 1313 and Juan León Mera Esquina; tel: 564565/230552/563380; fax: 502682; email: etnocru@uio.satnet.net Large conventional tour operator. They have several boats including two yachts. *Rembrandt Van Rijn* takes 32 people (3-, 4- or 7-night tour), and the *Mondriaan*, for 20 passengers (7-night tour). From US$200 per person per day.

Explorer Tours Reina Victoria 1227 and Lizardo Garcia; tel: 522220/508871; fax: 508872. Can book jungle lodges such as the **Sacha Lodge** which is 50 miles down the Napo River from Coca, on 3,000 acres of rainforest covering a variety of different habitats, mostly in primary jungle. Trained, English-speaking biologists provide an educational and rewarding learning experience. US$656 for 5 days starting Mon. US$525 for 4 days starting Fri. 10% discount for SAEC members. Prices include food, lodging, tours and guides. Highly recommended. Many other tours available.

FUNDEAL Reina Victoria 1227 and Calama, Quito; tel: 507284/507208; fax: 507245; email: fundeal@pi.pro.ec As well as supporting the sustainable development of indigenous groups, they organise 4- and 5-day tours based at their Choco Lodge. The tours visit the local Chachi people, giving an insight into their culture, and also visit the Cotacachi Cayapas reserve, where you have an opportunity to see the primary tropical rainforest of northwest Ecuador.

Kapawi Lodge Reservations at Carrión and Leonids Plaza, Ed. Libertador; tel: 220947; fax: 222203; email: eco-tourism@canodros.com.ec; web: mia.lac.net/canodros. US$140 per person per night plus US$275 for flights. This is the newest of the ecolodges in Ecuador. On the Pastaza River in the heart of Shuar Territory, it is accessible by small aircraft and motor canoe. The lodge was built in partnership with the indigenous organisation OINAE and offers programmes to suit. It was built in accordance with the Achuar concept of architecture, using typical materials, and uses solar energy, biodegradable soaps, and recycling.

Kleintours Av Shirys 1000 and Holanda; tel: 430345/461235; fax: 442389; email: kleintou@uio.satnet.net or ecuador3@kleintours.com.ec; web: www.galapagosecuador.com. Operate tours to the Galápagos on their yachts *Coral 1* and *Coral 2*, both of which take 22 passengers and depart on Sun and Wed, for 4, 5, or 7 days from US$200 per person per day. They also operate the *Discovery* with a capacity of 90, with departures Mon and Thur, slightly more expensive. The boats have air-conditioned cabins with private bathrooms.

Metropolitan Touring Amazonas 329 and 18 de Septiembre; tel: 506650/464780; fax: 560807. Jungle tours in the Cuyabeno area and many other tours all over Ecuador.

Native Life Calle Foch 167 and Amazonas; tel: 505158/550836; fax: 229077; email: natlife1@natlife.com.ec; web: www.natlife.ec. Programmes in the Cuyabeno Reserve from 3 to 7 nights, from US$60 per person per day. US$20 park entrance. 10% discount for SAEC members.

Neotropic Turis Calle Roblis 653 and Amazonas; tel: 527862/521212; fax: 554902; web: www.ecuadorexplorer.com/neotropic. Bookings for Cuyabeno Lodge.

New Life Travel Foch 713 and Juan León Mera; tel: 543956. Sell a wide range of flights and tours in Ecuador, for budget travellers. Very helpful.

Nuevo Mundo Expediciones Amazonas 2468; tel: 552617; fax: 565261. Tours to Cuyabeno.

Rolf Wittmer Turismo Galápagos Amazonas 621 and Carrión; tel: 553460/526938; fax: 228520; email: rwittmer@tiptop.com.ec; web: www.pub2.ecua.net.ec/rwittmer/index.html.

Safari Tours Domestic office: Casilla 17116060; tel: 234799/552505; fax: 223381. International office: Pasaje Roca 630 and Amazonas; tel: 220426; fax: 223381; email: admin@safari.com.ec ; web: safari.com.ec A reputable agency which can offer the full range of tours in Ecuador, from climbing, hiking and mountain biking to jungle tours in the Oriente, and the Galápagos. They will book Yutiri Lodge, Sacha Lodge, La Selva Lodge or Kapawi Lodge. They also operate a 5-day Cuyabeno camping tour (US$250) and 4–6 day tours to the Huaorani village of Nenquepare. Also Bellavista Forest Reserve.

La Selva Jungle Lodge 6 de Diciembre 2816 and Rivet; tel: 550995/554686; fax: 567297; email: laselva@uio.satnet.net; web: www.laselvajunglelodge.com They have a good quality lodge on the Upper Napo River 100km from Coca near the Yusuni National Park. From US$140 per day. Includes all meals, transportation from Coca, excursions, accommodation, English-speaking naturalist guides.

Tropic Ecological Adventures Contact Andy Drumm, Apt 1a, Ed. Taurus, Av República 307 and Almagro; tel: 225907; fax: 560756; email: tropic@uio.satnet.net Works closely with the Cofan, Sicoya and Huorani communities in conservation and sustainable use of the rainforest. Prices vary depending on length of trip, area accessed and group size. From US$50 per day. Local guides and bilingual naturalist guides accompany each group. Their main guide is Moi Enomenga, featured in Joe Kane's book *Savages*. They also work with Randy Borman in Zabalo.

Yachana Lodge is a project of the FUNEDESIN Fundación para la Educación y Desarrollo de las Nacionalidades Indígenas; Calle Andrade Marín 188 and Diego de Almagro; tel: 543851; fax: 220362; email: info@yachana.com; web: www.yachana.com or www.funedesin.org. US$77 per day includes 3 meals and guide; US$300 for 5 day package. 20% discount for SAEC members. All lodge profits support FUNEDESIN community development projects, which aim to protect the rainforest through protecting its people. You can visit the projects while at the lodge, which is 2 hours downstream from Misahuallí. Groups travel on Wed and Sat. Highly recommended.

Yacu Amu Rafting Baquedano E5-27 y Juan León Mera; tel/fax: 236844; email: yacuamu@rafting.com.ec; web: www.yacuamu.com.ec Canoeing and rafting of the tropical rivers of Ecuador, owned by Australian Steve Nomchong.

CERRO GOLONDRINAS CLOUDFOREST PROJECT

Based in northwest Ecuador, on the western slopes of the Andes, this project aims to conserve 25,000 hectares of highland cloudforest and introduce sustainable agroforestry techniques within the coming years. Many different skills are needed in order to fulfil the objectives of the project. Some are related to management of the forest and scientific research, others deal with education and administration. Additionally, the project is in constant need of manual labour. It has two field sites, the primary location being Guallupe. Guallupe village is located in the Mira Valley (1,000 m) surrounded by agricultural land, 1½ hours from the city of Ibarra. It is a deforested area. Lodging is provided in a house owned by the Foundation in the village centre with running water, a toilet, shower, electricity and telephone. Volunteers can expect to work in the following areas: agroforestry research and soil conservation techniques, re-introduction of local species, tree nursery, light construction, tree planting, weeding, creating fire breaks, environmental education, erosion prevention and land restoration. The second site is at El Corazón in the Golondrinas Valley (1,800 m), an isolated site in the middle of the forest. The ride from Guallupe to the trailhead in Las Juntas takes 1½ hours. From the trailhead it's another one hour walk to Santa Rosa, and about three hours to El Corazón. Horses for transporting luggage can be arranged with local farmers. Lodging in primitive housing is available. Activities include the further development of an existing

Yuturi Tur Amazonas 1324 and Colon; tel/fax: 504037/503225; email: yuturi1@yuturi.com.ec; web: www.yuturi.com. They have a lodge below Pañacocha on the Yuturi River. All meals, programmed excursions, bilingual guides, bottled water, accommodation in double huts, transportation by canoe. 4 days US$288; 5 days US$360.

Airlines

TAME Av Amazonas 1354 and Colón; tel: 509382; Av 10 de Agosto 239; tel: 583939; airport: tel: 287155.
SAN Santa María and Amazonas; tel: 564969.
SAETA Colón and Amazonas; tel:542148.

Shopping

Camping equipment

Camping, trekking and climbing equipment is increasingly available for rent in Ecuador. Quito has the greatest selection. Climbing gear including plastic boots in all sizes is generally easy to find, but tents and sleeping bags may be more difficult to get hold of. However, it is becoming much easier to buy decent mountaineering equipment which is imported or even made in Ecuador. Make sure you have a good look at any equipment you are thinking of buying or renting to check its quality before you hand over your money. The following shops tend to have a good selection:

Agama Expediciones Venezuela 11-63 and Manabí, Quito. Stoves, tents and sleeping bags for rent.
Altamontaña Jorge Washington 425 and 6 de Diciembre, Quito; tel/fax: 558380. SAEC discount 10%. Good climbing equipment for sale and rent.
Andísimo 9 de Octubre 479 y Roca, Quito; tel: 223030. SAEC discount 5% on rental equipment.

tree nursery, cutting climber weeds in plots of second growth forest, measuring the evolution of the recovery of these plots, pruning trees and cleaning existing trails. There is a minimum stay of one month for volunteers without experience, three months for those with experience in horticulture or permaculture. Basic Spanish is required. The cost is US$240 per month. Special financial arrangements can be made for people who wish to stay longer than three months. The minimum age is 17 years old. The project accepts volunteers year round, although three months' notice is required before arrival. Travel, visas, and health insurance must be arranged independently and are the responsibility of the individual. You can expect to use a machete and shovel a good part of your day; the work is laborious, the living conditions primitive, so be prepared to be challenged physically and mentally.

If you are interested in only obtaining a snapshot of the grassroots work you should consider joining the four-day **Golondrinas Trek** as an introduction to the project area. The trek crosses three ecosystems from 4,000m altitude to 1,000m. Malaria isn't a problem in the area, although all other inoculations normally recommended for Ecuador should be obtained. Items needed for a comfortable stay in the field include rubber boots, mosquito net, sleeping bag, light raingear, sandals, flashlight, sunscreen, canteen, knife, hat, repellent, working gloves, long trousers and long-sleeved shirts, personal first-aid kit.

Antisana Sport El Bosque Shopping Centre; tel/fax 467433. Good selection of boots and climbing gear for sale.
Camping Cotopaxi Av Colón 942 and Reina Victoria; tel: 5216261 fax 524644. Camping equipment for sale. 10% ISIC discount.
Campo Abierto Baquedano 355 and Juan León Mera, Quito; tel/fax: 524422; email: sinlimite@ecuaword.com Climbing and camping equipment for sale and rent.
Equipos Cotopaxi 6 de Diciembre and Patria, Quito; tel: 517626. Make their own equipment, including sleeping bags, backpacks, mittens, tents.
The Explorer Reina Victoria 928 and Joaquín Pinto, Quito; tel: 550911. SAEC discount 10%. Rentals and sales.
Kywi 10 de Agosto 2273 and Cordero, Quito; tel: 221832/221833; fax: 501723; email: kywi@pi.pro.ec Rubber boots, mosquito netting and ponchos for sale.
Los Alpes Reina Victoria 821 and Baquedano, Quito; tel/fax: 232326. SAEC discount 10% on cash transactions only. Rentals and sales.
Marathon Sports at shopping centres El Bosque, El Jardín, CCI, San Rafael, and Quicentro stock Columbia sportswear at reasonable prices.
Safari Sports 6 de Diciembre 2520 and Orellana, Quito; tel: 220647. Camping, fishing and hunting equipment, for sale only.

Maps and books

The **South American Explorers Club** has a good selection of books for sale. **Libri Mundi** on Calle Mera 851 is excellent also. **Libro Expresso**, Amazonas 816, stocks guidebooks and some maps. For good large-scale maps the **Instituto Geográfico Militar** is on Calle Paz on the hill above the Casa de Cultura; take your passport.

Money

There are many banks and change offices along Amazonas that change travellers' cheques and cash. There are also ATM machines.

Communications

Post office In the old part of town on Calle Espejo, or in the new town at Calle Colón and Reina, and also at the airport.
Phone office Calle 10 de Agosto and Colón, bus station and the airport.

Internet

There are dozens of Internet offices in the centre of Quito.

Basknet opposite Hostel Bask on Calle Lizardo García 537, is one of the cheapest at US$1.50 per hour.
CafeNet Reina Victoria and Cordero; email: dinosaur@mail.io.com. Open noon to midnight, Tue–Sun.
Cybercafe Cultural Juan Rodriguez 228 A and Reina Victoria; tel: 231656; email: wmaster@ecuanex.net.ec; web: www.cenfeil.org/uiocybl.htm. Open Mon–Fri 08:00–21.00, Sat and Sun 09.00–21.00.
Monkey Online Juan León Mera N 21-10 and J Washington; email: info@altesa.net; web: www.altesa.net/monkeyonline. Open Mon–Sat 08.00–22.00, Sun 10.00–20.00.
Netzone Café Reina Victoria 100 and Av. Patria; email: netzonecafe@netzone.com.ec; web: www.netzone.com.ec.
Papayanet Calama 413 Juan León Mera; email: papayanet@papayanet.com.ec; web: www.papayanet.com.ec. Open 09.00–24.00.

Consulates and embassies

Argentina Av Amazonas 477 entre Robles y Roca, Edif Banco de los Andes, Piso 5; tel: 562292
Bolivia Cesar B Lavayen 1222 and J P Sanz, Edif Vizcaya II, Piso 1; tel: 458863/868.
Brazil Amazonas 1429 and Colón, Edificio España, Piso 10; tel: 563086.
Chile J P Sanz 3617 and Amazonas, Piso 4; tel: 249403.
France General Plaza 107 and Pátria; tel: 560789.
Germany Av Pátria and 9 de Octubre, Edif Banco de Colombia, Piso 6; tel: 225660.
Israel Av Eloy Alfaro 969 and Amazonas; tel: 565510.
Italy La Isla 111 and Humberto Albornoz; tel: 561077.
Japan Juan León Mera 130 and Pátria, Edif de la Corporación Financiera Nacional, Piso 7; tel: 561899.
Panama Diego de Almagro 1550 and La Pradera, Piso 3; tel: 566449.
Paraguay Av Gaspar de Villaroel 2013; tel: 245871.
Peru Av Amazonas 1429 and Colón, Edif España, Penthouse; tel: 520134.
Spain La Pinta 455 and Av Amazonas tel: 564373.
Uruguay Tamayo 1052 and Lizardo García, Piso 5; tel: 561181.
UK Av Gonzalaz Suarez 111 and 12 de Octubre; tel: 560670/560755.
USA Av 12 de Octubre and Pátria; tel: 562890.
Venezuela Av La Coruña 1733 and Belo Horizonte; tel: 564626.

WHAT TO SEE AND DO

The best place to start a walk around the old town is in the **Plaza de la Independencia**, where you will find the **cathedral**, one of the first churches built in Quito, in the 16th century (Open Mon–Sat 08.00–10.00 and 14.00–16.00). The remains of Antonio José de Sucre are buried here and there are some interesting paintings by artists from the Quito school. **El Palacio de Gobierno** lines the west side of the square, and presidential business is still conducted there. There are often dozens of large cars parked round the side and a very high security presence in the square. Opposite the cathedral you can see the well-preserved buildings of what used to be the **archbishop's palace**. It's still possible to have a look inside some of the patios. From the plaza there is a clear view of El Panecillo, with the large statue of the Virgen Aklada del Panecillo. Don't walk up the Panecillo as the streets leading up to it are particularly dangerous; take a taxi.

Near the Plaza de la Independencia is **Plaza de San Francisco**, probably the most important plaza in Ecuador, having been witness to all important political meetings in the country since colonial times. The impressive **church of San Francisco**, the oldest church in Ecuador, is situated on the west side of the plaza. Construction of this church began soon after Quito was founded. The church displays some well-known paintings and sculptures by artists from the Quito school. You can sometimes find a guide to take you around the church. This plaza is at the heart of old Quito, with plenty of pedestrian traffic, and is the perfect place to sit for a while to watch people come and go. The **Centro Cultural Tianguez** (Fundación Sinchi Sacha) sells typical art from around the country and has a café overlooking the plaza.

Other churches in the old town include the **Santo Domingo church** in the busy **Plaza de Santo Domingo**, a brilliantly whitewashed 17th-century building. **La Compañía** is an 18th-century Jesuit church, one of the most beautiful churches in the city (currently being restored following fire damage). **San Agustín** on Calle Chile and Guayaquil is a monastery dating from the 16th century, where the first act of independence was signed. It has beautiful cloisters and paintings of San Agustín's life. **La Merced** on Calle Chile and Cuenca is early 17th century, built in honour of the Virgin Mary after the city survived Pichincha's eruption in the mid-17th century.

Museums

Museo de la Ciudad Located in the old hospital building of San Juan de Dios, opened in 1998 after extensive renovation work to the building. Calle García Moreno in the old town.

Museo Arqueológico del Banco Central Casa de la Cultura, Av Patria and 6 de Diciembre. Open Tue–Fri 09.00–18.00; Sat–Sun 10.00–15.00. US$2. Fascinating collection of prehispanic artefacts and detailed descriptions of prehispanic cultures. Art and furniture from colonial times, and contemporary.

Museo Nacional de Arte Colonial Calle Cuenca and Mejía. Open Tue–Fri 10.00–18.00; Sat 10.00–14.00. Housed in a 17th-century colonial house, this museum contains paintings from the Quiteño school by Miguel de Santiago, Bernardo Rodríguez, Manuel Samaniego, Bernardo de Legarda and Caspicara.

Museo de Ciencias Naturales Rumipamba 341 and Av de Los Shyris. Open Mon–Fri 08.30–13.00 and 14.00–16.30. Stuffed animals and birds of all shapes and sizes from all over Ecuador.

Mitad del Mundo, 35 mins by bus from Quito; get off the bus at the monument itself. There's a post office where you get a special stamp and a tour office for Calima Tours, trips to Pululahua crater and Rumicucho pre-Inca site (US$5 each, minimum 2 people).

Dance classes

Son Latino Calle Amazonas 232; tel: 565213. Can organise classes as a one-off or a course from US$5 per hour. Advance booking isn't usually necessary.

Prison visits

There are three prisons in Quito, with foreigners in all of them. Most of these prisoners will welcome visitors. Visiting the prisons is safe, but don't take your valuables. You can get a list of foreign prisoners who would like to be visited from the SAEC in Quito. Take your passport. Appreciated items include fresh fruit and vegetables, toiletries, water purification tablets, books, cassettes, writing materials, clothes, shoes, other food and cigarettes.

Carcel de las Mujeres Calle de las Toronjas. Wed, Sat and Sun 10.00–15.00. Take a bus on 6 de Diciembre to El Inca roundabout. Ask for the prison when you get off.
Penal Garcia Moreno Calle Rocafuerte and Chimborazo. About ten blocks from Plaza Santo Domingo in old Quito. Wed, Sat and Sun 09.00–17.00.
Carousel Municipal Calle Garcia Moreno. Wed, Sat and Sun 09.00–17.00.

The Andes

6

The Northern Highlands

To the north of Quito are the mountainous provinces of El Carchi and Imbabura. The province of El Carchi borders Colombia, and its capital is the town of Tulcán. Imbabura, known as the province of the lakes, has some beautiful and easily accessible scenic spots and the city of Otavalo, with its popular Indian market on Saturdays. Otavalo is home to one of Ecuador's most well-known ethnic groups, the Otavaleños, who are respected nationally and internationally for their entrepreneurial skills in promoting their handmade jumpers and other textiles. Cotacachi, to the north of Otavalo, is the leather centre of the north, and also near Otavalo is the jewel-like lake of Cuicocha. San Antonio de Ibarra is well known for its wooden sculptures and Ibarra itself is a small but interesting colonial city that deserves a visit, and is the gateway to the northwest coastal part of Ecuador.

OTAVALO

Telephone code 06

Otavalo is a small busy town of around 50,000 inhabitants, located at 2,530m, at the foot of the volcano of Imbabura and Cotacachi, and near San Pedro Lake. Otavalo's most well-known feature is its market. Although there are market stalls selling crafts every day in Plaza del Poncho in the centre of Otavalo, on Saturdays the market is also for livestock, when it is huge and creates quite an impression. It starts very early in the morning, from 05.00, as people come from the many scattered villages around to buy and sell their animals. The food market a block from the main plaza is interesting, great for colourful photos of produce and just to watch people. From Otavalo you can clearly see the volcanic peaks of Imbabura (4,580m) and Cotacachi (4,944m). Local legend claims that Imbabura is the father (Taita Imbabura) and Cotacachi the mother (Mama Cotacachi). Their son is the peak Urku Mojanda. Anything out of the ordinary that occurs in the Otavalo area is put down to the moods of the volcanoes, and the emotional state of their current relationship.

History

Otavalo is an exceptional area. There are approximately 40,000 Otavaleño indigenous Indians living in 75 communities throughout the valley. They are highly entrepreneurial and through the production and selling of their weaving they have become the most prosperous indigenous group in Ecuador. They maintain their own culture, speak Quichua and wear traditional clothes, but they are a part of the commercial world, travelling worldwide to sell their products.

The Otavaleños are descendants of the tribe known as Cara, which probably originally came from Colombia 1,000 years ago. They settled in the area to the north of Quito, hunting deer, rabbits and birds and growing a few crops such as potatoes,

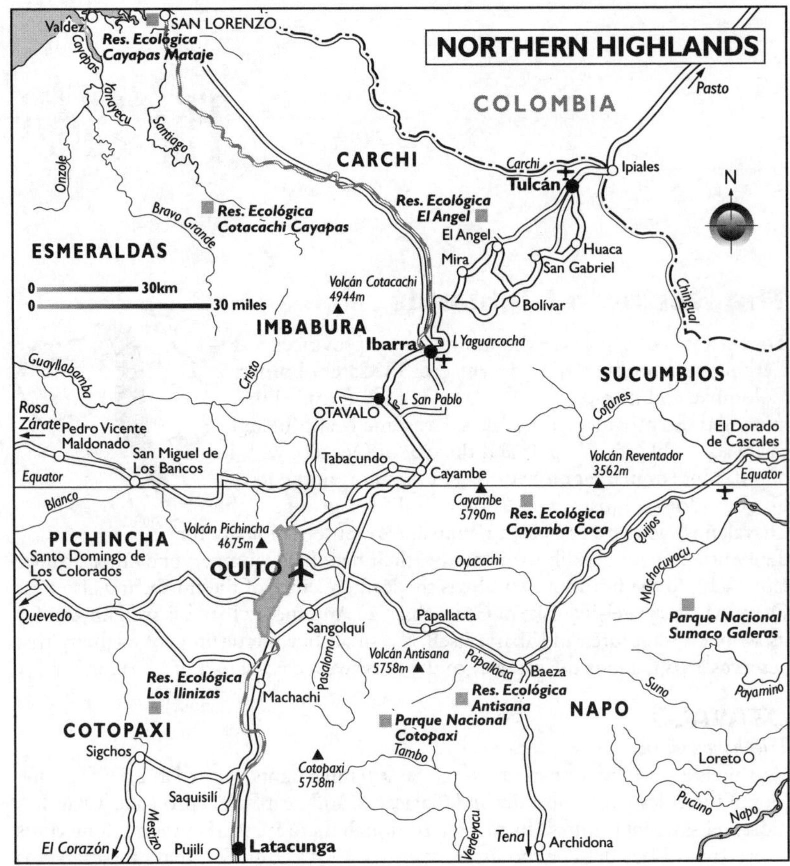

beans and corn. Cayambe, Otavalo and Caranqui were the principal towns. Textile production and trade were important even then; weavings were used for barter in exchange for products from other areas, *achiote* (a red dye), parrots, monkeys, cotton and food. Trading, then as now, was done by travelling merchants.

Weaving has always been important in Andean cultures, and some of the finest textiles ever found come from prehispanic Peruvian weavers. In Ecuador, because of the damp climate, far fewer textiles have survived from ancient times, but the fragments that there are suggest an equally rich and complex weaving history. The Otavaleños have been proficient weavers for thousands of years. In ancient times and to some extent still today an in-depth knowledge of spinning, dyeing, warping and weaving was an indication of social status, and these were considered essential skills for young girls.

The Inca conquest

The great emperor Tupac Yupanqui marched northwards in AD1455 in an attempt to expand the Inca empire into Ecuador. He was succeeded by his son Huayna Capac, who took 17 years to conquer the fiercely resistant Cara tribe. When Huayna Capac finally captured the town of Caranqui he slaughtered thousands by throwing them into a nearby lake. This lake is now named Yaguar Cocha, the lake

> **_THE OTAVALEÑOS_**
>
> The Otavaleños are distinctively dressed in finely made traditional clothing. One of the characteristic features of the men is their long hair worn in a braided pony tail known as a *shimba*. Even in the army Otaveleño men don't have to cut their hair. A felt hat is usually worn on top of the braid. Before Spanish colonialism the traditional men's shirt was a sort of tunic with an opening cut for the head and the side openings left unsown. Then a tailored shirt was adopted with a pleated front, made by hand from fabric woven on a floor loom and embroidered with stylised figures. Older men often still wear this shirt, worn outside the trousers and fastened traditionally by a woollen belt. Most younger men no longer wear these but use mass produced shirts. Traditionally white three-quarter length trousers were worn, but now there are many variations on these including white Levis. Most men wear ponchos (*ruwana*) which are predominantly dark blue in colour, with a few brightly coloured narrow stripes.
>
> Otaveleño women also wear their hair long, usually in a pony tail bound by a special hair wrap. They wear a white embroidered blouse and ankle length underskirt, both trimmed with lace. A white overskirt (*anaku*) is wrapped over the underskirt and on top of that a further blue or black *anaku* is added. A shawl is tied over the shoulders and the women are adorned with many necklaces.

of blood. Huayna Capac forced thousands more Cara people to move to Peru (this forced relocation is known as *mitmakuna*) and brought in loyal Quechua speakers to take their place. Further rebellion was quashed and the Cara people had to learn to comply with the Inca way of life. Because of its strategic location, on the main route north–south, Otavalo became a major Inca administrative centre.

Getting there and away

The bus station is on Calle Atahualpa a few blocks from the centre. There are frequent buses to and from Quito, 2½ hours. It's a good idea to get a bus with one of the companies that goes only to Otavalo, as they stop at the bus station in the town itself. Use Los Lagos or Transportes Otavalo. Other buses may drop you on the Pan American highway, some distance from the centre. If you are arriving after dark, there is a danger of being robbed on the way into town.

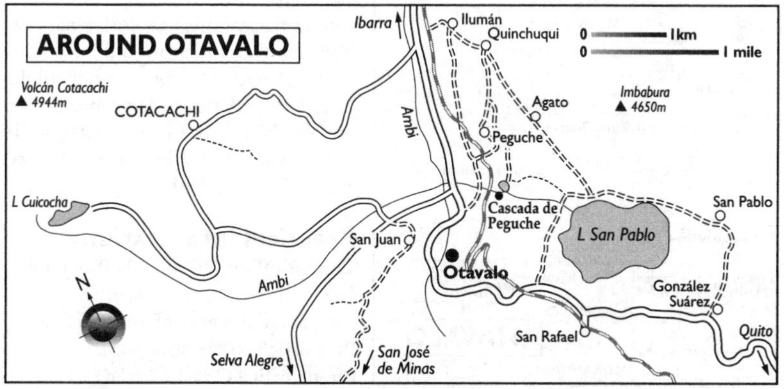

Where to stay and eat

There is plenty of accommodation in Otavalo itself to cater for the large numbers of tourists who stay here. If you are hoping to stay on a Friday night before the market you may have to book in advance, otherwise there are enough places for you to just turn up and find a bed. Outside the town there are several really nice places, within walking distance and perfect for relaxing or as a base for exploring the area, while quieter than being in town.

Inca Real Calle Salinas on the Poncho Plaza; tel: 922895. US$5 per person, great value, large clean rooms, newly opened, overlooks the market.
Hostal Riviera Sucre Calle Moreno 380 and Roca; tel: 920241. From US$3 per person, shared bath. This is popular and cheap, a rambling old colonial building with a courtyard, use of a kitchen and a variety of rooms. Recently renovated rooms with private bath.
Sumay Inn Abdón Calderón 1005 and Sucre. Tel/fax: 922871. From US$3 per person. Central, clean.
Hotel Otavalo Calle Roca 504. Tel/fax: 920416. US$10–17 with bath, very clean and comfortable, old colonial building, spacious.
La Luna Tel: 737415 for a free pick-up from town. A few km outside Otavalo, on the Laguna Mojanda road, this is a great place to spend a few days relaxing, reading, or walking. There is a choice of dormitory accommodation from US$3 per person (kitchen available), or cabins with shared or private bath, US$6/8 per person including breakfast. Restaurant, reading room, fireplaces.
Casa Mojanda Tel/fax: 731737; email: mojanda@uio.telconet.net; web: www.casamojanda.com. An extremely welcoming, beautifully located hotel and organic farm, with great food and a relaxing atmosphere. 10 mins by taxi, 30 mins walk from Otavalo. Bunk house with kitchen US$15 including breakfast, luxurious cottages from US$45 per person including breakfast and three course dinner. Perfectly situated for horseriding, mountain biking and trekking. Volunteer placements available.

In Peguche, a small weaving village 3km from Otavalo, there are a couple of places to stay: the **Hosteria Peguche Tio**, tel: 922619, or **Ayahuma Hostal**. This is particularly recommended at the weekend as there is often live folk music. You can walk along the railway track to get to Otavalo, which takes about 45 minutes.

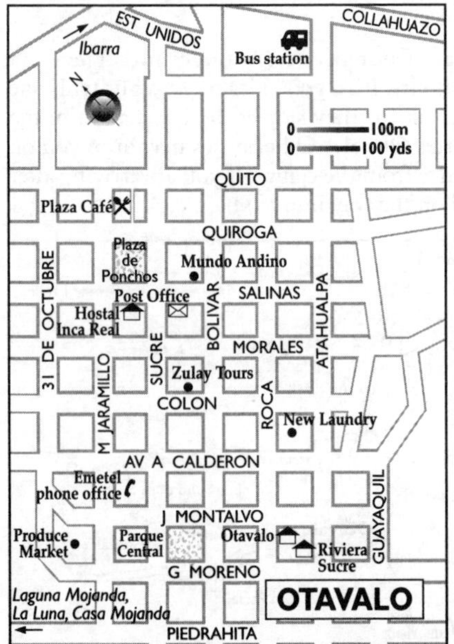

In Otavalo there is no shortage of places to eat and drink. There are several restaurants and coffee bars on Calle Bolívar and around the Poncho Plaza. If you go a bit further afield you will find more, local places. At the weekends there are *peñas* with live music on Calle Morales – try **Tuparina** and **Tukano**.

Practical information

Tourist office The official office is on Calle Bolívar. The travel agencies on Calle Sucre also give information freely.
Post office on the main plaza.
Phone office Calle Calderón.

Money Calle Sucre has several money change offices and there are banks on Calle Bolívar and Sucre. Changing travellers' cheques and cash is not a problem.
Travel agencies also on Calle Sucre. They organise one-day tours to the surrounding villages where you can see weaving, knitting, and other crafts. Alternatively there are horseback or trekking tours. Zulaytur Colón and Sucre 2nd floor; tel: 921176. Recommended, socio-anthropological tours, give a good insight into the way of life. US$10 per person, 08.00–14.30.
Internet Calle Sucre. Connections are made via Quito so it's expensive.
Spanish classes at Mundo Andino, Calle Salinas 404; tel: 921864; email: espanol@interactive.net.ec One to one, homestays, all levels.

What to see

Archaeology Museum Av de los Sarances, outside town, is worth a visit. Check with Zulaytur to see if it's open. Open Tue–Fri 08.00–12.00 and 14.30–18.30, Sat 08.00–12.00.

Laguna Mojanda You can walk or take a taxi (17km, taxi 40 mins each way, US$6) to this beautiful highland lake. Check locally for information on safety as there have been numerous reports of robberies from walkers near the Laguna. Local communities have organised watchmen to prevent robberies and the situation is apparently improving. Check locally.

Laguna Cuicocha is 17km from Otavalo. It was formed by the collapse of a volcanic crater, and is now a picturesque blue lagoon of 3km diameter, within Cotacachi–Cayapas National Park. You can walk around the lake, about 8km; allow 4–5 hours. However, there have been reports of robberies and armed hold-ups in this area, so go in large groups or on a tour. Ask in town for the latest safety reports.

IBARRA

Telephone code 06

Ibarra is a charming colonial town, with many historical churches. It's a tranquil place with wide streets and well-tended plazas. The countryside around Ibarra is green and pretty, with several volcanoes near enough to climb. The majestic volcano of Imbabura is nearby; though not to be taken lightly, it is good for acclimatising if you are thinking of climbing more later on. One of the great things about Ibarra is the natural fruit ice-cream, called *helado de paila*. Nougat and thick blackberry syrup are also typical local produce.

Getting there and away

Most buses leave and arrive at their own offices, which tend to be near the railway terminal. There are sometimes trains from here to San Lorenzo on the north west coast, but in recent years this service has become somewhat erratic beacause of landslides and the construction of a new road.

Where to stay and eat

There are plenty of cheap hostels near the bus and train stations, but they tend to be very basic.

Hostal Imbaburra Calle Oviedo 9–33; tel: 950155. US$2 per person. Lovely place, very friendly, large colonial building, big rooms, with central courtyard.
Hostal Blue Lake Pedro Moncayo and Bolívar; tel: 641851.

For restaurants the best streets are Calle Moncayo, Olmedo and Bolívar. There are a variety of restaurants to suit most tastes.

Practical information

Tourist office The CETUR office is at Calle Rivadeneiro and Mariano. Open Mon–Fri, helpful.
Post office Calle Salinas.
Phone office Calle Sucre.
Money There are several banks on Calle Olmedo for changing money. Casa de Cambio Imbacambios, Calle Oviedo 7, will cash travellers' cheques.
Travel agencies Nevitur, Calle Bolívar and Oviedo; Delgado, Calle Moncayo and Bolívar.

What to see

The nearby village of **La Esperanza** (10km south), with the hostels **Casa Aida** and **Café Maria**, is a good base for walks, and the place to start to climb Cubilche or Imbabura volcanoes. Take a taxi from Ibarra or a bus from Parque Grijalva. For wood carvings visit **San Antonio de Ibarra**, where there are several shops and workshops. A taxi from the centre of Ibarra takes just a few minutes.

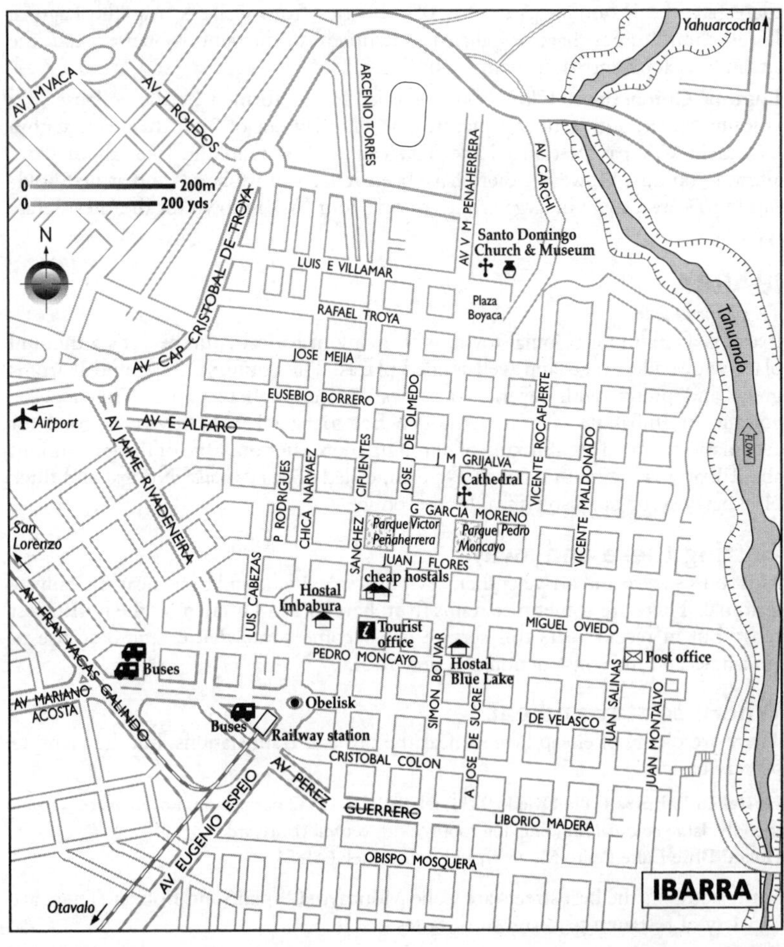

NORTH OF IBARRA

The Pan American highway continues north to Tulcán and the Colombian border.

About 100km north of Ibarra is the entrance to the **Reserva Ecológica El Angel**. From Bolívar or San Gabriel on the Pan American highway take a truck or bus to the village of El Angel (20km). Trans Espejo also run a bus from Ibarra (4 hours), from behind the train station. This is a small place, with some basic accommodation, **Hostal El Angel** and **Viña del Mar**. Beyond El Angel there is no public transport, so you will have to look for a pick-up or jeep to hire (US$40 to get to El Volader and back).

Reserva Ecológica El Angel

The Reserva Ecológica El Angel has magnificent stands of frailejon (*Espeletia pycnophylla*), which grow up to 7m tall with long, feathery leaves at the crown. There is some native forest left in and around the reserve, including some polylepis trees. The area has suffered as a result of pressure on the land from nearby farmers, together with the widespread practice of burning of the high *páramos*. Many of the animals that should be plentiful in the reserve area have also suffered, as a consequence of heavy hunting.

The climate here is quite extreme, with an average temperature of only 8°C, and a daily variation of 18°. From June to October there are strong winds, sunny days and freezing nights, while from November to May mist and even snow are common, and visits can be wet and muddy. For further information visit the local office of **INEFAN**, which is at Calle José Grijalva 04–26. Guides can be contacted at this office. For possibilities of tours or voluntary work in this area contact the Cerro Golondrinas Cloudforest Conservation (see pages 68–9). Their protected forest is west of El Angel.

TULCÁN

Telephone code 06

Tulcán is a busy commercial town, with under 40,000 inhabitants, near the Colombian border. It can get quite busy at weekends with Colombians, who come here to shop. There is not a great deal to do here other than cross the border to Colombia. The town centres around the streets of Bolívar and Sucre, and this is where you will find most of the hostels, restaurants, post office and shops.

Getting there and away

By bus

There is a central bus terminal, about 2km south of the centre. Buses from Quito take 5–6 hours and leave frequently. There are also buses to Ibarra, Otavalo, Guayaquil and Huaquillas. To get to the border take a minibus from Parque Ayora in the north part of town, or a bus from the terminal (6km).

By plane

There are daily flights to Quito with TAME, and international flights to Cali in Colombia. The airport is on the edge of town, 3km from the centre.

Where to stay and eat

There are plenty of cheap hostels to choose from. Calle Sucre has several reasonable places such as the **España**, tel: 983860, the **Florida**, tel: 983849, and the more basic **Quillasinga**, tel: 981892.

Calle Sucre and Bolívar have several places to eat. For vegetarian food try **Café Mexico**, Calle Bolívar 49–095.

Practical information

Money There are money changers in the main plaza. Banks include Filanbanco, Calle Sucre, which will do foreign exchange. It's best to change pesos and sucres into US dollars when crossing between countries.

What to see

Tulcán is famous for the **topiary** at its cemetery, begun in 1936. The cemetery is 2km from the centre to the north; take a taxi.

Crossing the border

The border at Rumichaca is open 06.00–21.00, and crossing is usually quick and straightforward. Make sure you get your passport stamped. There are money changers at the border who usually give a good rate, but check their calculations carefully. The nearest Colombian town is Ipiales, a few kilometres from the border.

The Central Highlands

The central highlands, also known as the Valley of the Volcanoes, include the provinces of Cotopaxi, Tungurahua, Bolívar and Chimborazo. This is one of the most spectacular parts of the country, particularly attractive to mountaineers and walkers as it contains some of Ecuador's highest peaks: El Altar (5,319m), Cotopaxi (5,857m), Illinizas (5,767m), Tungurahua (5,016m), Carihuayrazo (5,020m) and Chimborazo (6,310m). Indian markets are held regularly at the towns of Salasacas, Saquisilí, Latacunga, Pujilí and Ambato and many festivals are colourfully celebrated in the mountainous towns and villages. This is an area rich in contemporary culture and there is also a wealth of pre-colonial and colonial treasure to discover. At the heart of the province of Cotopaxi is the imposing snow-capped volcano of the same name, a tempting climb even for the inexperienced mountaineer. The scenery is wild and dramatic, and the national park of Cotopaxi is worth a visit even if you don't fancy the climb or the weather is too inclement to permit an attempt. The cities of Latacunga and Ambato are not particularly special, but there are interesting things to see nearby. Near Latacunga is the Quilotoa Lagoon, good walking country, and the town itself has a few colonial buildings still standing, and the wonderfully colourful festival of Mama Negra at the end of September on the day of the Virgin de Mercedes. Around Ambato fruit, vegetables and flowers are grown, and the celebration of the year, in February, is the Festival of the Fruit and Flowers. The main town in Chimborazo province, which lies at the foot of the highest volcano in Ecuador, is Riobamba. Riobamba is the starting place for the famous spectacular train ride down the mountain pass of the Devil's Nose. The volcano of Chimborazo, the highest mountain in Ecuador, is on the doorstep, so climbs, treks and jeep tours often start from here.

LATACUNGA

Telephone code 03

Latacunga is a pretty city of colonial buildings, only busy on Saturdays, and quiet the rest of the time. It's the capital of Cotopaxi Province, with a population of 40,000, situated at 2,850m with an annual average temperature of only 12°C. The most interesting part of the city is the colonial core around the Parque Vicente León. The beautifully restored cathedral dates from the early 19th century, while the narrow streets are lined with low houses with patios. If the weather is clear there are good views of several volcanic peaks around the city.

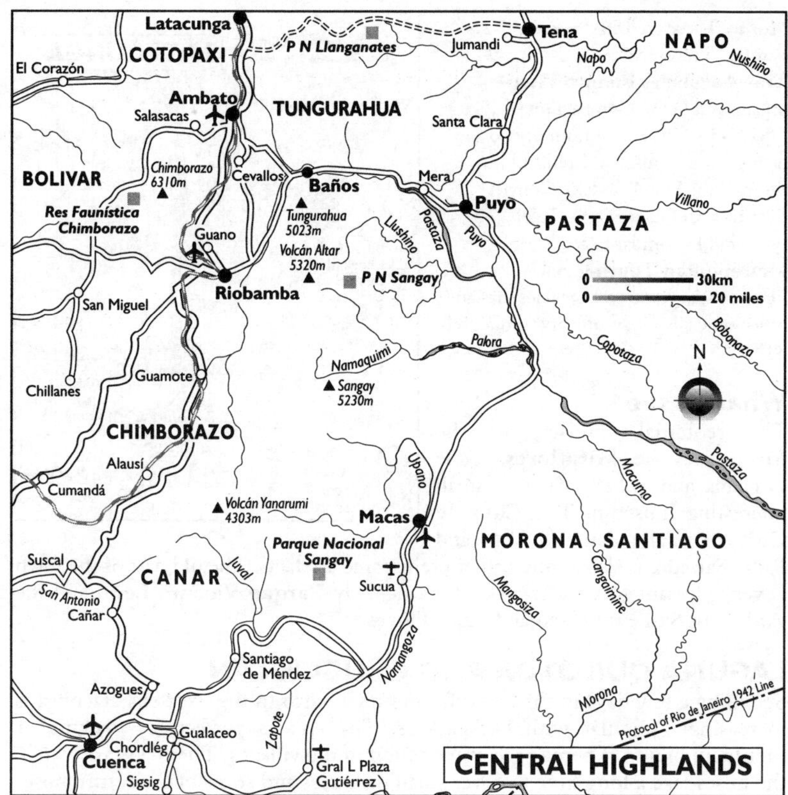

Getting there and away

There is no central bus terminal in Latacunga, though most buses leave from one of the streets bordering the market or along the Pan American highway across the river. If you are going north or south along the Pan American highway you can wave down the buses as they pass. Buses to Chugchilán leave daily from Calle Melchor de Benavides (daily, 11.00), and some from Calle 5 de Junio (Fri, Sat, 10.30). Buses to Zumbahaua on Calle 5 de Junio run every few hours.

Where to stay and eat

There are lots of cheap places to stay near the market, but the nicer hostels are in the old part of the town a few blocks to the east.

Hotel Estambul Calle Quevedo 6–46 and Salcedo; tel: 800354. From US$5, a popular budget choice. Large old colonial building, comfortable, good value, central.
Hotel Rosim Calle Quito 16–49 and Padre Salcedo; tel: 802172. From US$8, great value, big rooms, private bath, TV, comfortable.
Hotel Rodelú Calle Quito 1631; tel: 800956; fax: 812341; email: rodelu@uio.telconet.net From US$10–13 with bath. Central, friendly, good restaurant.

Practical information

Post office on Calle Quevedo and Maldonado.
Phone office near the post office.

Money There are banks on the plaza, Parque Vicente León.

Travel agencies Ramiro Viteri organises tours to Cotopaxi for US$25–30 with a minimum of two people, or to Quilotoa. Contact him through the Hotel Rodelú. Contact **Fausto Batallas** through Hotel Estambul for similar tours. **Metropolitan Touring**, one of Ecuador's largest travel agencies, has an office on Calle Guayaquil and Quito; tel: 803985.

What to see

The colonial house of the **Marquéses de Miraflores**, Calle Orellana and Echeverría, is a small interesting museum. The **Casa de Cultura**, Calle Antonio Vela and Padre Salcedo, is also a museum of prehispanic artefacts. The old part of the town is very pleasant to wander around, particularly **Parque Vicente León** and the gardens of **San Francisco** and **Lago Flores**.

LAGUNA QUILOTOA AND CHUGCHILÁN

Spending a few days in the beautiful mountain area to the west of Latacunga is increasingly popular with backpackers. The area is perfect for walking or mountain biking. There is accommodation in the villages. The roads are rough, the buses take a long time to cover small distances and some of the return buses leave in the middle of the night.

Probably the easiest route is to take the bus to **Zumbahua** (80km from Latacunga), where there are several hostels. Hostal Cóndor Matzi on the plaza is the nicest. There is occasional transport to **Quilotoa** from here, check locally for the times. From Zumbahua it is 12km along the road to the crater lake of Quilotoa, where there are three basic but warm and friendly places to sleep. From the crater it is 22km to **Chugchilán** by road or 11km cross country, a good walk passing through the village of Huayama. At Chugchilán you can stay at the Black Sheep Inn, a great place, warm, friendly and ecologically run. Breakfast and dinner included, and there are hot showers, maps and information on nearby hikes. Hostal Casa Mama Hilda is also recommended, and offers dorm rooms, shared bathrooms and food. Travel back to Latacunga (4 hours minimum) through **Sigchos** with its Saturday market and **Saquisilí**, with its famous Thursday market.

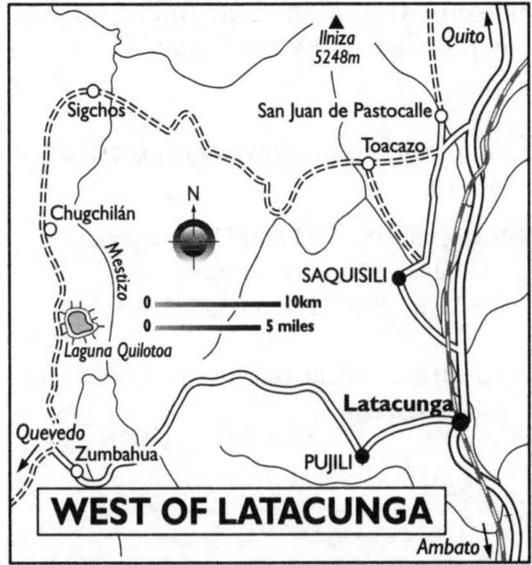

COTOPAXI NATIONAL PARK

The Cotopaxi National Park is dominated by the magnificent peak of the cone volcano of Cotopaxi (5,897m), the second highest mountain in Ecuador after Chimborazo. Cotopaxi is one of the highest active volcanoes in the world. It last erupted at the beginning of the 20th century, with over 20 eruptions between 1532 and 1904. The area was declared a national park in 1979 to protect the geological formations and to maintain and sustain the flora and fauna of the area, while allowing controlled access. The volcano, a perfect cone, has a base diameter of 20km and is glacier covered above 4,800m. Many people visit the park to climb Cotopaxi. The best way to do this is through a specialist climbing agency with a professional guide, such as Safari (see page 67). There are designated camping areas within the park. If you don't have your own transport the best way to see the national park is on a tour, as it's too big an area to make access easy on foot, and there's no public transport.

AMBATO

Telephone code 03

Ambato is a large market town of over 150,000 inhabitants. Most of the city was destroyed in 1949 by an earthquake, and has since been rebuilt. The buildings are quite modern and not of any interest but the streets are lined with trees, and the parks well cared for. On Mondays Ambato is heaving with people as it is market day, and this is one of the biggest markets in Ecuador. Produce is brought from far and wide to be sold here, and the banks are apparently the busiest in the country. In February, often coinciding with carnival, Ambato celebrates its Festival de Frutas y Flores. The festival consists of parades, music and dancing, bullfighting and general revelry. Finding a hotel room during the festival can be impossible.

Getting there and away

Ambato has a large bus terminal a few blocks from the centre of town. There are frequent buses to Quito (3 hrs), and to Baños (1 hr), Riobamba (1 hr), Puyo (3 hrs), Guaranda (1 hr), Latacunga (1 hr), Guayaquil (7 hrs), Tena (6–7 hrs), Macas (6–7 hrs), Esmeraldas (8–9 hrs), Loja (12 hrs) and Machala (7 hrs).

Where to stay and eat

There are plenty of hostels in the centre of the city. The cheapest are to be found around the Parque 12 de Noviembre. Near the bus station is **Hostal Madrid**, Calle Juan Cajas and Cumandá; tel: 828798. Shared or private bath. **Hostal Portugal** is also near at Calle Juan Cajas and 12 de Noviembre; tel: 822476. Private bath. **La Casa Blanca**, Luis Cordero 2–10 and Los Shyris, Ambato; tel: 844448; fax: 844512; email: adventures@ecuaworld.com US$7–10 with breakfast in a family house. Climbing, trekking and other trips organised with qualified guides. English speaking.

Practical information

Tourist office The CETUR office is at Calle Guayaquil and Rocafuerte; tel: 827800.

Post office Calle Castilla and Bolívar.

Phone office Calle Castilla and Rocafuerte.

Money There are several banks in Ambato. Cambiato, Calle Bolivár, is good for travellers' cheques and foreign currency. Banco del Pacifico, Calle Cevallos and Lalama. Banco de Guayaquil, Calle Sucre and Mera.

Airlines TAME has an office in town at Calle Sucre and Guayaquil. SAETA has its office at Calle Bolívar.

Travel agencies Surtrek, Calle Los Shyris 2-10 and Luis Cordero; tel: 844448, is a reputable agency for climbing and trekking. Metropolitan Touring, Bolívar and Castillo, is one of Ecuador's largest agencies.

What to see

Museo de Ciencias Naturales, Calle Sucre and Lalama. Open Mon–Fri 09.00–12.00 and 14.00–18.00. Displays many stuffed animals. Interesting photographs.

It's worth walking through the town to the southwest along Avenida Bolívar, to the suburb of **Miraflores**, which is good for shopping, especially for leather.

GUARANDA

This is a quiet and pretty town a bit off the beaten track and worth a visit if you have a couple of days to spare, especially for the Friday and Saturday markets. It is the capital town of the province of Bolívar. It is a beautiful bus ride from Riobamba (2–3 hours), and for spectacular road little can beat the journey from Ambato (2 hours), which goes up to 4,400m with great views of Chimborazo and the other surrounding volcanic peaks. Be prepared for cold nights, and take plenty of warm clothes. During the dry season there is transport to the coast from Guaranda. If you happen to be in Ecuador for carnival in February this is one of the best places to go, for dances, parades and lots of water. There is a weekly market here on a Saturday.

There are quite a few small hotels, the nicest are **Hotel Bolívar** (tel: 980547), and **Hotel Cochabamba** (tel: 981958), from US$7 per person.

BAÑOS

Telephone code 03

Baños has become one of the most popular tourist spots in Ecuador. It has almost enough hostels, cafés and travel agencies to rival Quito. The town itself is quite small, and it is beautifully set at 1,800m surrounded by steep, patchwork green mountainsides. There are dozens of day walks, and longer hikes and climbs you can do on your own or through a specialised agency. Horseriding, mountain biking and rafting are also available through the agencies in town. The hot springs, after which the town is named, are very busy at weekends but worth visiting during the week at quieter moments. Baños has a subtropical feel to it, with a nice climate, but its rainy season is different from other parts of the country. In Baños July and August are the wettest months, and from May to October is rainy season.

Getting there and away

Baños has a bus terminal within easy walking distance of the centre. There are frequent services to Ambato (1 hr), Quito (3–4 hrs) Riobamba (1 hr), Latacunga (2–3 hrs), and Puyo (2 hrs).

Where to stay and eat

Baños has dozens of hotels, almost all of which you can walk to in just a few minutes from the bus station. Calle Eloy Alfaro and Calle 16 de Diciembre have a high concentration of hostels. In carnival, like everywhere, most places fill up fast and charge considerably more than normal.

Pensión Patty Calle Eloy Alfarro 556. From US$2 per person. Cheap, basic accommodation, small rooms, kitchen and tourist information. Popular with backpackers, central.

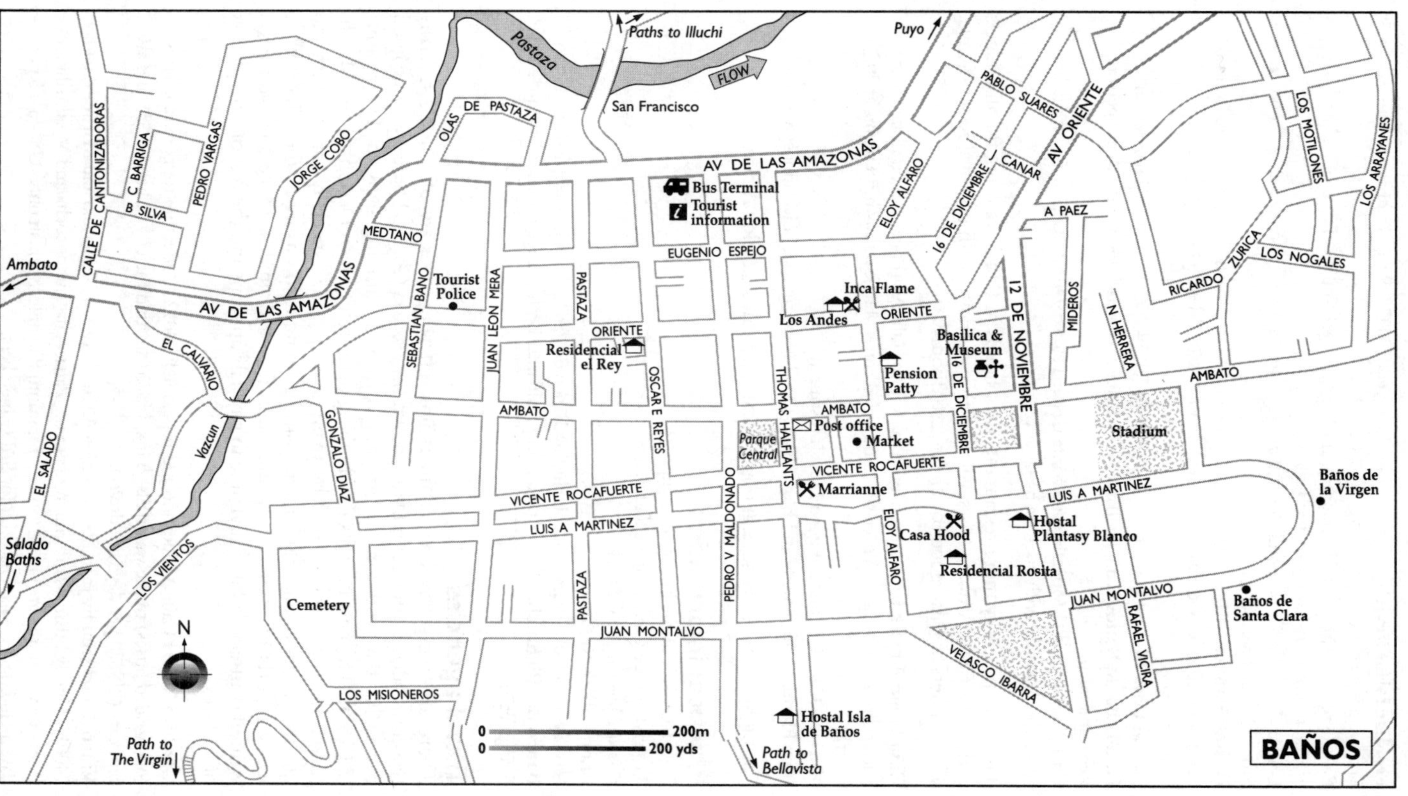
BAÑOS
Paths to Illuchi
Puyo
Pastaza
FLOW
San Francisco
Ambato
Bus Terminal
Tourist information
Tourist Police
Inca Flame
Los Andes
Residencial el Rey
Basilica & Museum
Pension Patty
Post office
Market
Parque Central
Stadium
Marrianne
Casa Hood
Hostal Plantasy Blanco
Residencial Rosita
Baños de la Virgen
Baños de Santa Clara
Salado Baths
Cemetery
Hostal Isla de Baños
Path to The Virgin
Path to Bellavista
Vazcun
N
0 200m
0 200 yds
CALLE DE CANTONIZADORAS
C BARRIGA
B SILVA
PEDRO VARGAS
JORGE COBO
OLAS DE PASTAZA
AV DE LAS AMAZONAS
ELOY ALFARO
16 DE DICIEMBRE
J CANAR
PABLO SUARES
AV ORIENTE
LOS MOTILONES
LOS ARRAYANES
A PAEZ
LOS NOGALES
ZURICA
RICARDO
MEDTANO
EUGENIO ESPEJO
SEBASTIAN BANO
JUAN LEON MERA
PASTAZA
ORIENTE
12 DE NOVIEMBRE
MIDEROS
N HERRERA
AMBATO
EL CALVARIO
OSCAR E REYES
THOMAS HALFLANTS
EL SALADO
GONZALO DIAZ
VICENTE ROCAFUERTE
LUIS A MARTINEZ
PEDRO V MALDONADO
LOS VIENTOS
JUAN MONTALVO
RAFAEL VICIRA
VELASCO IBARRA
LOS MISIONEROS

Residencial El Rey Calle Oriente and Reyes; tel: 740322. Basic, but friendly and clean. From US$2 per person.
Residencial Rosita 16 de Diciembre and Martínez; tel: 740396. From US$2 per person, private rooms or flats for four with kitchen.
Los Andes Calle Oriente and Eloy Alfaro; tel: 740838. Small, friendly, clean, good value. From US$2.50 per person.
Hostal Plantas y Blanco Calle 12 de Noviembre and Martínez; tel: 740044. From US$6 with bath. Good restaurant, nice rooms, clean, friendly, rooftop terrace. Recommended.
Hostal Casa Blanca Maldonado and Oriente; tel: 740092. From US$2 per person.
Hotel Isla de Baños Calle Halflants and Montalvo; tel: 740609. US$6–10 per person. Recommended.
Café Cultura Calle Montalvo and Santa Clara. Tel/fax: 740419. US$46–58; upmarket, very nice. Also café with book exchange.

There are probably more restaurants than hotels in Baños, catering for all budgets and tastes. Calle Ambato has several local restaurants, with good value set menus. The markets are also good for cheap tasty food.

Casa Hood A block behind the central market on Calle Martínez, also on Calle 16 de Diciembre and Martínez. Vegetarian food, good coffee, books, films most nights at 20.30 for free.
Mariane Calle Martínez. A good French restaurant.
Inca Flame Calle Oriente and Eloy Alfaro. Good Mexican food, nice atmosphere.

For nightlife there are several popular bars and cafés on Eloy Alfaro.

Practical information

Tourist office at the bus terminal upstairs.
Tourist police Calle Oriente and Baños.
Post office Parque Central.
Phone office Rocafuerte and Halflants.
Money There are several banks including Banco de Pacífico, Calle Montalvo and Alfaro.
Banco del Pichincha, Calle Ambato and Halflants. Both change travellers' cheques and foreign cash.

Travel agencies

There are many travel agents in Baños, offering a variety of tours. Especially recommended is mountain biking down the Pastaza Gorge. There are some good day walks that you can do on your own and climbing trips to Tungurahua (5,016m). The best months for climbing here are between December and March. Jungle tours are also offered by many agencies. Be especially careful with the quality of guides and equipment you are going to be using as there have been many reports of poor quality and unprofessional guides. Make sure you get a written contract and it is advisable to pay half up front and the rest on completion of services.

Córdova Tours Calle Maldonado and Espejo; tel: 740923. Offer fun tours in rancheros (open-sided buses) to the waterfalls (5 hrs, US$5), around the city (2 hrs, US$3), and also rent cars (US$70 per day with driver).
Vasco Tours (run by Juan Medina) Eloy Alfaro, between Montavalo and Martinez; tel/fax: 740017. Family business offering tours to the Pañacocha, Limoncocha and Misahualli area. Prices vary with the area to be toured, minimum 8 people. Spanish only. US$45–55 per day, including 3 meals. Discount for SAEC members.

Julio Verne Calle Oriente 11–69 and Alfaro; tel: 740253; email: julver@interactive.net.ec Recommended Ecuadorian and Dutch travel agency. Climbing trips with good quality guides and equipment. They sell treks, jungle trips, rafting and the Galápagos.
Rainforestur Ambato and Maldonado; tel: 740743. Good, knowledgeable guides.
Río Loco Calle Maldonado and L A Martínez; tel/fax: 740929; email: rioloco@ecuadorexplorer.com; web: www.ecuadorexplorer.com/rioloco. A Swiss Ecuadorian agency that organises rafting, mountain biking and horseriding trips.
Selvanieve Expediciones Montalvo and Halflants; tel: 740335. Climbing and trekking trips and jungle tours.
Yawa Jee Fundación Indigena Av Oriente and Eloy Alfaro; tel/fax: 740957; email: yawajee@gye.satnet.net An indigenous foundation run by Shuar Indians to protect and conserve the indigenous communities and their natural resources. Operates trips into the jungle.

Spanish classes

Centro de Español y Ingles Oriente and Alfaro; tel/fax 740360; email: jbariio@uio.satnet.net.
Elizabeth's School Calle 13 Julio Cañar and Av Oriente; tel: 740632. US$5 per hour.
Raíces Spanish School Calle 16 de Diciembre and Pablo A. Suárez; tel/fax: 740090; email: RACEFOR@hotmail.com. First hour free.

Internet

There are a couple of internet offices in Baños, but connections are made through Quito so are expensive at US$12 per hour: **C@fé** at 12 de Noviembre and Oriente, and **Cyber** at Calle Maldonado and Rocafuerte.

What to see

The **basilica and museum** on Calle Ambato are worth visiting. The basilica has some interesting paintings of miracles.

The baths

There are five different hot pools you can visit in Baños. The most convenient and nicest are the following. They do get very busy especially at weekends, and if you want peace its best to go early in the morning.

Baños de la Virgen in town, open 04.30–17.00.
El Salado, 2km west of the centre of town, probably the nicest. Follow Calle Martínez past the cemetery. Open 04.30–17.00.

Walks

Don't take valuables with you or walk alone if you can avoid it, as there have been reports of robberies on the trails out of town. Around the town there are some beautiful walks: the easiest and most obvious, taking less than an hour, takes you to the statue of the virgin that overlooks the town. Head for the cemetery and there is a path from there. Alternatively you can cross the Pastaza River by San Francisco bridge and head up any of the many trails into the hills beyond.

LLANGANANTES NATIONAL PARK

Llanganantes is believed to be where Atahualpa's general Rumiñahui hid the Inca treasures so they didn't fall into the hands of the Spanish conquistadors. Since colonial times numerous expeditions have attempted to find this mythical gold, but so far without success. The national park was established in 1996 to protect the Cordillera de los Llanganantes. It is a remote and inhospitable area, and though full of interesting flora and fauna, a trip there should not be treated lightly. Only go with an experienced local guide who knows the area well as there is a very high danger that you will get lost, and there is no infrastructure within the park. Contact INEFAN for detailed information and to find out about experienced guides.

EAST FROM BAÑOS

The road from Baños down into the Oriente is one of the most dramatic in the country. Any Baños to Puyo bus will drive this route, through the deep canyon of the River Pastaza.

RIOBAMBA

Telephone code 03

Riobamba was founded by Diego de Almagro in 1534. It is a busy commercial highland town, with many markets to which people come from villages all around. The setting is quite unique with magnificent views of Chimborazo, Carihuairazo, Sangay, Altar and Tungurahua, on a good clear day. The main attractions of the town are the train ride down the zigzag track to Durán, and the close access to Chimborazo, Ecuador's highest mountain.

Getting there and away

By bus

Riobamba has a central bus station only 1km from the town centre. There are frequent services to Quito (4 hrs), Cuenca (5–6 hrs), Guayaquil (4–5 hrs) and Ambato (1 hr). Buses to Guaranda take 2–3 hrs, depending on the road condition.

By train

The train station is right in the centre of town. Trains run several times a week to Huigra, and sometimes at weekends to Quito. Ask for the latest times and prices. Severe weather problems affected the train line in 1998 and in 1999 sections were still closed, so the full route from Riobamba to Durán was not open. Trains are currently (late 1999) only operating between Riobamba and Huigra and only run on a Wednesday, Friday and Sunday leaving Riobamba at 07.00, but days and times change, so check in advance. You can get your tickets the day before in Riobamba or from 06.00 on the morning of travel. Tickets cost US$15 from Riobamba to Sibambe (at the bottom of the section of the Nariz del Diablo) or US$12 from Alausí to Sibambe (the section of the Nariz del Diablo). Make sure you get the

right ticket, in dollars only. If you have a large backpack ask the guard to lock it up inside the train so that you can sit on the roof. From Alausí you can catch a bus to Guayaquil or back to Riobamba. Alausí has accommodation, Hostal Panamericano; tel: 930156 from US$2.

Where to stay and eat

Hostal Imperial Calle Rocafuerte 22–15 and 10 de Agosto; tel: 960429. From US$2.50, comfortable but can be noisy. Organises tours through Alta Montaña, and the owner does car tours up to Chimborazo 07.00–14.00, from US$8.

Hotel Manabi Calle Colón 19–58 and Olmedo; tel: 967967.

Hotel Tren Dorado Calle Carabobo 22–35 and 10 de Agosto; tel/fax: 964890. From US$5, with private bath. Friendly, central and clean, café.

Café El Delirio, Calle Constituyente and Rocafuerte, has good food at US$3 per main dish; there is a **vegetarian restaurant** next to Hotel Tren Dorado. The **Casa de Cultura** on 10 de Agosto has a bar with music at weekends, and other night spots include **La Casa Vieja**, Calle Orozco and Tarqui.

Practical information

Tourist office Calle 10 de Agosto 25–33; tel: 960217.

Tourist police Calle España 20–50.

Post office 10 de Agosto and Espejo.

Phone office Av de Policia and La Paz.

Money There are several banks in the centre of town including Banco del Pacifico, Calle Garcia Moreno, and Casa de Cambio at 10 de Agosto and España for travellers' cheques and cash.

Internet Email and Internet at Banana Net, Calle 10 de Agosto, US$3 per hour. Also book exchange and tourist information. There is also an Internet café on Calle Rocafuerte and 10 de Agosto, opposite the Hotel Imperial.

Travel agencies

Alta Montaña Daniel León Borja 37-17 and Diego Ibarra; tel: 963694; fax: 942215; email: aventura@exploringecuador.com Organise climbing, trekking and horse riding trips.

Andes Calle Espejo 24–43; tel: 966344. Have been recommended.

Andes Trek Colón and 10 de Agosto; tel: 940964. Organise treks and climbing trips, equipment to rent.

AGIG (Asociación de Guías Indígenas Guarguallá) 1430 Casa Indígena. Guayaquil and Juan de Velasco; tel: 941728. For an English-speaking guide contact Hotel Canadá diagonally across from the bus station; tel: 946677. They organise horseriding and trekking to the basecamp of Sangay. 5 days from US$175.

What to see

Riobamba is an elegant city with several interesting plazas and many colonial buildings. **Parque Maldonado** is the main square in the town. It has the **cathedral** and **Palacio Municipal** on two sides and arcaded colonial houses on the other two. There is a statue of Pedro Vicente Maldonado, a locally born scientist, in the square. **Parque Sucre**, with the **Colegio Maldonado** along one side and the **Fuente de Neptuno** in the centre, is an impressive plaza. The **Museo de Ciencias Naturales** is inside the Colegio Maldonado. The **Covento de la Concepción** now houses Riobamba's Religious Art Museum (Calle Orozca and España; open Tue–Sat 09.00–18.00; shut lunchtime). Wednesday and Saturday are the best days for markets in Riobamba.

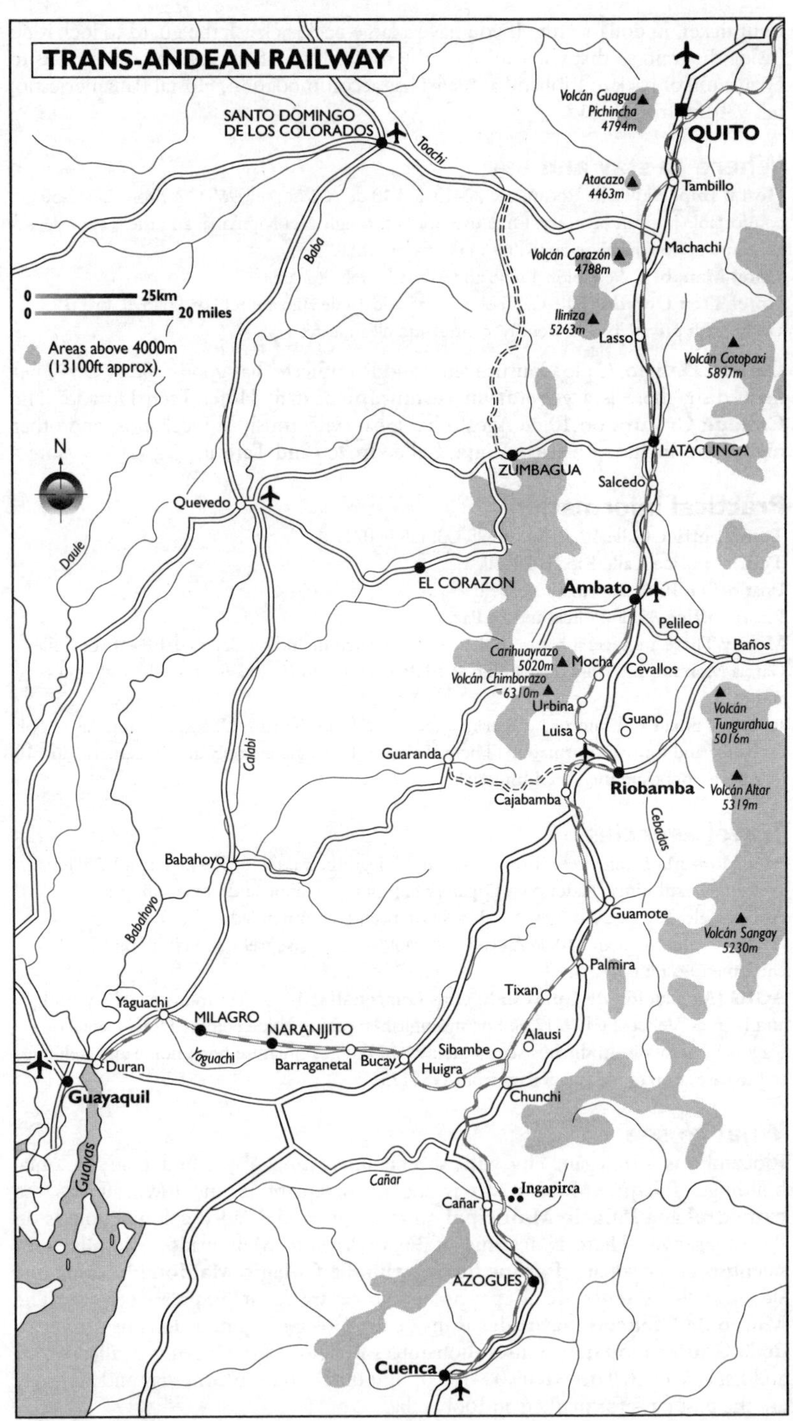
TRANS-ANDEAN RAILWAY
SANTO DOMINGO
DE LOS COLORADOS
Toachi
Volcán Guagua
Pichincha
4794m
QUITO
Atacazo
4463m
Tambillo
Machachi
Volcán Corazón
4788m
Baba
0 25km
0 20 miles
Areas above 4000m
(13100ft approx).
Iliniza
5263m
Lasso
Volcán Cotopaxi
5897m
N
LATACUNGA
ZUMBAGUA
Salcedo
Quevedo
Daule
EL CORAZON
Ambato
Pelileo
Baños
Carihuayrazo
5020m
Mocha
Cevallos
Volcán Chimborazo
6310m
Urbina
Volcán
Tungurahua
5016m
Guano
Luisa
Calabi
Guaranda
Riobamba
Volcán Altar
5319m
Cajabamba
Cebadas
Babahoyo
Guamote
Volcán Sangay
5230m
Babahoyo
Palmira
Tixan
Yaguachi
MILAGRO
NARANJITO
Alausi
Sibambe
Yaguachi
Barraganetal
Bucay
Huigra
Duran
Guayaquil
Chunchi
Guayas
Cañar
Ingapirca
Cañar
AZOGUES
Cuenca

THE TRANS-ANDEAN RAILROAD

In 1860 the first plans were made to build a train line from Guayaquil to Quito. However, it wasn't until 1895 that Eloy Alfaro, the then president, made contact with some North American technicians, Archer Harman and Edward Morely, and an agreement was reached, which signified the beginning of construction. Many lives were lost during construction, especially in the section known as La Nariz del Diablo, the Devil's Nose, where space for the line had to be carved from the rock. In 1902 the train line reached Alausí and in 1905 Riobamba. From there on construction was a bit easier, and in 1908 the train line finally reached Quito. Between 1915 and 1965 the line was extended to Cuenca.

Chimborazo

Chimborazo is Ecuador's highest mountain at 6,310m. Agencies in Quito and Riobamba organise mountaineering trips up the mountain, for experienced climbers. **Hostal Imperial** organises day tours up to one of the refuges on the mountain, worth it for the views if the weather is good.

SANGAY NATIONAL PARK

The National Park of Sangay includes within its boundaries the volcanoes of Sangay (5,230m), Tungurahua (5,016m) and Altar (5,319m). It covers a broad range of altitudes from 900m to 5,219m, encompassing lowland tropical rainforest and highland páramo. Access to Tungurahua is usually from Baños (3,200m below it), where you can find agencies with experienced guides. This is a non-technical climb, but due respect should be given to the mountain; it is high, and you will need to acclimatise fully at reasonable altitudes before attempting a climb. El Altar is one of the most difficult of Ecuador's peaks. Sangay is infrequently climbed as it is continuously active and throwing out burning volcanic material. This national park was once home to many mountain tapir (*Tapirus pinchaque*). This animal is now endangered due to illegal poaching which it seems little is being done about, despite the protected status of the park. In addition, areas of the park are repeatedly burned by farmers, to provide foraging for cattle. The park is most readily accessed from Riobamba, and there is an administration office and ranger station at Alao.

For further details contact INEFAN through their Quito office or at Riobamba Oficinas de MAG, Circunvalación, Riobamba; tel: 03 963779. Best to be at the office early in the morning.

The Southern Highlands

CUENCA

Telephone code 07

Cuenca stands out as one of the most impressive cities in Ecuador. It is Ecuador's third largest city with a population of 240,000 inhabitants. A lively place, it has a historical centre more extensive than any of Ecuador's other cities. Even so, everything of interest in the city is within walking distance. Around the city, within a day's journey there are a number of places that merit a visit: the small town of Baños with its hot baths (not to be confused with Baños in Tungurahua); the national park of El Cajas; and the archaeological site of Ingapirca. Cuenca has a considerable population of foreigners, especially English teachers, and is a popular tourist destination. There are numerous hostels, bars, cafés and Internet offices, catering for backpackers. Located at 2,500m, Cuenca has an average temperature of 14°C, which varies little throughout the year but a lot throughout the day (by up to 12°C). There is quite a marked rainy season from October to May. Cuenca's official name is Santa Ana de los Cuatro Ríos de Cuenca, the four rivers being Tomebamba, Yanuncay, the Tarqui and the Machángara. The Tomebamba is the river that runs right through the centre of town, and there is a nice walk along its banks.

History

The provinces of Azuay and Cañar were home to one of the most important prehispanic cultures of Ecuador, the **Cañari**. The Incas arrived under Tupac Yupanqui in the 15th century and in the same place where Cuenca stands today, they built the magnificent city of **Tomebamba** (the remains of the Inca city can be seen in part at the Museo Banco Central). This was possibly the second most important city in Tahuantinsuyo (the Inca empire), covering 40 hectares, with temples to Viracocha and Coricancha (sun temple). The Incas themselves destroyed this city rather than let it fall into the hands of the advancing Spanish conquistadors. In 1557 the Spanish founded the city of Cuenca on this well-chosen site, a fertile open valley irrigated by four rivers, and of temperate climate.

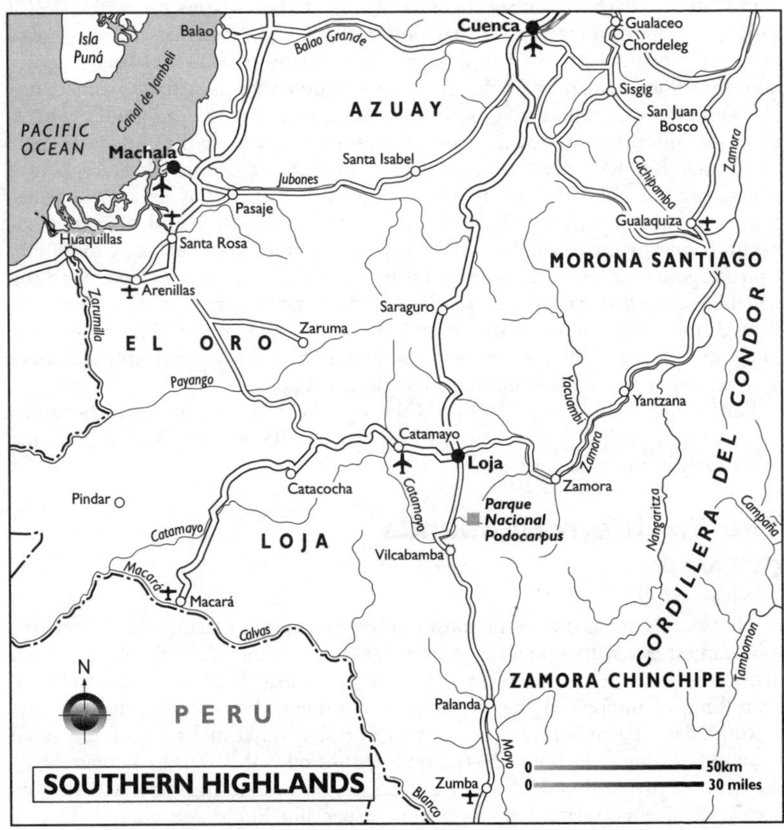

By the 17th century the city had grown substantially and already had several churches and a hospital. The economy was based on agriculture, mining and artisan work. In colonial Cuenca, as in all colonised Andean cities, the Spanish ruled and controlled all the top positions in the city. They made up approximately 10% of the population. The church was also powerful and at the top of the social hierarchy. The *criollos* (of Spanish descent, but born locally) had lesser administrative roles; they acquired land and became traders. There was an increasing number of *mestizos* (22% of the population), mixed race children from legitimate and illegitimate relations. The most numerous sector of the population were the indigenous people (67%). They had to suffer the injustices of the system, paying tributes to their conquistadors by working in mines, and as slave farmers on large hacienda estates. There were also a small number of black slaves (1%), mostly put to work on the sugar plantations of Gualaceo, Paute and Santa Isabel. Cuenca was an important commercial city and trade was done with Quito, Guayaquil and Lima. A journey to Lima could have taken 30 long and arduous days.

Getting there and away

By road

There are frequent buses from Cuenca's new and efficient bus terminal to Guayaquil (240km), Quito (440km), Machala (220km) and Huaquillas (270km).

By air

SAN and TAME fly to Cuenca from Quito. The airport is just a few kilometres from town past the bus terminal.

Where to stay

There are several really nice hostels in the old part of town. General Torres and Padre Aguirre have a high concentration of cheap and basic places.

Hotel Pichincha Calle General Torres 6–84; tel: 823868. From US$3 per person. Clean, large, central place, basic.
Hostal Rex Calle Tarqui 601; tel: 838352. From US$3 per person. Cheap and very basic.
El Cafecito Honorato Velasquéz 7–36 and Luis Cordero; tel: 832337. $5 per person. Colonial building with nice décor, sunny courtyard, unlimited hot water, good breakfast. Popular café with live music, can be noisy.
Hostal Chordeleg General Torres and Gran Colombia; tel: 824611; fax: 822536. From US$5 per person with bath and breakfast.
Hostal Macondo Calle Tarqui 11–64 between Lamar and Sanguirema; tel: 831198. From US$7 per person. Big rooms in a beautiful colonial building. Kitchen, garden, information and tours available.
Hostal La Orquidea Borrero 9–31 and Bolívar; tel: 824 511. $13/25 with bath and breakfast.
Hostal Caribe Inn Gran Colombia 10–51 and Padre Aguirre; tel: 835175/834157. $10–15 with bathroom and breakfast. Clean, attractive, colonial building.
Posada del Sol Calle Bolívar 5–03 and Mariano Cueva; tel: 838695. US$15–20 (+20% tax) with bath and breakfast. Also offer trekking, horseriding and bike tours. Beautiful hotel and very helpful staff.
Inca Real Torres 8–40 and Sucre; tel: 823-636. US$25–30 (+20% tax) with bath. Central location, beautiful building. All rooms on the courtyard.
Cabañas Yanuncay Take a taxi (or Baños bus) from Av Loja, then take the first right after the 'Arco de la Luz', or get off the bus there. Go 200m along the river to number 2–149. Tel: 883716/810265; fax 819681. US$8–12 single with breakfast. Country setting on the Yanuncay River, 10 minutes from downtown Cuenca. Rooms in chalet style houses.

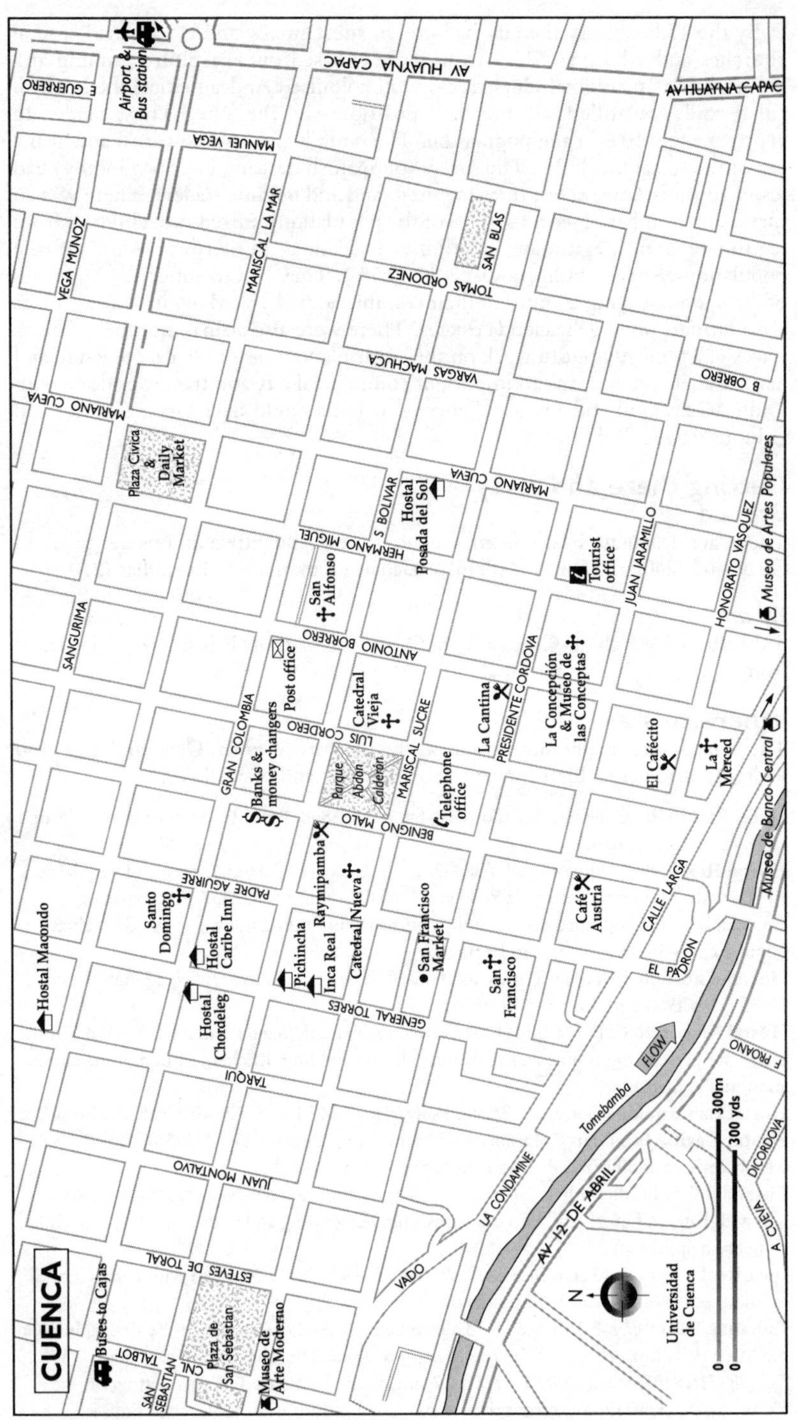
CUENCA
Buses to Cajas
Plaza de San Sebastian
Museo de Arte Moderno
SAN SEBASTIAN
CNL TALBOT
ESTEVES DE TORAL
JUAN MONTALVO
TARQUI
GENERAL TORRES
PADRE AGUIRRE
GRAN COLOMBIA
LUIS CORDERO
ANTONIO BORRERO
HERMANO MIGUEL
MARIANO CUEVA
VARGAS MACHUCA
TOMAS ORDONEZ
MANUEL VEGA
E GUERRERO
AV HUAYNA CAPAC
Airport & Bus station
VEGA MUNOZ
MARISCAL LA MAR
SAN BLAS
B OBRERO
Plaza Civica & Daily Market
SANGURIMA
S BOLIVAR
MARISCAL SUCRE
PRESIDENTE CORDOVA
JUAN JARAMILLO
HONORATO VASQUEZ
CALLE LARGA
EL PADRON
BENIGNO MALO
Hostal Macondo
Santo Domingo
Hostal Caribe Inn
Hostal Chordeleg
Pichincha
Inca Real
Raymipamba
Catedral Nueva
San Francisco Market
San Francisco
Banks & money changers
Post office
Parque Abdon Calderon
Catedral Vieja
San Alfonso
Hostal Posada del Sol
Telephone office
La Cantina
La Concepción & Museo de las Conceptas
Tourist office
Café Austria
El Cafécito
La Merced
Museo de Artes Populares
Museo de Banco Central
Tomebamba
FLOW
AV 12 DE ABRIL
LA CONDAMINE
VADO
F PROANO
DICORDOVA
A CUEVA
Universidad de Cuenca
N
0
300m
300 yds

Where to eat

Vegetarian restaurant on Calle Tarqui 9–21 and Bolívar.
Good food at **El Dorado** on Gran Colombia and Luis Cordero.
El Tequila Gran Colombia and Unidad Nacional. Good typical food.
Café Inca General Torres 8–40 between Sucre and Bolívar.
La Cantina Calle Borrero and Córdova.
Picallilly on Borrero and Córdova.
Café Austria on Calle Malo and Jaramillo.
Wanderbar on Hermano Miguel and Calle Larga.

Practical information

Tourist office Calle Hermano Miguel 6–86. They have maps of the city and can help with information on museums, local buses, hotels etc. The airport and bus terminal also have information offices.
Post office Calle Gran Colombia corner Borrero.
Phone office Calle Benigno Malo 7–26.
Money All the major banks have offices in the centre of the city. Open Mon–Fri, 09.00–13.30. Banco de Azuay, Calle Bolívar corner Borrero. Banco del Austral, Calle Sucre corner Borrero. Exchange offices Calle Sucre corner Borrero, open all day.
Airlines TAME, Gran Colombia and Hermano Miguel. SAN/SAETA, Benigno Malo and Pres Córdova.
Travel agencies Metropolitan Touring, Calle Sucre 6-22; tel: 831185, organise day trips to Cajas and Ingapirca and other more traditional services. Calle Sucre and Calle Gran Colombia also have a number of travel agents. Club de Andinismo/Club Sangay, Gran Colombia 7-39 and Luis Cordero, Ed Alfa, Of E; tel: 836758; fax: 829958, organise regular walks.
Internet There are several internet offices around the centre of Cuenca. Café on Hermano Miguel and Vásquez.
Language classes CEDEI (Fundación Centro de Estudios Interamericanos), Gran Colombia 11-02; tel: 839003; fax: 833593; email: compulab@cedei.org.ec

What to see

The **Parque Calderón** is right in the heart of old Cuenca. In the centre of the park there is a statue of Abdón Calderón, independence hero and native of Cuenca. There are eight pine trees in the park, brought from Chile by the president Luis Cordero. Around the square you will see a real mixture of buildings, marble, brick, stone, cement and adobe. The cathedrals, both old and new, the seminary, university and municipalidad are all of different ages, styles and materials. Nearby in the **Plaza de las Flores** all sort of flowers and plants are sold. For a look at normal Cuenca life visit the **Mercado of San Francisco**. It sells everything except food, which is sold in the **Mercado Diez de Agosto**. For crafts, from ceramic pots to basket work, furniture, weavings, stone and metal work, don't miss the **Plaza Sangurima**. Calle Gran Colombia has many shops selling art and crafts too.

Churches

The **new cathedral** was started at the end of the 19th century and finished in the 1960s. It is a tremendous building, 200m tall, with three blue-tiled cupolas in the roof. Various styles are represented: the overall appearance is romanesque, the towers and windows are gothic, and the rooftop with its three cupolas is Renaissance, reminiscent of the style of St Peter in Rome. The façade of the cathedral features the main door, in Renaissance style, flanked on each side by a series of marble columns decorated with the busts of the 12 apostles amidst bunches of grapes. In the centre of the façade there is a large round window with the bust of Christ and two angels just below. The top of the façade is dominated by two unfinished towers with a statue of Saint Ana and the Virgin between the two.

The **old cathedral** was the principal place of worship for the Spanish during colonial times, while San Sebastian and San Blas were for the indigenous people. The foundations of this cathedral were built using stones from the ruined Inca city of Tomebamba.

San Blas was built in the second half of the 16th century, also using stone from Tomebamba. The church has undergone considerable reconstruction in the 20th century, including the cupola and the roof. It is the only church in Cuenca built in the shape of a cross.

The **Convent Church of Las Conceptas** was built in the 17th century and was the first cloistered convent in Cuenca. Part of the adobe and wooden building has been restored and now contains religious art from the 17th century onwards. Calle Hermano Miguel 6–33; open Mon–Fri, 09.00–17.30, Sat 10.00–13.00. US$2.

The **Convent and Church of Carmen de la Asunción** was founded in 1682, and contains a wealth of religious art and artefacts, including an 18th-century fresco in the refectory.

There are many other churches which may be of interest to you including San Sebastian, San Francisco (19th century), Santo Domingo (20th century) and the colonial constructions of Todos Los Santos, San Roque, El Vecino, La Merced and Nuestra Señora de Guadalupe in Baños.

Museums

Museo de Arte Moderno Calle Sucre 15–27. Open Mon–Fri 09.00–13.00 and 15.00–19.00, Sat 09.00–12.00. Free. Set in a beautifully restored 19th-century building, this museum is dedicated to contemporary art.

Museo Banco Central Calle Larga and Avenida Huayna Capac. Open Mon–Fri 09.00–18.00, Sat 09.00–13.00. US$1. This museum has a collection of ethnography, archaeology and colonial art as well as temporary exhibitions, and the *in situ* site of Tomebamba.

Museo de Artes Populares Calle Hermano Miguel 3–23. Open Mon–Fri 09.30–13.00 and 14.30–18.00. Free. This is an interesting small museum of typical crafts, music, traditional tools etc.

There has been a considerable amount of architectural restoration in Cuenca in recent years, including the **Casa de la Familia Carrión**, the **Banco del Pacífico**, and many other houses and private buildings. **La Casa Azul** on Calle Gran Colombia with its shops and art galleries is one restored building you can get inside to appreciate.

Parque Nacional El Cajas

This national park is just 29km from Cuenca, and is one of Ecuador's most accessible and appealing. A national park since 1996, it protects 29,000 hectares of mostly páramo moorland, *stipa* grass, and glaciated valleys (*cajas*) of the Ecuadorian Andes (3,000–4,700m). Despite being so close to Cuenca the park receives relatively few visitors and those who do go tend to be quite unadventurous, so it's easy enough to get away from them and find some lovely unspoiled landscapes. There are almost 300 lakes in the park, formed from retreating ice flows, and dozens of smaller ponds. You can camp anywhere in the park for free, or stay in the refuge. Take all supplies with you, and be prepared for warm, sunny mornings, cloud and rain in the afternoons and cold nights. The best time to visit the park is between September and January. The bird, plant and animal life in the park are an additional attraction, with the possibility of seeing Andean condors, deer, foxes and rabbits. To get there from Cuenca take the morning bus from San Francisco market (06.30). The bus returns from the park at 15.00 (bus company San Sebastián or Turismo Occidental). There is an entry fee of US$10. Several travel agencies offer one-day tours to the park.

The small town of **Baños** is just 8km from Cuenca, overlooking the city. It has hot springs, where you can bathe, and several good restaurants and hotels. The thermal waters of Baños come up from below the earth's surface through a geological fault, which can be seen clearly in Baños, a 400m long 10m high rock dyke. There are several establishments with hot pools to choose from.

INGAPIRCA

Ingapirca (meaning wall of the Inca) is the most important Inca archaeological site in Ecuador today. It is strategically located at 3,100m on a rocky promontory, 80km from Cuenca. Take any northbound bus to Guayaquil, Riobamba or Quito to El Tambo or a direct bus with Transportes Cañar from the bus station in Cuenca. From El Tambo there are frequent buses to the site, 8km away. Access is from the villages of Cañari or Tambo. Many years before the Incas built on this site in the 15th century, the Cañari people used it for their own purposes. Many thousands of pieces of ceramics found here can be attributed to the Cañari people. Despite recent excavations and studies, we do not know exactly what function each part of the construction had. It is thought that Ingapirca was a temple to *Inti* (the sun) and the Inca's supreme deity.

The main building in the site is the *Adoratorio* or sun temple. This is the best preserved of all the buildings because of its solid construction, elliptical in shape, 3–4m high, 37m long, with an east–west orientation. The style and quality of the construction is typically Inca, with tightly interlocking stones and trapezoidal doorways and niches. To the south of the sun temple are several constructions which were probably the houses of the priests, and an open area, probably the principal plaza where meetings would have been held. To the east of the plaza is the area named after an 18th-century archaeologist, Condamine. There are varying opinions as to its purpose – it was possibly a *tambo* (resting house), or home of the virgins of the sun, or even a cemetery, maybe all three. To the southeast of the *Adoratorio* on a small hill is the part of the site known as *Pilaloma* (meaning small hill). From archaeological evidence unearthed here it is probable that this area was a Cañari ceremonial centre. It is a semi-elliptical construction of rooms, perhaps for priests, around a plaza. Throughout the complex there is evidence of Inca roads, store rooms, more houses and protective walls.

AZOGUES

This is one of the centres of the Panama hat industry, where you can see them being made. There are a couple of cheap and basic places to stay here: Hotel Charles or Residencial Tropical. Azogues is 31km north of Cuenca. To get to Azogues take any northbound bus from the bus station.

LOJA

Telephone code 07

This is a large town of just over 100,000 people, a gateway to the southern Oriente and to the Peruvian border at Macará. There are some interesting colonial buildings in the centre of town. There are two universities and a music academy. Most people go straight to Vilcabamba and on to the southern Oriente or head south for Peru. If you decide to stay in the town there are plenty of hostels and restaurants.

Getting there and away

By bus

Loja has a modern terminal for all buses on the northern edge of town. There are buses to Macará (6 hrs), best with Loja International, to Quito (14 hrs), Guayaquil (9 hrs), Cuenca (5 hrs), Huaquillas (8 hrs) and Zumba (7 hrs). Buses run every 30 mins to Vilcabamba. The bus station has an information office, shops and restaurants.

By air

There are daily flights to Quito some days via Guayaquil (Tue, Thur and Sat). TAME office Calle Zamora and 24 de Mayo; tel: 570248.

The airport is 30km from Loja. There are shared taxis into town.

Practical information

Post office on Calle Colón.
Phone office on Calle Rocafuerte and Olmedo.
Money There are a couple of banks on the main plaza, Filanbanco and Banco del Azuay.
INEFAN office Calle Azuay 12-44, Loja; tel: 563131. Contact for information on Podocarpus National Park.

VILCABAMBA

Telephone code 07

This small peaceful town is a haven from the hassle and exhaustion of travelling. It doesn't have the attraction of high snow-capped volcanoes, but rather of gently rolling, vegetation covered hills, flower filled valleys and a comfortably warm climate (1,600m, average temperature 20°C). There are several really nice places to stay with swimming pools and hammocks, spectacular views of the surrounding forested mountains, and good food. There are an infinite number of walks, or horseback rides, in the mountains from the town, and Vilcabamba is the gateway to the natural wonder of Podocarpus National Park. Major floods in 1999 caused water and road problems in the town, with the River Chaupi seriously changing course and washing away most of the road bridge on the east side of town.

History

Vilca means sacred and *bamba* valley, hence the name Vilcabamba; for the Incas and their predecessors this valley was sacred. A significantly high proportion of the inhabitants of this sacred valley supposedly live to be over a hundred years old, keeping in good health. It could be the water, the diet, the use of medicinal plants, the good clean air or the generally relaxed attitude to life.

Getting there and away

By road

There are buses every half hour to Vilcabamba from the bus terminal in Loja. Several companies ply the route, which takes under an hour. Buses run 05.00–21.00. From Vilcabamba buses and shared taxis run to Loja. There are also buses to Zumba, and Gualaquiza in the Oriente. From Loja bus terminal there are buses to Quito (14 hrs), Guayaquil (9 hrs), Cuenca (5 hrs), Huaquillas (8 hrs), Machala, and Macará (6 hrs, departures at 09.00, 10.00, 23.00). The best company for Macará is **Loja International**.

By air

There is an airport near Loja (30km) from where there are flights to Quito (Mon, Wed, Fri) and Guayaquil (Tue, Thur, Sat). TAME office in Loja Calle Zamora and 24 de Mayo; tel: 570248.

Where to stay and eat

Hostal Mandango at the bus station is the cheapest place in town, and reasonable, from US$2 per person.

The Hidden Garden Calle Sucre, just off the plaza; tel: 580281. From US$6 per person. Very central, friendly and clean, good food, swimming pool, kitchen.

La Posada Real Calle Agua del Hierro. From US$6 per person. Interesting place, friendly, quiet and comfortable, good views, good food.

Las Ruinas de Kinara Tel: 580314. From US$6 per person. New hostel with large pool, hammocks, good food, friendly. 10 mins walk from the centre of the town.

Cabañas Río Yambala 8km from town, take a taxi. From US$2 per person. Cabins for 3–6, great views, kitchen, restaurant. Treks organised.

The Pole House Lodge is just out of town, over the river. They have a variety of accommodation, from the Pole House itself, a wooden stilted house, with room for 4 people, and a fully equipped kitchen and bathroom (from US$4 per person, US$16 for the house). Also several self-contained, charming adobe houses with great views, kitchen, hammocks, US$3–4 per person. Ask at Primavera shop on the square for directions. Tel: 637186.

There's a good vegetarian restaurant behind the Plaza on Calle Piscobamba. There are several places to eat around the square, and on Diego Vaca de la Vega after you cross the river Chaupi.

Practical information

Gregorio's Book Exchange, across the river and keep walking. Won't change anything but good quality.

Travel agencies Orlando Falco is highly recommended as a naturalist guide to Podocarpus, US$25 for a day tour. Ask at Primavera shop on the plaza for details. Ask for Luis or Ramon, on the plaza, for horse tours, usually 4 hours, US$1 per hour.

Internet Vilcanet, with just one computer, is just off the plaza next to Restaurant Orquídea.

What to see

Podocarpus National Park

Podocarpus is unrivalled for its richness and variety of plants and animals. It was created in 1982 and covers an area of 146,280 hectares, over 1,400km^2, ranging from 950m to 3,700m. It was created to protect the two species of Angiosperms found here in large numbers, *Podocarpus rospiglios* and *Podocarpus oleifolius*, which have given their name to the park. The vegetation in the park consists of páramo at higher altitudes and elfin forest, temperate forest and subtropical forest as you descend on either side of the Andes, which traverse the park. Mammals found here, though somewhat elusive, are puma, spectacled bear, fox and the páramo wolf. There are well over 500 bird species in the park, which are considerably easier to see than the mammals. The ones you are most likely to see include tiger heron, torrent duck, Andean cock-of-the-rock, toucan, parrot and hummingbird. There are over a hundred lakes in the park, left by glaciers, and dozens of beautiful streams and cascading waterfalls.

To visit the park you will need good warm clothing, a map, compass, torch, repellent, waterproofs and boots and all your food supplies. You can camp or stay at the refugios, US$2 per person. For further information and a map contact INEFAN office at Calle Azuay 12–44, Loja; tel: 593 7563131. The conservation group **Arco Iris** does a lot of work to help preserve the forest of Podocarpus; their office is at Calle Valdivieso 03–26, Loja; tel: 593 7572926; email: fail@fai.org.ec.

MACARÁ AND THE BORDER WITH PERU

It is very straightforward to cross into Peru at Macará, much nicer, quicker and less stressful than at Huaquillas. You can get from Vilcabamba or Loja to Piura in a day quite easily, thereby avoiding having to stay in Macará or Sullana, neither of which is particularly pleasant. A 6-hour bus journey from Loja, through dramatic mountain scenery, brings you to Macará, a small border town. Landslides often affect this road in the rainy season, so check beforehand. You have to visit the immigration office in a concrete building in the centre of town. There are several cheap and nasty places to stay. **Espiga de Oro**, near the market is reasonable. Where you get off the bus there will be taxis or pick-ups to indicate the way. Get your exit stamp and then take a taxi or truck to the bridge (5 mins, US$1). Walk over the bridge and at the far side go through Peruvian immigration. The border is open daily 08.00–18.00. This is usually quick and hassle free. There is nowhere official to change money here but there is often someone hanging around willing to exchange a few dollars. Take a *colectivo* taxi to Sullana (135km), and ask the driver to let you off at the right place in Sullana to catch the bus to Piura (40km, 45 mins) if that's where you're going. Sullana is not a good place to stay, as there's nothing there. Watch out for bag snatchers and pickpockets.

Southern tamandua

7 The Coast

Esmeraldas Province

The northernmost province on the coast of Ecuador is Esmeraldas, which is the poorest province in Ecuador. South of the town of Esmeraldas there are some good beaches, while to the north the natural vegetation is lush, with extensive tropical forests of *tierra firme* and marshy flooded areas of mangrove trees which reach to the water's edge. This is an interesting area for animal and plant life, though actually getting off the main route and into the interesting areas requires patience and enterprise as there are few tourists in this part of the country and very little provision for them.

The best route to take to the northwest coast of Ecuador is from Ibarra, by a beautiful and spectacular train or bus journey. The trip takes you down the western slopes of the Andes through verdant cloudforest, into the mangrove swamps and river deltas of the Pacific coast.

Today most of the inhabitants of the province of Esmeraldas are Afroecuadorians. They are descended either from shipwrecked slaves, or from slaves brought here by the Spanish conquistadors to work on plantations. Slavery wasn't abolished until the 1850s. There are also indigenous Indian communities of the Cayapa or Chachi tribe and of the Awa people.

Inland from the coast there was once just thick forest. Just a fraction of this remains as large tracts of forest have been cut down for farming. Agriculture is important in this province and crops such as tobacco, coffee, cocoa, cotton and bananas are grown for export, while for local consumption maize, beans, rice, and other fruit are grown. You'll see various types of tropical cattle being farmed, Swiss Brown, Brahman, Holstein and Santa Gertrudis. There is some industry in the province, principally oil related and fish processing.

The River Cayapas-Santiago drains the northern part of the province and the River Esmeralda in the south. The climate in this area is quite uncomfortably hot and sticky most of the time. Average rainfall on the northern coast is 3,000mm, most of which falls between December and June. Temperatures vary little throughout the day or year, the average being 25°C. High humidity and overcast days are common.

HISTORY

The first settlers here were of the Valdivia (3,500–1,500BC) and the Chorrera cultures (900–300BC). Later the Atacames, Tolas and Cayapas lived in this part of the country. The La Tolita (600BC–AD400) culture inhabited the whole of the coast from Esmeraldas in the south to the Bay of Buenaventura in Colombia in the north. The name given to this culture comes from large, earth funerary mounds known as *tolas*, characteristic of this tribe. The fine ceramics left by the Tolita people have given archaeologists an insight into their way of life, religion and

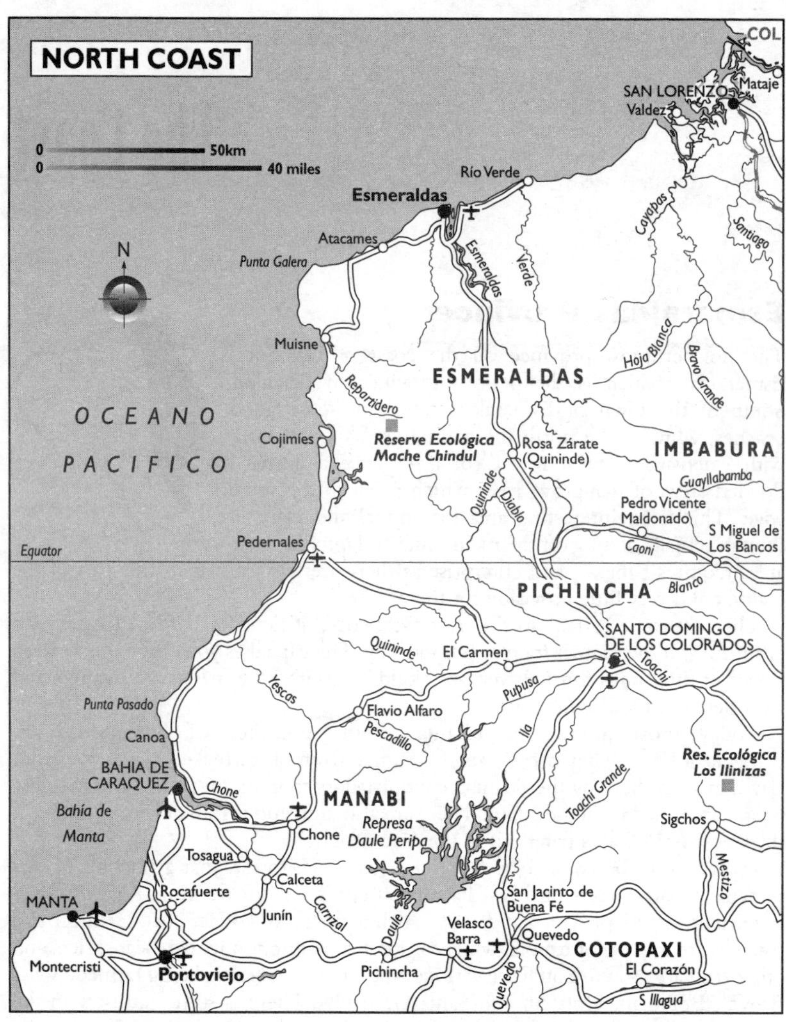

symbolism. The world depicted on their pots shows the use of sacred plants. Feline figures are particularly prominent, and probably served as an image for worship, representing one of the most powerful deities of the Tolita. Other anthropomorphic figures commonly represented on ceramic objects are serpents and birds. The principal site of the Tolita is on an island near the town of La Tola, accessible only by boat from La Tola. There isn't much to see today, but it is worth a visit if you are particularly interested in archaeology.

The Cayapa

About 4,000 **Chachi** or **Cayapa Indians** live in the northwest part of the province of Esmeraldas, a tropical, wet and fertile area. Their villages are along the banks of the Santiago, Cayapas, Onzole and San Miguel rivers, and they live by hunting, fishing and small scale agriculture. Their land is communally owned and its use determined by the needs of the tribal people living there.

There is no commercial exploitation, which so far has helped protect the forest. The people travel the extensive coastal waterways and the open sea in small canoes hollowed from wooden logs. Their houses are simple constructions, platforms with partition walls, hammocks made of bark and palm leaf thatch roofs. There are ceremonial centres on the Cayapas River where important events are held, to which all the Chachis travel. Their language, which has been transmitted orally through generations, is *Cha'apalachi*. The Chachis struggle to keep their culture alive but it is constantly under threat from the intrusions of the modern world.

SAN LORENZO

Telephone code 06

The town of San Lorenzo is right on the coast, only 25km from the border with Colombia. It is quite distinct from anywhere else in Ecuador. The population (15,000) is mainly of Afroecuadorians, descended from black slaves, who have a very different culture from the rest of the country. This is apparent in the music and dancing of the area. San Lorenzo is a lively town especially at weekends when dancing, often in the street, goes on into the small hours. The typical instruments you may see here are African in origin, the *marimba*, the *guasa hembra* and *guasa macho* (sugarcane with seeds inside), and various sorts of drums. The people make a basic living from fishing and small scale agriculture, but this is one of the poorest parts of Ecuador. As soon as you arrive in San Lorenzo, whether by train, bus or boat, you will probably be adopted by a local kid, who will want to show you around, for a small tip. There is not a lot to do in the town, but you can take a tour into the Reserva Ecológica de Manglares, or hire a canoe to explore the area.

Getting there and away

By road

The roads in this part of Ecuador are not too good, and are prone to landslides during the wet season (December to June). You can get a bus to San Lorenzo from Esmeraldas through Borbón (172km). There are buses from Ibarra (178km, 4–5 hrs) to San Lorenzo on a new road. Buses leave Ibarra every couple of hours from 05.00 from one of the companies with offices behind the market. They usually stop en route at a roadside restaurant.

By rail

The railway journey from Ibarra to San Lorenzo is truly spectacular (293km, minimum 8 hrs). However, it is also prone to landslides and for that reason is often not operational.

By boat

Motorised canoes operate like taxis up and down this northern stretch of the coast, connecting remote, sometimes isolated settlements. The size and speed of these craft vary enormously, and they may be weather protected, covered over, with reasonably comfortable seats for up to 30 people. Some boats are small and unstable, with wooden boards balanced between one side and the other, where you perch with your knees squeezed to your chest and without moving for fear of capsize.

There are several motorised canoes a day to La Tola (2 hrs, US$3), passing through Limones; departures from San Lorenzo 05.00–15.30. Limones has a couple of very basic hostels if you really want to stay here. The journey is quite fun, and a good way to see the mangrove forest and river deltas. From La Tola there is road transport to Esmeraldas; it is 45 mins to the main road and then a further 3 hrs to Esmeraldas. From San Lorenzo there are boats to Borbón and daily boats to the Colombian border, but you have to get your passport stamped in Esmeraldas or Quito, and this is a very rarely travelled route for tourists.

Where to stay and eat

There are three or four reasonable hostels in town to suit the budget traveller.

Gran Hotel San Carlos Calle Imbabura; tel: 780267. This is the nicest and the best value at US$5.
Hotel Continental Calle Imbabura; tel: 780126. This is a good budget choice at US$5. Rooftop terrace, safe, central.
Ballet Azul serves good fresh fish at very reasonable prices. **Estancia** is also a good, though expensive restaurant.

Practical information

Tourist office There is an INEFAN park information office on the plaza, next to the port. They can give you help and information on how to visit the Reserva Ecológica Manglares Cayapas Mataje.
Phone office on the main street, Calle Imbabura.
Money You can exchange dollars at some of the hotels but it's probably best to travel with sucres through this part of Ecuador.
Travel agencies Jaime Burgos runs Estancia Tours and restaurant, and organises local excursions into the reserve or to the local indigenous communities; email: ecumater@uio.satnet.net

What to see

Reserva Ecológica Manglares Cayapas Mataje, established in 1996 and lying to the north of San Lorenzo, is mostly mangrove swamps. Access is not easy and the best way to visit is by hiring a boat from the port in San Lorenzo to take you up some of the nearby inlets of the river deltas to see the forest. There are several different types of mangrove tree supporting a variety of wildlife and birds. The manglar rojo is one of the tallest mangrove species, some trees reaching a height of 68m. The area is rich in crustaceans, fish and reptiles. Further inland in the drier areas there a number of mammals too such as the anteater (*Tamandua mexicana*), white-throated capuchin (*Cebus capucinus*), kinkajou (*Potos flavus*), tayra (*Eira barbara*), and paca (*Agouti paca*).

Tayra

Borbón is four hours from Esmeraldas by ranchera or bus. There are several basic hostels here and it is a good starting point for trips up the Santiago River. A 5 hr boat trip from Borbón will bring you to Playa de Oro, which has a lodge operated by SUBIR, an organisation concerned with sustainable development (visit their office in Borbón for details or email: subir@care.org.ec). To visit the lowland part of the Catacachi Cayapas Reserve access is from San Miguel on the River Cayapas. There is a daily boat from Borbón. A trip into this river network is highly recommended to glimpse the way of life of the indigenous and the Afroecuadorian river communities. There is an INEFAN office in town.

Reserva Ecológica Cotacachi Cayapas This reserve area covers 204,000 hectares. The lowland area of the reserve lies within the Chocó biogeographic area, which extends from the Darien Gulf in Panama to the Toisán Mountains in Ecuador. It is an area of very high biodiversity, and with a remarkably large number of endemic species. Six hundred and thirty bird species have been registered here. The typical forest of the area is wet and tropical, characterised by trees, which can be 60m tall, such as chanul (*Humiriastrum procerum*), guadaripo, sande and guayacán. These trees are draped in epiphytes, with beautiful orchids and bromeliads.

FUNDEAL works with indigenous communities to support alternative development, and is concerned with research and conservation of nature. They have a lodge, Verdes Trópicos Chocó, and organise 4–5-day tours from Quito visiting the Chachi people and Cotacachi Cayapas. Contact their office in Quito at Calle Reina Victoria 1227 and Calama; tel: 507284/507208; fax: 507245; email: fundeal@waccom.net.ec

ESMERALDAS

Telephone code 06

Esmeraldas itself is an unappealing town, one of the poorest in Ecuador and consequentially with probably one of the highest chances of being robbed. It is an important port, with a population of over 100,000. Most people who come here go straight through to the resort area of Atacames, and this is undoubtedly the best thing to do rather than stay in Esmeraldas itself.

Getting there and away

By bus

There are frequent buses from Esmeraldas to Santo Domingo, Quito (hourly, 6 hrs), and Guayaquil (7 hrs). There isn't a central bus terminal in the town – companies are scattered around the centre, within a couple of blocks of the plaza. Use taxis to get from one bus office to the other, especially after dark.

By air

TAME has a daily flight from Quito. A taxi from the airport costs US$5.

Where to stay and eat

Ambato Av Kennedy and Guerra; tel: 721144. Good budget choice.

Sandry Av Libertad and Montalvo; tel: 726861. Good budget choice.

El Galeón Piedrahita and Olmedo; tel: 723818. From US$8 per person, with fan or air conditioning.

Hotel Esmeraldas Calle Libertad 407 and Ramon Tello; tel: 728703. Has a casino and piano bar, air conditioning, TV etc.

For food, **Más o Menos Supermarket** has a good selection of American and Colombian goods. **La Sultana de la Valle**, Calle Libertad on the way to Las Palmas, has good seafood. Calle Cañizares has several reasonable places. Cine Esmeraldas is the best cinema in the city.

Practical information

Police Calle Cañizares and Bolívar.
Money It is possible to exchange money at Filanbanco and Banco Popular between Cañizares and Piedrahita on Bolívar. Money exchange is upstairs in both banks.

ATACAMES

Telephone code 06

Atacames is one of the most popular beach resorts near Esmeraldas (25km to the south). Prices go up considerably during high season, from December to March. Weekends can also be busy. As all along the coast, be very security aware, make sure your room locks properly, don't carry any more valuables than you have to, and don't walk around at night away from lit areas.

Where to stay and eat

The German-run **Hostal de Manglar** has been recommended; tel: 731464.
Villas Arco Iris. Tel: 731069; fax: 731437. From US$5 at low season for clean cabins with all facilities.
Cabañas Rogers south of Atacames is a quiet place with beautiful grounds, but bring a mosquito net.

For food try **Paco Foco** for good seafood, or the Italian pizza place; for dancing **Ludo's disco** and **San Baye disco**. Things change rapidly so ask around for the latest recommendations on places to stay, eat and go out at night.

MUISNE

Muisne is a small, quiet fishing community on an island connected by a ferry service. It is a popular backpacking destination and just 30km beyond Atacames, 1 hour by bus.

It is possible to travel on from Muisne to Canoa by boat. It is also possible to combine small boats and open sided buses south along the coast from Muisne to Cojimíes (30km). I wouldn't recommend walking along these beaches on your own, particularly for women as there have been many cases of theft and muggings. Check locally for the latest on safety in the area. **Hostal Calada** is cheap and safe, from US$5 for a double; **Playa Paraíso** is recommended, a small pink hotel, right on the beach with hammocks. From US$2 per person. There are reasonable places to eat in the village itself, and the kiosks on the beach have good seafood.

Manabí Province

BAHÍA DE CARÁQUEZ

Telephone code 05

This is a small commercial town with nice beaches. It tends to be full of Ecuadorians at weekends and pretty quiet during the week. On the north side of the River Chone the busy village of San Vicente is interesting to visit.

Where to stay and eat

Bahía Bed and Breakfast Calle Ascázubi; tel: 690146. From US$2 per person with fan.
La Querencia Malecón; tel: 690009. From US$3 per person with private bath.
La Herradura Tel: 690446. From US$9 per person.

Practical information

The agency **Guacamayo Tours** arranges fishing trips to suit you. Av Bolívar and Arenas; tel: 691412. It can reserve hotels along the coast and advise on itineraries. Owned by an Ecuadorian and a New Zealander, the agency aims to promote ethical tourism and has set up several environmental projects including a school, organic farm, recycling project, and an organic eco-friendly shrimp farm. Volunteers with a minimum of a month are welcome on their projects. Contact Nicola and Dario at email: ecopapel@ecuadorexplorer.com or tel: 690597.

Bahía Dolphin Tours Calle Salinas; tel: 692097/84/86. Offers tours to Chirije archaeological site, Cerro Seco dry forest, Isla de los Pajaros, shrimp farms, Monte Cristi, where Panama hats are made, and nearby beaches and caves.
CETUR tourist office is at Malecón between Octavio and Arenas; tel: 691124.

NORTH OF BAHÍA

The beaches between Bahía and Pedernales are some of Ecuador's best. Santo Domingo to Pedernales is 3 hours by bus or *ranchera* (open-sided bus).

Canoa

Canoa has one of the best beaches on the whole coast. It's 17km from San Vicente and is a quiet fishing village with a clean beach and friendly people. From Pedernales or Portoviejo you can take a bus to Canoa.

Where to stay and eat

Hotel Bambú, tel: 09 753696, is right on the beach. It is run by Dutch people and is clean, comfortable and peaceful with hammocks, a balcony overlooking the beach and good food. From US$5 per person. **La Posada de Daniel** off the beach is friendly with a nice restaurant, and a pool. From US$7 per person. Reserve through Guacamayo Tours, tel: 691412. **El Torbelino** has good-value typical food.

Pedernales

Pedernales is a small commercial town. There are a few places to stay, though very few people stop here.

Cojimíes

If you're travelling north from Pedernales you can stop off at the tranquil and rustic beach hotel of **Coco Loco** (from US$10 per person) between Pedernales (26km) and Cojimíes (14km). Book through Guacamayo Tours (tel: 05 691412).

SOUTH OF BAHÍA

Cruzita

This is a small fishing village with great beaches, 45 minutes from Portoviejo. There are several budget hostels and good seafood restaurants. Try **Residencial Rosita** or **Hotel Hippocampo**.

Santa Domingo

This modern town has few attractions, but you may have to travel through it to get from one part of the coast to another.

Getting there and away

Santo Domingo has a well-organised bus terminal on the edge of the town. Buses to Esmeraldas are frequent (3 hrs, US$3). A taxi into town from the terminal is less than US$1, or there are local buses passing the terminal. Buses to Portoviejo (7 hrs, US$3).

Where to stay and eat

Hostal Geneva, 21 de Mayo; tel: 02 759694, from US$3 per person, is clean and reasonable. Calle 25 de Mayo has dozens of small restaurants.

Manta

Manta is quite a large port city, but it does have a good safe swimming beach, popular with locals, called Tarqui. The beach is also a good place to see the fishing boats come in early in the morning. You'll see sharks, swordfish, dorada and dozens of other sorts of fish. A recommended hostel is **Villa Eugenia** on the Malecón, which is family run, safe and overlooks the sea. **CETUR tourist office** is at Paseo Egas, Calle between 13 and 14, tel: 05 622944.

Few backpackers spend much time in Manta, but generally prefer to head south to the coastal area of Machalilla. Passing through Portoviejo and Jipijapa the vegetation is quite unique, dry tropical forest, with bizarre shaped kapok trees. There is little of interest for tourists in either of these two towns, though you may have to change buses. Puerto Lopéz is the best place to head for, with plenty of hostels and restaurants, a nice beach, and easy access to the gems of the Machalilla National Park.

PUERTO LÓPEZ

Telephone code 05

Puerto López is a small fishing town of around 10,000 inhabitants. It has a very ramshackle appearance at first sight, but it's quite charming, and grows on you. The town is at its most active from 07.00 in the morning when the fishing catch is brought in. If you go down to the beach you will see an amazing range of Pacific fish, of all shapes and sizes, including hammerhead sharks. A market is set up on the beach and various stalls sell fish for breakfast. You can swim from this lovely long golden beach too, but don't leave your belongings lying around on their own, as thefts are becoming more common. There are a couple of nice hostels in the town and the surrounding national park of Machalilla has several attractions well worth a visit. The fresh fish restaurants, which line the beach, are excellent, and very good value.

History

Like the other towns along the coast Puerto López was an important urban centre and prehispanic port during the Bahía (500BC–AD650) and Manteño (AD500–1532) periods. It was a centre for the collection and processing of the spondylus and *concha perla*, as was Salango and also Machalilla. There has been very little excavation in Puerto López and the new town has probably been built right on top of any pre-existing settlement.

Getting there and away

By bus

There are early morning and evening **buses** to Quito, and several buses a day along the coast to Jipijapa, Manta and Portoviejo (2 hrs). Reina del Camino or Panamericana are recommended bus companies, coming from Quito. Going south there are pick-up trucks and buses to coastal villages and towns, if the roads are open. After the 1998 El Niño and rains the following year large tracts of the road south of Puerto López were washed away entirely. From Guayaquil, Panamericana or Transporte Ecuador are recommended.

Where to stay and eat

Residencia Tourisma on the seafront is cheap and basic.

Hostal Villa Colombia Tel: 604105. One block inland from the main street, this is a great hostel, with lots of space, hammocks and a kitchen available. Friendly and relaxing. From US$3 per person.

Hostal Tuzco Tel: 604132. A couple of blocks from the market, inland; reasonable and clean. From US$3 per person.

Practical information

Police on the main street, a one man office, helpful if somewhat laid back.

INEFAN Park Office for Machalilla National Park and information centre, very helpful, sell entrance tickets to the park for US$20, valid for one week. Located just off the main street.

Travel agencies Several travel agents sell trips out to the island of La Plata from US$45, including the park entry fee of US$20. They also organise tours to other parts of the park.

Machalilla National Park

This is one of the most visited of all Ecuador's national parks. It's easily accessible from the town of Puerto López, which is the centre of operations for the park (see above) and the departure point for boat trips out to the islands. The climate and vegetation of the national park are determined by the convergence of two powerful currents of water in the Pacific, the cold Humboldt current from the south and the warm Panamá current from the north. Most of the year it is sunny and hot, but there is a marked rainy season from January to May, and a dry season from June to December. This part of the Educadorian coast has the only dry tropical forest of South America, with strange-looking trees of bulging trunks. Typical trees of this forest include *algarrobo* (carob), laurel, and kapok. Further inland on the slopes of the Cordillera Chongón-Colonche is a rich humid tropical forest. The national park also protects the marine area just off the coast of Puerto López and the island of La Plata.

Agua Blanca

When the Spanish arrived here in the 16th century they found that the local inhabitants lived in a highly organised society. Using balsa rafts they sailed up and down the Pacific coast as far north as Mexico, and south to Chile trading the spondylus (*Spondylus princeps*) shell. Their capital city of over 600 buildings was known as Salangóme. The remains of this city can be seen at Agua Blanca, just to the north of Puerto López.

There is a good archaeological museum and a guided trail around the reasonably well-preserved extensive site, where you can see a complex of terraces and platforms with adobe and stone walls. Open daily 09.00–17.00. US$1.50. Take any of the coastal buses or pick-ups from the main street in Puerto López going north and ask to get off at the turn-off for Agua Blanca. Walk 5km along the road to reach the site. There is a shop at the site and a small village. Tours can be organised to San Sebastián; talk to the guards at Agua Blanca.

San Sebastián

Approximately 10km beyond Agua Blanca, further inland, after hiking through the dry forest you reach the humid tropical forest of San Sebastián. This is great for seeing orchids, birds and monkeys. You will need at least a couple of days to appreciate this part of the park. Talk to the guards at Agua Blanca, who can arrange accommodation and horses. Take all supplies with you. US$20 per day for a guide, US$3 per mule.

Los Frailes

This is a series of gorgeous beaches and cliffs reached by walking along a 4km track, through dry tropical forest. It is one of the most beautiful parts of the park, just 10km north of Puerto López. Take a pick-up or any northbound bus and ask to be dropped off at Los Frailes.

La Isla de la Plata

This island lies 37km off the coast, around 1½ hours by boat. It has colonies of three sorts of boobies, blue-footed, red-footed and masked, and you will see numerous other seabirds, such as pelicans, terns and frigate birds. There are sealions on the island and you are likely to see dolphins, rays and whales (from June to September). Take plenty of water and sun protection with you as it can be very hot and dry on the island. On most tours you will spend 1½–4 hours walking on the island. Tours cost US$25 in addition to the park entrance fee of US$20.

THE HUMPBACK WHALE

The humpback whale is a regular visitor to the Ecuadorian coast, and the waters off the province of Manabí, now protected by the national park of Machalilla, are breeding grounds for this magnificent whale. There are frequent sightings from June to September. The female whales are larger than the males and can weigh up to 40 tonnes, reaching 16m in length. The whales migrate from the Antarctic, approximately 8,000km from their breeding ground off Ecuador. They probably migrate here to breed as the water is warmer and safer, away from the cold Antarctic waters and their main predators, the Orcas and sharks. The only other known breeding ground of the humpback whale is off the Colombian coast.

Yaqu Pacha is a non-governmental organisation founded in 1992 in Germany. Its main goals are the conservation of aquatic mammals in South America. The name Yaqu Pacha comes from the Quichua Indians and means water world. Yaqu Pacha gives support to scientific investigations that produce valuable information to help the protection and conservation of endangered aquatic mammals. In Ecuador, Yaqu Pacha is involved in two projects. One is the Sacha Pacha project in the Ecuadorian rainforest, where the organisation is trying to protect river dolphins, manatees and the otter. The second project, begun in 1996 and growing ever since, is the humpback whale project. Studies include photo-identification of the individual animals by the distinct fluke patterns they show when diving; general habitat use; and the influence of commercial whale-watching on the behaviour of the whales. Much effort goes into environmental education of the local people and involvement of Ecuadorian biologists in the project, in the hope that they, together with the tourist agencies, fishermen and park rangers, will help protect the whales in the future.

Information provided by Meike Scheidat; email: Mscheidat@aol.com

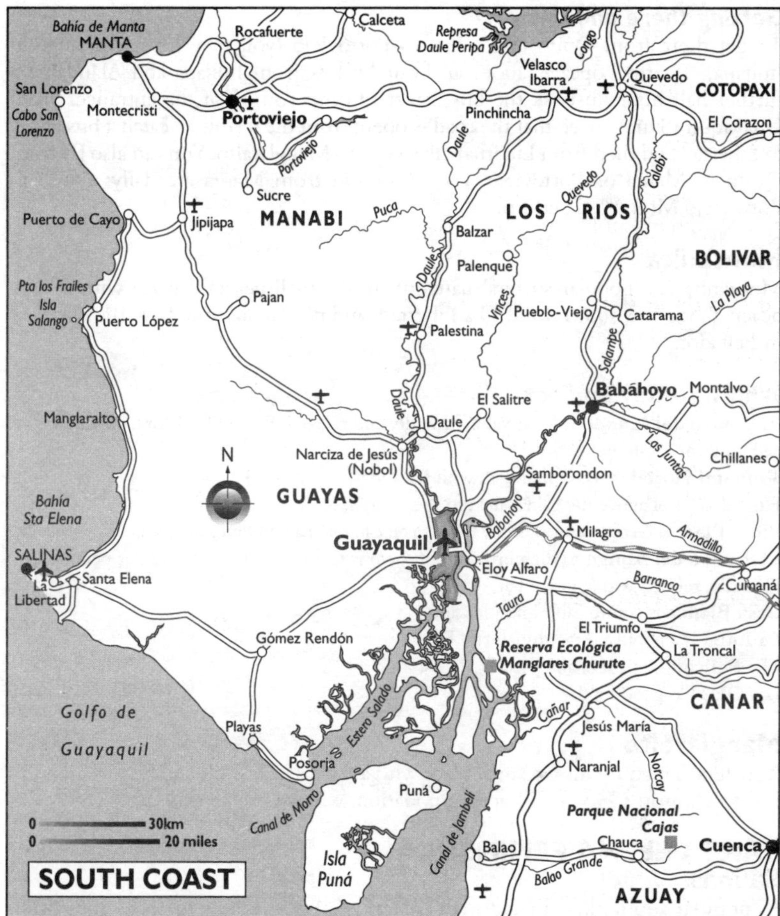

Salango

The port of Salango, 10km to the south of Puerto López, has an excellent small museum with information on the intrepid sailors of prehispanic times. It contains artefacts from many of the different cultures that have inhabited coastal Ecuador from the Valdivia to the present day. There is a decent restaurant here, **Delfín Mágico**, and you can walk along the beaches. Take a pick-up or bus from Puerto López heading south.

SOUTH OF PUERTO LÓPEZ

Alándaluz

Fifteen kilometres from Puerto López to the south is **Alándaluz**, an amazing ecological hotel, with beautiful cabins, a private beach, great seafood and vegetarian cuisine. It is a bit expensive for the budget traveller but you could always stay here and eat out in one of the nearby villages. For reservations, tel: Quito 505084; fax 543042; Baquedano 330 and Reina Victoria, 2nd floor; in Puerto López (05) 604103. They also organise tours to Machalilla National Park including the Isla de la Plata, dry forest, Agua Blanca and Montecristi.

Getting there and away

To get there from Quito take a bus to Portoviejo (you may have to change in Jipijapa). Puerto López is about an hour by bus from Jipijapa and Alándaluz a further half hour; just ask the bus driver to drop you off at the entrance. From Guayaquil (8 hrs) check that the road is open; from the terminal, catch a bus going to Libertad and then from Libertad take a bus to Manglaralto. You can also fly from Quito to Manta or Portoviejo. Flights to and from Manta are daily; Quito to Portoviejo Mon, Wed and Fri.

Montanita

Montanita is a popular surfers' hangout. It's a small peaceful place with a large beach about one hour north of La Libertad, and it's supposed to have the best surf in Ecuador.

Where to stay and eat

El Centro del Mundo is good value, friendly and relaxed. From US$1 for a dormitory bed with mosquito net.

Tsunami Hostal is recommended, with a sea view. From US$1.

Hostal Brezel above the baker, next to the church, is clean.

Vito's Place is recommended, from US$3. You can pitch a tent here. Boogie boards available.

El Rincón del Amigo to the north end of town is recommended at US$2 per person. Friendly, relaxed with a beach bar.

Casa Blanca is comfortable and pleasant.

La Luna is a popular Argentinian run bar.

The **Pelicano** for pizza and pasta.

Las Olas has good food.

Manglaralto

A surfers' hangout, this is a small place with a few basic hostels and restaurants. Try **Señor Ramon's House** for accommodation, which is clean and safe.

SANTA ELENA PENINSULA

Salinas

A popular upmarket Ecuadorian resort, Salinas is overpriced and often overcrowded. Swimming is safe. Try the **Hotel Yulee**, Diagonal Iglesia Central, Avenida 2 and Calle 14; tel: 772028; from US$4. Cheap surfer shops along the Malecón. **Pesca Tours** organises fishing trips.

Playas

This is the nearest beach area to Guayaquil and can become unbearably overcrowded at weekends and during holidays. It's a good beach for surfing and the area has plenty of birdlife. There are frequent buses to Guayaquil (2 hrs).

Where to stay and eat

There are several reasonable places to stay, mostly within easy walking distance of the bus station Try **Hotel Playas** on the Malecón; tel: 04 760121. Further east along the seafront there is **La Gaviota**, **El Delfín** and **Los Patios**. The cheapest place is **Miraglia** just off the beach near Playas. This is where most surfers stay. There is good food available from the many places along the beach front.

Practical information

The **post office**, **phone office** and **Banco de Guayaquil** are in the centre of town.

GUAYAQUIL

Telephone code 04

Guayaquil is Ecuador's largest city with a population of nearly two million. It's not a particularly attractive city and during the late 1990s has had a particularly bad reputation among tourists and locals alike for crime. It's not unknown for curfews to be imposed after dark. On top of that the climate is particularly hot and humid, and during the wet season, January–April, it is almost unbearable. Even the locals try to get out of the city then, often heading for the coastal resorts. Avoid walking around any part of the city after dusk, leave your valuables at the hotel and use taxis.

Guayaquil lies at the confluence of the Rivers Guayas, Daule and Babahoyo. The city has been an important port since it was founded by Francisco de Orellana in 1537. Most of the area around the city is filled with vast plantations of bananas, covered in blue plastic bags. The Gulf of Guayaquil is used for shrimp farming, which is very important to the Ecuadorian economy. Unfortunately there is a lot of pollution in the Gulf, primarily from the pesticides used on the bananas. This is forcing shrimp farmers to move their farms to the northern province of Esmeraldas.

Getting there and away

By bus

There is a large bus terminal with departures to most other towns in Ecuador. There are numerous companies with varying times, prices and quality of service for each destination. The bus station is several kilometres from the centre of the city, so take a taxi or local bus into town. Taxis are around US$4, but negotiate.

By plane

There are frequent flights to Quito, Cuenca, Loja, Machala, and Galápagos. The airport is a few kilometres north of the city centre. Taxis into town should be US$4. There are no meters so negotiate before you get in. The airport has an information office, money changing facilities, a café and post office.

By train

Currently (1999) the train from Guayaquil to Riobamba is not running the full length of the line, but only between Riobamba and Huigra. There have been landslides on the line between Durán and Huigra, and it's not known when this section will be reopened.

Where to stay and eat

It's a good idea to book ahead in Guayaquil, or at least phone before you go to a hotel. Check the prices and that tax is included.

Youth Hostal Sauces I, Av Isidro Ayora (opposite Banco Ecuatoriana de la Vivienda); tel: 248357; fax 248341; email: youthhost@telconet.net From US$8. Near the airport. Open to non-members. Discount for ISIC card holders and YHA members. Call ahead to be picked up from bus station or airport. Friendly, helpful, recommended.

Residencial Metropolitana Rendón 120 and Panama 4th Floor; tel: 305250/565250. US$12 per person. Clean and safe, luggage storage, recommended.

Tangara Guest House Block F House 1, Ciudadela Bolivariana, Manuela Sáqenz and O'Leary; tel: 284445; fax: 284039. US$33–45 with bath. Between the airport and bus station, in a safe residential area. 10% discount for SAEC members

Hotel Plaza Chile 414 and Clemente Ballén; tel: 327140/324006. From US$9 per person including tax and breakfast. Good restaurant and international papers.

Hotel Palace Chile 214 and Luque; tel: 321080. US$65–80. Business hotel. Good restaurant.

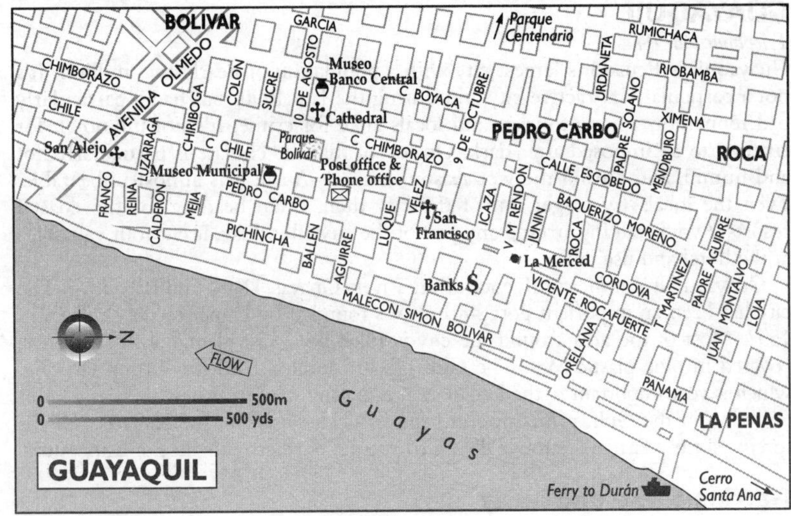

Durán is the suburb of Guayaquil from which you could once take the train to Alausi and Riobamba. The train left at 06.00 for the 464km journey up to the highest point at Urbina (3,610m). Hotels in the area include:

Hostel Londres, Baquerizo Moreno 501 and Torras Martinez; tel: 309666. US$6 double room. This is near the ferry that takes you across the river to Durán.
Residencial Paris, Loja y Yaguachi; tel: 810732, from US$6, is two blocks from the train station.

Most of the restaurants are in the centre of town or in the districts of Albaroda or La Garzota, which are safer than downtown. There is a wide variety to suit all tastes and budgets.

Practical information

Tourist office Calle Aguirre 104 and Malecón; tel: 326312. Open Mon–Fri 08.30–17.00
Post office Calle Pedro Carbo and Aguirre.
Phone office Calle Pedro Carbo and Aguirre.
Money Calle 9 de Octubre has a number of banks and exchange offices. There are also money changers on the same street who give decent cash rates.
Books Librería Científica, Calle Luque 223 and Chile.
Airlines TAME, Calle 9 de Octubre 424; tel: 561751. SAETA and SAN, Calle 9 de Octubre 2002 and Los Ríos; tel: 200600/200614; email: ehbuzon@saeta.com.ec
Internet At the youth hostel. There are Internet cafés throughout the city.

Travel agencies

There aren't as many travel agents as in Quito but there are enough concentrated in the centre of the city.

Canodros Calle Urdaneta 1418; tel: 285711. Operate the Kapawi Lodge in the southern Oriente.
Galasam Calle 9 de Octubre 424; tel: 306289. Cheaper Galápagos tours.
Metropolitan Touring Calle Antepara 915; tel: 330300.

What to see

The heart of the city is between Av Olmedo and Calle 9 de Octubre. The **Malecón Simon Bolívar** runs along the riverfront beginning at Av Olmedo where you will find the statue of José Joaquin de Olmedo, an eminent citizen who fought for the independence of Guayaquil. At the northern end of the Malecón is the neighbourhood known as **Barrio de las Peñas**, which has coastal colonial architecture. There are good views of the city from the top of the hill Santa Ana in this neighbourhood. It is not currently safe to walk up these streets, as the danger of mugging is high. The main street in the neighbourhood is Calle Numa Pompilio Llona. During Guayaquil's fiestas around July 24 and 25, a lot of art work is exhibited in this part of the city. The **church of Santo Domingo**, at the foot of Santa Ana hill, is one of Guayaquil's oldest churches, dating from the 16th century. However, the current building is 20th century.

The main square in the city is **Plaza Centenario** on Calle 9 de Octubre. The **Parque Bolívar** (better known as Parque Cemenario) is an historical park with land iguanas and small tortoises, in front of the **Gothic cathedral**, which dates from the end of the 19th century. The districts of **La Garzota**, **Sauces** and **Alborada** near the bus station and airport are safer than the centre, with all the same facilities. They have plenty of restaurants and hotel accommodation. The northern part of Guayaquil has new shopping centres, Mall del Sol and Policentro, if you want cinemas, shops, and fast-food restaurants.

The **Botanic Garden** is located at the foot of Cerro Colorado hill on Av Francisco Orellana. There are many interesting varieties of plants.

Museums

Museo Municipal Calle Sucre and Chile, has history, art and archaeology collections. Open Tue–Sat 09.00–16.00.
Museo del Banco Central Calle Anteparra 900 and 9 de Octubre, has an interesting archaeology collection. Open daily 10.00–18.00, closes earlier at the weekend.
Casa de Cultura Calle 9 de Octubre and Moncayo has gold and archaeology. Open Tue–Fri 10.00–17.00, Sat 10.00–15.00.

Outside Guayaquil

The nature reserve of **Cerro Blanco** is 15km along the coast road, a great example of tropical dry forest and good for birdwatching. Open Sat and Sun, just turn up. Other days book in advance at La Cemento Nacional, Multicomercio, Oficina 91, Eloy Alfaro and Cuenca; tel: 871900. Nearby is **Puerto Hondo**, 17km along the coast road, where there is some mangrove forest and the archaeological site of Palombamba of the Huancavelica culture. Booking as for Cerro Blanco.

Manglares Churute Reserve, covering nearly 123,000 acres (50,000 hectares) is 35km from Guayaquil. You really have to go on a day tour as there is nowhere to stay at the park. The vegetation is mangroves on the coast and inland there are stands of laurel, balsa, silk cotton and oak, with many orchids and bromeliads. It's a good place for birdwatching, with horned screamers, ducks, herons and woodpeckers. There are also mammals in the park, though these are obviously harder to see, such as howler monkeys, agouti, paca, and anteaters. You can take canoe trips through the mangroves and there are trails through the forest. For further details contact INEFAN at Av. Quito 402 and Solano; tel: 397730.

SOUTH FROM GUAYAQUIL TO THE PERUVIAN BORDER

Heading south from Guayaquil to the border can be a long hot journey through banana plantations and then increasingly scrubby bush vegetation. This is one of the least attractive parts of the country. The large city of Machala (4 hrs from Guayaquil), with a population of almost 200,000, doesn't have much to offer, but does have plenty of hostels and restaurants if you need to stay here. As you get towards the border there are increasing numbers of police checkpoints, where you have to get out of the bus and sign a list. An hour beyond Machala is Huaquillas, a busy, typical border town with lots of shops, market stalls and people trying to make a bit of money from passing trade. In Ecuador you have to go through immigration about 3km before the border, then through customs at the border, then walk over the bridge. The border is open daily 08.00–18.00, and closes at 16.00 on Sundays. Make sure you get your passport stamped. You can change money here, but watch out for dodgy notes and inaccurate accounting.

8 The Oriente

The Oriente is Ecuador's Amazon region. It covers around 40% of the total land area of the country. The Oriente is subdivided into the Northern Oriente which includes the provinces of Sucumbíos, Napo and Pastaza, while the Southern Oriente includes the provinces of Morona–Santiago and Zamora–Chinchipe. Travel to the northern Oriente is relatively straightforward and the area is pretty geared up for tourist visits, with a wide variety of tours available to suit all tastes and budgets. The Oriente is an incredibly biodiverse and fascinating part of the country. The main towns in the region are all quite small and relatively new. They have grown to support the mass influx of people into the area, which has occurred as a direct result of the oil exploration that has been going on here since the early 1970s. They are ugly unattractive places in themselves, with little of interest to hold you there for more than a few hours. You may end up spending a bit of time in one of these jungle towns as tours inevitably start from Lago Agrio, Coca, Tena, Misahuallí, Baños, Puyo or Macas.

GEOGRAPHY AND CLIMATE

The immense Amazon Basin stretches for 3,000km east–west and 1,000km north–south. The Amazon River is 6,448km long from the source, high up in the Peruvian Andes, to its mouth in the Atlantic Ocean. It is the largest river in the world and runs through the world's largest tropical rainforest. In Ecuador about half of the total land area is taken up by the Amazon Basin. The Napo, Pastaza and Putumayo are the major rivers in Ecuador's Amazon area. They flow eastwards into the Amazon.

Rainy season in the jungle is most of the year, with January and February being marginally less wet, and April to July the wettest months. The temperature in the Amazon area is usually 23–26°C, and there is very little seasonal or daily variation. Even though the temperatures are quite high it can feel cool in the evenings because of the dampness, so bring a warm sweater.

HISTORY

The Amazon was first discovered by the Spanish, arriving from Ecuador in 1541. The first European to sail all the way down the river was Francisco de Orellana, cousin to the Pizarro brothers, and founder of Guayaquil. In 1540 Gonzalo Pizarro had been sent by his older brother Francisco, then in Cusco, to be governor of Quito in place of Orellana. There had been rumours of a pending expedition to search for the mythical El Dorado and of a land of spice, especially cinnamon. Spices were particularly prized at that time in Europe. Orellana, a veteran explorer, joined the expedition team. In February 1541 Pizarro and his large accompanying

entourage of guides, porters, dogs to ward off Indian attack, pigs and llamas, set off to the east. Orellana missed the departure and followed rapidly with just a few men. The journey across the Andes was gruelling, and many men and animals were lost. By the end of the year, many people had died, nothing of great interest had been discovered, and there was little to eat, so Pizarro decided to build a boat. This was duly done and Orellana was given command. He set off with 60 men, leaving Pizarro and a few other starving people behind. Orellana was never seen by Pizarro again. Pizarro and his men took six months to struggle back to Quito, outraged at the behaviour of Orellana in abandoning them. In August, round about the time Pizarro arrived back in Quito, Orellana and his men sailed out of the mouth of the mighty Amazon into the Atlantic Ocean.

TOURS TO THE ORIENTE

Arranging a visit to the Amazon is straightforward. The best way to enjoy the jungle and see it to its full potential is to go on an organised tour through a reputable travel agent in Quito, Tena, Baños, Coca, Puyo or Misahuallí. There are generally two tour options: one is to be based at one of the many high quality jungle lodges; and the other is to participate in a tour visiting various places, usually more basic than the lodges and involving camping. As well as the reputable agencies, there are many freelance guides offering tours into the jungle. Some are registered and professional, but many aren't. Remember that you are visiting remote areas, where incompetence on the part of your guide could have dire consequences. Before you agree anything check your guide's papers and permits and always try to get recommendations from other backpackers. Some tours offer you the opportunity to visit indigenous communities.

Jungle lodges

Lodges such as Yuturi Lodge, Sacha Lodge, La Selva Lodge and Kapawi Lodge are the most comfortable option for visiting the jungle. They are equipped with cabins with private bathrooms, mosquito nets and running water. The price, usually between US$60 and US$150 per person per day, includes transport from the local airport or a local office, an abundance of good food, bottled drinking water and a full programme of activities and excursions with naturalist guides. Most of these lodge tours have to be booked in Quito directly with the lodge office or through a travel agent (see page 66–7).

What to take

Long cotton dense weave trousers, T-shirts and long-sleeved dense-weave shirts, shorts, swimming costume, socks, rubber boots, sandals, sunhat, towel, sunglasses, waterproof coat or poncho, torch, penknife, binoculars, sunblock, insect repellent, biodegradable soap, camera and lots of film, a daysack, and thick plastic bags for all your belongings.

Visiting indigenous communities

If you are interested in visiting the few indigenous communities that remain in the Oriente you must be very aware of the impact you are making. You should only visit communities with guides from those communities, and ensure that your guide is licensed and has permission to visit the community. You may be approached by freelance guides in Baños, Coca or Misahuallí, offering tours. They aren't necessarily bona fide guides, nor do they necessarily have permission or the local community's best interests at heart. The Organización de Nacionalidades Huaorini de la Amazonia Ecuatoriana (ONHAE) gives permission to certain guides to enter Huaorini territory, but others do so illegally and are not welcome.

PEOPLE OF THE ORIENTE

The **Sionas** and **Secoyas** live in the northeastern part of the Ecuadorian Amazon, bordering Colombia. They have close ties with the neighbouring indigenous groups in Colombia. Their land, and much of their traditional way of life, have been devastated by oil exploration and the trappings of the oil industry. In 1993 the Sionas and Secoyas sued Texaco for environmental abuse of their territory, including massive dumping of oil products into their lagoons.

The **Shuar** are the second largest Amazon group remaining in Ecuador. They live in the remote southeastern Ecuadorian Amazon area between the Pastaza and Marañón rivers. This area is quite isolated with many unnavigable rivers to the east and the high Andes to the west, so the Shuar have been relatively free from outside interference. They used to have a reputation for being an aggressive group of savages and headhunters. In 1964, the Shuar were the first Ecuadorian group to found a federation to protect their culture from intrusion: **Federación de Centros Shuar–Achuar**, Domingo Comín 17–38, Sucúa, Morona–Santiago; tel: 07 740108.

The **Huaorani** are Ecuador's most isolated indigenous group. They used to be known as Aucas, meaning savages. They earned this name because of their reputation for being hostile warriors, similar to the Shuar. They once attacked intruding outsiders, killing anyone who set foot in their territory. Today there

CAPIRONA

The following code was drawn up in 1992 by an indigenous Quichua community in the Ecuadorian Amazon. It stresses the communal nature of tribal life and the ecologically fragile nature of this, and similar destinations. Capirona is a Quechua community near Tena, and is a participant in the RICANCIE (Red Indigena Comunidades del Alto Napo para la Convivencia Intercultural y Ecoturismo) programme to promote community tourism projects (see page 127).

Before you visit indigenous areas, whether with a tour or independently, consider:

- Who operates the programme? Is it run by local people? If so, is it operated communally, or do only a few individuals or families profit?
- If it is not operated by indigenous people, do local communities receive an equitable share of the profits or any other direct benefits, such as training? Or do only a few individuals or families benefit?
- Learn as much as you can about the local culture and customs. Visit local indigenous federation offices for information and materials with an indigenous perspective.
- Do not take photographs without asking permission.
- If you want to offer a gift, make it a useful gift to the community rather than to an individual. Most indigenous communities function communally. Gifts for the local school are much appreciated and shared by all.
- Refrain from tipping individuals. If you are with a group, everyone can contribute to a gift for the community.
- Be aware of the boundaries of individual homes and gardens. Never enter or photograph without permission.

are approximately 1,600 Huaorani living in around 25 communities, three of which are in the Yasuni National Park. The largest community is Toñampari on the Curaray River. Most of the other Huaorani communities lie within the Huaorani Ethnic Reserve, an area bordering the Yasuni National Park, defined and demarcated in 1983 as a protectorate and added to in 1990. This is within the provinces of Napo and Pastaza in the Upper Amazon. The Huaorani culture is continually under threat from outside influences, such as oil exploration and tourism. In 1990 they formed the Organización de Nacionalidad Huaorani de la Amazonía Ecuatoriana (ONHAE) to try to protect themselves and maintain their culture in the face of modern intervention and exploitation.

The **Amazon Quichuas** are a large ethnic group of 30,000–40,000. There are two subgroups, the Napo Quichuas of the Upper Napo River area, and the Canelos Quichuas in the province of Pastaza. The language they speak is Quichua which, although originally an Andean language, was introduced into the Oriente by traders and missionaries in the 17th century.

The **Cofan** traditionally lived in communities along the rivers of the northwest Ecuadorian Amazon, bordering Colombia. They speak a language known as A'lngae, and characteristically decorate their bodies with feathers and flowers. They were warriors and traders who travelled along the tributaries of the Amazon to exchange their stone axes, knives and canoes for cloth, salt and sea shell beads. From a thriving population of several thousand before contact with whites, by the early 20th century disease had reduced their population to just a few hundred. Smallpox, measles, polio, whooping cough and cholera wiped out whole villages

- Bring your own water purification tablets. Do not rely on boiling water exclusively as it depletes scarce fuelwood or contributes to forest destruction.
- Take out what you take in (especially non-biodegradable items such as plastic water bottles). Use biodegradable soaps.
- Be sensitive to those around you. Use headphones with tape/cassette-players.
- Do not make promises you cannot or will not keep – for example, sending back photographs to local people.
- Do not collect plants or plant products without permission.
- Wear appropriate clothing. For example, many cultures are offended by women in shorts even though they may go topless.
- Respect local residents' privacy and customs. Treat people with the same respect you would expect from visitors to your own home.

To visit Capirona and experience the Quichua culture and rainforest ecology, contact **CONFANIAE** (Confederación Nacionalidades Indigenas Amazonia Equatoriana) in Quito; tel: (02) 543973 c/o FOIN, Tarquino Tapuy, Calle Augusto Rueda, CP 271, Tena, Napo, Ecuador; tel: (06) 886288. From US$35/day. Spanish only.

For further information on sensitive tourism contact **Tourism Concern**. This is a UK-based organisation that aims to promote greater understanding and awareness of the impact of tourism. They promote sustainable, responsible tourism and travel with critical insight and understanding, and are working for change in current tourism practice. They can be contacted at Stapleton House, 277–281 Holloway Rd, London N7 8HN; tel: 020 7753 3330; email: tourconcern@gn.apc.org

throughout the Amazon. Tuberculosis and malaria also claimed many lives. The Cofan have an intricate knowledge of medicinal plants.

The Cofan were relatively isolated until the 1950s, but since then have suffered hugely from the ruthless exploration of oil companies, the first of which was Shell, followed by Texaco and Gulf in the 1960s. At the time oil companies started work in the area there were thought to be about 500 Cofan people living along the banks of the rivers Guamues, San Miguel and Aguarico of southern Colombia and northern Ecuador. The arrival of the oil companies also meant the building of roads, airstrips and pipelines, and an influx of oil workers. Oil exploration was carried out with no regard for the indigenous people living in the area, devastating their traditional lifestyle. In 1966 good quality oil was found, the Lago Agrio road was built, and colonists moved in, encouraged by free gifts of parcels of land, to be cleared of forest. This land and forest was the home and livelihood of the Cofans. Throughout the 1990s the Cofan have attempted to battle against the further invasion of their land by oil companies, which were often there without authorisation and within supposedly protected national park land.

Dureno is the largest Cofan community, with over 300 inhabitants. The land titles were given to the people there in 1977, but a shortage of forest resources has forced most people out of subsistence hunting and farming into some form of commercial agriculture, coffee and fish being a source of revenue. The Cofan culture, although constantly under threat, remains and the language is intact. In 1984 the Cofan founded a new community at Zabalo where around 100 people now live, making a living from ecotourism while being involved in forest conservation (see pages 67 and 123).

The Northern Oriente

Getting there and away

By bus

The **northern Oriente** is readily accessible from the highlands; there are frequent buses from Quito to Lago Agrio and Coca, and from Baños to Puyo and Tena. The roads over the Andes and down into the Oriente are not always in a good state of repair, especially during the highland wet season in the months of January and February, so be prepared for delays. However, the journeys are spectacular, whichever route you choose.

By air

There are daily flights to Coca from Quito with TAME at US$60 each way, and you can also fly to Shell–Mera, just 10km from Puyo, and to Lago Agrio and Coca.

LAGO AGRIO (Nueva Loja)

Telephone code 06

Lago Agrio is the capital of the province of Sucumbíos, which lies in the northernmost part of the Ecuadorian Amazon. An unexciting fast-growing oil workers' town, it is the gateway to the northern Oriente, particularly the indigenous community of Dureno and the Cuyabeno Reserve. Unless you are coming here to start a tour it is one of those places there is little reason to visit and so is probably best avoided. There's nothing much to do except look at the trappings of the oil industry.

Getting there and away

By bus

There are frequent buses from Quito and Coca. The bus takes up to 10 hrs from Quito, 3 hrs from Coca and 9 hrs from Tena.

By plane

Flights to Lago Agrio from Quito cost approximately US$110 return. There are usually two a week with TAME.

Where to stay and eat

There are plenty of cheap and basic *residencias* centred around the main road through town, Av Quito. For somewhere a bit more upmarket try **Hotel Lago Imperial** on Av Quito; tel: 830453, from US$11; or **Machala** on Av Colombia 122; tel: 830073, from US$10 per person. For jungle lodges, see opposite.

Practical information

There are **money changers**, a **post office** and **phone office**, all in the centre of town.
Airlines TAME office is on 9 de Octubre and Manabí; tel: 830981/830982.

What to see

The Cofan village of **Dureno** is 21km east of Lago Agrio. Conditions are basic but accommodation is available. It is advisable to take a hammock, mosquito net, food, cooking equipment etc. You can find guides here for trips into the jungle, from US$30 a day. **Zabalo** is also a Cofan community, about 130km down the Aguarico

River. For information on visiting the communities contact **Randall Borman**, Comunidad Cofan Zabalo, Casilla 17 11 06089. Quito; tel: 02 446270; fax: 02 446270.

Jungle lodges accessible from Lago Agrio

Cuyabeno Lake Lodge A lodge working with local guides, and bilingual naturalist guides. Seven thatched cabins, natural materials, on the Cuyabeno Lake. Book through Neotropic Turis in Quito, Calle Roblis 653 and Amazonas; tel: 527862/521212; fax: 554902; web: www.ecuadorexplorer.com/neotropic

Flotel Orellana, **Imuya Camp** and **Iripari Camp** Metropolitan Touring organise trips on their floating hotel and to the quite basic but perfectly located and well-designed Imuya and Iripari camps. The camps are several hours by boat downstream from Lago Agrio, in the River Agauarico area. Communities of Siona, Secoya and Cofan inhabit this area and are now involved in tourism. Tours visit some of their projects. Imuya Camp is set amongst a network of blackwater rivers and lakes known as Lagartococha, while Iripari Camp is in *terra firme* forest. Great opportunities for birdwatching, boat trips and trekking through primary rainforest. The Flotel Orellana is a floating hotel that sleeps 48 in comfortable cabins and travels up and down the River Aguarico in the Lower Cuyabeno Reserve.

Native Camp Programmes in the Cuyabeno Reserve from 3 to 7 nights, from US$60 per person per day. US$20 park entrance. 10% discount for SAEC members. Book through Native Life Quito office at Calle Foch 167 and Amazonas; tel: 505158/550836; fax: 229077; email: natlife1@natlife.com.ec; web: www.natlife.ec

Cuyabeno National Park

Cuyabeno is one of the world's most biodiverse spots, with an incredible array of plant life and birdlife. It covers 604,400 hectares of lowland tropical rainforest in the provinces of Sucumbios and Napo in northeast Ecuador. Access is from Lago Agrio by boat. There are Siona, Secoya and Cofan communities within the reserve.

COCA (Puerto Francisco de Orellana)

Telephone code 06

Coca, a port on the River Napo, is easily accessible and many expeditions into the jungle start from here. It is the nearest town for some of the best lodges. The town itself is not very interesting – it is supported by oil workers and tourism and also has a military base. There is one surfaced main road, which runs from the bus terminal to the port, where you can find the Capitanía and the tourist office; along the road are various bars and restaurants, several bus company offices, shops chemists etc. The rest of the town has dusty or muddy (depending on the weather) unsurfaced roads and ramshackle buildings.

Getting there and away

By bus

Buses leave several times a day from Quito and the total journey time is a minimum of 11 hours. The journey is spectacular, as you climb out of Quito over the high altitude páramo and then plunge into cloudforest and jungle lowlands. From Coca to Lago Agrio takes 3 hours by bus. To Tena, there are 6 hours of bumpy jungle road, with amazing vegetation and oil pipelines alongside. This is a fascinating journey and, though it will be hot and probably crowded in the bus, the local people are usually friendly and helpful.

By plane

There are daily flights to Coca from Quito with TAME. The return flight is around US$120.

Where to stay and eat

As in most of the jungle towns there is plenty of very basic and cheap accommodation to cater for the oil workers who frequently come here. This is fairly horrendous and best avoided. There are some very reasonably priced tourist hostels, which are much nicer.

Oasis Hotel up river from the main road; tel: 880164. US$2 per person. Double rooms with fan and bath, but not much character.
Hotel Auca Calle Napo; tel: 880600. From US$4 per person. Central, popular budget hostel. Fans, private bath, garden with hammocks, restaurant/café, plenty of other tourists.
Hostería Amazonas downriver from the main road on Calle Espejo; tel: 881215/880444. Recently completed, from US$4 per person, fan, bath, good beds, comfortable, garden, games room, overlooking the river.
La Misión upriver from the main road; tel: 880544; fax: 880263. Smartest place in town US$9–13. Swimming pool, restaurant, disco etc. Credit cards accepted. Spacious rooms, clean.

The **market** has all sorts of fruit juices and a variety of tasty local dishes such as *corvique* (green banana with cheese), from 08.00 in the morning. The restaurants at the Auca and Misión hotels are reasonable.

Practical information

Tourist office and **Capitanía** down by the river. **Bank** and **phone office** in the centre.
Airlines TAME office on Calle Napo opposite the Hotel Auca.

PAÑACOCHA

Lisa Crampin

My rainforest trip started in Coca, one of the frontier towns on the edge of the forest. In February there are only a few travellers, but groups of oil workers waiting to go back to the oilfields which are being developed to the consternation of conservationists. After breakfast in the food market I sat at the pier watching my boat being filled with supplies for the next five days.

Dense vegetation means travelling is by water – six hours by motorised canoe down the River Napo before turning into a network of smaller rivers heading for the lodge on Pañacocha (lake of the pirañas). The lodge consisted of several sleeping huts on stilts and a large kitchen/dining hut in a clearing on the edge of the lake. There was no electricity so we used candles and torches at night, there was running water pumped from the lake with the only generator, and sheets and mosquito nets were provided.

Each day we set off on tracks through the forest or in the canoes. The variety of vegetation is amazing. I saw plants that have been used by the Indians for generations, which have medicinal properties: the sap of the Dragon's Blood Tree which cures a variety of ailments, and Curare from which part of the modern anaesthetic is derived. I experienced a lot of new tastes: chewing the bark of the cinnamon tree and sucking seeds from the cocoa pod, which have a sweet and sticky covering. On another trip we fished for pirañas by attaching lumps of meat to hooks and lying back in the boat waiting for a bite. I caught a pacu, a fruit-eating piraña which was cooked for our dinner and delicious.

The lodge has an observation tower, a platform 80 feet high on a tall Ceiba tree, with stunning views across the lake and over miles and miles of primary

Travel agencies and guides

Amasanga The office is at the dock in Coca. Cost varies according to trip and group size. Quichua people who offer a variety of trips.

Expediciones Jarrin Calle Napo; tel: 880251. Organise trips to Pañacocha Lagunas, 6 hrs by boat from Coca. From US$30 per day. Tours are usually 4–5 days and depart with a minimum of 4 people. Local indigenous guides are used.

There are independent guides who organise trips, usually for a minimum of three people, with a tailor made itinerary according to what you want to do. Cost is from US$30 per person per day, all inclusive. Trips from 4–8 days deep into the jungle. Ask at the Hotel Auca.

Ernesto and Patricio Juanka Coca; tel:880275. US$35–45 per day. The Juankas are Shuar Indians who lead trips into the Tiputino and Pañacocha areas. 2–8-day tours for groups of 4–7 people. Spanish only.

Wymper Torres Coca; tel: 880336; fax: 880118 to contact Wymper directly. US$40 per day, including 3 meals plus US$20 park entrance, US$30 Laguna Verde. 4 people minimum. Specialises in Río Shripuno and Pañacocha areas. Spanish only.

Jungle lodges accessible from Coca

Pañacocha Amazon Lodge On the shores of Pañacocha Lake, 5 hours from Quito by boat. Book through Ecotours in Quito.

La Selva Lodge Good quality, beautifully situated lodge on the Upper Napo River 100km downriver from Coca near the Yusuni National Park. From US$140 per day. Includes all

rainforest. You can sit there with just the vultures for company watching for any movement in the forest below.

Because the forest is so dense most wildlife you can see is in the air or on the ground and most of it moved too fast to take photos; there were toucans and macaws darting across the sky or butterflies and snakes moving through the trees. The highlight for me was watching the river dolphins swim around our canoe as we paddled across the lake. The closest I came to wildlife was making friend with the tarantula who lived in our hut – you can let them walk over your body, and they will only push their poisonous hairs into you if you frighten them.

We were brilliantly looked after by two Quichua speaking guides and two English speaking guides, between six tourists. They guided us everywhere, cooked three marvellous meals a day and told us about all the flora and fauna surrounding us. The only time they had me worried was ten minutes after leaving Coca when the canoe sprung a leak and they needed my pen knife and gaffer tape to carry out a hasty repair.

When I arrived back in Coca it had turned into the Wild West. It was the end of carnival, when Ecuadorians throw water over each other, but in Coca the whole thing gets a bit crazy. We had to flatten ourselves to the walls to miss being hit by the water, flour and salt being thrown from windows and avoid the trucks tearing along the main street full of people throwing mud at everyone. As I sat on the bus, exhilarated, damp and covered in flour, waiting for the ten hour trip back to Quito, the peace of the rainforest already seemed miles away. But, I can still remember it all: laughing as we trudged through the swamps in the torrential rain, swimming in the lake in the blazing sunshine, lying in my hammock listening to the sound of the birds and the monkeys in the forest.

meals, transportation from Coca, excursions, accommodation, English-speaking naturalist guides. Book at Quito travel agents or at their office in Quito at Calle 6 de Diciembre 2816 and Rivet; tel: 02 550995/554686; fax: 02 567297; email: laselva@uio.satnet.net; web: www.laselvajunglelodge.com

Sacha Lodge A comfortable lodge, 3½ hours by boat from Coca, 85km downstream. Reputedly one of the best lodges, set in 3,000 acres of rainforest. Great for birdwatching, excursions, viewing platform, trails. From US$525 for 4 days. Book through Quito travel agent Explorer Tours at Calle Reina Victoria 1227 and Lizardo Garcia; tel: 02 522220/508871; fax: 02 508872.

Yuturi Lodge The lodge is set in one of the largest private reserves of the Oriente and consists of 15 cabins, with a total of 40 beds, with nets. It is surrounded by primary rainforest typical of the lowland Oriente. Good local food, comfortable place. Guided hikes, boat rides, birdwatching, trips to the Samona indigenous communities, night hikes. Reservations can be made through the Quito office: Amazonas 1324 and Colon; tel/fax: 02 504037/544166/503225; email: yuturi@yuturi.com.ec; web: www.yuturi.com Coca is next to the Oasis Hotel. Prices from US$288 for 4 days, US$360 for 5 days, 20% discount for SAEC members, if reserving in Quito. Tours from Coca are Mon–Fri or Fri–Mon. **Yarina Lodge**, which is nearer Coca (1 hour down river) is run by the same people, with departures daily. From US$40 per day.

Yasuni National Park

Yasuni is a UNESCO Biosphere Reserve located in the northeast of Ecuador close to the borders with Peru and Colombia. The reserve is accessible from the Río Napo, approximately 4 hours by boat from Coca. The reserve is world renowned for its high biodiversity, with over a hundred species of mammal, several hundred of bird and also of fish, and a huge variety of vegetation, typical of tropical lowland rainforest. The area is supposedly protected from any exploitation, but has incurred damage from oil exploration companies, and its future is not totally secure. The park is also home to some of the Huaorani tribal groups (see pages 19–20).

TENA

Telephone code 06

Tena is the capital town of the province of Napo, and lies on the Pano and Tena rivers. The town has a dramatic setting with the forested lowland foothills of the Andes as a backdrop.

Getting there and away

By bus

There are frequent buses to Quito (5 hrs, US$3). To Coca is 6 hrs, US$4, several a day. To Baños there are several buses a day (2 hrs), to Misahuallí at least one an hour 06.00–18.00.

By plane

There are flights from Quito to the airstrip at Shell-Mera. Take a bus from there to Tena.

Where to stay and eat

Hostal Cambahuasi opposite the bus terminal; tel: 887438. Popular with backpackers, canoeists and rafters. The agency Ríos Ecuador is based at the hostel. Rafting is US$50 for a one-day trip. Kayaks for rent.

Hostal Travellers Lodging Av 15 de Noviembre 438; tel: 886372. From US$4. The most popular backpackers' hostel. Recently expanded, a variety of rooms. Good restaurant next door.
Hostal Amazonica Av Amazonas and Abdon Calderón; tel: 886487. From US$4 per person. Central.

For food try the place next to Travellers Lodging. The main street in town also has several reasonable eating places.

Practical information

Tourist office Calle Bolívar and Amazonas; tel: 888536.
Post office Calle Olmedo just off Amazonas.
Phone office Calle Olmedo just off Amazonas.

Travel agencies and nearby lodges

FOIN Tarquino Tapuy, Calle Augusto Rueda, CP 271; tel: 886288.
RICANCIE (Red Indigena Comunidades del Alto Napo para la Convivencia Intercultural y Ecoturismo) Indigenous organisation involving a network of ten communities promoting community tourism projects, including Capirona. 3–6-day tours for a minimum of 3 people from US$25 per day. Contact: Tarquino Tapuy or Edwin Cerda, Bellavista Baja, Calle Atahualpa and 9 de Octubre 435, Tena; tel/fax: 06 887 406/886614; email: RICANCIE@aanapo.ecx.ec In Quito contact Judith Guerra.
Sacharicsina Tel: 886250/802608. From US$25 per day. Indigenous family (Familia Cerda) provides tours of various lengths, camping or staying in cabins with Spanish- and German-speaking guides. One-day motorised canoe tours from Misahuallí to Huabuno US$30 per person.
Amarongachi Tel/fax: 886372. Arrange through the Travellers Lodging. From US$30 per day, includes transport, food, accommodation with the option of cabins or staying with an indigenous family. They also work alongside Fundación Amazonia Viva who work closely with local people.
Cabañas Pimpilala Tel: 886434/886-088 or make reservations in Quito through Natural Life, Calle Reina Victoria and Foch. US$30 per day, includes transport, food, accommodation. Tours 2–4 days.

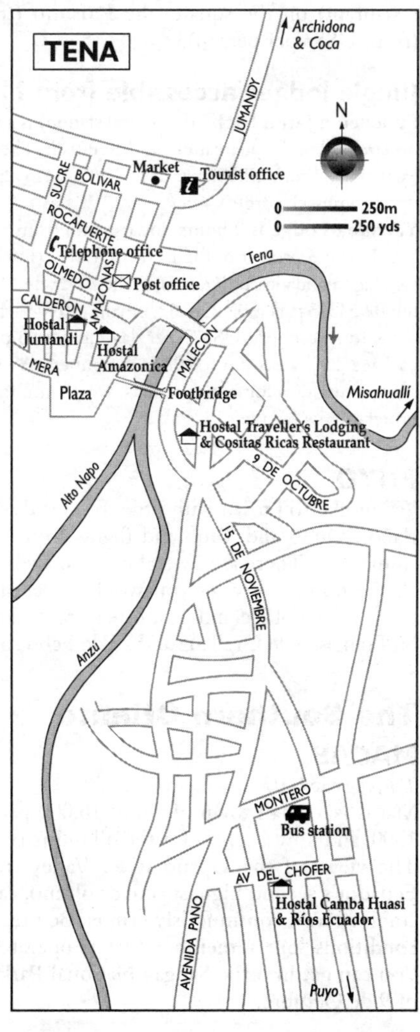

Ríos Ecuador Tel/fax: 887438 (Quito tel/fax: 02 558264); email: info@riosecuador.co They operate rafting and canoeing trips on the upper Napo River (class 3) and the Misahuallí River (class 4 and 4+). Trips for beginners and experienced people in good shape. As they operate in jungle areas the vegetation and wildlife is beautiful.

MISAHUALLÍ

An hour by bus from Tena, this small town on the River Napo is a popular place for backpackers to pick up a cheap jungle tour to the Upper or Lower Napo. Buses leave the Tena bus station for Misahuallí at least once an hour 06.00–18.00. There are a number of agencies around the main square that offer a variety of tours, usually US$30–40 per person per day. You can also organise day trips from here down the river: a motorised canoe is around US$40 per day for the boat, split between the number of passengers. Try asking around to find other people who are interested. There are several hostels: the **Posada** (which also has a reasonable restaurant) on the square, the **Paisano** (from US$3 per person) and **Marana** (from US$3 per person).

Jungle lodges accessible from Misahuallí

Fundación Jatun Sacha (biological station) is a tropical rainforest reserve of 2,000 hectares 10km downstream from Misahuallí. There are wooden cabins for guests, and excursions. From US$50 per day. Tel/fax 441592; email: jatsacha@jsacha.ecuanex.net.ec or info@jatunsacha.org

Yachana Lodge is 2 hours downstream from Misahuallí. Groups travel on Wed and Sat. This is a project of the FUNEDESIN (Fundación para la Educación y Desarrollo de las Nacionalidades Indígenas). Calle Andrade Marín 188 and Diego de Almagro, Quito; tel: 02 543851; fax: 02 220362; email: info@yachana.com; web: www.yachana.com or www.funedesin.org US$77 per day includes 3 meals and guide, US$300 for 5-day package. 20% discount for SAEC members. All lodge profits support FUNEDESIN community development projects, which aim to protect the rainforest through protecting its people.

PUYO

Yet another oil town with little to offer the passing tourist. There are buses from Baños, Quito and Teno and flights from Quito to Shell-Mera airport, 30 mins from town. There are several cheap hostels and some more upmarket hotels, and all the normal services you would expect in a town of 25,000 inhabitants. The bank, phone office and post office are in the centre of town. The tourist office is on Francisco de Orellana and 27 de Febrero; tel: 03 883227.

The Southern Oriente

MACAS

Telephone code 07

Macas is a small town of about 10,000 people, founded as a mission station in 1590, and now a centre for the oil industry in the southern Ecuadorian Amazon. The views of the Upano River Valley from the town are beautiful. Sangay, Ecuador's second highest active volcano, can sometimes be seen in the distance, smoking as it continuously erupts. Be prepared for wet weather and hot humid conditions, but remember that temperatures can drop considerably at night. You can get into the Sangay National Park from Macas, by going to the village of 9 de Octubre.

Getting there and away

By bus

Buses from Quito take about 11 hours as do buses from Cuenca. Either way the journey is bumpy and uncomfortable. It's a good idea to break the journey in Baños or Puyo.

By plane

You can fly from Quito to Macas in about 40 minutes for US$55 with TAME, or from Cuenca for US$25.

Where to stay and eat

The best budget hotel is **Peñon del Oriente**, good value at US$3–5 per person; Calle Domingo Comín 837 and Amazonas; tel: 700124; fax: 700450. There are other cheap hostels including **Residencial Macas** on Calle 24 de Mayo. The **Orquídea** on Calle 9 de Octubre is reasonable and helpful. Also good is **Esmeraldas**, Calle Cuenca 6–12; tel: 700160.

The **Big Chifa** is a reasonable restaurant, and there are several decent cafés on Calle Amazonas – try **El Jardín** and **Eros**. For vegetarian food try the **Prashada**. **La Randimpa** on 24 de Mayo is also good. Don't drink the tap water here without treating it first.

Practical information

Post office, **phone office** and **bank** in the centre of town.

Travel agencies Aventura Tsunki, Calle Bolívar; tel: 700464; email: tsunki@cue.satnet.net; web: www.tsunki.com.ec Run by a north American, a Chilean and a Shuar Indian, this agency has been recommended for trips into the jungle around Macas. From US$15 per day.

What to see and do

Try climbing to the **Voz del Upano** radio station, just a few minutes' walk from the bus station or airport, for great views. The **cathedral**, finished in 1922, is worth a visit. To the north of the cathedral there is a **park and botanic garden** with a reconstruction of a Shuar Indian home and an orchid garden. Near Macas you can swim in the Upano River, but ask the locals for the best places and be careful of strong currents.

GALÁPAGOS ISLANDS
0 50km
0 30 miles
KEY
Settlement
Airfield
Visitor site
Major snorkelling site
Peak
PACIFIC OCEAN
Equator
Isla Wolf (Wenmen)
Pinta (Abingdon)
Cabo Chalmers
Cabo Ibbetson
Punta Mejía
Marchena (Bindloed)
Punta Montalvo
Punta Espejo
Playa Negra
Punta Calle
Genovesa (Tower)
El Barranco
Darwin Bay
Punta Albemarle
Punta Flores
1660m
Cabo Marshall
Volcán Wolf
Cabo Berkeley
Punta Vicente Roca
Volcán Darwin 1330m
Punta Espinosa
Cabo Douglas
Volcán La Cumbre
Fernandina (Narborough)
Cabo Hammond
Tagus Cove
Urvina Bay
Volcán Alcedo 1125m
Isabela (Albemarle)
Punta Mangle
Elizabeth Bay
Punta Moreno
Volcán Santo Tomás 1490m
Tomás de Berlanga
Punta San Juan
Punta Cristóbal
1689m
Volcán Cerro Azul
Puerto Villamil
Punta Essex
Cabo Rosa
Buccaneer Cove
Espumilla Beach
Puerto Egas
Canal de Isabela
Punta Córdova
920m
Cerro Cowan
Santiago (James)
Sullivan Bay
Bartolomé
Sombrero Chino (Chinese Hat)
Beagle
Rábida (Jervis)
Bahia Cartago
Daphne Major
Seymour Norte
Isla Mosquera
Baltra
Bachas Beach
Guy Fawkes
Caleta Tortuga Negra
South Plaza
Pinzón (Duncan)
Los Gemelos
Media Luna
Santa Rosa
Bellavista
Santa Cruz (Indefatigable)
Tortoise Reserve
Los Tuneles
Punta Ballena
Puerto Ayora
Charles Darwin Research Station
Tortuga Bay
Punta Davis
Los Cuatro Hermanos
Punta Veintimilla
Tortuga
Santa Fé (Barrington)
Cerro Pan de Azúcar
Punta Pitt
Cerro San Joaquin
896m
La Galapaguera
León Dormido
Roca Este
Lobos
El Junco Lagoon
Cerro de las Tijeretas
San Cristóbal (Chatham)
Pto Baquerizo Moreno
El Progreso
Punta Sur
Post Office Bay
Punta Cormorant
Puerto Velasco Ibarra
Campeón
Punta Ayora
Caldwell
Punta Ensillada
Gardner
Santa María (Floreana/Charles)
Punta Sur
Española (Hood)
Punta Suárez
Gardner Bay

9 The Galápagos Islands

The Galápagos Islands are undoubtedly Ecuador's most well known tourist attraction. They really are amazing and quite unique, and should not be missed if you can help it. Even non-wildlife enthusiasts will not cease to be amazed by the animals, birds, vegetation and scenery of these truly enchanted islands. The archipelago consists of 13 large islands, six smaller ones and many little rocky outcrops, situated 1,000km off the coast of mainland Ecuador. The Equator runs through Isabela Island. The Galápagos are the most diverse and complex island group in the world in terms of their relatively pristine conditions, where the flora and flora were able to evolve without being threatened by introduced species.

BACKGROUND INFORMATION

History

As early as the 14th century the Galápagos Islands were known about. The Bishop of Panama, Fray Tomás Berlanga, came across the islands accidentally when he was becalmed and swept out to sea on his way to Peru. He wasn't very impressed by the lack of sorely needed water. From the 16th century the Galápagos began to appear on maps and were used habitually by sailors, buccaneers and whalers as a stopping off place and for restocking with food and water. The first resident of the islands was an Irishman, a man named Patrick Watkins, probably a victim of a shipwreck. He lived on the islands for two years before escaping in a stolen whaler's boat. In 1832 Colonel Ignacio Hernández claimed the islands for Ecuador, and a small settlement was established on Floreana. Three years later Charles Darwin visited the islands during his voyages on the *Beagle*. His observations led him to develop his theory of evolution. Within a few years settlers began to arrive. The population has risen now to around 20,000 with the principal concentrations in Santa Cruz and San Cristóbal. It has undoubtedly been beneficial to the survival of the wildlife that most of the islands are not suitable for habitation, because of the lack of fresh water. The people who did settle introduced a number of threats to the native fauna, such as goats, donkeys, cats, dogs, pigs, rats and numerous plant species. Conservation attempts are focussed on attempting to remove introduced species.

Galápagos National Park

The Galápagos National Park was established in 1936 to include all the islands that had not at that time been colonised. This was Ecuador's first national park. In 1968 the boundaries were extended so that 96% of the land of the islands now falls within the national park. Only the populated areas of Santa Cruz, San Cristóbal, Isabela, Floreana and Baltra are excluded. In 1978 the Galápagos were put on the World Heritage List and internationally recognised as a biosphere reserve. In 1986 the Marine Resources Reserve was established to include all the waters within 15 miles of the islands. In 1996 this was upgraded to a Biological Reserve of Marine Resources.

Climate

The climate in the islands is strongly influenced by the presence of oceanic currents, the relatively cold Humboldt current and the warm tropical current from the Gulf of Panama. These currents converge north of the islands, but the meeting point moves south from January to April and the warmer current flows round the islands. There are two marked seasons in the Galápagos: the warmer months with occasional heavy rain from January to May/June, and the cooler drier months from May/June to December, caused by the presence of the Humboldt current. During the cooler months there are overcast skies and little rain in the lowlands, but considerable *garúa* (mist) and rain in the highlands. February is the hottest month of the year and August and September the coolest when you may need a jacket in the evenings. The seas are choppy in the cooler months when southeast winds prevail, and sea temperatures are also cooler, around 20°C. From January to June the average sea temperature is around 25°C. The weather between the two marked seasons is generally somewhat unpredictable, and also varies from one part of the archipelago to another. Rainfall at sea-level is less than 350mm, while in the highlands it can be over 1,000mm.

Wildlife

The Galápagos Islands are oceanic islands formed from submarine volcanoes, which emerged lifeless from the ocean millions of years ago. The great distance of approximately 1,000km between the Galápagos Islands and the mainland continent has acted as a natural barrier to animals and plants populating the archipelago. The range of plants and animal species found on the Galápagos has been determined by the fact that the islands have never been connected to the mainland. Originally their ancestors all had to make the journey across the Pacific Ocean. It is striking that amongst the wildlife found on the Galápagos there is a predominance of reptiles and seabirds, there are very few mammals or land birds, and no amphibians or freshwater fish. Butterflies, moths and beetles are the predominant insects found on the islands, and there are far fewer species than would be expected in a comparable area on mainland Ecuador.

Vegetation

Around the coast there are mangrove swamps in protected coves and lagoons, and behind that an arid zone where the dominant plant is cactus. There is then a transition zone and beyond that a humid zone of plants such as scalesia. On the mountain summits there is a zone of ferns, grasses and moss.

Fauna

There are 11 subspecies of Galápagos giant tortoise, all of which are endangered, terrestial iguanas, marine iguana, lizards and geckos. There are 57 species of resident bird, 26 of which are endemic and 31 regular migrants. Native mammals include the Galápagos sealion and Galápagos fur seal, rats, and bats. There are also several species of shark, ray and cetacean. There are green turtle and hawksbill turtle in the waters around the islands.

Transportation of flora and fauna

The presence of a particular plant species on the Galápagos is determined by its ease of dispersal. There are no plants with large flowers or heavy seeds, while the lighter ferns, grasses, and composites are relatively common. There are three possible means for flora and fauna to arrive on the islands: across the water; through the air; or carried by another organism. Seeds float or can be carried by natural raft. Prevailing oceanic winds blow towards the Galápagos from the east, and the oceanic currents can also sweep organisms along with them. Reptiles, along with sealions, fur seals, sea turtles and penguins, swim well and travel with the help of the currents. Most insects probably come by air. Transport via other organisms, particularly birds, is also common. Among 607 species of plant found in the Galápagos, it has been estimated that 40% were transported by birds, 32% by man, 22% by wind and 6% by flotation.

Adapting to the environment

Once on the islands the plants and animals must find a suitable environment in which to establish themselves. The presence of suitable food and nesting material influences which birds or animals can survive. Seabirds that nest on the ground, were probably the first colonists as they need no vegetation, and so have no problem reproducing. Red-footed boobies, pelicans and frigate birds, which nest in trees, cannot have colonised the islands until there was suitable vegetation, even if there was food available. Likewise, insects, iguanas, and seed-eating finches needed plants for food, while hawks, flycatchers, snakes, and lava lizards could not establish themselves until there was suitable prey.

Many of the plants found in the islands are weed types with a high tolerance of inhospitable conditions and an ability to adapt. The first colonisers would have been plants needing little or no soil, such as lichens. Most of the plants are wind pollinated as those depending on pollination by specific insects or certain bird species would have a more difficult time surviving. There are very few Galápagos plants with large attractive flowers – they tend to be small and not colourful.

The pressures of man

Since the first human contact with the islands in the 16th century man has played a central role in the introduction of plants and animals. People have, both inadvertently and deliberately, introduced dozens of weeds and exotic plants and numerous domestic animals, which have since become feral. Given the increasing number of visitors and yachts to the Galápagos Islands as a result of tourism (an influx of over 60,000 people per year), the danger of further species being introduced remains a real one, continually threatening the survival of the endemic species. Special legislation for the Galápagos Islands passed recently has recognised the danger of the presence and introduction of alien species, and provides a programme for the control and eradication of such species. The 20,000 resident population of the Galápagos, most of whom live on Santa Cruz, San Cristóbal, Isabela and Floreana, earn their income from tourism, cattle grazing and fishing. Immigration to the islands is now controlled, but uncontrolled fishing remains a major threat.

Geology

The Galápagos are volcanic islands which are similar to other oceanic islands such as the Canaries, Hawaii, and the Azores, in that they have arisen from the sea, rather than separating from a land mass. In geological terms the islands are young, only three to five million years old. They are formed from the action of mantle plumes, columns of hot rock rising from deep within the earth as much as 1,000km down. The plumes rise because they are hotter and less dense than the rock around them. As the plumes rise they begin to melt because of the lower pressure around them. The rising plumes become trapped by the lithosphere, the cool and rigid outer layer of the earth's surface, and spread into magma chambers several kilometres beneath the earth's surface. Sometimes the magma trapped in the chamber forces itself upwards and bursts out in a volcanic eruption. This is how the Galápagos Islands have formed. The islands we can see above the sea are only the tips of the volcanoes – the bulk is below sea level.

As the magma forces its way up in a volcanic eruption, the lithosphere is also pushed upwards. This and the crystallisation of magma beneath the volcanic eruption have led to the forming of the Galápagos Platform, the raised sea bed on which the islands are located. The ocean depth around the platform is 2,000–3,000m, while most of the platform is only 400m below the surface.

The Galápagos Islands, although not entirely linear, have two major axes running east–northeast and north–northwest. The islands are older to the southeast. Española is the oldest island at 3.25 million years, while Isabela and Fernandina are only 700,000 years old. The oldest islands are found to the south–southeast because of the effect of plate tectonics. The Galápagos Islands are on the Nazca Plate, which is moving east–southeast. The movement of the plate carries a volcano away from the magma source, so that it eventually becomes extinct. As it moves away from the magma source it begins to cool and contract. As a result of this contraction, the volcano slowly sinks beneath the sea, eventually creating submerged extinct volcanoes known as seamounts. There is a seamount in the Galápagos thought to be eight million years old. It is now 1,500m below sea-level, but has a flat top and rounded stones on the top shaped by wave erosion. Some scientists think the Galápagos mantle could be 90 million years old and that there have been islands in the locality for that long.

Volcanoes of the Galápagos

The Galápagos Islands are an unusually active volcanic area. In the last 10,000 years there have been volcanic eruptions on Volcán Darwin, Volcán Ecuador, Genovesa, San Cristóbal and Santa Cruz. In the more distant past there have been eruptions on several other Galápagos volcanoes including Fernandina, Volcán Wolf, Alcedo, Sierra Negra, Cerro Azul, Santiago, Pinta, Floreana and Marchena.

There are two types of volcano in the Galápagos Islands. On the younger islands, including Isabela and Fernandina, the volcanoes are large with rounded tops and deep *calderas* or craters, formed by the collapse of the upper part of the volcano into the magma chamber from which the magma has retreated. The caldera of Fernandina is now over 1,000m deep measured down from the rim of the crater. The latest collapse was in 1968 when, accompanied by several earthquakes and the dramatic release of gases and magma, the floor of the crater fell a further 300m. In the eastern islands the volcanoes tend to be smaller shield volcanoes with gentler slopes and rounded tops. In both cases the volcanoes are the result of successive eruptions and lava build-up. The islands reflect a variety of types and ages of volcanic activity. Characteristic volcanic features of the islands include crater lakes, fumaroles, lava tubes, sulphur fields and a variety of lava, pumice, ash and tuff.

Española and Santa Fe are parts of extinct volcanoes. Both the volcanoes have been extinct for millions of years, and large portions have eroded away. Pinzon and Rabida are shield volcanoes, which have been extinct for a million years. Santa Cruz and San Cristóbal, although they are still active volcanoes, have some parts which are extinct and considerably older, more than a million years in the case of Santa Cruz and nearly 2.5 million years in the case of San Cristóbal.

THE ISLANDS

Telephone code 05

There are designated visitor sites on each of the islands, where boats can land or approach, and where there are defined trails to follow. This is to reduce impact from the masses of tourists who arrive on the islands each year.

The larger islands within the Galápagos archipelago are Isabela (458km^2), Santa Cruz (986km^2), Fernandina (642km^2), Santiago (585km^2) and San Cristóbal (558km^2). Brief descriptions are given of the islands most commonly visited on boat tours. Santa Cruz and San Cristóbal are the most populated, and have airports to which there are daily flights from mainland Ecuador.

Santa Cruz (Indefatigable)

This is the most populated of the islands. Puerto Ayora, the main town on the island, is probably where you will start your tour if you are booked on one already, and the best place to start looking for one if you haven't booked anything before you arrive. A sizeable town, it has all the amenities you would expect to service the large number of tourists passing through, as well as the resident population. The **Charles Darwin Research Centre** (see box) is within walking distance of the town, and definitely worth a visit. Here you can see the giant land, or Galápagos, tortoises, which once roamed the islands. In the 19th century their populations were severely reduced as whalers would capture them and keep them on board as a fresh meat supply. Also from Puerto Ayora you can walk the 3km to **Turtle Bay**, just southwest of town. A trip to the interior of the island to see the twin craters **Los Gemelos** in the highland Scalesia forest is fascinating. This lush forest is found above the dry zone on Santa Cruz, and receives most of its moisture from the *garúa*, a mist often present in the highlands particularly during July and December. About 10km from Puerto Ayora there are several **lava tubes** you can go inside. These are characteristic of volcanic scenery, and are formed when the outer layer of flowing lava cools; the molten lava inside flows away, leaving a space behind it and creating a tunnel. You can also visit the **Tortoise Reserve** near Santa Rosa.

Getting there and away

The airport is actually on Baltra Island, and you need to take a bus to the ferry, then a further bus to Puerto Ayora (total time 1½ hrs). Daily flights with TAME from the mainland. Student discounts. Make sure you reconfirm your return flight.

Where to stay and eat

Estrella del Mar Av Charles Darwin and 12 de Febrero; tel: 526427. From US$3 per person, nice rooms, sea view.
Hotel Lirio del Mar Calle Bolívar Naveda and Tomás de Berlanga; tel: 526212. From US$5 for a double.
Hotel Lobo del Mar Calle 12 de Febrero; tel: 526569; email: lobomar@uio.satnet.net US$10–20. Also organises boat tours.
Hotel Salinas Tomás de Berlanga and Bolívar Naveda; tel: 526107. US$10 for a double with bath, good-sized rooms, comfortable.
La Peregrina Av Charles Darwin; tel: 526323. US$15 for a double includes air conditioning, private bath and breakfast.

There are restaurants all along the main street which generally serve fish and seafood of a high quality. There is quite a selection of bars and salsa clubs including **Barbara Negra**, **Bar Frank** and **Galápason**.

Practical information

Tourist office Av Charles Darwin.
Post office Calle Los Colones.
Phone office Calle Padre Herrera.

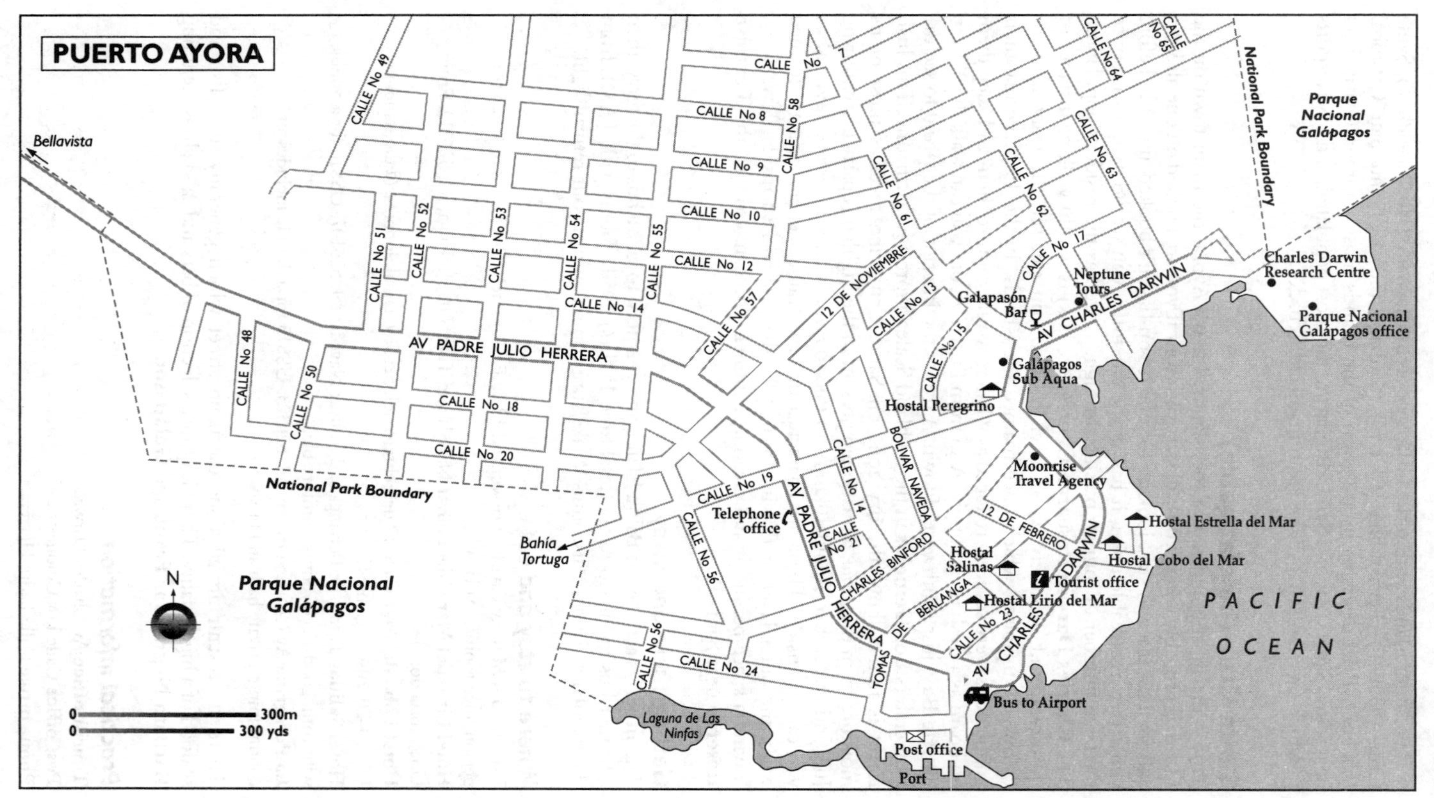
PUERTO AYORA
Bellavista
Parque Nacional Galápagos
National Park Boundary
Charles Darwin Research Centre
Parque Nacional Galápagos office
Neptune Tours
Galapasón Bar
AV CHARLES DARWIN
Galápagos Sub Aqua
Hostal Peregrino
Moonrise Travel Agency
Hostal Estrella del Mar
Hostal Cobo del Mar
Hostal Salinas
Tourist office
Hostal Lirio del Mar
PACIFIC OCEAN
Bus to Airport
Post office
Port
Laguna de Las Ninfas
Telephone office
Bahía Tortuga
National Park Boundary
Parque Nacional Galápagos
N
0 300m
0 300 yds
AV PADRE JULIO HERRERA
12 DE NOVIEMBRE
12 DE FEBRERO
BOLIVAR NAVEDA
CHARLES BINFORD
TOMAS DE BERLANGA
CALLE No 7
CALLE No 8
CALLE No 9
CALLE No 10
CALLE No 12
CALLE No 13
CALLE No 14
CALLE No 15
CALLE No 17
CALLE No 18
CALLE No 19
CALLE No 20
CALLE No 21
CALLE No 23
CALLE No 24
CALLE No 48
CALLE No 49
CALLE No 50
CALLE No 51
CALLE No 52
CALLE No 53
CALLE No 54
CALLE No 55
CALLE No 56
CALLE No 57
CALLE No 58
CALLE No 61
CALLE No 62
CALLE No 63
CALLE No 64
CALLE No 65

Money The Banco del Pacífico on Av Charles Darwin has an ATM, and changes travellers' cheques and dollars for cash.
Airlines TAME office Av Charles Darwin.
Servicio Parque Nacional Galápagos Puerto Ayora.
Charles Darwin Research Centre Puerto Ayora; tel: 593 5 526146/7; fax: 593 4 564636; email: cdrs@fcdarwin.org.ec; web: www.Galapagos.org

Travel agencies

The following is a list of some registered travel agencies, most of which offer a variety of boat and land tours and diving. Whenever you book a tour be sure to read the contract and check carefully exactly what is included each day. Don't forget to take an underwater camera, at least two rolls of film per day, snorkel gear, suncream, a raincoat and some extra snacks. Some landings on the islands are wet so you need shoes that you don't mind getting wet and that will dry reasonably quickly.

Andando Tours is a family operated and owned business with 25 years' experience in the Galápagos. Office in Quito and Santa Cruz at Calle Moisés Brito; tel/fax: 526308; email: andando2@ecnet.ec or andando1@ecnet.ec.
Encantour Av Charles Darwin, tel: 526187. Boat trips and diving.
Ensueños de Galápagos Av Charles Binford; tel: 526593; fax: 526419. Various tours offered.
Ensugal Av. Charles Binford; tel: 526593; fax: 526419. Boat tours.
Galápagos Discovery Padre Julio Herrera; tel/fax: 526245. Boat trips, day tours, diving, mountain bikes, horseriding.
Galápagos Sub-Aqua Av Charles Darwin; tel: 526350. Boat tours and diving.
Moonrise Av Charles Darwin 160; tel: 526402/526348/526589; fax: 526403; email: sdivine@ga.pro.ec Contact for details of last minute bookings.
Servicios Navieros de Galápagos Av Charles Darwin; tel/fax: 526186.
Turismo del Pacífico y Galápagos Av Charles Darwin; tel/fax: 526581; email: aaagalap@uio.satnet.net; web: www.galapagostour.com Boat tours in the *Pulsar*, with departures on Thurs and Sun, for 10 passengers. Low season from US$335 for 4 days, US$595 for 8 days; high season from US$370 for 4 days, US$655 for 8 days. Snorkelling equipment for rent US$5 per week. Diving, US$70 per dive including full equipment.

Boats

Below is a list of boats that have been recommended, but crews, costs and itineraries change, so this list should only be treated as a guideline. It's best to ask around until you find something that suits your itinerary, time and budget. There are three categories of boat, and the approximate prices are given, but are seasonal. Low season is usually early September to mid-December and mid-January to mid-June, except for Easter. High season is mid-December to mid-January, Easter and mid-June to the end of August. Boats are usually categorised as follows: Economic, from US$50 per day, usually for 10–12 people; Tourist, from US$65 per day, usually for 16 people; Large, from US$85 per day, for 40-plus people. Some of the boats give last minute special offers and that way you could end up paying considerably less than if you book from Quito, but obviously there's no guarantee of a place.

M/S Tropic Sun from US$85 per day. A large boat, that takes 48 people, plenty of food, hot water, spacious and comfortable with good service.
M/V Sulidae from US$750 (tourist class) for 8 days, a vintage sailboat beautifully restored, takes 14 maximum, good food. Calle Charles Binford; tel: 526295; fax: 526294.
Yate Flamingo from US$520 for eight days, maximum 12 people, small cabins, plenty of deck space. Tourist class. Calle Tomás de Berlanga; tel: 526556.

THE CHARLES DARWIN RESEARCH CENTRE

Information provided by the Charles Darwin Research Station

The Charles Darwin Research Station (CDRS) is the operative branch of the Charles Darwin Foundation for the Galápagos Islands, an international, non-governmental, scientific, non-profit organisation dedicated to the protection of the Galápagos Islands since 1959. As part of a formal agreement with the Government of Ecuador, CDRS conducts and facilitates research in Galápagos to supply information and technical assistance to the Galápagos National Park Service and other branches of the government. CDRS also provides environmental education to island communities and schools and to the visitors who come to Galápagos each year. Ecuadorian university students receive hands-on training in science, education and conservation at CDRS through volunteer and scholarship programmes. The principal focus of CDRS is scientific research by staff, scientists and consultants, directed mainly toward the conservation and management of Galápagos National Park and the Galápagos Marine Resources Reserve. Visiting scientists from all over the world come to Galápagos to perform research on a wide variety of topics, such as evolutionary biology, geology, ecotourism, climatology and population genetics.

CDRS promotes research programmes and cooperative research agreements with both national and international scientific research institutions. The information generated by this research is provided to decision makers of the government of Ecuador, published in refereed scientific journals and internal reports, and interpreted for visitors and environmental education programmes in the islands. The major physical plant of CDRS is located on Santa Cruz Island, and is reached by air from the airport on Baltra Island, north of Santa Cruz. The station facilities include a library, museum, herbarium, marine laboratory, darkroom, computer centre, research boat *Beagle*, and forestry nursery. There is accommodation for visiting researchers, students, and staff; office and laboratory buildings; and a public area which constitutes an official Visitor Site of

Aida María from US$95 per day. Tourist class boat for 16 passengers. Av Padre Julio Herrera; tel: 526117; fax: 526333.

Reina Silvia From US$900 for 8 days. Expensive but recommended. A first-class yacht for 16 passengers. Tel: 526210.

For diving

Galápagos Sub-Aqua Charles Darwin Av, Puerto Ayora; tel: 526350; email: sub_aqua@pa.ga.pro.ec

Scuba-Iguana Hotel Galápagos, Santa Cruz; tel: 526296; email: hotelgps@pa.ga.pro.ec. Own two boats and the Hotel Galápagos.

Seymour

This is an uplifted island, which is quite flat. There is a trail to follow which takes you through palo santo forest, past colonies of blue-footed boobies, frigate bird colonies and beaches with marine iguanas and sealions.

Santa Fé (Barrington)

This island is only 20km from Santa Cruz, so can be visited in a day trip. It is very pretty with some dramatic giant cacti (*Opuntia*) and endemic land iguanas. There

Galápagos National Park, where visitors can view young and adult giant tortoises in the breeding and rearing centre. CDRS also has representatives on San Cristóbal and Isabela Islands, who offer support to researchers and perform environmental education.

The station's principal partner, the Galápagos National Park Service, is the government institution responsible for the Galápagos National Park. By conducting applied research on key problems affecting the Galápagos ecosystem, the CDRS assists the park service in design, planning, and implementation of conservation programmes. The partnership between the two institutions has produced some highly successful programmes, such as captive breeding of endangered tortoises and iguanas, eradication of introduced mammals in certain islands, the rescue of near-extinct plants, and important advances towards effective conservation of the marine environment, which has come under much pressure recently. Current areas of conservation research by the station include improvement of reptile breeding, tortoise health, methods to counter threats to endangered birds, monitoring and protection of endangered plants, methods to control introduced plants, monitoring and control of introduced insects, marine biodiversity studies, biology of exploited marine species, fisheries monitoring and ecological monitoring. The station is or has also been directly involved in providing technical guidance on the training of tourist guides, introduction of a quarantine system, the development of improved agricultural land management (free of aggressive introduced species), the drafting of a special law for Galápagos, and other important elements of a conservation strategy for Galápagos.

By becoming a Friend of the Galápagos you can help to further the work of CDRS. You will receive two reports per year about up-to-date research. Contact email: darwin@Galápagos.org

Charles Darwin Research Station, Isla Santa Cruz, Galápagos, PO Box 17-01-3891; tel: 526146/7; fax: 564636; email: cdrs@fcdarwin.org.ec; web: www.Galápagos.org.

is a trail leading up the cliff which overlooks the southern part of the bay. There are plenty of sealions in the bay, and snorkelling here is fun.

South Plaza

This is an uplifted island with a large sealion colony. It is near enough Santa Cruz to be visited on a day tour. There is a trail through the *Opuntia* cactus forest, where you may see land iguanas, to cliffs on the south side where you can see swallow-tailed gulls, red-billed tropic birds, and Audubon shearwaters.

San Cristóbal (Chatham)

This island is the second most populated in the archipelago after Santa Cruz. The main town is **Puerto Baquerizo Moreno**, capital of the province of Galápagos. The town has several hotels, restaurants, shops and bars, and has become a popular departure point for boat tours. There is an airport near the town, with frequent flights from the mainland with SAN. The airport is within walking distance of the town. It is possible to pick up a boat tour here, but departures are much less frequent than from Santa Cruz.

San Cristóbal is one of the oldest islands. In the north of the island you can see eroded volcanic peaks. You can take a bus from the port to **El Junco**, a freshwater lake with interesting birds such as white-cheeked pintails. **Punta Pitt**, at the northeast of the island, is a visitor site where you can see red-footed, blue-footed and masked boobies. A couple of hours by boat from San Cristóbal is **Leon Dormido**, also known as Kicker Rock, the remains of a tuff cone, split in two; small boats can sail through the crack. There is good snorkelling here too.

Where to stay

A couple of recommended places to stay for budget travellers include:

Hostal San Cristóbal Puerto Baquerizo Moreno; tel: 520338.
Pensión Islas Galápagos Puerto Baquerizo Moreno; tel: 520203.

Española (Hood)

This is the oldest of the islands, and it has eroded away to such an extent that it is quite small and flat, with no visible volcanic crater. There are two places to visit on the island, Gardner Bay on the east and Punta Suárez on the western side. **Gardner Bay** has a long white sandy beach which is a nesting area for marine turtles, and is also used by sealions. Snorkelling is good, and you may see turtles and sharks. Near **Punta Suárez** is the only colony and nesting site of the waved albatross on the Galápagos. Approximately 12,000 pairs come to the island to breed between late March and December. In addition there are many other interesting species of wildlife to be spotted here including an endemic marine iguana, Hood mockingbirds, lava lizards, cactus finch, blue-footed boobies, masked boobies, swallow-tailed gulls, red-billed tropicbirds and oyster catchers. Beyond the waved albatross colony there is a spectacular blowhole, at its best in heavy swell, when it spouts water 20m into the air.

Floreana (Charles)

There are three areas to visit on Floreana Island, Post Office Bay, Devil's Crown and Punta Cormorant. **Post Office Bay** is the site of the original post office barrel placed by British whalers to send letters home in 1793. The barrel today isn't the same one but you can still leave letters here in the hope that another passing tourist will pick them up and take them to their destination. **Punta Cormorant** has two contrasting beaches. You land at a dark coloured beach with olivine crystals, and then walk, past a salt lagoon where you may spot wading birds including flamingos, pintails and stilts, to a fine golden sandy beach which is a nesting site for green sea turtles. You may also see stingrays in the water. You cannot go in the water here. Just offshore from Punta Cormorant lies the **Devil's Crown**, which is a collection of rocks, a half-submerged crater. The snorkelling around here is excellent with plenty of fish and the chance to play with young sealions. The rocks themselves are a popular roosting site for boobies, pelicans, and frigates. Red-billed tropicbirds can also be seen and sometimes nest in crevices in the rocks.

Where to stay

Pension Wittmer Calle Ignacio Hernández; tel: 520150.

Santiago (James)

James Bay, on the west side of the island, has several sites to visit: Espumilla Beach, Puerto Egas, Bucaneer Cove and a salt crater. At **Espumilla Beach** there is a lagoon where you may see stilts, flamingos, waders and ducks. **Puerto Egas** is a black sand beach that was the site of a salt mining industry in the 1960s. From here there is a trail to the salt crater, where you may see several land bird species such as Darwin's finches, doves and hawks. There are feral goats here too. Follow the trail south from Puerto Egas to a fur seal grotto, passing marine iguanas and sealions. **Buccaneer Cove** is north of James Bay, and a scenic spot. On the east side of the island is **Sullivan Bay**, where lava from 1897 covers a large area. There is little vegetation, but the pahoehoe lava itself is quite amazing to walk over, with its obvious ripples and swirls.

Bartolomé

This is a small island off Santiago Island. The beaches are white sand, with mangroves fringing the edges. There are two trails, one to the summit, from the easternmost beach, which gives great views towards Santiago. There is also a trail from the beach to the south, through mangroves and dunes. **Pinnacle Rock**, just offshore is the remains of a tuff cone. It is a good place to spot the Galápagos penguin.

Genovesa (Tower)

This island is low lying, with a large cove, probably a breached caldera, on the south side, where boats often anchor. The two sites you can visit are Darwin Bay and Prince Phillip's Steps. **Darwin Bay** is a coral beach which attracts vast numbers of great frigate birds, red-footed boobies, swallow-tailed gulls and storm petrels. There is a trail leading round the bay to the east to **Prince Phillip's Steps**, at the top of a cliff, and ideal for sighting storm petrels. The cliffs are a breeding ground to thousands of band-rumped storm petrels. On the way you can probably spot tropicbirds, great frigate birds, red-footed and masked boobies, and doves and finches. Occasionally you can spot short-eared owls hunting the nesting storm petrels.

Rábida (Jervis)

This island has red coloured cliffs, volcanic slopes and sand. You can land on the beach, where there are usually plenty of sealions, and walk inland on a short trail observing finches, doves, warblers and mockingbirds. There's a salt water lagoon with occasional flamingos. There is good snorkelling off the spit east of the beach, and nesting pelicans west of the beach.

Isabela (Albemarle)

This is the largest island in the Galápagos archipelago, nearly 5,000km^2, and 112km from end to end. It is one of the youngest islands and consists of a series of five volcanoes connected by their lava flows. The highest of all Galápagos peaks is found here, Volcán Wolf (1,707m). The latest eruption in the Galápagos was on Isabela Island when Cerro Azul volcano began erupting. This was the first eruption in the Galápagos for 20 years. Isabela is one of the most dramatic of all the islands, with some superb volcanic scenery. There are several interesting sites to visit on Isabela including Alcedo volcano, Elizabeth Bay, Tagus Cove and Urvina Bay. There are five distinct subspecies of the Galápagos tortoise on Isabela.

The **Alcedo volcano** is one of five shield volcanoes on the island. It is a 4–6 hour strenuous trek to get to the rim of the crater. The views inside and outside the crater are outstanding. There are steaming fumaroles and Galápagos giant tortoises of the Alcedo subspecies. It's a good idea to spend a night in this area if you have time, and there are several places to camp, at the beach, on the way up and around the crater.

Elizabeth Bay is a good place to see marine turtles, flightless cormorants and rays. **Tagus Cove** was popular with pirates and whalers, and some of the names of the many ships that visited the cove are painted on the cliffs. On land you can see a salt water lagoon and the lava fields of Darwin volcano, while along the cliffs from the sea you may find the elusive Galápagos penguin, the flightless cormorant, and other seabirds.

Urvina Bay, on the west side of the island, is the remains of a coral reef uplifted from the sea in 1954. The area is good for seabirds, especially flightless cormorants and brown pelicans. You can also find an endemic marine iguana, rays and marine turtles.

The crater of **Sierra Negra volcano** at the southern end of Isabela measures 10km across. It is possible to visit this area and also the area just to the north known as Volcán Chico. This comprises a groups of craters where you can see fumaroles.

On the southeast of the island is **Puerto Villamil**, a small fishing village with about 500 inhabitants. A road with good views of the southern Galápagos Islands goes from here towards Sierra Negra. Near Puerto Villamil there are lagoons and mangrove forests with flamingoes and other wading birds. There is also an experimental station near the port of Villamil, where the Galápagos National Park are doing experiments to aid reproduction of the subspecies of *Geochelone elephantopus gunteri* (tortoise). Las Tintoreras, just a few minutes by boat from the port of Villamil, is a good place to observe the white-tipped shark.

Where to stay

Hotel Ballena Azul Calle Conocarpus, Puerto Villamil; tel/fax: 529125; email: isabela@pa.ga.pro.ec; web: www.pub.ecua.net.ec/isabela.
Hotel Tero Real Puerto Villamil; tel: 529106; fax: 529103.
Hotel Loja Av 16 de Marzo, Puerto Villamil; tel: 529174.
Pensión la Casa de Marita Calle Conocarpus, Puerto Villamil; tel: 529238; fax: 529201; email: hcmarita@ga.pro.ec On San Cristóbal Island, tel/fax: 520036; in Guayaquil, tel/fax: 593 4 304488. From US$10 per person with breakfast. Day tours from US$10 and sea tours from US$45 per person per day.

Fernandina (Narborough)

Fernandina is the youngest of the Galápagos Islands, and it is also the most active volcanically, with frequent eruptions. It is one of the least contaminated islands in terms of introduced species. You can visit Punta Espinoza, where there are marine iguanas, flightless cormorants, sealions, penguins, and Galápagos hawks on the relatively young lava landscapes.

WILDLIFE

Seabirds

There are 19 resident species of seabird on the Galápagos, five of which are endemic, and many passing migrants, which are regularly recorded. There are as many as 750,000 seabirds at any one time in the islands. Blue-footed boobies, red-footed boobies and masked boobies are particularly prominent and possibly the most well-known species. They are a delight to watch as they preen their plumage, wave their feet around while trying to keep cool, and display in a curious sort of dance.

Galápagos penguin

This is the most northern of all penguins and one of the smallest, standing only 35cm tall. The Galápagos penguin (*Spheniscus mendiculus*)is one of the five endemic species of seabirds in the islands, and lives and breeds here all year round. The penguins normally breed on the western side of Isabela and on Fernandina, though they are sometimes seen on Bartolomé. Black on the back and with white underparts, and a stripe round the chest and face, the penguins spend most of the day out swimming in pursuit of fish. They can reach speeds of 40km/h when chasing shoals of fish, by porpoising through the water. The penguins have a mate for life and nest in crevices, small caves and holes in the rock, laying one or two eggs, which they then take it in turn to watch over for the five weeks before hatching.

Waved albatross

The waved albatross (*Diomedea irrorata*) is the largest bird to be seen on the islands with a wing span of over 2m and weighing up to 5kg. Almost all of the world's population of 12,000 pairs nest on Española Island. From January to March there are few waved albatross on the island, the males arriving from the end of March and their mates for life arriving shortly afterwards. They lay their eggs during May and June, each pair laying one egg that is then incubated for two months. The eggs are not laid in nests, but on open ground and are frequently rolled around by the parent birds. It isn't known why they do this but it seems to increase the chances of hatching. The young continue to grow, fed up to 2kg at a time of an oily liquid manufactured in the parents' stomach, until in January they are full size and able to leave the nest. They may not return for four or five years after leaving. October is the best month for watching the elaborate and spectacular courtship ritual, up to 20 minutes of extraordinary displaying.

True petrels and shearwaters

The dark-rumped petrel (*Pterodroma phaepygia*) and Audubon shearwater (*Puffinus lherminieri subalaris*) are resident in the Galápagos although other non-resident members of the family are also often seen. The dark-rumped petrel, larger than the shearwater, has long narrow wings, a white forehead and a characteristic swooping and banking motion when seen flying out at sea. It is an endangered species in the islands and commonly nests in earth burrows in the highlands. The Audubon shearwater is a smaller black and white bird widespread throughout the islands. It nests in burrows or holes but is most frequently seen as it feeds at sea, characteristically skimming the waves as it catches crustaceans and fish larvae from the surface of the ocean.

Storm petrels

There are three commonly seen storm petrels in the Galápagos. They are all small birds, the largest being only 20cm long, about swallow size. The birds are dark with a white rump, short black bills and a strange erratic flight. You may see them at the back of your boat weaving through the air in search of food morsels.

White-vented storm petrel (Elliot's) (*Oceanites gracilis galapagoensis*) This is most commonly seen around yachts looking for scraps. It has a white line running round its breast and under its tail, and its feet project out behind when it flies. It is not known where these birds breed.

Wedge-rumped storm petrel (Galápagos) (*Oceanodroma tethys tethys*) This is a slightly larger bird with a larger triangular white rump patch. It is active at the nesting area during the day unlike the other storm petrels, and feeds at night.

Band-rumped storm petrel (Madeiran) (*Oceanodroma castro bangsi*) This is the largest of the three and its white rump marking is a band. It has the most widespread distribution, and there are two breeding populations which take turns to use the same nests. November to January and May to June are the egg-laying periods.

Both of the latter are found breeding on Genovesa Island in crevices in the rock, flying above their breeding area in huge bewildering flocks. The short-eared owl is a predator, taking the birds from their nesting burrows.

Red-billed tropicbird

The red-billed tropicbird (*Phaethon aethereus limatus*) is a truly beautiful seabird with long white tail streamers and a coral red bill with black eye stripe. The birds have a wing span of just over a metre, and are extremely graceful in flight, flapping, gliding and occasionally uttering a high pitched screaming call. They are strong birds, flying far out to sea to dive and feed on fish and squid. They breed throughout the year on most of the islands, nesting on cliffs and steep slopes, carefully guarding their nest sites.

Brown pelican

The brown pelican (*Pelecanus occidentalis urinator*) is an easily recognisable and widespread bird with its large characteristic pouch used for scooping fish from the water in an ungainly shallow dive. In flight the birds are graceful, skimming in unison, rising and falling over the ripples of the ocean's surface. The adults develop chestnut and white markings on their heads and necks at the start of the breeding season, in stark contrast to the dull brown of the rest of the year. They build nesting platforms of twigs in mangrove forests or on low shrubs, usually in small colonies and all year round. They incubate the eggs for four weeks, both parents feeding the fledglings for about ten weeks when they are ready to learn to fend for themselves, not an easy task to master. It is thought that many young die of starvation before they master the pelican style dive.

Boobies

The boobies are one of the most popular and characteristic seabirds of the Galápagos. They are approachable and entertaining on land and incredible to watch as they plunge dive into the ocean for fishing at breakneck speed. There are four recorded species of booby, three of which nest on the Galápagos. They resemble gannets, with long pointed beaks, elongated narrow wings up to 1.5m from tip to tip and standing nearly a metre off the ground. They are often seen hunting in groups, bills pointed down towards the surface of the sea, wings tucked in as they then rocket into the water after the sighted prey. They all live in the islands in colonies of varying sizes, and incubate their eggs on the webs of their feet maintaining a constant temperature of 39°C.

Blue-footed booby (*Sula nebouxii excisa*) This is the most commonly seen of the boobies and is easily distinguished by its white body, brownish head and wings and of course its bright blue feet. The females are slightly larger than the males, with a larger pupil, while the males have a longer tail which enables them to dive closer to the shore, in water as shallow as half a metre. There are large colonies on Española and Seymour, where the elaborate courtship dance ritual can be observed at any time throughout the year. Nests are really only patches of dusty ground scraped bare and one to three eggs are laid and incubated for 40 days, by both parents. In a good year all three chicks may survive, but more often the oldest and strongest one will out compete the others.

Masked booby (*Sula dactylatra granti*) The largest of the boobies, the masked booby has a pure white body with black wing markings, and a blue-black face mask surrounding its orange bill. Its feet are grey and it is less theatrical in its courtship dance than the other boobies. It also nests on the ground, but usually nearer to the sea on slopes where its heavier body can take off. The masked booby has an annual breeding cycle unlike the others, but timings vary from island to island. As the cycle is nine months, each colony is away at sea for three months of the year. Two eggs are laid but only one bird will ever survive, the older and stronger bird usually forcing the other out of the nest where it will die from starvation, or temperature extremes. On Genovesa the birds arrive in May, eggs are laid from August and most of the young are fledged by February. On Española most eggs are laid from November.

Red-footed booby (*Sula sula websteri*) This, the smallest of the Galápagos boobies, has impressively bright red feet and a blue bill. Most of the adult birds are brown, but about 5% are white. The red- footed booby is only found on outlying islands, so despite being the most abundant it is the least seen. This booby nests in trees and shrubs, laying only one egg in a flimsy nest, and fishes much further out to sea than the other two. The breeding cycle is 12 months and eggs can be laid in any month.

Flightless cormorant

Found only on the coast of Fernandina and Isabela, the flightless cormorant (*Nannopterum harrisi*) is the only seabird other than the penguin which has lost its ability to fly. The adult bird has turquoise eyes and is black and brown on the body, the male being noticeably taller than the female, reaching up to 90cm. The flightless cormorant is a remarkable swimmer and swims and dives in the surf of the shallows, where it feeds on bottom-living fish and octopus. The cormorants have no predators on land and generally its feeding grounds are nearby, so that it doesn't have any need to fly. Most birds lay their eggs between March and September in large seaweed or flotsam nests in rocky coastal areas. The eggs are incubated for 35 days by both parents. Once hatched the female may leave the young, go off to find another mate and breed again.

Frigatebirds

The frigate bird is an extremely distinctive large black bird with long wings, a large hooked beak and forked tail. The birds are scavengers, and often to be found flying at the back of boats looking for scraps. They steal food from other birds and pick up fish from the surface of the sea. There are two species of frigatebird in the Galápagos, the great frigatebird (*Fregata minor ridgwayi*) and the magnificent frigatebird (*Fregata magnificens magnificens*). Genovesa and San Cristóbal are the places to see the great frigatebird, while the magnificent frigatebird is found on North Seymour and San Cristóbal. During the breeding season the red pouch which the male bird has on its neck inflates as it sits in a tree trying to attract the attention of a passing female. They build nests in scrubby trees and lay just one egg, which is incubated by both parents for up to eight weeks. The chicks do not fly for five months, and then take several years to mature.

Swallow-tailed gull

This is an attractive grey and black gull (*Creagrus furcatus*) with a red eye ring and red feet, endemic to the islands. It feeds at night, catching fish and squid off the surface of the ocean. Swallow-tailed gulls are found on all the islands, although when not breeding they tend to fly to other waters off Peru and Ecuador.

Lava gull

This rare gull (*Larus fuliginosus*) is only found in the Galápagos, and in very small numbers. It is a dark grey colour with a black hood on its head, and a white eye ring. You are most likely to see it in Academy Bay, scavenging from the waste in the harbour.

Flamingos

The greater flamingo (*Phoenicopterus ruber*) is found throughout the islands in salty lagoons, where it feeds on insects and shrimp. Flamingos build their nests out of mud and lay one egg on the top of the nest.

Herons

There are several species of heron, quite common in the coastal areas and in the lagoons. They catch their food, usually fish, crabs, lizards, insects and even young birds and iguanas, by remaining motionless until the prey approaches, then stabbing rapidly with their sharp beaks.

Landbirds

There are 29 resident species of landbird on the Galápagos, 20 of which are endemic. The most noticeable feature of the birds is how tame they are.

Galápagos hawk

A dark brown bird of prey, the Galápagos hawk (*Buteo galapagoensis*) preys on young iguanas, lizards, rats, doves, and other small birds, and scavenges on dead animals.

Owls

The Galápagos barn owl (*Tyto alba punctatissima*) and short-eared owl (*Asio flammeus galapagoensis*) live on the islands. The barn owl is nocturnal and the short-eared owl tends to hunt during the day.

Galápagos mockingbird

The ubiquitous mockingbird (*Nesomimus trifasciatus*) is found on almost all the islands. There are nine distinct subspecies on different islands, with no overlapping of territory. Mockingbirds will eat young birds, insects and eggs, and the remains of anything left by any other predator.

Darwin's finches

There are 13 species of these little sparrow size brown-black birds. They are not easy to tell apart from one another, though each specialises in one thing or another, some eating seeds, some insects, some flowers, some insect larvae, some tics from tortoises and iguanas. The sharp-billed ground finch feeds on the blood it manages to extract from boobies by pecking at the base of their feathers. It has evolved by specialising in a food resource so that it can survive during harsh conditions.

Mammals

Galápagos sealions

Found around most of the islands, especially on sandy beaches, these sealions (*Zalophus californianus wollebacki*) are a subspecies of the Californian sealion. They are very playful and fun to watch. The males can weigh up to 250kg, and are quite distinctive from the females with their thick necks and the bump on their forehead. The bulls are territorial and the females come and go. Be wary of the males, which can be very aggressive when guarding their territory. Females usually give birth to one pup after nine months of gestation, during the dry season. The pups become at least partially independent after five months, living up to 20 years.

Galápagos fur seals

Found in rockier areas than the sealions, the fur seals (*Arctocephalus galapagoensis*) are smaller with smaller, broader heads and pointed noses. They have larger ears, eyes and flippers and thicker and denser fur. Because of the high quality of their fur they were hunted almost to extinction in the 19th century. As with sealions the bulls are territorial. Most pups are born in October and are not fully independent for two to three years. Genovesa and Santiago are good places to see the fur seals.

Dolphins and whales

Several species of whale are seen regularly in the Galápagos Islands: the blue, fin, sperm, humpback, sei, minke, pilot and orca. The bottle-nosed dolphin and the common dolphin are seen frequently, often at the bow wave of the boats.

Reptiles

There are five families of reptiles on the islands: tortoises, marine turtles, lizards and iguanas, geckos and snakes.

Giant tortoise

The giant tortoise (*Geochelone elephantopus*) is probably the most well-known Galápagos animal. It weighs up to 250kg and measures 150cm across the curve of the shell. There are 11 subspecies of the giant tortoise left, out of a probable 14. In the 18th and 19th century many tortoises lost their lives to the whalers and sealers who based themselves on the islands. On Floreana they were hunted to extinction. They were taken on board ship where they were kept alive, for up to a year, until they were needed as meat. Five of the 11 subspecies live on the distinctive volcanoes of Isabela Island, and the others are found on James, Santa Cruz, San Cristóbal, Pinzón, Española and Pinta. The Charles Darwin Research Centre is the best place to see these gentle giants, or alternatively the tortoises reserve on Santa Cruz Island. Lonesome George is the most famous of the tortoises, the last remaining example of his subspecies from Pinta. He lives at the Charles Darwin Research Centre so far resisting attempts to have him breed with members of a different subspecies. It is thought that giant tortoises live for 150 years.

Marine turtles

Marine turtles are most often spotted as you snorkel, or close to some of the beaches where they come to breed, around February. The Pacific green turtle (*Chelonia mydas agassisi*) is the only resident turtle, though the leatherback and hawksbill are occasionally seen. The turtles breed on sandy beaches, usually above the high tide line. They lay over 70 eggs at a time and may lay several times over a period of two to three months. They weigh up to 150kg, and little is known about where they swim to between breeding cycles.

Snakes, geckos and lava lizards

There are three species of snake on the islands, all small and brown. They eat lava lizards, geckos, the young of marine iguana and bird nestlings. They are not often seen. Geckos are active at night. They are often seen scaling the walls of houses in residential areas, and are easily recognisable by their large eyes and webbed feet.

There are seven endemic species of the small lava lizard (*Tropidurus* spp). Size and markings vary but generally the males are larger than the females and more brightly coloured. Their colours change according to their temperature and mood.

Marine iguana

The marine iguana (*Amblyrhyncus cristatus*) is the only one of its kind in the world, a sea-going lizard. The larger, stronger iguanas dive for up to an hour at a time to feed on algae, while others feed on intertidally exposed areas. When you see marine iguana sneezing what they are actually doing is excreting salt from the salt glands above the eye. Like all reptiles the iguana has to control its body temperature through its behaviour, so they spend a considerable amount of time sunbathing, panting to lose heat when it gets too hot. They only go into the ocean at midday after heating up for a considerable time, and then return to sunbathing to restore the high body temperature. At night the iguanas cluster together to keep warm. Mating occurs at different times of the year on different islands; eggs are laid in a sandy nest and take two months to hatch.

Land iguana

There are two species of land iguana (*Conolophus* spp), which grow up to a metre in length and are yellow and brown. They eat the fruit and pads of the prickly pear, sometimes swallowing the spines, and may also eat some insects. They live on Santa Fé, Isabela, Santa Cruz, Fernandina, Seymour and South Plaza. They live up to 60 years. The females lay up to 25 eggs in a burrow; they take up to four months to hatch and then the young have to dig their way out of the burrow. You may see birds cleaning parasitic insects off the iguanas.

Further information

Galápagos Wildlife: A Visitor's Guide by David Horwell and Pete Oxford, Bradt 1999, covers the wildlife and natural history of the Galápagos in full colour, and has details of all the island trails.

Part Three

Peru

Hoffman's two-toed sloth

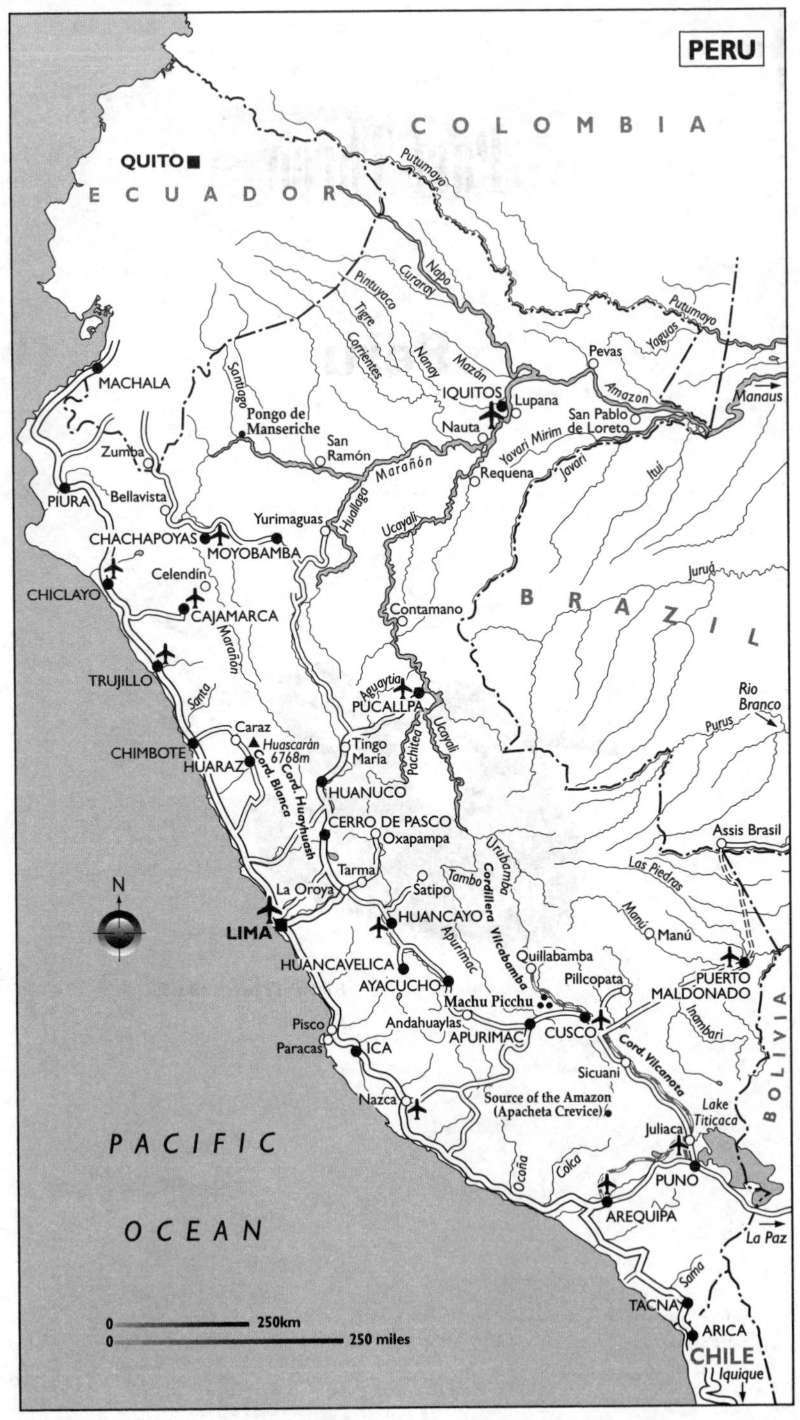
PERU
COLOMBIA
QUITO
ECUADOR
BRAZIL
BOLIVIA
CHILE
PACIFIC
OCEAN
Putumayo
Napo
Curaray
Pintuyaco
Tigre
Corrientes
Nanay
Mazán
Yaguas
Pevas
Amazon
Manaus
IQUITOS
Lupana
Nauta
San Pablo
de Loreto
Yavari Mirim
Javari
Ituí
Requena
MACHALA
Santiago
Pongo de
Manseriche
San
Ramón
Marañón
Zumba
PIURA
Bellavista
Huallaga
Ucayali
Yurimaguas
CHACHAPOYAS
MOYOBAMBA
Celendín
CHICLAYO
CAJAMARCA
Juruá
Contamano
TRUJILLO
Santa
Aguaytia
PUCALLPA
Rio
Branco
Purus
Caraz
Huascarán
6768m
CHIMBOTE
HUARAZ
Cord. Blanca
Cord. Huayhuash
Tingo
María
Pachitea
HUANUCO
CERRO DE PASCO
Oxapampa
Assis Brasil
Urubamba
Cordillera Vilcabamba
Tambo
Las Piedras
Tarma
La Oroya
Satipo
LIMA
HUANCAYO
Apurimac
Manú
N
HUANCAVELICA
AYACUCHO
Quillabamba
Pillcopata
PUERTO
MALDONADO
Machu Picchu
Pisco
Andahuaylas
APURIMAC
CUSCO
Paracas
ICA
Inambari
Cord. Vilcanota
Sicuani
Nazca
Source of the Amazon
(Apacheta Crevice)
Lake
Titicaca
Juliaca
Ocoña
Colca
PUNO
AREQUIPA
La Paz
Sama
TACNA
ARICA
Iquique
0 250km
0 250 miles

The Country

An increasingly popular country with travellers, Peru offers a stunning range of things to see and places to visit. Culturally, historically and in wildlife it is one of the richest countries in the world. Echoes of the past can be seen all around, in the buildings of colonial cities and in the present day life of the Peruvian people, whether on the coast, in the Andes or in the jungle. Peru has some great museums and art collections, some superb Inca and pre-Inca archaeological sites and endless opportunities for trekking, rafting and climbing. It is a country of great geographical contrast: scenically little can surpass the magnificent mountains of the Andes, but the coast and jungle have their hidden treasures too. As for getting around, things are now relatively well organised and tend to run fairly smoothly. Backpacking through Peru is a wonderful way to see the country and given a bit of time and adventurous spirit you can easily get to know some of its more interesting and remote corners.

GEOGRAPHY AND CLIMATE

Peru is the third largest country in South America (1,285,216km^2), and with 24 million inhabitants, the fourth most populated. Peru borders Ecuador in the north, Colombia and Brazil to the east and Bolivia and Chile in the south. It comprises three major geographical areas: a narrow belt of desert along the Pacific coast; the steep, high Andes mountains; and the eastern slopes of the Andes, blending into the lowlands of the Amazon basin. Although it lies within the tropics, because of its great geographical diversity you can experience a full range of climates, from extremely hot and sunny in coastal areas to very cold mountain conditions in the Andes.

FACTS AND FIGURES BOX

Area 1,285,216 km^2
Population 24 million
Capital Lima, population 8 million
Borders Ecuador, Colombia, Brazil, Bolivia, Chile
Largest towns Arequipa, Chimbote, Chiclayo, Tacna
Official time GMT – 5hrs
Languages Spanish, Quechua, Aymara
Currency nuevo sol
Head of state Alberto Fujimori

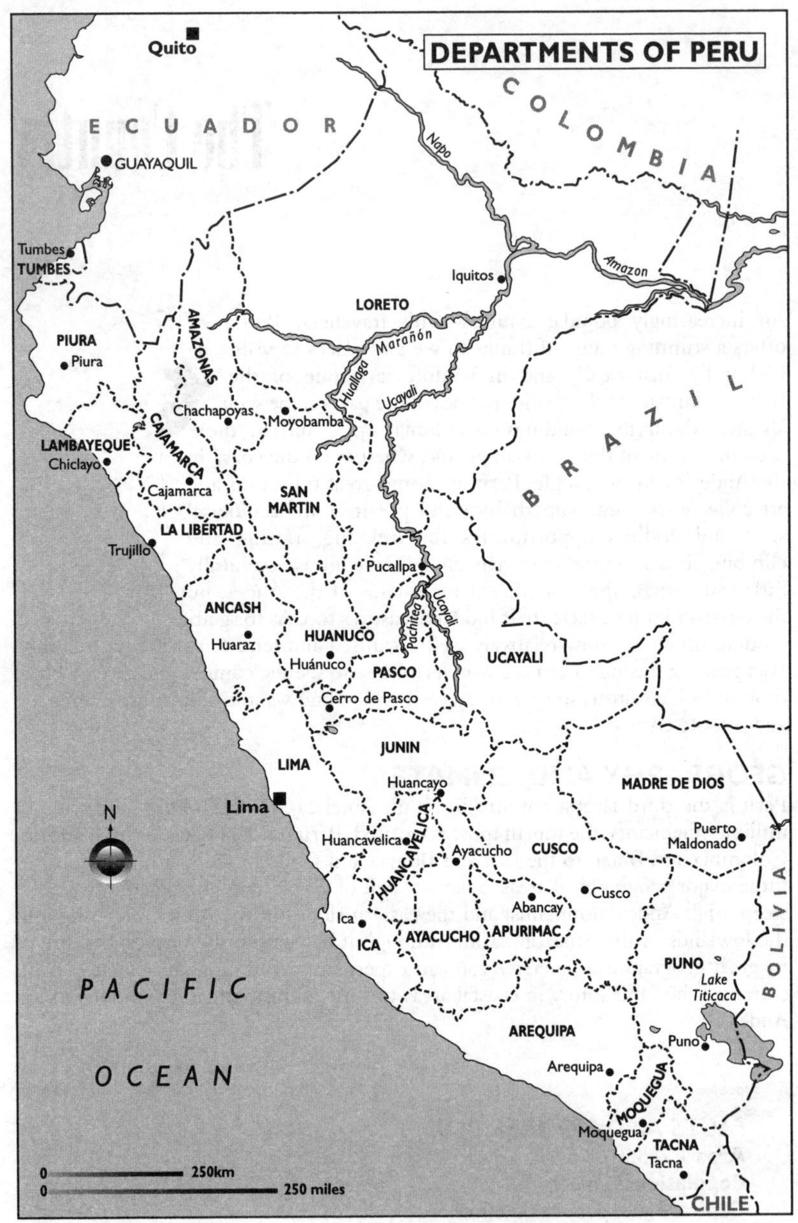

The coast

Peru has 2,500km of coastline. The coastal area is a dry barren desert strip, the width of which varies from 200km at its widest in the north, in the Sechura Desert, to a mere 40km wide in the south, where the Andes are very near the sea. The temperatures on the coast are not as high as you might expect (19–22°C), because of the influence of the Humboldt current, an upwelling of cold, nutrient rich waters influencing life all along the eastern Pacific coast of South America. The climate is extremely dry, with virtually no rainfall at any time in the year, except once every three to seven years during El Niño, when ocean temperatures heat up and storms ravage Peru's coast. The El Niño of 1997–8 deranged weather patterns around the world, and in Peru many people had never seen so much rain. Hundreds lost their homes and dozens were killed, entire villages were swept away in landslides and roads suffered major damage, all at an immense cost.

Over 50 river valleys cross the desert strip carrying meltwater from the Andes to the Pacific Ocean. Most of these rivers have a seasonal flow, but surprisingly they provide enough water for the coastal population, which is over 50% of Peru's total. Modern technology, coupled with complex irrigation systems, allow the farming of a variety of crops, including cotton and sugar, two important exports. Each river valley tends to have its own speciality. In the winter months, April to November, some sections of the coast may experience a coastal mist, *garúa*, until midday, though once it lifts the days are warm and sunny. Lima suffers from this mist for most of the year, making it particularly grey and cool. In the summer months, December to March, the weather on the coast is usually hot and sunny.

The Andes

The Andes run the length of Peru, but are split into several separate mountain ranges, the most well known of which are the Cordillera Blanca, Huayhuash, Vilcanota and Vilcabamba. They form an immense barrier between the coast and the jungle, the highest point of which is Huascarán (6,768m) in the Cordillera Blanca, near the town of Huaraz. In this mountain range there are 33 immense peaks towering above 6,000m. The remote Cordillera Huayhuash, four hours by bus from Huaraz, has seven summits over 6,000m – the highest is Yerupajá at 6,634m. The Cordilleras Vilcabamba and Vilcanota are in the Cusco area, and boast a network of interconnected Inca trails linking enigmatic ruins.

In the south of Peru and also covering a considerable area of Bolivia there is a large plateau known as the altiplano. The landscape of the altiplano is dramatic in its bleakness, vast open spaces and lack of trees, just *ichu* or scrubgrass. Very little grows at this altitude and the climate is inhospitably cold. There are two distinct seasons, the wet from October to April and the dry from May to September. During the rainy season it can rain every day, and generally does at least in the afternoons. Day temperatures don't change much throughout the year – most days are sunny and comfortably warm in the strong sun. The air temperature, however, really is quite cool, so out of the sun or in the wind you definitely need extra layers of clothing. The average temperature is only 10°C. Night temperatures in the dry season can drop well below zero, especially in the Puno area and around Lake Titicaca. This, the largest lake in South America at 3,820m, is 170km long and dominates the southern Peruvian altiplano. Puno is the main Peruvian town on the shores of the lake.

Rainforest

The eastern slopes of the Andes are steep, with deep valleys and high ridges, plunging away to the vast Amazon lowlands. Peru's main rivers flow into the gigantic basin of the Amazon, the largest in the tropical world. Together they form a characteristic flat landscape of giant meanders, lakes, marshes and frequently flooded forest. The climate is warm (average 28°C), wet and humid, generally quite uncomfortably so. Rainfall is 1,900–3,200mm per year. In the rainy season, from November to May, you are likely to get daily afternoon downpours, but be prepared for rain at any time of year. Iquitos is the entry point to Peru's northern lowlands, and is easily accessed by plane. For access to the southern Peruvian lowlands travel from Cusco into Manu National Park or Tambopata Reserve.

HISTORY

Although exact dates aren't known, there is evidence to suggest that the first people arrived in Peru over 20,000 years ago, before agriculture or farming techniques were known. These people lived in small tribal groups and survived from hunting and gathering, following a semi-nomadic way of life dictated by the climate on the coast, but with a more stable way of life in the highlands. Here cameloids were abundant, providing plentiful meat and clothing. Birds and rodents were also hunted and tubers and fruits gathered. Archaeologists have found tools suggesting that in approximately 6,000BC agriculture was adopted on the coast and in the sierras. There was a gradual change in the way of life, as settlements became more permanent, llamas and alpacas were bred from the wild guanacos and vicuñas, the population increased, and weaving was taken up. Archaeological evidence indicates that over the ensuing centuries there were great advances in agricultural farming techniques, such as the adoption of irrigation and the development of new crops such as maize, squash, beans and fruits. There is evidence of the first solid buildings, which may have been used as houses and meeting places. The earliest pottery also dates from this time. Farming was collectivised and the important social unit was the clan or Ayllu based around extended families. This is still the case in Andean communities. As production intensified and the quantities became more than adequate to feed the population, time was released for pursuing other activities. The social structures of communities changed, and there is evidence of larger settlements, elaborate religious architecture in the form of temples and *huacas* (sacred sites), more advanced woven textiles and fired pottery.

Chavín

The Chavín culture, beginning around 1,000BC, was probably the first to embrace the whole of Peru. At that time there was a period of intense integration of the tribal groups of the coast and the sierras, an exchange of knowledge and skills, and simultaneously a rapid increase in the overall population. The result of this assimilation of different groups was the formation of a state structure with ceremonial centres, a class structure and a non-productive section of the population, generally religious leaders and artisans. The complex nature of this society and the belief system which it developed are reflected in the architectural design of its buildings and the imagery found within them. Characteristic of this time are ceremonial centres with sunken circular courtyards, U-shaped temples and the widespread adoption of jaguar and snake images. Representations of the jaguar and snake were used by many subsequent cultures in their artwork and architecture.

The principal religious centre for the Chavín culture was in the Callejon de Conchucos, in the Cordillera Blanca, midway between the coast and the jungle. This is a site which, despite centuries of neglect, is still worth visiting. The easiest option is to take a full day tour from Huaraz.

Regionalisation

A period of regionalisation followed a gradual loss of power of the Chavín culture. This may have been the result of an increasing regional specialisation in the development of agricultural techniques. People were learning to take advantage of their particular climatic conditions or land fertility to maximise production of suitable crops. Buildings were made of adobe clay or stone depending on the availability of materials, and wool or cotton dominated textiles, again depending on what was most widely available. The predominant regional cultures to develop were: **Moche** on the north coast; **Lima** on the central coast; **Paracas** and **Nazca** on the south coast; **Cajamarca** and **Ayacucho** in the central highlands; and **Titicaca** or **Tiahuanaco** on the altiplano. In all of these cultures cities and urban centres developed and grew, ever increasing in importance as the power centres for religious leaders. By the 6th century AD Peru was characterised by prestigious cities, high agricultural production even in seemingly impossible desert conditions, complex irrigation systems, and water channels connecting one valley to another.

Tiahuanaco-Huari

From AD500–800 a new dominant culture emerged across the country, known as **Tiahuanaco–Huari**. This culture emanated from two distinctive centres, Tiahuanaco near Lake Titicaca on the Bolivian altiplano, and Huari in the Ayacucho Valley in the Peruvian highlands. It looks as though the two existed as a unified empire while each maintained its own power centre. It is possible that a prolonged drought in the 6th century initiated the demise of the water dependent coastal cultures and saw the rise of an Andean people who had started to use canals and agricultural terracing in the highlands to increase the amount of productive land. Because of this agricultural development the Tiahuanaco–Huaris had the potential to feed a population of many thousands, which gave them the opportunity to spread their culture. Tiahuanaco grew to be an immense city with an estimated population of 50,000 inhabitants, covering 10km^2. The Tiahuanaco stone masons were so revered that they were later adopted by the Incas to work on their ceremonial centres. The high quality Inca stonework, so typical of their palaces and temples and famous throughout the world, is attributable to the skills of the Tiahuanaco stone masons. Tiahuanaco can easily be visited on a day trip from La Paz. The Huaris were less expert stone masons, and better known for their tapestries, particularly their tunics of intricate abstract design.

Regional cultures

Distinct regional cultures re-emerge after the fall of the Tiahuanaco–Huari empire in the 11th century. The north coast of Peru saw the rise of the **Chimú**, best known for its immense adobe ceremonial centre of Chan Chan. Pachacamac was an important independent centre near present-day Lima, while the **Ica** culture flourished on the south coast. It seems that this was a time when the population was concentrated into large urban units in coastal areas.

Chan Chan in the north was an impressive site with high boundary walls, streets, reservoirs, pyramids and temples. You can visit the site from Trujillo in half a day. The northern valleys had their own similar, though smaller, constructions. There are some excellent examples of textiles and metalwork from this period, demonstrating a high level of skill. **Pachacamac** in the Lurin Valley was a large pyramid temple, and similarly the valleys of Chancay and Rimac in the central coastal area had their own urban centres. No great cities are known in the Ica culture, but there are well preserved adobe constructions in the southern coastal areas, such as **Tambo Colorado** near the town of Ica, a large administrative centre with storehouses and residences. In the highlands at this time there is less evidence of the growth of large cities. The *chullpas* or funerary towers found around Lake Titicaca, which date from this time, demonstrate a high level of skilled stone masonry, which is also characteristic of the later Inca period.

The Incas

Inca history begins in AD1100 according to the legend of the mythical Inca king Manco Capac and his sister queen Mama Occllo. The two, supposedly children of Inti, the sun god, rose out of Lake Titicaca with a quest: to civilise the earth. Manco carried a long golden staff, with which he tested the richness of the earth he stood on. When his travels brought him to the site of modern Cusco, he was able to plunge the staff deep into the earth, a sign that this would be the place to build his capital. According to the legend, the staff is still buried in the main square of Cusco.

In reality, the Inca culture probably evolved from an alliance of small tribes living in the Cusco area. It seems from their high-quality stone masonry that they were strongly influenced by the Tiahuanaco culture.

Archaeological evidence, and the writings of the chronicles, suggest that the Incas remained in the valley of Cusco, just defending their boundaries from attack from neighbouring tribes, without any great ambitions of expansion until 1420. It wasn't until the ninth Inca king, whose name was **Pachacutec**, assumed power in 1438, that Cusco became the centre of a quickly expanding empire. Pachacutec pushed the frontier of the Inca territory outwards, while at the same time masterminding the design of his imperial city, Cusco. Pachacutec (1438–71) and then his son **Topa Inca** (1471–93) expanded the empire to the north as far as the border of Ecuador and Colombia, and to the south as far as central Chile.

It seems that the Incas assimilated the accumulated knowledge of the many cultures that surrounded them as they conquered their land and subjugated their people. They used a system known as *mitima* to forestall rebellion, which involved separating tribal groups and sending them to work in different geographical areas. Topa Inca was responsible for the enlargement of the great monolithic site of Sacsayhuaman, for carrying out the first census, and for setting up a system of officials to keep accurate records. He also started the custom of *yanacona* and *mamacuna*, a class of chosen men and women who served the Inca. He died at the age of 81 leaving two royal heirs by his sister, and 60 sons and 30 daughters by other women.

Huayna Capac (1493–1525) succeeded Topa Inca, and a period of unrest began as the empire was by now too large for one person to handle, even with the tight control of the Inca. When Huayna Capac died without naming his successor, there was a huge battle at Riobamba between his son Huascar and Huascar's half-brother, Atahualpa, who was victorious. There were several further battles between the two brothers, Atahualpa always winning and Huascar retreating southwards to Cusco. It was during the civil war that rent the Inca Empire after Huayna Capac's death that the Spanish arrived on the scene.

The Inca trails

The Inca roads ran along two longitudinal axes, one from northern Chile to Tumbes and the other linking Cusco with Quito along the backbone of the Andes. They were well used by Inca nobility, armies, public officials and runners (*chasquis*). Generally the roads were 3m wide, big enough for the llama trains that passed through loaded with food and supplies. They were sophisticated in their design, usually lined with stones and containing bridges, stairways and drains. Sometimes a dirt track ran alongside the main road for the servants and messengers of the Incas. The construction and maintenance of the roads was organised throughout by the *mita* system, which was the obligation of all members of the population to work for the state for a certain period of the year. All along the roads are *tambos* (in Quechua *chaskiwasis*, literally houses of the *chaskis* or runners), approximately every 33km. These were places for the travellers to rest after each day's journey. Some of the *tambos* are considerably grander than others, with storerooms, meeting rooms and more extensive accommodation.

In some areas of the Andes there was already an intricate network of roads before the Incas. In other areas the Incas had to build their own routes. The hanging bridges, necessary in some of the steep mountain areas, are well known as incredible feats of engineering. They were made from the hand-twisted fibres of the maguey plant to form enormously thick rope cables, which were suspended from stone towers across tremendous gorges and great canyons such as the Apurimac. Supports were hung down from the suspended cables and wooden planks were attached to these. These bridges were meticulously maintained and survived 500 years of foot and mule traffic.

The Spanish Conquest

The conquest of Peru and the Inca people was a long, treacherous and bloody battle. It began in 1532, when Francisco Pizarro and 180 men marched from Ecuador down into Peru looking for the riches of the new world. This arrival had been prophesied by the Incas, who had foreseen the coming of fair-haired, fair-skinned, bearded gods on floating houses. The Incas were thoroughly unprepared for the reality of what was to happen to them.

Francisco Pizarro was born in 1477 in Trujillo, an illegitimate son and an uneducated man who worked as a swineherd. The only way to make money and rise socially in those days was through warfare or marriage, so he decided to try his hand in the new world. He joined the Spanish army at the age of 19 and first sailed to the Americas in 1502. He fought in the Dominican Republic and Haiti and was soon in demand as a battle-hardened young veteran. He became one of the first citizens of Panama in 1519 and was granted land and slaves in recognition of his achievements. By then he was a 50-year-old Spanish soldier, respected and rich, but not content to retire, so in 1524 he sailed from Panama in command of the first of three expeditions of discovery.

Pizarro decided to go in search of Peru as rumours had been heard that there were riches to be found there. In 1527, after a run of bad luck and with only 13 of his men still alive, and having spent the previous ten months sickly and near starvation on an uninhabited island off the Pacific coast, Pizarro finally reached the city of Tumbes on the northwest coast of Peru. He took some items of gold, silver and other evidence of the advanced civilisation he had found, and returned to Spain to ask for a licence entitling him to conquer and settle Peru.

By this time a hardened conquistador, he set sail again in 1530 with his partner Diego de Almagro, 180 men and 27 horses. Almagro was also a veteran explorer and had worked with Pizarro for many years. He too was of a lowly background and had fled Spain as a fugitive from justice but, like Pizarro, had managed to achieve status in the new world. The relationship between the partners was tinged with friction as Almagro resented Pizarro being granted such extensive rights in Peru, and he was unhappy about Pizarro inviting along his four half-brothers and a large number of friends from home.

Pizarro and the major expeditionary force landed in Ecuador and set off on foot to search for the hub of the Inca Empire. They were plagued by harsh conditions, disease and Indian attacks as they marched down the tropical Pacific coast, but they were lucky as the empire was in disarray and they were able to advance almost unnoticed into its heart. It had taken them almost two years since they set off from Panama to get this far.

At the time Pizarro and his men arrived in Cajamarca, now with reinforcements, there was a civil war in the empire. The Inca emperor, Huayna Capac Inca, had been killed by a smallpox epidemic in 1525. He had ruled from the north of his huge kingdom in what is now Ecuador. Two of his sons, **Huascar**, who ruled the southern part of the empire from Cusco and **Atahualpa** a half-brother, who ruled the northern part from Quito, couldn't agree over who was to be his successor.

At the time of Pizarro's appearance on the scene Atahualpa was winning strength and power in the north and his troops held Huascar prisoner in Cusco in the south. Atahualpa was heading south at Cajamarca with his army when Pizarro and his men attacked. Atahualpa had a huge army of thousands of men, which filled the plains around the town. Pizarro installed himself in the town centre with his small, but significant, army of 60 horsemen and 100 foot soldiers. After they had settled themselves in, Pizarro sent some of his men to meet Atahualpa who was bathing at hot springs nearby. Atahualpa agreed to come into town and meet Pizarro the next day. He was carried into the central square in a fine litter made of silver and timbers, accompanied by many of his warriors. But the Spaniards had hatched a murderous plan, and the central square of Cajamarca was ideally suited to their plot. Pizarro's men were able to hide themselves and their horses in the buildings opening out on to the plaza, effectively surrounding it. As the Spanish Catholic priest spoke to a bemused Atahualpa of their god and the requirement to submit to the pope and the king of Spain, Spanish horsemen charged from their hideouts and fell upon the Incas in a murderous spree. The Incas were taken totally by surprise, and offered little resistance. Thousands of Indians were brutally slain and Atahualpa was taken prisoner and locked up. With their leader captured, the vast empire was paralysed.

Atahualpa offered Pizarro a huge ransom for his release, a room full of gold and twice as much silver. This was collected from throughout the land and brought to Pizarro who melted it down, divided it between his men, himself and the Spanish crown, to which he had to give a fifth. Atahualpa thought he could buy his way to freedom and then attack and kill Pizarro at a later date. He ordered the murder of Huascar so there would be no possibility of his brother taking advantage of Atahualpa's unfortunate captivity. It took several months to amass the ransom payment, and the waiting made Pizarro understandably nervous. When Almagro arrived with reinforcements and to share the gold booty, he pressurised Pizarro to kill Atahualpa, rather than risk allowing him to be free. Pizarro conceded and Atahualpa was killed by a rope around the neck in 1533 in the same square in which he had been captured.

Pizarro and his men then marched to Cusco. Many battles were fought on the way, but against the well-equipped conquistadors the Indians were a poor match. The Spanish had swords, lances and daggers of Toledan steel, chain mail, protective leather clothing, crossbows, guns and horses. The Indians had only wooden helmets, battle axes and maces of stone and copper; they fought by hurling darts and firing stones. A victorious Pizarro finally marched into Cusco on November 15 1533. There he appointed **Manco**, brother of Huascar, as the Inca successor, but he was really only a puppet ruler, to be used by Pizarro to help subjugate the Incas. In 1535 Pizarro decided to build a new capital as Cusco was too isolated and far from the coast. He chose the mouth of the Rimac River, and on January 6 1535, Lima was founded.

Relations between the Incas and the conquistadors had deteriorated rapidly as the Incas realised the true intentions of the Spaniards. The promised gods were ruthless tyrants. They desecrated temples, melted down the gold and generally made life difficult for Manco. The Incas were treated like slaves, their chiefs tortured, their women raped, and no laws were respected. The Inca population fell catastrophically as their irrigation and food storage systems were abandoned. For a while Manco went along with the Spaniards while working on his own schemes. His ambition was to be rid of them and restore himself as the new Inca emperor. But in 1536 he realised that getting rid of the conquistadors was not going to be easy, so he persuaded Pizarro to let him go, supposedly to worship and collect gold from distant temples, but in reality to amass an army of 100,000 men.

From 1536 to 1572, 36 long years, there was resistance to the Spaniards, led first by Manco and then by his sons. Manco laid siege to Cusco, burnt large parts of it and only after almost a year was finally forced to retreat to Ollantaytambo. The Spaniards followed and managed to capture several thousand llamas and men. Manco retreated further to the jungle-clad hills of Vilcabamba and the Spaniards, lulled into a false sense of security, went back to Cusco.

Relations between Almagro and the Pizarro brothers had gone from bad to worse, and a new civil war now broke out in Peru, this time between the Spanish themselves. Almagro was strangled in Cusco by Hernando Pizarro in 1538, and the Pizarros became the lords of Peru. Then in 1541 Almagro was revenged by the murder of Francisco Pizarro, who was hacked to death at his palace in Lima by Almagristas. The Spanish crown sent a royal official out to Peru to march with the Pizarro supporters and defeat the Almagristas. There followed a period of further instability and infighting, Gonzalo Pizarro still fighting until he was put to death in 1548.

Meanwhile, Manco still had an Inca camp deep in the jungle around the Vilcabamba Valley. He had been joined by some fugitives from the Pizarro regime. The Spanish soldiers taught the Incas horsemanship, but they became bored by life in the jungle, so planned to leave when the opportunity arose. News reached them of the viceroy's clash with the brothers of Pizarro and the chance of a pardon. They killed Manco and attempted to return to Cusco, but were killed on the way by retaliating Incas.

Tupac Amaru was the last free Inca. He lived in Vilcabamba and continued to fight against Spanish rule. In 1572 a messenger was sent from the viceroy in Lima but was murdered en route. Enraged, the viceroy decided to capture Tupac Amaru. Tupac fled deeper into the jungle but was betrayed, captured and returned exhausted to Cusco to be beheaded.

Independence

Peru was declared independent on July 28 1821 by Simon Bolívar. This was the culmination of years of unrest by the locally born descendants of the Spanish conquistadors, the *criollos*, who no longer wanted to be ruled from Spain. But although the declaration was made on that date, the final decisive battle was not won until December 9 1824, on the plains above Ayacucho.

Independence did not bring about radical change, but merely passed the power into the hands of an élite few. There were endless power struggles between the liberal and conservative parties which emerged from among the prominent military leaders (*caudillos*). A liberal constitution was adopted in 1828 but that did not stop General Agustín Gamarra taking power a year later. General Felippe Salavery wrested power for himself in 1835. In 1845 General Ramón Castilla seized power and remained on the scene until 1862.

In the 1840s Peru began to export guano, bird produced fertiliser from the islands along the Pacific coast. This provided a welcome boost to the flagging economy, as taxes were controlled by the government. Castilla abolished payments of tribute from Indians and ended slavery in Peru, but landowners on the coast were able to import thousands of Chinese labourers to work on coastal plantations instead. In 1864 when the Spanish decided to try to reclaim Peru for themselves, their attempts were thwarted by determined opposition, but at huge financial cost to Peru.

Between 1879 and 1884 Peru was at war with Chile in the **War of the Pacific**. The war was caused by rivalry over nitrate beds in the Atacama Desert. It was won by Chile, whose army invaded as far as Lima, looting and pillaging as they went. Peru and Bolivia both lost significant amounts of land to Chile, and after the war Peruvian debt was at such a high level that they agreed to allow their creditors to manage the railways and guano mines. In the 1890s there was a considerable swing in Peruvian politics, and for a change a relatively orderly political system prevailed. There was a steady increase in production and strengthening of the economy, which lasted until 1919. The then president Agusto Leguía, in his second term, began to run up massive debts in attempting to finance wide-scale development. However, there was increasing social unrest and he turned his political rule into a dictatorship, repressing all opposition.

In 1924 APRA (Alianza Popular Revolucionaria Americana) was formed by Victor Haya de la Torre, then in exile. The party supported the end to exploitation of the Indian people through nationalisation and anti-capitalist, anti-imperialist means. At the same time Peru's Communist Party was born, inspired by Marx and started up by José Carlos Mariategui. Both these parties had a far-reaching influence on Peru's future. In the 1930s an era of military rule began and APRA was brutally repressed after an uprising in Trujillo in 1932. Hundreds were murdered by the army and a deep hatred formed between the party and the military.

There followed a succession of dictatorships until in 1963 a civilian government was elected to power with Belaúnde Terry at its head. He had great plans for social and economic reform and wanted to build a highway connecting Colombia, Venezuela and Bolivia, and to colonise the Amazon. Under a minor land reform in 1964 some land was returned to the Indians, community development projects were started up, and irrigation schemes financed. Again, debt caused the fall of Belaúnde Terry and the reinstatement of a military leader, Juan Velasco. He took over the oil installations of the US-owned International Petroleum Company and also expropriated various of the powerful mining giants and the Paramonga chemical and paper complex owned by W R Grace, also a US interest. He also instigated major land reform, breaking up the haciendas and returning land to the Indians. However, the reforms were not as effective as he had hoped; Velasco became more and more authoritarian and unrest grew again.

In 1975 there was yet another military coup, and its right-wing leadership provoked widespread demonstrations and protests. Belaúnde was returned to power in 1980, this time with more conservative plans following the IMF austerity philosophy. Recession hit the country and it spiralled into deeper debt and poverty. In 1985 Alan García, elected for APRA, seemed to offer a brighter future for the country. The last five years of the 1980s turned out to be even worse than before, with inflation again rising rapidly and wages devalued, basic goods in short supply and costing the earth. The military seemed to be out of control as the war waged on with *Sendero Luminoso* (see page 230). Thousands of people disappeared.

The economy in the 1990s

Since the election of Alberto Fujimori to the presidency in 1990, a radical restructuring of the economy was begun to try to reduce the massive inflation and stabilise the economy. Subsidies and import duties were cut, and many state-owned companies privatised in an attempt to open up the economy to private and especially foreign investment. In 1992 Fujimori carried out a self coup to rid himself of the parliament and judges who did not give him full support in his radical reform.

By the late 1990s over US$7 billion of Peruvian goods were exported annually, 105% more than in 1990. Most of these are primary exports including mined metals, fishmeal and fish oil, coffee, cotton and sugar, and oil and its by-products. The rest of the exports include a wide range of industrial manufactured goods.

In 1997 an agreement was made to restructure Peru's debt to the financial institutions of the first world. In effect, this means that Peru has ended up having to pay back almost 2 billion dollars annually, a large proportion of export earnings. In 1998 there was a fall in exports due to El Niño and the Asian crises. In order to honour its debt payment, Peru has to continue to push up production and exports. Increased investment in mining is planned, with continued exploitation often in environmentally sensitive areas. There is also investment within the fishing industry. Within agriculture improved technology and seed quality receive investment. There are USAID projects to increase coffee production in coca areas in conjunction with the Illegal Crops Eradication Programme and the government plans to continue to improve roads, ports and airports.

On October 26 1998 after lengthy negotiations, a peace agreement was signed between Peru and Ecuador by Presidents Alberto Fujimori and Jamil Mahuad. This means the end of the battle to delineate the border between Peru and Ecuador, which has gone on throughout this century since the end of the War of the Pacific. This peace agreement should make a big difference to both countries, not only allowing a massive saving in defence spending, but also the possibility of joint ventures and increased trade. Until 1998 only a tiny percentage of Peru's exports went to Ecuador, but trade has been increasing since peace talks began. There are plans to open up several new border crossings in addition to the existing crossings at Aguas Verdes to Huaquillas and La Tina to Macará.

However, despite all this apparent improvement in the economic situation of the country, a high proportion of Peru's population, as much as 50%, still lives in poverty. Over 30% of the population works in agriculture, living from subsistence farming. In the cities huge numbers of the residents survive from reselling whatever trinkets they can afford to buy in the streets. There is also a large proportion dependent on the illegal, but economically important, coca industry.

NATURAL HISTORY

The geographical characteristics of Peru, climatic variations and immense range of habitats are matched by a diversity of flora and fauna as great as anywhere else in the world: it has 361 mammal species, 1,780 bird species, 4,000 butterflies, 20,000 moths and over 1,300 orchids! If you are interested in natural history I recommend getting hold of one of the specialist books on the subject as it is impossible to do justice here to the richness of Peru's wildlife.

The desert coast

The greatest concentration of coastal wildlife is in or on the shores of the Pacific Ocean. There are dozens of species of seabird, including Chilean flamingos, Peruvian boobies, Peruvian pelicans, Humboldt penguins, guanay, red-legged or neotropic cormorants, black skimmers, Inca terns and various gulls. The Paracas Reserve is a good place to watch birds. There is a great variety of marine life too, particularly sealions, dolphins and migrating whales.

The Andes

As you move inland from the coast you reach the western slopes of the Andes, which are generally dry and barren, except in some of the cultivated river valleys. As you get higher and moisture levels increase, life is somewhat more prolific, and the land supports grasses and shrubs. Climatic conditions change but are equally inhospitable, and plants and animals have had to evolve to cope with these. The typical animals of the mountainous areas are the cameloids, including the wild vicuña, and the domesticated versions, the llama and alpaca. These animals have evolved to live at altitudes of over 3,500m, grazing on low-protein vegetation. Viscachas, a large rodent similar to a rabbit, are also commonly seen in rocky areas, and foxes, puma and white-tailed deer are also rumoured to live in the mountains but are almost impossible to see.

Typical plants found in the harsh mountainous conditions are the impressively tall (up to 12m), *Puya raimondii*, *ichu* (scrub grass) and various cacti such as the prickly pears known locally as *tunas*, found abundantly in the central Andean valleys. A plant used by the Incas in bridge construction for the strength of its fibres is the maguey or cabuya, a cacti found growing at altitudes up to 3,600m. Typical of the highlands is the cushion-like yareta (*Azorella yareta*), a very slow- growing, compact circular plant often used for firewood because of its high concentration of oils and heat value. You may see the hats of the Indian women decorated by a brightly coloured flower, which is known as cantuta (*Cantuta spp*). Growing up to nearly 4,000m, this tubular-shaped red, orange or violet flower is used as decoration by single women to show their unmarried status. There is very little in the way of tree life other than the introduced and now ubiquitous eucalypt and the native, attractive red-barked polylepis, known commonly as *queñual*. This tree, found at altitudes as high as 4,500m, has numerous layers of dark red flaky bark, small wax-covered leaves to prevent evaporation and twisted trunks to capture humidity. Small copses of forest provide a haven for some of the mountain wildlife such as deer, foxes and pumas.

Bird life is plentiful, particularly on the mountain lakes. The Andean condor (*Vultur gryphus*), the largest flying land bird in the world, is frequently spotted in the cordilleras as it soars the peaks looking for prey. Other raptors often seen are various hawks, falcons and kestrels. Hummingbirds are plentiful on the Andean slopes.

The high jungle and lowland forest

As you descend the lower eastern slopes of the Peruvian Andes there is a vegetation gradation from tropical cloudforest to rainforest and what is known as the high jungle, or *seja de selva*, literally the eyebrow of the jungle. The cloud forests, clinging precariously to steep, rugged slopes, are densely vegetated and rich in flora and fauna. This is one of the world's most biodiverse areas. Within the tropical lowland rainforest of eastern Peru there are three types of forest: dry, seasonally flooded and occasionally flooded. The diversity of tree species is astonishing, the most common being myrtles, laurels, acacias, cedrelas, cecropias, rosewoods, Brazil nuts, rubber trees, figs and palms. At ground level small plants and ferns are dominant, at the next level

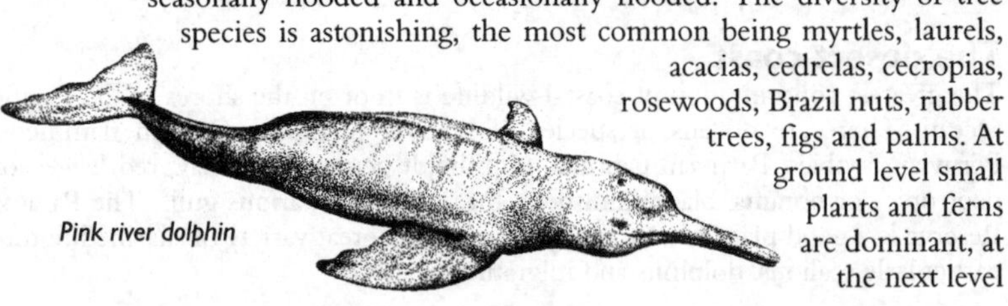
Pink river dolphin

THE ALPACA

The alpaca is a domesticated vicuña and cousin of the llama, itself a domesticated version of the guanaco; all four are members of the cameloid family. They come in a variety of colours from white through a full range of browns to jet black. They have large expressive eyes, a short muzzle, a frizzy fringe of hair over the brow, and particularly fine wool. A fully grown adult can weigh 150 pounds and can live 20 years or more. A female alpaca gives birth to one young a year after an 11-month gestation period. The young are usually born during the rainy season, when temperatures are slightly warmer than in the dry season. Alpacas are grazers and browsers with efficient digestive systems, doing well on low-protein, good-quality grass.

There are two breeds of alpaca: the Huacaya, comprising about 90% of all alpacas, and the less common Suri, forming the other 10%. The Huacaya's fleece looks crimped, while the Suri has a shiny fine fibre that has no crimp, but grows in defined, tightly twisted locks. Alpacas are normally shorn every year, each producing approximately eight pounds of fine wool, used to make the very cheap alpaca wool products found extensively throughout the Andes, or exported as fibre or high quality woollens.

Alpacas and llamas have been domesticated for thousands of years. They played an integral part in the prehispanic civilisations of South America. The alpaca's fleece was used for clothing while the larger llama was used to transport cargo. Currently there are about 1.5 million alpacas in South America with the heaviest concentration in the altiplano, or high regions of southern Peru, Bolivia and Chile.

are taller plants and bushes; then shade-loving trees, often covered in epiphytic and parasitic plants; and finally the canopy which consists of the forest giants, huge trees dominating the skyline.

Animal life is also very diverse with, amongst others, puma, jaguar, ocelot, margay, giant otters, anteaters, sloths, river dolphins, numerous primate species, and 1,800 bird species. Unless you have plenty of time and patience, you are less likely to spot mammals than the thousands of species of beautifully coloured butterflies, moths and other insects.

Protected areas

Peru has eight designated national parks covering a total area of 2,381,126 hectares, but there are also several other categories of protected areas. In total national parks, reserves, sanctuaries and monuments protect nearly 5% of the land mass and coastal zones of Peru. They are administered by INRENA (Instituto Areas Naturales Protegidos de Flora y Fauna Silvestre), Calle 17, 355 Urb. El Palomar, San Isidro, Lima; tel 01 2243298. Entrance fees are charged at Huascarán (US$20), Pacay Samiría (US$10) and Machu Picchu (US$10).

Giant otter

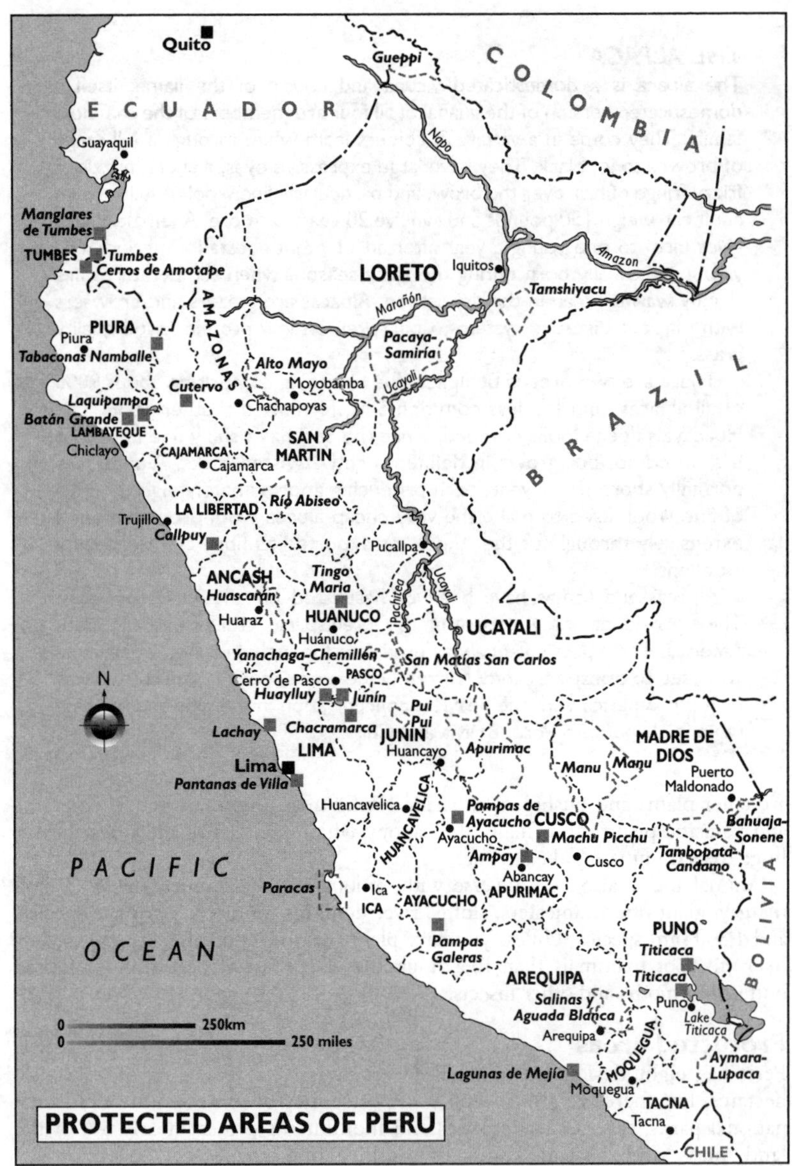

National parks

These areas have complete protection, and entry permits are required by visitors and local people. The park administrators are primarily concerned with the protection of environments which are home to many rare and endangered species, the control of deforestation, and the incorporation of sustainable resource management as a basis for maintenance and future growth. Local people have the right to continue to use the resources in protected areas only if the resources are an integral part of their culture.

Protected area	*Date established*	*Department*
Bahuaja-Sonene	1996	Madre de Dios and Puno
Cerros de Amotape	1975	Tumbes, Piura
Cutervo	1961	Cajamarca
Huascarán	1975	Ancash
Manu	1973	Madre de Dios, Cusco
Río Abiseo	1983	San Martín
Tingo Maria	1965	Huánuco
Yanachaga-Chemillén	1986	Pasco

National reserves

A second category of protected areas, *reservas nacionales*, cover a further 2,946,686 hectares in eight reserves. Wildlife is preserved and protected and the government allows use of the resources by local people.

Protected area	*Date established*	*Department*
Calipuy	1981	La Libertad
Junín	1974	Junín, Pasco
Lachay	1977	Lima
Pacay Samiría	1982	Loreto
Pampas Galeras	1981	La Libertad
Paracas	1975	Ica
Salinas y Aguada Blanca	1979	Arequipa, Moquegua
Titicaca	1978	Puno

National sanctuaries

The third category of protected areas, *santuarios nacionales*, cover an area of 150,223 hectares. These areas are protected for their wildlife or a particular feature of scientific or geographic interest.

Protected area	*Date established*	*Department*
Ampay	1987	Apurímac
Calipuy	1981	La Libertad
Huayllay	1974	Pasco
Lagunas de Mejía	1984	Arequipa
Manglares de Tumbes	1988	Tumbes
Tabaconas Namballe	1988	Cajamarca

Historical sanctuaries

Places of special historic or archaeological interest are designated as historical sanctuaries (*santuarios históricos*).

Protected area	*Date established*	*Department*
Chacamarca	1974	Junín
Machu Picchu	1981	Cusco
La Pampa de Ayacucho	1980	Ayacucho

There are several other protected areas, covering 3.5 million hectares, and known as *zonas reservadas*. They are protected areas awaiting further scientific study, after which they will be categorised.

BIRDWATCHING IN PERU

Barry Walker

Paracas National Reserve Paracas is a paradise for inshore birds thanks to the Humboldt current. The Pisco marshes are crowded with herons and waders, and the surrounding grassy fields hold specialities such as dark-faced ground tyrant, tawny-throated dotterel and Peruvian thick-knee. On the adjacent rocky coastline of Lagunillas, surfbirds abound during the northern winter and surf cinclodes can be seen searching amongst the seaweed. The mudflats of Paracas Bay host thousands of North American waders, especially during the northern winter, and Chilean flamingos during the northern summer. The nearby Ballestas Islands are a nesting site for thousands of seabirds. Almost all of these are Humboldt current specialists, and they include the dazzling Inca tern and Peruvian booby. During the boat ride, many pelagic (offshore) species may be spotted, including albatrosses, petrels and shearwaters.

Lomas de Lachay National Reserve About 90km north of Lima, and a convenient place for a day trip, this small reserve, holding several important species, is typical loma habitat, a type of vegetation formed during the winter months by dew falling from the coastal fog banks. It is home to the endemic Raimondi's yellow-finch and thick-billed miner.

Marcapomacocha An area of high *puna* grass and bogland, this is about four hours' drive east of Lima, at 4,500m. Besides regular high Andean species such as ground-tyrants, seed-snipes and sierra-finches, the main reason for birding here is twofold: the diademed sandpiper, a rare, almost mythical wader of the mineral-rich marshes, and white-bellied cinclodes, perhaps the prettiest and one of the rarest of the furnarids. With luck, both can be seen here. Other highlights include giant coot on the lake at Marcapomacocha, and the smart black-breasted hillstar, a hummingbird endemic to Peru.

Along the central highway from the Marcapomacocha turn-off, the well-paved road continues another 120km to **Lake Junin**, where, with prior arrangement, it is possible to hire a boat to see the endemic Junin flightless grebe. This lake is also a fantastic place to see all the highland waterbirds and raptors, and the surrounding fields abound with sierra-finches and ground-tyrants.

A further 180km along the highway brings you to **Huánuco**, the base for exploring the Carpish Tunnel area. About one hour's drive northeast of Huánuco, the road passes through the Carpish range, and birding either side of the tunnel can be very productive. Powerful woodpecker, sickle-winged guan and large mixed feeding flocks appear out of the mist in the epiphyte-laden cloudforest.

Huascarán Biosphere Reserve Situated in the central Andes, Huaráz is the starting point to explore the more remote areas of the mountains, such as the lakes of Llanganuco. In the surrounding high Andean woodlands, many little-known and interesting birds can be seen, including that rare mistletoe specialist, the white-cheeked cotinga, or the endemic plain-tailed warbling finch, whilst a check on the skyline will surely produce an Andean condor soaring against the 6,000m snow peaks.

Chiclayo-Cajamarca circuit Starting at the coastal city of Chiclayo, a tough but rewarding trip can be made into the deep Marañon valley and its environs. On this route, some of the most sought after and spectacular of Peru's birds can be found – legendary species such as the marvellous spatulatail, marañon crescent-chest, long-whiskered owlet, and buff-bridled Inca finch, to name but a few. Many of the species on this circuit have been seen by only a handful of ornithologists.

Iquitos From this city it is possible to visit a number of rainforest lodges. For the birder, two lodges stand out above the rest: Explorama and ExplorNapo. These lodges are quite expensive but very comfortable. ExplorNapo has a canopy walkway, which is superb for observing tree-top birds. Both lodges are excellent for Amazon birds, especially for the many species that are not seen south of the Amazon River.

Machu Picchu and Abra Málaga The bamboo stands surrounding the ruins provide good opportunities for seeing the Inca wren. A walk along the tracks near the railway station can also produce species which are difficult to see elsewhere: this is the place to see white-capped dipper and torrent duck.

From Ollantaytambo, on the way to Machu Picchu, it is only two hours' drive to one of the most accessible native polylepis woodlands in the Andes, whilst the humid temperate forest of **Abra Málaga** is only 45 minutes further on. In the polylepis, some very rare birds can be located without too much difficulty, including royal cinclodes and white-browed tit-spinetail (the latter being one of the ten most endangered birds on earth). The humid temperate forest is laden with moss and bromeliads, and mixed species flocks including multicoloured tanagers are common.

Manu Biosphere Reserve (see also page 254) The variety of birds here is astounding; the reserve holds over 1,000 species, significantly more than the whole of Costa Rica and over one-tenth of all the birds on earth. Although access to Manu is limited, there are adjacent areas where one can see all the Manu bird specialities and an astounding variety of other wildlife. Driving down through the cloudforest, every 500m loss of elevation produces new birds. This is the home of the Andean cock-of-the-rock, and a visit to one of its leks (courtship sites) is one of the world's great ornithological spectacles. There are also two species of quetzal here; in fact, these humid montane forests are home to a mind-boggling variety of multicoloured birds; a mixed flock of tanagers, honeycreepers and conebills can turn any tree into a Christmas tree!

In Manu the forest is intact, and species such as the Amazonian umbrellabird, and blueheaded and military macaws, can be found. The beaches are packed with nesting birds in the dry season; large-billed terns scream at passing boats and Orinoco geese watch warily from the shore. Huge colonies of sand-coloured nighthawks roost and nest on the hot sand.

As you leave the foothills and reach the untouched forests of the western Amazon, you enter jungle with the highest density of birdlife per square kilometre on earth. However, only strange calls betray their presence – until a mixed flock comes through, containing an astonishing 70-plus species; or a brightly coloured group of, say, rock parakeets dashes out of a fruiting tree. This forest holds such little-seen gems as black-faced cotinga and rufous-fronted ant-thrush. Antbirds and furnarids creep in the foliage and give tantalising glimpses until, eventually, they reveal themselves in a shaft of sunlight. For the birder who craves the mysterious and rare, this is the site.

Tambopata-Candamo Reserved Zone This area is accessible via the Tambopata River. A number of jungle lodges offer excellent lowland rainforest birding, providing a reasonable alternative for those who do not have the time or money to visit Manu.

Arequipa The best birding route is the road to Laguna Salinas, a large salt lake which regularly holds three species of flamingo (Chilean, Andean and Puna). Andean avocet and Puna plover are also common here. Between Arequipa and the lake, the polyepis-clad slopes and arid scrub can produce various earthcreepers and canasteros not found elsewhere, and this is one of only two locations for the Tamarugo conebill. A highlight of this region del Condor, the world's deepest canyon. This viewpoint overlooks a spot where condors roost and in the mornings they soar upwards on the thermals, passing startled observers at point blank range.

BIRDS

Barry Walker

Peru has more bird species than any nation on earth except Colombia, and stands at the top of the international birder's agenda. Its varied geography and topography, and its wildernesses of so many different life zones, have endowed Peru with the greatest biodiversity and density of birds on earth. About 1,780 bird species occur in Peru; 18.5% of all bird species on earth, and 45% of all neo-tropical birds. For ornithologists, it doesn't come more exciting than this: eight species new to science have been discovered in Peru in recent years, four of them so new they have not yet been given scientific names. Unlike other top-ranking neo-tropical birding destinations, such as Ecuador and Costa Rica, Peru has vast tracts of forest and wilderness untouched by civilisation; two-thirds of the Manu Biosphere Reserve, for example, is completely unexplored.

If you are new to neo-tropical birding, Peru's potential can be daunting (see box on page 166); a four-week trip can produce over 750 species, and some of the identifications can be tricky! Unfortunately, there is no single field guide that covers all the birds of Peru, and some species are not illustrated anywhere. However, taking a combination of a few books will ensure that 90% of your sightings can be identified.

PRACTICAL INFORMATION

Accommodation

Finding accommodation in Peru is rarely a problem. All the major cities have dozens of places to choose from to suit all budgets. Popular tourist destinations like Lima, Arequipa, Puno, Cusco and Huaraz have good backpackers' hostels, which are useful for meeting other travellers and swapping stories. Small, less touristy places usually have some choice, though they may be pretty basic. Even in remote villages you can usually find someone willing to put you up. Prices throughout Peru are cheap, though less so than Bolivia or Ecuador. A hotel will set you back over US$10 a night, more if you want a private bathroom, while a *residencial* or *hostal* will be from US$5 per person. A *pension*, *hospedaje* or *casa familiar* may be even cheaper. The cheapest places are usually concentrated around bus and train stations. Shared rooms are always cheaper, and unfortunately people on their own often have to pay considerably more. Expect a hot water problem, and sometimes no water at all; always look at the room, and do try negotiating prices out of season. It is a good idea to have a lockable bag for your valuables or to use the hotel safe box, depositing items of value against a receipt; don't leave valuables lying around the room, at least pack them at the bottom of a rucksack out of sight. Generally speaking you don't have to book accommodation in advance, but if you are travelling in peak tourist season, July–August, it is wise to book ahead, and definitely reserve ahead of time if you are going to be in a town during any of their *fiestas*. You can get information on affiliated youth hostels from YHA-Perú (Asociación de Albergues Juveniles), tel: (511) 242 3068; fax: (511) 444 8187; email: hostell@mail.cosapidata.com.pe.

Books, newspapers and maps

For books in English there are several bookshops in Lima: try the South American Explorers Club (SAEC), and the bookshops in Miraflores or downtown Lima (see page 182). Cusco also has a wide range of books available in the shops around the Plaza de Armas. For novels the best bet is to trade with other travellers or look for some of the hostels or cafés which do book exchange. There are a couple of English language newspapers, the *Lima Times* and the *Lima Herald*. Also worth looking out for is the free, monthly *Peru Guide*, with useful listings for the whole country. There are numerous daily newspapers in Spanish, the best being *El Comercio*, *El Expreso* and *La República*. They are all online. For online news, try **El Comercio**, www.elcomercio.com.pe/; **Expreso**, www.expreso.com.pe; **Gestión** www.gestion.com.pe/; **La República**, www.republica.com.pe; and **Travel Update** (Travel news), www.travelupdate.limaperu.net.

For maps, try the Instituto Geográfico Nacional at Aramburu 1198, Surquillo; Touring y Automóvil Club del Perú; tel: (511) 221 2432; fax: (511) 441 0531; email: touring@hys.com.pe; web: www.hys.com.pe/tacp; South American Explorers Club, www.samexplo.org/maps.htm

Health and safety

Crime in Peru is not as bad as it was even five years ago, but you should still take normal care to avoid potentially dangerous places and situations. Try not to arrive in a new place after dark and if you do, take a taxi to a hotel. Don't walk the streets with your rucksack on – again, take a taxi. Taxi prices are low and you are at your most vulnerable when carrying all you own, so it's worth being cautious despite the extra cost. Pickpockets and bag snatchers are rife, so keep your money in a money belt or a secret pocket, and never put your bag down on the ground nor take your eyes off it. Bus and train stations are particularly risky as you are easily distracted, so be attentive when boarding trains or buses or whenever there are a lot of people milling around. It's a good idea to leave valuables locked up in your hotel, in the safe or in a lockable bag, carry only what you may need and don't wear jewellery or flash money or cameras around. You must carry your passport with you, but make sure you have a photocopy somewhere safe in case you need to get a replacement. Beaches seem to be a particular danger hotspot for theft, so don't ever leave anything on a beach unattended. Arequipa and Cusco have also seen a few incidents of tourist muggings in recent years, generally late at night, so use taxis. Bags under tables in restaurants are not safe from theft. The situation changes, so it's best to check for any particular danger spots with the Foreign Office or South American Explorers Club in Lima and with other travellers.

Food and drink

The food in Peru is as varied as the geography and climate. The markets are filled with fresh produce from the whole country, including a huge variety of quality fruit and vegetables. Most Peruvians eat a large meal at lunchtime and eat very little in the evenings. This is reflected in the availability of cheap set menus in most restaurants from midday to early afternoon, usually excellent value (from US$1 for the most carbohydrate-loaded to US$4 for high-quality excellent food). The good thing is that you know it has been freshly prepared. There are regional variations in food, and cultural influences from the Spanish, indigenous people, Negroes, Asians and even Europeans. A classic dish eaten widely is *ají de gallina*, made from potatoes, a sauce with chillis, groundnuts and breadcrumbs, and finely shredded chicken. A similar sauce flavours the tasty dish *papas a la Huancaina* consisting primarily of boiled potatoes. All along the coast fish and shellfish are good and cheap. The typical dishes are *ceviche* (marinated fish served with chilli peppers, cooked corn on the cob and sweet potato) and *sudado* (steamed fish). Also popular is *causa*, a cold dish made with mashed potatoes, shrimps, avocados, eggs and mayonnaise. A *chupe* is any sort of thick soup, particularly good when made from freshwater shrimps, *camarones*. In the mountains the main ingredient of any dish is potatoes, which in tourist restaurants usually come as chips. Chicken and chip restaurants are everywhere. There are literally thousands of varieties of potato, hundreds of which form part of the Peruvian diet. The freeze-dried version, *chuño*, is often used in soups and stews. Other tubers which are also quite common include *camote* (sweet potato), *olluco* (a small yellow potato) and *yucca*. In the jungle the food is totally different: bananas and rice are prevalent over potatoes, and there is an unending variety of tasty river fish. The Chinese influence is seen in the large number of 'Chifa' restaurants, serving cheap, adapted Cantonese dishes. There are Japanese restaurants in Lima too and an increasing international representation in most major cities. See also *Appendix 1*, page 370.

Getting around

By road

Except in inaccessible jungle areas, where boats must be used to get around, public buses are the most popular form of transport. Long-distance buses are frequent and usually in fairly good condition: some even have air conditioning, heating, video entertainment of dubious quality, reclining seats and hostess service. They stop every few hours at roadside restaurants. The larger companies such as Ormeño, Civa, Oltursa and Cruz del Sur are the most recommended, but there is still no guarantee of safety and accidents are frequent. It's a good idea to buy your ticket a day in advance to ensure you get the seat of your choice. Be careful with your bags at the bus stations, and when checking in your luggage make sure you get a receipt. Put your rucksack into a plastic bag or flour sack of some kind if you want to prevent it getting covered in dirt, dust, rain and other muck. For short distances there are minibuses called *colectivos*, which are usually in poor condition and for the average European or North American are far too tight a squeeze for comfort. Of course there are taxis in all towns and cities, which are usually very cheap, and the main tip here is to negotiate a price before you even open the car door. In rural areas pick-up trucks and lorries are the normal mode of transport, and function as buses.

Road conditions vary enormously. The Pan American highway, running down the length of Peru's coast, is all tarmac as are several of the roads connecting the coast to the highlands, including the roads to Huaraz, Huancayo, Huánuco, Ayacucho and Arequipa. The roads within the highlands and down to the jungle are not in good condition and especially during the rainy season can be closed altogether. Long delays should be expected if you are trying to get to remote places between November and April – bridges may be down or avalanches may block the route. If this is the case you may have to wait for a vehicle coming the other way into which everyone will transfer with all their belongings after scrambling over the obstruction.

Cruz del Sur Tel: 511 424 1005; web: www.protelsa.com.pe/cruzdelsur.
Ormeño Tel: 511 427 5679/427 1710; fax: 511 426 3810; email: ormeno@ascinsa.com.pe; web: www.ascinsa.com.pe/ORMENO.

By train

The only train lines currently in operation in Peru are: Puno to Cusco; Arequipa to Puno; and Cusco to Machu Picchu. In the central highlands there is a train from Huancayo to Huancavelica and the Lima–Huancayo train now runs again about once a month.

By boat

In the jungle lowlands sometimes the only way to travel is by boat. Luxury tourist cruise boats ply the Leticia–Iquitos section of the Amazon, but other than that most boats cater for cargo and locals and are far from luxurious. You will need your own hammock and mosquito net as well as food and water to supplement what you may be given. Despite the unsavoury sounding conditions boat trips can be a lot of fun, allowing you a real insight into life on jungle rivers.

By air

Internal flights within Peru are cheap, especially out of season when the airlines tend to have a flat fare special of around US$40 per flight. You can usually buy tickets from airline offices or travel agents, except in July and August, at several days' notice. Once a ticket is bought, changing the date is not a problem. Aero Continente have offices in all major cities, including several in Lima. Lan Peru and TANS started operating services from Lima in 1999. Check travel agents for details.

AeroContinente Tel: 511 2424260/2213449; fax: 511 4467638/2418098; email: aerocont@aerocontinente.com.pe; web: aerocontinente.com.pe
AeroCóndor Tel: 511 4411354/4425663; fax: 511 4429487; email: acondor@ibm.net; web: www.ascinsa.com.pe/AEROCONDOR/index.html
Aero Ica Web: www.peruhot.com/nazcaline/hotel.html
Helicusco Web: ekeko.rcp.net.pe/HELICUSCO.
Airport Lima Jorge Chávez; tel: 511 575 0912.

Money

The currency of Peru is the nuevo sol, at the time of writing the exchange rate was S/3.4 to the US dollar. The exchange rate has been quite stable since 1992. US dollars are accepted in hotels and restaurants in the cities, but you will need local currency for everything else. You can only change good quality dollar bank notes with no tears or writing on them. There are money changers in most cities, both offices and people on the street, who will give you the official rate. Check the rates with several people before changing in the street and always calculate how much you should get before doing any transaction. Watch out for forged sol notes, as there are plenty around. Banks will also change money and travellers' cheques: try Banco Weiss, Banco de Crédito and Interbanc; and remember that changing travellers' cheques is not easy away from the main commercial centres. You can use ATM cards to get cash from the machines, using Plus, Cirrus or Link system.

Post, telephone and email

Post offices in the main cities and towns open daily Mon Sat, 08.00–20.00 and Sun 08.00–15.00. Letters can take weeks to reach European destinations, and cost approximately US$1 each. There are telephone offices in all except the most remote settlements, and you can dial directly overseas (open daily 07.00–23.00). There are phone boxes in the large cities too, which take coins or phone cards. In many shops there are also small green phones which only take coins.

The international code for Peru is 51. When dialing from overseas to a Peruvian destination dial 00 51 then the local area code without the zero. To call internationally from Peru dial 00 then the country code. Local area codes are: Arequipa 054, Ayacucho 064, Andahuaylas 084, Cajamarca 044, Cusco 084, Chiclayo 074, Iquitos 094, Juliaca 054, Piura 074, Pucallpa 064, Puerto Maldonado 084, Rioja 094, Tacna 054, Tarapoto 094, Trujillo 044, Tumbes 074, Yurimaguas 094. Email has become an increasingly popular way to stay in touch, and as in Bolivia and Ecuador, Peru is well stocked with Internet cafés, each major town or city having a choice of cheap places.

Business hours

Most businesses are open morning and afternoon and shut for lunch, usually 14.00–16.00. Banks don't usually shut for lunch and are open Mon–Fri 09.30–16.00 and Sat mornings. Most public office are open weekdays from 09.00–15.00.

Public holidays

1 January	New Year's Day
End of February	Carnival
April	Holy Thurday, Good Friday, Easter
1 May	Labour Day
15 May	Independence Day
29 June	St Peter & St Paul
28-29 July	Independence Day Celebrations
30 August	St Rosa of Lima
8 October	Battle of Angamos
1 November	All Saints Day
8 December	Immaculate Conception
25 December	Christmas Day

Some local festivals with fixed dates

January

7	Anniversary	Tumbes
15	Fiesta del Niño Perdido	Huancavelica.
18	Anniversary of the Foundation of Lima.	

February

2	Fiesta de la Virgen de la Candelaria	Puno, Ayacucho, Huancayo, Cusco, Lake Titicaca
Last week	Verano Negro	Chincha

March

8	San Juan de Dios	Puno
19	San José	Chiclayo, Lambayeque
31	Domingo de Ramos en Porcón	Cajamarca

April

15–23	Official Contest of Paso Horses	Lurín, Lima
Easter week	Holy week	Ayacucho
Last week	Anniversary of the Political Formation of Apurimac	

May

2–4	Velacuy Cross	Cusco
2–5	Feria de las Alasitas	Puno
3	Fiesta de las Cruces	Ayacucho
10	Señor de la Asunción	Ayacucho
13	Virgen de Fátima	Ayacucho, Concepción, Huancayo

June

2–3	Señor de Qoyllur Rit'i	Cusco
24	Inti Raymi	Cusco
24	San Juan	The Selva and the Sierra
Mid June	Corpus Cristi	Cusco
Last Sun	Ollantay Raymi	Cusco
28	San Pedro	

July

12	Aniversario Puerto Maldonado	Madre de Dios
16	Virgen del Carmen	Paucartambo (Cusco)
24	Fiesta de Santiago, Junín	Huancavelica
28	Independence day	throughout Peru
31	San Ignacio	Cajamarca

August

5	Virgen de las Nieves	Cerro de Pasco, Parinacochas (Ayacucho), Sihuas (Ancash)
12–20	Anniversary	Arequipa
15	Virgin of the Ascension	Cangallo, Ayacucho

September

5	Anniversary of Chachapoyas	Amazonas
7-8	Baños del Inca	Cajamarca
8	Virgin of Guadalupe	Nazca, Ica
24	Virgin of las Mercedes	Ancash, Junín, Piura, Puno
Last week	Primavera International Festival	Trujillo

October

1st week	Virgin of the Rosary	Apurimac, Ancash, Cajabamba, Cajamarca, Cusco
8–10	San Francisco de Borja	Yunguyo, Puno
12–20	Anniversary of Pucallpa	Ucayali
18–28	Lord of the Miracles	Lima
17	Señor de Luren	Ica

November

1–2	All Saints and All Souls	throughout Peru
1–8	Anniversary of Abancay	Apurimac
3	Festivity of San Martín de Porres	Lima
25	Anniversary of Moquegua	Moquegua
27	Anniversary of Cerro de Pasco	Cerro de Pasco

December

1st week	Celebrations for the Battle of Ayacucho	
7–10	Immaculate Conception	Paucartambo, Pasco
24	Santuranticuy	Cusco
26	Anniversary	Madre de Dios

Tourist information offices

The principal organisation dealing with tourist information is called PROMPERU. Its head office is in Lima, Calle 1, Urb. Córpac, San Isidro, and is open to the public Mon–Fri 09.00–18.00. There is a 24-hour hot line for tourist complaints run by INDECOPI (Servicio de Protección al Turista), tel/fax: (511) 224 78888/2248600 or freephone: 0800 42579; email: postmaster@indecopi.gob.petel

GIVING SOMETHING BACK

If you are interested in voluntary work in Peru contact any of the organisations listed below, who would be happy to hear from you. Supporting the local charities is a good way to repay some of the hospitality you receive in Peru while helping the people who most need it. The South American Explorers Club have an information pack for potential volunteers and can also give you further information about local charities.

Fundación Peruana para la Conservación de la Naturaleza (FPCN) Postal address: Apartado 18-1393 Lima; tel: 442-6616; fax: 4427853. Peruvian Foundation for Conservation of Nature; focuses on protecting habitat, scientific research, public policy and environmental education.
The Mountain Institute Av Ricardo Palma 100, Huaraz; postal address: Apartado 01, Alameda Grau 1028, Huaraz, Peru; tel: 044 721884/723446; fax: 044 725996; email: tmi@mail.cosapidata.com.pe A non-profit scientific and environmental organisation committed to preserving mountain environments and advancing mountain cultures throughout the world. Peruvian activities are presently focused on Parque Nacional Huáscaran.
Niños Calle Meloq 442, Cusco; tel: 084 235183; email: Jolanda Van Den Berg and Titus Bovenberg ninos@correo.dnet.com.pe A lovely hostel run by a Dutch couple who have adopted street children in Cusco. The children help out in the hotels and are trained in tourism related skills. A very worthwhile project to support and lovely place to stay.
Pro Natureleza Parque Blume No 106 con Av Gral Cordova 518, Miraflores, Lima 18; tel: 441 3800; fax: 441 2151; email: fpcn@mail.cosapidata.com.pe Contact: Andrew Halliday. This organisation is involved in environmental work all over Peru, including collaborative work with the national parks and many foreign agencies.
Takiwasi, located in Tarapoto, is a drug rehabilitation centre which also does research into traditional Amazon medicines. It was founded in 1992 and is run by a French doctor. Volunteers able to offer some useful skills, technical or medical are welcome for a maximum of six months. For further information contact: Dr Jacques Mabit, Director, Prol Alerta 466, Tarapoto, Peru; tel/fax: (51 94) 525479/522818; email: takiwasi@sm.itdg.org.pe

Lima is not the most attractive of cities and this is compounded by the fairly awful climate. The place seems to be perpetually damp with a sort of grey mist that hangs over the city most of the year, except in January and February when the sun shines. The temperature is around 15°C in winter months and 25°C in the summer. However, there are some redeeming features. The many museums have some of the best collections in Peru and are worth a visit to give you an insight into the prehispanic cultures that occupied Peru. Each district of the city is quite distinct, and some still have a certain colonial charm, particularly the centre of Lima and Barranco. Miraflores is now the commercial centre of the city. Many banks, businesses and boutiques have moved here for safety. Security is tight and affluence obvious. When you are walking around Lima it is a good idea to leave all your valuables locked up in the hotel and be wary of pickpockets and bag snatchers.

HISTORY

Francisco Pizarro founded the city of Lima on January 6 1535. The climate of this coastal area is ugly, but the Rimac Valley was chosen because it is one of the few river valleys on the coast with permanent water. There is a large natural harbour at the mouth of the river, and reasonably good access to the Andes. By the 1550s the town had grown to a considerable size and was the powerful and important viceroyalty capital for the Spanish conquered countries of Peru, Ecuador, Bolivia and Chile.

The 17th century was Lima's most prosperous era. The population was then 26,000, of which 40% were black slaves, 38% Spanish, 8% pure Indian, and the rest a mixture. The centre of the city was crowded with exotic trading posts. In 1746 a large earthquake shook the city, leaving only 20 houses standing and killing thousands. The 19th century saw a large expansion and the growth of the suburbs of Barranco, Miraflores and Magdalena. Originally several kilometres from the centre, these suburbs have now been swallowed up. Throughout the 20th century the population of the city has continued to grow, from 30,000 in the 1930s to 3,500,000 in the 1970s and around 10 million today. There have been attempts to clean up the city, install sewage systems, electricity and clean water, and more recently to move street sellers off the central streets. However, many of the city's inhabitants are still marginalised, living any way they can by selling on the streets to scrape a few sols together. Although difficult to assess, estimates put as many as 80% of the population as unemployed.

GETTING THERE AND AWAY

By bus

Getting a bus out of Lima is easy once you know where your bus goes from. There is no bus terminal – each company has its own departure and arrival depot. There

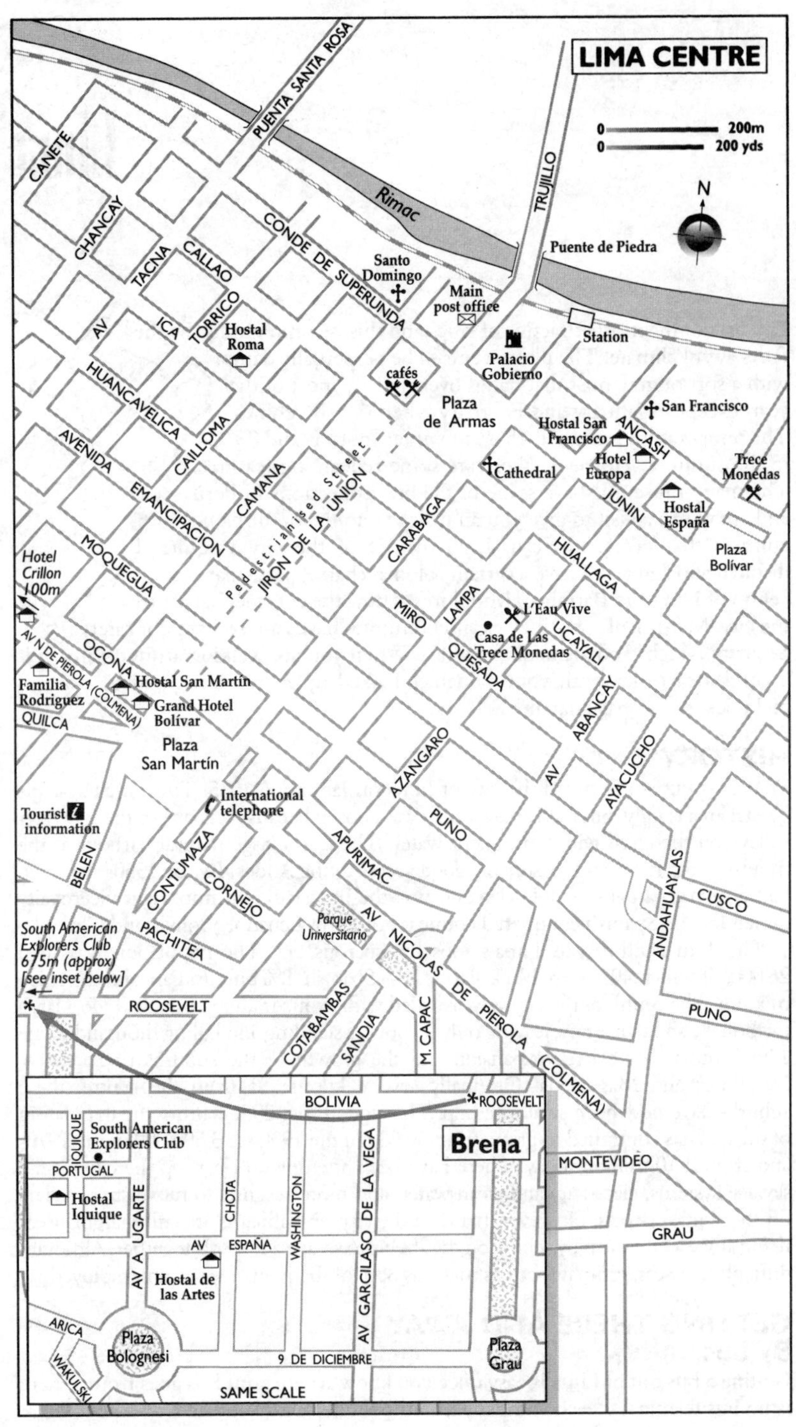
LIMA CENTRE
0 200m
0 200 yds
N
Rimac
PUENTA SANTA ROSA
TRUJILLO
Puente de Piedra
CANETE
CHANCAY
AV
TACNA
CALLAO
CONDE DE SUPERUNDA
Santo Domingo
Main post office
Station
Palacio Gobierno
ICA
TORRICO
Hostal Roma
cafés
Plaza de Armas
San Francisco
Hostal San Francisco
ANCASH
Hotel Europa
Trece Monedas
HUANCAVELICA
CAILLOMA
AVENIDA
EMANCIPACION
CAMANA
Pedestrianised Street
JIRON DE LA UNION
Cathedral
CARABAGA
JUNIN
Hostal España
Plaza Bolívar
HUALLAGA
Hotel Crillon 100m
MOQUEGUA
MIRO
LAMPA
L'Eau Vive
Casa de Las Trece Monedas
UCAYALI
QUESADA
AV N DE PIEROLA (COLMENA)
OCONA
Hostal San Martín
Grand Hotel Bolívar
Familia Rodriguez
QUILCA
Plaza San Martín
AZANGARO
AV
ABANCAY
AYACUCHO
International telephone
Tourist information
PUNO
BELEN
CONTUMAZA
APURIMAC
CORNEJO
ANDAHUAYLAS
CUSCO
South American Explorers Club 675m (approx) [see inset below]
PACHITEA
Parque Universitario
AV
NICOLAS DE PIEROLA (COLMENA)
ROOSEVELT
COTABAMBAS
SANDIA
M. CAPAC
PUNO
BOLIVIA
ROOSEVELT
IQUIQUE
South American Explorers Club
Brena
PORTUGAL
Hostal Iquique
AV A UGARTE
CHOTA
WASHINGTON
AV GARCILASO DE LA VEGA
MONTEVIDEO
GRAU
AV
ESPAÑA
Hostal de las Artes
ARICA
WAKULSKI
Plaza Bolognesi
9 DE DICIEMBRE
Plaza Grau
SAME SCALE

is talk of building three new terminals but no action as yet. Most of the companies' offices are in the centre of the city, around Calles Montevideo, Graú, Abancay and Zavala, and the best thing is to look them up in the phone book. Be particularly wary around the bus stations as they are rife with thieves and bag snatchers. The biggest companies with countrywide destinations include **Ormeño** (Calle Carlos Zavala 177; tel: 4275679 and Av Javier Prado Este 1059; tel: 4721710), **Cruz del Sur** (Quilca 531; tel: 4249643), **Oltursa** (Av Graú 617; tel: 4282370) and **Civa** (Montevideo 500; tel: 4264926), with offices next to each other. For Huancayo the best is **Mariscal Caceres** (Calle 28 de Julio 2195; tel: 4747850).

There are services to Arequipa (12 hrs, US$10), Tacna (22 hrs, US$13), Juliaca (24 hrs, US$17), Cusco (24 hrs, US$22), Nazca (8 hrs, US$5), Ayacucho (12 hrs, US$8), Puquio (13 hrs, US$8), Chimbote (6 hrs, US$4), Trujillo (7 hrs, US$6), Chiclayo (12 hrs, US$8), Piura (15 hrs, US10), Tumbes (22 hrs, US$13) and Huaraz (8 hours, US$7).

Ormeño have an international service including the following destinations: Guayaquil (US$50, 29 hrs), Quito (US$60, 38 hrs), Cali (US$120, 56 hrs), Bogota (US$130, 3 days), Caracas (US$160, 4 days), Santiago (US$75, 54 hrs), Mendoza (US$120, 3 days 6 hrs) and Buenos Aires (US$140, 3 days 18 hrs). You should reserve several days in advance. Pay in cash with dollars or sols.

By air

Lima airport is about 30 minutes by taxi from the centre of town or from Miraflores or Barranco, if there isn't too much traffic. You should allow an hour to be on the safe side. From Miraflores take a minibus from the Ovalo to outside the airport. Taxis are usually around US$7 from town and US$12 from the airport to town. There is just one airport building with domestic departures at one end and international at the other. The airport has a bank, post office, café, 24hr left luggage, Internet and phone office. When you arrive in Peru you are given an entry slip, which you need to keep to get out again. International departure tax is US$25 payable in sols or dollars. The national departure tax is US$5.

By train

The tourist train between Lima and Huancayo has started running again, but only about one day a month. It costs US$20, departs from Lima at 07.40 and arrives at Huancayo at 18.00.

WHERE TO STAY

Telephone code 01.

There are dozens of cheap hotels and a couple of particularly popular backpackers' hostels in downtown Lima. Alternatively Miraflores and Barranco are quieter, with a good variety of accommodation. Wherever you decide to stay it is safest to use taxis at night and when carrying your luggage.

Hostal de las Artes Jr Chota 1454, near Av España, Breña; tel: 4330031; email: artes@telematic.com.pe From US$4 per person. Friendly owners, close to SAEC near the centre of town, nice clean rooms.

Hostal Iquique Jr Iquique 758, Breña; tel: 4334724. From US$4 per person. Use of kitchen, central and close to SAEC.

Hostal Residencial Kori Wasi Av Washington 1137, Santa Beatriz; tel: 4338127. From US$4, nice, safe and friendly.

Familia Rodriguez Nicolas de Pierola 730, 2nd floor; tel: 4236465. US$6 per person in dorm. Family house, good information, friendly and safe, recommended. Very central.

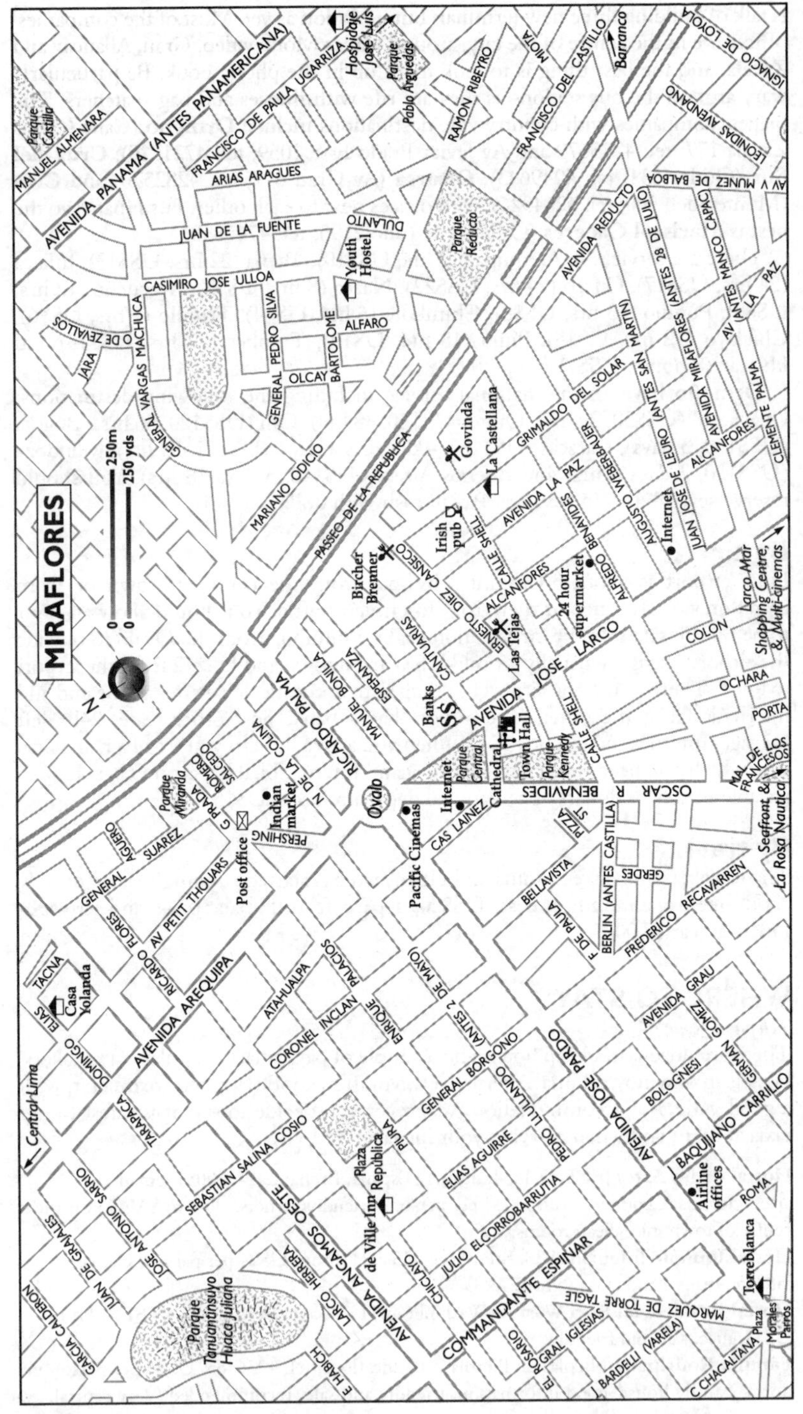
MIRAFLORES
0 250m
0 250 yds
N
AVENIDA PANAMA (ANTES PANAMERICANA)
MANUEL ALMENARA
Parque Castilla
FRANCISCO DE PAULA UGARRIZA
Hospidaje José Luis
Parque Pablo Arguedas
RAMON RIBEYRO
MOTA
FRANCISCO DEL CASTILLO
Barranco
IGNACIO DE LOYOLA
LEONIDAS AVENDANO
AV V MUNEZ DE BALBOA
ARIAS ARAGUES
JUAN DE LA FUENTE
DULANTO
Youth Hostel
Parque Reducto
AVENIDA REDUCTO
CASIMIRO JOSE ULLOA
O DE ZEVALLOS
JARA
GENERAL VARGAS MACHUCA
GENERAL PEDRO SILVA
BARTOLOME
ALFARO
OLCAY
MARIANO ODICIO
PASSEO DE LA REPUBLICA
Govinda
La Castellana
GRIMALDO DEL SOLAR
AVENIDA MIRAFLORES (ANTES 28 DE JULIO)
AV (ANTES MANCO CAPAC) LA PAZ
AUGUSTO WEBERBAUER (ANTES SAN MARTIN)
JUAN JOSE DE LEURO
ALCANFORES
CLEMENTE PALMA
Internet
Irish pub
AVENIDA LA PAZ
CALLE SHELL
Bircher Brenner
DIEZ CANSECO
ERNESTO
24 hour supermarket
ALFREDO BENAVIDES
Larco Mar Shopping Centre, & Multi-cinemas
COLON
OCHARA
PORTA
MAL DE LOS FRANCESOS
Las Tejas
AVENIDA JOSE LARCO
CANTUARIAS
Banks $$
ESPERANZA
MANUEL BONILLA
RICARDO PALMA
Town Hall
Cathedral
Parque Kennedy
Parque Central
Internet
BENAVIDES
OSCAR R
Seafront & La Rosa Nautica
COLINA
N DE LA
Ovalo
Pacific Cinemas
CAS LAINEZ
PIZZA ST
Indian market
Post office
PERSHING
Parque Miranda
SALCEDO
ROMERO
G PRADA
AGÜERO
GENERAL SUAREZ
AV PETIT THOUARS
BELLAVISTA
BERLIN (ANTES CASTILLA)
GERDES
FREDERICO RECAVARREN
F DE PAULA
TACNA
ELIAS
Casa Yolanda
RICARDO FLORES
AVENIDA AREQUIPA
ATAHUALPA
PALACIOS
(ANTES 2 DE MAYO)
CORONEL INCLAN
ENRIQUE
AVENIDA GRAU
GOMEZ
GERMAN
DOMINGO
TARAPACA
Central Lima
GENERAL BORGONO
PEDRO LUJLANDO
AVENIDA JOSE PARDO
BOLOGNESI
J BAQUIJANO CARRILLO
SEBASTIAN SALINA COSIO
Plaza de Ville Inn
Plaza Republica
PIURA
ELIAS AGUIRRE
Airline offices
ROMA
JULIO ELCORROBARRUTIA
CHICLAYO
SARRIO
JOSE ANTONIO
JUAN DE GRAVALES
GARCIA CALDERON
Parque Tahuantinsuyo Huaca Juliana
AVENIDA ANGAMOS OESTE
HERRERA
LARCO
F HABICH
COMMANDANTE ESPINAR
MARQUEZ DE TORRE TAGLE
Torreblanca
Plaza Morales Parros
EL ROSARIO
GRAL IGLESIAS
J BARDELLI (VARELA)
C CHACALTANA

Hostal España Jr Azángaro 105; tel: 4285546. From US$3 per person, in dorms or private rooms. Very popular with backpackers. Restaurant, videos.
Hostal Roma Jr Ica 326; tel: 4277576. From US$6 per person. Popular with backpackers, safe and very central.
Albergue Malka Los Lirios 165, San Isidro (just off block 4 of Javier Prado Este); tel: 2225589; email: alberguemalka@hotmail.com. US$6 per person, including breakfast. Clean, run by climbers, climbing wall in the garden.
Hotel Renacimiento Parque Hernan Velarde 52-54; tel: 4332806. US$15–25. Colonial building, nice rooms, quiet.
La Posada del Parque Parque Hernan Velarde 60, Block one of Petite Thours; tel: 4332412; email: monden@telematic.com.pe. US$25–45. Very clean restored house in quiet street off Petit Thours. All rooms have private bath and cable TV.
Hotel San Martín Av Nicolas de Pierola 882, 2nd fl; tel: 4285337. US$30–42. Includes all taxes and a continental breakfast. Clean, safe, modern, friendly.

In Barranco

Mochilero's Backpackers Hostel Av Pedro de Osma 135, Barranco; tel: 477 4506/477 0302; email backpacker@amauta.rcp.net.pe or backpacker@lanet.com.pe. US$10 per person, shared bath. Comfortable hostel in the centre of Barranco, large, nicely renovated post-colonial building. 50 beds total, 8 per room, lockers.

In Miraflores

International Youth Hostel Casmiro Ulloa 328; tel: 4465488. From US$10. You do not have to be an IYHF member. Clean, safe, garden.
José Luis Hostal Calle Paula Ugarriza 727; tel: 4441015; fax: 4467177; email: hsjluis@telematic.edu.pe. US$12 per person for private bath and breakfast.
La Castellana Grimaldo de Solar 222; tel: 4443530. US$45–55. 10% discount for SAEC members; friendly, safe, nice colonial house, restaurants, courtyard.
Torreblanca José Pardo 1453; tel: 4479998. US$40–50 with breakfast. Near the waterfront, quiet and safe.
De Ville Inn Jr Chiclayo 533, Miraflores; tel: 4474325. US$30–40. Very clean, newly restored hotel. Private bath and cable TV. Central Miraflores.

WHERE TO EAT

Finding somewhere to eat in Lima is never a problem, as the choice is great. Typical food in this part of Peru is fish and seafood. *Cebiche*, which is marinated raw fish, is delicious at lunchtime with a cold beer. Eating raw fish is not dangerous as long as it's fresh, so choose your restaurant carefully. There are numerous dishes of cooked fish, such as *a lo macho* which is with a seafood sauce and *a la chorillana*, with tomatoes and onions. Chicken is widely available as everywhere in Peru; a good dish is *aji de gallina*. *Lomo saltado* is stir-fried beef and usually served with rice; *anticuchos* are kebabs. Fixed menus are usually excellent value – you get three courses for just a few dollars.

In the centre

El Conquistador Plaza de Armas. Great location.
La Naturaleza Jr Lampa 440. Open daily until 19.00. Good vegetarian food.
L'Eau Vive del Perú Jr Ucayali. French food, good value, served by nuns.

Miraflores

La Rosa Nautica Costa Verde, on the seafront. This is a great place for cocktails and dinner for a treat. Lovely atmosphere, credit cards accepted. Expensive, but worth it.

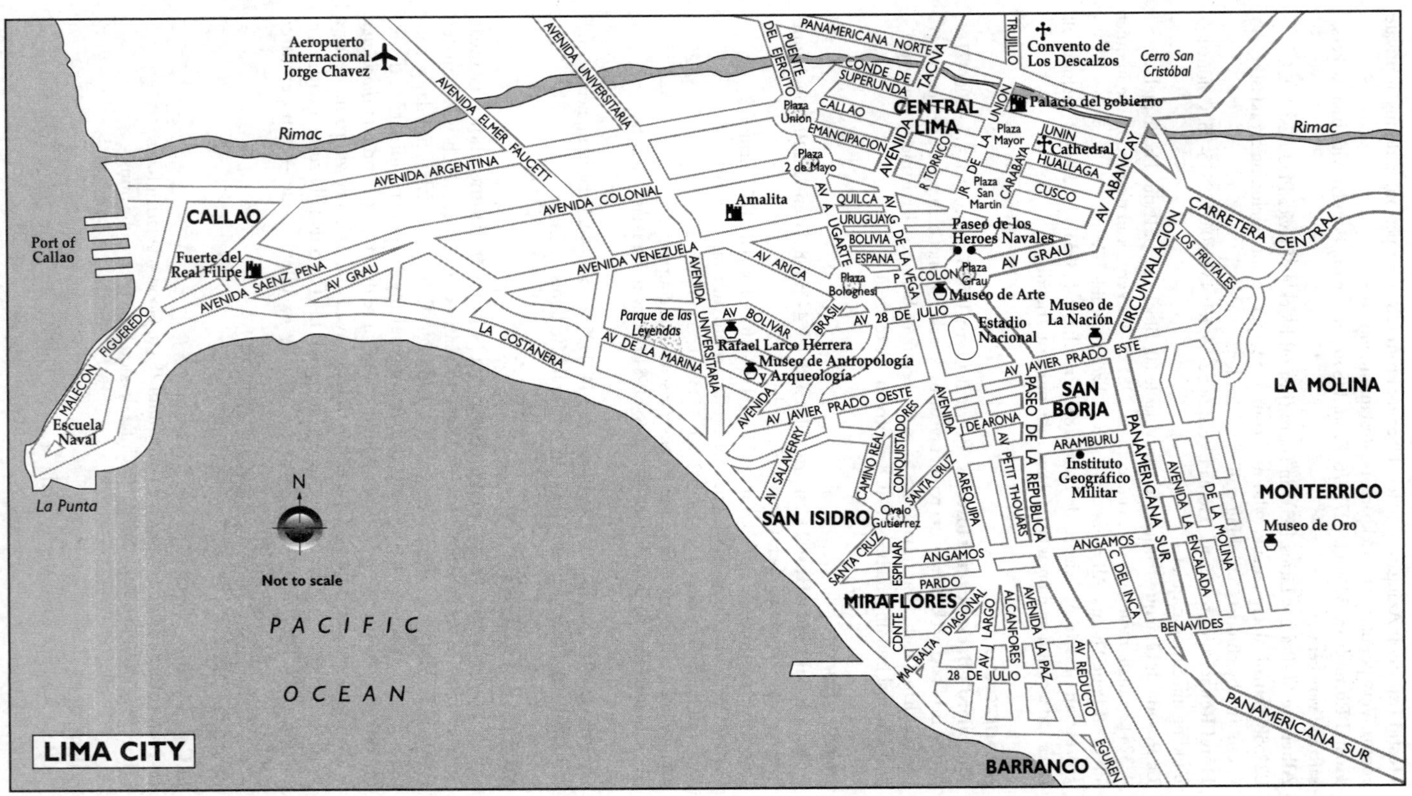
LIMA CITY
Not to scale
N
PACIFIC
OCEAN
CALLAO
Fuerte del Real Filipe
Port of Callao
Escuela Naval
La Punta
MALECON FIGUEREDO
AVENIDA SAENZ PENA
AV GRAU
Aeropuerto Internacional Jorge Chavez
Rimac
AVENIDA ARGENTINA
AVENIDA ELMER FAUCETT
AVENIDA UNIVERSITARIA
AVENIDA COLONIAL
AVENIDA VENEZUELA
AVENIDA UNIVERSITARIA
LA COSTANERA
AV DE LA MARINA
Parque de las Leyendas
Amalita
AV BOLIVAR
Rafael Larco Herrera
Museo de Antropología y Arqueología
AV ARICA
AV SALAVERRY
AVENIDA BRASIL
AV JAVIER PRADO OESTE
SAN ISIDRO
MIRAFLORES
BARRANCO
PUENTE DEL EJERCITO
Plaza Union
Plaza 2 de Mayo
PANAMERICANA NORTE
CONDE DE SUPERUNDA
CALLAO
EMANCIPACION
AVENIDA TACNA
CENTRAL LIMA
AV A UGARTE
QUILCA
URUGUAY
BOLIVIA
ESPANA
Plaza Bolognesi
AV G DE LA VEGA
AV 28 DE JULIO
P COLON
Plaza Grau
Museo de Arte
Paseo de los Heroes Navales
R TORRICO
JR DE LA UNION
CARABAYA
Plaza San Martin
Plaza Mayor
TRUJILLO
Convento de Los Descalzos
Palacio del gobierno
Cathedral
JUNIN
HUALLAGA
CUSCO
AV ABANCAY
AV GRAU
Cerro San Cristóbal
Rimac
CARRETERA CENTRAL
CIRCUNVALACION
LOS FRUTALES
Museo de La Nación
Estadio Nacional
AV JAVIER PRADO ESTE
SAN BORJA
LA MOLINA
MONTERRICO
Museo de Oro
DE LA MOLINA
AVENIDA LA ENCALADA
PANAMERICANA SUR
BENAVIDES
Instituto Geográfico Militar
ARAMBURU
PASEO DE LA REPUBLICA
AV PETIT THOUARS
DE ARONA
AVENIDA AREQUIPA
ANGAMOS
C DEL INCA
AV REDUCTO
EGUREN
AVENIDA LA PAZ
ALCANFORES
AV J LARGO
28 DE JULIO
DIAGONAL
MAL BALTA
CDNTE ESPINAR
PARDO
SANTA CRUZ
Ovalo Gutierrez
CAMINO REAL
CONQUISTADORES
PANAMERICANA SUR

EL CEBICHE

Cebiche, or *ceviche*, is one of Peru's great culinary delights. It is a delicious plateful of marinated fresh fish or shellfish, eaten all along the coast and even in the highlands, in fact, wherever fresh fish is available. The best *cebiche* is made only from the freshest ingredients: good quality fish (*pescado*), which could be *lenguado* (sole), *corvina* or *cojinova* (white sea fish) or shellfish (*mariscos*); freshly squeezed lemons (*limones*) and hot chilli peppers, known locally as *ají*. Toasted corn (*cancha*), sweet potato (*camote*) and boiled potato or yucca are eaten together with the *cebiche*.

Las Brujas de Cachiche Bolognesi 460. Good food, creole style.
Calle de Las Pizzas off Diagonal. Many pizza places.
La Tranquera José Pardo 285. Steaks.
La Tejas Diez Canseco 340. Good value Creole food.
El Trapiche Larco 1031. Good food.
Govinda Vegetarian restaurant on Calle Schell near Vía Expresa. Great value Krishna place.

The cafés around the Ovalo in Miraflores are great for watching life go past.

ENTERTAINMENT

Try to pick up a copy of the booklet *Peru Guide* or the *Lima Times* for useful information on what's going on, current exhibitions, concerts etc.

Lima has lots of cinemas mostly showing original versions of the latest Hollywood movies. Check in *El Comercio* or *La República*, the local newspapers, for what's on guides. Barranco has a thriving nightlife. There are dozens of bars and clubs centred around the pedestrian street Los Pasos. Try **La Noche** (Calle Bolognesi 317), a huge bar which often has live music. **Bar Kitsch** (Bolognesi 743) is relatively new, stays open late, has good music, and the clientele is not quite so young as many of the other places. **Noctambul** on Graú 627 is also a popular bar/disco. In the centre of town the place for live folk music is **Las Brisas de Titicaca** (Walkuski 168). There is an entry fee.

TOURIST INFORMATION

Tourist office Calle Santa Rosa, Plaza de Armas. There's a kiosk in Parque Kennedy, Miraflores; email: postmaster@foptur.gob.pe. The Promperu tourist office is in Edificio Mitinci, Piso 13, Calle 1, Corpac, San Isidro; tel/fax: 2243113; 224312; email: postmaster@promperu.gob.pe; web: www.promperu.org

South American Explorers Club Av República de Portugal 146, Breña, Lima; postal address: Casilla 3714, Lima 100, Peru; tel/fax: 4250142; member email: memberlima@amauta.rcp.net.pe; administrative email: montague@amauta.rcp.net.pe Open 09.30–17.00 weekdays.

Trekking and Backpacking Club Jr Huascar 1152, Jesus Maria; tel: 4232515; email: tebac@hotmail.com

Tourist police Museo de La Nación, Javier Prado and Aviación; tel: 4767708. Open 08.00–20.00. There is a 24-hour tourist complaints line: tel: 2247888/2248600.

Immigration Av España and Jiron Huaraz; tel: 3304114. Mon–Fri 08.00–12.00.

Travel agents

Ayllu Viajes Calle Chiclayo 562B, Miraflores; tel 4459639/9787060. Packages, tickets, hotels, transfers, Galápagos. English speaking.

Chavín International Av Pardo 620, Miraflores; tel: 2410991.
Coltur Av José Pardo 136, Miraflores; tel: 4477790.
Explorandes San Fernando 320, Miraflores; tel: 4458683/4450532. Adventure tourism.
Huaraz Chavín Tours Miguel Dasso 126, San Isidro; tel: 4421514. Conventional and adventure tourism. Also have an office in Huaraz.
Lima Tours Jr de la Unión 1040, centre of Lima; tel: 4276624. Long standing conventional professional travel agent.
Trekkandes Av Benavides 470B, Miraflores; tel: 4478078.

Airlines

Aero Continente José Pardo 651; tel: 2424260/2424242.
Aerolinias Argentinas José Pardo 805, Floor 5, Miraflores; tel: 4440810.
Alitalia Camino Real 497, San Isidro; tel: 4428507.
American Airlines Juan de Arona 830, Floor 14, San Isidro; tel: 2117000.
Avianca Paz Soldán 225, Office C5, San Isidro; tel: 2217822.
British Airways Andalucia 174, Miraflores; tel: 4226600.
Iberia Camino Real 390. Floor 9, San Isidro; tel: 4214616.
KLM José Pardo 805, Floor 6, Miraflores; tel: 2421241.
Lan Chile José Pardo 805, Floor 5, Miraflores; tel: 2415522.
Lloyd Air Boliviano José Pardo 231; tel: 2415210.
Lufthansa Jorge Basadre 1330, San Isidro; tel: 4424466.
Saeta Andalucia 174, Miraflores; tel: 4220889.
Varig Camino Real 456, Floor 8, San Isidro; tel: 4424361.

Shopping

Crafts

For craft markets the widest selection is on Calle La Marina, on the way to the airport, or Petit Thouars 5321 in Miraflores. This has rugs, jumpers, T-shirts and crafts from all over Peru.

Maps

You can get 1:50,000 maps of most of the country from the **Instituto Geográfico Nacional** on Calle Aramburú 1198. Take your passport with you. Open Mon–Fri 08.00–16.00. Maps are US$6 each. The **South American Explorers Club** has a wide range of maps for sale too.

Books

Try **Epoca**, José Pardo 399, Miraflores or Jr de la Unión 1072 in the centre of Lima. **Studium**, on Larco 720, also has a wide selection. The **SAEC** has most South American guidebooks and a book exchange.

Money

In the centre of Lima: **Banco Wiese**, Jr Cusco 245; Interbanc, Jr de la Unión 499. Money changers in Jirón Ocoña. In Miraflores: **Interbanc** and **Banco de Crédito** on Av Larco, **Banco Weise** on Pardo and Diagonal. There are many money changers on the streets of Diagonal and Larco in Miraflores.

Communications

Post office The main post office is on the Plaza de Armas. In Miraflores there is one on Calle Petit Thours 5201.

Phone office You can use coins or phone cards in the Telefónica phone boxes found all over the city, for national or international calls. The central phone office is on Plaza San Martín, open daily 08.00–21.00.

Internet

Dragon Fans Calle Tarata 230, Miraflores. US$2 per hour. Internet phone also. Open 08.00–23.00, Sun 09.00–22.00.
Phantom Café Diagonal, Miraflores. Open 09.00–01.30.

Consulates and embassies

Argentina Pablo Bermúdez 143, Jesus María; tel: 4335709.
Bolivia Los Castaños 235, San Isidro; tel: 4228231.
Brazil José Pardo 850, Miraflores; tel: 4462635.
Chile Javier Prado Oeste 790, San Isidro; tel: 4407965.
Ecuador Las Palmeras 356, San Isidro; tel: 4424184.
France Arequipa 3415, San Isidro; tel: 4704968.
Germany Av Arequipa 4202, Miraflores; tel: 4457033.
Great Britain Plaza Washington (corner of Arequipa – 5th block); tel: 4335032.
Italy Av G Escobedo 298, Jesús María; tel: 4632727.
Japan Av San Felipe 356, Jesús María; tel: 4630000.
Spain Jorge Basadre 498, San Isidro; tel: 4705600.
United States Av Encalada, block 17, Monterrico; tel: 4343000; fax: 4343065.

WHAT TO SEE

City centre

In recent years a lot of effort has been put into doing up the centre of Lima. It is much more pleasant than it was and quite a few interesting buildings are worth seeing. The Plaza de Armas, the administrative and political centre of the city since it was founded, is dominated by the **Palacio del Gobierno** on the north side. This was Pizarro's Lima home and then home to subsequent viceroys of Peru. Today this is the presidential palace, home of Alberto Fujimori. You can watch the changing of the guard here at 11.45 each morning. The **City Hall**, **cathedral** and **archbishop's palace** are also around the Plaza de Armas. The 18th-century cathedral houses the remains of Francisco Pizarro and a museum of religious art (Open Mon–Fri 10.00–14.00–17.00, weekends 10.00–16.00). You'll see a statue of Pizarro on horseback in a corner of the square, a replica of one in his home town of Trujillo in Spain. The other principal squares in the centre of the city are **Plaza San Martín** and **Plaza Bolívar**. There are some interesting examples of 17th- and 18th-century colonial architecture with some typical façades and balconies: **Palacio de Torre Tagle**, which has intricately carved wooden balconies (Jr Ucayali), **Casa Pilatus** (Jr Ancash 390), **Casa de Oquendo** (Jr Conde de Superunda 298) and **Casa de la Riva** (Ica 426). **San Francisco Convent and Church**, a couple of blocks from the Plaza de Armas, is one of the most attractive religious buildings in Lima. It dates from the 16th century, although most of it had to be rebuilt after an earthquake in 1672. There is a series of underground crypts that served as Lima's cemetery until 1808, and it is believed that around 25,000 people are buried here. Guided tours available. Open Mon–Fri 09.30–18.00.

Museums

Museo del Oro (Gold Museum) Monterrico; tel: 4350791. Open daily 11.30–19.00. Large private collection, haphazardly arranged, but dazzling. US$5.
Museo de Arqueología, Antropología e Historia (Anthropology and Archaeology Museum) Plaza Bolívar, Pueblo Libre; tel: 4635070. Open Mon–Sat 09.00–18.00, Sun 10.00–17.00. Excellent displays of objects from prehispanic Peruvian civilisations. Includes the Tello Obelisk and Estela Raymondi from the site of Chavín de Huantar.

Museo de la Inquisición (Museum of the Inquisition). Junín 548; tel: 4270365. Open daily 09.00–18.00. Dungeon and torture chamber of the Spanish Inquisition from 1570 to 1813.
Museo de la Nación Javier Prado 2465; tel: 4769875. Open Tue–Fri 09.00–18.00, Sat 10.00–18.00. Modern museum with many scale models of sites in Peru.
Museo Larco Herrera Av Bolívar 1515, Pueblo Libre; tel: 4611312. Mon–Sat 09.00–18.00, Sun 09.00–13.00. Quite incredibly extensive archaeological exhibition, with thousands of ceramic pots of all shapes and sizes including a room full of erotic Moche ceramics.
Museo de Arte Paseo Colón 125; tel: 4234732. Tue–Sun 10.00–13.00 and 14.00–17.00. Artwork from Chavín times to the present day.

Coati

North of Lima

The North Coast

The north coast of Peru has a lot to offer if you have the time and energy to explore the area's myriad archaeological sites. The north coast was the setting for the development of many prehispanic cultures, including the Huaca Prieta civilisation, which is more than 5,000 years old, and the Cupisnique, more than 3,000 years old. The first culture to expand out from its core area was the Moche culture, which dominated the area from AD200 to AD900.

The lively colonial city of Trujillo or the nearby beach resort of Huanchaco are the best places to stay for exploratory forays to visit the Moche sites (Huaca del Sol, Huaca de La Luna), and also for Chan Chan, the vast adobe city of the Chimú culture. From Trujillo northwards is desert, interrupted by the cities of Chiclayo, Piura and Tumbes. Don't miss Lambayeque with the fascinating find of the Señor de Sipán, or the ruined city of Túcume. When you've had enough of archaeology, the warm waters of the Pacific are readily accessible at the many beach resorts all along the northern coast.

TRUJILLO

Telephone code 044

Trujillo is an interesting city to spend a few days in. The climate is good and the city is lively and fun. Its centre is of pastel-painted colonial buildings, very different from the other Peruvian cities. The city is ideally located for visiting the archaeological sites of Chan Chan and the *huacas* (temples) of the sun and the moon. It is also close to Huanchaco, the small fishing village where you can still see *totora* (reed fishing boats). Trujillo has two main festivals, the Marineras in the last week of January and the spring festival in September. They are both very popular with Peruvians and the city can get very busy at these times.

History

Following the Moche culture, the Chimú developed from AD1100 to AD1400. Their capital was Chan Chan, the largest adobe site in South America. The Chimú are also known for their advanced metalwork techniques, especially in gold, and their extensive network of aqueducts. They were conquered by the Incas in the 15th century. Under the Spanish the city of Trujillo was one of the most important in the viceroyalty. It was founded in 1534 and named by Diego de Almagro after Francisco Pizarro's home town in Spain. The Moche River valley was chosen because of the extensive irrigation networks already established by the Chimú people. The Spanish were able to plant sugarcane and wheat, which brought them enough wealth to build the many fine colonial mansions and churches in the city.

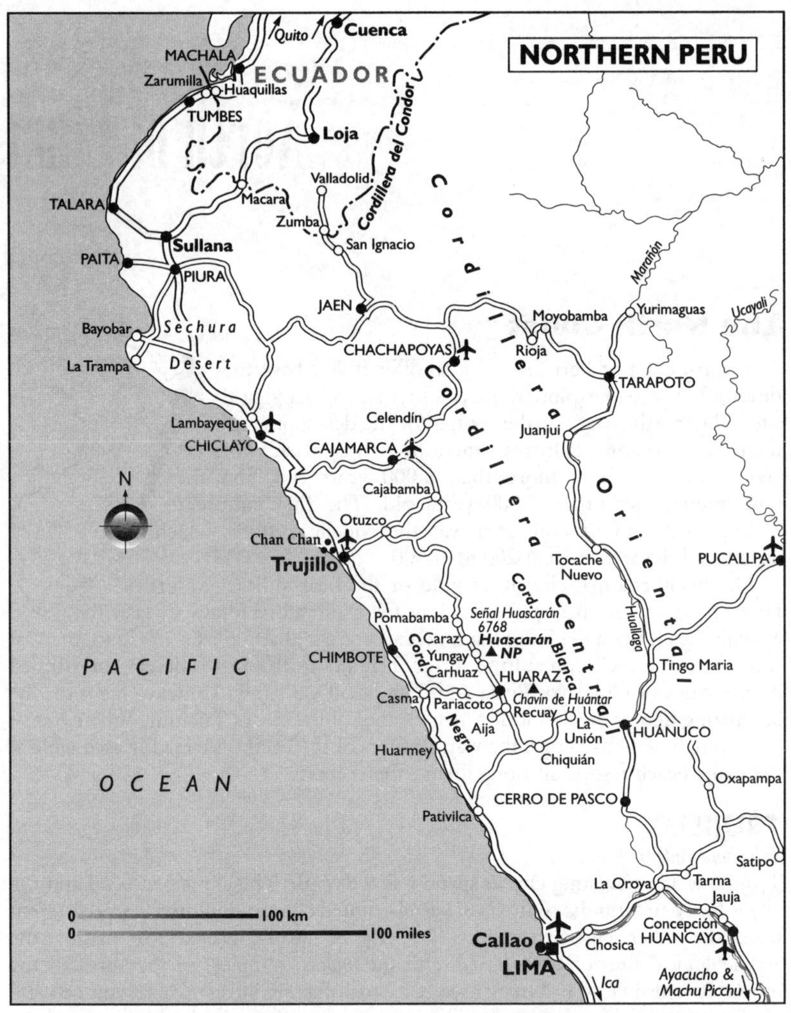

City walls were built to protect Trujillo from marauding pirates, and in 1619 a major earthquake destroyed much of the city, so it had to be rebuilt. Trujillo was the first city of the north to proclaim independence on December 29 1820. The aristocracy became leaders of the republic.

Getting there and away

By bus

Trujillo is well connected to the other cities along the coast. It is 560km to the north of Lima, and 209km from Chiclayo. Operators are: **Cruz del Sur**, Av Del Ejército 285 (to destinations on the Pan American and Huaraz); **Oltursa**, Av Del Ejército 342 (between Lima and Piura); **Tepsa**, Jirón Almagro 849 (destinations on the Pan American); **Comité**, 14 Av Moche 544 (to Huaraz). Opposite the stadium in Calle Mansiche there are several company offices with buses to Chiclayo and Cajamarca. Buses for Huanchaco go from Av España corner Av Industrial.

By plane

The airport is on the Huanchaco road a few kilometres from the city centre. Take a taxi or a Huanchaco bus and walk 500m.

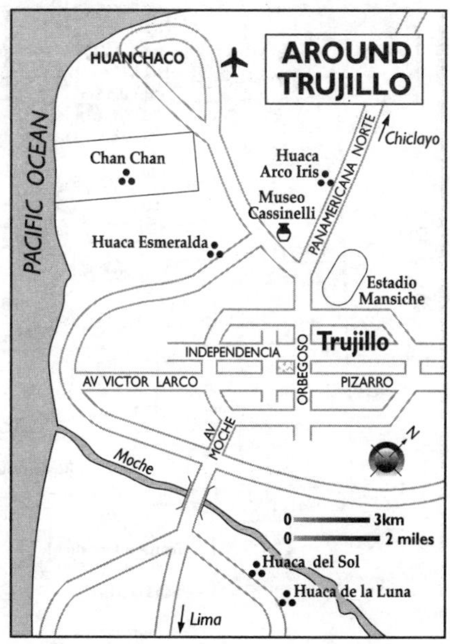

Where to stay and eat

The cheapest places include **Hostal Lima** (tel: 233569) and **Hostal Central** (tel: 246236) on Calle Ayacucho, but they are basic and don't have hot water.
Hotel Americano, Calle Pizarro 792; tel: 241361, is similarly cheap and basic, a huge place that often has school parties; good location.
Los Escudos Jr Orbegoso 676; tel: 255691. Colonial building with patio, nice rooms.
Hostal Recreo Estete 647; tel: 246991. Private bathrooms, TV.

Calle Pizarro has a couple of good places to eat:

Restaurante Romano and **Restaurante Asturias** do tasty food at a reasonable price.
There are several restaurants in **Plazuela del Recreo** and this is a popular place for sitting outside with a beer.
The most popular pub is right on the corner of the Plaza de Armas, **Las Tinajas**.

Practical information

Tourist office Av España 1800; tel/fax: 245794. Open Mon–Fri, 09.00–17.00. Or Calle Independencia 628.
Post office Jirón Independencia 286.
Telephone office Bolívar 658.
Money Banco Weiss, Jirón Pizarro 314; Banco de Crédito, Jirón Gamarra 562; Interbanc; Jirón Gamarra 471. Money exchange on the Plaza de Armas.
Airlines Aero Continente, Av España 305.

Travel agencies

Ama Tours Jirón Bolívar 535; tel: 2574141. Local excursions.
Condor Travel Jirón Pizarro 547; tel: 244658. Local excursions.
Guía Tours Jirón Independencia 519; tel: 234856. Experienced professional guides for local sites.

What to see

The streets between the Plaza de Armas and the Plazuela de Recreo are the centre of the colonial town.

Museo Arqueológico de la Universidad de Trujillo, Jirón Pizarro 349. Open Mon–Fri, 08.00–13.00. This is a good museum with examples of ceramics, textiles and metalwork from various prehispanic cultures.

Colección José Cassinelli is a fascinating, extensive private collection of ceramics, at the corner of Av Mansiche and Víctor Raúl Haya de la Torre (underneath a petrol station).

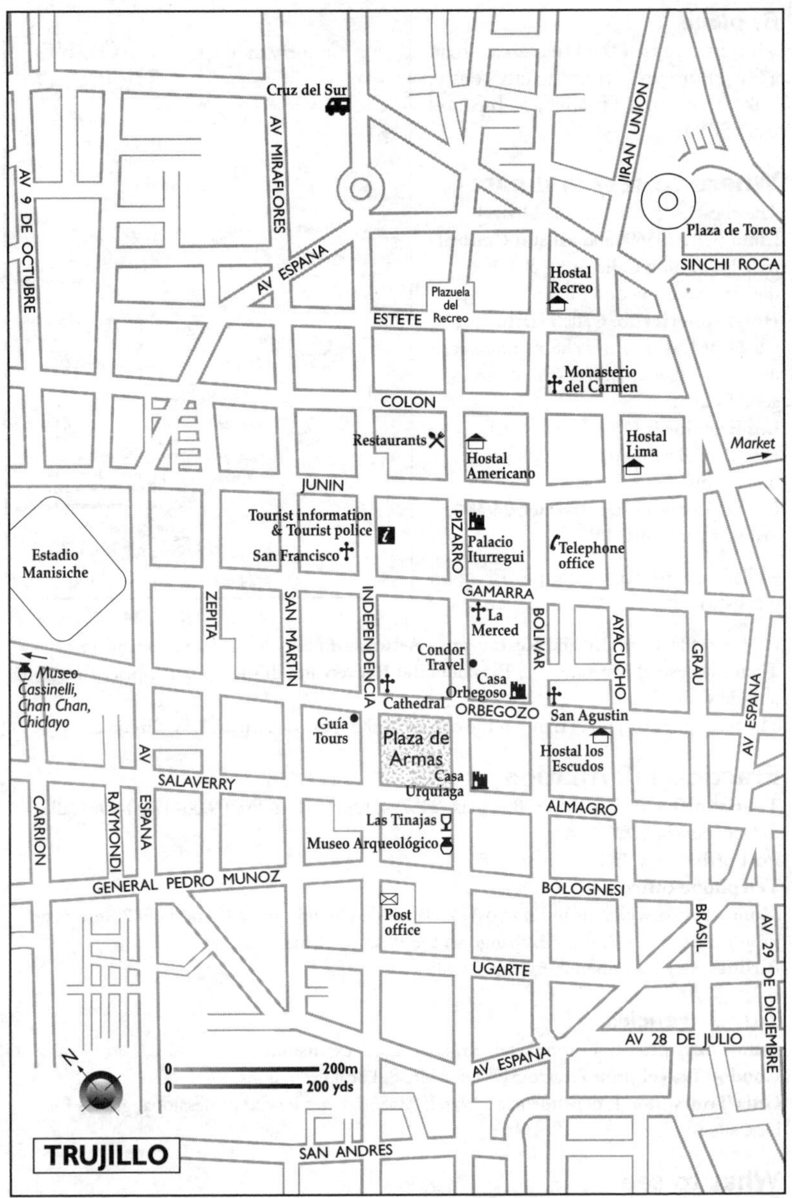

Churches

The **cathedral** is on the Plaza de Armas, and dates from 1666. It has some interesting paintings and religious sculpture. Open daily 06.00–21.00, closed lunchtime.

The **Monasterio del Carmen**, on the corner of Calle Colón and Bolívar, is one of the most beautiful buildings in the city. It was built in 1759 and boasts a fine collection of paintings and sculptures and a beautiful altar. **San Agustín** on Jirón

Mariscal de Orbegozo is a 17th-century church with a gold leaf altar and carved pulpit. Other churches you may want to visit are **San Francisco** on Calle Vallejo and **La Merced** on Jirón Francisco Pizarro.

Colonial houses

Because Trujillo was an important colonial city there are some impressive mansion houses which are interesting to look at if you like colonial architecture. It is usually best to visit these houses in the mornings as many close at midday. They include: **Palacio Iturregui** in Jirón Pizarro; **Casa del Mayorazgo**, between Calle Pizarro and Bolognesi; **Casa Urquiaga** and **Casa Bracamonte** in the Plaza de Armas (both open mornings); **Casa de la Emancipación** in Jirón Pizarro 610, where Torre Tagle formalised independence for the city in 1820 and was the seat of the first congress and palace of the government; **Casa Calonge** on Jirón Pizarro 446, now the Banco Central, a museum with Chimú and colonial objects; **Casa Orbegoso**, Jirón Orbegoso 553, open Mon–Sat 09.00–17.00. This impressive colonial house was once the home of Orbegoso who became the president of Peru in 1833.

Around the city

Chan Chan

This huge prehispanic city made of millions of adobe bricks is just a few kilometres from the centre of Trujillo. It was the capital of the Chimú culture. It covers an area of 20km^2 and probably had a population of more than 40,000 people. You need several hours to visit the site, and I recommend you go with a guide to get the most out of your visit. There are guides at the site, generally Spanish speaking. You can only visit a small area of the site as much of it is closed off in order to protect it.

The site, which was occupied from AD1000 to AD1470, consists of houses, storerooms, decorated walls, pathways and pyramidal temples. There were probably around 40,000 people living here at its peak. The city was built on the coast because of the dependency of the Chimú people on the sea: seabirds, fish and seaweed figure in their decorations. All levels of social class lived in the city, and three notably different complexities of architecture reflect the class of the inhabitants: popular, intermediate and monumental. Monumental is characterised by the nine palaces where the lords of the Chimú lived. There are large plazas and reservoirs, and the whole site is underlain by a labyrinth of aqueducts bringing water from great distances to this dry desert city. The only such palace of the nine in the city which is open to the public is Tschudi. Much of it is reconstructed – only 5% is original. Wandering around the palace will give you an insight into the way of life of the people that lived here.

Complejo Arqueológico El Brujo

In the Valley of Chicama there are three temples (*huacas*) of great historical importance, all built several thousand years ago: the Huaca Prieta, which is around 5,000 years old, the Huaca El Brujo and the Huaca Cao Viejo. Check with the tourist office about access, as permission to visit the sites may be needed.

Huaca del Sol and Huaca de la Luna

Just 5km south of the city of Trujillo next to the River Moche you will find two impressive Moche temples, the Huacas of the Sun and the Moon. Take a bus from Calle José Gálvez in Trujillo. The temples are at Cerro Blanco, the Moche culture's principal administrative and religious centre. The Huaca de la Luna is pyramidal and a stepped construction of multiple levels, which was once 50m tall.

It is a giant structure made of innumerable adobe bricks, imprinted with the mark of their makers, who probably worked in labour groups to construct this amazing temple. The construction of such huge temples was only possible because of the control over water and labour held by the Moche leaders. Unfortunately the ravages of natural disasters and human predation have left little of this city. The Huaca del Sol, which was even bigger than the moon temple, is not in good condition, and large sections were washed away when the Spanish diverted the River Moche in 1602 to erode the temple and find treasure.

THE SEÑOR DE SIPÁN

Sandra Araujo

Peru has always been a country with many interesting archaeological sites, not least of which is the north coastal area, a great centre of prehispanic cultures. In Peru's vast territory, international and national archaeologists compete to find the hidden treasures of history. However, the presence of abandoned, unprotected riches has attracted unscrupulous collectors and scavenging grave robbers, who have unearthed and removed invaluable objects, unwittingly disturbing many sources of information. Alerted by a major *saqueo* (robbery) at the beginning of 1987 a group of Peruvian archaeologists, led by Walter Alva, made one of the greatest archaeological discoveries of recent times in the deserts of the north coast of Peru. They found the Señor de Sipán.

Sipán

Sipán is the name of a small village, 26km southeast of the city of Chiclayo in the department of Lambayeque, 770km from Lima and 580km from the Ecuadorian border. Just 1km from this small village is the archaeological site where the Lord of Sipán was found, *Complejo Arqueológico de Sipán*. The site was named Sipán after the village, which means 'house of the moon' in the Muchik language of the Mochica people.

The Moche culture

The Moche culture flourished in the north coastal area between the first and eighth centuries. The Moche empire was not geographically extensive, only 550km from the Piura Valley in the north to the Huarmey Valley in the south, and 50–80km from the eastern edges in the Andes to the sea shore of the Pacific.

Before the Moches, minor regional cultures had occupied this coastal area, known for their architectural achievements, distinctive ceramics and advanced metalwork. The Moche consolidated the skills and characteristics of their forebears and added their own special touches, becoming one of the most distinctive of all prehispanic cultures. They were a dynamic and expressive culture, building 40 defensive fortifications in the Santa Valley alone, constructing the largest adobe building in the continent, making thousands upon thousands of creatively decorated ceramic pots, and building extensive irrigation canals.

Physical characteristics of the Moche people

Archaeological studies of the bones of the Moche people indicate that they

CHICLAYO

Telephone code 074

Chiclayo is the capital of the department of Lambayeque, approximately 700km north of Lima, 209km north of Trujillo and 270km south of Piura. It is one of Peru's largest cities with a population of over 600,000. A thriving commercial centre, Chiclayo itself doesn't have a lot to offer the passing tourist, but is a good place to base yourself for a couple of days while visiting the archaeological and historical gems of Lambayeque (12km north), Túcume, Sicán and Sipán.

were of Asiatic or Oceanic origin. Their faces usually had prominent cheekbones, but there were also quite angular faces with short noses and oblique eyes, and faces dominated by long pointy noses, wide foreheads, thin lips and large eyes. Generally the Mochica were of short stature with wide chests, short thick arms and short strong legs.

Food

The Moche people had a diet of seafood, and also farmed maize and domestic animals such as birds, guinea pigs and llamas. Maize formed 60% of the diet, prepared in various ways, including the drink *chicha*, made from fermented maize and rather like a very yeasty beer. Maize is still widely consumed in all of Peru in many of the same dishes, over a thousand years later.

Clothes

Cotton was grown for the weaving of clothes, and is still a major crop in northern coastal areas. Vicuña and llama wool were also used. To colour the wool and cotton, natural organic and mineral dyes were used: cochinilla and cinabrio for reds, seashells for purples, copiapita for bright orange, and from plant sources (taya, nogal and quinua) shades of brown and black.

The style and elegance of dress depended on social class, but generally men wore tunics with ornate decoration while the women wore simpler less decorated clothing. The way the women wore their hair indicated their marital status: if married, plaits went behind, and if they were single, plaits were worn to the front. This is still the case today.

Architecture

The building of the great pyramids was done for political, religious and military reasons, and they also provided a place for the elite to live, with the rest of the population spread in the surrounding area. The main building material used was adobe bricks, a sort of mud mixture with clay and ground-up shells. The bricks were made by the villagers and given as a tribute for the construction of the temples of their gods.

Religion

The main gods of the Moche people were the sun, the moon and the sea. Ceremonies were conducted to venerate the gods, often involving offerings and sometimes sacrifices. There is evidence to suggest that human sacrifices were made to the gods, and it is thought this was seen as an honour by the victim. Sacrifice and death was just one step into the next life, so death was seen as a privilege.

THE SEÑOR DE SIPÁN

Sandra Araujo

The excavation

From the tomb of the Señor de Sipán, and the great testimony it left to life 1,700 years ago, archaeologists have been trying to piece together clues to the complex Moche culture. When the excavation first began the surface of the ground around the tomb was littered with fragments of jugs, a crown and a mask. This encouraged the archaeologists and they continued to excavate, finding 1,137 ceramic vases containing the remains of maize, *chicha* and dried meat. This was an indication of something important lying below, and soon the tomb itself was found, bordered by adobe bricks. The first person to be found was a soldier, carrying a shield and wearing a gold helmet. A few centimetres further down were wooden supports made from carob (*algorrobo*) wood, a typical tree in the north of Peru, placed parallel to each other to form a roof, below which lay the tomb itself. Cleaning away the accumulated layers of dirt, archaeologists came upon the first wooden coffins found in American archaeology.

As the rotting trunks were removed, a small figure of gold and turquoise shone up at them, one of the most beautiful of the objects found. They continued to excavate, finding many more amazing ornaments, and finally the deteriorated body of the Señor de Sipán, which can now be seen in the Museo Brüning in Lambayeque.

The Señor de Sipán

Thanks to the analysis by John Verano, physical anthropologist at the Smithsonian Institute, we know that the Señor de Sipán died at between 35 and 45 years old. There are no indications of a violent death, but it is possible that he was afflicted by an epidemic that may have affected the whole coastal region in AD250–350, caused by the famine and drought following an El Niño weather

Getting there and away

By road

Chiclayo doesn't have a central bus station, but most companies have bus depots on Av Bolognesi.

Cruz del Sur Av Bolognesi 751; tel: 242164. Regular departures for Lima, Piura, Tumbes and Trujillo.
Civa Av Bolognesi 757; tel: 242488. Departures for Lima, Jaén, Pedro Ruiz and Chachapoyas.
El Cumbe Av José Quiñones 425; tel: 231454. Departures for Cajamarca and Jaén.
Vulcano Av Bolognesi 638; tel: 233497. Departures for Trujillo, Piura, Cajamarca and Lima.
The coast **minibuses** leave from Calle Vicente de la Vega or 7 de Enero corner Amazonas.
Buses to Lambayeque leave from Calle San José every 20–30 minutes.
Buses to Túcume leave from Av Angamos every 20–30 minutes.

By air

The airport is 2km to the southeast of the centre on Av Bolognesi. There are daily flights to Lima, and several a week to Piura, Tarapoto, Tumbes and Iquitos.

phenomenon. The Señor de Sipán was 166cm tall, which was probably more than average for that time. He was not a muscular man, indicating that he did not perform physical work. He had a small flat area on the top of his skull, caused by the practice of the time of placing young children in short wooden cots. His teeth were in good condition, with little wear, indicating a diet of soft foods, carefully selected to suit him, as his status dictated.

The tomb

The Señor de Sipán was buried in the central part of the tomb suurounded by large pieces of gold, silver, copper, and gold-plated objects, to take with him into the next life. He took what he thought he would need, as well as the objects, and eight people were found entombed with him. Next to him, on the left side, was a standard bearer, who had by his side a dog, thought to be the guide to show the way into the next life. On the Señor's right lay the Jefe Militar (military chief), armed and with one foot amputated. This symbolised immobility in the next life. At the head of the Señor there were two women, in coffins, one on top of the other. They were possibly concubines or servants. At the foot there was another woman wearing a copper crown, who may have been the principal wife. There was a child of between eight and ten years old in the tomb, probably a symbol of purity and regeneration. The young soldier in the tomb, the guardian or watchman, also had his feet amputated. The eighth person was found in a seated position. Around the *cámara* were five niches which contained items of food.

All of the bodies were found approximately 5m underground, and the Señor de Sipán was aligned with his right side towards the rising sun, and his left side towards the setting sun. The Moche culture, in accordance with many other ancient cultures, believed strongly in the dual forces of nature, good and bad, day and night, sun and moon, man and woman. Many Moche ornaments are made in gold and silver, also representing this duality.

Where to stay and eat

Plaza de Armas and Calle Pedro Ruiz have several hotels.

Hotel Lido Calle Elias Aguirre. US$4 per person. Reasonable budget hotel.
Hotel Royal San José 787, on the plaza; tel: 233421. US$8 double room with bath. Good budget option, central.
Hotel Sol Calle Elias Aguirre 119; tel: 232120. US$18–25. Opposite the post office, safe, clean, hot water, restaurant, pool and garage.
Café D'Kaly, San José 728, has been recommended for lunches.
The chain **Las Tinajas**, Calle Elias Aguirre 957, 139 and several others, are recommended for good Peruvian food.

Practical information

Tourist office on the plaza is very helpful with good information on the sites and how to get to them.
Airlines Aero Continente, Plaza de Armas; tel: 209916.
Money Try Av Balta or the Parque Central for banks. For changing cash money changers are usually on Av Balta corner Elías Aguirre.
Indiana Tours Calle Colón 556. Very helpful specialists in adventure travel and tours of

the local sites. English speaking guides, US$100 between four for a one-day tour including entrance fees.

What to see

The **Mercado Modelo**, Calle Arica, is well worth a visit to see the many plants and pieces of animal used in witchcraft or *brujería*, which is particularly prominent in northern Peru.

A visit to the **Museo Brüning** in Lambayeque, approximately 12km from Chiclayo is highly recommended to see the contents of the tomb of the Señor de Sipán. Take a minibus (*combi*) from the bus stop in Chiclayo, on Calle San José near Plaza Aguirre. Open daily 0900–18.00 (US$1.50).

Just north of Chiclayo is the site of an archaeological complex known as Valle de las Pirámides (Valley of the Pyramids) or the Pyramids of Túcume. There is evidence that several successive pre-Inca culturally advanced civilisations inhabited this area. The most impressive pyramids can be seen well from the top of Cerro La Raya, a small hill at the heart of South America's largest group of pyramids. The site is open daily 08.30–16.30 (US$1.50), there are frequent minibuses from Chiclayo to the plaza of Túcume, a tiny village on the Pan American highway (1 hr), and further buses from there to the site (2km).

Santa Rosa and **Pimentel** are interesting coastal towns only a short bus ride from Chiclayo. Pimentel (14km) is popular with Chiclayo residents in the summer months and quiet the rest of the year. It is the most resort-like with a nice beach, modern buildings and good restaurants. Santa Rosa is a fishing village where you can still see *totora* or reed boats. **Monsefú**, where you can stop off on the way back, is famous for its craft work, baskets, carved wood, and straw hats.

PIURA

Piura has a dry tropical climate with an average annual temperature of 24°C. It is a city of 280,000 inhabitants set in the middle of the driest part of Peru, the Sechura desert (5,240km^2). The city is quiet with several colonial buildings in the centre. It lies at the centre of a region rich in mineral reserves: nearby is the petrochemical complex at Talara. The Pacific fishing off Piura has broken world records for black marlin and swordfish, and surfers also are attracted to the warm waters of northern Peru. Within easy reach of Piura there are some good beaches, which are becoming more and more popular with national tourists. Around Piura some of the best cotton in the world is grown, and there is also rice and fruit production.

History

The most important culture of the Piura area was called Vicus, known for its high quality metalwork and ceramics. In 1532 Francisco Pizarro arrived here on his way

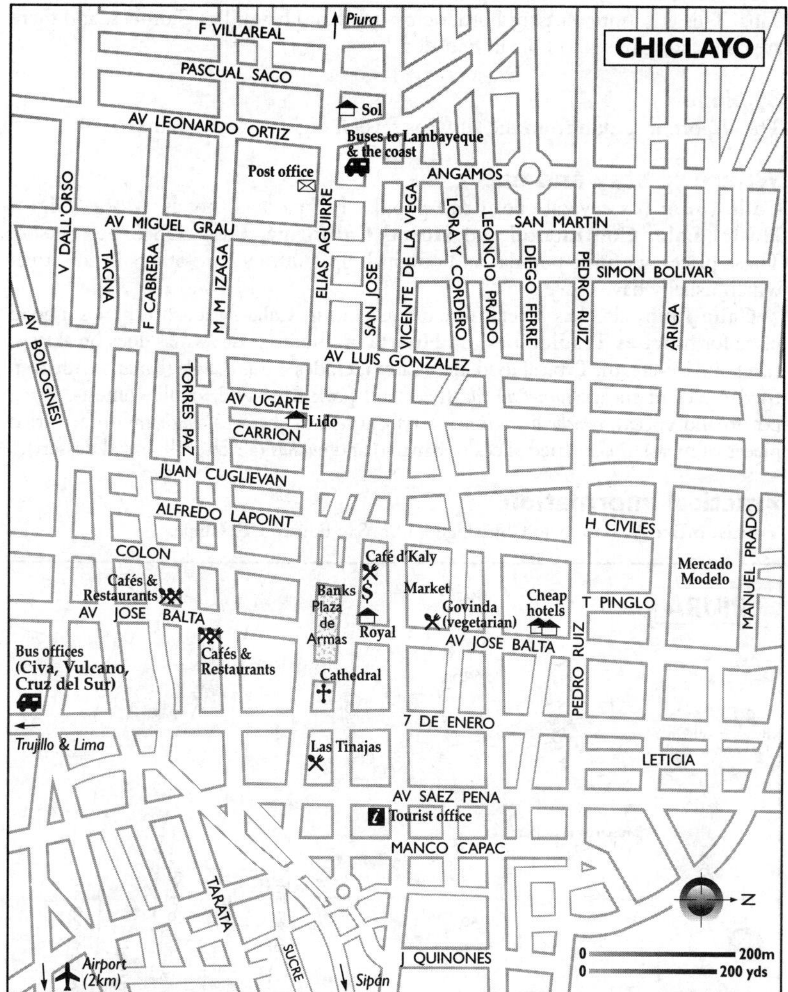

south from Tumbes. He founded a city, 40km north of Piura today, and gave it the name of San Miguel de Piura. Some of the conquistadors remained there while the others continued southwards. Forty years later the residents of the settlement decided to move somewhere less inhospitable, and resettled by the sea in what today is Paita. However, they were attacked by pirates so had to move again, this time to the present-day location of Piura, naming the city San Miguel de Piura del Villar. Miguel Graú, hero of the Pacific War with Chile, was born in Piura, and you can visit his house which is now a museum.

Getting there and away

By bus

Piura is 16 hours by bus from Lima along the Pan American highway (about 1,000km), 280km south of Tumbes, 210km north of Chiclayo and 420km north of Trujillo. It is about three hours from the Ecuadorian border, via Sullana and La

Tina. This is a more pleasant border crossing than Huaquillas–Tumbes, and there are connecting buses to Loja in Ecuador.

By plane

The airport, just 2km from the city, has several flights a day to Lima.

Where to stay and eat

Calle Junín has several cheap and popular backpackers' hotels, **Moon Night**, **Hostal Lalo**, **Continental** and **Hostal California**. From US$5 per person. These places are quite popular and often fill up, but there are others in the street which usually have space.

Calle Junín also has several restaurants, and in Calle Ayacucho there's a good place for fish, **Las Tradiciones**. **La Huerta** on the Plaza de Armas does breakfasts, cakes and ice-cream. Typical food in this area includes *seco de chavelo* (banana with deep fried pieces of meat); *carne aliñada* (beef and pork fried with chillis, onions, sweet potato and yucca); *cebiche de cachema*, a typical fish of the area; *chicharrón* (deep fried pieces of meat); *chifles* (fried slices of banana) and *natillas* (a rich milk based dessert).

Practical information

Tourist office Av Fortunato Chirichigno, Urb. San Eduardo, El Chipe.

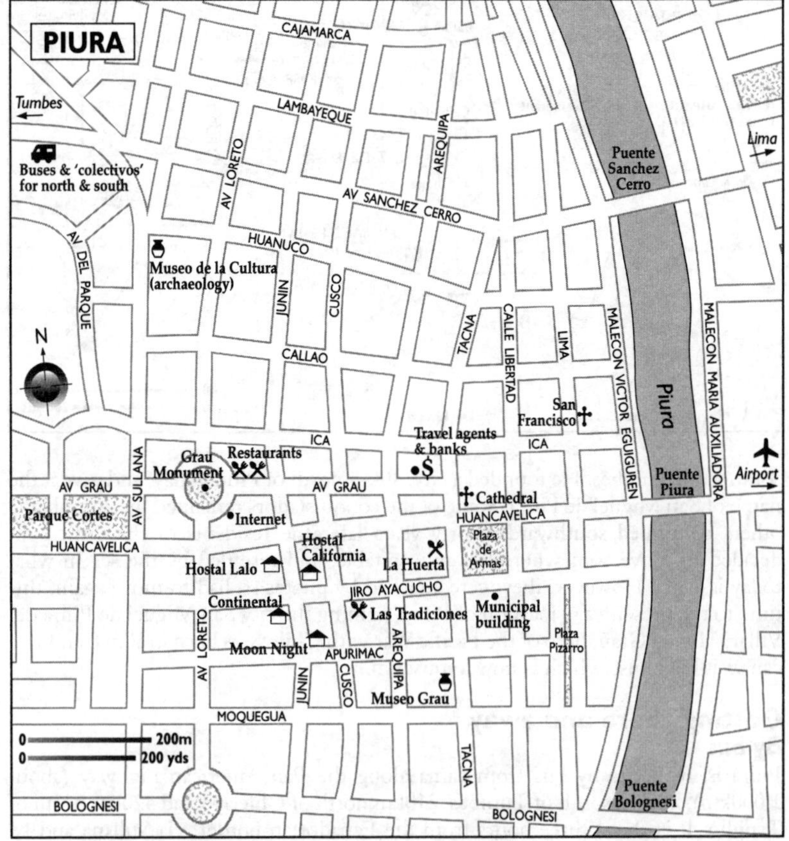

What to see

The **cathedral**, on the shady and peaceful Plaza de Armas, was built in 1588, and has a collection of paintings by Ignacio Merino, a 19th-century local painter. **San Francisco** church is the oldest in the city and is where independence for Piura was proclaimed in 1821. The **Archaeology Museum**, Av Sullana corner of Jirón Huánuco, contains a collection of ceramics and other objects from the Vicus culture; and the **Casa Museo del Almirante Miguel Graú** on Jirón Tacna, the birthplace of Miguel Graú, is now a museum.

Around the city

Catacaos (10km) is a small village of traditional crafts, weavings, gold and silver work, and also for leather and wood objects and Panama hats. You can see and buy this craftwork in Calle Comercio. There are several good places for food too at the local Picanterías. Take a minibus from Plaza Pizarro in Piura.

In the highlands of the province of Huancabamba, 214km from Piura at 1,953m, is **Las Huaringas**, a series of small mineral rich lakes. This is considered to be the capital of *brujería* (witchcraft) in Peru.

Vicus is the centre of the Vicus culture, one of the oldest of the Peruvian coast. It is 56km southeast of Piura on the Pan American highway.

Cabo Blanco is famous for the size of *merlin negro* fished here. The largest was fished in 1952, weighing 752kg. Ernest Hemingway used to visit for the fishing. **Paita** is the main port of Piura (57km), with nearby beaches, such as Colán just to the north of town. It's an interesting place to visit from Piura, with basic accommodation. To the north of Piura there are great beaches of white sand, many are very popular with surfers. Other good beaches are: **Laguna San Pedro**, 55km south of Piura (near Sechura), very attractive, with many flamingos and herons – you can camp but take all supplies; **Laguna San Pablo**, a long sandy beach, 50km from Piura; and **Matacaballo**, 67km from Piura a calm sandy beach. 200km to the north of Piura is **Punta Sal**, a resort becoming increasingly popular with tourists from Lima.

TUMBES

Telephone code 074

Tumbes is set in the wide green valley of the Tumbes River. It is becoming increasingly popular with Peruvian tourists for its warm waters and white sandy beaches. The weather is generally sunny all year round, with summer temperatures of around 30°C and winter temperatures of 20°C. The town itself is not very inspiring, although the Plaza de Armas is quite pleasant.

In pre-colonial days there was a flourishing population of hunters, farmers and traders in the Tumbes area. They were seafaring people who traded the highly prized pink shell of the *Spondylus princeps*. The port of La Leña was Francisco Pizzaros's entry point into Peru in 1532.

Getting there and away

By bus

Tumbes is on the Pan American highway and connections to the north and south are good. Buses to Lima take 22 hours to cover the 1,320km. There is no central bus station, most buses go from Calle Tumbes. *Colectivos* (minibuses) go from Calle San Martín.

Border crossing to Ecuador

The border with Ecuador is just 26km from Tumbes at Aguas Verdes. This is not the best place to cross the border, as so many people hassle you – kids, taxi drivers

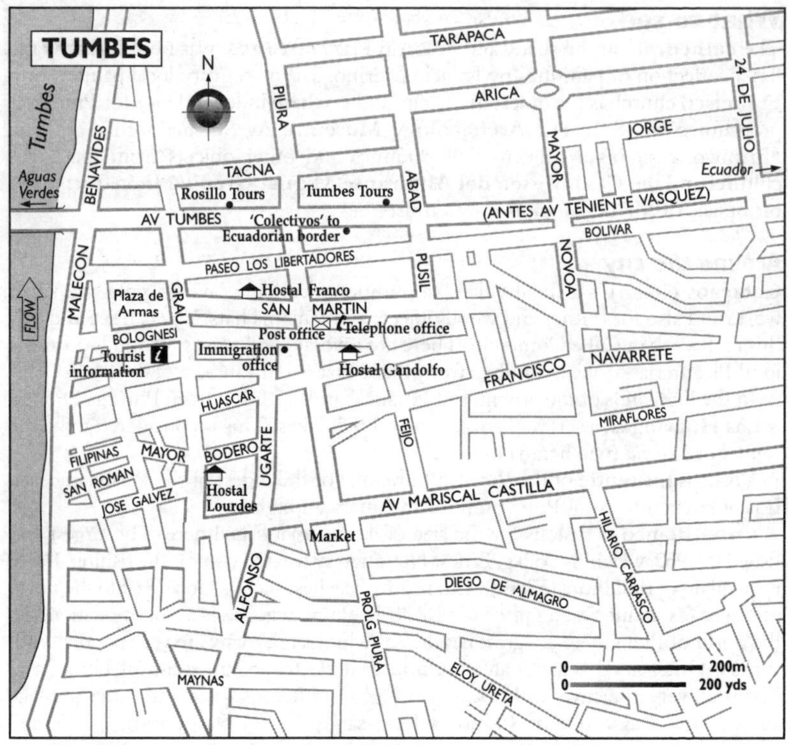

and money changers. To reach the Ecuadorian border take a shared taxi for US$2 per person or a minibus. You then go through the immigration office, continue 1km to the bridge over the River Zarumilla at the border and walk across into Ecuador. From the bridge on the Ecuadorian side it is 3km to the immigration office at Huaquillas, where there are numerous taxis waiting to take you. You can change money here at the border, but to avoid being ripped off make sure you know the exchange rate beforehand.

By plane

The airport is 15km from the city.

Where to stay and eat

Hostal Gandolfo Calle Bolognesi 420; tel: 522869. US$4–6 shared bath. Probably the cheapest but very basic.

Hostal Franco Calle San Martín just off the Plaza; tel: 525295. From US$6 per person; this is a bit better.

Hostal Lourdes Mayor Bodero 118; tel: 522126. From US$10. Cafeteria, private bath, TV, fan.

The Plaza de Armas has several reasonable restaurants.

Practical information

Tourist office Centro Civico José Jiménez, 2nd floor, Plaza de Armas; tel: 524940.

Post office and **phone office** are on Paseo de La Concordia.

Travel agencies Tumbes Tours, Av Tumbes Norte 341; tel: 522481, organise local excursions. Manglares Tours and Rosillo Tours, also on Av Tumbes Norte, sell flight tickets and also offer day trips.

What to see

The most popular beaches are Puerto Pizarro to the north of the city, and Playa Murmova, Caleta la Cruz, Puerto Loco, Santa Rosa and Zorritos to the south of the city. Punta Sal still further to the south is considered the best beach. Local buses go to these places from the market area.

The department of Tumbes is an ecologically important area for its forests, which stretch from the sea as far inland as 100–150km. The **national park of Cerros de Amotape** protects the dry equatorial forest of northern Peru. These forests are well adapted to high temperatures and severe lack of water. Typical trees of this forest are the carob and the ceibo or *palo borracho*, a strange-looking tree with a bulging trunk, in which it accumulates water. The wildlife found in the forests is surprisingly diverse: there are species from dry areas, tropical forests and mountainous areas, including parakeets, parrots, white-necked squirrels, white-winged guan, the grey deer and the coastal fox. The **tropical mangrove forest** of the Pacific coast is the only mangrove forest in Peru. It consists primarily of four species of mangrove, and is rich in aquatic life, alligators and waterbirds. This is the wettest part of the Peruvian coastline and many of the animals have come from the Amazon area or the dry equatorial forest mentioned above. It supplies water to the cities and agricultural areas along the coast and is a reserved zone. There are boats from Puerto Pizarro up the River Tumbes.

The Cordillera del Condor, although not a high mountain range, stretches 250km southwest to northeast along the Peruvian and Ecuadorian frontier. Because of the remoteness and isolation of this area it is extremely species rich and contains many unknown plants and animals. This mountain range cuts through the plateau known as Cerro Machinaza, which forms the headwater for the Cenepa and Comainas rivers flowing into Peru and the Coangos River, which flows into Ecuador.

The Northern Highlands

CAJAMARCA

Telephone code 044

Cajamarca is a colonial town similar in many ways to Cusco. The centre has attractive colonial buildings with red roofs, wooden balconies and white painted façades. The plaza, with the imposing San Francisco Cathedral, is well cared for and a relaxing place to sit and watch life go by. It's lively in the evenings with lots of people wandering around and plenty of shops, bars and restaurants.

History

Although this area has a long history of settlement, it is best known historically as the setting for one of the most momentous events in Peru's history, the beginning of the end for the Incas. It was here that Atahualpa was captured and put to death, in July 1533, at the hands of the Spanish conquistador Francisco Pizarro. Before Inca occupation there is evidence of early settlers from around 1,500BC. Cave paintings in the Cumbemayo area date from this period and the Lanzón culture (500–200BC) was a strong regional tribe with its political, economic and religious centre at a temple near Cajamarca. The Chavín influence is evident in the stonework from this time. A regional culture, known as the Cajamarca culture,

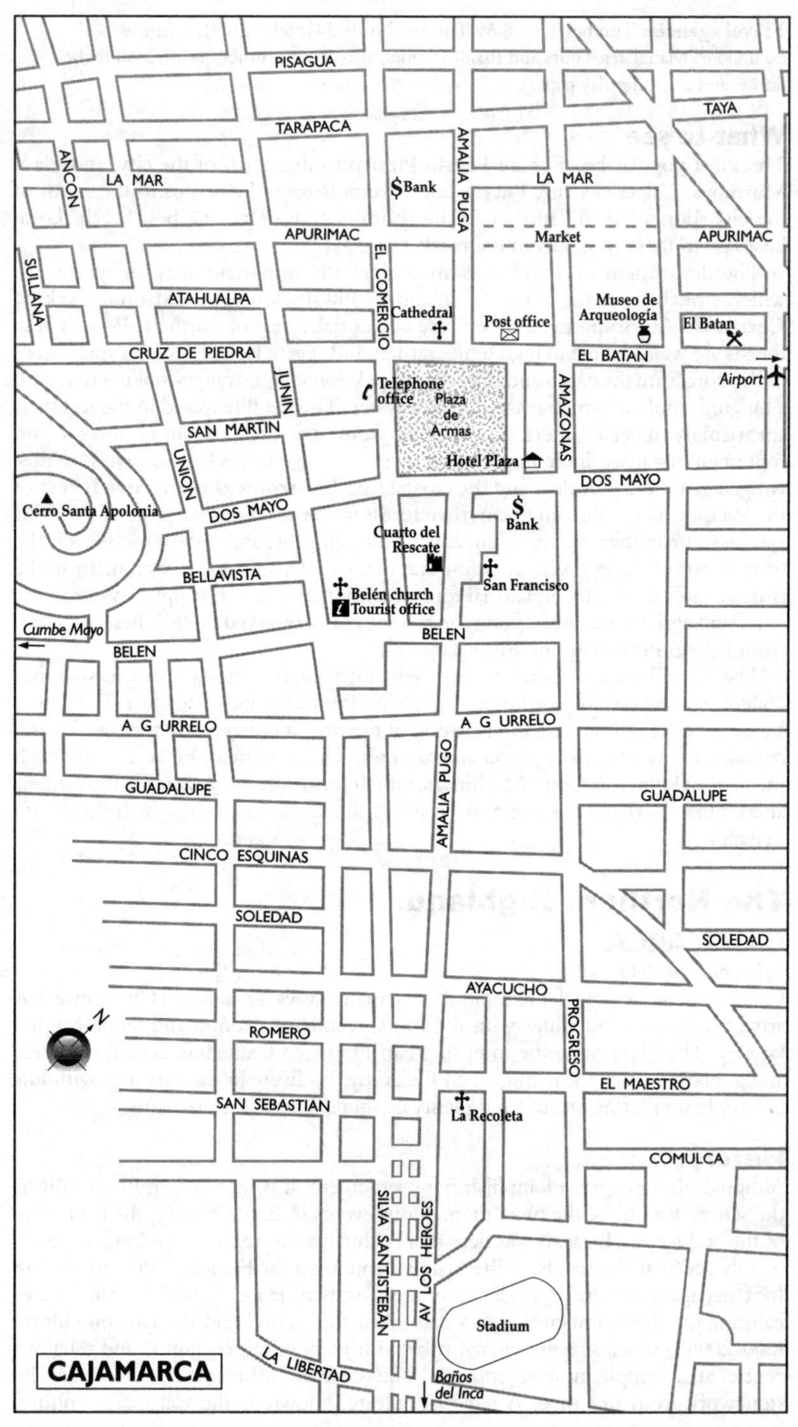

PISAGUA
TARAPACA
TAYA
ANCON
LA MAR
LA MAR
AMALIA PUGA
$Bank
APURIMAC
EL COMERCIO
Market
APURIMAC
SULLANA
ATAHUALPA
Cathedral
Post office
Museo de Arqueología
El Batan
CRUZ DE PIEDRA
JUNIN
EL BATAN
Airport
Telephone office
Plaza de Armas
AMAZONAS
SAN MARTIN
UNION
Hotel Plaza
DOS MAYO
Cerro Santa Apolonia
DOS MAYO
Bank
Cuarto del Rescate
BELLAVISTA
San Francisco
Belén church
Tourist office
Cumbe Mayo
BELEN
BELEN
A G URRELO
A G URRELO
AMALIA PUGO
GUADALUPE
GUADALUPE
CINCO ESQUINAS
SOLEDAD
SOLEDAD
AYACUCHO
PROGRESO
ROMERO
EL MAESTRO
SAN SEBASTIAN
La Recoleta
COMULCA
SILVA SANTISTEBAN
AV LOS HEROES
Stadium
CAJAMARCA
LA LIBERTAD
Baños del Inca

began to develop around 200BC and existed in the valley until the 15th century, when the Incas arrived. Although Huari influence is evident during this time it is not known to what extent the Huaris dominated this regional tribe. Many ceramics and the Ventanillas de Otuzco (see page 202) have been left by the Cajamarca culture. Cajamarca is currently a rich agricultural area producing huge quantities of milk and dairy products for the national market. The largest gold mine in Peru is also near the city.

Getting there and away

By bus

There are frequent services to Lima (22 hrs, 856km, US$11) – for the best views sit on the right; also to Trujillo (295km) and Chiclayo (260km). For Chachapoyas (336km) you have to go first to Celendín or via Chiclayo. From Cajamarca to Celendín (5 hrs, US$3). Most bus companies have their offices in Calle Ayacucho: for Lima, Chiclayo or Trujillo try **Atahualpa**, **Sudamericano**, **Mercurio** or **Vulcano**, and for Celendín and Cajabamba try **Palacios**.

By air

Aero Condor fly several times a week from Lima. Calle Dos de Mayo 323; tel: 922813.

Where to stay

Hostal Sucre Calle Amalia Puga 815. Cheap, backpackers' hostel.

Hostal Prado Calle La Lar 582. US$3 per person, shared bath.

Hostal Plaza On the plaza. US$12 for double with small bathroom. Noisy, rambling building with character.

Hostal Yusovi Calle Amazonas 637; tel: 922920. One block from the Plaza de Armas. US$6 double, clean and friendly. Good views from the roof.

Casa Blanca Calle Dos de Mayo 446; tel: 822141. US$20 double with bath.

Hotel Cajamarca Calle Dos de Mayo; tel: 822532. US$25 double with bath.

Where to eat

Casa Blanca, **Restaurant Grand Plaza**, **Los Faroles** and **Los Altos de Hatuchay** on Jirón Dos de Mayo are good, as is **Salas** on the Plaza. There are a couple of good, local restaurants on Calle Amazonas; at 616 is **La Casita del Cuy**. For an arty atmosphere **El Batán**, Jirón Batán 369, is a gallery, meeting place, restaurant etc. The **market** on Calle Amazonas has an excellent selection of fresh fruit, vegetables and bread. Cajamarca produces huge amounts of cheese and honey, *manjar blanca* (sweet caramel paste for putting in cakes or on bread) and corn biscuits (*galletas de maíz*). Typical dishes include *sopa verde*, a soup made from eggs, cheese and herbs, *humitas*, hot pasties of ground maize and *cuy*, guinea pig.

Entertainment

For nightlife at weekends and holidays, try **Usha Usha**, Jirón Cruz de Piedra, **Éxodus** in the Cajamarca Turistas Hotel on the Plaza, **Las Cascadas**, Pasaje Soledad, **Up and Down**, Jirón Tarapacá 890, and **La Casita** on the Plaza de Armas.

Practical information

Tourist office In the Belén complex; tel: 822997; fax: 822903. Open Mon–Fri 09.00–13.30 and 16.00–18.00.

Tourist police Plaza Amalia Puga corner Ayacucho.

Post office Plaza de Armas.

Phone office On the Plaza de Armas.
Money Banco de Crédito, Jirón del Comercio 679. Interbanc, Plaza de Armas. Banco Continental Tarapacá 725. Try the Plaza de Armas for money changers too.

Travel agencies

Atahualpa Inca Tours Jirón Amazonas 760; tel: 927014. Local tours and also tours of several days to Kuélap.
Aventuras Cajamarca Jirón Dos de Mayo 446, Plaze de Armas; tel: 922141. Local and longer tours including treks.
Cumbemayo Tours Plaza de Armas, for local day tours.
Inca Bath Tour Company Jirón Puga 653; tel: 921828. Recommended for local tours.

What to see

The **Baños del Inca** are communal or private pools, of varying standard, but generally clean and fun. US$1.50 entrance. Take a minibus from Plaza de Armas.

The **Cumbemayo forest of stones (*bosque de piedras*) 'Los Frailones'** are best visited on a short tour from Cajamarca (3–4 hrs, US$5). This is an amazing rock outcrop dramatically located high above the town on the *ichu* (grass) covered windy moorland). The rocks have been shaped by erosion into weird contorted figures. There are also some pre-Inca remains, including a very impressive aqueduct carved out of the stone and cave paintings. The aqueduct is nearly 8km long, half of which is carved from solid rock. The canal carries water from the Pacific side to the Atlantic side of the mountains. The 3–4-day walk from Cumbemayo to the village of San Pablo is a lovely trek, through cultivated valleys and small adobe villages, surrounded by lofty mountains – well worth it if you have the time and inclination. (See Bradt guide to *Backpacking and Trekking in Peru and Bolivia*.)

You can walk or take a bus or taxi to **Ventanillas de Otuzco**, a pre-Inca funerary site 7km from the city. There are dozens of niches thought to have been for burying mummies, carved out of the solid rock. It is possible to walk from here along the riverbank to the Baños del Inca (6km). Ask the site warden for details.

Cuarto del Rescate is right in the centre of the city on Calle Amalia Puga. This is the room where Atahualpa was held hostage while gold was collected for a ransom. Open except Tues 09.00–12.00 and 15.00–17.00. The only Inca building in the city, it has been restored and is a popular spot for national and international tourists.

Colonial buildings

Cajamarca has a number of colonial houses and churches which dominate the central part of the city. They are open to the public and worth looking at. The complex of Belén includes the 17th-century church with a richly decorated façade, the 18th-century men and women's hospitals, archaeology museum and also the *Instituto Nacional de Cultura*. Open except Tues 09.00–12.00 and 15.00–17.00. Other religious buildings include the 17th-century church and convent of **La Recoleta**,

17th-century church, convent and catacombs of **San Francisco** and the 18th-century cathedral of **Santa Catalina**. Santa Catalina stands on the northeast side of the Plaza de Armas, an imposing building built in part with stones from Inca temples, and a volcanic rock façade. There is a valuable collection of paintings in the church and some quite oddly decorated columns. There are dozens of colonial **doorways** throughout the city, concentrated in the central streets of Dos de Mayo, Bellavista, Junín, Apurímac, José Galvez and Amalia Puga.

Crafts

Cajamarca is well known for its craft work in wool, leather, wood, clay, straw and stone. Typical objects include ponchos, all sorts of crochet work, leather bags, belts and wallets, baskets and ceramics.

Festivals

There are dozens of festivals in the Cajamarca area, the most important in Cajamarca itself being carnival in February, Easter week and Corpus Christi in May or June. It's worth trying to time your visit to coincide with one of these times, although you should book accommodation in advance. They are a great opportunity to see local typical dances and to join in the partying.

CHACHAPOYAS

Telephone code 074

Chachapoyas is the capital of the department of Amazonas, in the northeast of Peru. It is a remote area of subtropical valleys, halfway down the eastern slopes of the Andes with vegetation typical of *ceja de selva* ('eyebrow of the jungle'). The jungle is impenetrable, dense with low trees, bromeliads, bamboos, orchids and mosses. Despite its remoteness Chachapoyas is becoming increasingly popular with backpackers, who come to see the archaeological remains of Kuélap from the prehispanic Chachapoya culture which managed to survive in such apparently unsuitable surroundings. Be prepared for long hard journeys to get there, but a friendly welcome, amazing archaeological sites and a botanical paradise.

History

Amazonas was the seat of the Chachapoya culture until it later became a part of the Inca Empire under Inca Túpac Yupanqui, and was then conquered by the Spanish. The city of Chachapoyas was officially founded by Alonso de Alvarado in 1538 and was the centre for the Spanish incursions into the jungle.

The Chachapoya culture developed in this area around AD800. There are numerous sites left by this culture that give some indication of the way they lived. There is evidence that they lived in villages of up to several hundred people, in circular houses. Archaeologists have found tombs on inaccessible clifftops, and ancient agricultural terraces. The Chachapoya lived in small independent groups, fighting each other for resources. They built their cities on ridges in the cloudforest, and put their dead in cliff top mausoleums together with ceramics, textiles and other objects from their culture.

Getting there and away

By road

Travelling from Cajamarca (225km) you have to go through Celendín (4 hrs). From Celendín to Chachapoyas there are only a couple of buses a week, currently Sun and Thur at 13.00 (13 hrs, US$6); with return buses Tue and Fri at 03.00. Try to get a seat on the right. This is a daily service and the easiest way to go. For local minibuses, go to Calle Grau, near the market. Chachapoyas to Chiclayo is 455km, 12 hrs, US$8 with Civa, Olano and Transportes Kuélap.

By air

Several small airlines fly from Lima to Chachapoyas, usually only Sat and only during the dry season. US$55 each way. The airport is 4km from Chachapoyas.

Where to stay and eat

Hotel El Dorado Ayacucho 1062; tel: 777047.
Hostal Kuélap Amazonas 1057. US$7–10. Central, basic, clean.
Hostal Amazonas Plaza Grau; tel: 777199. US$10 double. Good budget choice.
Gran Hotel Vilaya Jirón Ayacucho 755; tel: 777664. US$15–18.
Choctamal Lodge near Choctamal. US$10 with dinner. An American-run place (Charles Motley), good guide, good as a trekking base. Situated on the road up to the Kuélap site.

For food try **Chacha**, Plaza de Armas, or **Matalache**, Jirón Ayacucho.

Practical information

Tourist office (INC) Plaza de Armas. MITINCI (tourist office), Triunfo 582. Information on guides. Both very helpful.
Recommended guides include Martín Antonio Olivi (San Juan de Libertad 361), Charles Motley (at Choctamal Lodge), and Martín Chumbe (Jirón Pivre 909).
Travel agents Karajia Tours, Amazon Tours on the plaza.

What to see

The city still has many beautiful old Spanish-style houses with large gardens and tiled roofs. The **Plaza de Armas** has a colonial bronze fountain in the centre. There are two colonial churches and you can walk to the *mirador* of Cerro Luya Urco. Ask at the tourist office for details of other sites: Karajia, Pueblo de los Muertos and Laguna de los Condors.

KUÉLAP

About 37km from Chachapoyas is the small village of Tingo. From here it's a steep 4–5-hour walk (1,500m) to the site of Kuélap, which is situated at an altitude of 3,100m, overlooking the River Utcubamba. The whole site is 600m long, an almost impregnable fortress surrounded by strong back-filled defensive walls. There are narrow entrances, just wide enough for one person, through these thick walls. Inside the walls lies the rest of the site, a maze of round stone houses, watchtowers and stairs, now crumbling, and overgrown with ever-advancing cloudforest. Despite the impressive size and location of this pre-Inca site it is still visited by very few tourists and relatively little is known about it. It was first found in 1843. There is a US$3 entry fee, and the site is at its most beautiful in the early morning light. Open 08.00–18.00. Restoration is being carried out from time to time. A taxi to the site itself costs US$40 from Chachapoyas.

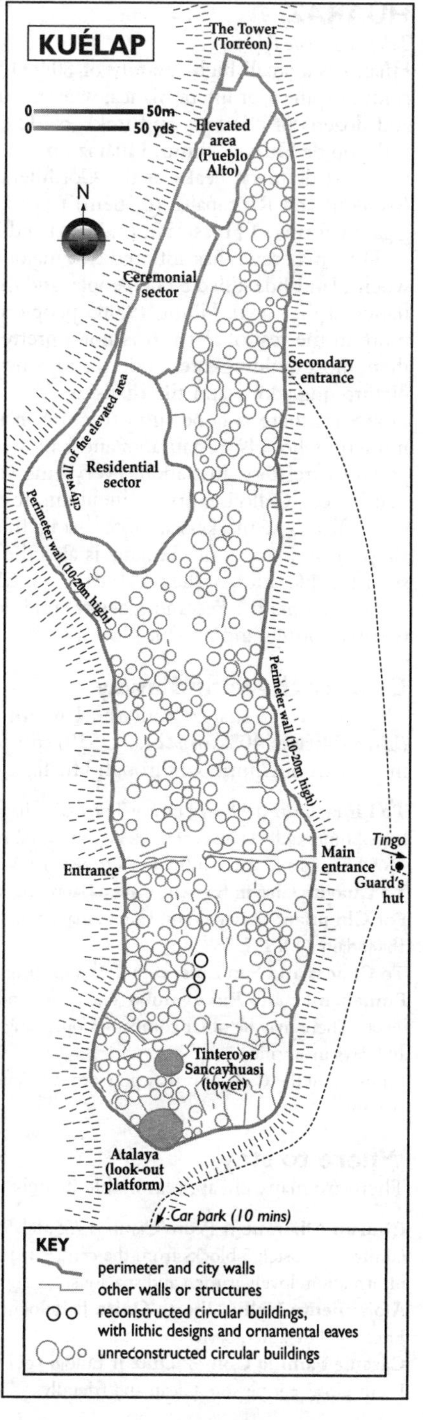

Where to stay

The **Albergue de Kuélap**, the last house on the left before the ruins, has friendly accommodation for US$2 per person. It is run by the guardian of Kuélap, who can also guide you round the site. The police in Tingo can sometimes provide you with a bed and store your luggage while you go to the site. There is also basic accommodation at **Hotelito Tingo** or **Albergue Leon**, Jirón San Juan, in Tingo or **Chcotamal Lodge** near Kuélap.

In Celendín

Hostal Celendín is clean and friendly, from US$4 per person.
Hostal José Galvez also recommended basic, but OK, US$2.5 per person.

HUARAZ

Telephone code 044

Huaraz is a small highland city of 80,000 inhabitants, the trekking and climbing centre for the Cordillera Blanca, where you will find most of Peru's highest peaks and dozens of climbers and trekkers. The town itself is spectacularly set in the Callejón de Huaylas. From Huaraz on a cloudless day you can clearly see some of the most dramatic peaks of the Cordillera Blanca, Mounts Palcaraju, Tocllaraju (6,034m) and Ranrapalca (6,162m) towering over the city and, to the north, the gigantic forms of Huascarán (6,768m) and Huandoy (6,395m).

This small town has suffered two major disasters this century, the first in 1941, when a landslide killed 5,000 people, and the second the earthquake of 1970 which flattened the town, killing 19,000 people in Huaraz alone, and many thousands more in the rest of Peru. It is not a pretty place, having been completely rebuilt then: most buildings are modern and concrete, and there are no longer any of the picturesque adobe and tile mansions that once lined the narow winding streets. However, there is good infrastructure in the town to cater for the tourists, and numerous hostels, restaurants and bars where you can meet other travellers and potential trekkers. Just about everything you are likely to need is on or near the main street, Calle Luzuriaga, including restaurants, outdoor shops, banks and the post office. The markets are interesting, full of local produce, and the best place to shop for trekking food. Huaraz is also the perfect base for less physical activities such as exploration of the pre-Inca site of **Chavín de Huántar**, or bus-based tours to the mountain lakes and glaciers, traditional villages with their lively markets, thermal springs and pre-Inca history.

Getting there and away

The routes to Huaraz from the Pan American Highway are through Pativilca (Lima–Huaraz 408km, 9 hrs, US$8); through Casma (Casma–Huaraz 150km, 7 hrs); or from Chimbote through Huallanca and Caraz to Huaraz (185km, 9 hrs).

To Lima: Cruz del Sur, Lucar y Torre 573, have a special rapid service without stops (7 hrs). Empresa de Transportes 14, Av Fitzcarrald 216, to Lima, Chimbote and Trujillo. Móvil Tours and Ancash (part of Ormeño) are on Av Raymondi.
To Chavín: Chavín Express, Calle Cáceres 338, or D'Walthers Tours, Av Tarapacá.
For Chiquían: El Rápido on Calle Huascarán, not very rapid but scenic; 08.00, 14.00 and 18.00 daily (4 hrs, US$2.50).
To Chacas and San Luis: with Transuir, Jirón Caraz 604, leaves at 07.00 daily, to **Pomabamba and Piscobamba** Tue, Thur and Sat at 06.00 and to **Sihuas** Tue and Fri at 09.00. There may be other companies operating these routes, so ask around. Check times and days in advance.
Buses along the Callejón valley go from Av Centenario from early morning until late evening.

Where to stay

There are many cheap, reasonable hostels in the centre of town.

Churup Albergue Jr Pedro Campos 735; tel: 722584. From US$3 per person. A friendly family run hostel, 5 blocks from the centre in a quiet residential area, hot water, laundry, information, lovely garden and spacious.
Alojamiento Nelly Alberto Quito Jr Bolognesi 507; tel: 724021. From US$3 per person. Friendly, hot water, basic.
Casa de Familia Gomez Diaz Jr Eulogio del Río 1083, just off the Plaza de Armas. From US$3 per person. Clean and friendly.

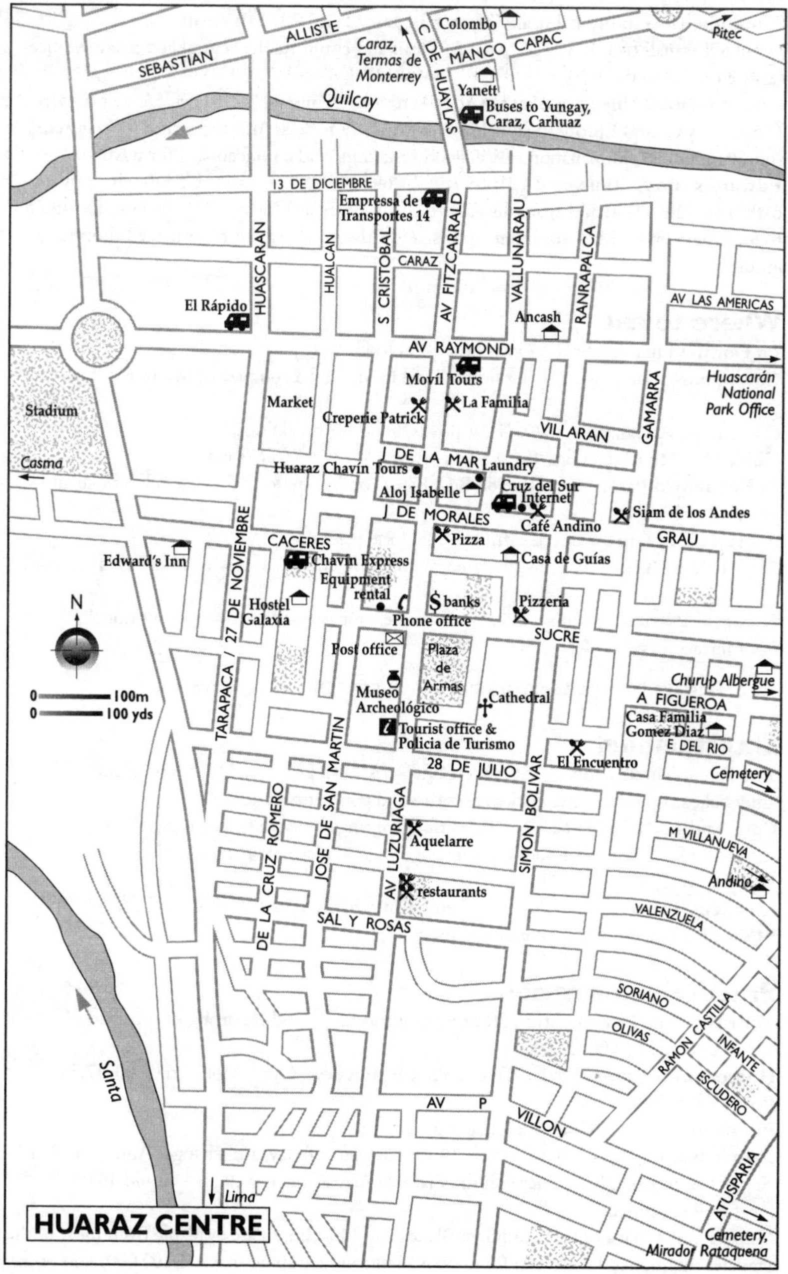

Hostal Soledad Amadeo Figueora 1267; tel. 721196. From US$3 per person. Clean, basic hostel.

Hostal Galaxia Juan de la Cruz Romero 638; tel. 722230. From US$3 per person. Central, clean and popular hostal.

Alojamiento Isabelle Jr Lucar y Torre 538; tel: 726367/721203; email: ysamb@hotmail.com US$5 per person. Clean and comfortable, central and friendly, nice terrace on the roof.
Casa de Guías/Albergue Alpes-Andes Parque Ginebra; tel: 721511. US$5 per person. Clean, very central European style hostel, dormitory rooms. Also the centre for registered mountain guides, information office, good restaurant and a noticeboard for travellers.
Edward's Inn Av Bolognesi 121; tel/fax: 722692. US$$7 in dorm, US$10 with private bath. Friendly, clean and spacious. There is a noticeboard for trekkers looking for others to join them and with recommendations, and Edward is also an experienced mountain guide.

Where to eat

La Familia Luzuriaga 431. Good cheap local food.
Campobase, Luzuriaga 407, 1st floor. Good food, criolla and pizzas, live music, reasonable prices.
Chez Pepe Av Luzuriaga 570. Great pizzas, good for breakfasts.
Chifa Min Hua Luzuriaga 424. Large portions of typical chifa food.
El Encuentro Parque Sebastian de Beas 856. Good value local food, quick service and plentiful helpings.
Pizzeria Landaura Plaza de Armas. Great local pizzeria.
Siam de Los Andes Av Agustín Gamarra 560. Not cheap but fresh and delicious genuine Thai food.
Crêperie Patrick Luzuriaga 422. Great coffee, crêpes and French food but not cheap. Roof terrace.

Av Luzuriaga beyond the plaza has a high concentration of restaurants.

Entertainment

The Bar Julian de Morales 759. Open 11.00–15.00 and 18.00–24.00. Good pizzas, sandwiches and salads, also cocktails, coffee and good atmosphere.
Café Andino Julian de Morales 753. Friendly gringo café/bar, good atmosphere, great coffee and large library of books to exchange, a good place for hanging out.
Aquelarre Calle Uribe. Climbers' bar.
Amadeus Taberna Plaza de Armas behind Interbanc, a popular disco and bar.
El Tambo Jaré de la Mar. Popular night club/peña.

Practical information

Tourist police Plaza de Armas, for tourist information and reporting of robberies. Open 09.00–13.00 and 16.00–19.00.
Huascarán National Park office, Calle Las Americas. Open Mon–Fri 08.00–17.30.
Post office On the plaza.
Phone office Several on Calle Luzuriaga.
Money Banco de Crédito, Luzuriaga Block 6 is open all day, and changes Amex travellers' cheques. Interbanc, Jirón Sucre on the Plaza de Armas, open 08.00–14.00 and 16.00–19.00, for travellers' cheques.
Maps Tourist maps of the Cordillera Blanca and Huayhuash are available from most of the agencies mentioned below, but for good walking and climbing maps (1:100 000) you need to go the South American Explorers Club, or the ING in Lima.
Internet Andes on Line, Julian Morales 759, 2nd floor. US$2 per hour. Also offers coffee etc and has a hostel with shared rooms, hot water, videos. Universidad Nacional de Ancash, Instituto Superior, Av Centenario 200 (an extension of Luzuriaga) is the cheapest in town, at less than US$2 per hour. Open 08.00–20.00.

Travel agencies

Chavín Tours Luzuriaga 502; tel: 721578; email: chavin@telematic.edu.pe Very professional agency that rents equipment and organises excursions.

Baloo Tours Simon Bolívar 471. Rents climbing and trekking equipment and organises excursions.

Casa de Guías Parque Ginebra 28-G; tel: 721811. Open 09.00–13.00 and 16.00–20.00. Excellent information on trekking and climbing, transport, prices, guides etc. Quality equipment to rent, rescue team, qualified guides.

Mountain Bike Adventures, Julio Olazo, Jirón Lucar y Torre 530, PO Box 111, Huaraz; tel: 724259; fax: 724888; email: Olaza@mail.cosapidata.com.pe. Quality bikes for hire at $20 a day, organised excursions in the Cordillera Blanca and Negra, book exchange, books for sale, maps and information.

Montrek Luzuriaga 646. Rent equipment, organise trekking and climbing excursions.

Pablo Tours Luzuriaga 501. Organise conventional tours and adventure trips, mountain biking, rafting, trekking, climbing etc.

Pyramid Adventures Luzuriaga 530. Organise conventional tours and adventure trips.

What to see

The **Museo Archaeológico**, Plaza de Armas, has a good collection of Recuay ceramics and monolithic sculptures, enthusiastic guided tours, videos of the 1970

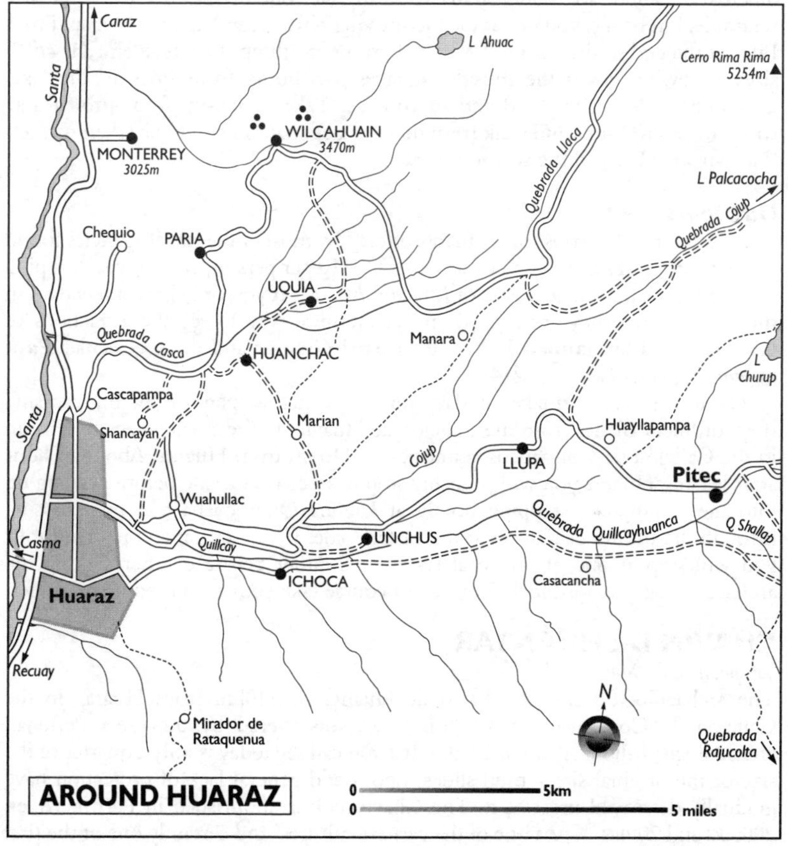

earthquake, and photos showing Huaraz as it was. Open Mon–Sat 09.00–18.30, Sun 09.00–12.00.

The **hot springs of Baños de Monterrey** are just 5km from Huaraz and great for relaxing after a trek. There is one large pool and several smaller private ones. Take a bus from Av Luzuriaga right to the gate. Open daily 08.00–18.00.

There are a couple of nice upmarket hotels here, **El Patio** and **Baños Termales Monterrey**.

The **Foto Galería**, Pasaje Cayetano Requena Mz 36, is a good place to buy photos of the Cordillera Blanca if yours didn't come out, and has some lovely shots. **Jr José Olaya**, a narrow street of adobe houses with wooden balconies, is testimony to the old city of Huaraz before it was destroyed by the 1970 earthquake.

Day walks

The Casa de Guías has maps and up-to-date information. There have been reports of robbery on some of the trails around Huaraz, so be careful: don't take valuables and always go in a group. For a short warm-up walk (3–4 hrs) with great views from Huaraz, head out past the cemetery and up to the white statue of Christ on the hill, then continue upwards and along the ridge to the south, coming back down into Huaraz a few kilometres further on.

For a full day's walk nearby, start from the hamlet of Pitec at 3,850m just west of Huaraz. There are several trails you can take: one of the nicest is a bit of a scramble, but brings you out at the picturesque blue-green Laguna Churup. From Pitec at the end of the road follow a path to the north up the left side of the small stream flowing down the hillside. It takes 2–3 hours from Pitec to the lake, depending how acclimatised and fit you are. Take a pick-up from Jirón Caraz (from 07.00) to Llupa and walk from there or negotiate a price to be taken further. You can walk back all the way to Huaraz.

Day tours

There are three day-trips from Huaraz offered by most of the travel agencies found in the centre of Huaraz, each of which is US$10 per person, with prices dropping outside the main tourist season of July and August. If you only have a few days in the Huaraz area they are a good and economical way to see the attractions of **Chavín**, the **Llanganuco Lakes**, **Pastoruri Glacier** and the spectacular ***Puya raimondii*** plants (see page 214).

The tour to **Chavín** takes all day, much of which is spent on the bus crossing the Cordillera Blanca from the Callejón de Huaylas to the small village of Chavín in the Callejón de Conchucos, a journey of 115km from Huaraz. About an hour after leaving Huaraz you will probably stop in Recuay at a café before heading up into the mountains, stopping briefly at Laguna Querococha and then passing through the tunnel of Kawish to the eastern side. If you are on an organised tour you will stop at one of the local restaurants either before or after visiting the archaeological site, for lunch. You can of course take your own food if you prefer.

CHAVÍN DE HUÁNTAR

Telephone code 044

The archaeological site of Chavín de Huántar is 110km from Huaraz in the Callejón de Conchucos at 3,150m. It was discovered by the great Peruvian archaeologist Julio C Tello in 1919. What you can see today is only a quarter of the size of the original site – mud slides, floods and general lack of protection have gradually destroyed most of it. The Chavín culture flourished in Peru between 2000BC and 200BC. It was one of the earliest cultures, and certainly one of the first

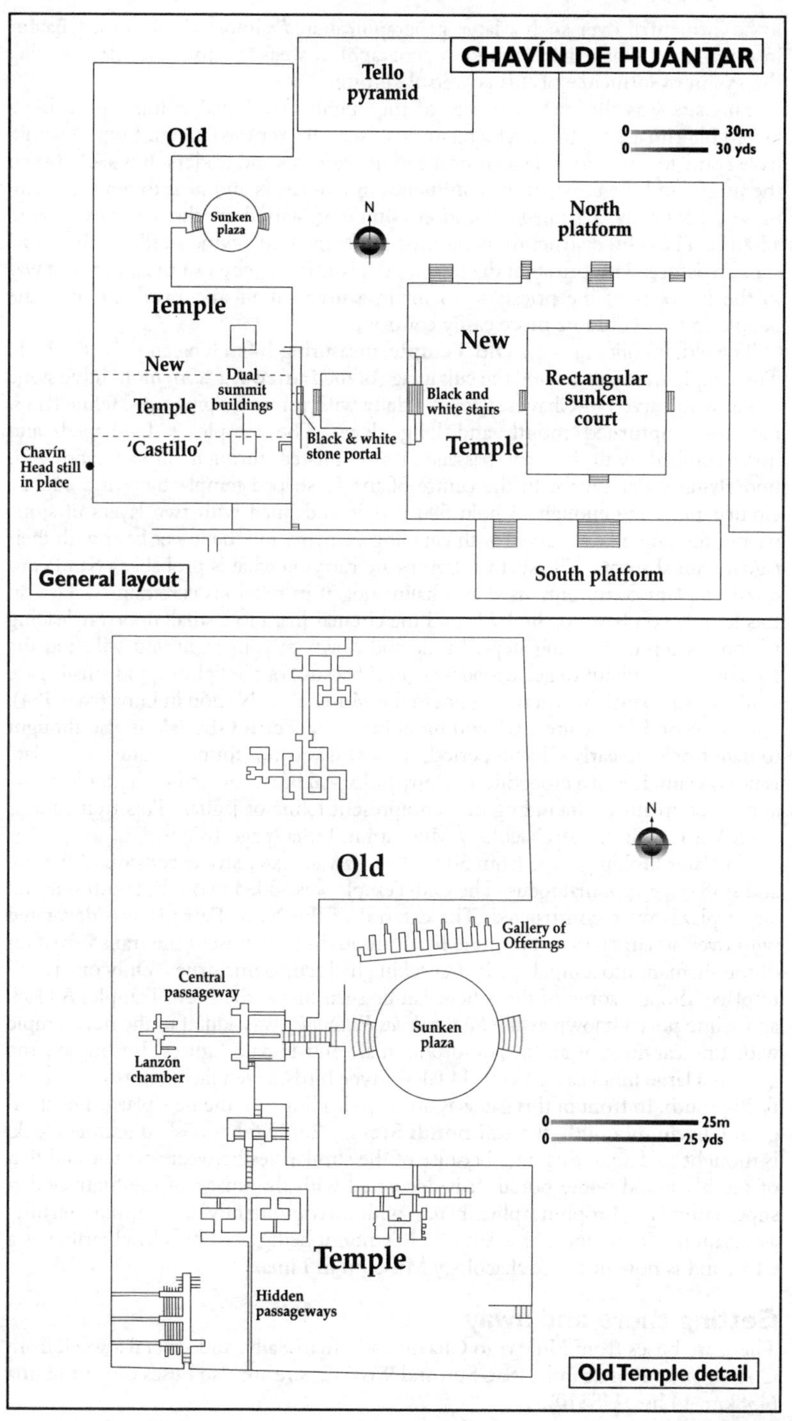
CHAVÍN DE HUÁNTAR
Tello pyramid
0 30m
0 30 yds
Old
Sunken plaza
N
North platform
Temple
New
New
Dual summit buildings
Rectangular sunken court
Temple
Black and white stairs
'Castillo'
Black & white stone portal
Temple
Chavín Head still in place
General layout
South platform
N
Old
Gallery of Offerings
Central passageway
Sunken plaza
Lanzón chamber
0 25m
0 25 yds
Temple
Hidden passageways
Old Temple detail

to be influential over such a large geographical area, almost all of Peru. Chavín-inspired objects have been found in geographical areas far from the site, showing the extent of influence of this powerful culture.

This site was the seat of power of this highly developed culture, probably a sacred pilgrimage centre to which citizens from all over the Chavín Empire would have come to worship and pay homage to their priests and leaders. It is set between the jungle and the coast, at the confluence of two rivers and near to ten mountain passes, obviously a strategic location. Building started in the temples around 1300BC. The whole structure is built on different levels which reflects the social class structure, with priests at the top and the common people at the bottom. It was in the interests of the priests to maintain a mystical air and instil fear into the people so they could be more easily controlled.

The oldest building is the **Old Temple**, measuring 100m long and 11–16m high. The temple was built around the cult image of the **Lanzón**, a 4.5m monolithic stone monument carved in Chavín style, of a deity with round bulging eyes, feline fangs, flat nose, upturned mouth and long claws. The temple is U-shaped, and honeycombed with internal passageways ventilated through airways and with underlying water canals. In the centre of the U-shaped temple there is a sunken circular plaza big enough to hold 500 people and lined with two layers of stone panels, the upper layer carved with parading shamans and the lower layer with their jaguar animal spirits. The shaman figures are carrying what is probably a San Pedro cactus, a plant commonly used as a hallucinogen in religious ceremonies. To visit this temple you have to climb beyond the circular plaza to a small doorway leading to some steep descending steps. Inside and down to your right you will find the Lanzón. It is difficult to get a good view of it because of the lighting and small space available, so if you can visit the replica in the Museo de la Nación in Lima (page 184).

The second of the great Chavín monoliths, the **Tello Obelisk**, is also thought to date from the early Chavín period, though it was not found on site so the date is not certain. It is of a crocodile-type mythological beast covered with jungle plants and other creatures, including the omnipresent feline or jaguar. This tremendous obelisk is now in the Archaeology Museum in Lima (page 182).

The later building stage from 500–200BC saw an extensive expansion of the site and shift of ceremonial focus. The Old Temple was added to on the south side and larger plazas were constructed. The exterior of the **New Temple** was decorated with over 40 larger-than-life stone heads, thought to represent the transformation of the shaman into animal spirit after taking hallucinogenic drugs. Only one is still in place, though some of the others can be seen inside the New Temple. A black and white portal known as the *Pórtico de las Falcónidas* was added to the new temple with fine carvings of anthropomorphic male and female figures. Resting on the posts is a large lintel carved with 14 falcon-type birds, seven facing north and seven facing south. In front of this gateway are steps leading into the new plaza. The third great Chavín monolith, the **Raimondi Stela**, a 2m highly polished granite block, is thought to date to this time because of the similarities between its style and that of the black and white portal. It is decorated with the image of the Staff God, a supernatural anthropomorphic being with predominantly agricultural fertility associations. It was found by Antonio Raymondi being used by a local farmer as a table, and is now in the Archaeology Museum in Lima.

Getting there and away

There are buses from Huaraz to Chavín and Huari daily, and several a week from Chavín on to Pomabamba (Sat, Sun and Wed). There are also buses direct to Lima (438km, 14 hrs, US$10).

Where to stay

There are several basic hostels in Chavín, the best of which are:

Hostal Chavín San Martin 141; tel: 754055. From US$3 per person. A clean hostel with hot water and some rooms with private bathrooms.
Hostal Rickay Jiron 17 de Enero 172; tel: 754068. US$7 per person. Hot water, private bath.

CALLEJÓN DE HUAYLAS

The Callejón de Huaylas is the wide valley that runs north–south for approximately 200km between the Cordillera Blanca and the Cordillera Negra. It is one of the finest areas in South America for its mountain views. The River Santa, which rises in Lake Conococha at 4,100m, flows through the valley from south to north. There are several towns along the valley on the banks of the River Santa, each with its own spectacular view of the snow-capped peaks of the Cordillera Blanca to the east. The main towns are Recuay, Huaraz, Carhuaz, Yungay and Caraz. The Callejón has a rich history, as the seat of the Chavín culture and later where the Recuay or Huaylas culture flourished.

Typical dishes

The most popular dishes from this area, seen at festivals and in some local restaurants are: *picante de cuy* (guinea pig), *charqui de chancho* (pork), *chancho asado al horno* (roast pork), *tamales* (maize pasties), *pachamanca* (a mixture of roast vegetables and meat), *puchero* (mixed soup/stew) and *chicharrón con mote* (fried pork with corn). These are often accompanied by locally produced cheese, honey, ham, butter, *manjar* (thick sweet caramel), jams and various fruits such as *capulí*, *lúcuma*, *granadilla*, *chirimoya*, *guayaba* and *tuna*.

Festivals

There is an important festival in the valley almost every month. The festivals are usually a riot of colour, with much drinking, eating and dancing. The main festivals everywhere are carnival in February and Easter celebrations in March or April. In Huaraz May is the festival of Señor de la Soledad, patron saint of Huaraz, and the first week of June is Semana del Andinismo. July sees the festival of Santa Isabel in Huaylas and the festival of Santa María Magdalena en Casma (17–24th), the Virgen del Carmen in Chavín (18th) and civic week in Huaraz (20–30th). August is the festival of the Virgen de la Asunción in several villages and of Santa Rosa, patron of Chiquián (30th). September (24th) is the festival of the Virgen de las Mercedes in Carhuaz. In October there is the Virgen del Rosario in Huari. December is the festival of the Virgen Inmaculada Concepción in Taric.

Getting there and away

For buses into the Callejón from the Pan American highway, see page 177. There is a frequent minibus service along the valley from early in the morning until late in the evening. Recuay to Huaraz 27km, 1 hr; to Catac 11km more; to Pachacoto 9km more.

What to see

Lake Parón, 100km to the north of Huaraz and just 32km from Caraz, is the largest lake of the Cordillera Blanca (4,200m). It is a deep sky-blue colour and provides excellent views of the snow-capped peaks of Pirámide de Garcilaso, Huandoy Norte, Pisco, Chacraraju and Paria.

Just 80km north of Huaraz and 25km from Yungay are the green-blue lakes of

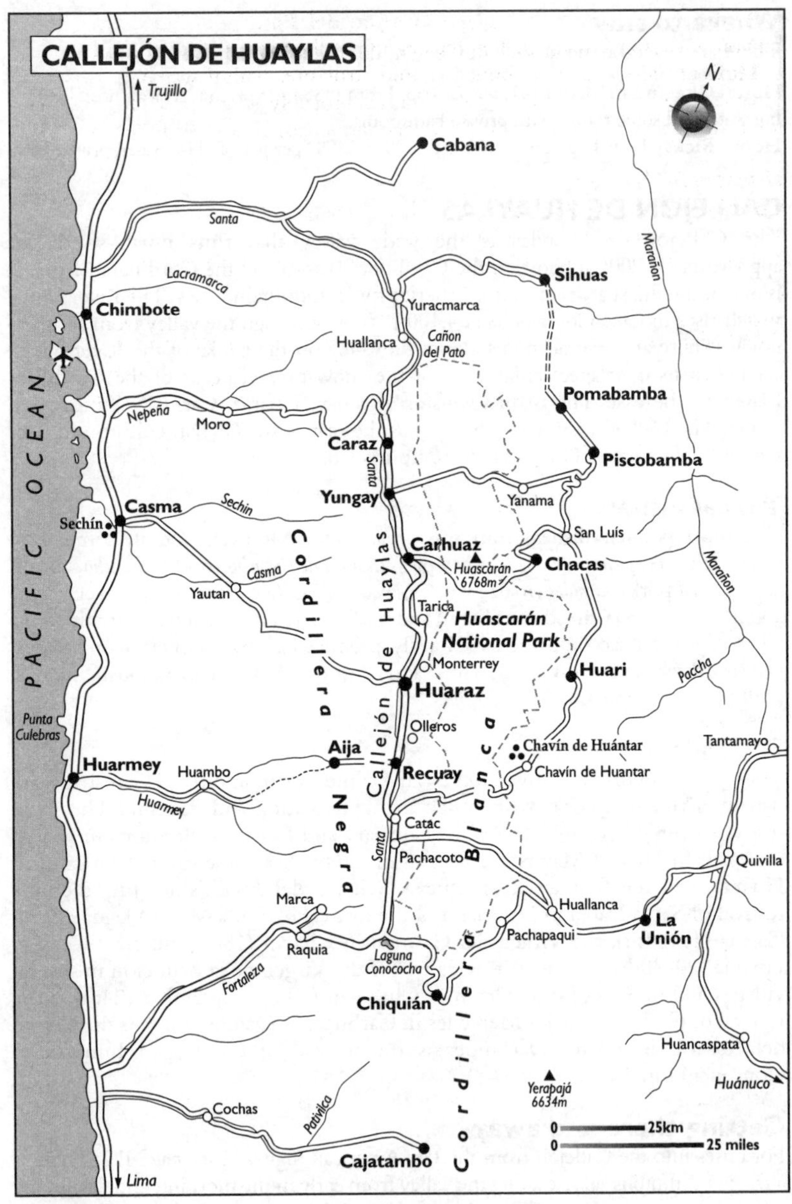

Llanganuco, **Chinan Cocha** and **Orcón Cocha**. From the lakes there are great views of some of the range's most impressive snow peaks, Chopicalqui, Huascarán, Huandoy, Pisco, Chacraraju and Yanapaccha.

Quebrada de Pachacoto, the valley of Pachacoto, 57km to the south of Huaraz, is the best place to go to see the 12m-high *Puya raimondii* plants. There are mineral springs here too alongside the River Pumapampa and great views of the snow peaks of Murruraju, Paria and Huarapasca and Caullaraju.

At the north end of the Callejón, **Cañón del Pato** is an impressive narrow canyon only 5m wide, created by the erosion of the torrential River Santa.

Huilcahuain is a stone-built pyramid structure, within walking distance of Huaraz (7km) which dates to AD900 and was probably built by the Huaris. Take a torch with you to see inside the chambers on the various levels of the pyramid.

Huascarán National Park

Covering an area of 340,000 hectares, this spectacular national park was created in 1975 to preserve the natural landscapes of the area and to protect the abundant flora and fauna. There are seven life zones within the park. Nearly 800 species of high Andean flora, 112 species of birds (see page 166) and more than ten species of animal have been identified. Animal species which are in danger and have been found in the park include mountain cats (*Felis colocolo* and *Felis jacobita*), spectacled bear (*Tremarctos ornatus*), taruca (*Hippocamelus antisensis*) and the vicuña (*Vicugna vicugna*). Others you may see are deer (*Odocoileus virginiansus*), vizcacha (*Lagidium peruanum*) and foxes (*Pseudalopex culpaeus*). Road access to the park is from the Llanganuco Lakes or the Nevado Pastoruri, though if you are walking there are many other access points with no control gates. You should get a permit from the National Park office in Huaraz if you intend to visit the park through some other entrance. The weather is suitable for trekking and climbing in the dry season between April and November. The permit cost for one day is US$5; for longer a flat charge of US$20 is payable at the entrance gates.

Towns in the Callejón

Recuay (3,394m) is 25km to the south of Huaraz, a small village dedicated to mining and agriculture. **Carhuaz** (2,688m), 34km to the north of Huaraz, is a small quiet town with a Sunday market. Trucks go from here into the Quebrada Ulta. There are several cheap hostels and restaurants here. **Yungay** (2,458m) is 55km to the north of Huaraz (about 1 hr by bus), situated right at the foot of Huascarán. It is a town that became known worldwide for the tragedy that occurred there in 1970 when a huge landslide, set off by an earthquake, buried the whole town, killing almost all of its 18,000 inhabitants. There is a memorial park to the dead with a large white statue of Christ and a few palm trees remaining from the original town. There are several cheap hostels including Hostal Yungay, Hostal Sol de Oro and Hostal Gledel, all of which are reasonable. Tourist minibuses will take you up to Llanganuco Lakes. Check the price before you go. There are also pick-up trucks and buses going right over to Yánama.

Caraz

Caraz (2,285m) is a small, quiet town about 67km north of Huaraz. It is a good place to stay away from Huaraz, and a perfect base for treks into the Alpamayo area, or visits to the Cañon del Pato or Laguna de Parón.

Getting there and away

Moreno has daily buses to Chimbote (7 hrs) at 08.00 and **Turismo Chimbote** has a night service to Chimbote and Trujillo. There are local buses to the Cañon del Pato and frequent buses along the Callejón de Huaylas. Pick-up trucks leave for Cashapampa.

Where to stay

There are several hostels and some excellent restaurants nearby. Try **Hotel Walter**, Calle San Martín 1135, from US$7. Also reasonable are **El Regina** and

Los Olivos or the **house of Señor Caballero** (ask at Pony's), which is friendly and comfortable.

Practical information

Pony's Expeditions owned by Alberto Cafferata, Jirón Sucre 1266, Plaza de Armas Caraz; tel: 791642; email: ponyexp@mail.cosapidata.com.pe Organises treks and climbs, rents equipment, sells maps. Also a shop and café.

Chiquián

This small highland village, 110km to the southeast of Huaraz, is the starting point for the 160km (100 mile) Huayhuash Circuit, a beautiful trek around the remote Cordillera Huayhuash (see *Backpacking and Trekking in Peru and Bolivia* for a full description).

Getting there and away

There are several buses daily from Huaraz, and also buses direct to Lima and inland to Huallanca and La Unión.

Where to stay

Hostal San Miguel Jirón Comercio 233; tel: 044 747001. US$3 per person. Basic, limited hot water, but probably the best in town.
Hospedaje Doña Victoria Calle Leoncio Prado 270; tel: 044 747158. US$3 per person.

Hoatzin

13 The Central Highlands

Very near to Lima, yet worlds apart, the central highlands contain some of Peru's richest mineral deposits, very productive agricultural land and lively peasant and labour movements. The Mantaro Valley is Lima's breadbasket, supplying the capital's ever-increasing demand for food. Thanks to the plentiful supply of agricultural work and mining jobs, the people are a bit better off here than in other highland areas, and the infrastructure reflects this. There are good roads and a constant stream of trucks, buses and taxis between the towns. If you travel from Lima you climb quickly out of the smog and endless shanty towns through dry rocky landscapes until reaching La Oroya, a bleak and dirty place dominated by its smelting plant. From there, dropping into the central highland valleys is a pleasant surprise; the land is green and obviously fertile, planted extensively with potatoes, maize and beans.

HUÁNUCO

Telephone code 064

This town of 119,000 inhabitants is situated on the banks of the River Huallaga, which flows into the Marañon, amid rolling Andean valleys at 1,912m above sea-level. It is a good place to break a long journey between the coast or central highlands and Pucallpa in the jungle. There are still very few tourists here, the people are friendly and the climate neither too hot and sticky like the jungle, nor as cold as the highland towns.

History

This part of Peru has been populated for 10,000 years, initially by hunter-gatherers. The Kotosh culture, one of the oldest in Latin America, developed here between 2000BC and AD200. The Temple of Kotosh, also known as *Las Manos Cuzadas* (the crossed hands) dates from then. Later there were a number of other tribes until the Incas came to predominate. Huánuco lies on the main Inca highway, which runs between Cusco and Cajamarca. The amazingly intact archaeological site of Huánuco Pampa (near La Unión) was one of the provincial cities of the Cusco-centred Inca Empire. It was probably one of the major outlying administrative centres and *tambos*, or resting places on the long journeys the Incas made through the empire. The Spanish founded the city of Huánuco in 1539 in its current location, a more hospitable environment.

Getting there and away

By road

Huánuco is 105km from Cerro de Pasco, 235km from La Oroya, 375km from Pucallpa and 410km from Lima. There is no central bus station. Shared taxis are the

best way to get to Tingo María from just over the bridge Puente Calicanto. Recommended bus companies to Lima and Pucallpa are **León de Huánuco**, Malecón Aromía Robles 821; **Trans Mar**, Calle Abtao 889; **Trans Rey**, Jirón 28 de Julio 1215, or **Trans Inter**, Crespo Castillo 690. To get to Huancayo by day you have to change buses in Cerro de Pasco; there is a direct night service. Calles Huallayco and Tarapaca have a concentration of bus companies going south and north. There are buses to La Unión and on towards Tantamayo or Huallanca; although the roads are terrible, this is really off the beaten track and the scenery is spectacular. La Unión has basic hostel accommodation.

Where to stay and eat

For some unknown reason, there are many hotels in Huánuco, and very few tourists. The hostels are generally of pretty poor standard, a bit dark, dreary and not always too clean. There are several cheap hostels right on the Plaza de Armas.

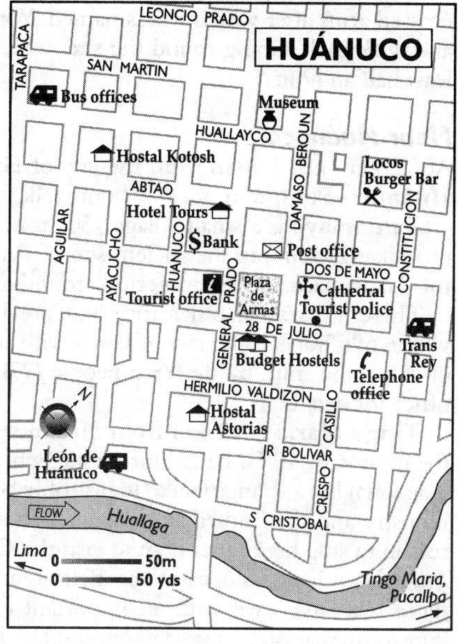

El Paraíso Plaza de Armas; tel: 514773. From US$4, cheap, basic, central, no hot water.

Hostal Cancún and **Hostal Lima** (tel: 514773) Also on the square. Reasonable.

Hostal Kotosh Calle Ayacucho. At US$5 per person it is good value, clean and with hot water.

Hostal Astoria Calle Prado 984; tel: 512310. Large old building, shared bath, no hot water.

Hotel Tours Calle Abtao corner Huánuco. US$13 for double with bath and TV. Nice place.

There's a small vegetarian place on Calle Dos de Mayo 751; a popular fast food burger bar called **Locos Burger Bar** on Abtao 102 with quite good food and not bad beer; several Chifas on Calle Beraun and bakeries on Calle Dos de Mayo. Around the town there are popular weekend restaurants that serve the typical dishes of the area such as *locro de gallina* (an all-in-one chicken dish), *picante de cuy* (guinea-pig served with a chilli and peanut sauce), *picante de carne* (beef, pork or lamb served with a chilli and peanut sauce) and *pachamanca* (chunks of marinated meat and vegetables cooked on hot stones under the ground).

Practical information

Tourist office Plaza de Armas, Jirón General Prado. Open Mon–Fri 09.00–15.00.
Tourist police Jirón 28 de Julio.
Post office Plaza de Armas.
Phone office Calle 28 de Julio 1170.
Money Banco de Crédito, Jirón Dos de Mayo 1005; Interbanc, Dos de Mayo 1151. Money changers on the Plaza de Armas.

What to see

The **cathedral** on the Plaza de Armas holds an interesting collection of paintings from the Cusco school. Other churches of interest include 16th-century **San Francisco**, 17th-century **San Sebastián** at the entrance to the town and 16th-century **La Merced**, which holds the original Spanish Virgin de las Mercedes given by the Emperor Charles V. **San Cristóbal** has some original wooden figures of the Virgin of Asunción, San Agustín and la Virgen Dolorosa.

The **Museo de Ciencias**, Calle General Prado 495, is a highly recommended small museum managed by the enthusiastic Néstor Armas Wenzel, who will show you around.

Kotosh, a site which is more than 4,000 years old, is just 5km from Huánuco on the road to La Unión. It is not the most well-maintained of sites but it is well worth a visit if you are particularly interested in pre-hispanic cultures. There is evidence of settlement 4,000 years ago, and several separate periods of habitation since. The temple of **Los Manos Cuzadas** now contains a reproduction of the crossed arms after which it was named. You can walk out to the site or take a taxi and walk back. Going round the site, which is open from dawn to dusk, takes at least half an hour.

Near Huánuco

At 3,200m, just 144km from the city of Huánuco is the remains of an Inca city, **Huánuco-Pampa**. It is a 2–3-hour walk from La Unión.

Tantamayo is a small village 150km north of Huánuco. From the village you can hike (2–3 hrs) to the ancient site of Tantamayo, which is though to date from the Tiahuanaco and Huari period around AD1000.

There are several other Inca and pre-Inca sites around Huánuco. Near the village of Choras is the city of **Garo** with some 10m buildings still standing, built of stone and mud by the Yaro people (77km from Huánuco). Ask at the tourist office for details.

Tingo María is 129km from Huánuco on the River Huallaga surrounded by the mountains of La Bella Durmiente, which have the form of a sleeping woman. The town has a strange feel to it, probably because of its involvement in the cocaine industry and the immediate suspicion attached to foreigners. There is very little reason to stop here other than to visit the **Cave of the Lechuzas** (*La Cueva de las Lechuzas*). On the slopes of the Bella Durmiente, only 6km from Tingo María, there is a large cave with an important colony of oilbirds (*Steatornis caripensis*), known in Spanish as *guácharos* or *santanas*. There are several hotels and restaurants in the town, if you do end up staying.

Cerro de Pasco is a large mining settlement of 63,000 people, 105km (4 hrs by bus) from Huánuco at 4,338m. It is interesting only to see how a mining settlement works, but is a bleak, cold and dirty place, especially in the rainy season. There is a bus terminal in the town.

La Oroya has a similar feel to Cerro de Pasco. It is an industrial town at 3,700m with nothing to recommend it to the tourist.

HUANCAYO

Telephone code 064

Huancayo is a busy highland city in the fertile Mantaro Valley, at 3,249m. A functional commercial city, it is not particularly attractive. However, there is plenty to see and do in the surrounding area and there are still very few tourists here compared to the Huaraz area or southern Peru. Huancayo is a good place to start if you want to make an exploratory visit to the high jungle area beyond Tarma or do some trekking in the mountains. In day trips from the city you can see weavers at work, carving of gourds and silver filigree, and ceramics being made, or do some great day hikes. Don't miss the Sunday market in Huancayo itself or the train journey to Huancavelica. The overland route to Ayacucho and Cusco, though long, is scenically dramatic.

History

The Mantaro Valley was the seat of the Huanca people, a tribe of hunters and shepherds, who flourished until conquered by the Incas under Pachacutec in 1467. It became one of the main Inca routes to the north.

Folklore

Huancayo and the whole Mantaro Valley are well known for their festivals and dances. The principal festivals are February 2, the celebration of the *Virgen de la Candelaria*; *Semana Santa* which is Easter May 1–4; *Fiesta de Las Cruces*; and July

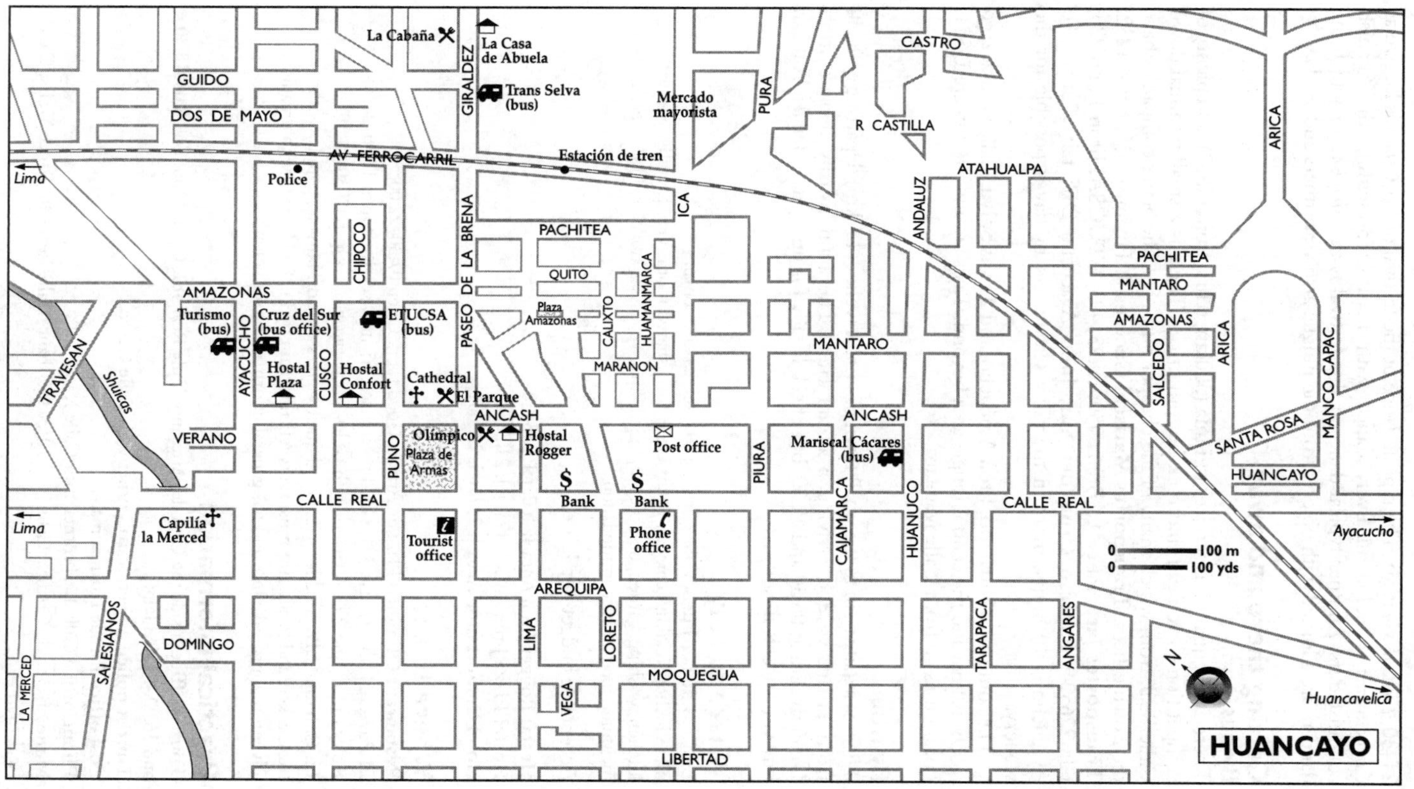
La Cabaña
La Casa de Abuela
GUIDO
GIRALDEZ
Trans Selva (bus)
DOS DE MAYO
Mercado mayorista
PURA
CASTRO
R CASTILLA
ARICA
AV FERROCARRIL
Estación de tren
Lima
Police
ATAHUALPA
ANDALUZ
ICA
PASEO DE LA BRENA
CHIPOCO
PACHITEA
QUITO
HUAMANMARCA
PACHITEA
MANTARO
AMAZONAS
Plaza Amazonas
CALIXTO
AMAZONAS
Turismo (bus)
Cruz del Sur (bus office)
ETUCSA (bus)
AYACUCHO
CUSCO
MANTARO
SALCEDO
ARICA
MANCO CAPAC
MARANON
TRAVESAN
Shuicas
Hostal Plaza
Hostal Confort
Cathedral
El Parque
ANCASH
ANCASH
SANTA ROSA
VERANO
Olímpico
Hostal Rogger
Post office
Mariscal Cácares (bus)
Plaza de Armas
PUNO
PIURA
HUANCAYO
Bank
Bank
CALLE REAL
CALLE REAL
CAJAMARCA
HUANUCO
Lima
Capilía la Merced
Tourist office
Phone office
Ayacucho
0 100 m
0 100 yds
AREQUIPA
SALESIANOS
DOMINGO
LIMA
LORETO
TARAPACA
ANGARES
N
LA MERCED
MOQUEGUA
VEGA
Huancavelica
LIBERTAD
HUANCAYO

24–30, *Fiesta de Santiago*. The typical dance of the festival of *Las Cruces* is known as *Chonguinada*, a colourful lively dance with masks representing the Spanish conquistadors. Another typical dance at this festival is the *Shapish*, for which the dancers are adorned with objects from the jungle: arrows, feathers and seeds.

Getting there and away

By bus

There are frequent bus services to Lima (300km, 6 hrs, from US$3), and plenty of competition so you can find rock-bottom prices. There is a small terminal down Calle Real, from which many of the cheaper buses go. The better companies have their own offices: **Transportes Mariscal Cáceres**, Jr Huánuco 350; tel: 231232; **Transportes Jara**, Paseo La Breña 350; tel:231493; **ETUCSA**, Jirón Puno 220; tel: 226524; **Expreso Cruz del Sur**, Jirón Ayacucho 287; tel: 235650. To Ayacucho is 10 hours, more in the rainy season. Go by day if possible for the scenery.

The companies **Turismo**, Jirón Ayacucho, and **Trans Selva**, Calle Giraldez, go to Oxapampa and the central jungle area beyond. Taxis around the city are US$1. Local buses go from Calle Mantaro.

By train

There is a daily train to the small town of Huancavelica (147km) departing at 06.30 from Huancayo and arriving 5 hours later. The train usually departs from Huancavelica at 06.30 and 12.30, but check locally for up-to-date details. You can buy your tickets in advance.

Where to stay

La Casa de la Abuela Calle Gíraldez 691; tel: 234383; email: inca&lucho@mail.hys.com.pe. From US$5 for a shared room. Very friendly, popular, kitchen, washing, garden, breakfast included. Spanish classes available, US$20 per day including food and accommodation.

Acceptable budget hotels are:

Hostal Rogger Jirón Ancash 460; tel: 233488.
Hostal Plaza Jirón Ancash 171; tel: 210509.
Hotel Confort Jirón Ancash 237; tel: 233601.

Where to eat

Restaurant Olímpico Plaza de Armas. Good food. Open 07.30–22.00.
El Parque Calle Ancash 391. Good meat place, friendly service. Open 17.30–24.00.
Koky Jirón Puno 298. A bakery with tables, great *empanadas*. Open 07.30–21.30.
La Cabaña Calle Giráldez 652. Good quality pizzas, salads, burgers, popular with backpackers and locals, live music at weekends. Run by Lucho Hurtado who organises adventure tours, bike hire and has general information (see below).

Practical information

Tourist office Inside the Casa del Artesano, Calle Real 481. Open Mon–Fri 08.00–13.30 and 16.00–18.30. Helpful.
Tourist police Av Ferrocarril corner with Calle Cusco.
Post office Parque Huamanmarca.
Phone office Calle Real corner with Calle Ica.
Money Banco de Crédito, Calle Real 1013; Interbanc, Calle Real 646; Banco Weiss, Calle Real 750.

Travel agencies There are several travel agencies in Calle Real in blocks 500 and 600, try Huancayo Tours at Calle Real 517; tel: 233351. For adventure tours and treks talk to Lucho at Incas de Peru Calle Giráldez 652; tel: 223303; email: inca&lucho@mail.hys.com.pe
Internet office Calle Puno.

What to see

The city was founded at **Plaza Huamanmarca** in 1572. Today it houses many public buildings. **Plaza Constitución** is the main square. The neoclassical **cathedral**, built from stone and adobe, dates from 1799. **Capilla La Merced**, a colonial building, has been declared a historic monument because the political constitution of Peru was signed here in 1839.

In Avenida Huancavelica there is a large **Sunday craft market** (*Feria Dominical*) of locally produced artefacts: *mates burilados* (carved gourds) depicting legends and everyday life; *bordados* (embroidery) – the typical clothing in this area includes beautifully embroidered skirts, blankets and jackets; *cerámica* (pottery); *peletería* (leather work) using the skins of sheep, alpaca, and rabbit; *tapicería* (weaving) of very high quality from San Pedro de Cajas, Tarma and Hualhuas, made from sheep and alpaca wool and some artificial fibres; and *platería* (filigree work with silver).

While you are exploring the city don't miss **Cerrito de La Libertad**, a small hill and lookout just 1km from the centre of the city at the end of Calle Giráldez. One kilometre beyond that is the area known as **Torre Torre**, weird rock formations eroded by wind and rain.

Warivilca is the archaeological remains of one of the principal Huari economic, administrative and religious sites, 6km from Huancayo. It covers 10km^2 and is thought to be as much as 3,000 years old.

In many of the surrounding villages you can see local artefacts being crafted. **Huancán**, **Huayucachi** and **Viques**, 9km from Huancayo, are the centres for embroidery. **Cochas**, **Cochas Chico** and **Cochas Grande**, 11km from Huancayo, are an excellent place to go to see the carving of gourds (*mates burilados*). You can visit the houses to see them carved with small chisels and then burnt with electrically heated instruments, to depict elaborate scenes from legends or daily life. **Hualhuas**, 12km from Huancayo, is a small community where you can see the whole weaving process from the teasing, spinning, and dyeing of wool with natural plant dyes, to weaving. This is a fascinating experience and a good place to purchase blankets, rugs etc. If you are interested in silver and gold filigree work you can see the craftsmen at work in **San Jerónimo de Tunán**, 16km from Huancayo.

Ingenio, 30km from Huancayo, is an area specialising in trout farms and a nice place for walking, with several good country restaurants. Also great for walks is **Cordillera de Huaytapallana**; its snow-capped peaks lie to the northeast of Huancayo, approximately 25km away.

Concepción is a small colonial village 22km from Huancayo. Interesting for a visit and possibly a stay in the hostel on the plaza. It's a quiet and flower-filled sort of village, very restful.

Convento de Ocopa, a fascinating monastery 30km from Huancayo, was built in 1725 by Franciscan monks on an evangelical mission to 'civilise' and convert the indigenous people of Peru to Catholicism – some things change little, Franciscans still train here. There are five cloisters, religious artwork, and an impressive library with 20,000 books dating from the 16th century. None too good guided tours only. Open 09.00–12.00 and 15.00-18.00, daily except Tues.

Jauja, the first capital of Peru, founded by Francisco Pizarro in 1534 and the nearby **Laguna de Paca**, 42km (1 hr) to the north of Huancayo are worth a visit. There are good walks in the hills around the Laguna. Accommodation is available in the small, very busy market town of Jauja. The local people here are very chatty and still quite unaccustomed to seeing tourists.

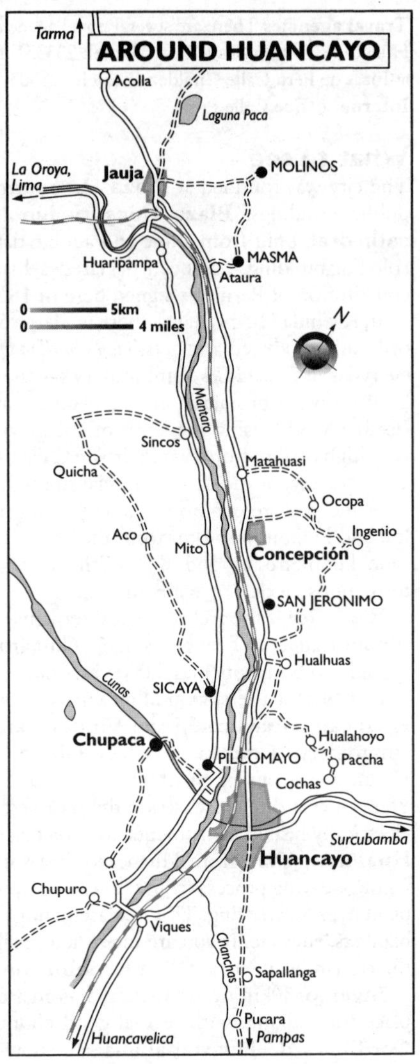

FROM HUANCAYO TO THE EAST

From Huancayo you can travel by local transport to Tarma and down to the Chanchamayo Valley, San Ramón and La Merced, or take the spectacular 12-hour journey to Satipo, and you can then continue through the high jungle on narrow winding roads to Oxapampa and Pozuzo. Tarma is a pleasant mountain town, with several hostels. Few tourists ever make it this far, and for many years it was advisable to stay away because of terrorist activity, but this is no longer a problem. The main problem now is the poor condition of the roads, particularly in the rainy season. Also recommended are the weaving and textile villages of Palcamayo (at 3,200m, 1½ hrs from Tarma) and San Pedro de Cajas (4,040m, 20km from Palcamayo), between Junín and Tarma. Take a bus from Tarma. The area is good for walking, caves and archaeological sites, and although there is little transport between the two villages the people are friendly and you should be able to get a lift. Take warm clothes, food and water in case you have to walk. From San Pedro you can walk back to the main La Oroya road (7km) and pick up transport there.

San Ramon and La Merced

These small settler towns in the Chanchamayo Valley mark the beginning of the Amazon basin. This was an area until recently occupied only by the Ashaninka Indians. The road down is dramatic, passing through verdant cloudforest. Both towns have cheap, basic accommodation and plenty of restaurants.

Satipo

This town supplies the thousands of settlers who have moved into the area from the central Andean valley of Jauja in recent years. You will also see Ashaninka Indians here who come to trade and shop. There are a few basic places to stay, and this town has a fascinating frontier feel to it.

THE ASHANINKA

Peru's Amazon territories are home to some 300,000 native people from 65 different ethnic groups. Fifty-five thousand of these people are Ashaninka, the largest indigenous group in the Peruvian Amazon. The Ashaninka face constant threats to their survival. During the rubber boom of 1839–1913 an estimated 80% of the Ashaninka people were killed, and since then their settlements have been systematically destroyed and their territories reduced. In recent years, the presence of guerrilla groups and coca producers has caused the death of several thousand Ashaninka, the forced recruitment of thousands of young men into rebel ranks and the displacement of some 10,000 people from nearby communities. Colonisers, generally from the central highland valleys, who had themselves been displaced from their homelands by guerrillas, are authorised to live on Ashaninka ancestral lands in the central forests of Peru and now threaten the survival of these native people. The Ashaninka have held on to their social organisation, their forms of self-government and their determination to defend their ancestral lands. They even formed the *Ovayeriite*, their own army, to free captives and recover their land. But the problem lies in the different treatment of the land by the colonisers and the Ashaninka. New techniques put the land at risk and resettlement programmes favour new settlers who are relocated on Ashaninka land without regard to prior habitation by Amazon groups.

HUANCAVELICA

Telephone code 064

This is a charming, friendly small town, with lovely hills all around, perfect for walking.

Getting there and away

By train

The train to Huancayo usually leaves at 06.30 and 12.30 taking a minimum of 5 hours.

By road

There are plenty of buses to Huancayo. It is possible to find transport from Huancavelica to Santa Inés, but it will probably be an old bus or open truck and the road isn't too good, so be prepared for long waits and cold conditions. Take warm clothes and food.

Where to stay and eat

There are several cheap hostels in Huancavelica:

Hostal Camacho Calle Carabaya 481. US$4 for a double.
El Milagro Calle Carabaya. Next door to Camacho, with sauna.
El Cinabrio Jirón Manco Capac 580. A good bar for the evening, with good food during the day.
Viña del Mar near the plaza is reputedly good for fish.

Practical information

Tourist office Jirón Nicolás de Piérola 180 or contact Jorge Salas Guevara at Restaurant Sideral.

What to see

Huancavelica boasts some interesting churches, hot springs, and a good Sunday market, even more interesting than in Huancayo. The **Museo Archaeologicó** just off the square is interesting, and guides are available. Visit the small, friendly Yauli market on Saturdays and the nearby archaeological sites of Uchkus and Inkañan.

AYACUCHO

Telephone code 064

Ayacucho is in the southern central highlands, a small, attractive city of 120,000 inhabitants with many well-maintained colonial churches. The city became famous in the 1980s as the home of Abimael Guzmán, a philosophy professor at the university in Ayacucho and leader of Peru's Communist Party and terrorist organisation known as *Sendero Luminoso* (the Shining Path). Ayacucho was out of bounds throughout the 1980s, the centre of violent terrorist activity, and many thousands of local people were forced to leave the region. This was the case until Guzmán's imprisonment in 1992. Now, although you may still notice a high security presence, it is just as safe as anywhere else, and an interesting area to visit which still doesn't receive many tourists. The city is near enough Lima to make it worth going to if you have a few days to spare, and is a good alternative overland route to get to Cusco. The rainy season is from November to March and the rest of the year is dry with an average temperature of 17°C. *Semana Santa* (Easter week) in Ayacucho is a very popular festival.

History

Ayacucho was the seat of the Huari culture which flourished in Peru from AD500 to AD1,000. This culture was a fusion of several regional cultures that came about through social, economic and cultural interaction. In the Huari culture you can see the influence of the Nazca people, the Tiahuanacos and local regional tribes such as the Huarpas. The Huaris were imperialistic and, unlike the Incas, they destroyed the cultures they dominated, imposing their own regime. They built administrative centres around their empire to control local populations, including the site of Pikillacta near Cusco. The Huaris were responsible for the building of a major road network throughout their empire, which was later adopted and further developed by the Incas. During colonial times Ayacucho was an important trading centre, lying halfway between the cities of Quito and Cusco, and between the Andean altiplano and the northern provinces of Argentina. Thousands of pack mules would have passed through daily on their way to or from the Pacific coast. Money from the silver mines financed the growth of the city and it became a popular residence for colonists until its demise in the 18th century when the mines dwindled. On December 9 1824 colonial rule came to an end when royalist forces were defeated at the battle of Ayacucho by Antonio José de Sucre.

Getting there and away

By bus

Ayacucho is 585km from Lima, 393km from Abancay, 316km from Huancayo and 590km from Cusco. There are daily buses from Ayacucho to these destinations, the highland routes taking you over wild, desolate, windswept mountains and through dramatic gorges. The road to Lima via Pisco is tarmac and generally in good condition and is also a beautiful journey. Transport can be severely disrupted in the rainy season between November and March. The principal transport companies are **Molina** and **Lobato** in Manco Capac, **Huamanga**, **Transmar** and **Chancas** in Av Mariscal Cáceres and **Libertadores**

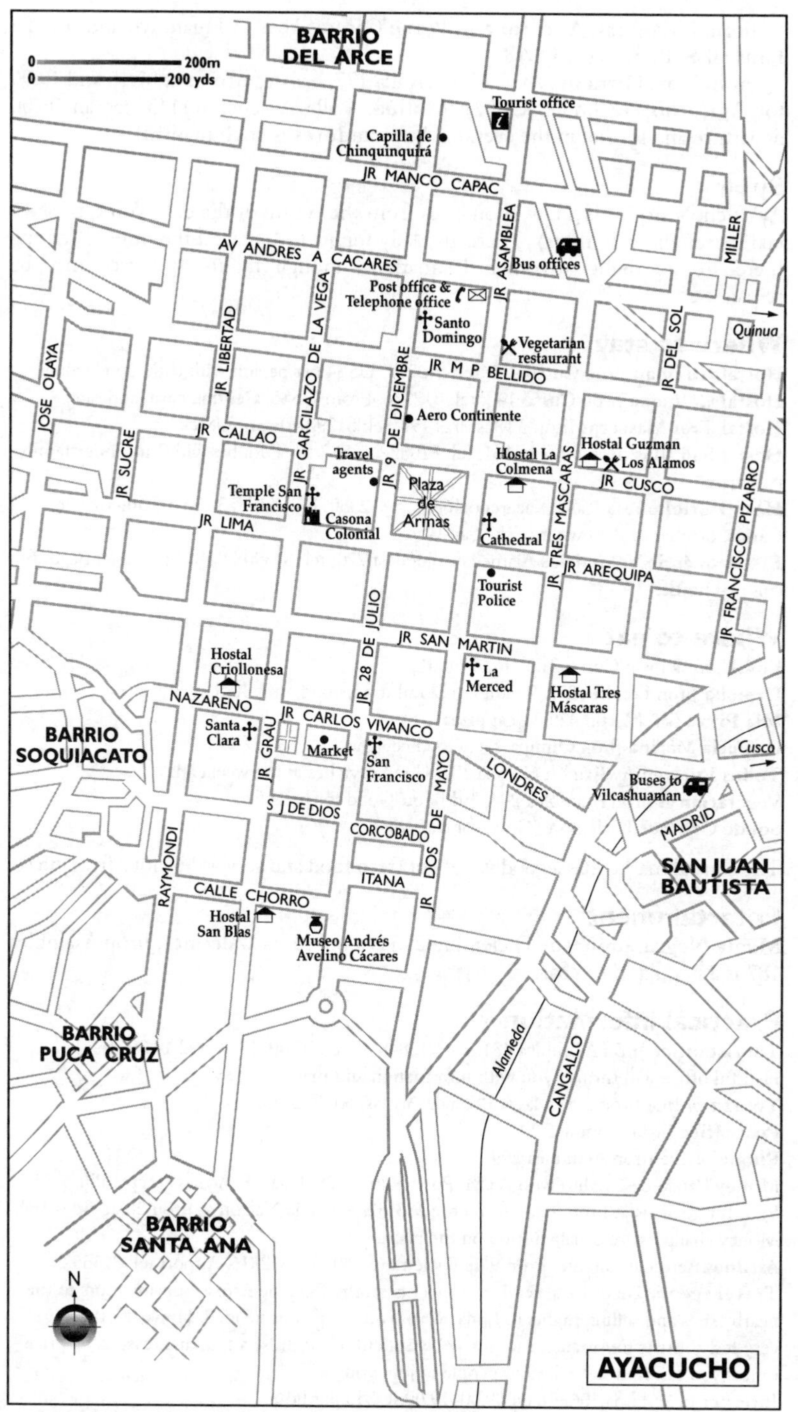
BARRIO DEL ARCE
0 200m
0 200 yds
Tourist office
Capilla de Chinquinquirá
JR MANCO CAPAC
JR ASAMBLEA
Bus offices
MILLER
AV ANDRES A CACARES
Post office & Telephone office
Santo Domingo
Vegetarian restaurant
JR DEL SOL
Quinua
JR LIBERTAD
JR GARCILAZO DE LA VEGA
JR 9 DE DICIEMBRE
JR M P BELLIDO
JOSE OLAYA
Aero Continente
JR CALLAO
JR SUCRE
Travel agents
Hostal La Colmena
JR TRES MASCARAS
Hostal Guzman
Los Alamos
JR CUSCO
Temple San Francisco
Plaza de Armas
JR LIMA
Casona Colonial
Cathedral
JR FRANCISCO PIZARRO
JR AREQUIPA
Tourist Police
JR SAN MARTIN
Hostal Criollonesa
JR 28 DE JULIO
La Merced
Hostal Tres Máscaras
NAZARENO
JR CARLOS VIVANCO
BARRIO SOQUIACATO
Santa Clara
JR GRAU
Market
San Francisco
LONDRES
Cusco
Buses to Vilcashuaman
S J DE DIOS
JR DOS DE MAYO
MADRID
CORCOBADO
RAYMONDI
SAN JUAN BAUTISTA
ITANA
CALLE CHORRO
Hostal San Blas
Museo Andrés Avelino Cáceres
BARRIO PUCA CRUZ
Alameda
CANGALLO
BARRIO SANTA ANA
N
AYACUCHO

in Jirón 3 Máscaras. **Antezana** in Pasaje Cáceres goes to Huancayo and Ica. To Lima takes 10 hrs, cost US$8.

From Lima **Ormeño**, Av Carlos Zavalla 177, has departures at 07.15 and 19.00 for Ayacucho (12 hours, US$7). **Molina**, Calle Ayacucho 1145 has an 08.00 departure and several in the evening. **Libertadores** is at Grau 491.

By air

Ayacucho's airport is a few kilometres from the centre of the city. You can take a taxi there (allow 10 mins). There are daily flights to Lima. At the time of writing there are no flights to other destinations, though flights to Cusco may be reinstated.

Where to stay

Hostal Guzman Jirón Cusco 241; tel: 812284. US$4 per person with bath, good value.

Hostal Colmena Jirón Cusco 140; tel: 812146. From US$5. Central, clean and safe.

Hostal Tres Mascaras Jirón 3 Máscaras 194; tel: 812921. From US$5.

Hostal San Blas Jirón Chorro 161; tel: 810552. US$7 for a double with bath. Nice family-run place.

Hostal Criollonesa Calle Nazareno 165; tel: 812350. From US$3. Interesting owner, Carlos, brother of the owner of the San Blas.

El Marqués de Valdelirios Alameda Bolognesi 720; tel: 813908. US$12 double. Beautiful colonial house.

Where to eat

Los Alamos Jirón Cusco 215. Good food.

Urpicha Jirón Londres 272. Traditional local food, good, only lunch.

Mia Pizza San Martin 420. Great pizza.

La Perla Marina Jirón Quinua 236. Good ceviches.

Todos Vuelven Av Ramón Castilla 307. Good ceviches at the weekends.

Vegetarian at Jirón Asamblea 204, 3rd floor. Good for breakfast.

Sol de Oro 9 de Diciembre. Good for *anticuchos*.

The central market has a good variety of fresh food and serves delicious fruit juices.

Entertainment

Magía Negra, Jirón 9 de Diciembre 293 is a pub; **Los Balcones,** Jirón Asamblea 187 is a popular disco bar.

Practical information

Tourist office Jirón Asamblea 481; tel: 912848. Open 07.00–13.00 and 14.30–16.45. Helpful office will furnish you with information and maps on the area.

Tourist police Jirón 2 de Mayo, Plaza de Armas; tel: 812179.

Post office Jirón Asamblea 293.

Phone office Jirón Asamblea 299.

Money Banco de Crédito with ATM, Portal Union 28, Plaza de Armas accepts Plus and Visa; Interbanc is at Jirón 9 de Diciembre 183; Banco de la Nación at Jirón 28 de Julio 167. Money changers are usually found on the plaza.

Airlines Aero Continente, Jirón 9 de Diciembre 160; tel: 812816. Airport tel: 813552.

Travel agents There are several travel agents on the Plaza de Armas offering tours to the nearby sites and selling flights to Lima. Wari Tours is recommended. However, there are very few tourists to Ayacucho so it may be difficult to organise a tour at a reasonable price unless you can find several other people to join you.

Internet Jirón Lima 106. Open 09.00–19.00, US$3 per hour.

What to see

Climb to the Mirador for great views over the city. The Plaza de Armas is one of the most beautiful and well kept in Peru, with a lovely peaceful garden in the centre and arched walkways all the way round with many colonial mansions, the cathedral, town hall and other public buildings.

Churches

There are over 30 churches in Ayacucho, many of which are not open other than for mass, but the façades are generally original colonial and beautifully made. The 16th-century church of **Santo Domingo** (Jirón 9 de Diciembre) still has its original façade, and the **Compañía de Jesus** (Jirón 28 de Julio) has an original pink and grey stone baroque façade. The altar has flora and fauna motifs and the chapel has a carved stone floral frieze. The **cathedral** on the Plaza Mayor took 59 years to build; it has three naves lined with wooden and gold-plated carvings, and a baroque style façade of pink stone with grey towers. The **Monastery of Santa Teresa** (Jirón 28 de Julio), founded in 1688, is a single-nave church which has a beautifully made altar and a mother-of-pearl inlaid high choir. There are still cloistered nuns here who sell sweets to the public. Around the Plaza de Armas and in 28 de Julio and 2 de Mayo there are several colonial *casonas*, mansion houses.

Crafts

Ayacucho is a major craft centre, with a distinctive style of work distinguishing it from other parts of the Andes. You can walk or take a taxi to the neighbourhood of **Santa Ana** to see weavers at work. Many extremely high quality rugs and blankets are made here and end up in art galleries around the world. The prices are good and there is plenty of variety of colours, sizes and designs. Ayacucho is also the centre for the production of finely carved *retablos*, also known as Cajónes de San Marcos (Saint Mark's boxes), which are brightly painted portable boxes crowded with figures and scenes, often representations of Andean festivals or particular customs. It is more difficult to find the workshops of these craftsmen – ask at the tourist office. Very creative ceramics are made near Ayacucho in **Quinua** (see below).

Museums

Museo de Antropología y Arqueología Av Independencia. Mostly Huari ceramics.
Museo Andrés Avelino Cáceres Calle 28 de Julio. In the beautiful colonial mansion Casona Vivanco. Open Mon–Sat 09.00–18.00, for a wide collection of colonial paintings and furniture.

Outside the city

The crumbling remains of what was once the capital of the **Wari** or **Huari** empire, with a thriving population of 60,000, lie 22km north of the city. Take a local bus from Av Centenario, or a tour with one of the travel agents.

Quinua is a typical village 37km from Ayacucho which produces the ceramic figures, buses, bulls and other scenes so characteristic of Ayacucho. Just 1km above the village is the historically important Pampa de Quinua, where liberty was won for Peru in the battle of Ayacucho on December 9 1824 after three long centuries of oppression under Spanish rule. Take a local bus from Avenida Centenario, or a tour.

Vilcashuamán is a small village 120km (3-4 hrs by bus) south of Ayacucho, which was built on top of an important Inca administrative centre. The ruins of

THE SHINING PATH (SENDERO LUMINOSO)

The Shining Path grew out of the Maoist Peruvian Communist Party, *Bandera Roja* (Red Flag), which was founded in the 1960s by Abimael Guzmán, philosophy professor at the University of Huamanga in Ayacucho. Born in 1931 in Arequipa, Guzmán studied philosophy and law at university and then began working at the university in Ayacucho in 1962. He began youth work with the Communist Party, and by 1964 had formed *Bandera Roja*, a group inspired by Mao and the Chinese Communist Party and demanding military organisation. Guzmán travelled to China in the late 1960s where he trained in ambush, assault and demolition. In the early 1970s Guzmán, disillusioned with the politics of the *Bandera Roja*, led a breakaway faction known as *Sendero Luminoso* (the Shining Path).

From the mid 1970s the party began to work towards putting revolutionary theory into practice. They made use of the students and teachers trained by *Sendero* sympathisers and militants who had influential jobs in Huamanga's education department, creating the base needed for an armed struggle. A military-style training school was started in 1979 and by 1980 the armed struggle had been launched. Banks, pylons, public offices and police posts were bombed, the attacks spreading throughout the country. Government reprisals began and anyone suspected of collaboration could be detained. Initial tolerance of *Sendero* by normal people turned to disillusionment and fear as deaths mounted. Local authorities, peasant leaders, development workers and others considered to be agents of the state were brutally murdered by the terrorists. Over the next decade the war continued with terrorist attacks, and the armed forces and police striking back with similar brutality. In the cities the people had to adjust to bombings, blackouts and police roundups, while in the country the people were caught in the crossfire of *Sendero*'s military style campaigning and the retributive violence of the authorities.

The nightmare ended in the 1990s with the capture of Guzmán and the gradual reduction in terrorism in Peru since then. It is estimated that almost 30,000 people were killed in Peru during this war and that US$25 billion of damage was done.

the site are right in the centre of the village, and the temple of the sun is still very much apparent, with characteristic high quality Inca stone masonry, although a Catholic church dedicated to John the Baptist has been built on top of it. The site has several different architectural styles. There is a five-layered pyramid structure with a double throne at the top, similar to those built on the coast, and an area lined by trapezoidal Inca doorways and niched walls, thought to have been a ceremonial plaza. Unfortunately there is very little information about Vilcashuamán. There are several cheap and very basic hostels and restaurants around the square in the village, and nearby a further Inca archaeological site known as Intihuatana–Pumaqocha. You can walk to this site from the village of Vischongo, 20km before Vilcashuamán. From Vischongo you can also walk up behind the village to see the beautiful, 12m-high Puya Raimondii plants at Titankayuq (3 hrs walk from Vischongo). There are several buses a day to Vischongo and Vilcashuamán from Ayacucho, departing from Puente Nuevo or you can take a tour with one of the travel agents.

ANDAHUAYLAS

This small town is about halfway between Ayacucho and Cusco, and makes a good stopping-off place if you want to break a long journey. There are daily buses to Cusco (12 hrs, US$9) and to Ayacucho (10 hrs) from Malecón Grau. You usually have to change buses here for Ayacucho or Cusco. Local minibuses leave from Alfonso Ugarte for Laguna Pacocha, the local beauty spot.

Hostal las Américas, Calle Juan Francisco Ramos 410; tel: 084 721646 and **Hostal Cruz del Sur**, Andahuaylas 121 are near the bus terminals and reasonable.

ABANCAY

This is the capital of the department of Apurimac, 195km from Cusco (6 hrs) and 387km from Ayacucho.

There are several cheap hostels here and plenty of places to eat. Abancay is situated at the foot of the mountain Ampay (5,228m), around which is the **Santuario Nacional de Ampay**. This sanctuary has been a protected area since 1987, cared for by the Ministry of Agriculture through the Instituto Nacional de Recursos Naturales (INRENA). Very few people visit, but it is an excellent place for birdwatchers and walkers. The area has a great diversity of flora and fauna, and is noted particularly for its 600-hectare forest of *intimpa*, podocarpus (*Podocarpus glomeratus*), an endangered species. The reserve covers several different vegetation types including subtropical montane forest between 2,800 and 3,800m; subalpine subtropical páramo between 3,900 and 4,500m; and, above that, tundra-type high-altitude vegetation. The average temperatures are as varied as the altitudes from –1.5°C at glacier level to 12.9°C at 2,800m. A good map and plenty of supplies are needed for excursions into the sanctuary.

Near Abancay (45km on the Cusco road) you can visit the Inca site of **Conchasa**, where you will find large carved boulders quite similar to the Qenko site near Cusco. The principal monument is **Saihuite**, the Temple of Stone, a giant rock some 4m in diameter and 2.5m tall. This rock is carved into a model of Tahauntisuyo, the Inca Empire. It has been creatively sculpted into forms which represent the flora, fauna, customs and topography of Tahuantinsuyo. The trail to Choquekirau starts from here. Allow 2 days each way.

From Nazca to Abancay is a 16-hour journey. You can break the journey in Chalhuanca, which has a basic hostel called **Zegarra** (US$3 per person). There are only overnight buses from Nazca. This is a fantastic journey, but be prepared for cold and check for the latest recommendations, as there have been robberies on this route.

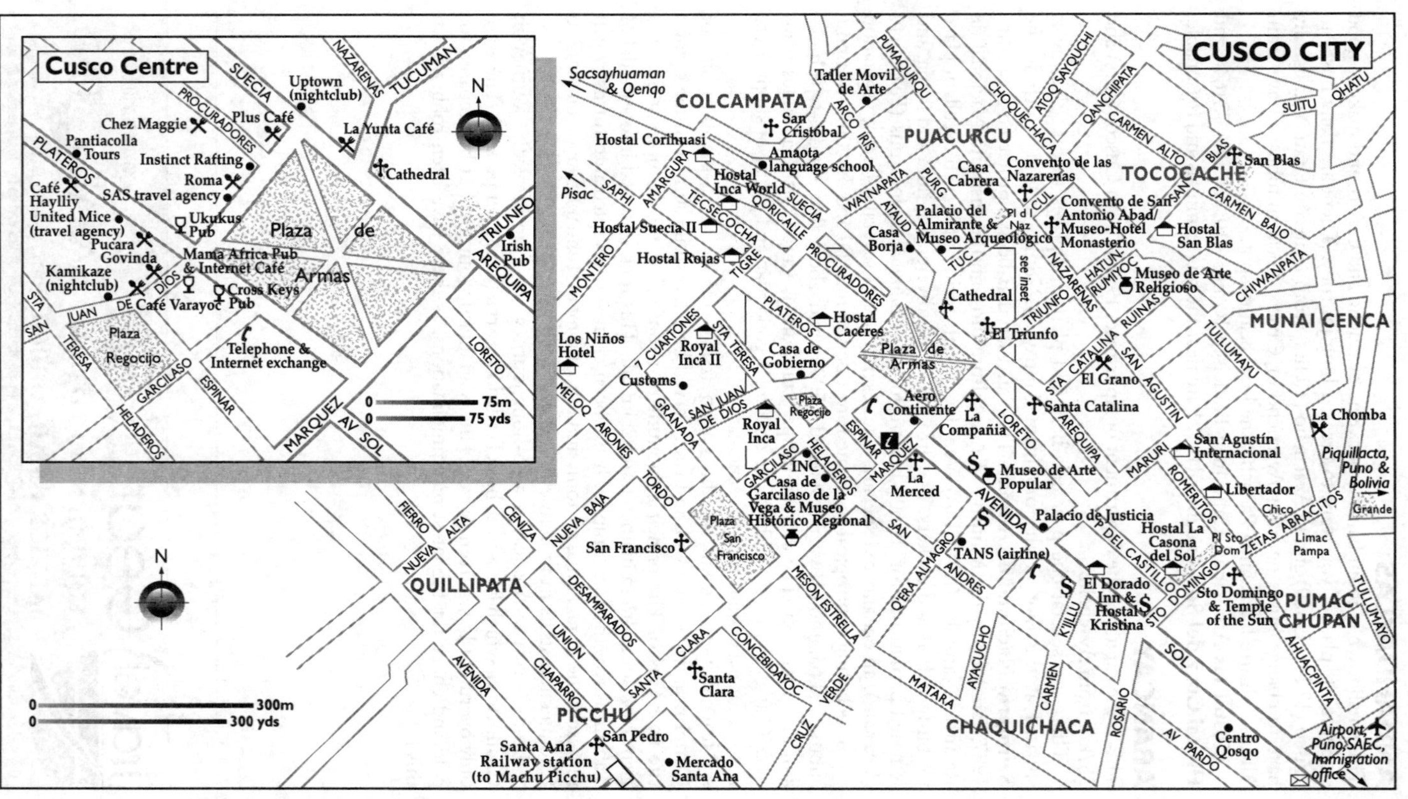
CUSCO CITY
Cusco Centre
TOCOCACHE
PUACURCU
COLCAMPATA
MUNAI CENCA
PUMAC CHUPAN
CHAQUICHACA
QUILLIPATA
PICCHU
San Blas
Hostal San Blas
Museo de Arte Religioso
Convento de San Antonio Abad/ Museo-Hotel Monasterio
Convento de las Nazarenas
Casa Cabrera
Palacio del Almirante & Museo Arqueológico
Casa Borja
Taller Movil de Arte
San Cristóbal
Amaota language school
Hostal Inca World
Hostal Corihuasi
Hostal Suecia II
Hostal Rojas
Hostal Caceres
Casa de Gobierno
Royal Inca
Royal Inca II
Customs
Los Niños Hotel
Cathedral
El Triunfo
see inset
Plaza de Armas
La Compañia
Aero Continente
La Merced
Plaza Regocijo
INC
Casa de Garcilaso de la Vega & Museo Histórico Regional
Plaza San Francisco
San Francisco
Santa Clara
Mercado Santa Ana
San Pedro
Santa Ana Railway station (to Machu Picchu)
El Grano
Santa Catalina
Museo de Arte Popular
Palacio de Justicia
TANS (airline)
Hostal La Casona del Sol
El Dorado Inn & Hostal Kristina
Sto Domingo & Temple of the Sun
Centro Qosqo
San Agustín Internacional
Libertador
La Chomba
Piquillacta, Puno & Bolivia
Airport, Puno, SAEC, Immigration office
Sacsayhuaman & Qenqo
Pisac
Limac Pampa
Chico
Grande
AV SOL
AV PARDO
AVENIDA SOL
0 300m
0 300 yds
N
Chez Maggie
Pantiacolla Tours
Café Haylliy
United Mice (travel agency)
SAS travel agency
Instinct Rafting
Roma
Plus Café
Uptown (nightclub)
La Yunta Café
Ukukus Pub
Mama Africa Pub & Internet Café
Cross Keys Pub
Café Varayoc
Pucara
Govinda
Kamikaze (nightclub)
Irish Pub
Telephone & Internet exchange
0 75m
0 75 yds

14 Cusco, Machu Picchu and Surrounding Area

This is indisputably the most popular part of Peru, with the splendid Inca site of Machu Picchu and bustling historical city of Cusco. There is plenty to see in the city and surrounding area, and this being the hub of tourist activity there are hotels, restaurants and an active nightlife to suit everybody.

CUSCO

Telephone code 084

Cusco is a lively and exciting city, with a resident population of 350,000 and a transient population of several thousand tourists. It is well geared up for the tourists, who are here all year round. The streets are lined with cafés, pizza and pasta restaurants and craft shops, interspersed with travel agencies offering the standard Inca Trail package, rafting, city tours and Sacred Valley tours. Cusco's main source of income now is from tourism, but it is also an important market town for the many farming communities all around. If you wander down to the markets you will see the huge range of products brought here to sell and trade from the highlands and the jungle.

Cusco is a beautiful city with a unique fusion of Inca stonework and elegant Spanish colonial architecture. There is always plenty going on, with the many churches and museums and nearby Inca sites to see and a seven-days-a-week buzzing nightlife. The altitude is 3,350m, so if you come from sea-level take it easy for a few days until you become acclimatised.

Just outside the town to the east and accessible on foot is the stunning monumental fortress of Sacsayhuamán, and other Inca sites of Tambomachay, Puca Pucara and Qenqo. Cusco is the gateway to the Urubamba Valley, known also as the Sacred Valley, one of the Incas' most important settled areas. The valley, a fertile agricultural area, with many key Inca sites, is easily reached by local bus from Cusco. At the southern end of the valley is the busy market town of Pisac with its tremendous Inca citadel. Downriver is the Inca town of Ollantaytambo, beyond which are the starting points for the Inca Trail to Machu Picchu.

History

Legend has it that Cusco was founded by the Inca king, Manco Capac and his sister queen, Mama Ocllo, in AD1100. Viracocha, the creator deity, placed these two children, son of the sun and daughter of the moon, in Lake Titicaca. Their mission was to found the Inca Empire, and civilise the earth. Manco Capac was given a long golden staff with which to test the earth he stood on. His travels took him to Cusco, where he was able to plunge the staff into the ground, which was the sign he needed to begin to build the Empire. According to legend the staff is buried deep underneath the main square of the city.

The reality is that the Incas evolved from a number of small tribes living in the valleys around Cusco. They were strongly influenced by the powerful Tiahuanaco culture centred around Lake Titicaca, and the many other cultures that preceded them. For the first few hundred years the Inca tribes remained within a short distance of Cusco, with little conquering ambition. In 1438, with the arrival of Pachacutec as the ninth Inca Emperor, things changed, and Cusco became the centre of a rapidly expanding civilisation. Pachacutec also masterminded the design of the imperial capital of Cusco. It was to be built in the shape of a puma, with the hilltop fortress of Sacsayhuamán at its head. The two rivers – Saphi, later called Huatanay, and Tullumayo – were channelled through the city, with their confluence at the puma's tail. The heart of the city was Huacaypata, a large central plaza which was the scene of all important ceremonies in the Inca calendar. This square was surrounded by the beautifully built palaces of the Inca kings. The characteristic interlocking stonework and trapezoidal doorways of these palaces is still in evidence today in many of the streets of central Cusco. Many of the foundations of Inca palaces were used subsequently by the Spanish invaders, in the construction of their own colonial buildings. See also page 158.

In 1650 a large earthquake shook the city, causing massive amounts of damage. The cathedral has a dramatic painting of the event. Bishop Mollinedo was responsible for the rebuilding, and under his influence the Cusqueño school of art emerged and flourished. The museums of Cusco hold many of the paintings by the indigenous Quechua and mestizo artists such as Quispe, Espinosa, Ruiz and Sinchi Roca.

Getting there and away

By road

Cusco has a new bus station (*Terminal Terrestre*) at the southeast end of town heading towards the airport. Almost all long-distance buses depart from here, although some companies still have their own depots. Departures include Puno (7–8 hrs, US$5), Arequipa (11 hrs, US$8) and Lima (24 hrs, US$18). Most buses to Abancay, Ayacucho, and to the west go from Arcopata at the northwest edge of town, although some now leave from the bus station. Buses to Urubamba leave from Calle Huascar and to Pisac from Calle Tullumayo, below Av de la Cultura.

By air

The airport in Cusco is about 5km from the centre of town, just over US$1 in a taxi. There are flights to Lima, Juliaca, Arequipa and La Paz. Internal flights are relatively cheap and there are often special offers available. There is a departure tax of US$5 national, US$25 international.

By train

To Machu Picchu

Unless you hike the Inca Trail the only way to get to Machu Picchu is by train. This beautiful journey across the plain of Anta and down the Sacred Valley takes 3½–4 hours. Check at the tourist office or railway station for the latest times and prices. In 1999 the train company was privatised and train services and prices are subject to change. Tickets for all classes except the local train to Machu Picchu are currently sold at the Puno railway station on Avenida del Sol. The trains leave from San Pedro station, which is open daily 08.00–11.00 and 15.00–16.00 (for local train ticket purchases). You can choose the type of train you travel in; times and prices for 2000 are:

Autovagon 06.00, US$55; return from Aguas Calientes at 15.00
Local 06.25, US$10 return from Puente Ruinas at 16.30

There is a new station at Aguas Calientes which the Autovagon uses; only the local train uses the main station in the centre of the town.

The local train used to go as far as Quillabamba but in 1998 heavy rains caused severe flooding and landslides at Santa Teresa, so this section of the line is now closed.

To Juliaca and Puno

Trains to Juliaca and Puno go from the station Av del Sol, five blocks from the Plaza de Armas. It's best to buy your tickets at least a day in advance for this dramatic journey across the altiplano. Trains depart from Cusco on Mon, Wed, Fri and Sat at 08.00. They arrive in Juliaca at 17.00 and Puno at 18.00. From Puno trains depart on Mon, Wed, Thur and Sat.

Económico US$8, non-reclining seats, crowded and uncomfortable
Turismo US$19, reclining seats, less crowded
Inka US$23, reclining seats, deluxe service

The train line splits at Juliaca, with part going to Puno and part to Arequipa. This means inevitable shunting of carriages and sometimes engine changes at Juliaca station.

Where to stay

The very cheapest hotels here are usually extremely simple with small, often internal rooms, and little in the way of furniture. Many also tend to be located in the least safe parts of town, by the stations or in San Blas, the area up behind the cathedral. In these hostels there are occasional reports of theft from rooms and left luggage. They are unlikely to have hot water; there is often a shortage of water in Cusco so unless a hotel has its own tanks there could be no water at all for parts of the day. In peak season, July and August, it can be difficult to find any room at all, so it is worth booking a few days ahead.

Huinariy Hostal Saphi 789; tel: 252400; fax: 252515. US$4–10 shared bath, US$5–15 with bathroom. Central, friendly, use of kitchen, hot water 24 hrs, safe and left luggage. Also operate treks to Ausangate and Camino Inca at competitive prices. Popular with Israelis.
Hostal Cáceres Plateros 368; tel: 232616. US$5–12 shared bathroom. Old colonial house with central patio, some interior rooms, others overlooking the busy street. Laundry, safe, left luggage. Free transfer if you advise of flight, train etc
Albergue Municipal Calle J Kiscapata 240, San Cristobal; tel: 252506. US$7 per person.
Hostal Rojas Calle Tigre 129; tel: 228184. US$8–10 shared bathroom, US$6–15 double with bathroom. Central, clean, quiet with interior patio garden, hot water, laundry, common room and cable TV.
Hostal Suecia 11 Tel: 239757. US$7–15 shared bathroom, US$10–23 private bathroom. Central, clean and friendly popular hostel in a colonial house with glassed-over courtyard.
Los Niños Hotel Calle Meloq 442; tel: 231424; email: ninos@correo.dnet.com.pe From US$10 per person, US$5 extra per room for a private bathroom. Immaculate, comfortable, beautiful old colonial house with central patio. Highly recommended. Café open all day. Part of a Dutch-run project to give a home to local street children.
Hostal Pankcha Real Calle Tandapata; tel: 237484. Friendly, clean place in the San Blas area.

Where to eat

There are dozens of restaurants in Cusco offering a wide variety of food. Many have adapted to the backpacker market so it's relatively easy to find pizza, pasta, burgers and vegetarian food. It is often much better value to eat a main meal at midday, when most restaurants serve cheap fixed-price lunches, usually about US$2. Calle Plateros and Procuradores off the Plaza de Armas are lined with restaurants offering good value international food. If you venture further afield you will find more local places. At lunchtimes try the *picanterías* of **La Chomba** in Calle Tullumayo or **Quinta Eulalia** in Calle Choquechaca for excellent local food.

Café Haylliy Plateros. Does good vegetarian food.
Govinda Calle Espaderos. Good cheap vegetarian food, wholemeal bread.
Greens Tandapata 700. Serves a Sunday dinner if you are missing home, also has curry, videos, cable TV and a big sitting room.
Kusikuy Calle Plateros 348. Serves typical Peruvian food including *cuy* (guinea pig), *anticucho* (kebabs), *chicharron* (deep-fried pork), *rocotto relleno* (stuffed peppers), *trucha* (trout), and *sopa criolla* (a typical soup). They have a fixed-price good-value lunch for US$2.
La Yunta, **Plus Café**, **La Tertulia**, **Globetrotter** and **Ayllu**, all around the Plaza de Armas, are great cafés also serving food.
Pucara Calle Plateros 309. Good food, set lunch excellent value. Japanese-owned restaurant, clean and good value.

Entertainment

The popular nightclubs in Cusco are **Ukukus**, Calle Plateros 316; **Kamikaze**, Plaza Recocijo; **Mama Africa**, Calle Espaderos 135 and **Uptown**, on the Plaza de Armas. These clubs often have live folk music or similar groups playing from about 22.00, and then from midnight they are discos. The **Cross Keys** pub on the Plaza de Armas is owned by English ornithologist Barry Walker, who also runs Manu Expeditions. It's a good place to meet other backpackers.

Ukukus and **Tumis**, both in Calle Plateros, show videos of original version films in the afternoons.

Practical information

Tourist office Plaza de Armas, Portal Belén. Give information and sell multi-entrance ticket for Cusco tourist sites, except Korikancha. US$10, valid 10 days.
SAEC Clubhouse Av del Sol 930; tel: 223102; email: saec@wayna.rcp.net.pe
Tourist police Av del Sol just outside Korikancha. Or Calle Saphi.
Immigration office Av del Sol. If you need to extend your tourist visa you can do so here.
Post office Av del Sol.
Phone office Av del Sol or Calle Garcilaso just off the Plaza de Armas.
Money Av del Sol has lots of places to change money and travellers' cheques, banks and change offices. The Plaza de Armas also has several money change offices.
Airlines Aero Continente, Plaza de Armas. TANS, Calle Almagro 133; tel: 242727.
Equipment rental For mountain bikes, boots, tents, sleeping bags, waterproofs and stoves try Soqllaq'asa, Calle Santa Teresa. Several of the trekking agencies on Plateros have equipment to rent, but do check the quality as it is usually pretty poor.
Laundry on Calle Siete Cuartones, Calle Teqsicocha 450, Saphi 578, usually US$1 per kilo, same day service.
Internet There are several Internet offices in Cusco, including: Av del Sol, Open Mon–Sat 08.00–22.00 US$2 per hour. The telephone office just off the Plaza de Armas Calle Garcilaso has lots of computers for Internet connections.
Spanish classes The best place for Spanish or Quechua classes is Amauta language school on Calle Suecia 480; tel: 241422. There is also a small school at Calle Purgatorio 395; tel: 235830/235903. US$5 per hour for one to one classes.

Travel agencies

Dozens of agencies in Cusco offer tours including a day trip to the Valle Sagrado from US$12, and city tours from US$8, 4-day Camino Inca tour from US$60. Others offer more specialist services such as mountain bike trips, alternative treks and paragliding, and horseriding, rafting and jungle expeditions. Watch out for cowboy travel agents. Competition amongst the agencies offering Inca Trail treks is high, and as a result prices are rock bottom. This means that the service you get can be miserly, with poor equipment, little food and unprofessional guides. During high season there is a danger that your agency will not take enough equipment on the trail and you may have to fight for a tent! Ask around for recommendations from other trekkers, and get a contract from the agency. Similarly, with rafting trips, competition has forced the prices down, the result being dangerous skimping on the safety side. In 2000 there is a move to regulate these agencies which may mean an end to cheap packages for backpackers.

Amazonas Explorer POBox 72; tel: 236826; email: info@amazonas-explorer.com. Safe and environmentally friendly rafting expeditions on Peruvian and Bolivian rivers, the Apurimac, Cotahuasi, Tambopata and Tuichi.
Ecoamazonía Lodge Plateros 351; tel: 236159. Bookings for their lodge in Puerto Maldonado.
Instinct Procuradores 50; tel: 233451. One of the original rafting companies.
Manu Ecological Adventures Plateros 356; tel: 261640.
Manu Expeditions Avenida Pardo 895; tel: 226671; fax: 236706; email: manuexpe+@amauta.rcp.net.pe Long standing experts in Manu trips. The most costly, but well worth it. 4-day tours from US$1,000. Owned by husband and wife team Barry Walker and Rosario Velarde, part owners of the Manu Wildlife Centre.
Mayuc Plaza de Armas; tel: 232666. One of the older rafting companies.
Pantiacolla Tours Plateros 360; tel: 238323. Reputable agency for Manu tours, medium price range. 5-day tour from US$725.
Peruvian Andean Treks Av Pardo 705; tel: 225701. Long-standing trekking agency.
Q'ente on Plateros and **SAS** on Plaza de Armas. A couple of the better Inca Trail agencies.
Tambopata Jungle Lodge Av Pardo 705; tel: 225701.
United Mice Plateros 348; tel: 221139. One of the better agencies for the Inca Trail.
Vilca Expediciones Calle Saphi. Reputable trekking agency, offering a variety of routes. Manu also, at the budget end of the market.

What to see

The **Plaza de Armas** lies at the heart of the city, and is the hub as far as most tourist activity goes. There are dozens of cafés, restaurants, craft shops, travel agents and just about everything else you need, clustered around the square. It is a wonderful place to sit and chat and watch life go by. Originally the central square was twice the size it is now, and used for all important Inca festivities; as the civic square of the Inca city, it was surrounded by the palaces of the successive Inca emperors. Paved roads converged on the square from the four corners of the huge empire of Tiahuantinsuyo. The **cathedral** stands on the northeast side of the square on the site of Inca Viracocha's palace, while on the adjacent south side of the plaza is **La Compañía**, a beautiful example of colonial architecture, built on the site of the palace where Huayna Capac once lived. The Pizzeria Roma stands where Pachacutec had his palace. During colonial times the square was the scene of executions, including that of the rebel Tupac Amaru in 1572.

Calle Loreto, which runs off the square on the adjacent side to the cathedral, is one of the finest for its intact Inca walls. On the right side was the Inca palace belonging to Huayna Capac, where the **Compañía** church is now. The courtyard of the palace was named Amarucancha, courtyard of the serpents, and you can still see carved serpents on the door lintel of the colonial entranceway halfway along the street. On the other side of Calle Loreto was the Acllahuasi, the House of the Chosen Women, or Virgins of the Sun. Here lived the carefully selected concubines of the Incas, beautifully attired and educated in the skills needed to serve their lords.

Hatunrumiyoc, is the street of the 12-angled stone. The wall forms a part of the original wall of Inca Roca's palace. The style is very different from Calle Loreto where the blocks are regularly shaped and fitted together in precise lines. This wall is made of massive polygonal stone blocks in an irregular pattern.

Churches

The cathedral and El Triunfo church

This impressive cathedral, built on the site of the palace of Inca Viracocha, dominates the Plaza de Armas. The first church in Cusco was the Triunfo, founded in 1536, and built to commemorate the Spanish conquerors' victory over the Incas. El Triunfo was built on the site of the Inca armoury, Suntur Wasi. During Manco Capac's siege of the city in 1536 the Spanish hid here, and when the Incas attempted to burn Cusco down the building would not catch fire. The Spanish declared that the Virgin had put out the fire and emerged from the armoury to retake the city.

After a certain amount of indecision about where to put it, the cathedral was added to this church between 1559 and 1654. Some of the stones for the cathedral came from the Inca palaces and some from the great monolithic construction at Sacsayhuamán. At the far end of the cathedral you can see the original wooden altar standing behind the silver altar which is used in its place. The choir is 17th century, made from ebony and cedar. Many of the paintings are from the Cusqueñan school, also from the 17th century. They are of typical Spanish religious style with local touches: look for the guinea pig being eaten at the last supper on the painting by local artist Marcos Zapata. Some of the faces in the paintings have typical Indian features. One of the most treasured features of the cathedral is the venerated Señor de Los Temblores, Lord of the Earthquakes. This figure, standing on a silver litter, was a gift from Carlos V in Spain. During the destructive earthquake of 1650 it was carried around the city square and was credited with ending the tremor. Each year on Easter Monday it is paraded through the square. In the sacristy there is a series of paintings of all the bishops of Cusco, starting with Pizarro's accompanying priest Vicente de Valverde who was heavily involved with the capture of Atahualpa at Cajamarca in 1532.

La Compañía de Jesús

Open Mon–Fri 09.00-11.00 and 15.00–18.00

This church was built by the Jesuits in the 16th and 17th centuries. It contains many notable paintings from the Cusqueño school. During its construction, there was much discussion about its size and grandeur; eventually the local bishop complained to the Pope in Rome that the church outshone the cathedral, but it was too late to halt construction. Friction continued between the two churches until the Jesuits were expelled from Peru in the 18th century.

La Merced Church, Convent and Museum

Open Mon–Sat 08.30–12.00 and 14.00-17.00

This church was originally built in the 16th century but was completely destroyed by the earthquake of 1650. It was rebuilt and contains the remains of Gonzalo

Pizarro and Diego Almagro (Francisco Pizarros's brother and his partner). There are some interesting paintings in the church and museum next to it, and a solid gold 12m-high altar encrusted with precious stones.

San Blas

Open Mon–Sat 10.00-11.30 and 14.00-17.30

This relatively simple church was built from adobe in the 16th century. The church has an intricately carved pulpit made from cedar wood, brought from the eastern Andean mountain slopes. The style is Spanish, but most probably a skilled local artist did the carving. At the base are flowers and fruits, then the figures of known heretics and enemies of the Catholic church, who carry the weight of the pulpit. Above them are seven gruesome faces, representing the seven deadly sins. The Virgin Mary and the four apostles, Matthew, Mark, Luke and John, also feature alongside columns and little angels. San Blas, the patron saint of the church, is on the back of the pulpit, and on the canopy there are similar designs to the base, fruit, flowers and angels, with the figure of Saint Paul, accompanied by five archangels. One of these archangels is holding several objects used in the crucifixion, and at his feet there is a human skull that may belong to the creator of the pulpit.

Santa Catalina Convent and Museum

Open Mon–Sat 09.30–17.30; Friday closes early.

This complex, which contains religious art and furniture, was built on the top of the residences of the Virgins of the Sun.

Santo Domingo and Koricancha

Open Mon–Sat 09.30-18.00

This was the site of the Inca Sun Temple, undoubtedly the most important ceremonial centre in the whole empire. The extremely high quality stonework reflects the importance of this holy site. It is likely that Inca marriages were held here, and mummies of the Inca kings may have been kept here, resting on golden thrones and brought out into the plaza only for major ceremonies. Ceremonies were held in Korikancha to worship the chief Inca god Inti, the sun. The moon and certain constellations were also sacred and worshipped, particularly at solstices and equinoxes. The temple consisted of a main hall dedicated to the Sun, and smaller rooms dedicated to the lesser gods, the moon and stars, thunder and rainbow. The walls of the main hall were once lined with gold plate and a huge round gold disc hung from the wall, representing Inti. When the Spanish took over the city they destroyed most of the temple and built the Dominican church of Santo Domingo in its place. This church fell in the 1650 earthquake and had to be rebuilt, and in 1950 some of the church and the tower again fell. Inside the church you find paintings including representations of dogs holding torches in their mouths. These are the guard dogs of god, in Latin Dominicanus, after which this religious order was named.

Museums

El Taller Móvil de Arte Calle Ladrillos 491. Open Wed–Sun 11.00–17.00. Art and paintings by children of indigenous communities around Cusco.

Arte Religioso Calle Hatunrumiyoc. Open Mon–Sat 08.00–11.30 and 15.00–17.30.

Histórico Natural Plaza de Armas. Open Mon–Fri 08.00–13.00 and 15.00–18.00.

Histórico Regional Open Mon–Sat 08.00–17.30. A chronological collection of artefacts from prehispanic cultures, in the house that belonged to Garcilaso, writer of chronicles and Inca historian. Includes objects excavated from Cusco and Machu Picchu in the last few years.

Arqueología Calle Tucumán and Ataud. Open Mon–Sat 08.00–17.00. An interesting collection of pieces, some of which you have to request to see, housed in an amazing old building. This museum is housed in the Admiral's Palace, one of the most sumptuous mansions in the city, and home to many influential people. The Inca Huascar, brother of Atahualpa, had his palace on this site, followed by Almagro until his murder by Pizarro. The Maldonado family then lived in the mansion, governors of Cusco and powerful in the armed forces. Many counts and bishops succeeded Admiral Maldonado after his death in 1643. It was the home of the last Spanish viceroy before independence and then of President Santa Cruz. In the 20th century it belonged to the university before becoming a museum.

Around Cusco

If you have a few free days in Cusco and feel like getting out of the town, there are plenty of things to do.

Sacsayhuamán, Qenqo, Puca Pucara and Tambomachay

These four impressive sites are within walking distance from Cusco. They are included on the multi-entrance ticket available for US$10 from the tourist office. Each of the sites is open daily 07.00–17.30. You can take a half-day tour from one

LOOKING FOR VILCABAMBA

Simon Calder

Looking for Vilcabamba is the title of a four-part BBC Radio 4 series that features a journey from Cusco to Vilcabamba, the last refuge of the Inca. It was a journey I made with chief producer Mick Webb, accompanied by our guide, Narciso Huaman. Narciso is an *arriero* who will provide travellers with an excellent guiding and cargo service. He lives just outside Huancacalle, and proved to be a superb horseman, an expert guide and a good companion on the three-day journey from Huancacalle to Vilcabamba. For his services, and those of his two horses, Castano and Beton, we paid a total of 240 soles (US$80: 40 soles per day for the six-day return journey). He can be contacted through Genaro, who acts as the INC chief/guide/top man in Huancacalle, and who is himself a good bloke. Note that Narciso, in common with most of the people you will meet along the way, speaks Quechua first, Spanish second and nothing else.

Travellers should not underestimate the journey from Vilcabamba to the roadhead at San Miguel/Chuanquiri. Some sources say the walk takes four hours; locals say five; but it took us six and proved one of the most demanding days we experienced.

At Chuanquiri, there are trucks daily from Friday to Monday. At other times you can charter a pick-up to Kiteni for around US$40–50, but work on the road may mean that the truck cannot get through. Despite advice to the contrary, the last microbus from Kiteni to Quillabamba departs around 15.00 or 15.30 and takes six hours.

Once in Quillabamba, steer clear of the literal fleapit that is the Hostal Cuzco; if the insects don't get you, noises from the urban farm next door will. And note that Selva Sur has the most aggressive sales team of all the four bus companies between Quillabamba and Cusco, and also the worst buses.

of the many agencies in Cusco, or visit the sites on foot, or by taxi. If you are walking, follow Calle Resbalosa or Calle Suecia upwards from the Plaza de Armas and you'll end up at Sacsayhuamán, the closest to Cusco.

Sacsayhuamán is a tremendous temple-fortress built of huge interlocking stone blocks. It apparently forms the head of the puma, the animal whose shape Cusco was designed to represent. Nobody really knows when the site was begun or for exactly what purpose it was built, but you'll hear a few theories if you take a tour. The site is centred around a large esplanade on the hillside above Cusco. Three layers of zig-zag walls line the esplanade, built from huge stones as big as 9m across and weighing up to 350 tonnes. How the Incas moved and cut these monoliths remains a mystery.

Much of the fortress has been destroyed, the lesser walls and buildings razed to the ground, or removed for the building of the city below. There were three towers on top of the walled area. One was Muyucmarca, circular in shape with walls adorned with gold and silver, and a water cistern fed by underground canals. The other two towers were for the soldiers garrisoned here. On the far side of the esplanade you can see the so-called Inca's Throne, where the supreme Inca supposedly watched parades going on below. Slightly beyond this is the sunken area known as Suchana, which was probably some sort of reservoir with ritual baths round about. The very popular and colourful midwinter festival of Inti Raymi is celebrated on the esplanade here every June 24.

The site of **Qenqo** lies beyond the large white statue of Christ (*El Cristo Blanco*), about 2km from Sacsayhuamán. It is a large chunk of limestone intricately carved with channels and animal shapes that enhance its natural shape. Qenqo was probably a sacred site, perhaps for sacrifices.

Puca Pucara means red fort. This fort that probably also served as a resting house (*tambo*) for visitors to Cusco or messengers stands on a promontary about 6km from Qenqo, overlooking the road into Cusco. It is not particularly impressive, but is worth a quick look. Just across the road are the Inca baths of **Tambomachay**, a beautifully designed and well-preserved site.

Chinchero

The Sunday market at Chinchero is less tourist orientated than Pisac market. The town has a church that is undergoing interior restoration to reduce further deterioration of its once beautiful interior paintwork. There are Inca buildings and fine carved stonework all around the town, and you can walk from here down the trails behind the town to the Urubamba Valley. Chinchero has a few restaurants serving *chicharron*, deep-fried pork. To get here take the Urubamba bus from Calle Tullumayo. The journey has one of the best views in all Peru with the Sacred Valley below and the Urubamba and Vilcabamba mountains in the distance.

Maras and Moray

Between Chinchero and Urubamba there is a turn off the road to the north leading to the village of **Maras**. From Maras you can take a trail heading down towards the valley bottom, passing through the amazing **salt mines** (*salinas*). This is a collection of cascading terraces of water-filled pools, encrusted with salt crystals. It is mostly women who have the heavy-duty work of digging up the crystals, loading them into sacks and then onto mules for the journey out to the road. The path takes you down the side of the terraces to the main Urubamba road, where you can wave down a bus. If you continue walking through Maras along the valley you come to the unique **Inca terraces of Moray**. These terraces take the shape of concentric circles sunk into the ground, presumed to be some sort of Inca agricultural growing station. The scale is immense, which you appreciate if you climb all the way down to the centre. You can walk from here down to the Urubamba Valley and pick up a bus on the road. Allow 2 hours to Moray and a further 2 hours from there to the road.

Tipón

Take the Urcos bus from Av La Cultura in Cusco and get off in the village of Tipón (23km from Cusco). From there walk up the road to the site (1 hr) or take a taxi. This is an impressive Inca site of extensive long terraces, with an irrigation system of deep-cut channels flowing down the edge of the terraces. There is a spring with a beautifully carved surround at the top end of the terraces, a fountain or bath, several buildings which were probably houses, and up on the hillside above the terraces, an aqueduct and a further collection of buildings.

THE SACRED VALLEY

The Sacred Valley of the Incas is the name given to the scenic Urubamba Valley, which was formed by the erosion of the Vilcanota River. This river is also confusingly called the Urubamba. The part of the valley which is referred to as sacred is a length of around 100km in which there are numerous villages that were significant during Inca times, as administration centres or places of ceremonial importance. The valley has a much warmer climate than Cusco – wealthy Cusqueños often have second homes there for weekends away. It also is extremely fertile, producing some of the best maize in all of Peru. The principal places of interest in the valley are the small towns of Pisac and Ollantaytambo.

Pisac

Pisac is 33km from Cusco, about an hour by local bus. As the road comes down into Pisac you can see the Inca ruins up on the hillside above the town. There are extensive terraces, probably used for growing maize but also built to prevent erosion, as a defensive wall and for aesthetic reasons. In the central square of the town there is a big market every Thursday and Sunday, for locals and tourists. The tourist part has bags, jumpers, woven rugs, woollen gloves, hats, socks and a variety of masks, pieces of stone, jewellery and other bits and pieces. The local market is mostly agricultural produce, much of which is brought here by mule from the highland villages in valleys of the Urubamba mountains behind Pisac. The clothes of the Indians from the Pisac area are distinctive, particularly the hats worn by the women.

Getting there and away

Take a local bus to Pisac from the bus station in Cusco on Calle Tulumayo. Buses to Calca go through Pisac. You can take a bus to Calca from Pisac and then continue down the Urubamba Valley to Urubamba or Ollantaytambo, and back to Cusco.

Where to stay

Samana Wasi on the plaza is a nice place to stay at US$3 per person; tel: 203018. There are a couple of other places – the Hotel Pisaq, tel: 203062, from US$10 per person and the Parador de Pisaq, tel: 203061, from US$5. There are several restaurants in and around the main square.

The ruins

To enjoy the site fully you need a full day. From the town head up the road to the left of the large Pisonay Tree in the square towards the terraces, or take a taxi from Pisac to the top, from where you can wander down. This is the best option if you

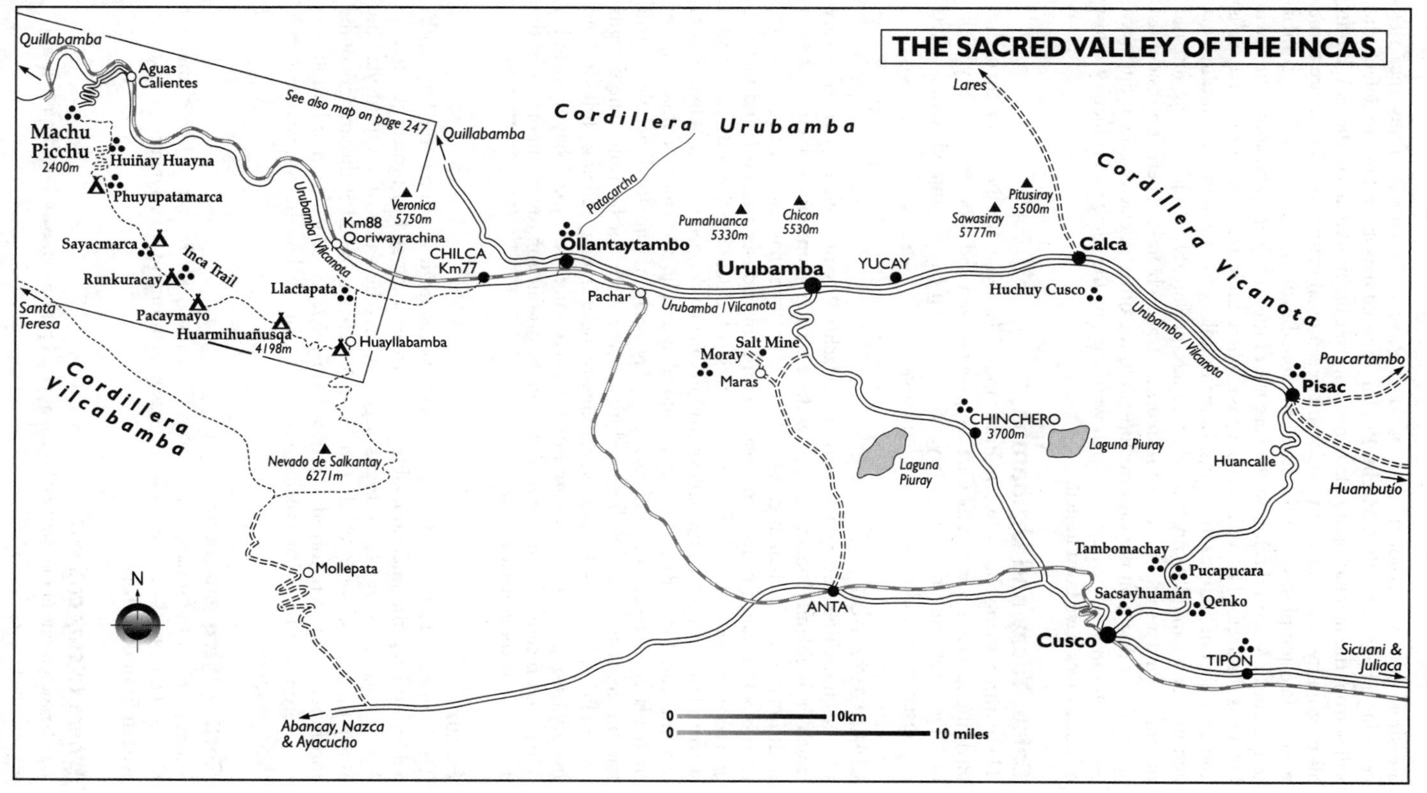
THE SACRED VALLEY OF THE INCAS
Quillabamba
Aguas Calientes
See also map on page 247
Machu Picchu
2400m
Huiñay Huayna
Phuyupatamarca
Cordillera Urubamba
Quillabamba
Patacarcha
Veronica
5750m
Km88
Qoriwayrachina
Urubamba / Vilcanota
Sayacmarca
Inca Trail
Runkuracay
CHILCA
Km77
Ollantaytambo
Llactapata
Pacaymayo
Huarmihuañusqa
4198m
Huayllabamba
Santa Teresa
Cordillera Vilcabamba
Nevado de Salkantay
6271m
Mollepata
N
Abancay, Nazca & Ayacucho
Pumahuanca
5330m
Chicon
5530m
Urubamba
Pachar
Urubamba / Vilcanota
Salt Mine
Moray
Maras
Laguna Piuray
ANTA
0 10km
0 10 miles
Lares
Sawasiray
5777m
Pitusiray
5500m
YUCAY
Calca
Huchuy Cusco
Cordillera Vicanota
Urubamba / Vilcanota
CHINCHERO
3700m
Laguna Piuray
Paucartambo
Pisac
Huancalle
Huambutío
Tambomachay
Pucapucara
Sacsayhuamán
Qenko
Cusco
TIPÓN
Sicuani & Juliaca

are short of time or not used to walking. Pisac is the largest of any Inca site, covering a bigger area than Machu Picchu. It could have been built to defend the valley from the marauding jungle tribes just over the mountains to the east, but in all probability it served as an important ceremonial centre too. There are some well-crafted temples within the site, ceremonial baths and an Intihuatana, similar to the one at Machu Picchu. At the very top of the site, over 400m above the town below, is the sector known as Kalla Q'asa, where there are strong protective walls and a number of baths or fountains. In the middle section you find the Intihuatana and the most carefully constructed buildings, presumably temples of the sun and the moon, and a series of fountains fed by a water channel. There is a residential sector lower down on the eastern slopes. On the other side across the Quitamayo gorge you can see some caves, which were used by the Incas as a cemetery. Most of these caves have been looted.

Calca, Yucay and Urubamba

These three towns lie between Pisac and Ollantaytambo. None of them has anything special to see, but they are all quite pleasant and good bases for day walks or longer treks into the valleys beyond. Each town has accommodation, markets and restaurants, and plenty of passing buses.

Ollantaytambo

On the train line between Cusco and Machu Picchu, Ollantaytambo is very much a highland Indian village with a strong community identity and a traditional, though changing, way of life. The town has an Inca street pattern, each block having a central courtyard with many houses around it and just one entrance onto the street. The great fortress of Ollanta still stands and is well worth a look around. In the valleys around Ollanta the people make a living from farming and the herding of llamas and alpaca. The weavings of this area are particularly well known and the everyday wear of the local people is still handmade, with special elaborate clothes being made for festivals. The designs are traditional, symbolic representations of flora, fauna, religion, folklore and history, though natural dyes are much less common now than they used to be. There has recently been a revival in pottery production, once important in the area, to feed the tourist market.

History

The impressive fortress of Ollanta was built at a strategic location in the Urubamba Valley, to keep the unconquerable jungle tribes away and to protect the trail to Machu Picchu. After Manco Inca's siege of Cusco he retreated to Ollantaytambo. When the Spanish approached to attack, they were astounded by the strength of the fortification and were forced to retreat hastily. Manco added to their humiliation by diverting the River Patacancha to flood the plains below the fortress, hampering their progress.

Getting there and away

Buses go from the square to and from Urubamba, where you have to change for Cusco. The Cusco–Machu Picchu trains pass through Ollantaytambo; the station is 1km from the village.

Where to stay and eat

La Miranda is one of the cheapest hostels at US$4 per person. Basic but adequate if you are on a budget.

La Chosa US$5 per person, not always open, basic but adequate.
Urpi Wasi Next to the station is US$7 per person. Nice place, garden, restaurant.
Hostal Las Orquídeas On the road to the railway station; tel. 084 204032. US$10 per person with breakfast. Nice rooms, comfortable, garden, clean, recommended. Dinner available.
El Albergue at the railway station is a great place, a bit more expensive than the others, but comfortable and very clean, handy for the trains.

There are a couple of restaurants, the **Alcazar** on Calle del Medio and the **Fortaleza** on the plaza. **Café Kapuly** and **La Ñusta** are nice cafés. Try the market for excellent fresh fruit juices.

Practical information

Ollantaytambo has a telephone office on the main square.

What to see

The site of the **fortress of Ollanta** at Ollantaytambo is one of the most impressive of all the Inca sites. It is open daily 08.00–17.00. There are several sectors to the site: the first area, beyond the entrance and up the steep flight of steps through the terraces, is the Temple of the Sun. The stonework is heavily influenced by the Tiahuanaco style, with straight-sided stones separated by strips of stone, and the step motif carved on the front. There is a residential area above this, and below is the tremendous wall of niches with typical Inca stonework. There are many blocks of stone that have never been put in their place – some never even made it to Ollanta and are lying by the roadside or between the site and the quarry, on the far hillside. At the bottom of the steps heading a little way up the valley you come to the Baños de la Nusta, or bath of the princess. On the rock wall which forms the side of the valley is a whole series of carvings, steps, niches and slabs.

A beautiful two-hour walk (each way) up the Patacancha Valley will take you to the little-visited Inca site of **Pumamarca**. The buildings were built between AD 1200 and AD1440, and there are some storehouses, canals and terraces. The site was strategically located to overlook an important trading route into the jungle. Salt, ceramics, maize and coca would have been transported along this route. To get there follow the road up the Patacancha Valley for just over 1km, then take a path going up the hillside steeply to your left to contour along the western slope of the valley.

CHICHA

Chicha is the main drink consumed by Indians all over the Peruvian Andes. It is made from maize, which is soaked overnight then placed in the sun wrapped in leaves to induce germination. This takes a week and produces *jora*. The *jora* is then boiled and placed in a basket lined with straw, which drains off the juice called *upi*. The maize is boiled up again producing *seque* which is then sieved. Sugar and flour are added and it's all reboiled. The *seque* and *upi* are then mixed to produce *chicha* and any residue is fed to the animals.

Any house with a long pole flying a piece of white cloth sells *chicha*, and it's also widely available at fiestas and in local restaurants and *chicha* bars. It tastes very yeasty and like home-brewed beer gone slightly wrong; sometimes fruit is added in the processing, which may change the colour and flavour. Try it!

The **Centro Andino deTecnología Tradicional y Cultura** is an excellent small museum packed with information about the culture of the local area. It is located in the old Parador just off the plaza, and highly recommended. Open Tue–Sun 10.00-13.00 and 14.00–16.00.

THE INCA TRAIL

The Inca Trail has become the most popular trek in South America, not surprisingly as it is the path to Peru's most well-known ancient site, Machu Picchu. The stunningly beautiful trail is 44km long, starting at the Inca town and terraces of Llactapaca, a couple of hours from Cusco by train. Any reasonably fit person can walk the trail. Recent privatisation of the trains has coincided with a change in management of the Inca Trail. It looks as if cheap backpacking packages will not be available for much longer. Prices have gone up and travel agencies are to be regulated. It is possible individuals will not be allowed to walk the trail, only groups.

Practical information

The trail fee is US$40 per person. Tens of thousands of tourists walk the Inca Trail every year. The pressure on the environment from that many people is enormous; the wear on the trail itself and the rubbish created, pollution by human faeces, and destruction of the stonework are just some of the problems. Make sure you don't add to the problems – carry everything out with you and make sure the agency carries everything out too.

The route

Take the local train to the trailhead at km88, around three hours from Cusco. Cross the bridge and turn left, heading up the Cusichaca Valley. You soon come to the ruins at Llactapata, where you can camp (but not in the ruins themselves). Follow the trail on up the valley to the village of Huayllabamba (3–4 hrs). There is camping here, but be careful of robberies, and don't leave anything outside the tent. Here the trail turns right up the Llullucha Valley, and this is the major climb of the trek (4–5 hrs, over 1,100m climb) to Huarmihuañusca, Dead Woman's Pass. There are a couple of campsites on the way up the pass at the Forks and at Llulluchapampa. This is the first pass and a good place to take a rest and enjoy the view. You can pick out your descent and next pass ahead. There is a campsite at Pacamayo (1–2 hrs) and another one at Runkuracay (45 mins beyond Pacamayo). There is an archaeological site here, which was probably a guard house and lookout post. From here to the top of the second pass is a short climb (1 hr), and the views surpass even those from the first pass. There is a steep descent down a stone path to Sayacmarca (1–2 hrs), a dramatically located site you shouldn't miss. The next few hours of trail take you through verdant cloudforest, with colourful flowers, birds and butterflies. It's a fairly level trail all the way to Phuyupatamarca (2–3 hrs), a good spot to camp although you have to climb down the steep stairs to the ruins to get water. The trail descends steeply from Phuyupatamarca to the hostel, shop and restaurant at Huiñay Huayna (2–3 hrs). The ruins of the same name are just a few minutes off the main trail. This is the last place on the trail where camping is possible. From here the trail contours around the hillside through the forest to reach Inti Punku, the Sun Gate and entrance to Machu Picchu (2–3 hrs). It is best to try to arrive at Machu Picchu early in the morning or after 15.00, in order to see the site without the hordes of tourists the train disgorges everyday. There are buses from the ruins down to the station 07.00–18.00 every day for a few dollars.

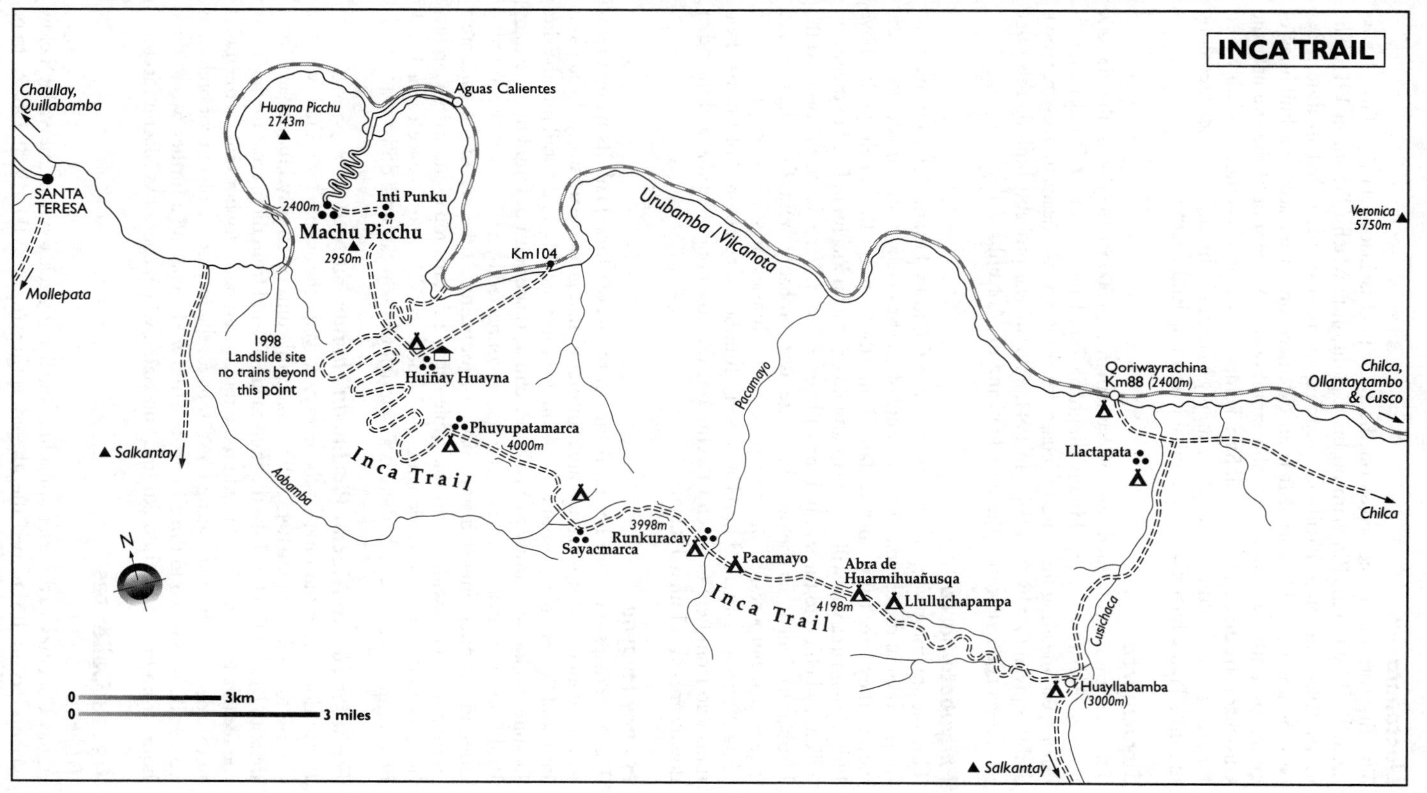
INCA TRAIL
Chaullay, Quillabamba
Huayna Picchu 2743m
Aguas Calientes
SANTA TERESA
2400m
Inti Punku
Machu Picchu
2950m
Mollepata
Km104
Urubamba / Vilcanota
Veronica 5750m
1998 Landslide site no trains beyond this point
Huiñay Huayna
Qoriwayrachina Km88 (2400m)
Chilca, Ollantaytambo & Cusco
Pacamayo
Phuyupatamarca
4000m
Salkantay
Inca Trail
Aobamba
Llactapata
Chilca
3998m
Runkuracay
Sayacmarca
Pacamayo
Abra de Huarmihuañusqa
4198m
Llulluchapampa
Inca Trail
Cusichaca
N
0 3km
0 3 miles
Huayllabamba (3000m)
Salkantay

Llactapata

The first site you come across on the Inca Trail is Llactapata (2,600m). It was discovered by Hiram Bingham on his expedition to Machu Picchu in 1911. The locals called the place Patallacta, meaning town in its place, but in time it has become known as Llactapata. It is an extensive site of terraces and buildings of quite unsophisticated style, probably storehouses. At the foot of the site near the Cusichaca stream there is a small Sun Temple. Llactapata was most probably used for growing agricultural products to supply Machu Picchu and the other sites along the Inca Trail which didn't have suitable farming land nearby.

Sayacmarca

The precipitously located site of Sayacmarca (3,600m) overlooks the densely forested Aobamba Valley. Hiram Bingham found the site in 1915 and named it *cedrobamba*, meaning the plain of cedars. Its present name means inaccessible town and was given to it by Paul Fejos in 1941. The site was probably built on this ridge to allow a good view over the Inca Trail and the Aobamba Valley.

Phuyupatamarca

This mountaintop site, at 3,800m, was also found by Hiram Bingham. Its name means town in the clouds, and it is quite often shrouded in mist. If you do see the views, they are truly spectacular. From the top of the small peak above Phuyupatamarca you will see the mountain of Machu Picchu in front to the north, Salkantay behind to the south, Pumasillo to the west, Veronica to the east and the Urubamba Valley far below. This site was probably built for religious and ceremonial purposes, as there seem to be no houses or storerooms. There is a natural spring channelled into baths, and a number of ceremonial platforms. Two trails lead from here to Machu Picchu, one directly along the ridge and the other downwards via Huiñay Huayna.

Huiñay Huayna

This is perhaps the most beautiful site on the whole Inca Trail. Its name means forever young, and it is named after an orchid that grows extensively throughout Peru and flowers all year round. Look out for these orchids on the trail into the site. Despite its close proximity to Machu Picchu, this site was not found until 1942 by Paul Fejos. It consists of a series of terraces, connected by a stone staircase, running alongside 19 interconnected stone baths or fountains. At the foot of the stairs are a number of houses with remarkable gable ends, and at the top of the stairs a circular building with windows overlooking the Urubamba Valley and the ice-capped peak of Veronica. Below the site there is a waterfall that you can walk down to.

From km104 to Machu Picchu via Huiñay Huayna

If you don't have the time or the energy to walk the whole Inca Trail, you can choose to walk from km104 to the wonderful ruins of Huiñay Huayna and from there to Machu Picchu. Take the train to km104 and from there cross the river, pay the fee of a few dollars and head up the trail. It can be a very hot walk as the trail is not shaded, but there are shaded rest stops on the way up. Look out for orchids as you walk. Allow two to three hours to Huiñay Huayna and a further two to three hours from there to Inti Punku (the Sun Gate), which overlooks Machu Picchu.

Aguas Calientes

Telephone code 084

Aguas Calientes is the ever spreading small rail track town in the valley below Machu Picchu. It is named after the hot springs (open 05.00--19.00, US$2), to be found at the top of the town, 15 minutes' walk from the railtrack, around which Aguas Calientes sprawls. The springs are best appreciated after you've walked the Inca Trail when you are more likely to be oblivious to the rather grotty nature of the place.

The springs seem to be in a state of constant refurbishment, but they never get any better. There are basic toilets and changing facilities. All the trains to Machu Picchu stop at Aguas Calientes and you get on a bus for the final few kilometres to the site itself. The first bus leaves at 06.30, and they continue to run all day until 17.00. The bus ride costs US$9 return; tickets are for sale at a small kiosk below the station. Guides to Machu Picchu are available from agencies along the railway track.

Where to stay and eat

Machu Picchu Hostal By the railtrack; tel: 211065. US$20–30, with bath and breakfast. Central, clean and comfortable.

Gringo Bills Tel: 211046. Just off the plaza. From US$10 per person. Friendly, characterful, rambling place. Clean and comfortable.

La Cabaña On the road to the hot springs; tel: 211048. US$15–20, with bath and breakfast.

Las Rocas Just before the hot springs; tel: 11049 US$10 per person with bath and breakfast. Pleasant rooms.

There are dozens of restaurants in Aguas Calientes, alongside the railtrack and up the hill towards the hot springs.

MACHU PICCHU

Entry to the site costs US$20.

Getting there and away

See page 234 and Aguas Calientes, above.

Where to stay and eat

See Aguas Calientes, above.

Discovery

The site of Machu Picchu first became known to the world in 1911 after it was found by the North American historian Hiram Bingham. There had been mention of a place known as Machu Picchu in some of the chronicles and rumours of this ancient city, but there was no realisation of the extent or importance of the site prior to 1911. Bingham was a professor of Latin American history at Yale University when he visited Peru to explore the old Spanish trade routes from Buenos Aires to Lima. On his arrival in Cusco he accepted an invitation to visit the distant Inca site of Choquekirau, where there were apparently treasures hidden amongst the ruins. Bingham was duly impressed by the Inca terraces and buildings, although they were largely covered by vegetation. He found no treasure but the adventurous trip on mule back along the narrow mountain trails whetted his appetite for the exploration of Inca ruins and their history.

In 1911 he mounted an expedition from Yale focusing on the land of the Incas. Bingham spent some time in Lima studying the chronicles written in the 16th and 17th century and, with the suspicion that there was a site to be found in the Urubamba Valley, he headed for Cusco. Helped by an Italian businessman resident in Cusco, Bingham set off down the Urubamba Valley. After a couple of days they reached the hamlet of Maquinayuj, now the site of Aguas Calientes, but

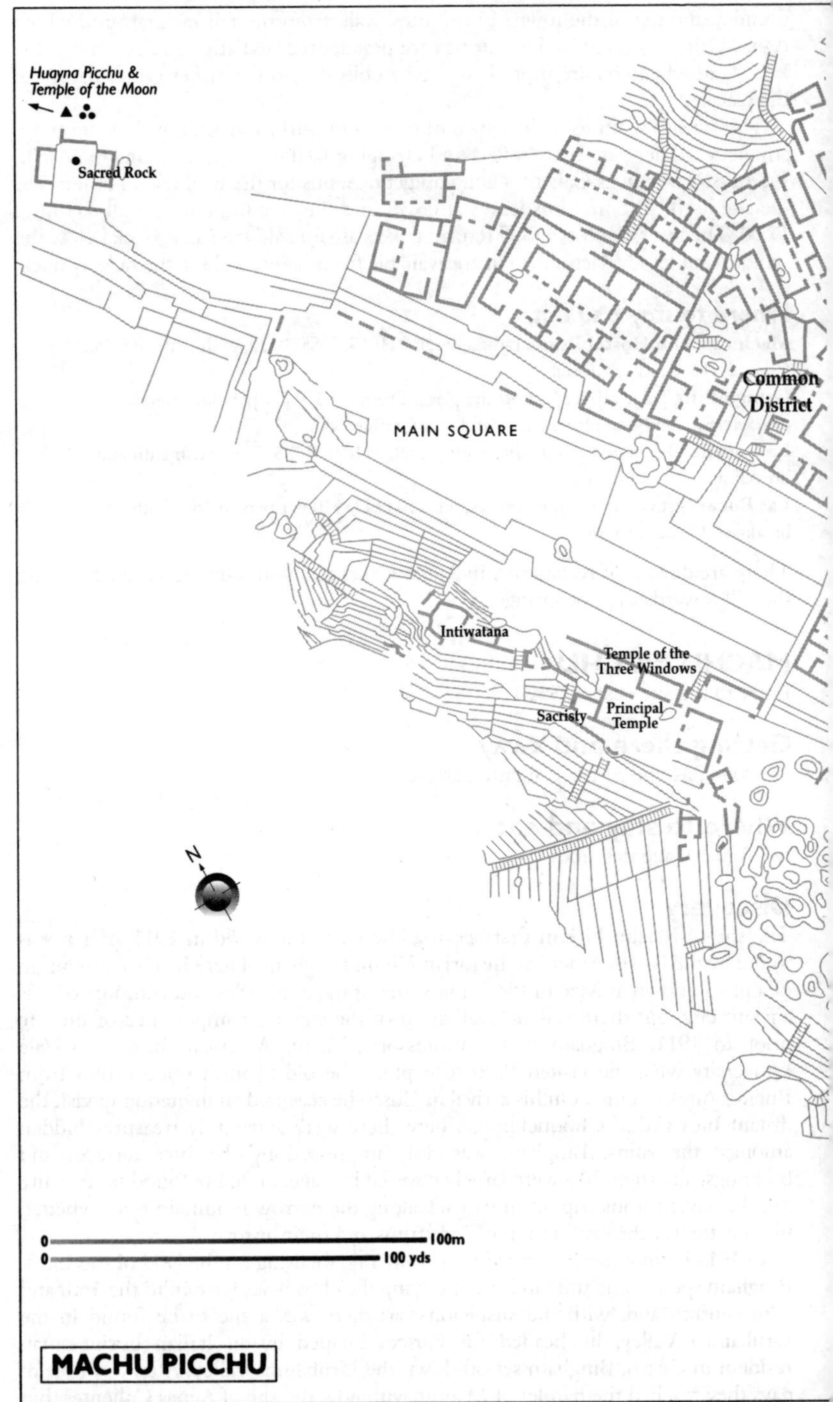

Huayna Picchu &
Temple of the Moon
Sacred Rock
Common
District
MAIN SQUARE
Intiwatana
Temple of the
Three Windows
Sacristy
Principal
Temple
N
0
100m
0
100 yds
MACHU PICCHU

KEY
Remaining walls
Flights of steps
Inca terraces etc
Mortar Building
Prison Group or Condor Temple
Ritual Baths or Fountains
Ritual Baths or Fountains
Royal Palaces
Principal Bath or Fountain
Temple of the Sun (Torreón)
Fountain Caretakers' Houses
Palace of the Princess
Quarry
Dry Moat
Dry Moat
Agricultural Sector
Agricultural Sector
Terrace Caretakers' Houses (Main Entrance)
Hotel Machupicchu & Road to Puente Ruinas, Aguas Calientes
Guard Post
Funerary Rock
Inca Bridge
Inti Punku & Inca Trail
Machu Picchu mountain

the local people were of little help, so he continued on to Mandorpampa, a single modest farmhouse. The owner of the house told Bingham, through a Quechua translator, of some ruins to be found on the mountain above the farm. He referred to the ruins as Machu Picchu, meaning old mountain. After spending the night in the farmhouse Bingham set off on the steep ascent through thick jungle vegetation to the ridge straight up, above the river. They arrived, somewhat exhausted, at a small hut, where two locals, Toribio Richarte and Anacleto Alvarez, gave them some water while they rested. Bingham was taken to see the ruins by a small boy, first seeing the agricultural terraces, some planted with corn by Richarte and Alvarez. They then pushed their way through the encroaching jungle vegetation to find the royal tomb, the stairway to the principal temple and the temple of the three windows – a spectacular discovery.

Bingham succeeded in raising sponsorship and was able to return to Machu Picchu the following year to begin the immense task of clearing it of vegetation. It took three long years to rid the site of the jungle vegetation. During that time they found tombs containing mummies. There were many ceramics, stone objects and the remains of animals. Most of these items were taken back to the United States.

Bingham began to write a book about the discovery, *The Lost City of the Incas*, which he finished in 1948 – the same year he returned to Machu Picchu to inaugurate the road up to the site that bears his name. Construction of the railway began in 1913, but it did not reach Aguas Calientes until 1928 and Puente Ruinas in 1948 to connect with the road to the citadel, 112km from Cusco.

In 1981 this whole area was declared a Historical Sanctuary by the Peruvian government, protecting an area of 325km^2. In 1983 the sanctuary was given the status of a World Heritage Site by UNESCO.

History

Machu Picchu was never known to the Spanish, making it likely that it was abandoned at the end of the 15th century or early in the 16th century. Most of the construction was done at Machu Picchu around AD1430 during the reign of the Inca Pachacuti. Nothing was written at the time about why the site was abandoned; it is possible that there was a deliberate evacuation. If the site was built for Pachacuti as his home, it may have been abandoned on his death and a new palace constructed for the next Inca, as was the custom. Another theory suggests that there was some sort of rebellion masterminded in Machu Picchu against the Cusco Incas, which had to be immediately put down, the perpetrators killed and all evidence wiped out in order not to encourage other rebellions. There are cases of this sort of happening in other parts of the empire, so it seems perfectly feasible. Other theories suggest that disease was responsible for the rapid decline in population and abandonment of the site, or that the water supply dried up in a drought, forcing the people to leave. Not really knowing what Machu Picchu was built for makes it harder to work out why it was abandoned. There were eight trails leading to Machu Picchu and it seemed to form an integral part of a busy, planned Inca province. Machu Picchu is not isolated, but forms part of a network of sites and trails that would have seen a vibrant, busy life during the 80-year period over which the area was populated. The construction work was of superb quality and many of the buildings obviously served a ceremonial function. The location, surrounded by sacred mountain peaks, also suggests a religious or ceremonial purpose, but also a defensive one, being on the edge of the unconquered eastern jungles with excellent lookout posts. Estimates put the population at between one and two thousand, with around 200 houses on the site. Machu Picchu was probably built for many different reasons but we may never know with accuracy. Its purpose remains a mystery.

The ruins

Hiram Bingham was the first to categorise the various sectors of Machu Picchu, based on his deductions from examining the structures and objects found in each area. The extensive terraced area at the south of the city was used for farming and it was named the **agricultural sector**. Some food would have had to be brought in from outside in addition to what was produced here, probably maize and potatoes. It is likely that some of the terraces were used for growing coca plants, its use controlled exclusively by the Inca nobles for its mild narcotic properties, and given as a gift to the gods during religious ceremonies. Beyond the terraces there is a large **central plaza** separating the eastern utilitarian part of the city, known as the **common district**, from the ceremonial and religious neighbourhood or **royal sector**. The plaza was undoubtedly used for gatherings.

At the top of the site there is a reconstructed roofed building enjoying the best view over the citadel. This was probably the **caretaker's house**, and lookout point over the city. Nearby there is a large carved rock, perhaps used for laying out bodies to dry, and the area known as the upper cemetery, where many of the mummies' remains were found.

Machu Picchu has its own quarry of white granite, the source of the stones used to construct the site. You can see one of the cutting techniques that the Incas may have used in a stone cut by a 20th-century Peruvian archaeologist, copying examples found in stones around Cusco.

The common district

Most of the stonework in this sector is of significantly lower quality than that of the royal sector. Its most impressive construction is the **Temple of the Condor**. Viewed from the front, the walls form the wings of this majestic bird and the head is the carved rock on the ground. The large niches around the temple were probably for mummies of important Incas. Near the Condor there is a small cave known as **Intimachay**, probably a solar observatory as the window is aligned with the rising sun. The other remarkable feature of this sector is the building containing two shallowly carved stone circles on the floor. These could have been mortars but were more likely for some astronomical purpose, for observing the movement of the sun or moon.

Royal sector

There are 16 connected fountains or baths, the first of which is just below the **Temple of the Sun**. This principal fountain has the finest stonework of all and was probably of great ceremonial significance because of its location next to the Sun Temple, and because water was venerated by the Incas. Next to the fountain is a house, used by anyone preparing to enter the Sun Temple. The **Sun Temple** itself is a remarkable construction, built around a sacred rock carved from the bedrock which forms its foundation. There are niches inside the temple used for ceremonial objects and idols. The windows in the temple are placed so that the sun's rays fall onto the central sacred rock at sunrise at the summer and winter solstices. Underneath the Sun Temple lies the **Royal Tomb**. Bingham found no bodies here, but gave it this name because of its location. There are many theories but no hard evidence about the function of this area, though its high-quality stonework and intricate step carving suggest some ceremonial use.

The other temples of the city are the Temple of the Three Windows and the Principal Temple located above the Sun Temple. There is a small plaza between the two, the Sacred Plaza. The **Temple of the Three Windows** has three windows in the eastern side and a small carved stone with the step design found

MANU NATIONAL PARK

Marianne van Vlaardingen.

Manu National Park is internationally recognised as one of the most pristine rainforests on earth, unequalled in species richness by any other park. Access is from Cusco with one of the recognised Manu agencies (see page 000). A minimum of five days is needed to visit Manu, but it is a truly unforgettable wildlife experience.

A road was built at the end of the 1960s to connect Cusco to the small village of Shintuya on the River Alto Madre de Dios. This opened up access to the jungle for loggers, who were after the valuable mahogany and cedar trees of the forest. It is thanks to a taxidermist Peruvian of Polish descent that the area was protected. Celestino Kalinowski became aware of the vast array of animal species in this area and put pressure on the government, who proclaimed the area a national park in 1973. Hunting, logging and agriculture were banned. As the international importance of Manu was realised, UNESCO decided that the Manu National Park and two adjacent zones, one a reserved zone for tourism, and the other a cultural zone for subsistence activities, would become Manu Biosphere Reserve. Ten years later in 1987, the International Union for the Conservation of Nature declared Manu a World Heritage Site, one of only about 200 representatives of important ecosystems on earth. Today it covers 1,881,200 hectares, or about the size of Wales in the United Kingdom or New Hampshire in the United States, and is one of the largest protected areas of rainforest on earth. It starts high up in the Andes mountains and goes down through elfin cloud and montane forest into the enormous lowland rainforest of the Amazon. It comprises two main rivers, the Alto Madre de Dios and the Manu River, as well as almost all their tributaries.

No other park in the world can equal Manu for species richness. Over 1,000 species of bird have been identified so far (see page 000), as well as over 15,000 species of plant, and 13 species of monkey, including the smallest monkey in the world, the pygmy marmoset, and the only nocturnal monkey, the night monkey. There are millions of insect species, of which only a tiny percentage have been named. In Manu there are healthy populations of jaguar, tapir, anteater and the endangered black caiman, and giant otter can still be found in undisturbed surroundings. The animals in Manu have not been subjected to widespread hunting as they have in many other jungle areas and are therefore less fearful of humans, increasing the possibility of actually catching a glimpse of them.

in many Tiahuanaco and Inca sites. The steps represent the future, present and past, showing the Incas' vision of the universe. The **Principal Temple** is one of the most impressive buildings on the site, although it has suffered from land subsidence. When Bingham found the temple he discovered that there was a layer of white sand on the ground. This was quite unusual but indicates a link between the veneration of water and mountain deities. In front of this temple there is a kite-shaped rock on the ground, representing the constellation of the southern cross. Behind this temple is the **Sacristy**, a logical place for priests to prepare before ceremonies in the temples nearby. A staircase leads upwards to **Intihuatana**, a sacred carved stone which is a common feature of Inca sites. This is one of the few that has survived. Intihuatana is usually translated as hitching

Practical information

A typical five-day camping tour into Manu Reserved Zone would set out from Cusco by bus, climbing over the Andes to a high point of almost 4,000m before descending to the cloudforest. You might explore the forest and spend the first night here. The following day would probably include a walk to one of the leks (courtship sites) of the incredible Andean cock-of-the-rock, to see the performance of the males. Afterwards you continue by bus to tropical lowland rainforest. Here, at 650m, you have to change your means of transport into a motorised dugout canoe to navigate down the turbulent Alto Madre de Dios River to Boca Manu, mouth of the Manu River. You then turn up the Manu River, where you will have great views of riverside birds, sunbathing caiman, and that enormous aquatic guinea pig, the capybara. It is possible to swim in the Manu River. That night you will camp deep inside Manu.

From here there are opportunities to hike through virgin forest and explore one of the most beautiful lakes of the Manu basin, Lake Salvador. There is a chance to see a huge variety of colourful birds, numerous species of monkey and with luck, a family of giant otters. You may hike through the forest to Lake Otorongo, where there is a 20m-high observation platform that overlooks the lake. At night it is possible to explore the forest by torchlight or go moonlight caiman spotting on the lake. Your return trip could be boat to Boca Manu airport, followed by a flight over the rainforest and the Andes to Cusco by light aircraft.

What to take

Rainforest expeditions are not comfortable tours, but with the following equipment you will get the best out of the forest and yourself: binoculars (imperative), flashlight with spare bulbs and batteries, sleeping bag, day pack, long trousers and long-sleeved shirts (thick and baggy fabric against mosquitoes), T-shirts, shorts, swimming costume, sweater or light jacket, two pairs of light shoes and long cotton socks, rain gear, rubber boots (only in the rainy season), sunhat, sunglasses, sunblock, insect repellent, with at least 25% DEET, afterbite and toilet-paper. Also bring plastic bags (to keep everything dry), a water bottle (with water for the bus ride into Manu) and copies of a valid passport, and yellow fever and tetanus vaccination certificates.

Health advice

There is an extremely low malaria risk in the Manu area and the occasional cases of malaria in the Alto Madre de Dios zone have proved to be completely curable. Use insect repellent and effective clothing to avoid being bitten.

post of the sun, which was the name adopted for these carved stone sites as late as the 19th century. It is unknown what the original name was, but Intihuatana seems appropriate given the speculative significance of this sacred place. The stone was carved in alignment with the sacred mountains visible in the distance. It was a sundial, indicating days and seasons, and was used for astronomical observations, indicating important days of the year. The shape of Intihuatana also reflects the form of Huayna Picchu, the shadows replicating those of the mountain; Intihuatana may have been used for paying homage to it. This is not unusual; there are many sacred stones throughout Peru that have been carved or placed in a certain way to represent mountain gods, and are worshipped because of this association with the mountains.

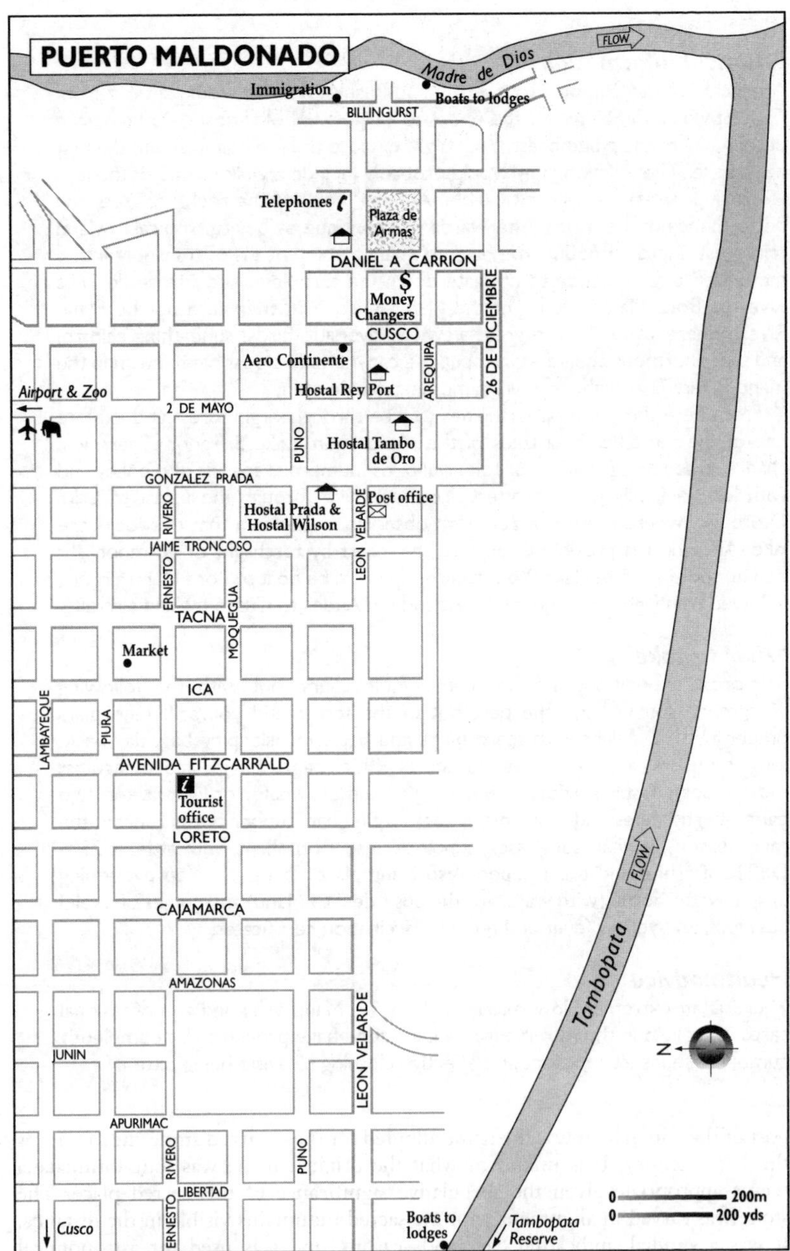

Huayna Picchu

The path up Huayna Picchu is steep, but the climb is well worth it for the tremendous views from the top. There are ingenious buildings and terraces near the top of the mountain, which may have served as a lookout post and sacred spot for worshipping Salkantay. Allow an hour to get to the top.

Temple of the Moon

This beautiful construction is found on the far side of Huayna Picchu mountain. It is finely constructed of high-quality stonework. The trail to the temple starts just up the Huayna Picchu trail. It is a lovely walk through verdant forest, and still relatively quiet compared to the main site.

THE SOUTHERN PERUVIAN AMAZON

Puerto Maldonado

Telephone code 084

Puerto Maldonado is situated at the confluence of the rivers Madre de Dios and Tambopata. It's a typical jungle frontier town with wide straight streets full of motorcycles and dust or mud depending on the season. Most people visit Puerto Maldonado with the intention of heading into the Tambopata–Candamo Reserve to stay at one of the lodges. You should book these in Cusco or Lima as it can be difficult to do in Maldonado. The town itself has little to offer.

Getting there and away

It is a long, hard 500km by road from Cusco, and not recommended unless you have plenty of time and are willing to put up with the poor road conditions and long bumpy truck journey. Trips can take 24 hours or more. The airport is 4km from town and well served by taxis. There are several flights a day to Cusco.

Where to stay and eat

Tambo de Oro Calle 2 de Mayo. Cheap and basic.
Hostal Wilson Calle Prada 355, central and good value.
Hostal Rey Port Av León Velarde 457; tel: 571177. Basic, central, reasonable.

Kristal Café is good for fruit juices; **La Mayuna** is recommended for *ceviche*. Discos **Waititi** and **Caiman** are reputed to be fun.

Jungle lodges

It is advisable to spend at least three nights in a jungle lodge because of the difficulties and time involved in getting to them. In order to connect with flights to Cusco you may arrive late on the first day and then have to leave your lodge ridiculously early in the morning on the final day. You can sometimes bargain for cheaper rates at travel agents in Cusco. Useful things to take with you are long, densely woven trousers, T-shirts and long-sleeved densely woven shirts, shorts, swimming costume, sunhat and cream, waterproof jacket or poncho, towel and malaria prevention. Don't forget binoculars, insect repellent, your camera and plenty of film, plus plastic bags to wrap everything in.

Tambopata Jungle Lodge Situated on the Tambopata River, 4 hours from Puerto Maldonado by boat. From US$180 for 4 days. Reasonable guides, comfortable.
Explorer's Inn on the Tambopata River. From US$180 for 3 days. Book through travel agents or direct to Av Garcilaso de la Vega 1334, Lima. 3 hours by boat from Puerto Maldonado. Comfortable lodge, good food, trails around the lodge, where you can see lots of birds, sometimes monkeys.
Cusco Amazónica Situated on the River Madre de Dios, 15km from Puerto Maldonado. Too near to town to see virgin jungle or much wildlife.
Tambopata Resource Centre US$550 for 5 days, very high quality remote lodge, 7 hours from Puerto Maldonado. Close to the macaw lick. Book through Rainforest Expeditions, Calle Galeon 120, Lima 41; tel: 511 4218347; email: rforest@perunature.com They also operate a second lodge together with the Ese'eja native community, Posada

Amazonas, which is cheaper. Attractions include a macaw clay lick, canopy tower, and good possibilities for observing harpy eagles and giant river otters.

Repeatedly recommended is the lodge belonging to **Hilmar and Tina Huinga**. US$15 to camp or US$20 for a bungalow. They are 6 hours upriver from Puerto Maldonado by boat taxi. Ask at Tambopata port before setting off to make sure they are around. Ask the boatman to let you off at Baujau lodge.

Practical information

Tourist office Av Fitzcarrald block 4, will give you a map.
Post office León Velarde 655.
Phone office Arica 249.
Travel agencies Transtours and Carolina Tours, both on Calle González Prada, sell plane tickets and can book some lodges.

What to see

Lago Sandoval can be reached by boat (1 hr) followed by a one-hour walk from the port Madre de Dios. Boat from US$3 per person. Lodge or camp.

Capybara

15

The Altiplano

The altiplano is the extensive highland plateau that covers a large area of southern Peru and also a considerable part of Bolivia. The landscape of the altiplano is dramatic in its bleakness and vast open spaces. There is little in the way of vegetation and very few trees, just *ichu* (scrubgrass) and a few planted crops of potatoes. Lake Titicaca is the major feature of the altiplano in Peru. This amazing, deep blue, high-altitude lake has a charm of its own and also supports many highland Indian communities on its islands and shores. The floating Uros Islands, although now somewhat commercialised, and the mystical islands of Amantani and Taquile are certainly worth a visit. You should try to allow at least two days on the islands, as the boat trips take several hours, and the islands are great for exploring and relaxing.

PUNO

Telephone code 054

Puno, at a breathtaking 3,830m, is the main stopping-off point for visiting the islands on the Peruvian side of Lake Titicaca. It is not an inspiring city, and most people don't spend any longer here than they have to, finding it rather cold and miserable. The average annual temperature here is only 7°C. You have no choice about staying here if you want to visit the fascinating islands in Lake Titicaca, and it is also the embarkation point for the spectacular train journey over La Raya pass (4,313m) to Cusco. Also while you are here don't miss the *chullpas* (funerary towers) of Sillustani or the small towns around the lakeshore. Puno is a good place for shopping for alpaca jumpers, possibly the cheapest place in Peru.

History

The ancient inhabitants of the northeastern part of Lake Titicaca, 1500BC, were the Pucara. They were followed by the Tiahunacos, who were dominant nationwide around AD500–1100. Later the Kolla culture established itself, an Aymara-speaking tribe governed by Kolla Kapac, who have been remembered primarily for their rite of worshipping deceased chiefs and burying them in *chullpas*, or funerary towers. In the 15th century the Kollas were conquered by the Incas, who continued the tradition of *chullpas*, perfecting the stonemasonry techniques.

The city of San Carlos de Puno was officially founded in 1668 by Viceroy Count of Lemos. Prior to that there had been a city nearby at a place called Laicacota, where in 1657 large amounts of silver had been found by the Salcedo brothers. The mine brought floods of people to the area in search of wealth, but it became a violent and conflict-ridden place. Consequently the viceroy had one of the Salcedo brothers killed and moved the whole body of mineworkers to the new city of San Carlos de Puno at its present location.

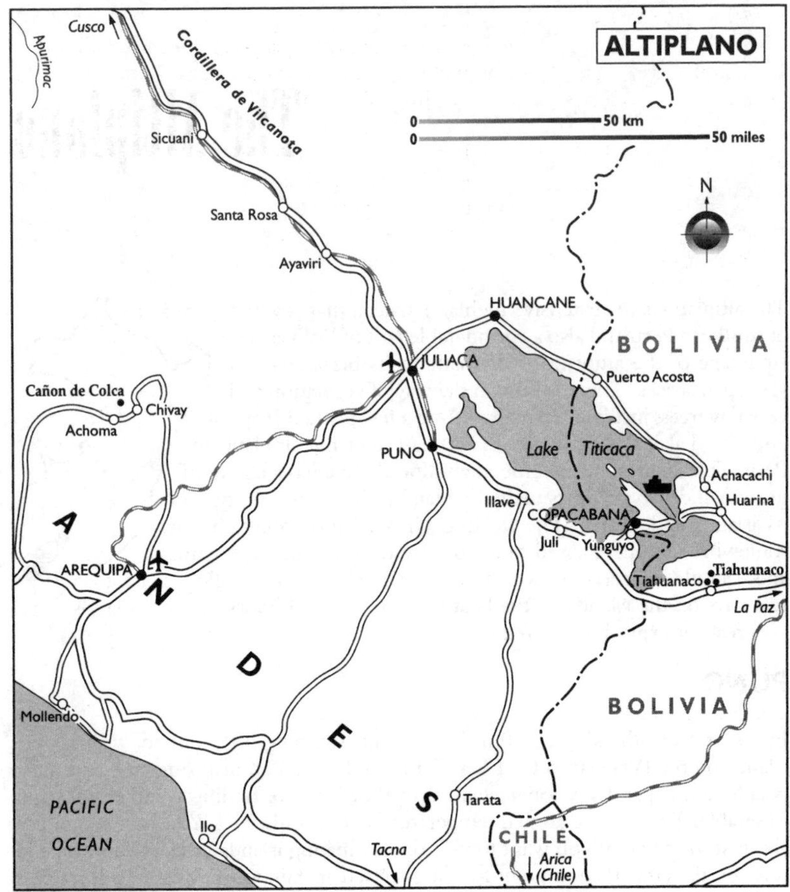

Folklore

Puno is the folk capital of Peru and celebrates local festivals in style. It is probably the city with most variety of dance, music and folk celebrations of one sort or another. Carnival in Puno is one of the best and wildest in Peru. The most well-known Puneña dances are *la wifala de asillo, el carnaval de ichu, la llamerada, el pujllay de Santiago, la khashua de Capachica, el machu-tusuj, el kcajelo, la diablada* and *la pandilla puneña*. The most important festivals are: January 18–20, San Sebastián in Juliaca and a ritual Andean ceremony in homage to Pachamama y Pachatata in Amantani; February, first two weeks, festival to the Virgen de la Candelaria, the patron of Puno, and the most important festival; May 2–4, festival of the cross in Puno and on Taquile weddings are held; July, festival of Santiago on Taquile; November 1–7: touristic week in Puno.

Getting there and away

By road

There is no central bus station in Puno, but most long-distance bus offices and departures are on Jirón Tacna or Jirón Melgar. The long-distance buses generally go overnight, leaving Puno from 16.00 to Cusco (389km, 7–8 hrs, US$7), Arequipa (323km, 10 hrs), and Tacna (376km, 11 hrs).

Border crossing

Backpackers travelling to La Paz generally go via Copacabana, where you have to change on to a Bolivian bus, and where most companies give an hour for lunch. Departures from Puno are at 08.00 on Jirón Tacna. You can stop off in Copacabana and continue travel at a later date, in which case it is easier to buy a ticket only as far as Copacabana, and not to La Paz. Slightly cheaper, though more hassle, is to go by *colectivo* bus to Yunguyo and there take a shared taxi to the border, walk through the checkpoints and pick up transport to Copacabana on the far side. *Colectivos* for Yunguyo leave from near the market in Puno. Alternatively, if you don't want to stop in Copacabana at all, you can go to La Paz via Desaguadero, which is several hours faster. Take a *colectivo* from the centre of Puno, go through the checkpoints at the border on foot and pick up a La Paz bus on the Bolivian side.

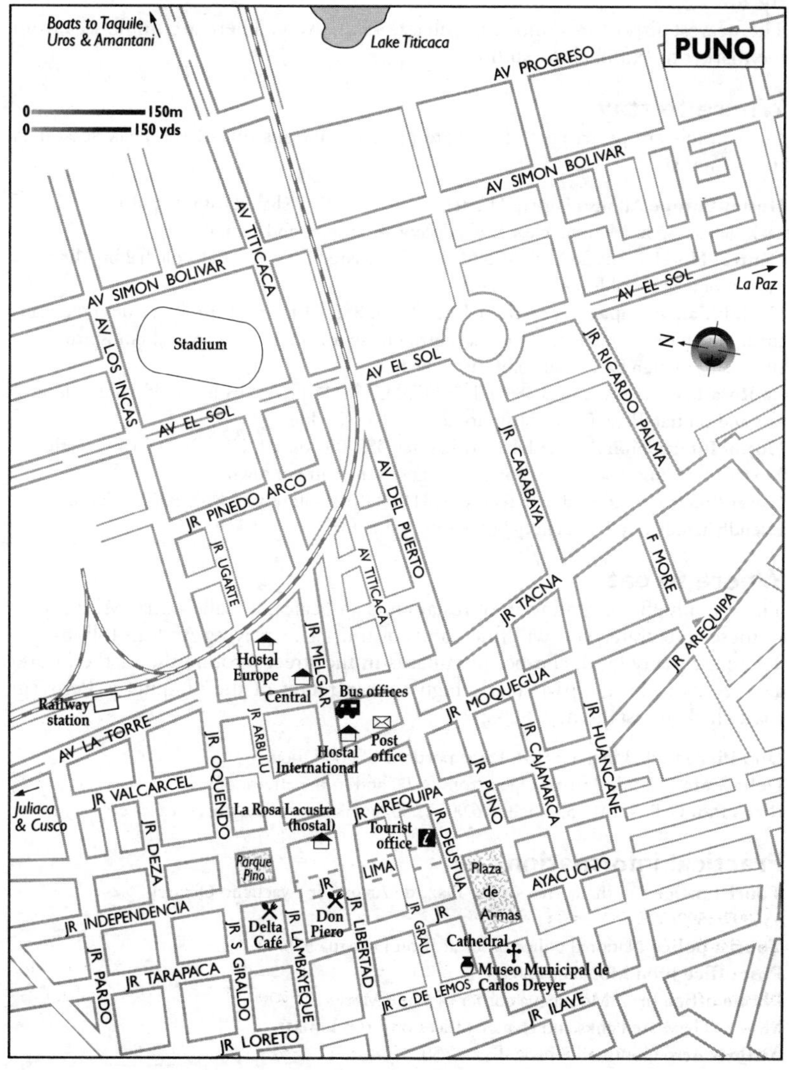

By train

There are two train lines, one from Puno to Cusco and the other from Puno to Arequipa. Trains to Arequipa leave Mon, Wed, Fri and Sat at 19.45, taking approximately 11 hours to reach Arequipa. The train ride to Cusco is beautiful, with many stops at small villages along the way, where you can get off the train if only for a few moments and buy food, drinks and crafts. These trains leave on Mon, Wed, Fri and Sat, leave around 07.30 and take a minimum of 10 hours. Buy your seat ticket in advance if possible: you can choose from Inca class (the most expensive, with reclining seats, comfortable, spacious and worth paying for), first (non-reclining seats, not much space) or second class (uncomfortable but very cheap).

By air

The nearest airport to Puno is in Juliaca, 45km away. There are minibuses from the market in Puno, allow an hour.

Where to stay

Most hotels are prepared to negotiate price reductions out of the peak season of June–August.

Hostal Europe Alfonso Ugarte 112; tel: 353023. US$5–7 shared bath. Popular backpackers' spot. Modern, clean, safe, decent size rooms and central.
Central Hotel Tacna 269; tel: 352461. US$5–8 shared bath. Central, colonial building, most rooms reasonable size, good beds.
Hostal Manco Capac Tacna 277; tel: 352985. US$6–11 private bath. Located on the main street but all rooms open onto internal corridors, so quiet if a bit dingy and uninspiring. Big rooms though basic, and comfortable beds.
La Rosa Lacustre Arequipa 386; tel: 355173. US$8–11 private bath. Comfortable, clean, safe and central. Breakfast and laundry service. Good value.
Hostal Internacional Calle Libertad 161; tel: 352109/366182. US$12–20. Private bath. Modern building, 3 star, impersonal large hostel in centre of town.
Hotel Pukara Jr Libertad 328; tel/fax: 368448. US$25–40 private bath and breakfast. Friendly family hotel, not cheap but worth paying for.

Where to eat

There is a high concentration of restaurants and cafés in Calle Lima. Most nights in these restaurants you will find bands of musicians playing Andean folk music. There are many local, cheaper restaurants in the streets around the market. Puno also seems to have a particularly high concentration of the ubiquitous Peruvian roast chicken restaurants.

Don Piero Calle Lima 348/364. Large portions of good food.
Delta Café Plaza de Armas. Open from 06.00 and in the afternoons.
Ricos Pan Calle Lima 357. Open 06.00–22.00, breakfast, coffee, juices, cakes etc.

Practical information

Tourist office On the corner of the Plaza de Armas, Jr Ayacucho 682; tel: 356097/351261.
Tourist police National police office at Jirón Deustua 536.
Post office Jirón Moquegua 269.
Phone office Jirón Moquegua corner of Calle Moré.
Money There are banks and change offices on Jirón Lima.
Airlines Aero Continente Jirón Tacna 330.

Travel agencies

There are many agencies offering similar excursions, to Sillustani, Uros and the islands of Amantani and Taquile. Talk to other travellers and check out a few options before committing yourself.

Instur Avenida La Torre 545; tel/fax: 351371. Organise tours from Puno.
Kontiki Tours Jirón Melgar 188; tel/fax: 355887/353473; email: Kontiki@unap.edu.pe
Pirámide Tours Jirón Tacna 305; tel/fax: 367302. Organise tours to the islands on Lake Titicaca.
Solmartur Jirón Arequipa 143; tel: 352901.
Turpuno Jirón Lambayeque 175; tel: 352001.

What to see

In the city

The 17th-century **cathedral**, located in the main square, is a typical example of the baroque mestizo style of southern Peru, with an interesting mixture of catholic and indigenous symbols.

Museo Municipal de Carlos Dreyer, Calle Conde de Lemos 289, open Mon–Fri 08.30–14.00, is a small archaeological museum with one room dedicated to the prehispanic cultures of the Puno area.

For good views of the city it's worth climbing to the large statue of Manco Capac dominating the town at the Mirador de Huaqsapata.

The Uros Islands

Although little is known about the history of the Uros people, it is thought that they are one of the oldest tribes in Peru, their ancestors having arrived on the altiplano several thousand years ago. A fishing and bird-hunting community until recently, now heavily supplemented by tourism and employment in Puno, the descendents of the Uros are now racially mixed through intermarriage with Aymara Indians. Some still live on Lake Titicaca on islands made from *totora* reeds. There are more than 300 families living within the Bay of Puno in extended family groups.

A visit to the islands can seem like a very commercial experience, with the islanders' only obvious interest being your money. However, given their extreme poverty and miserable living conditions, this is understandable. The way of life is obviously changing for the Uros people. Some of the islands now have primary and secondary schools, community centres, solar power and a telephone service. There are also small kiosks catering to the tourists. Try to look beyond the obvious commercialism to the culture and traditions of the islanders. Take a tour from one of the agencies in Puno or go down to the port in Puno and hop on a boat there (US$10, 2–3 hrs).

Sillustani

Sillustani, which is a sacred site of *chullpas* or funerary towers, is located on Lake Umayo just 35km from Puno. Sillustani was first written about in the 19th century when it was visited by a French tourist, who noted the funerary towers but no remains. It was not until the 1970s that excavation work began. The work revealed that the site had been occupied over thousands of years – there is evidence of hunters and gatherers living here 8,000 years ago. The Pucara culture also fished here and grazed their animals (200BC), then the site was occupied by the very powerful and extensive Tiahuanacos (AD700–1000), the remains from this time showing a high level of technological development. From AD1200–1450 the Kollas occupied the site, and there are some remains of adobe buildings thought to have been houses for the Kolla people. They inhabited one section of the site, using the other for sacred ceremonies. The two sections were divided by a wall.

The most impressive *chullpas* are those built during the time of the Incas of typically closely interlocking stone blocks. Under the emperor Pachacutec the Incas conquered the site in 1440. The inhabitants were moved out and the peninsula became an important graveyard for Inca nobles. When the Spanish arrived here only a century later they found many of the tombs unfinished and they remain that way today. Look for the stone ramps built to aid construction work on the *chullpas* themselves, and also look for the detailed carvings of animals on the outside of the towers.

It is well worth taking a tour here, and spending some time wandering around the site. The location is remote and starkly beautiful and its easy to see why this peninsula jutting into Lake Umayo was chosen for the final resting place of the Kolla chiefs. When the chiefs were buried, in ceremonies lasting several days, their women and animals were sometimes sacrificed with them, as it was believed that their spirits would live on. The lake has a wide variety of birdlife including flamingos, and all sorts of highland coots and ducks. The *totora* reed, which grows around the edge of the lake, is used to make boats and rafts and to thatch roofs and feed animals.

Lake Titicaca

Lake Titicaca is a truly amazing sight when you first set eyes on it, a huge inland sea covering an area of over 8,500km^2, 180km from end to end and on average 50km from one side to the other. Set at 3,800m in the Peruvian and Bolivian altiplano, Lake Titicaca is divided by a narrow strait into two bodies of water: the smaller, in the southeast, is called Lago Huiñaimarca, and the larger, in the northwest, is Lago Chucuito. From the northeast shore of the lake some of the highest peaks of the Andes rise to over 6,000m.

The lake averages 100m in depth, the bottom tipping sharply towards the Bolivian side. More than 25 rivers empty into it but only one small river flows out at the southern end, the Desaguadero. This empties only 5% of the lake's excess water, the rest being lost to evaporation under the fierce sun and high winds of the altiplano. The level of the lake fluctuates both seasonally (there is a 5m difference between the wet and dry season), and over a cycle of years. There are 41 islands, some of which, like Taquile and Amantani, are densely populated.

Archaeological remains around the shores attest to the many ancient civilisations that have thrived here: the ancient tribe of the Uros, the influential Tiahuanaco, Pucaras, and Kollas, and their descendants who live their lives around the lake today. The Aymara Indians still practise their ancient farming methods on the stepped terraces that predate the Incas. They grow quinoa, the potato, and endemic crops, and graze llamas and alpaca. Lake Titicaca itself is still highly respected and worshipped as the giver of life, the sacred mother, Mama Qota, provider of fish and birds.

Taquile

Taquile Island is one of the most unique and beautiful spots in all of Peru. It lies four hours by boat from Puno out in Lake Titicaca to the east of Peninsula Capachina and south of the island of Amantani. The island is only 4km long and on average 1km wide, but it supports a population of almost 2,000 Taquileños. There are several archaeological sites on the island, thought to be from the Tiahuanaco culture. However, it is the culture of the people living here today

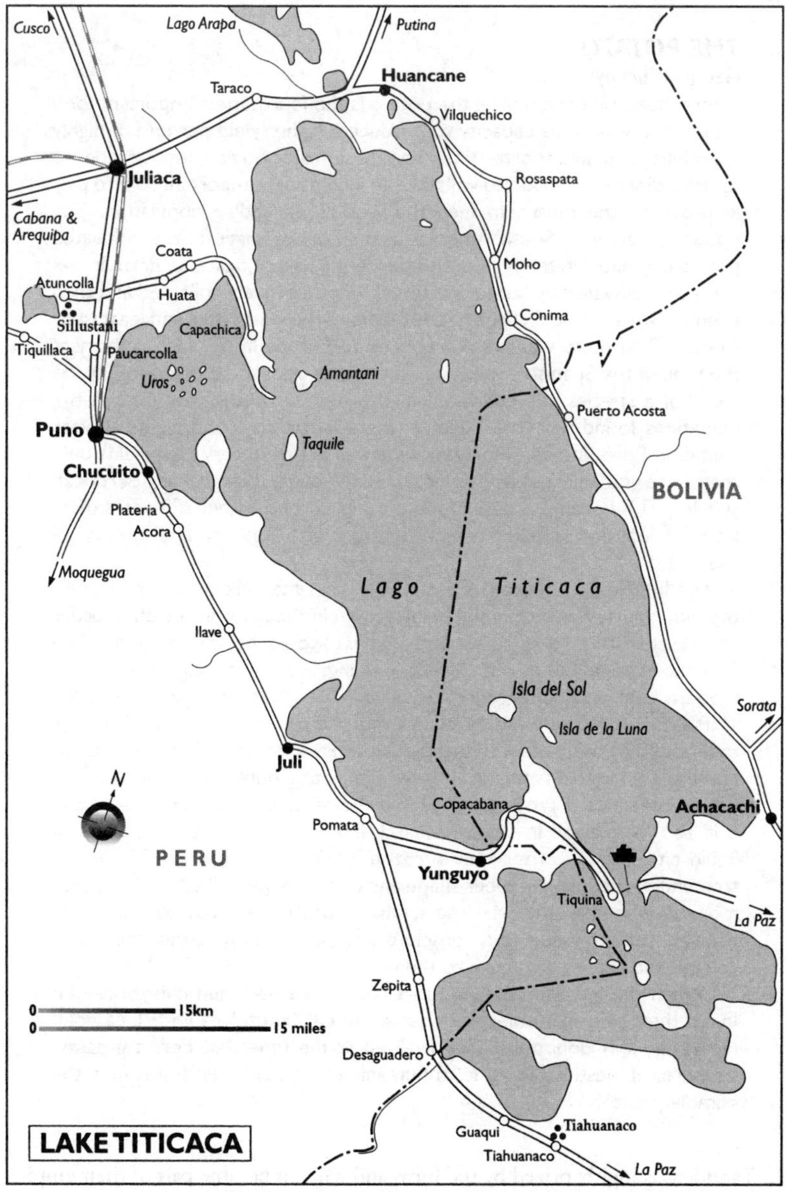

that makes it so interesting. The Taquile islanders have an intact culture far removed from our own. Taquile has become something of a tourist spot in recent years, with several boats making the long trip out and back in a day. You will find that by staying overnight, keeping away from the main square at midday, and taking the opportunity to explore the many trails leading away from the centre, you will be able to experience a unique island life unchanged in centuries.

THE POTATO

George Mackay

After wheat, rice and maize, the potato is the fourth most important food crop in the world. Its capacity to produce a higher yield per unit of highly nutritious food, in a shorter time than these major cereals, lends credence to the belief that the potato will have an increasingly important role to play in providing the means to feed the world's expanding population. The potato is native to South America, and evidence suggests the cultivated potato originates in the high Andes bordering Lake Titicaca, in Peru. It was probably cultivated by hunter gatherers who selectively collected and then eventually planted and cropped the tubers of the least bitter and least toxic clones. The potato was first introduced to Europe in the 16th century at the time of the Spanish conquests. The first species to be taken to Europe were of a species still cultivated in the Andes, which grew best in the conditions found near the Equator, equal length days and nights all year round. In Europe these short-day tubers didn't have very high yields until they were gradually developed into the day-neutral, high yielding European species. This became a staple food crop in Europe within 200 years of its introduction, and spread from Europe to North America and the rest of the world.

The International Potato Centre (CIP) in Lima collects and conserves the old strains of potatoes still being grown in the Andean region in order to preserve this genetic resource, which would be lost as and when farmers replace them with higher yielding, but genetically less diverse modern cultivars. CIP's collection of native cultivars originally exceeded 10,000 but, by careful study of the morphology of the plants and their tubers, and by using modern techniques, it has been possible to reduce this number to approximately 3,500, by eliminating duplicates. The centre's potato collection is grown each year at their field centre in Huancayo, and it is also maintained in Lima. Research into cyropreservation (the use of liquid nitrogen to conserve in a frozen state) is also ongoing. There is a tremendous variation in tuber shape and colour in this collection. It is much more diverse than the wild species from which the cultivated form has evolved, probably due to a conscious attempt by early farmers to select colours and shapes attractive to them.

When the Spanish conquistadors conquered Peru and overthrew the Incas, their principal objective was to enrich themselves with Inca gold. However, it is doubtful if they realised at the time that Peru's greatest treasure, of inestimable value to humankind, was *Solanum tuberosum*, the humble potato.

Taquile was highly prized by the Incas and when it became part of their empire the local Aymara-speaking Indians had to adopt the Quechua language. Likewise the Inca deity Inti (the sun) became their highest god, and Viracocha was worshipped as the creator. Under the Incas the island was divided into two *ayllus*, or sections: Uray Ayllu and Hanaq Ayllu. Each of the *ayllus* was further subdivided into three *suyos*. Today these divisions continue and the *suyos* are ruled over by six families who carefully control crop rotation and grazing on the steep terraced fields. A limited variety of crops are grown in each *suyo* – oca, potatoes, broad beans, maize, and wheat – and a few scraggy looking sheep and cattle are grazed.

Not much will grow here because of the altitude and harsh climatic conditions, but the diet is supplemented with eggs, delicious fresh lake fish and rice. During the coldest months from June to August the potatoes are repeatedly frozen outside overnight, trampled in the morning to squeeze out the water and hence made into *chuño*, the freeze-dried potato.

Folk dances, music and the islanders' traditional clothing have all survived the passage of time and many pre-Columbian festivities are still celebrated. I have never seen anything quite like the festival of Santiago, patron saint of Taquile. This is a week-long extravaganza, fuelled by sugarcane alcohol, in which the islanders dress in extremely elaborate and colourful costumes, complete with veils and head-dresses, to compete, one *suyo* against the other, in dance and music. Offerings are still made to the deities, and it is fascinating to see the traditional customs associated with coca leaves and *chicha*, a fermented corn beer which is poured on to the ground in the name of Pachamama before a drink is taken. Coca leaves are read to reveal the future, placed on different parts of the body for healing purposes, and chewed to ward off pain and hunger, and they play an important role in all ceremonies and fiestas.

Taquile is probably best known for the extremely high quality of its elaborate and sophisticated weavings. Both men and women weave from a young age, the women specialising in *chumpis* (wrap-round belts) made on ground looms, and the men in the black woollen trousers and waistcoats cut from cloth woven on treadle looms. From about six years of age boys are taught the complex designs used to knit *chullos* (hats) and *chuspis* (coca-carrying bags). The islanders spin, knit and weave whenever there is a free moment in the day or a quiet spell in the agricultural calendar, and they can be seen at this work as you wander around the island.

You can stay overnight on Taquile for a few dollars, and will be allocated a family to stay with when you arrive. There are now several basic restaurants around the square which serve simple but plentiful local food, and there are a couple of small shops that sell the most basic provisions and drinks, including water. At the island shops on the square you have the opportunity to buy woven or knitted items unique to Taquile.

Amantani

About 40km from Puno, over four hours by boat, lies the enigmatic island of Amantani. It's circular in shape, over 3km across, with a high point at a breathtaking 4,130m. The islanders live from farming potatoes, quinoa, oca, barley and beans, and grazing a few sheep and cattle. They also fish the lake for carachi, ispi and the introduced pejerrey and trout. The people of Amantani, like the people of Taquile, have very strong communities and deep beliefs in their gods, principally Pachamama, mother earth and Inti, the sun; they also carry out ritual ceremonies for good harvests, productive years, plentiful fishing, rainfall, and so on. They weave their own clothing too, and are highly skilled weavers.

Villages around Lake Titicaca

In the villages around the southern shore of Lake Titicaca there are some interesting colonial churches. The nearest to Puno is **Chucuito**, about 18km to the southeast, where you find the 17th-century church of La Asunción, and also a museum of phallic sculptures from an Inca fertility temple. There is an attractive hostel here, **Las Cabañas** (tel: 054 351276). Continuing on round the lake you come to **Juli** (81km from Puno), once a training centre for Jesuit missionaries destined for Paraguay. There are two interesting churches here: first, the richly decorated 18th-century San Pedro church in the main square, with a carved stone façade, a baroque altar and religious paintings from the Cuzqueño school. The second church of interest is San Juan de Letrán, a mestizo-Renaissance church which is now a religious museum. One hundred and eight kilometres from Puno is **Pomata** with its dramatically located Dominican church dating from the 18th century.

JULIACA

Telephone code 054

Very few people ever stay in Juliaca, though it is the largest city on the Peruvian altiplano with a population of 120,000, mostly highland Indians. It is a busy commercial city with a fascinating market; you can probably see this better from the train than anywhere else, as the train line runs right through the middle of it. Juliaca also has the only airport on the Peruvian altiplano and is where the Puno/Arequipa/Cusco trains intersect, so you might find yourself here even if only to catch a bus, train or plane out. If you want to travel around the northern shore of Lake Titicaca, Juliaca is the place to check out transport, though you still have to go to Puno to get an exit stamp. There is transport and accommodation, though very basic, but allow several days to get to Puerto Acosta, and several more days from there to La Paz.

Getting there and away

The airport is a few kilometres from the centre of the city – there are frequent minibuses from Juliaca and Puno. There are flights from Lima, Cusco and Arequipa to Juliaca. The railway station is right in the centre of Juliaca. Trains to Cusco currently run on Monday, Wednesday, Friday and Saturday. It is best to buy the ticket the day before you are due to travel.

Where to stay and eat

Juliaca has a range of hostels and hotels to suit most budgets., although there may be a hot water shortage in some of the cheaper places. The cheapest are near the train station.

Hostal Perú San Ramón 409;tel: 321510. From US$5. Probably the best budget option. Clean with hot water at times.

Yasur A few hundred metres from the station on Calle Nuñez 414; tel: 321501. From US$5. Popular budget option, clean, basic.

There are plenty of restaurants around the centre of Juliaca.

16 South of Lima

AREQUIPA

Telephone code 054

At the foot of three tremendous volcanoes: El Misti (5,821m), Chachani (6,075m) and Pichu Pichu (5,542m) sits the beautiful colonial city of Arequipa, built of *sillar*, a white pumice-type stone, testament to the long history of volcanic activity in the surrounding area. Arequipa is a city with many attractions of its own and is a good base for visiting the remarkably deep canyons of Colca and Cotahuasi and the Valley of Volcanoes, full of 200–300m high extinct volcanic craters. It is also the ideal base from which to climb the snow-capped volcanoes towering over the city. Arequipa is a popular stopping place for backpackers on the way to Puno and the altiplano. With a year-round springlike climate and guaranteed sunshine for 300 days of the year, it is the perfect place to begin acclimatising (at 2,325m) before continuing upwards.

History

Evidence suggests that there have been people living in the Arequipa area for six to eight thousand years. The early inhabitants probably survived by hunting wild animals. In the 7th century the Huari culture made an impact as did the later Tiahuanaco culture in the 10th century. The agricultural terraces around the city, in Carmen Alto, Paucarpata, Sabandía and Yumina, date from this time. Following the Tiahuanacos a regional culture named Juli flourished in the valley of Chili until the Incas arrived. Arequipa was officially founded by the Spanish in 1540, as a simple town of adobe and straw. The city grew and increased in wealth, benefiting in the 17th and 18th centuries from the silver mined at Potosí in Bolivia, and in the 19th century from the export of alpaca wool to England. New buildings were constructed, this time of the more earthquake-resistant *sillar*. Arequipa is in an earthquake hotspot, and has suffered many major earthquakes, the worst recent ones being in 1600, 1687, 1868, 1958 and 1960. Consequently very few of the original colonial buildings are still standing, but there are several later colonial churches and government buildings which are particularly impressive and worth a visit, the most well known of which is Santa Catalina Convent. Today Arequipa is an important commercial city of 650,000 inhabitants.

Getting there and away

By road

Arequipa has two bus stations right next to each other, 3km from the centre of town to the south. Take a taxi from the centre for US$1 or a local *terminal terrestre* bus on Calle Sucre heading south. There are frequent bus services to Lima (16 hrs), Nazca, Cusco, Juliaca and Puno, mostly overnight and also to

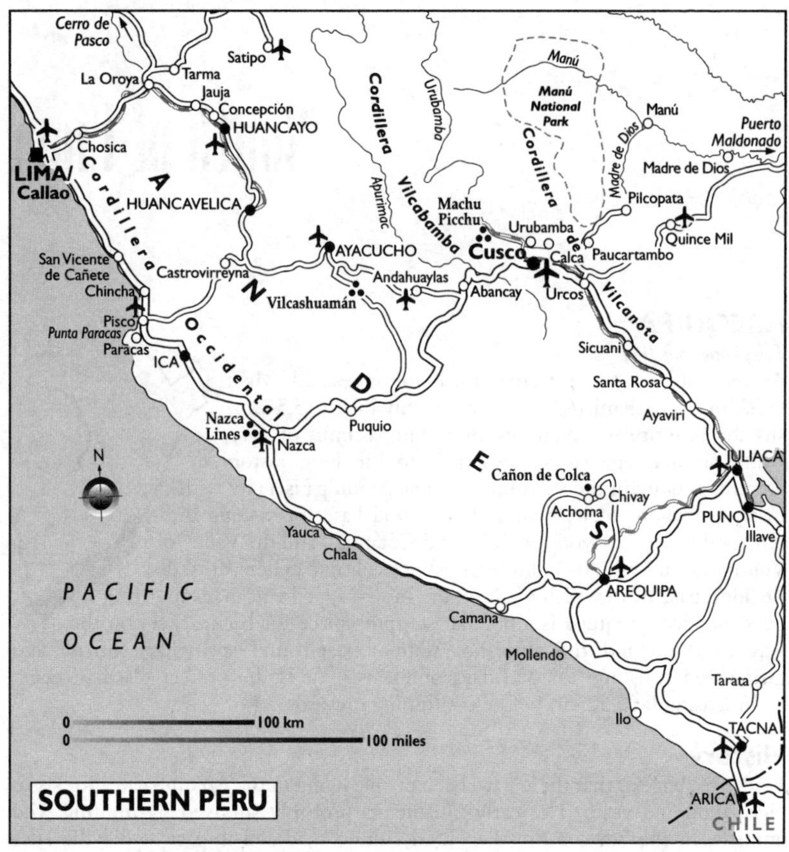

Mollendo (2½ hrs), Moquegua and Tacna (6 hrs). The best companies are Cruz del Sur, Ormeño and Oltursa, the most reliable and reputedly the safest. Bus companies Andalucia, Colca and Cristo Rey have daily buses to Chivay, Yanque, Achoma, Maca and Cabanaconde. Prado has buses to Cotahuasi (depart 15.00, 12–14 hrs). The bus station is well serviced, with a bank, change office, tourist information, telephone office, left luggage and several shops selling sandwiches, drinks etc.

By air

The airport is about 9km from the centre of town. There is no bus to the airport, but a taxi costs US$5. Aero Continente has several flights daily to Lima, Juliaca and Tacna, and some continue to Cusco.

By train

Trains for Juliaca and Puno depart from Arequipa Sun, Tue, Wed and Fri at 21.00 (11 hrs, US$6).

Where to stay

There are plenty of places to choose from in the centre of Arequipa, to suit all tastes and budgets.

Le Foyer Calle Ugarte 114; tel: 286473. From US$4 per person. Good budget option, central.
Hotel Regis Calle Ugarte 202; tel: 226111. US$5–10 shared bath, US$7–14 private bath. Clean, basic, terrace, popular with backpackers.
Colonial House Inn Puente Grau 114; tel: 223533; email: Colonialhouse@laRed.net.pe From US$6 per person with breakfast and private bath. Friendly, family run, tourist information, email.
Lluvia de Oro Calle Jerusalén 308; tel/fax: 214252. US$6 shared bath, US$9 private bath. Clean, terrace, café.
La Casa de Melgar Calle Melgar 108; tel/fax: 222459. US$17–26. Old colonial building, clean and comfortable, café, good coffee.

Where to eat

Vegetarian restaurants are **Govinda**, Calle Jerusalén 500; **Lakshimivan**, Jerusalén 402; **Mandala** in Calle Santa Catalina opposite the convent. Other restaurants worth trying are **Monza**, **Los Leños** and **Brocheta**. If you are looking for local specialities try the neighbourhood of Yanahuara where there are several *picanterías*, typical local restaurants, and the added bonus of great views of the city. The most typical dish of Arequipa is *rocoto relleno*, hot red peppers stuffed with mince meat, nuts, raisins, egg and olives. Other dishes you may see on the menu include: *chaque de cordero*, lamb with potatoes; *chairo* or *chupe de camarones*, fresh water shrimp soup; *cuy chactado*, guinea pig; *anticuchos* kebabs. Chilli, *chuño* (freeze dried potatoes), and *chicha* (maize beer) are ubiquitous – no *picantería* is complete without them. The most well-known *picantería* is **Sol de Mayo**, Calle Jerusalén 287.

Entertainment

Good bars for a drink in the evening are **Don Quijote**, Calle Moral, **The Blues Bar**, Calle San Francisco, and **Kibosh**, Plaza San Francisco.

Practical information

Tourist office Plaza de Armas. Open Mon–Fri 08.00–14.00.
Tourist police Calle Jerusalén 315.
Post office Calle Moral 118.
Money Banco Weiss, Calle Mercaderes 410, and Banco de Crédito, Calle San Juan de Dios 125, change travellers' cheques and give cash on credit cards. There are numerous change offices in San Juan de Dios and Mercaderes.
Airlines Aero Continente Plaza de Armas; tel: 219914. Servicios Aereos Arequipa, Calle Santa Catalina 210, organise flights over the Colca canyon, Cotahuasi and the Valley of Volcanoes for US$900 for a 6-seater plane, 1–2 hours. Atasur, Calle Jerusalén 303, also offer flights.
Internet Arequipa has many cyber cafés including Netmania, Santa Catalina 113, open Mon–Sat 09.00–23.00 and Sun 11.00–20.00; and Ciber Café, Calle Alvarez Thomas 219, open Mon–Sat 09.00–22.00.

Travel agencies

There is a high concentration of travel agents offering the standard tours to Colca, Cotahuasi and city tours, in Calle Jerusalén and Calle Santa Catalina.

Adventuranding Calle La Merced 125; tel: 234818.
Amazonas Explorer PO Box 333, Arequipa; tel: 212813; email: sales@amazonas-explorer.com Top-quality rafting trips.
El Giardino Calle Jerusalén 604; tel: 226461. Recommended for tours to Colca, around Arequipa and trekking trips.

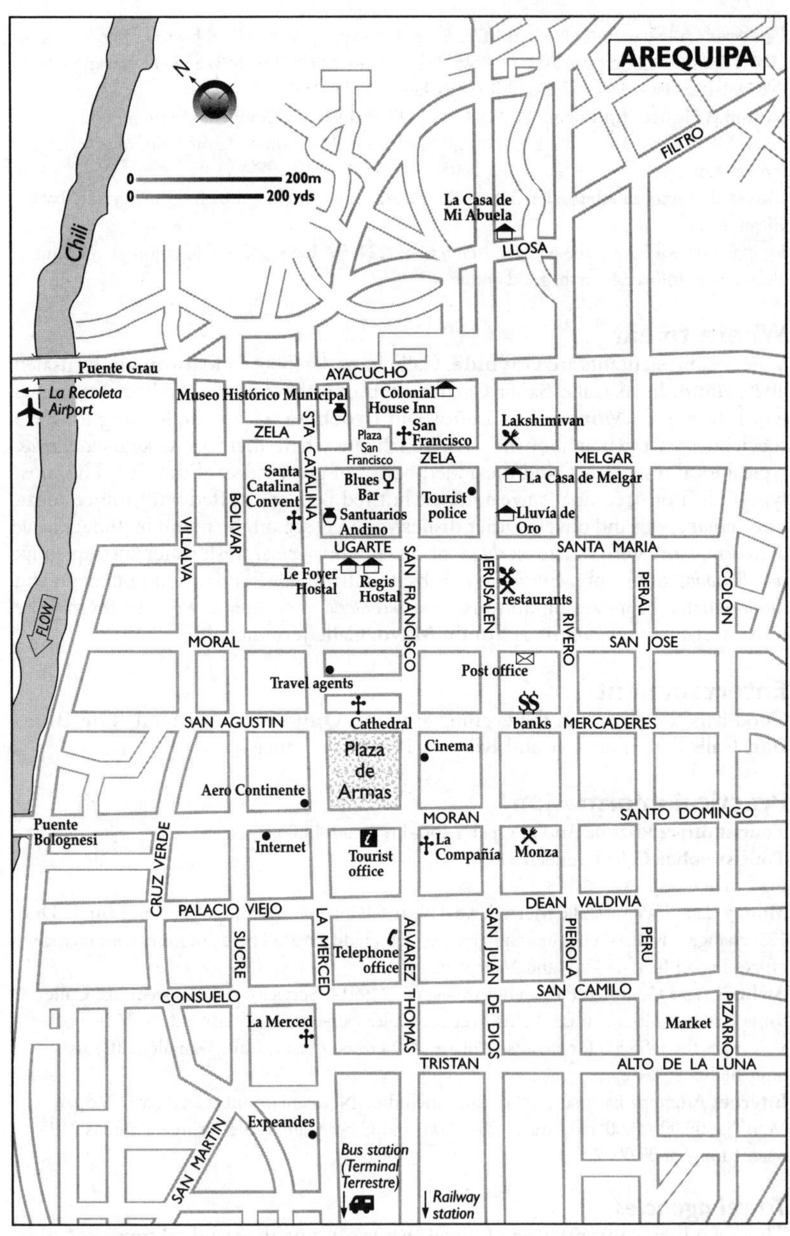

Expeandes Calle de La Merced 408; tel: 212888. Recommended for trekking and they have equipment to rent.

The most well-known trekking guide is **Carlos Zarate**, whom you can contact through the **Oficina de Guías**, Calle Alameda Pardo 117; tel: 231103 or tel: 263107. Other guides can be contacted through this office. For treks in Colca contact **Casa Colonial**, tel: 223533.

What to see

Arequipa has one of the most beautiful central squares of any Peruvian city. The **Plaza de Armas** is bordered on three sides by two-storey colonial buildings, with several restaurants on the balconies overlooking the square. The fourth side features the Renaissance façade of Arequipa's impressive **cathedral**.

Puente Bolívar, designed by Eiffel and built in 1882, was then the world's longest bridge at 488m.

Churches

The large **cathedral** which dominates the Plaza de Armas, was built of *sillar* in the 19th century after a fire destroyed the previous cathedral in 1844. Its principal altar is made from Italian marble, and the wooden pulpit was carved in France. It contains many important religious paintings. Open Mon–Fri 07.30–11.00 and 17.00-20.00; Sun 07.00–12.30 and 17.00-20.00.

Santa Catalina Convent, open daily 09.00-16.00, was founded in 1579 and closed to all visitors until 1970. This is a fascinating labyrinth of buildings, a city in itself. At one time up to 300 nuns lived here shut away from the world, with little more space than in a prison cell. A worthwhile (voluntary contributions) tour gives an impression of what life must have been like. Don't forget your camera.

La Compañía de Jesús, on the corner of Calle General Morán and Alvaro Thomas, is open daily 09.00–13.00 and 15.00-20.00. The sacristy is only open weekdays, and is well worth seeing for its profuse and colourful decoration. Built between 1654 and 1698, the church is typical of the baroque–mestizo style, high quality and very ornamental, with an elaborate façade and gold-plated altarpieces. The 18th century cloisters can also be visited.

La Recoleta (Recoleta 117, across the river; tel: 270966; open Mon–Sat 09.00–12.00 and 15.00-17.00) is a convent, museum and church. One of the most interesting and beautiful colonial buildings in the city, with an important collection of books and several cloisters with pre-Colombian pieces, religious art and Amazonian wildlife.

San Francisco, open Mon–Sat 09.00–12.00 and 15.00–1700, is in typical mestizo style with an elaborate façade carved in *sillar*. There is a 16th-century convent next door with religious art exhibits.

Museums

Museo Santuarios Andino (Universidad Católica-Cervesur) Calle Santa Catalina 210; email: santury@ucsm.edu.pe Open Mon–Sat 09.00–18.30. US$2 entry only, guide voluntary gratuity. Not to be missed, an excellent museum where you can see the mummy Juanita found at 6,380m on the volcano Ampato in 1995, other mummies and archaeological remains from the sacred sites. Guided tours only (French, German, English), video and tour 45 min total.

Museo Histórico Municipal Plaza San Francisco. Open Mon–Fri 08.00–19.30. An interesting museum dedicated to the history of the city of Arequipa.

Museo de la Universidad Nacional de San Agustín Av Independencia. Open Mon–Fri 08.00–15.00. Archaeological collection from Arequipa area with artefacts from prehispanic cultures, paintings from Cusco school and scale models of Arequipa.

Colonial houses

In addition to the churches there are a number of palaces and mansions dating from the 17th and 18th century which are within a few blocks of the Plaza de Armas and are open to the public: Casa de Moral, Calle Moral 318, is one of the

'JUANITA' LA DAMA DEL AMPATO

Sandra Araujo

The Incas had many traditions, often associated with sacred or religious beliefs. One such tradition was that of making human sacrifices or offerings. The chosen victims, those that were to be sacrificed, were educated in such a way that their own death was considered to be an honour. They were seen as intermediaries between the Inca and the creator god Viracocha, their role, to intercede on behalf of the Inca to ask for a favour such as water in the face of drought or good harvests. Between 1440 and 1450 when Inca Yupanqui, also known as Pachacutéc, was ruling the empire the sacrifice of Juanita, the recently found Dama de Ampato, was made.

El Capacocha was a ritual offering held every four to seven years. Four children, boys or girls, from the four corners of the empire would be brought to the main plaza in Cusco, where the Inca would await them. According to the chronicles the Inca would then embrace the children, in order to absorb their health, beauty, youth and perfection. From Cusco the procession to a designated sacred mountain site (Apu) began. In all the settlements they passed through gifts would be offered to the pilgrims. In the case of Juanita the chosen Apu was Ampato. A ceremonial platform and a tomb had been prepared on the mountain, *ichu* grass was placed on the ground to help during the climb. When everything had been prepared the ceremony of Capacocha could begin. The pilgrims began their ceremony early in the morning before sun rise. Juanita was dressed in a special robe (*acsu*), held by pins (*tupus*) with a belt (*chumpi*) with shoes (*polqos*) on her feet and a cloak (*lliclla*) around her shoulders. When everything was ready two priests gave Juanita *chicha* (maize beer) to drink, which would soon cause loss of consciousness. They then killed her by hitting her on the head with a carved granite stone called a *macana*. She was covered by a *nanaca* or funeral blanket and several other blankets to create a funeral bundle. She was then placed facing the east with her belongings, ceramics, cups, bags, small statues, and food, and left on the mountain as the other pilgrims descended.

Work that has been carried out on Juanita indicates that she was between 12 and 14 years old, of normal height, with no abnormalities and of a healthy diet. The stomach contents show that she had eaten approximately 6–8 hours before her death. She was 1.50m and weighed 35kg, and she was found in a sitting position, with her knees bent up and her arms crossed over her stomach. The skin on her body is completely intact, even the nails on her hands are still there. Her body underwent slow freezing after her death. The cold dry air at altitude served to preserve her body and clothing.

Juanita was found on the 8 September 1995 during the scientific expedition of North American anthropologist Johan Reinhard, veteran explorer with more than 18 years in the Arequipa area. Reinhard was accompanied by the climber Miguel Zarate, together with the rest of the team on the project Santuarios de Altura. Juanita was found on the mountain of Ampato at 6,380m. All of the objects found alongside Juanita are on display in the museum of Santuarios de Altura, de la Universidad Católica Santa Marìa in Arequipa. Her body is conserved in a Baltimore chamber in the museum at a temperature of –18°C.

finest of colonial houses; Casa Tristán del Pozo, Calle San Francisco 108, now a bank, has a magnificent doorway; Casa Irriberry, Calle Santa Catalina 101, an 18th-century building, is now a Law School; and Casa Goyeneche, Calle La Merced 20, 16th century, currently houses a museum of paintings.

Outside the city

If you have the time there are some lovely places worth visiting on a tour, by taxi or using local minibuses (ask at the tourist office for details), including: Sabandía for its 18th-century mill, terraces and hot springs; Socabaya, where you find the mansion of the founder of Arequipa; and Cayma, a small village with the imposing church of San Miguel Arcángel and an opportunity to see the ancient terraces of prehispanic civilisations.

Cotahuasi

Cotahuasi (2,684m) is 375km northwest of Arequipa, approximately 14–16 hrs by bus. The village itself is small with only basic amenities, but it does have several cheap hostels. Cotahuasi is reputed to be the deepest canyon in the world, but it is still a difficult place to get to although there are now tours with travel agents in Arequipa. Be prepared to rough it.

Valle de los Volcanes

Valle de los Volcanes is 377km to the northeast of Arequipa. There are several villages in this spectacular valley of volcanic cones. Andahua has a 17th-century church and nearby Inca archaeological remains. There is basic accommodation.

COLCA

A visit to the Colca Valley is well worth the two days for the conventional tour out of Arequipa, and longer if you can afford the time. There is plenty to see, great views on the way and once you get there, the impressive sight of dozens of beautifully constructed agricultural terraces which line the steep valley sides. There are also important archaeological remains, a variety of interesting flora and fauna including the majestic Andean condor, llamas, and vicuñas, and the people, whose customs and traditional costumes are generally unchanged since colonial times. The Colca Valley has its head at about 4,000m above sea-level. At this altitude very little grows and the land is only used for grazing. Lower down the valley, around Chivay (3,633m), the land is suitable for agriculture, and this is where you see the typical terraces. A few kilometres from Chivay the valley begins to narrow, and the sides steepen to form the Cañon de Colca, which has an average depth of 3,400m for over 100km.

Although there is evidence that people lived here several thousand years ago, the landscape owes its appearance to the pre-Inca tribes of Collaguas and Cabanas, great agricultural workers and the designers and builders of the characteristic irrigation canals and terraces of the Colca Canyon. The Collaguas and Cabanas used to practise head deformation, using wooden boards strapped to baby's heads to mould the skull into a particular shape. Their gods were the mountain spirits around the valley; the Hualqa-Hualqa mountain, 6,075m high, was worshipped for its power to control the water flowing into the valley.

From the time of the Cabanas until now, the Colca has been able to grow some of the best-quality agricultural products in all of Peru. The ancient cultures were important for the Incas, so much so that legend has it that Mayta Capac married a Collagua woman and built her a tremendous copper palace in Coporaque. When the Spanish conquistadors arrived they used the copper from this palace to make

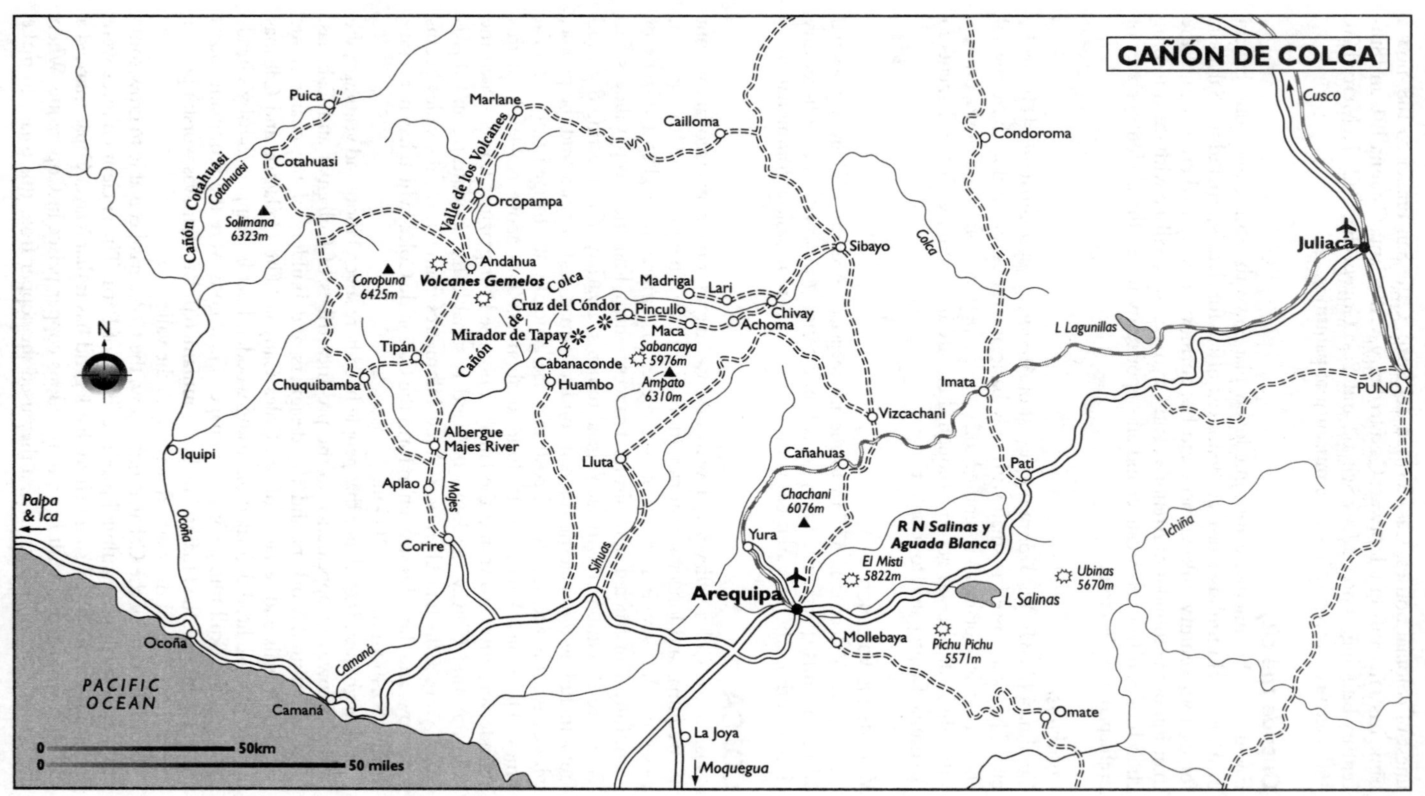

CAÑÓN DE COLCA
Cusco
Juliaca
PUNO
Condoroma
Cailloma
Marlane
Puica
Cotahuasi
Cañón Cotahuasi
Cotahuasi
Solimana 6323m
Orcopampa
Valle de los Volcanes
Andahua
Coropuna 6425m
Volcanes Gemelos
Colca
Sibayo
Colca
Madrigal
Lari
Chivay
Cruz del Cóndor
Pincullo
Maca
Achoma
Mirador de Tapay
Cañón de Colca
Tipán
Cabanaconde
Sabancaya 5976m
Ampato 6310m
Huambo
Chuquibamba
L Lagunillas
Imata
Vizcachani
Albergue Majes River
Iquipi
Lluta
Cañahuas
Pati
Aplao
Majes
Palpa & Ica
Ocoña
Chachani 6076m
R N Salinas y Aguada Blanca
Ichiña
Corire
Yura
El Misti 5822m
Ubinas 5670m
Sihuas
Arequipa
L Salinas
Ocoña
Mollebaya
Pichu Pichu 5571m
Camaná
PACIFIC OCEAN
Camaná
Omate
La Joya
0 50km
0 50 miles
Moquegua
N

shoes for their horses and the Catholic priest took some of the copper to make bells for his church, built at the end of the 16th century.

The volcanoes bordering the canyon are Coropuna (6,425m) and Ampato (6,320m). Parallel to the canyon is the Chila Cordillera. One of its peaks, Mismi (5,596m), is the source of the Amazon river.

The Colca Canyon continues to be exploited by man. Since 1975 there has been a major project to divert the abundant water supply of the River Colca to irrigate the desert and generate electricity. One hundred kilometres of tunnels and canals have been bored through the Andes, allowing 60,000 hectares of the Pampa of Majes to be cultivated. You see this incongruously green, intensively farmed area on the main road between Arequipa and the coast.

The River Colca is a great challenge to the canoeist or whitewater rafter. Because of problems in access and navigation it's not for the novice. Hikes and trips on horseback are a good option. Several days' trekking will show you the mystery of the hidden villages and tropical valleys inside one of the deepest canyons in the world.

The opportunity to see the Andean condor, giant among birds of flight and mythological symbol of ancient Andean civilisations, is one of the great attractions of the Colca Canyon. In spite of its large size, its weight of 10–12kg and a wing span of over 3m, the condor has managed to achieve an amazing efficiency of flight, which allows it, almost without moving its wings, to soar long distances at great altitudes. The Colca Canyon is one of the few places in the world where you are almost guaranteed to see these majestic birds flying just a metre or two in front of you.

Chivay

Telephone code 054

This is a small, traditional town, where most of the two-day tours spend the night. In the past few years several hostels, restaurants and even discos have sprung up to cope with the daily influx of minibuses from Arequipa. Chivay still manages to retain much of its charm, and if you take the time to walk around the market and the town's few streets, you'll get a feel for the traditional way of life of the people here.

Where to stay and eat

There are a surprising number of places to stay because of the influx of tourist minibuses each day.

Hostal Municipal On the plaza; tel: 521077. US$3–6 per person, private bath. Clean, hot water, recommended.

Hostal Colca Tel: 521088. US$5-6 per person with bathroom and breakfast. Clean and reasonable.

La Posada del Inca Next door to Hostal Colca, similar.

Practical information

Tourist office Plaza de Armas. Very helpful, and also has a small museum with interesting photos.

Money There is a bank in Chivay but it does not change cash or travellers' cheques. A couple of the shops will change US dollars cash.

What to see

The **thermal pools** of Chivay are 2km from the town, 30 minutes' walk. There are several pools and showers. Open daily 06.00–19.00. US$1.50.

Cabanaconde

Cabanaconde is a small village in the canyon. It is the best place to stay if you are not with a tour, for access to the canyon. You can take the bus from Arequipa or pick it up in Chivay. The village has two hostels, **Valle del Fuego** and **Virgen del Carmen**; both are cheap (from US$3 per person) and basic. From here it is a two to three hour walk to the bottom of the canyon.

NAZCA

Telephone code 034

Nazca is not an appealing town, and were it not for the intriguing and world-famous Nazca Lines there would seem little reason to visit. However, the Nazca civilisation was one of Peru's most important and influential and in addition to the lines the archaeological remains, mummies and ceramics are fascinating. Nazca has a rather run-down look and feel about it, partly because of the dry, warm climate, which obviates the need to construct solid buildings, and also because it has suffered considerable damage from earthquakes, the most recent of which was in November 1996. It flattened most of the city's adobe houses, which are still undergoing reconstruction.

History

The Nazca culture is closely related to the Paracas culture from which it developed in the 3rd to 7th century AD. The Nazcans were expert artists, craftsmen and engineers, creating an ingenious system of hydraulics which enabled them to survive in the arid coastal plains of the Peruvian desert, where it virtually never rains. The administrative centre of the civilisation is thought to have been at Cahuachi, which is 20km from where Nazca is today. Nazca artwork, with its many symbols of war including trophy heads, sling shots, and depictions of fighting, indicates that they were a warrior people. However, a wide representation of animals, birds, and stylised figures seen in the Nazca Lines, textiles and ceramics indicates a more complex society with an intricate religion and system of beliefs.

Getting there and away

The only way to get to Nazca is by road. All the bus companies travelling between Lima (440km, 7 hrs, US$6) and Arequipa (10 hrs, US$8), Tacna (14 hrs), Abancay (17 hrs), and Cusco (via Arequipa) stop in Nazca. There is also a bus to Puquio daily at 16.00 and 19.30 (US$4). There is no central terminal, but the bus offices are concentrated around the Ovalo on the Pan American highway, which is very near the centre of the town and most hotels and restaurants. There are frequent departures from Nazca for destinations mentioned above, generally late afternoon and evening. The road to Abancay is much less frequently travelled than the others and there have been reports of robberies, so check for the latest information. For Ayacucho it's best to go to Ica (130km) and take a bus from there.

Where to stay

There is a good selection of reasonably priced places to stay in Nazca. It is worth negotiating prices out of season.

Hostal Estrella del Sur Calle Callao 568; tel: 522764. US$7–11. All with bath, fans and breakfast. Clean, safe, good beds, hot water, recommended.

Hostal Alegria Jirón Lima 168; tel/fax: 522444; email: info@nazcaperu.com From US$5 per person, various standards of room. Very popular with backpackers, café, video, arranges flights tours etc.

Sol de Nazca Calle Callao 586; tel: 522730. US$8–13 with private bath. Clean, good beds, hot showers.

El Mirador Plaza de Armas. From US$5 per person. Clean, central, good value, great views from the 3rd floor lookout room.

Where to eat

El Griego Calle Bolognesi 287. Run by Orlando Aragonéz, who speaks English and French. Good value, local and international food.

La Cañada Calle Lima 160. Large, good restaurant popular with backpackers, English spoken. Internet available.

La Taberna Calle Lima 321. Reasonable value, long-standing restaurant.

Hotel de Las Lineas Plaza de Armas.

Pinpoint Jirón Lima is a good coffee bar.

Practical information

Tourist office Arica 386.

Tourist police Avenida de Los Incas.

Post office Jirón Lima 816.

Phone office ENTEL is on Calle Lima.

Money Banco de Crédito, Interbanc and money changers are all on Jirón Lima.

Swimming pool The Nazca Lines Hotel, Calle Bolognesi 1; tel: 522293. Has a swimming pool that you can pay to use, or use for free if you have lunch in their restaurant, a wonderful place to relax.

Internet Alegría Tours and La Cañada restaurant have Internet access (08.00–22.00, US$1.50 per hour).

Travel agencies

If you want to take the 40-minute flight over the Nazca Lines, you can book through one of the following agencies or take a taxi along the Pan American to the aerodrome (2km, US$1). There are now at least half a dozen companies offering flights and the prices are competitive, from US$35. The following agencies also offer three alternative tours, each one 2–4 hours: Chauchilla Nazca cemetery, a ceramic workshop and visit to a yard to see gold extraction; the archaeological site of Paredones and the aqueducts; or Estaquería, Pueblo Viejo and Cahuachi (US$5–7).

Alegría Tours Jirón Lima 168; tel/fax: 523775/522444; email: info@nazcaperu.com They can also arrange to fly the lines from Ica for US$140 per person. Credit cards accepted.

Nazca Travel Jirón Lima 438; tel: 522085.

Tour Perú Calle Arica 285; tel: 522481.

What to see

The Nazca Lines

On the Pampas de Nazca, covering an area of 350km², are the world-famous Nazca Lines. Something of an enigma, the lines consist of huge etchings of animals and geometric shapes stretching out as far as the eye can see across the desert pampa. They have been protected and made famous by Maria Reiche, a German-born mathematician. She carried out tireless investigations of the lines, surveying and measuring the figures and trying to correlate the lines with the rising and setting sun, moon and stars. She lived in Nazca from the 1940s until her recent death in 1998. Since the lines were first spotted from the air early this century there has been endless speculation as to their purpose, especially as they cover too vast an area to be appreciated from the ground. They were mostly made by the Nazcans over a period of time from AD500, by the simple technique of scraping away the dark red-brown topsoil and lining the scraped out yellow-white subsoil with small stones. Some of the figures may be much earlier, as many as 2,000 years old. It's possible the shapes were used for ritual or religious purposes, processions of people tracing their outline, or shamans following the lines on drug-induced spiritual journeys. Many of the animals depicted are frequently used spirit helpers to jungle shamans today. One of the largest figures is of the Andean condor, 110m long and with five straight lines crossing its body. There are 18 bird figures in total and many other animals such as the monkey, dog,

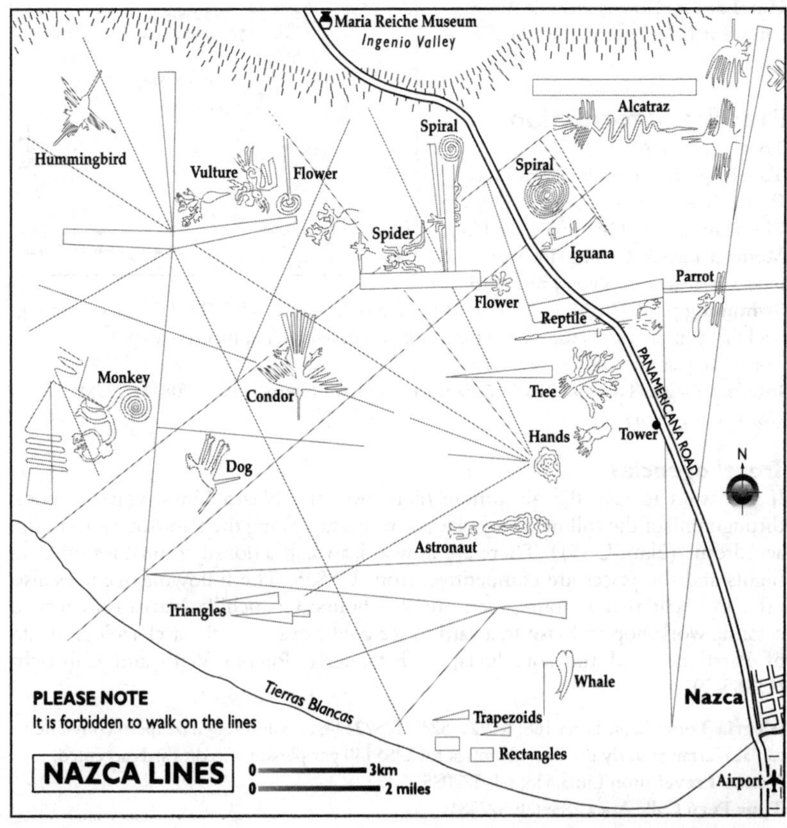

whale, spider and lizard. Just as impressive are the large numbers of straight lines and trapezoids, which cover the pampa every which way, ignoring the topography in their straightness, and defying explanation.

Cementerio de Chauchilla

Twenty-eight kilometres to the south of Nazca on the Pan American highway is this Nazcan cemetery which has been ravaged by *huaqueros* (grave robbers), leaving only bits of mummies and fragments of pots lying around the desert. It is still worth seeing as it is quite an incongruous sight, and a little disturbing.

Aqueducts of Cantalloc

These intriguing spiral rock-lined holes in the ground are 4km from the centre of Nazca. They give access to the network of underground aqueducts built by the ancient Nazcans to irrigate their crops. This hydraulic system was known as *puquio*. The channels were roofed with stones and planks of wood and every 10–20m eyes were built which permitted cleaning of the channels and access to the water. These channels were up to 10m underground and an average of 500m long. There are 30–40km of rock- and wood-lined tunnels running through the valley.

Paredones

Thought to have been a Nazcan temple, this adobe site is now in poor condition with very little to see. In a shed next to the entrance there is a private collection of craniums and pieces of mummies and ceramics collected from the site (US$1). The site is just 2km from the centre of town.

Museo de Maria Reiche

On the Pan American highway, 27km from Nazca, is the house of Maria Reiche, the German mathematician, protector and researcher of the lines. She died in 1998 and her tomb is next to her house, which is now a museum (US$1). Take a taxi from Nazca (US$12), or any bus heading north.

Lomas

This small seaside town is 90km south of Nazca. It is a good beach for swimming and popular with the people from Nazca at weekends and in summer months. There are buses from El Ovalo in Nazca with Cuevas.

Cahuachi

Near the River Nazca, 27km south of the lines, are the archaeological remains of what was probably the principal city of the Nazca culture, a ceremonial centre including 40 temple mounds and vast plazas. Nearby is the Estaquería where you see *huarango*, wooden stakes up to 2m tall, probably used as some sort of supporting structure or even a solar observatory. There are several cemeteries in this area too.

PISCO

Although not a particularly interesting town, Pisco is the most convenient place to stay if you want to visit the wildlife reserves of the Ballestas Islands and the Paracas Peninsula. This can easily be done on a one-day tour from Pisco. Around Pisco there are several fishmeal factories, which you'll probably smell. They grind up anchovies, caught by the fishing fleets you may see off the coast, exporting fishmeal mostly for chicken food. The Paracas Peninsula was central to the influential regional Paracas culture which developed after the demise of the Chavín culture. The Julio Tello Museum on the peninsula itself is fascinating and contains some good examples of the amazingly complex Paracas textiles, and interesting recontructions of the tombs where the mummies of the Paracas people were buried. Nearby, Ica is the centre of the Peruvian wine and *pisco*-making industry, and a visit to a vineyard is feasible. Also increasingly popular is a visit to the peaceful desert oasis of Huacachina, with the opportunity to sandboard down the golden dunes, swim or just relax in the sun.

History

Until the start of the 20th century nobody knew that the drifting desert sands of the coastal lowlands covered remains of a once powerful pre-Inca culture. The Paracas culture was prominent in this region between 600BC and AD200. It was a village culture now well known because of its high-quality textiles and high-prestige burial customs. The Paracas people lived on the inhospitably hot, dry, windy peninsula, fishing from the plentiful fish stocks and trading spondylus shells, furs and feathers with seagoing cultures from the north.

Thanks to the extremely dry climatic conditions many of the impressive artefacts of the Paracas culture have been preserved and have given us an insight into this fascinating culture. In the 1920s its true richness was discovered with the unearthing by Julio Tello, the father of Peruvian archaeology, of several hundred textile-wrapped mummies. The first ones he found were in shaft, or Cavernas, bottle-shaped tombs on Cerro Colorado (500–300BC) and the later ones in square

chamber, or Necropolis, tombs (300BC–AD200) in the nearby Arena Blanca, on the Paracas Peninsula. A normal burial involved the wrapping of the body in simple cotton before placing it several metres underground. A high-prestige burial would involve wrapping the body in several layers of plain and heavily embroidered textiles creating a bundle of up to seven metres diameter, also containing offerings of shells, ceramics, gold, feathers and skins. Often dozens of bodies were placed together in family tombs, and many of the skulls found in these tombs have been trepanned and deformed, a common practice at the time. Many of the textiles are exquisite in their design and detail, measuring several metres, and involving hundreds if not thousands of hours of hard labour to create a variety of fish, seabird, geometric and anthropomorphic multicoloured figures. Examples can be found in the Tello museum on the peninsula and in the Museo Regional in Ica, which are both well worth a visit.

The Paracas Peninsula is of more recent historical importance as the place where General San Martín landed in 1818 and which he used as a base for the war that eventually liberated Peru from Spain.

Getting there and away

Pisco is 250km south of Lima just off the Pan American highway. It is 60km from Ica and 20km from the Paracas Reserve. Ormeño operate a frequent service to Lima (4 hrs) from their office just off the plaza. There are also minibuses to Ica about every half hour (1 hr) from where you can catch long-distance buses to the south. There are frequent buses to Puerto Paracas too.

Where to stay and eat

Hostal Pisco On the plaza. US$7 double. Popular with backpackers, varying quality of rooms. Café.
Hostal San Jorge Calle Juan Osores 267. US$10–15 with bath, new, modern and clean.
Hostal San Francisco Calle San Francisco. US$10 double with bath, TV, fan. Clean and safe.
Hostal Embassy Plaza de Armas. US$10 double with bath.
Posada Hispana Calle Bolognesi 236. US$12 double with bath. Nice place.

Calle Comercio has several good restaurants. For fresh fish the seafront restaurants in Puerto Paracas are great value.

Puerto Paracas has several fairly expensive hotels including the Mirador (US$25 per double with bath and breakfast) and the Paracas Hotel (US$45 per person) which has bungalows, a good restaurant, bar and swimming pools.

Practical information

Tourist information Available from travel agents.
Tourist police In the plaza.
Post office Calle Progreso.
Phone office Calle Bolognesi.
Money There is an Interbanc on Calle San Martín.

What to see

Paracas Reserve

This was established in 1975 to protect the ecosystems of this coastal area and the wildlife thriving within it. The total area protected is 335,000 hectares, of which one-third is land and two-thirds ocean. The water is particularly rich in plankton, on which the wildlife feeds because of the influence of the cold

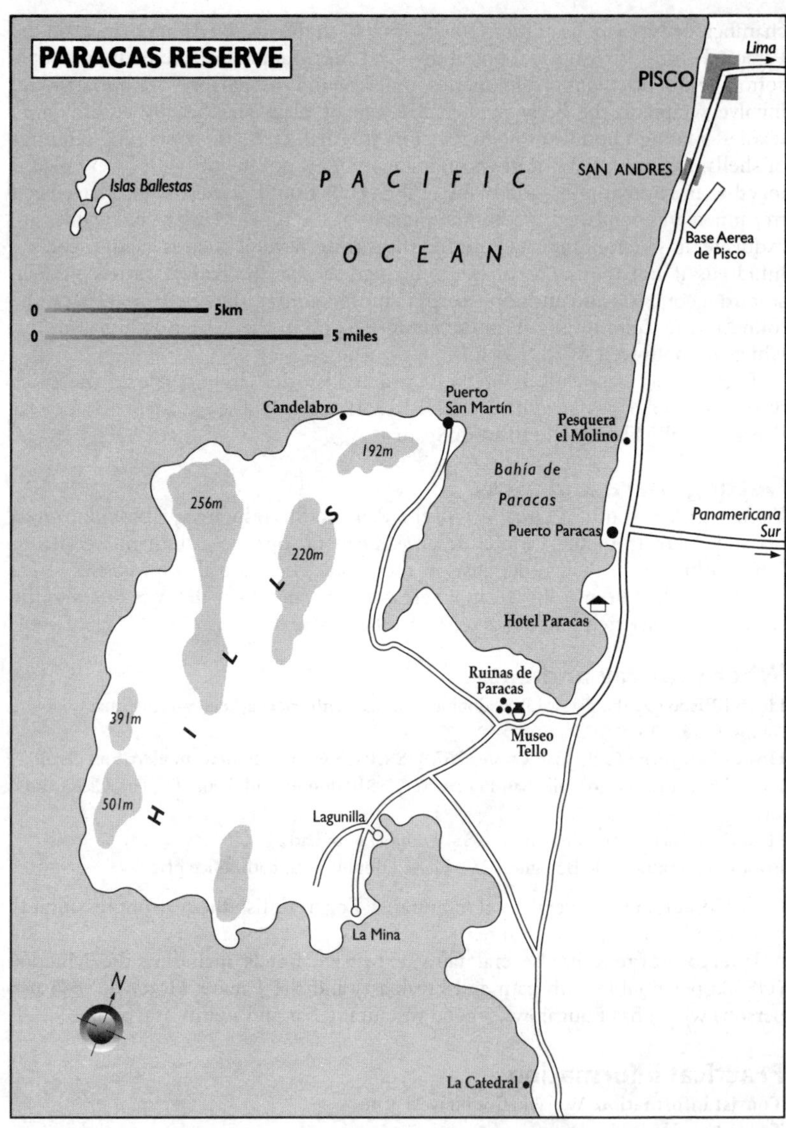

Humboldt current and the oceanographic characteristics around here. Birds you are likely to see are Chilean flamingos, Peruvian boobies, Peruvian pelicans, Humboldt penguins, Guanay, red-legged and neotropic cormorants, black skimmers, Inca terns, diving petrels and various gulls. On the Ballestas Islands and on the peninsula itself there are large breeding colonies of sealions; there are passing dolphins and sometimes you can spot migrating whales. The best way to visit the reserve is on one of the many day tours from Pisco as access is difficult by public transport and the area to cover is large. It is possible to camp on the peninsula, but carry everything you need with you and beware of theft and strong, dangerous ocean currents.

Ballestas Islands

These are three islands, 16km offshore, which are a part of the Paracas Reserve, and host a large breeding colony of sealions. Boats leave from the Puerto de Paracas (10km from Pisco) every morning if the sea is calm, from 08.00 for the tour to the islands. The length of time it takes to get there depends on the quality of the boat, but it is usually a minimum of an hour each way and an hour drifting around the islands looking at South American fur seals, sealions and the myriad seabirds. You can arrive at the port and pick up a tour or come on an organised tour from Pisco. The boat trip is about US$5, or US$10 if you go by speedboat from the Paracas Hotel. On the way to the islands look out for the **Candelabra** figure on the peninsula, a mysterious etching in the desert sand of the peninsula. On the islands, apart from the amazing wildlife, you can still see the remains of the machinery from the days of guano mining in the 19th century.

Museum of Julio C Tello

This is at the entrance to the Paracas Peninsula and is open every day except Monday, 09.00–17.00. A small but well laid-out museum with fine examples of Paracas textiles, trepanned skulls, and the instruments used, and reconstructed burial chambers.

ICA

Ica is a busy commercial town of 250,000 people approximately 50km inland from the Pacific coast and high enough to avoid the *garúa*, or sea mist. It is worth stopping off here to visit the regional museum, the vineyards, the oasis of Huacachina and to buy the pecan sweets typical of the area, known as *tejas*.

History

The River Ica is one of the few Peruvian rivers flowing into the Pacific Ocean that has a flow of water all year round, and in addition it runs parallel to the coast for a considerable distance, allowing its water supplies to be fully exploited. There is evidence to suggest that the valley has been inhabited for 10,000 years, the existence of water and a good, sunny climate (average summer temperature is 27°C, and winter 18°C) making conditions perfect for prehispanic settlements. The Paracas, Nazca, Huari, Ica and Inca cultures have all used this valley, developing irrigation systems to help in crop productivity. When the Spanish conquistadors settled here they found conditions in the region suitable for growing grapes. Thanks to the ancient Peruvian irrigation techniques they were able to adapt introduced plants as well as developing new varieties. They began to produce *pisco*, a grape brandy made from distilled fresh wine. There are four types: pure *pisco*, made from non-aromatic grape varieties; scented *pisco* with the additional flavour of fig, mango, cherry, lemon, or chirimoya; acholado *pisco* made from a mix of grape juices; and green *pisco* or Mosto Verde, made by distilling partially fermented juices. *Pisco* is usually served as *pisco sour*, a cocktail made by blending *pisco*, lemon juice, sugar and egg white with ice, which is highly potent and delicious. It is also added to tea or coffee or drunk neat. During colonial times *pisco* was widely exported from the port of Paracas to other ports in the Spanish viceroyalty. Independence, the War of the Pacific and a grape plague put paid to this and the area in production declined, with new crops such as cotton and pecans being planted instead.

Getting there and away

Ica is 300km from Lima and 140km from Nazca. There is no central bus station but Ormeño and Cruz del Sur have their offices on Calle Lambayeque as do many of the other bus companies. There are frequent departures to Pisco (1 hr), Nazca (3 hrs), Arequipa (15 hrs) and Lima (5 hrs). Buses also go from here to Huacachina.

Where to stay and eat

Ica's budget hotels are a couple of blocks from the plaza on Independencia and Castrovirreyna.

Hotel Siesta Calle Independencia 160 and 194; tel: 034 231045/233249. US$12/18 with private bath.

Try Calle Lima and the plaza for restaurants. **El Peñoncito**, Calle Bolívar 255, is recommended, and **La Achirana** and **El Velero Azul**, also Calle Bolívar.

Practical information

Tourist office Av Grau 150; tel: 034 233416. Just off the main square.
Tourist police Calle Lambayeque.
Post office Av San Martín 398.
Phone office Calle Huánuco 289.
Money Interbanc on Calle Ayacucho and Grau; Banco de Crédito on the plaza.

What to see

The **cathedral** of Ica, Calle Bolívar, dates from the 18th century.

Santuario del Señor de Luren, Calle Ayacucho and Calle Piura. El Señor de Luren is the patron saint of Ica. His image is taken out of the church and paraded through the streets at Easter and in the third week of October.

The **vineyards** of El Catador, Tacama, Vista Alegre or Ocucaje, are all located in the Ica valley, within a few kilometres of the city. Wine production in Peru is not big, and the wines are nothing like as good as in Chile or Argentina, but a visit to a vineyard is interesting to see how *pisco* is made. All the vineyards are open to the public and El Catador is also open Friday and Saturday evenings as a disco. If you don't have private transport ask a taxi driver. The tourist office can give you details of how to get there.

Museo Regional, Av Ayabaca; tel: 234383 is open Mon–Sat 08.00–19.00 and Sun morning. US$1.50. It is near the centre of Ica – take a mototaxi. Excellent displays of Paracas textiles, Nazca pots, mummies, trepanned and deformed skulls, and *quipus* (counting system of knotted strings).

Just 5km from Ica is the small desert oasis resort of **Huacachina**. It used to be a popular *balneario* where people came to bathe themselves in the curative waters of the lagoon. Now it's better known for the beautiful sand dunes surrounding the oasis and the opportunity to try sandboarding off the top of the dunes. You can rent boards, and go prepared to get covered from head to foot in hot sand. Good shoes are necessary, and water, and sun protection. There is a swimming pool at the **Hotel Mossone**, tel: 231651/236136, US$30/40, with bath. **Hostal Salvatierra** and **Huacachina** are much cheaper, from US$4 per person.

Folklore

The Ica area is the centre for the increasingly popular Afro-Peruvian music. Frequent festivals and concerts are held in Chincha and Ica. Cockfighting is also very popular as is betting. The village of Cachiche and the rural areas around are well known for their traditional medicine and the skill of their local healers.

17

Northern Peruvian Lowlands

The jungle of Peru covers over half the total land area of the country. Access to organised tours and jungle lodges is best through Iquitos in the north or Maldonado in the south. However, don't discount the busy jungle town of Pucallpa, which is accessible from the central highlands. If you are visiting jungle areas it's a good idea to keep your baggage to a minimum, pack light, drip-dry clothes, long sleeves, hiking boots, tennis shoes, waterproof jacket or poncho, insect repellent, sunglasses and sun protection, hat, binoculars, camera with 800ASA film and 200mm lens, and a torch. If you are not going to a lodge but travelling independently, you will probably also need a hammock, fishing gear, water sterilisation tablets, mosquito net, tent and plastic bags. Don't forget your passport. Wrap everything in plastic to keep it dry.

PUCALLPA

Telephone code 064

Pucallpa is one of the most important jungle towns in Peru, with a population of approximately 200,000. There isn't a lot for the passing tourist to do here, but if you want just a taste of jungle town life it is a good place to spend a few days, with busy markets and plenty of action at the port on the River Ucayali. The people are friendly and fairly laid back, quite different from in the highlands. This is also a good place to pick up a boat down the Ucayali to Iquitos. Pucallpa is surrounded by flat Amazon jungle but the drive here from Tingo María is spectacular, passing through the dramatic 5km-long canyon of Boquerón del Padre Abad, with towering walls more than 2,500m high and numerous waterfalls.

History

This area has been inhabited for centuries by the Shipibo Indians. The town was founded in the 19th century and at that time it was a centre for fishing, hunting and rubber tapping. Today its economy is based on small industries and its river port.

Getting there and away

By road

There are several bus companies operating services to Lima (22 hrs, US$7) via Tingo Maria (255km) and Huánuco (375km). There is only one road out of Pucallpa. **Transportes Rey** is one recommended bus company, Calle Raimondi corner 7 de Junio. **León de Huánuco**, Calle Tacna 657, is also a good company. Most departures are early morning, from 07.00. There are many police control points on this road, especially between Pucallpa and Tingo María, and until the early 1990s this was one of the most dangerous in Peru thanks to the terrorist

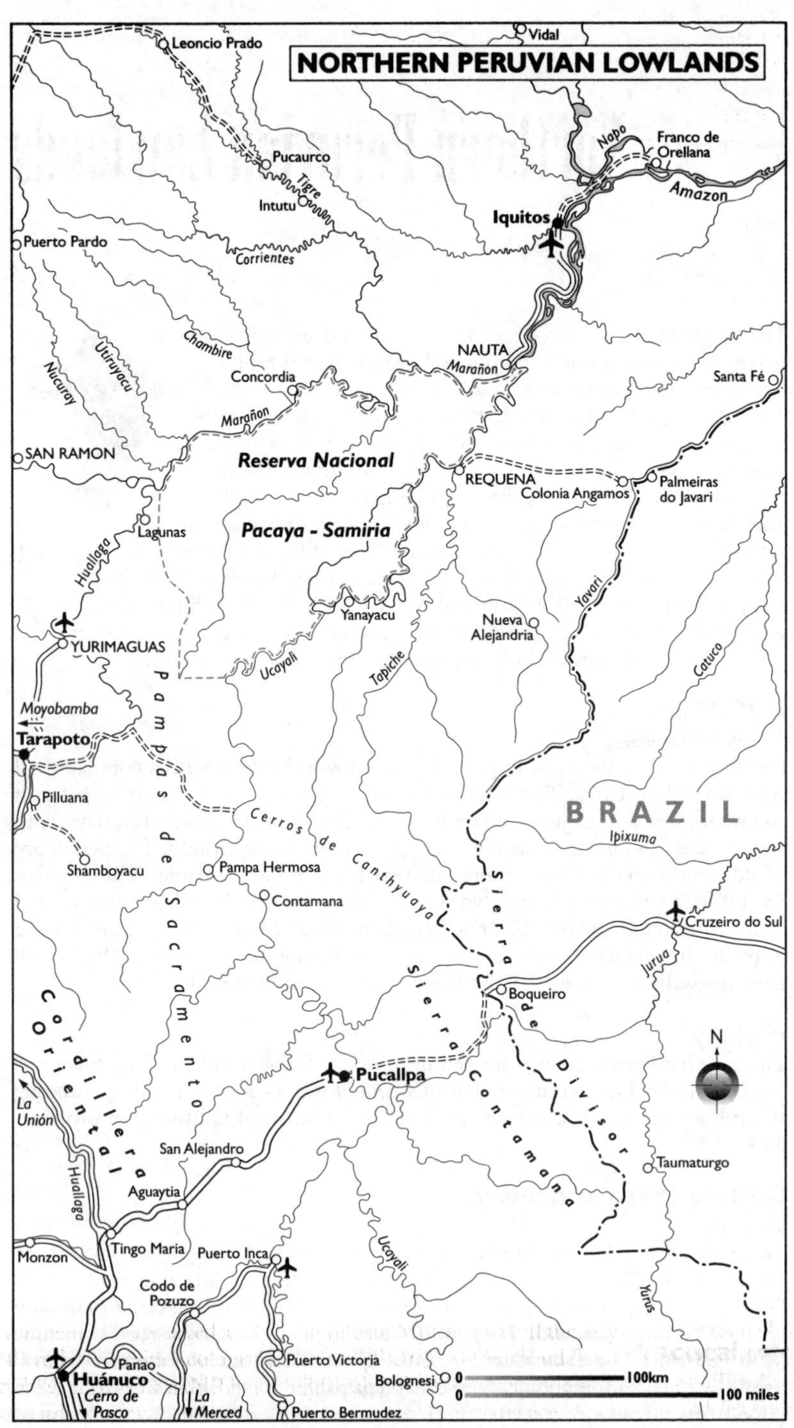
NORTHERN PERUVIAN LOWLANDS
Vidal
Leoncio Prado
Napo
Franco de Orellana
Amazon
Pucaurco
Tigre
Intutu
Iquitos
Puerto Pardo
Corrientes
Chambire
Utiruyacu
Nucuray
NAUTA
Marañon
Concordia
Santa Fé
Marañon
SAN RAMON
Reserva Nacional
REQUENA
Colonia Angamos
Palmeiras do Javari
Lagunas
Pacaya - Samiria
Huallaga
Yavari
Yanayacu
Nueva Alejandria
YURIMAGUAS
Ucayali
Tapiche
Catuco
Moyobamba
Tarapoto
Pampas de Sacramento
Pilluana
BRAZIL
Cerros de Canthyuaya
Ipixuma
Shamboyacu
Pampa Hermosa
Contamana
Sierra de Divisor
Cruzeiro do Sul
Jurua
Boqueiro
Sierra Contamana
Cordillera Oriental
N
Pucallpa
La Unión
San Alejandro
Taumaturgo
Huallaga
Aguaytia
Tingo Maria
Monzon
Puerto Inca
Ucayali
Codo de Pozuzo
Yurus
Puerto Victoria
Panao
Huánuco
Bolognesi
0
100km
0
100 miles
Cerro de Pasco
La Merced
Puerto Bermudez

activities of *Sendero Luminoso* (see page 230). Make sure you have your passport to hand. In the rainy season this section of road can become impassable.

By air

Pucallpa airport is 5km from the town centre, US$1.50 by taxi or take a mototaxi from outside the airport for under US$1. There are daily flights to Lima.

By boat

Boats take from four to six days to get to Iquitos, at a cost of US$10 per day. They are not particularly comfortable, but the journey can be fun and a good way to meet local people, who travel a lot by river. There are three ports in Pucallpa, water levels determining which is in current use, so ask. In the rainy season water levels are high enough for boats to depart from the port right in the centre of town, otherwise you may have to go 2–3km up river. Bring your own hammock (which you could get here at the market), toilet paper, mosquito net, insect repellent, water and some food to supplement the basic provisions you will get on board.

Where to stay and eat

Pucallpa has many cheap and basic hostels, most of which look particularly unsavoury – I wouldn't recommend them. It's probably worth paying a bit more to sleep somewhere safe and clean.

Hostal Richard Av San Martín 350; tel: 064 572242. US$5–8 private bath. Very basic, but clean and central.

Hostal Peru Av Raymondi 639; tel: 578128. US$5–10 basic, clean.

Hotel Kombi Calle Ucayali 360; tel: 571184. US$10–13 private bath, fan, TV, nice swimming pool, worth paying for.

Happy Day Calle Huascar 440; tel: 572067. US$11–15 private bath and breakfast. Clean, modern, email available.

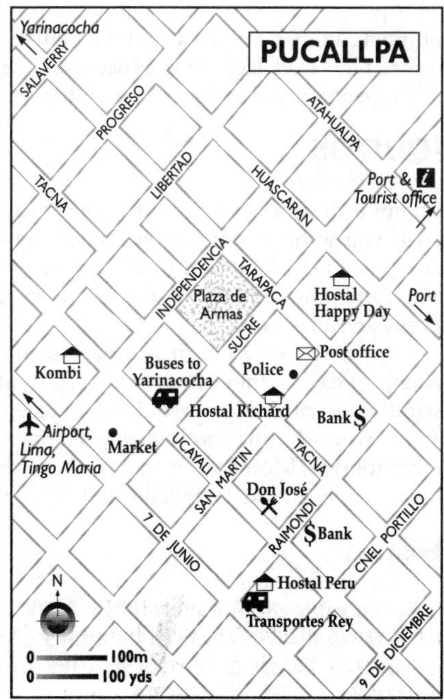

The food in Pucallpa is typical of jungle towns, and a nice change from highland food. Fish fresh from the rivers is generally excellent: try *palometa*, *boca chico*, *sungalo*, *maparate*, *bagre*, *chiu chiu*, *paco* and *paiche*. It is almost always eaten with some form of banana or rice, not potatoes. *Tacu tacu* is rice with beans, *inchicapi* a soup made from maize and peanuts, *jwanes* are leaf-wrapped rice packages with a bit of meat, *cecina* is smoked pork, *chonta* is palm heart. The best place for good value local food is **Don José** on Calle Ucayali. Try Calle Inmaculada for pizzas, chicken or Chinese food.

Practical information

Tourist office Next to the market in the Municipalidad building. A helpful office.

Police Av San Martín.
Post office Av San Martín 418.
Phone office Jirón Tarapacá on the plaza.
Money Banco de Crédito and Interbanc on Calle Raymondi.
Airlines Aero Continente, Jr 7 de Junio 861; tel: 575643.
Festivals June 18–24, San Juan and regional fiesta, October 12–20.

What to see

Yarinacocha

The beautiful oxbow lake of Yarinacocha is 10km from Pucallpa – take a bus from Calle Ucayali. Puerto Callao on the lake is an interesting little port with some good restaurants, which are popular with local people at weekends. Several boat owners will be more than happy to take you out on the lake (US$3 per hour), or you can take a *peque peque*, a river taxi up to the Shipibo community of **San Francisco** (1 hr each way). This is home to a large community of Shipibo Indians, with schools, health care and workshops. Ask for Las Mujeres, a group of women craft workers from whom you can buy the typical Shipibo cloth, ceramics, necklaces of seeds and beads and various other souvenirs. Just pottering along the edge of the lake makes it possible to see a variety of wildlife. Look out for dolphins. Staying out here is a good option, rather than in Pucallpa: there are a couple of basic hostels (**El Delfín** and **El Pescador**) and the more expensive Swiss-owned **Cabaña** for US$10 per night plus food. This is on the far shore of the lake, a few minutes' boat ride away. Negotiate a price. **Pablito Tours** do two-day jungle trips from here for US$60 for two people; check to see if it's what you want.

Parque Natural de Pucallpa

This park-cum-zoo is 4km from town on the Lima road. It has a large collection of jungle animals and birds, not particularly well housed but less depressing than most. The small **Regional Museum** is also set in the park and has interesting ethnographical and anthropological displays; open 08.00–17.30, US$1.

IQUITOS

Telephone code 094

Iquitos is the northern gateway to the Peruvian Amazon basin. It is a good place to go if you want to explore the jungle, travel the mighty waters of the Amazon downriver to Colombia or Brazil or upriver towards Pucallpa. Manu National Park and Tambopata Reserve are the best access points to visit the southern part of the Peruvian Amazon Basin.

If you are interested in getting into the jungle you should allow yourself a couple of days to find exactly what you want. You will have to decide exactly what standard of comfort you require, how deep into the jungle you would like to go, and how much time and money you are prepared to spend. Shop around and ask other tourists. Most tour operators offer trips of at least two days, a blend of jungle lodge, camping, jungle trekking and canoe trips.

History

Iquitos was founded by the Jesuits in 1757 but did not really grow much until the boom in rubber exploitation of the 1860s. Evidence of the wealth created during this time is all around you in the centre of the city. Portuguese tiles were used to decorate the homes and offices of wealthy rubber barons. A walk along the Malecón Tarapaca, lined by once elegant mansions, gives some idea of this former affluence.

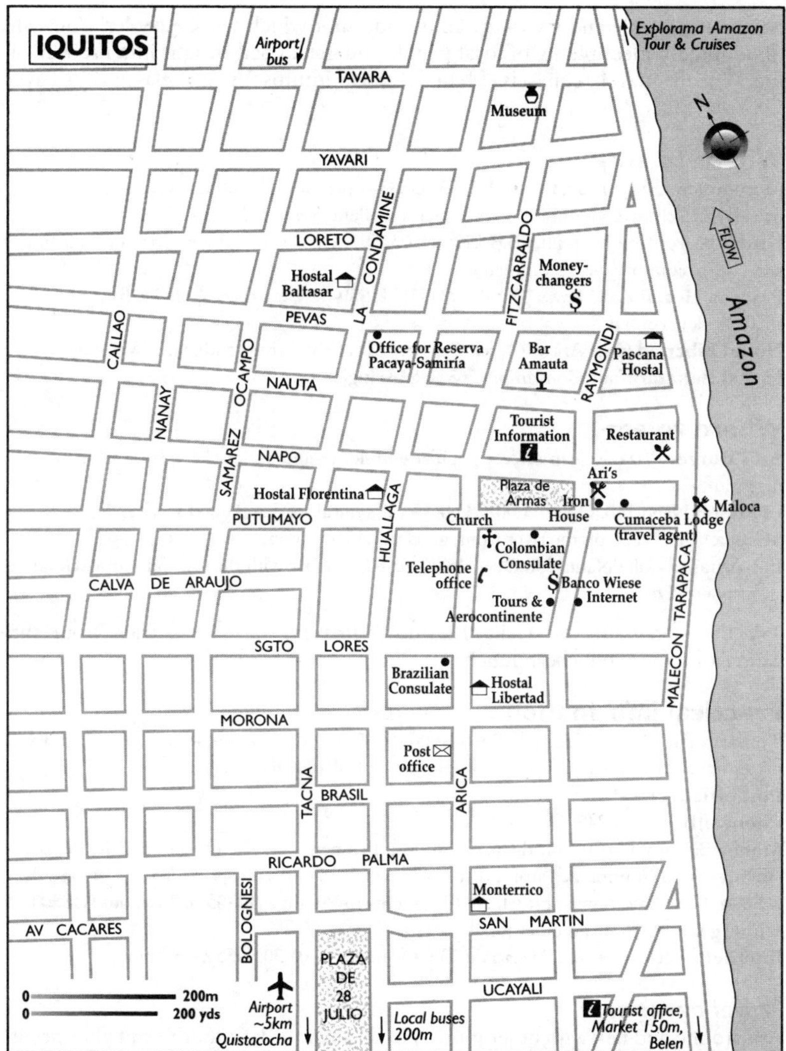

Getting there and away

By air

The airport is 5km from the centre of town, US$2 by *motocarro*, a three-wheeled bike-cum-rickshaw. There are daily flights to Lima. *Motocarros* are the best bet for getting around the city; the flat fare is 1 sol.

By boat

Rivers take the place of roads in this part of the world. There are local services to the settlements along the riverbanks, usually pretty basic boats costing around US$10 per day including food, but not necessarily the sort of food you would like to eat. They can take a long time so take a good book and be prepared to be uncomfortably cramped. Bring a hammock to string up, keep away from the engine if possible and try to get an outside spot which will be cooler. You will undoubtedly meet plenty of local people and get a good insight into the way of life. Yurimaguas–Lagunas is 14 hrs, US$5; Iquitos–Yurimaguas is 2½ days, US$10.

Where to stay

Monterrico Calle Arica 633; tel: 235395. US$5–7 private bath and fan. Good beds, friendly and clean. Café connected, try their excellent *ceviche de Paiche*.
Hostal Florentina Jirón Huallaga 212; tel: 233591. US$11 for a double, private bath and fan. Clean, comfortable, recommended.
Pascana Hostal Calle Pevas 133; tel: 231418. US$9–12 basic rooms, private bath, fan, small garden, central.
Hostal Libertad Calle Arica 361; tel: 235763. US$14–30. Private bath, fan, TV. Good value.
Hostal Baltasar Calle Condamine 265. US$8 single.

Where to eat

Ari's Burger Plaza de Armas. Very popular with locals and backpackers, reasonable food, nice spot.
El Meson Napo 116. Open 11.00–23.00. Good, typical food and good service.
Maloca Calle Napo on the river front, good value local food.
Bar Amauta Calle Nauta 250 Open 18.00–05.00, café bar with theatre and music. Good atmosphere. Disco.

Try the restaurants on Calle Ricardo Palma several blocks back from the waterfront, for good, cheap lunches.

Practical information

Tourist office Plaza de Armas. Open 07.00–14.45. Information on licensed guides, lodges, places to visit etc. There is also a tourist office on Calle Hurtado 654.
Post office Arica 402.
Phone office Arica 249.
Money Banco Wiese just off the plaza on Jirón Prospero. Change offices on Calle Pevas.
Airlines Aero Continente, Jirón Prospero 331; tel: 235990. Transporte Aéreo Nacional de la Selva, Calle Sgto Lores 127; tel: 234632; flights to Pucallpa (US$59), Tarapoto (US$60), Yurimaguas (US$60) and other jungle towns.
Internet Cybercafé, Calle Fitzcarrald 335. Open 08.30–01.30, US$2 per hour.

Travel agencies

Ask around and talk with other tourists to find out the best tour to suit your needs and budget.

Amazonia Expeditions Tel: 261439; fax: 232974. US$30 per day. Guide Pedro Marin has been recommended, speaks some English, and takes people to Samiría Pacaya Reserve. Departs Mon, Tue, Fri, and Sat.
Amazon Tours and Cruises Calle Requena 336; tel: 233931/231611; fax: 231265. Operate cruise boats including *Río Amazonas* and the *Arca*, which travel between Leticia and Iquitos. Depart Iquitos Sun at 07.00, arrive Leticia Wed 14.00, then return to Iquitos Sat morning. US$595 one way, US$1,095 full week. Good quality boats, private cabins, air conditioning, nice food, relaxing trip, but expensive. Day walks in the jungle and visits of local villages.
Andres Peña Calle Piura 162; tel: 253082; fax: 231111. US$40–50 per day. Recommended guide, with good English and knowledgeable, organises hiking, and camping at his own camps. Will meet you at the airport.

Cumaceba Lodge Calle Putumayo 184; tel: 232229. Daily departures for their lodges. From US$45 per person per day. Not primary rainforest but has been recommended.
Explorama Box 446, Av La Marina 340; tel: 252526; fax: 252533; email: amazon@explorama.com or explora@telematic.edu.pe From US$90 per day. Have several lodges: the nearest, Explorama Inn, is only 25km away, and the most well known at 160km has a canopy walkway, an amazing 500m suspended walkway 35m up in the trees. They use local, highly professional guides.
Paseos Amazónicos Calle Pevas 246; tel: 233110; fax: 231618. From US$25 per person per day to stay in their Sinchicuy Lodge. Recommended as good value for money.

What to see

Just a few blocks from the Plaza de Armas is **Belen**, Iquitos' market and floating neighbourhood. The market is fascinating to walk around; you'll see dozens of kinds of fish, bits of turtle, cigarettes in the making, intriguing bottles of potions for medicinal purposes, and a collection of tropical fruits, most of which you have probably never seen before. From the market, walk down to the water where you can pick up a dugout canoe to take you on a tour of the floating city. It's a poor part of town, where you should take particular care of your belongings, but is unlike anywhere else in Peru and leaves an impression. Literally everything gets thrown into the river, while people wash in the same dirty water, drink it and use it for cooking. There are even schools, health centres, churches, petrol stations, and lines of street lights sticking up through the muck.

Quistacocha

Take a bus from Calle Grau 1200, 20 mins to this small zoo and park on the edge of Lake Quistacocha. This is quite a nice place to relax for the afternoon, but watch out for mosquitoes.

Pacaya–Samiría Reserve

This is the most extensive of Peru's reserves, covering over 2 million hectares of species-rich tropical forest. Notable wildlife found here includes *paiche*, armour-plated lung fish (*Arapaima gigas*), one of the world's largest freshwater fish, giant river turtles (*Podocnemis expansa*), the Amazon manatee (*Trichechus inunguis*), the pink dolphin (*Inia geoffrensis*) and grey dolphin (*Somalia fluviatilis*), the black spider monkey (*Ateles paniscus*), common woolly monkey (*Lagothrix lagothricha*) and the giant otter (*Pteronura brasiliensis*).

Black spider monkey

Check with Oficina Reserva Pacaya–Samiría (Calle Pevas 363) or INRENA in Lima (see page 163) regarding requirements for entering the reserve; there is an entry fee (US$10) and permits may be needed though they are not usually required for tourists. It is best to visit the reserve from **Lagunas**, a small basic town on the River Marañon. The best route to Lagunas is by boat from Yurimaguas (US$5, 14 hrs). Lagunas has very little in the way of tourist infrastructure; there are basic hostels and restaurants but bring your own jungle supplies. Repeatedly recommended guides are Job and Luis Gongora who charge US$10 per day plus food (Tel: 352888 and leave a message).

BRADT TRAVEL GUIDES

Part Four

Bolivia

Jaguar

BOLIVIA
0 200km
0 200 miles
BRAZIL
PERU
CHILE
PARAGUAY
ARGENTINA
Fortaleza
Guayaramerín
Riberalta
COBIJA
Orthón
Porvenir
Madre de Dios
Beni
Madidi
Mamoré
Itenez (Guaporé)
N
Ixiamas
Magdalena
Santa Ana
Llanos
San Miguel
Paragua
Rurrenabaque
San Borja
TRINIDAD
JULIACA
Sorata
Santa Ana
Lake Titicaca
Coroico
PUNO
Copacabana
Chapare
Grande (Guapay)
Concepción
San Ignacio de Velasco
Orientales
LA PAZ
Yungas
Desaguadero
Pto Villaroel
Montero
COCHABAMBA
Epizana
Sajama 6542m
Desaguadero
SANTA CRUZ de la Sierra
San José
ORURO
Aiquile
Poopó
Lake Poopó
Abapo
ARICA
Challapata
SUCRE
Puerto Suárez
Chaco
POTOSI
Corumbá
Río Mulato
Valles
Salar Uyuni
Altiplano
Uyuni
Boyuibe
Asunción
Iquique
Camargo
Villamontes
Ollagüe
TARIJA
Tupiza
Villazón
Yacuiba
Bermejo
Tocopilla & Antofagasta

18 The Country

Bolivia is a landlocked country, in the heart of South America, which borders Brazil, Argentina, Chile and Peru. It is a great country for backpacking with a wealth of history and tradition, an endless number of interesting places to explore and things to see. The distances are huge so journeys can be long and arduous, but the scenery is spectacular and the variations in climate, people and their way of life is enough to entertain you on those long bumpy bus rides. A month is really the minimum time to spend here to do full justice to such a fascinating country.

GEOGRAPHY AND CLIMATE

Geographically Bolivia is a country of extreme and dramatic contrast. Three-fifths of the total area of Bolivia is taken up by vast lowland plains, which cover the northern and eastern sections of the country, known as the Oriente, while the western part, known as the altiplano, is one of the highest inhabited areas in the world.

The Andes and the Altiplano

The Andes, which run the length of the South American continent, are at their widest in Bolivia, where they divide into two parallel ranges, called *cordilleras*, the Cordillera Oriental to the east and the Cordillera Occidental to the west. The Cordillera Occidental boasts the highest of the Bolivian peaks, Sajama, a volcano of 6,542m. Between these two cordilleras lies the vast bleak plain of the altiplano, a relatively flat, inhospitable and mostly treeless area, between 3,600 and 3,800m above sea-level, 800km long and in places over 100km wide. Well over half of Bolivia's population live on the altiplano, mostly in the northern part. The

FACTS AND FIGURES

Area 1,098 581km^2

Capital Sucre is the constitutional capital and La Paz the seat of the government, ie: the executive and legislative capital

Borders To the north and east Brazil, to the southeast Paraguay, to the south Argentina, to the southwest Chile and to the northwest Peru

Largest cities La Paz, Santa Cruz

Official time GMT –4 hours

Population 7.5 million

Official languages Spanish, Aymara, Quechua

Currency Boliviano

Head of state President Hugo Banzer Suárez

southern part of the altiplano is starkly beautiful, with a unique luminosity and beauty of light caused by the thin and dry air. It is almost empty of human habitation; conditions are extreme, with low rainfall, high evaporation and sudden temperature drops, strong winds, thin soils and limited opportunities for making a living. This is one of the poorest parts of the country. Around Lake Titicaca in the north, conditions are marginally better; the weather and soils are more suitable for human life, and this is home to Bolivia's Aymara-speaking Indians, whom you will see farming small plots or herding their flocks of sheep, alpaca and llamas.

On the altiplano the climate changes considerably throughout the year. There is a marked wet season between late September and April when you can expect some cloudy days and daily rains. Day temperatures vary little throughout the year, most days being sunny and feeling pleasantly warm. Step out of the sun and into the wind, though, and you will soon feel how cool the air temperature really is. The average temperature is only 10°C. Night temperatures are considerably cooler in the dry season, especially July and August when it can drop well below freezing and you will need extra layers of warm clothes for evenings and early mornings. The cities of La Paz, Oruro and Potosí are on the altiplano.

The majestic high peaks of the Cordillera Real and Oriental rise spectacularly to the east of the altiplano. The most impressive peaks are Illampu, Huayna Potosí and Illimani, which dominates the skyscape over La Paz. Obviously the climatic conditions in the cordillera are extreme, and you should be suitably equipped before attempting any trekking or climbing. The best time for trekking is in the southern hemisphere winter, from May to September, with June, July and August the months with the most stable weather conditions.

The Yungas

In between the high peaks of the cordilleras and the flatlands of the Oriente are the eastern slopes of the Andes. In the north this area is known as the Yungas, where Coroico is the main town of interest to tourists. It is typically rugged terrain of deep gorges with precipitous densely forested slopes, separated by high ridges. Further south the mountains slope more gently to the plains. Above 2000m the climate is temperate to subtropical, with an average temperature of 15°C. Below 2,000m the climate is tropical in the valleys of these eastern slopes, with high rainfall from December to March and an average temperature of 25°C with little variation. Rainfall is high, between 800 and 5,000mm per year. The principal cities in this southern valley region are Cochabamba, Tarija and Sucre.

The Oriente

The Oriente is composed of lowland swamps at or near sea-level, seasonally flooded savannahs, immense lowland forests and very hot semi-desert. The average temperature of the Oriente is 25°C. The Pando and northern Beni departments in the north and northeast Oriente are typified by low wet plains, most of which are covered by tropical forest, periodically flooded between November and May. Central Beni is typified by vast pampas. The main river in the northern Oriente, which eventually flows into the Amazon, is the Beni and its major tributaries the Madidi, Tuichi and Mapiri. Further south is the department of Santa Cruz, where the northern part is better drained lowland forest while in the extreme southeast lies the Bolivian Chaco, part of the Argentinian Gran Chaco, a hot dry semi-desert, of thorn-bush and scrubland. Near the Brazilian border in the extreme east of Bolivia is the western edge of the swamplands of the Pantanal, which when flooded create the largest wetland in the world.

HISTORY

Prehispanic civilisations

It is possible that parts of Bolivia have been inhabited for 20,000 years, but it wasn't until AD200–300 that there were important established concentrations of people and highly developed civilisations, 3,000 years later than in Peru. Archaeological remains at the great Tiahuanaco site near the shores of Lake Titicaca suggest that from the 7th to the 11th century this was the centre of the first Andean civilisation to extend over the Peruvian and Bolivian highlands and the Peruvian coast. The textiles, ceramics, buildings themselves and surrounding evidence of agricultural practices would imply a technologically advanced culture that sustained a large population. For some unknown reason the Tiahuanaco culture died out around AD1,200.

Despite the demise of the Tiahuanaco culture, the large population living on the altiplano remained there and flourished, but as smaller units. By the 15th century there were various powerful Aymara-speaking kingdoms around Lake Titicaca controlling this highland region. They lived in a way not dissimilar to the way people in the same area live today, farming alpaca and llamas and growing a limited range of crops, mostly potatoes. The Aymara societies were centred around clans, known as *ayllus*, which maintained a very strong sense of identity, such that the Aymara language and culture managed largely to survive the Inca conquest and imposition of Quechua, and the Spanish conquest. Today both Quechua and Aymara are still spoken widely in Bolivia, Quechua more so than Aymara. The Incas succeeded in incorporating most of highland Bolivia into their empire, but not without resistance. The valleys and eastern lowlands were not subjected to Inca rule because of the natural difficulty in access which they presented to the invaders.

The Spanish conquest

Under the Spanish the highlands of Alto Perú (as the Spanish referred to Bolivia) became one of the wealthiest parts of their whole kingdom, financing wars in Europe. The indigenous Indians were forced to work in the silver and tin mines at Potosí, open from 1545, and Oruro from 1606, and also on the large farming estates called *haciendas*. This system of forced labour was called *mita*. The cities of La Paz, Chuquisaca (now Sucre) and Cochabamba provided support services to keep the whole system functioning. Thousands of Indians perished because of the appalling working conditions and new diseases introduced from Europe.

Independence

In 1809 the first signs of rebellion against Spanish rule began to appear, in Chuquisaca (Sucre) followed shortly by La Paz. However, independence was late coming to Alto Perú. In 1825 Antonio José de Sucre was made first president of what was now La República de Bolivia. By then the riches of the mines had been virtually exhausted, leaving little but economic depression. There were many border disputes and political problems beset the country. From being the wealthiest country in South America Bolivia became one of the poorest, as silver reserves were exhausted. Direct taxes of the indigenous population were the only source of government revenue as there was little to export and the costs of transportation were too high to make much export worthwhile. Political life was ruled by the élite and powerful landowners, who exploited the Indians in a semi-feudal system of labour.

The War of the Pacific

Until the War of the Pacific (1879–84) Bolivia owned a huge tract of land along the Pacific coast. Through a lack of resources newly independent Bolivia was unable to exploit the wealth of nitrates and guano in this coastal area. Investment had been by the English, Peruvians, Chileans and North Americans, and little by little Chile began to expand along the coast. When Peru and Bolivia decided not to renew the Chileans' licence to mine their nitrates, Chile invaded Bolivia and started a war, which became known as the War of the Pacific. Chile succeeded, through a combination of diplomatic pressure and finally outright war, in claiming this land for itself, thereby rendering Bolivia landlocked. Not only did Bolivia lose its access to the sea, but through a series of other wars, disputes and trade-offs, it managed, within just over a hundred years of independence, to lose over half its original territory. By 1935 Argentina, Brazil, Peru and Paraguay had all acquired Bolivian territory.

20th century

At the end of the 19th century, after the loss of the Bolivian littoral to Chile, there was a change in the politics of Bolivia. The military leaders or *caudillos* who had held the country in their hands lost power and two political parties, the Liberal and Conservative parties, took over. Until the 1930s there was a period of relative political peace, economic development and modernisation in the mining sector. The Indians were still excluded from political life, and in reality a small upper class urban set ruled, their success dependent on knowing the right people. Tin became an important export at this time, as the world silver market, which had experienced a brief revival, again collapsed. By 1900 tin accounted for over 50% of Bolivia's exports; both foreigners and Bolivian entrepreneurs were involved in tin mining and several families became extremely wealthy on the profits of the tin mines. Eighty per cent of tin production was in the hands of three giants, Simón Patiño, and the Aramayo and Hochschild families. This boom only lasted until the 1930s, and since then the costs of production have steadily increased and the quality of ores has decreased.

In the 1930s Bolivia suffered a further setback when the **Chaco War** broke out. The border with Paraguay at the eastern edge of Bolivia had never been exactly defined, and on the discovery of oil in the Bolivian Chaco border disputes erupted into full blown fighting. The war lasted from 1932 to 1935 and cost Bolivia dearly in terms of money, human life and land. The civilian government was overthrown and military rule resumed. A further consequence of the war was that thousands of Indians, who had survived the fighting, refused to return to serfdom, but settled in towns and there played an important role in the raising of political awareness and the forming of civilian dissident groups. The groups formed two political parties which presented a challenge to the old regime, the MNR (Nationalist Revolutionary Movement) and the PIR (Party of the Revolutionary Left). Both managed to gain seats in congress in the 1940s.

In the elections of 1951 Victor Paz and the MNR won the presidential elections. The existing government refused to accept the result and transferred power to a military junta. Revolution broke out, and given the high level of support throughout the country, after three days the army surrendered and Victor Paz became president. What followed was one of the most profound **social revolutions** in Latin America of the 20th century. In 1952 the government introduced some important and far-reaching reforms. They nationalised 80% of the mines, incorporating them into the state-owned mining corporation of COMIBOL. Universal suffrage was declared with the abolition of literacy requirements and the power of the armed forces was reduced. The government also approved an agrarian reform, which changed the way Indians had been forced to live since colonial times, gave them land rights and freed them from labour obligations. The MNR had the difficult task of constructing a new system to push forward economic and social development and social justice. After

Paz stood down in 1956 and Siles Zuazo replaced him, most of the advanced social programmes were stopped and Bolivia re-entered the international market. An IMF (International Monetary Fund) plan was adopted. This plan sought to stabilise the economy, reduce the high inflation that had occurred since the revolution, abolish subsidies and encourage foreign investment. The consequent freezing of wages and removal of subsidies caused inevitable suffering for the poorer sector of the population. The miners' objections were put down using military force. There was a split in the MNR and gradually the party lost its strength. For 12 years MNR managed to hold onto power, until yet another military coup ended single party rule in 1964.

The 1960s and 1970s saw many more coups and military governments until 1982. General Barrientos was the first of many military leaders. Others followed, and in 1972 Hugo Banzer Suárez appeared on the scene, ending a period of military populism, with a violent and bloody coup, lasting three days. He led the country from 1971 until 1978 under an oppressive regime in which the labour movements were banned and many people were jailed, exiled or killed. For the miners the situation was appalling with strikes violently put down by the army, and many miners were killed. Trade unions were banned, and wages were worthless. Despite initial economic growth, massive amounts of money were borrowed and levels of international debt rose and rose. Banzer Suárez' regime was supported by the USA and Brazil. He was finally forced to call elections in 1978 after a massive hunger strike protest. From 1978 to 1982 there was a period of political instability with a total of seven military and two civilian governments. These were crisis years for most Bolivians with high inflation, unemployment, poverty and the growth of debt. The growth of coca for the cocaine industry provided the major source of income.

The 1980s and 1990s

The 1980s saw a return of democratic rule to Bolivia. In 1982 Hernán Siles Zuazo was elected followed by a return of Paz Estenssoro. The economy was bankrupt by the time Siles Zuazo became president. The early 1980s were characterised by endless strikes, demonstrations and protests at the hyperinflation, high cost of living and food shortages faced by most Bolivians. Jaime Paz Zamora (1989–93) followed as president and adopted a severe IMF policy of radical economic reform. In 1984 many mines that had been operating at a loss were closed. A few were privatised, but thousands of miners lost their jobs and were forced to move to seek work in the eastern lowlands, in the coca production areas or in the towns. Many miners started working for themselves in cooperative groups in extremely dangerous conditions. Most of the rural population lived in conditions of extreme poverty. By 1993 inflation was under control. Gonzalo Sánchez de Lozada was president from 1993 to 1997 and on June 1 1997 Hugo Banzer Suárez was re-elected to the Bolivian presidency.

THE PEOPLE

Much of Bolivia's political turmoil is rooted in the ethnic, racial and geographical diversity found within the country. The population of Bolivia, 7.5 million, is small relative to the size of the country, just over a million square kilometres. More than 50% of the people live in rural areas, and less than 25% live in the eastern lowlands, which cover 60% of the land area.

Racially 60% of the population is Indian, of whom 50% are Quechua Indian, 40% Aymara Indian and the other 10% lowland indigenous groups. Thirty per cent of the population is mestizo, and less than 10% of white origin. It is the whites who dominate political life.

NATURAL HISTORY

Altiplano

On the altiplano, known in Quechua as the *puna*, the environment is very heavily influenced by the presence of the highland Aymara Indians. Natural vegetation is scarce. The most common plant is a coarse bunched grass known as *ichu* (*Stipa ichu*). This grassland is probably the result of thousands of years of habitation by man, and grazing by domestic animals. There are also some other plants such as thola (*Baccharis thola*) which is a thorny bush, yareta (*Azorella yareta*), a very slow growing, dense low-level green plant and cactus. These are plants which have adapted to the harsh highland environment and can survive grazing. The *puna* used to support small forests of polylepis, which is the tree that grows at the highest altitude in the world (4,000-4,500m), but few trees remain now as they have mostly been cut for firewood and replaced by the cold and desolate steppe. Eucalypts have been introduced and grow extensively on the northern part of the Bolivian altiplano. Above 4,600m there are almost no plants at all. The most striking wild animal is the vicuña, a member of the cameloid family, the wild version of the alpaca. You are also likely to see the viscacha, a large rodent related to the chinchilla. The female is much smaller

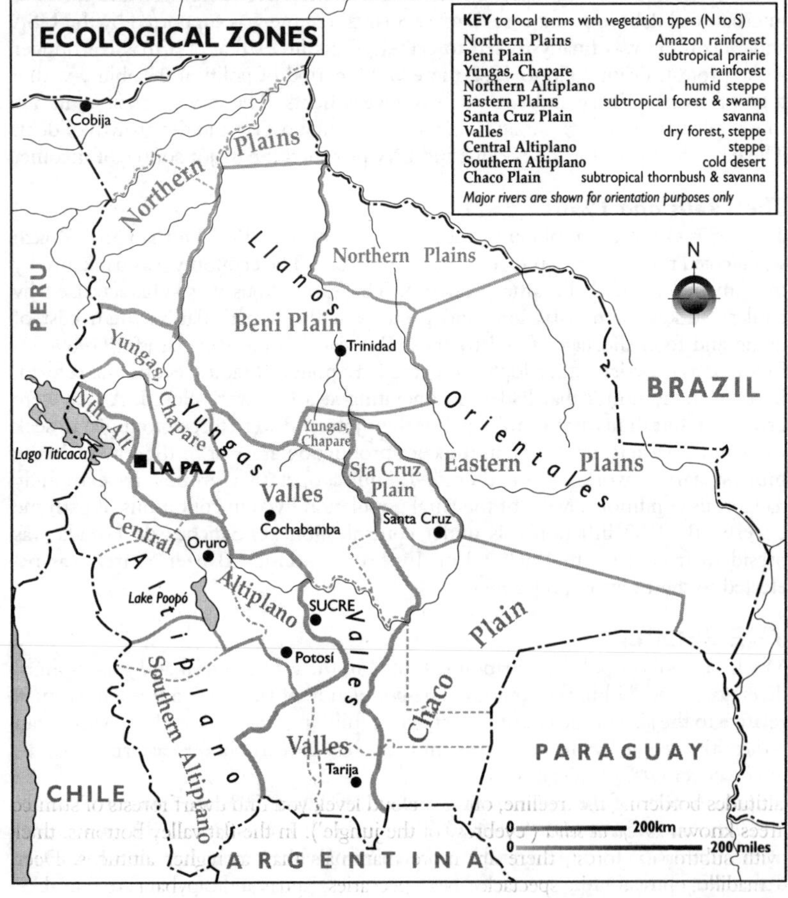

than the male, which is the size of a large rabbit. Viscacha live in groups in areas of boulders and are most easily seen at dawn and dusk. There are plenty of birds around the lakes of the altiplano, including coots, ducks, geese, gulls, flamingos and gulls, and the Andean condor, largest land bird in the world, is often seen flying in the cordilleras.

Yungas

The Yungas is an area of temperate subtropical forest which is very rich in biodiversity. Fortunately, because of the difficulties caused by climate and topography, there has been little clearing of these forests in Bolivia. Tree species include cedar (*Cedrela*), mahogany (*Swietenia macrophylla*), walnut (*Juglans*), laurel (*Cordia alliodora*), jacaranda, ceiba which yields kapok, caucho, cinchona (a source of quinine), palms, dyewoods, many aromatic trees and shrubs and numerous fruit trees. Sugarcane, coffee, tobacco and coca are planted and grow well at lower altitudes. At higher altitudes bordering the treeline, often at cloud level, you find dwarf forests of stunted trees known as *ceja de selva* ('eyebrow of the jungle'). In the flat valley bottoms, thick with subtropical forest, there are more mammals than at higher altitudes. Deer, armadillo, opossum, the spectacled bear, peccaries, jaguar and capybara are found.

Lowland forest and savanna

The Oriente comprises several vegetation types, from the dense tropical forest of the north to the Chaco plains of the south, and boasts a variety of animal life to match. In the northeast snakes, caiman and lizards are common as are salamanders, frogs and toads. Of the mammals there are sloths, monkeys, jaguars, ocelot, opossum, tapir, capybara, peccary, armadillo and anteaters. Insects and birds are also found in great variety and abundance. Vultures, parrots, macaws, toucans and hornbills are the most easily spotted.

Typical of the Bolivian Chaco is semi-deciduous forest with many leguminaceous trees, savannah grassland and large cacti. Maned wolves and pampa foxes are found in this area, both of which eat small mammals but in times of drought will also eat reptiles, birds, insects and fruit. There are several species of skunk and armadillos, anteaters and burrowing birds all root out insects to feed on. Snakes, jaguars, puma and deer also inhabit the grasslands and scrub forest. Noticeable among the birds are rhea, storks and a large number of waterbirds.

Pantanal

In the southeast corner of Bolivia in the vicinity of the River Paraguay, which is part of the La Plata drainage basin, is the area known as the Pantanal. The whole Pantanal, only one-third of which is within Bolivian boundaries (the rest is in Brazil), is a huge basin at only 150m above sea-level, which covers an area of 200,000km^2. For half the year this flatland is submerged beneath the floodwater spilling from the myriad rivers criss-crossing the area, filled beyond capacity by the heavy annual rains which fall between November and April. This is an area of sparse human settlement but abundant wildlife including caiman up to 2.5m long, the large rodent capybara, water birds such as egrets, herons, ibises and wood storks, limpkins and jabiru storks. The savannah grasslands of the Pantanal in the dry season support pampas deer, marsh deer, peccaries and rheas, ground birds, rodents and the maned wolf. Ants and termites nesting there attract anteaters and armadillos. During the rains up to 3m of water covers the grassland and all these animals have to retreat to higher land.

Nine-banded armadillo

PRACTICAL INFORMATION

Accommodation

Every Bolivian town has cheap accommodation of some description, and the cities of La Paz, Potosí, Sucre, Oruro, Santa Cruz, Trinidad, Cochabamba and Tarija have many options of all standards. Popular tourist destinations like Copacabana, Coroico, Rurrenabaque, Sorata and Uyuni have several good backpacker hostels often run by expats. Smaller less touristy places usually have some choice although the accommodation is often very basic, and even in villages you can sometimes find locals who will give you a bed for the night. Prices throughout Bolivia are cheap, a hotel from US$10 per person, *residencial* or *hostal* usually US$5–10 per person and the cheapest option, an *alojamiento*, from US$3 per person. The cheapest places are usually concentrated around bus and train stations. You should book ahead during festivals, when prices are likely to rise considerably, but otherwise it isn't usually necessary and at off-peak times prices can generally be negotiated down.

Books, newspapers and maps

A good weekly paper in English is the *Bolivian Times,* web: www.latinwide.com/boltimes; email: boliviantimes@latinwide.com. Books in English are not very easy to get hold of, though several of the backpacker hostels and some cafés do book swaps. It is best to buy all the maps you need in La Paz at the Instituto Geográfico Militar or one of the large bookshops such as Los Amigos del Libro.

Health and safety

The main problem with crime in Bolivia seems to be bag snatching and pickpockets, particularly around bus and train stations. Unlike in Peru or Ecuador I haven't come across or heard of any violent crime or muggings. But you should in any case take normal precautions, try not to arrive anywhere after dark and if you do, take a taxi to a hotel. Watch your bags like a hawk and never put them down on the ground while you buy tickets unless you have some means of securing them to your body. Use a secret money belt of some description for valuables and your passport. Look out for scams, a particularly common one in Santa Cruz being false 'policemen' trying to get you to go in a car with them to a 'police station'. Lock your luggage when flying as things tend to go missing from checked-in bags.

Although tap water is treated in most of Bolivia's cities, if you are only going to be in Bolivia for a few weeks it is worth sticking to bottled water. Outside the cities you should only drink bottled or treated water. Avoid unpeelable fruit, vegetables and salads and only eat freshly cooked food. Personal hygiene is also very important in keeping healthy, though often made difficult by a lack of water and absence of soap. Always carry your own toilet paper and soap.

Entry formalities

British, European Union and USA passport holders don't require a visa and on entering Bolivia will be given an entry stamp usually with permission to stay for three months. Work permits and temporary residence permits are only available from Immigration Offices in Bolivia. In 1999, Irish nationals were being asked for visas.

Food and drink

The food varies considerably throughout Bolivia, depending on whether you are in a highland or lowland area, or somewhere in between. The best value meals are the set menus served at lunchtime (*almuerzos*) from 12.00 and in the evenings from 18.00 (*cenas*). For just a few bolivianos you can get a two- or three-course meal. The quality is reflected in the amount you pay, the cheapest being very much starch and carbohydrate based meals. Lowland jungle areas have a predominance of fresh fish and tropical fruits, with yucca, rice and bananas the staple carbohydrates. Chicken is the predominant meat served in lowland areas. In the highlands there tends to be more meat, usually pork, sometimes beef, with potatoes or quinoa as the staple to accompany the meat. Wherever you go you can buy *salteñas*, a sort of meat pastie, often quite spicy, and you can usually get *ají*, a chilli based spicy sauce to hot up whatever you're eating. Vegetarian food is not widely available, other than in La Paz, though most markets have a plentiful supply of fresh fruit and vegetables, so you can prepare your own food. It is best to be cautious when eating Bolivian food until your stomach adapts to the local bacteria. Wash all fruit and vegetables and if you are eating market food, make sure it is well and freshly cooked and hasn't been standing around. As for drinks, you can get reasonable lager type beer (*cerveza*) all over the country, and all the usual soft drinks. Typical local drinks are *chicha*, made from fermented maize, *singani*, made from distilled wine, primarily in the Tarija area, and *api*, a thick purple-coloured hot drink made from maize and often served for breakfast in markets. You can also get a variety of fresh fruit juices, which are widely available and delicious.

Getting around

By road

Bolivian roads are notoriously bad, mostly unsurfaced (96%!), dusty if dry, potholed and in the rainy season thick with mud, sometimes blocked by rivers in spate, fallen trees, avalanches or crashed vehicles. The bus service is pretty good, however, with frequent regular departures between all cities and large towns. Most buses (called *flotas*) leave on time. Some have heating, some have reclining seats, some have videos, and on major routes you may have a choice of service and price, but generally speaking the bus and the service are basic. It is a good idea to buy your ticket in advance to ensure you get the seat you want, and to take food and water with you. Most buses will stop every few hours for refreshments and toilet breaks, but you may not want to eat what is on offer, and it is quite possible you will be delayed in the middle of nowhere where nothing is available. Keep a careful eye on your luggage but not to the point of being paranoid. Minibuses (*micros*) are sometimes used on shorter routes or very twisty roads like the ones to Sorata and Coroico. City buses are called *trufis*.

By train

Bolivia has the following functioning train lines at the moment: from Oruro to Villazón; from Uyuni to the border with northern Chile; from Santa Cruz to the Brazilian border (Puerto Suarez); and from Santa Cruz to Yacuiba on the Argentinian border. Details of services are given in the relevant chapters, but check at stations for current times and prices as services are continually being changed and some are under threat of closure.

By boat

It is possible to travel by boat in the lowland areas of Bolivia – there are 14,000km of navigable rivers. There are boats, every few days, up and down the River Mamoré between Puerto Villarroel, Trinidad and Guayaramerín. Check at the Capitanía del Puerto for details. Prices (from US$7 per day) and quality vary considerably, but conditions are usually pretty basic and it's best to take your own food and water to keep you going. Trips at lower water in the dry season can take twice as long as during the wet season. It is also a good idea to bring along plenty of insect repellent, a mosquito net and your own hammock.

By air

Lloyd Air Boliviano (LAB) and Aero Sur fly between the major Bolivian cities, La Paz, Cochabamba, Sucre, Tarija, Santa Cruz, Trinidad and Cobija. TAM, the military airline, flies passenger services to more than 20 regional airports. LAB have a toll free number for information: 0800 3001/0800 4321 and Aéro Sur is 0800 3030.

Money

The boliviano is the local currency. The exchange rate is fairly stable, with approximately 5.4 bolivianos to the US dollar. There are ATM machines (Cirrus and Plus) in all the cities, from which you can get cash. Banks and change offices exchange other currencies as well as US dollars, but it is always easiest to bring dollars. US dollar travellers' cheques are changeable in banks in cities; you need your passport and often proof of purchase too. Credit cards are accepted in larger hotels and some restaurants only. It is perfectly legal, and often the easiest option, to change money (US dollars cash, good quality notes only) on the street and the exchange rate is the same as in money change offices, *casa de cambio*, or banks.

Post, telephone and email

International post is reasonably cheap and pretty slow, but seems to be reliable. Allow several weeks for letters to arrive. Most towns and all cities have ENTEL phone offices (Open 08.00–23.00) where you can make local and international calls direct or send faxes. You can usually see the cost of the call as you make it. BT chargecards are usable. There are also phone boxes which take phone cards or special tokens called *fichas*. Email is now widely available in Bolivia as it is in Peru and Ecuador. It is cheap to use at around US$2 per hour, and usually connections are good.

The country code for Bolivia is 591. The city codes are: La Paz 02; Cochabamba 042; Pando 0842; Oruro 052; Potosí 062; Santa Cruz 03; Sucre 064; Beni 046; and Tarija 066. Other codes are given in the relevant chapters.

Business hours and public holidays

Most businesses are open Mon–Fri 08.00–12.00 and 14.00–18.00. Some are also open Sat mornings. Banks are usually open Mon–Fri 08.30–11.30 and 14.30–18.30, although some don't close for lunch.

Public holidays are New Year's Day, Monday and Tuesday of Carnival, Good Friday, May 1st which is Labour Day, Corpus Christi in June, Independence Day on August 6, All Saints' Day on November 1 and Christmas Day. Each of the nine departments will also celebrate its own Independence Day.

Tourist information offices

The main tourist information office for Bolivia is at Calle Mercado 1328, Edificio Mariscal Ballivían, Floor 18, La Paz. You can get information specifically on La Paz from the helpful office in Plaza Estudiante. There are regional offices in all the main cities, most of which are useful despite having extremely limited resources.

GIVING SOMETHING BACK

There are plenty of opportunities for volunteer work in Bolivia, including the following organisation. For further possibilities contact the South American Explorers Club who have a special information pack for volunteers available for US$6.50.

Conservation International, tel: (591) 2-323975, has an office in La Paz but is based in the United States. This organisation has a far-ranging 'Andes Region' programme which includes a Rapid Assessment Program of endangered areas, habitat conservation, and development of eco-tourism projects owned and operated by the indigenous communities they are designed to benefit.

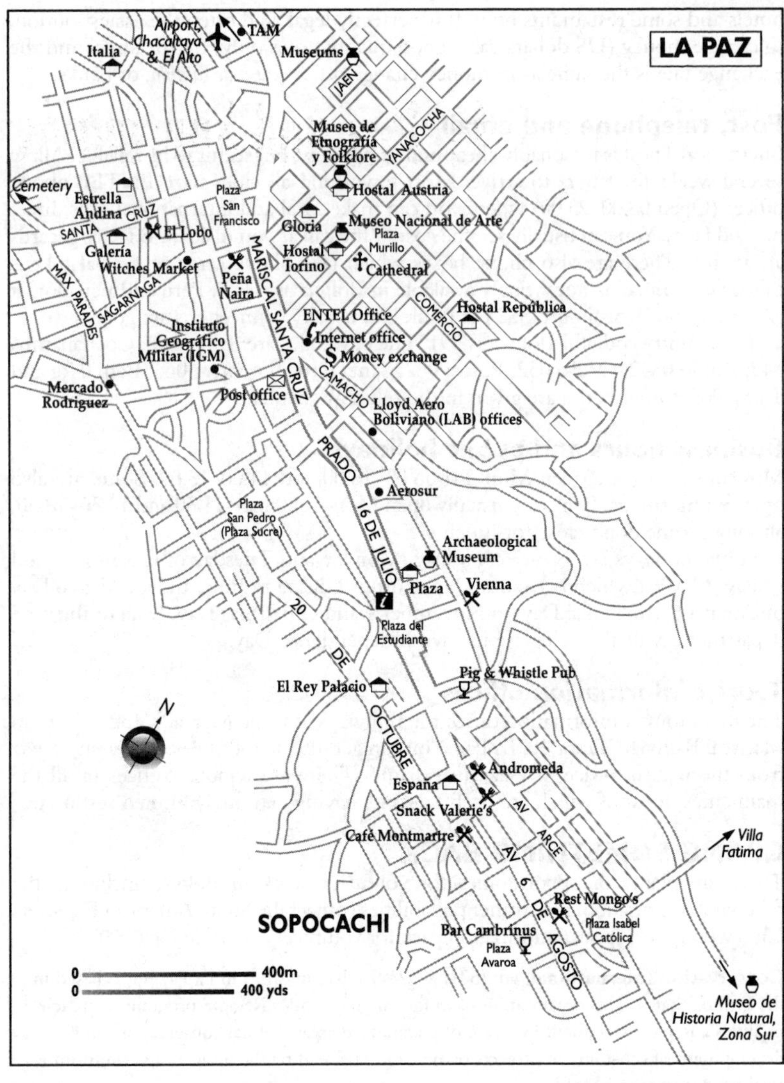
LA PAZ
Airport, Chacaltaya & El Alto
TAM
Italia
Museums
JAEN
Museo de Etnografía y Folklore
YANACOCHA
Cemetery
Estrella Andina
Plaza San Francisco
Hostal Austria
Gloria
Museo Nacional de Arte
Plaza Murillo
SANTA CRUZ
El Lobo
Galería
Hostal Torino
Cathedral
Witches Market
MAX PARADES
SAGARNAGA
Peña Naira
MARISCAL SANTA CRUZ
COMERCIO
Hostal República
ENTEL Office
Internet office
Money exchange
Instituto Geográfico Militar (IGM)
Mercado Rodriguez
Post office
CAMACHO
Lloyd Aero Boliviano (LAB) offices
PRADO
Aerosur
Plaza San Pedro (Plaza Sucre)
16 DE JULIO
Archaeological Museum
Plaza
Vienna
20 DE OCTUBRE
Plaza del Estudiante
Pig & Whistle Pub
El Rey Palacio
N
Andromeda
España
Snack Valerie's
AV ARCE
Café Montmartre
Villa Fatima
AV 6 DE AGOSTO
Rest Mongo's
Plaza Isabel Católica
SOPOCACHI
Bar Cambrinus
Plaza Avaroa
0 400m
0 400 yds
Museo de Historia Natural, Zona Sur

19 La Paz and Surrounds

LA PAZ

Telephone code 02

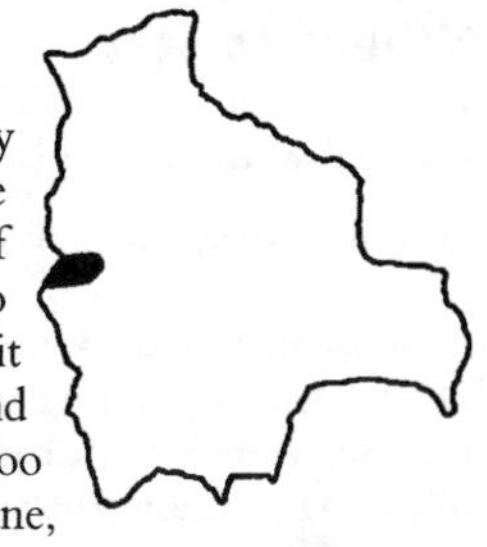

La Paz (3,600m), with a population of 854,000 in the city itself and over 500,000 more in El Alto, is one of the world's most dramatically located cities. It's also one of the highest, and *soroche* (altitude sickness) is something to watch out for if you aren't already acclimatised. Take it easy for your first few days at altitude, avoid alcohol and rich food, drink plenty of water and don't move around too fast. Whether you arrive by road from the north or by plane, the first views of the city are unforgettably striking. La Paz sits in a deep canyon off the altiplano, at the foot of the great snow-covered mountain peak of Illimani. The city has a very high proportion of indigenous Indians, and is a fascinating place to spend a few days, just wandering around the many markets and steep city streets watching local life. It is also a good place for shopping: jumpers, hats, bags and weavings are sold here at reasonable prices in all colours, shapes and sizes. It is a fairly easy city to find your way around as all roads lead steeply downhill to the central square of Plaza San Francisco and the main road running between there and Plaza Estudiante, Avenida Mariscal Santa Cruz or Prado.

Getting there and away

By road

La Paz has a large and central bus station (*terminal terrestre*) from which long distance buses run to the south and east of the city. There are daily buses to Potosí, Sucre, Santa Cruz, Oruro and Cochabamba. There are international services to Arica (11 hrs, 430km), Iquique (10 hrs), Buenos Aires (2–3 days), and Puno (297km via Copacabana, 325km via Desaguadero). You won't get one bus all the way through on these services – expect to have to change at the borders. Sometimes it is easier and more flexible just to buy tickets in stages. Other buses, generally to the north to destinations like Sorata and Desaguadero, leave from the cemetery area. Buses and jeeps to Coroico and the Beni go from Villa Fatima. You can take taxis or minibuses from the centre of La Paz to these neighbourhoods.

By air

La Paz's airport is at El Alto, on the altiplano above the city. Flying in or out of El Alto gives you a stunning view of the nearby ice-capped peaks of the Cordillera Real. The airport is modern and efficient with a café, restaurant, bank with ATM machine, phone office with Internet and a few kiosks selling trinkets. Transport to the airport is easy: taxis cost US$7, or there is also a local *combi* (minibus) No 232

'Aeropuerto' to and from Av Mariscal Santa Cruz, US$1, allow 30 mins. When leaving from La Paz you have to pay an airport tax, which is US$10 national and US$20 international.

By train

La Paz's train station is at the west end of the city just a few blocks from San Francisco square. Trains used to run from here to Uyuni and Villazón (920km), but those trains now go from Oruro. There is a connecting bus service from the bus station in La Paz to the Oruro train station. Trains to Camana, Chile, now run from Uyuni.

Where to stay

La Paz has no shortage of places to stay. There are dozens of hotels in the centre of town from the very basic to five star.

Hostal Austria Calle Yancocha 531; tel: 351140. From US$3. A very popular place, 26 beds, some shared rooms, 3 bathrooms, full most nights, clean, safe, cheap and good for meeting other backpackers. It's a good idea to book ahead and arrive early.

Hostal Torino Socabaya 457; tel: 341487. From US$5 per person. A large colonial building centrally located, good café/restaurant next door of the same name (open 07.00–23.00). Clean, variety of rooms, all shapes and sizes. Book exchange. Popular with backpackers.

Hotel Italia Calle Manco Kapac 303; tel: 325101. US$7–9 with shared bath. Popular with locals, noisy at weekends, clean and comfortable.

Estrella Andina Av Illampu 716; tel: 350001. US$9–17 with shared bath. Rooms with bath available. Family run, clean, central hotel. Nice rooms, modern bathrooms, includes breakfast.

Hotel Sagárnaga Calle Sagárnaga 326; tel: 350252; fax: 360831. US$12–16 without bath, US$20–27 private bath. Central, TV, clean and safe.

Hotel España Av 6 de Agosto 2074; tel: 354643; fax: 342329. US$20–28 with private bath, includes breakfast.

Where to eat

As with hostels there is no shortage of restaurants in the centre of La Paz. On Prado itself there are all sorts of places to eat, from upmarket steak houses to the popular fast food **Eli's**. Around Calle Illampu and Sagárnaga there are places catering for tourists, cafés and a few vegetarian restaurants. **El Lobo** serves huge portions on Calle Illampu and Santa Cruz upstairs. Vegetarians can eat well at Manantial, **Hotel Gloria**, Calle Potosí, Mon–Sat 07.00-23.00. Other veggie places include **Café El Layka**, Calle Sagarnaga 288. **Café Torino** (next door to Hostal Torino Socabaya 457) does good breakfasts, muesli, fruit juices and coffee.

South of Plaza Estudiante in Sopocachi is a student area, with several good bars and places to eat. **Mongo's** is particularly good for tasty burgers and a variety of international food, and is a popular place with expats and young Paceños; Calle Hermanos Manchego, open 17.30–01.00. Also in this area is the **Café Montmarte**, Calle Fernando Gauchalla next to the **Alliance Française**, with live music and exhibitions. They serve French food. In Calacoto, at the south end of town, there are several good restaurants and bars. Take a taxi or bus (marked Calacoto) to this upmarket part of La Paz. It could be any modern city and is worlds away from the centre of town, with big international supermarkets, fast food restaurants and young wealthy Paceños hanging out. Some of the restaurants worth trying are the Chinese **Puerto del Sol** (Calle 11), **Los Patos** at Calle 14 for

Bolivian food, Italian at **Tratoria Tiberius**, meat at **Abracadabra**, Mexican at **Pueblo Viejo**.

The markets in La Paz offer a wide variety of very cheap food. If your stomach is adapted to the local bacteria and you are on a tight budget these are the best places to eat. For just over a dollar you can get soup and a full plate of chicken or fish with rice, chips and some vegetables. *Almuerzos* and *cenas* are usually available. Most markets open about 06.00 for tea, coffee, *api* (a sort of thick purple maize drink) and various pastries.

Entertainment

For nightlife try the lively salsa club **El Loro en su Salsa**, Calle Rosendo Gutiérrez corner 6 de Agosto; Tue–Sat from 20.30. A great salsa club, it goes on all night. The biggest disco is **Forum** at Calle Sanjines 2908, open until the early hours. Thursday, Friday and Saturday nights are the big nights for nightlife, while the rest of the week is quiet. **Calacoto** has some popular up and coming bars from Calle 8 onwards; take a taxi or minibus from the centre marked Calacoto. There are several Peñas where you can see live folk music – **Nairas** on Calle Sagárnaga 161 and **Los Escudos** on Mariscal Santa Cruz are the most well known. There is usually a small entrance charge to see the show.

La Paz has several cinemas with most films in original versions with subtitles. Sitting in the cinema is a good way to acclimatise, not too energetic, and selections are usually no worse than anywhere else. The best cinemas are on the main road near the Plaza del Estudiante: **Cine 16 de Julio**, **Cine 6 de Agosto**, **Cinemateca Boliviana** on Calle Pichincha (tel: 325346) which often has alternative films. The **British Council** (Av Arce 2708) also shows films from time to time.

Tourist information

Tourist office Calle Mercado 3423, Edificio Mariscal Ballivían, Floor 18; tel: 367441/367463; email: mceiyturismo@mpoint.com.bo
Tourist police Plaza del Estadio, Miraflores; tel: 225016.
Immigration Calle Gosálvez between Arce and Calle 6 de Agosto.

Travel agencies

Andean Summits Calle Sagárnaga 189; tel: 317497. A trekking agency. Specialises in renting and selling equipment. Experienced guides.
Andino Calle Sagárnaga 372; tel: 228924. Trekking and climbing.
Bolivian Journeys Calle Sagárnaga 363; tel: 357848. A trekking agency, sells maps and rents equipment.
Colibrí Calle Sagárnaga 309; tel: 371936. Climbing, trekking, safaris. Rents camping equipment and has jeeps with drivers for hire.
Colonial Tours Hostal Austria, Calle Yanacocha; tel/fax: 316073. All sorts of tours, and transport to Copacabana.
Crillon Tours Av Camacho 1223; tel: 374566. Conventional travel agent.
Diana Tours Calle Sagárnaga 328; tel: 350252; fax: 360831. Popular tours of La Paz, Tiahuanaku, and transport to Copacabana. Credit cards accepted.
EcoBolivia Foundation Tel: 315974; fax: 325776; email: ECOB@megalink.com Organises trips to Madidi National Park (see page 367).
Fremen Tours Calle Pedro Salazar 537, PO Box 9682, La Paz; tel: 414069; fax: 417327; email: vtfremen@caoba.entelnet.bo Tours throughout Bolivia, including Flotel floating hotel from Trinidad, and El Puente jungle lodge near Villa Tunari. Offices in Santa Cruz, Cochabamba and Trinidad.

Magri Turismo Calle Capitan Ravelo 2101 and Murillo; tel: 434747/434660; email: magri_emete@megalink.com This agency has many years' experience of organising everything from day tours to treks and climbs in the Cordillera Real and expeditions into the Amazon.
Refugio Huayna Potosí Calle Illampu 626, Hotel Continental; tel: 323584; fax: 378226.

Airlines

Aero Sur Av 16 de Julio; tel: 313233/08003030.
Aerolíneas Argentinas Av 16 de Julio; tel: 351711.
American Airlines Plaza Venezuela 1440; tel: 351360/353804.
LAB Av Camacho 1456; tel: 374032/367707.
Lufthansa Av 6 de Agosto 2512; tel: 431717.
TAM (Transporte Aero Militar) Av Montes; tel: 379286. Military airline, which flies to regional airports in the eastern lowlands including: Rurrenabaque, Trinidad, Guayaramerín, Yacuiba and Villamontes.

Shopping

Camping equipment

Camping Caza y Pesca Handal Centre on the corner of Socabaya and Mariscal Santa Cruz. Good for any camping equipment you may need and camping gas.

Maps

You can purchase 1:50,000 maps of most of Bolivia from the **Instituto Geográfico Militar (IGM)** at Calle Juan XXIII 100, Oficina 5, behind the main post office off Calle Rodriguez. Open Mon–Fri 09.00–11.00 and 15.00–17.00. You must take your passport. Maps are US$7 each or US$5 for photocopies.
Amigos del Libro Calle Mercado 1315. Sells books and some maps.
Club Andino Boliviano Calle México 1638; tel/fax: 324682. Some maps and equipment, call for opening hours.

Money

Banco Unión Potosí 911, Amex travellers' cheques, US$2 commission.
Casa de Cambio Hotel Gloria, Calle Potosí 909, open 09.30–12.30 and 14.30–18.30, changes many different currencies and cheques.

Communications

Post office Av Mariscal Santa Cruz and Oruro. Open Mon–Sat 08.00–20.00.
Phone office ENTEL, Calle Ayacucho 267. Open 08.00–23.00. You can buy phone cards and use them in the newer phone boxes now found in some hotels and shopping centres.

Internet

Angelo Colonial Linares 922; tel: 360199; email: AngeloColonia@hotmail.com Open 08.30–21.30, book exchange, café with old artefacts, good coffee. US$3 per hour.
Café Torino Socabaya 457. US$5 per hour. Open 09.00–19.00.
Café Cultural on San Francisco square, Av Camacho 1377. Internet open 08.30–23.00. US$2 per hour.

Embassies

Argentina Calle Aspiazu 497; tel: 369266/353233
Brazil Av 20 de Octubre 2038l tel: 352175/352108
France Av Hernando Siles 5390; tel: 786125/786138

Germany Av Arce 2395; tel: 430850/431851
Great Britain Av Arce; tel: 432397/433424
Israel Av Mariscal Sta. Cruz 1285; tel: 374239/371287
Italy Av 6 de Agosto 2575; tel: 364211/361129
Japan Calle Rosendo Gutiérrez 497; tel: 373151/366859
Perú Av 6 de Agosto; tel: 353550/352352
Spain Av 6 de Agosto 2827; tel: 431203/430118
United States Av Arce 2780; tel: 430251

What to see

Most of the interesting buildings in La Paz are within a few blocks of **Plaza San Francisco**, which lies at the heart of the city. The plaza is always busy with street sellers offering a variety of drinks and snacks, there are often live musicians busking, and there are always loads of kids willing to clean your shoes for a boliviano. The second most important centre of the city is the **Plaza Murillo** just north of the Prado. This is where you will find the government buildings, the cathedral and the colonial heart of La Paz. **Calle Jaén** has the best examples of colonial architecture in La Paz, and is worth wandering down.

The **markets** in La Paz are fascinating. You can buy anything, from coolboxes to domestic appliances, bikes, computers, cheap Raybans and jeans, perfumes, sports shoes, and more. There is also a large area dedicated to food of various sorts and the well-known **witches' market** where you can buy any number of lucky charms, llama foetus, or natural medicines. The witches' market is in Calle Linares and the other markets are on up the hill filling the streets around Calle Max Paredes. For souvenirs the best area is around Calle Sagárnaga.

Churches

The plaza of San Francisco is dominated by the very fine **San Francisco Church**, which was built in 1549. The façade is of baroque style and was added in 1790. The church is beautifully decorated and contains a collection of religious art.

Museums

Museo Nacional de Arte Calle Commercio corner Socabaya. Open Tue–Fri 09.00–12.30 and 15.00–19.00, weekends 10.00–13.00. A large collection of paintings, including some from the Paceña school of art and contemporary Bolivian artists, in a very fine colonial building.
Museo de Etnografía y Folklore Calle Ingavi 916. Open Mon–Fri 08.30–12.00 and 14.30–1800. Small permanent collection on Tarabuco, video room with good variety of material available to watch, and centre for meetings.
Museo Nacional de Arqueología Calle Tiwanaku 93. Open Tue–Fri 09.30–12.30 and 15.00–19.00, weekends 10.00–12.30. Interesting collection of archaeological pieces from prehispanic Bolivian cultures.
Museo de Historia Natural Calle 26, Cota-Cota. Open Mon–Sun 08.30–16.00.

Calle Jaén has the **Museo de Instrumentos Musicales de Bolivia, Museo Casa de Murillo**, a museum of colonial art, artefacts and belongings of Bolivia's presidents from the 19th century, **Museo de Metalles Preciosos**, and **Museo del Litoral Boliviano** featuring the War of the Pacific. Open Tue–Fri 09.30–12.30 and 15.00–19.00; weekends 10.00–12.30.

AROUND LA PAZ

From La Paz there are several trips worth making into the surrounding area.

Chacaltaya

Chacaltaya is the highest ski resort in the world and is offered by travel agencies as a day trip. If, and only if, you are acclimatised and the weather is fine, this is a good day out, with superb views of the Cordillera Real and over the altiplano and La Paz. It involves driving to the ski lodge (2 hrs) and walking from there to the top of Chacaltaya at 5,600m (1 hr). It isn't a hard walk if the altitude poses no problem, but shouldn't even be attempted until you have spent at least four days at altitude. Bring warm clothes and your own food and drink.

Tiahuanaco

The pre-Inca site of Tiahuanaco is definitely worth a visit. It was the centre of the Tiahuanaco culture, a flourishing altiplano civilisation, and the population were expert stone masons and farmers. The Tiahuanaco culture was at its most powerful between AD400–1000 and then, for some unknown reason, it lost its power and began to subdivide into smaller groups of Aymara kingdoms. If you are short of time the best way to get to the site is on a tour from La Paz. If you have more time or an aversion to tours you can go on public transport easily enough.

The site of Tiahuanaco covers an area of 10km^2 and is thought to have housed a population of between 30,000 and 60,000 people at its grandest. The original name for the site was *Taypikhala*, an Aymara word meaning stone in the centre. The city is in the centre of the altiplano, with the mountains of the Cordillera Real to the east dominated by Illimani; through the mountains are the paths to the fertile lowlands, and to the west lie Lake Titicaca and the pasture lands for llamas and alpaca. The location was undoubtedly considered sacred, being in a central position geographically and with clear views of the rising and setting sun.

Such large populations were sustained through innovative agricultural irrigation practice. Water was channelled from the lake to a system of raised fields. You can still see this raised field system on parts of the altiplano today. The way it works is

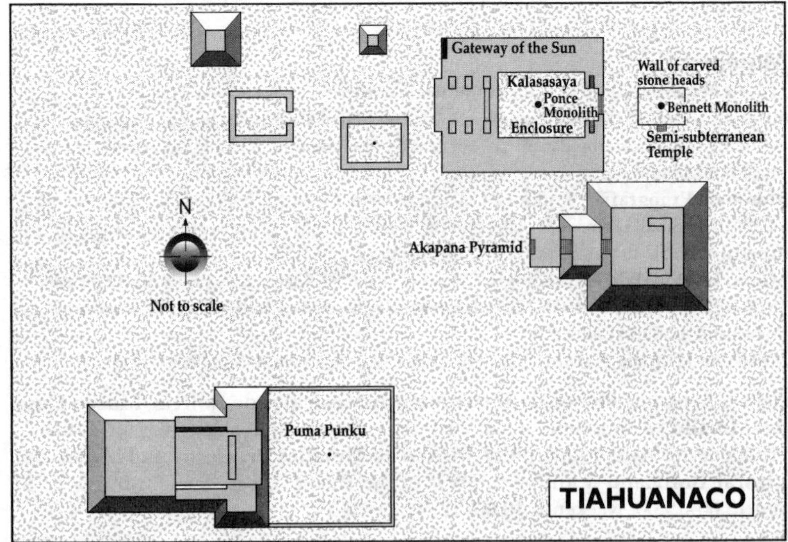

that the earth is dug out to create long ditches on either side of a mound. The salt from the brackish water then leeches out and the water content of the soil remains constant. The soils resist frost and the silt from the ditches is periodically spread on the mounds.

The high-quality stonework at Tiahuanaco is its most striking feature. There are all sorts of buildings within the site, but there are three principal temples. The main ceremonial building is a pyramid construction called **Akapana**, which may have been constructed to reflect the shape of the Andes in the distance. This structure was 17m high and over 200m along each side. It was made of earth and clay and faced with large stone slabs, the higher levels also having carved feline and human tenon heads. Within the pyramid, cut from the top layer, was a sunken courtyard with what are presumed to have been priests' houses inside. Burial remains have been found in the pyramid. A complex network of drains and fountains ran within the whole pyramid, thought by some to reflect the water courses on the mountain of Illimani.

On the north side of Akapana there is a sunken courtyard, a semi-subterranean temple, and nearby the huge enclosure of the Kalasasaya Temple. The sunken courtyard is lined with stones studded with further tenon heads, mostly human. This courtyard contained a number of stone sculptures within it, including one of a figure known now as the **Bennett Monolith**. The area was probably used for ritualistic meetings. The Bennett Monolith was over 7m tall and an impressive sight. Together with the Ponce Monolith, it is typical of Tiahuanaco figure carving. The decoration on the stonework is finely detailed, with similar patterns to those found on textiles from the same time.

The **Kalasasaya Temple** has at its entrance the great doorway seen from the sunken courtyard, now reconstructed, made from tremendous blocks of stone. This was a large courtyard for mass meetings.

In a corner of this temple is the intricately carved monolithic portal known as the Sun Gate. It is not known where this gate would originally have stood, but it may possibly have been at the Puma Punku Temple, 1km south of its present day location.

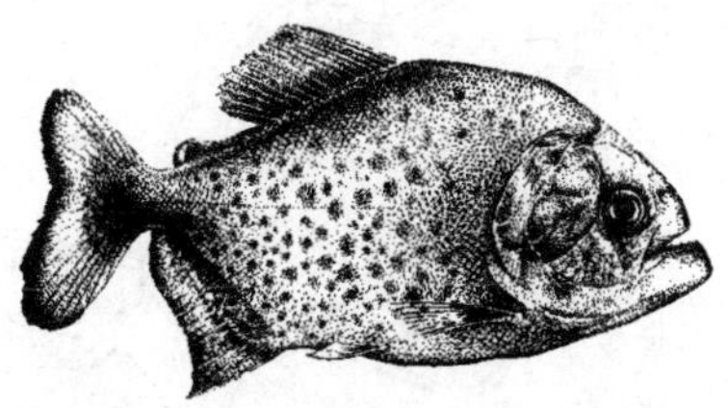

Red-bellied piranha

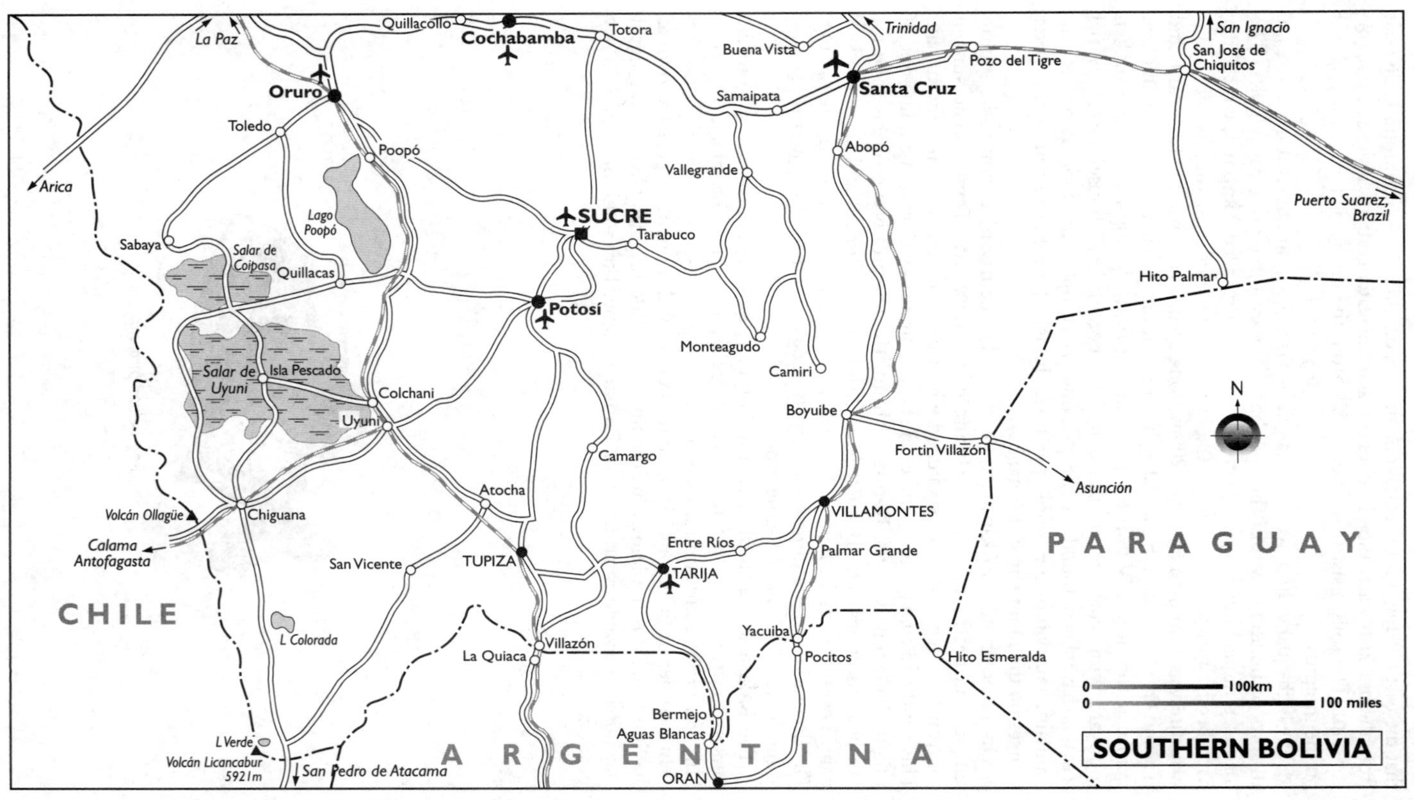
SOUTHERN BOLIVIA
0 100km
0 100 miles
N
PARAGUAY
ARGENTINA
CHILE
La Paz
Quillacollo
Cochabamba
Totora
Trinidad
Buena Vista
Santa Cruz
Pozo del Tigre
San Ignacio
San José de Chiquitos
Puerto Suarez, Brazil
Oruro
Toledo
Poopó
Arica
Lago Poopó
Samaipata
Abopó
Vallegrande
SUCRE
Tarabuco
Sabaya
Salar de Coipasa
Quillacas
Potosí
Hito Palmar
Monteagudo
Camiri
Salar de Uyuni
Isla Pescado
Colchani
Uyuni
Boyuibe
Fortin Villazón
Camargo
Asunción
Atocha
Volcán Ollagüe
Chiguana
VILLAMONTES
Calama Antofagasta
Entre Ríos
Palmar Grande
San Vicente
TUPIZA
TARIJA
L Colorada
Yacuiba
Villazón
La Quiaca
Pocitos
Hito Esmeralda
Bermejo
Aguas Blancas
L Verde
Volcán Licancabur 5921m
San Pedro de Atacama
ORAN

20 South from La Paz

The area of the altiplano from La Paz southwards has a wealth of history and is of great scenic beauty. The cities of Oruro, Potosí and Sucre reflect Bolivia's past, the indigenous way of life, mining industry and colonial heritage. They are fascinating to visit: Oruro for its cultural history and carnival; Potosí, once the largest and wealthiest city in South America, for the chance to visit the mines of Cerro Rico; and Sucre for its grandeur and colonial majesty. Towards the Chilean border there are no more cities; the land is inhospitable and sparsely settled. This is the poorest part of Bolivia, where just surviving is a daily battle. The scenery is wild and dramatic, with salt lakes, volcanic peaks and remote, windswept high desert landscapes. Travelling through this part of Bolivia, where there is so much to see, is very rewarding and relatively straightforward. The roads are not bad and there is frequent public transport, bus, train and plane.

POTOSÍ

Telephone code 591

Founded in 1545, Potosí was to become one of the world's richest cities. It lies at 3,977m at the foot of Cerro Rico, the mountain rich in the silver that transformed Europe. The beautiful colonial buildings in the centre of Potosí reflect this wealthy past, but the outlying adobe slums, which house most of the city's 112,000 inhabitants, give a greater indication of the current economic situation and the poverty in which most people in Potosí now live. In the 16th century thousands flocked to the city, lured by the glimmer of silver. However, it didn't last and the depletion of the silver in the 19th century, coupled with recent drops in world mineral prices, have left most Potosí miners and their families with very little income, forcing many people to migrate to lowland regions in search of work. Although Potosí is a fascinating city to visit, it can be very cold and conditions for the local residents are miserable. The city comes to life in the afternoon and evening when hundreds of people emerge on to the streets to shop and wander around with their friends.

History

Silver was first found on Cerro Rico by the Indian Diego Huallapa in 1545. The first mine was established and just one year later the city of Potosí was founded. It grew fast and by the end of the 16th century it was one of the largest cities in the world with a population of 160,000. However, it was not until the visit of the Viceroy of Toledo in 1572 that some order was put into the planning of Potosí, the streets widened and the Plaza Mayor designed and built. The first mint was built in Potosí in 1573.

Enough silver was mined from Cerro Rico to finance the Spanish economy for 300 years, but this wealth came at a bitter price for the people forced to work in the mines. In the haste of the Spanish to mine the precious metals many millions of altiplano Indians and black slaves were forced to live and work underground in the most horrific conditions. In 1572 the Viceroy of Toledo introduced a law forcing the miners to work 12-hour shifts and remain underground, without seeing the light of day or breathing fresh air, for four months at a time. Many miners could not survive and between 1545 and 1825 an estimated eight million people died in the mines. Since then conditions have improved only a little and 15,000 miners still trudge into the mines daily in a struggle to make a living from the minerals of Cerro Rico. Children as young as 12 can be seen at work, generally pushing the huge carts that bring the ore out of the tunnels.

Getting there and away

By bus

There is a bus terminal 20 minutes' walk from the centre of town (US$0.50 by taxi). Be very careful in and around the terminal, as it is notorious for bag snatchers; don't put your rucksack on the ground. There are daily buses to La Paz (11 hrs) and Oruro (7 hrs) early morning and evening. To Sucre there are frequent departures (3 hrs). There are also buses to Uyuni (6 hrs), Cochabamba (12 hrs), Villazón (11 hours), Santa Cruz (18 hrs), and Tarija (12 hrs). Check at the terminal for times and prices.

By plane

Potosí airport is on the Sucre road, 5 km outside the city. Aero Sur fly daily to La Paz. Take a taxi, allowing 20 mins.

Where to stay

There is a reasonable choice of accommodation in Potosí ranging from cheap budget hostels to four star hotels. The centre of the city is quite small, so it's easy to wander around until you find somewhere you like.

Hostal María Victoria Calle Chuquisaca 148; tel: 22132. US$4 per person. Shared rooms, clean and recently refurbished. Popular with budget travellers.
Hostal Central Calle Bustillos 1230. US$4. A bit gloomy and hot showers only in the morning.
Alojamiento Ferrocarril At train station; tel: 24294. US$3–4 single/double. Good for budget travellers.
Residencial Felcar Calle Serudo 345; tel: 24966. From US$4 per person. Central, popular.
Hostal Carlos V Calle Linares; tel: 25121. From US$4 per person.
Hotel Jerusalén Calle Oruro 143; tel: 22600. US$4–6 without bathroom; US$9–13 with bathroom.
Hotel El Turista Calle Lanza 19; tel: 22492. US$12–18 single/double. Large place, courtyards, reasonable size rooms, comfortable.
Hotel Colonial Calle Hoyos 8; tel: 24265. US$30–40. Clean, pleasant.
Libertador Hostal Calle Millares 58; tel: 27877; email: Hostalib@cedro.pts.entelnet.bo US$30–40. Very comfortable, colonial building.

Where to eat

The centre of Potosí has many places to eat from the market to quite upmarket restaurants. The market on Calle Bolívar is open 06.00–18.00 for good breakfasts and other meals.

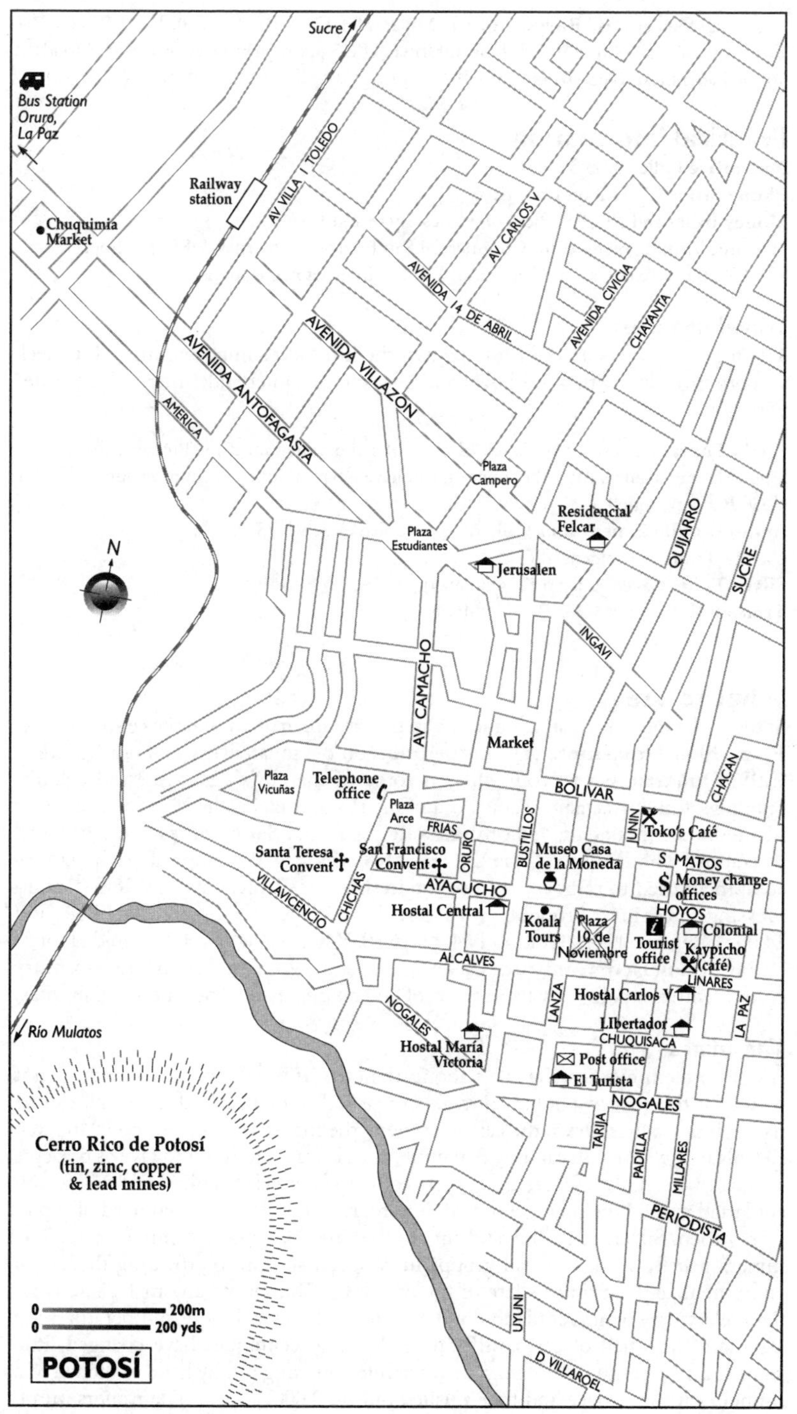
Sucre
Bus Station
Oruro,
La Paz
Railway
station
Chuquimia
Market
AV VILLA I TOLEDO
AV CARLOS V
AVENIDA 14 DE ABRIL
AVENIDA CIVICIA
CHAYANTA
AVENIDA VILLAZON
AVENIDA ANTOFAGASTA
AMERICA
Plaza
Campero
Residencial
Felcar
Plaza
Estudiantes
Jerusalen
N
QUIJARRO
SUCRE
INGAVI
AV CAMACHO
Market
CHACAN
Plaza
Vicuñas
Telephone
office
Plaza
Arce
BOLIVAR
FRIAS
BUSTILLOS
JUNIN
Toko's Café
Santa Teresa
Convent
San Francisco
Convent
ORURO
Museo Casa
de la Moneda
S MATOS
VILLAVICENCIO
CHICHAS
AYACUCHO
Money change
offices
Hostal Central
Koala
Tours
Plaza
10 de
Noviembre
HOYOS
Tourist
office
Colonial
Kaypicho
(café)
ALCALVES
LINARES
Hostal Carlos V
NOGALES
LANZA
LA PAZ
LIbertador
Río Mulatos
Hostal María
Victoria
CHUQUISACA
Post office
El Turista
NOGALES
TARIJA
PADILLA
MILLARES
Cerro Rico de Potosí
(tin, zinc, copper
& lead mines)
PERIODISTA
UYUNI
0 200m
0 200 yds
D VILLAROEL
POTOSÍ

Vegetarian food at **Café Kaypichu** Calle Millares 24. Open 07.00–13.00, 16.00–21.00.
Tuko's Café Calle Junin 9, 3rd floor. Internet (US$3 per hour), travel agent, good food, try the llama meat. Open 07.00–23.00.

Practical information

Post office Calle Lanza 3.
Phone office ENTEL on Plaza Arce.
Money Banks and change offices on Calles Sucre and Bolívar.
Internet Virtu@l Net Centro Commercial San Francisco, Internet, US$3 per hour, 09.00–22.00. Tuko's Café at Calle Junín also has Internet connections.

Travel agencies

The following agencies offer tours down the mines. It's important that you check you are provided with good boots and a jacket, a helmet and lantern. Take water with you.

Koala Tours Calle Ayacucho 5; tel: 22092. Offer the mine tour daily. Probably the most reputable tour agency. After the tour you can have a typical lunch of quinoa soup and llama meat. Recommended.
Andes Braulio Expeditions Calle Alonso de Ibañez 3; tel: 25175.
Carola Tours at Residencial Felcar.
Silver Tours Calle Quijarro 12; tel: 23600.
Transandino Tours Calle Bustillos 1078.
Victoria Tours at the Hostal María Victoria.

What to see

Some of the most interesting buildings in the city are in or around the central square, **Plaza 10 de Noviembre**. The **cathedral** is on the square itself, and northwards is **Calle Quijarro**, where you will find some of the city's best preserved colonial buildings. Calle Ayacucho, leading out of the Plaza, contains the **Museo Casa de la Moneda**, the Jesuit church **Compañía de Jesús**, and **Santa Teresa convent and museum**. The **Museo Casa de la Moneda** has the original 16th-century equipment used to mint coins from the freshly mined silver and the 18th-century pressing machines brought from Seville. Open Tue–Fri 09.00–12.00 and 14.00–17.30; Sat 09.00–12.00 and 14.30–16.30. You have to take a 2 hr guided tour.

San Francisco Convent, Calle Tarija and Nogales, has an 18th-century church with a superb view from the roof and an interesting collection of paintings.

The mines

A visit to the mines usually takes about six hours. It is well worthwhile, though it is not for the claustrophobic or weak stomached – the heat and the smell can be nauseating at times. From the centre of town, the first stop is at the miners' market, El Calvario, where you can buy dynamite, coca leaves, and water to give as presents to the miners. This is where the miners come to buy their supplies. From here you get kitted up with helmet, rubber boots, lantern and jacket and then head off up to Cerro Rico. Silver, lead, zinc and tin are the principal products mined here. The miners usually work in small groups in cooperative mines, providing their own equipment, and earning a share of the profit. Conditions are abysmal: there is no light, electricity or air ventilation in the mines and no machinery, temperatures are high and the smell of gases suffocating. Mining techniques have changed little since the 16th century: minerals are dynamited and dug out by hand, winched to a tunnel near the surface and then pushed out on 2,000kg carts. The miners numb their senses by continually chewing wads of coca leaves; they typically die in their early forties, usually from silicosis or in accidents which kill about 20 miners a year.

Mine tours cost about US$8, some of which goes to the miners. Most agencies offer a very similar service. Independent guides will also tout their business. The advantage of an agency is that you are more protected should something go wrong. Check that you are provided with the necessary equipment (see above).

Tarapaya thermal baths

This is a popular spot only 25km from Potosí where you can swim in the hot pools, known to have been used by the Incas. The surrounding scenery is beautiful and this is a relaxing way to spend a few hours after the mine tour. The crater lake is a public bathing pool about 100m across, with water at 30°C, and there are additional private pools. To get here, take a bus from Av Universitaria.

SUCRE

Telephone code 064.

Sucre, the official capital city, is without doubt Bolivia's most beautiful city. It has many well-preserved brilliant white colonial buildings, set around a particularly well cared for Plaza de Armas. Sucre is a university town, attracting masses of students from all over South America. The streets are full of young people and there is a flourishing nightlife, with some lively bars and cafés. As well as the opportunity to visit the many colonial buildings and museums, Sucre is a good city to relax in and recharge before continuing your journey. The average temperature is a pleasant 18°C and the altitude is 2,800m. Nearby, the Sunday market at Tarabuco is one of the greatest cultural attractions of Bolivia, where you can see splendidly dressed indigenous people exchanging their agricultural produce with each other and selling their intricate weavings.

History

Sucre was founded in 1540 by the Spaniard Captain Pedro Anzures, one of Gonzalo Pizarro's men. Before the Spanish conquest the area was the seat of the Charca Indians, thought to have numbered at least several thousand. The Spanish first gave the city the name La Villa de Charcas and later changed it to La Plata when Cerro Rico, the source of silver in Potosí, was discovered. The name Sucre wasn't adopted until 1825, in honour of José Sucre becoming first president of the Republic of Bolivia. Throughout the 16th, 17th and 18th centuries Sucre was the most important Andean city, providing judicial and administrative services to Potosí and the whole area known as the Audencia de Charcas. Sucre has a special place in history as the place where the fight for independence was sparked. The University of San Francisco de Xavier was founded in 1624, and was to become the source of unrest that led to a rebellion on May 25 1809, and the beginning of the fight for independence. Independence was declared in Sucre on August 6 1825.

Getting there and away

By bus

Most buses leave from the Terminal Terrestre, which is 3km from the centre on Calle Ostria Gutièrrez; take minibus (*trufi*) 3 from the centre. Some companies go direct to La Paz (14 hrs), or change at Cochabamba (11 hrs to Cochabamba, 19 hours total). There are also daily departures to Santa Cruz (leaves 17.00, 15 hrs) and Tarija (leaves 12.00, 18 hrs). Long-distance buses usually leave early evening so most journeys are overnight, which is a shame as the scenery around Sucre is worth seeing. There are frequent departures for Potosí throughout the day.

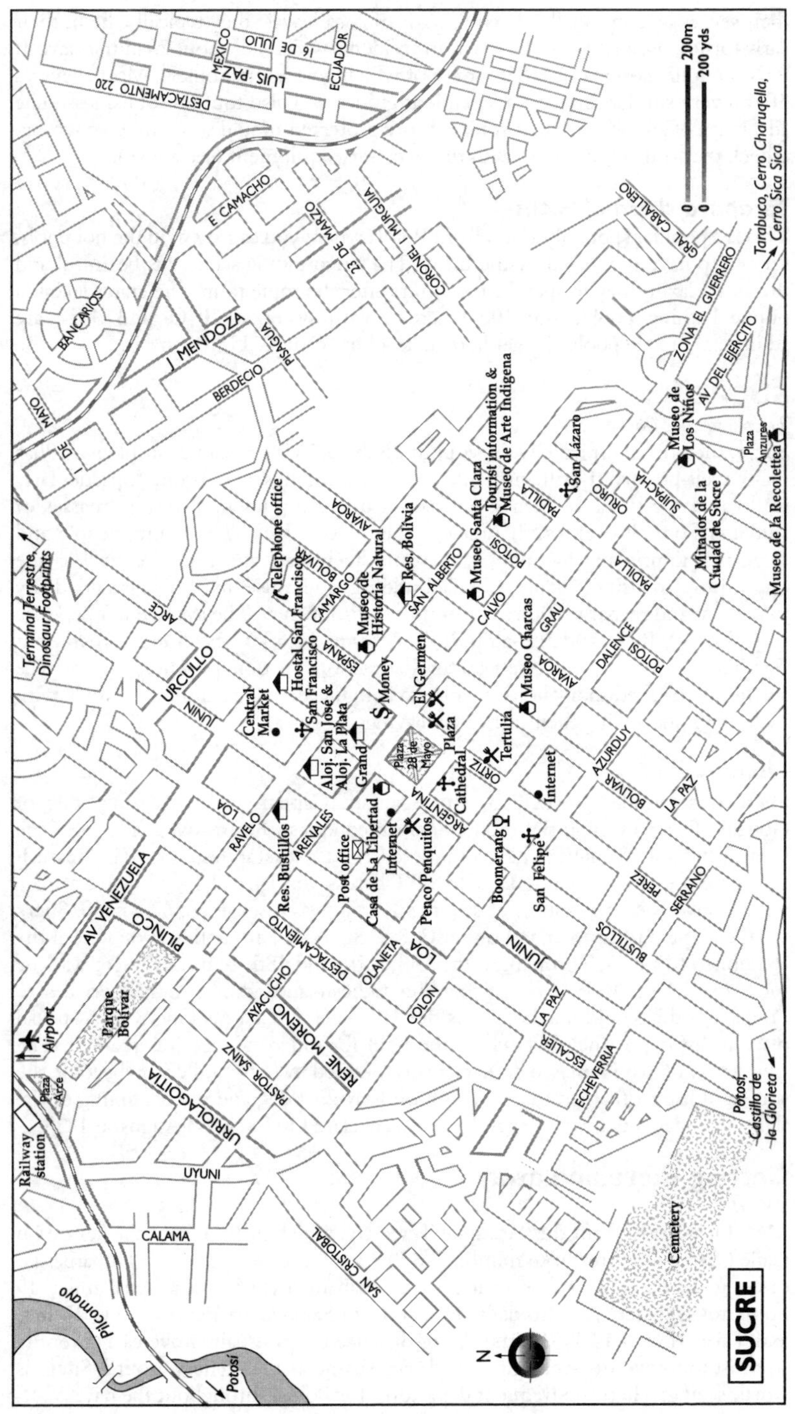
SUCRE
0 200m
0 200 yds
Tarabuco, Cerro Churuqella, Cerro Sica Sica
Terminal Terrestre, Dinosaur Footprints
Potosí, Castillo de la Glorieta
Potosí
Pilcomayo
Railway station
Plaza Arce
Airport
Parque Bolívar
Cemetery
Central Market
San Francisco
Hostal San Francisco
Telephone office
Museo de Historia Natural
Res. Bolivia
Museo Santa Clara
Tourist information & Museo de Arte Indigena
San Lázaro
Museo de Los Niños
Mirador de la Ciudad de Sucre
Museo de la Recoletea
Plaza Anzures
Res. Bustillos
Aloj. San José & Aloj. La Plata
Grand
Money
El Germen
Plaza
Plaza 28 de Mayo
Cathedral
Tertulia
Museo Charcas
Post office
Casa de La Libertad
Internet
Penco Penquitos
Boomerang
San Felipe
Internet
AV VENEZUELA
URCULLO
ARCE
J MENDOZA
BERDECIO
PISAGUA
E CAMACHO
23 DE MARZO
CORONEL I MURGUIA
BANCARIOS
I DE MAYO
DESTACAMENTO 220
LUIS PAZ
MEXICO
16 DE JULIO
ECUADOR
GRAL CABALLERO
ZONA EL GUERRERO
AV DEL EJERCITO
JUNIN
LOA
RAVELO
ARENALES
BOLIVAR
CAMARGO
ESPAÑA
AVAROA
SAN ALBERTO
CALVO
POTOSI
PADILLA
ORURO
SUIPACHA
GRAU
DALENCE
AZURDUY
LA PAZ
PEREZ
SERRANO
BUSTILLOS
ORTIZ
ARGENTINA
OLANETA
COLON
DESTACAMIENTO
AYACUCHO
PILINCO
RENE MORENO
PASTOR SAINZ
URRIOLAGOITIA
UYUNI
CALAMA
SAN CRISTOBAL
ESCALIER
ECHEVERRIA
N

By air

Sucre's airport is 6km to the north of the city; take minibus (*trufi*) F from Hernando Siles and allow 30 mins. LAB and Aero Sur fly daily to La Paz, Cochabamba, Santa Cruz and Tarija.

Where to stay

Sucre has dozens of hotels of all standards to suit all budgets. They are mostly within a couple of blocks of the main square, conveniently located close to the centre of town.

Alojamiento San José Calle Ravelo 62. US$3 per person. Basic, old building, small hostel.
Alojamiento La Plata Calle Ravelo 32; tel: 52102. US$5–8 shared bath. Small rooms, basic but central, clean and cheap.
Residencial Bustillos Calle Ravelo 158; tel: 51560. US$6–10 shared bath, clean.
Residencial Bolivia Calle San Alberto 42; tel: 54346. US$6–11 single/double, rooms with bath a bit more. Spacious rooms, includes breakfast, comfortable, good value, set around large patio gardens.
Hostal Vera Cruz Calle Ravelo 158; tel: 51560. US$11–21 private bath, TV, roof terrace. (same building as Bustillos).
Hostal Charcas Calle Ravelo 62. US$7–11 shared bath and US$11–17 with private bath and breakfast. Comfortable, clean and light with roof terrace.
Hostal San Francisco Calle Ancieto Alerce 191; tel: 52117. US$11–18 with bathroom and breakfast. Light, spacious and comfortable.
Hostal Los Pinos Calle Colón 502; tel: 54403. New building, clean with nice garden. US$20/27 single/double.
Grand Hotel Calle Ancieto Arce 61; tel: 52104. US$20–22 single/double with bathroom and breakfast. Friendly, clean, large patios, big comfortable rooms, cable TV, popular with groups.
Paola Hostal Calle Colón 138; tel: 41419. Newly opened restored colonial building; big, comfortable rooms with bath US$25–35 includes breakfast.

Where to eat

Penco Penquitos Calle Estudiantes. Good coffee and bakery. Open Sundays. Other cafés along this street are popular with students.
Café Tertulia Calle Ortiz. Good coffee/wine bar with food. Several restaurants and bars along this street.
Restaurant Plaza 25 de Mayo 34. Balcony overlooking the square, good value set menu. Friday peñas.
Boomerang Calle Dalence 69. Popular bar, club that comes to life after midnight.
Bibliocafé Calle Nicolás Ortiz 42. Live music some evenings.
Vegetarian restaurant **El Germen** Calle Calvo 7. German run, book exchange, nice atmosphere, good food.
Alliance Française Calle Anciete Arce 35. Nice food, courtyard bar, cultural events.

The market in Sucre is centrally located and good for fresh fruit juices, local food and a wide variety of fresh local produce. Typical food in this part of Bolivia includes *ckocko de pollo*, chicken cooked in chicha; *surubí*, a lowland river fish; *sullucka*, beef with corn and potatoes; *picante mixto*, chicken, tongue, chilli peppers, *chuño*, and potatoes; and *singani*, distilled wine.

Practical information

Tourist office Calle Potosí 102 next to the ASUR museum is helpful. Open Mon–Fri 08.30–12.00 and 14.30–18.30. Try also the Casa de Cultura, Calle 25 de Mayo, and the

tourist office at Calle Ortiz 182.
IGM (for maps) Calle Dalence between Ortiz and Bustillos.
Post office Calle Ayacucho and Junín.
Phone office ENTEL, Calle España 271.
Money Calle España, just off the main plaza, has several banks which will change cash and travellers' cheques.
Airlines Aero Sur, Calle Arenales 204; LAB, Calle Bustillos 127.
Internet Cybercafe, Calle Estudiantes 79. US$3 per hour. Open 09.00–12.00 and 14.00–21.00.

Travel agencies

Sur Andes Calle Nicolas Ortiz; tel: 59164. Organise treks, city tours, horseriding tours.
Seatur Plaza 25 de Mayo 25; tel: 62425. City tours, flights etc.
Candelaria Tours Calle Audiencia 1. Tours and flights.

What to see

The historical centre of Sucre is quite compact, which means exploring its narrow whitewashed streets is easy on foot. Most of the buildings of interest are within a few blocks of the shady Plaza de Armas.

Museums

Casa De La Libertad On the plaza. The Independence Act was signed here in August 1825. A fascinating museum, which gives a summary of the history of independence in Bolivia. Guided tours only, English speaking guides. Open Mon–Fri 09.00–11.30 and 14.30–18.30; Sat 09.30–11.30.
Museo de la Recoleta Plaza Pedro Anzurez, a 20-min walk uphill from the plaza. Good views over Sucre from the Mirador. Open Mon-Fri 09.00–12.00 and 15.00–16.30.
Museum of Religious Art Beautiful cloisters and patio at the Recoleta Monastery founded in 1600. Guided tours only.
Museo de Historia Natural Calle San Alberto 156. Currently undergoing restoration.
Museo Charcas Calle Bolívar and Dalence. Several collections including colonial and contemporary art, archaeology, anthropology and ethnography at this museum belonging to the university. Open Mon–Fri 08.30–12.00 and 15.00–18.00; Sat 08.30–12.00.
Museo Santa Clara Calle Calvo 212. An interesting collection of paintings by some of Bolivia's finest artists, together with religious artefacts. Open Mon–Fri 09.00–12.00 and 15.00–18.00 and Sat 09.00–12.00.
Museo de Arte Indígena Calle San Alberto 413; email: asur@mara.scr.entelnet.bo Excellent collection of textiles, some from 2,000 years ago, and contemporary clothes of diverse local indigenous groups, very well displayed with detailed explanations. The institution of **Antropólogos del Surandino**, ASUR, which runs the museum, was set up to revive indigenous handicraft production and to aid local economies by generating employment and income. You can watch weavers at work and purchase their high quality designs in the museum shop. Highly recommended. Open Mon–Fri 08.30–12.00 and 14.30–18.00; Sat 09.30–1200.
Museo de Los Niños Email: wawas@mara.scr.entelnet.bo. This is a centre for the children of Sucre, where they can attend art and theatre workshops. There is a café, and volunteers are welcome to help with all activities. Email or drop in for details.

Churches

The **cathedral**, built in 1559, has a museum containing religious art, with some fine examples of the work of Melchor Perez Holguin. Open Mon–Fri 10.00–12.00 and 15.00–17.00; Sat 10.00–12.00. Other churches worth a visit include the 16th-century **San Lazaro**, Calle Calvo and Padilla, the 17th-century **San Felipe Nery**, Calle Colón and Ortíz, and the 16th-century **San Francisco**, Calle Ravelo and Arce.

Other places of interest

A short walk of a couple of hours close to the city, a steep climb up the hills to the south of Sucre gives great views. One of the hills (**Cerro Churuquella**), which has a clear path all the way up, has a statue of Christ on the top, and the other, with aerials, involves a bit of a scramble (**Cerro Sica-Sica**).

To see the **dinosaur footprints** at the cement factory, take bus (*micro*) A from Calle Hernando Siles behind the market to the end of the line (5km, 20 mins). Walk for 30 mins along the road, to the entrance to the cement factory. The guards will let you in and for a small fee take you up to the wall at the back of the factory, where in 1996 fossilised footprints of 15 different types of dinosaur were found criss-crossing what was once a swamp, but is now a flaking vertical wall. They are 68 million years old.

Local people bring their produce from miles around to the famous **Tarabuco Sunday market**. It is a good place to see the traditionally dressed indigenous

THE JALQ'A AND TARABUCO TEXTILES

The area around Sucre is rich in indigenous culture, and the textiles produced here are some of the most beautiful of all Andean weavings. The highly technical designs you see woven into the clothing reflect the complex creative thinking of the tribal people. Quite typical of the area and on display in the ASUR museum (see above. page 324) are the intricate **Jalq'a** designs. These are not geometrical, but a profusion of richly coloured figures and animals on a dark background. They are characterised by the designs particularly of animals: *uywas*, which are domesticated animals; *saxra pallay*, the Andean demon; *khurus*, strange, real and imaginary wild animals; and *saxra*, the master of the *khurus*. The ASUR project has served to revitalise the textile economy, by helping communities to recover traditional techniques and designs and to express the present in new designs.

As with many of the indigenous groups around Sucre, the **Tarabuco** people still wear very distinctive traditional clothes. The men wear a rainbow-coloured poncho. They also wear *monteras*, a Spanish style helmet shaped hat, while women wear a black felt top hat decorated with multi-coloured sequins. The principal piece of female clothing is the *axsu*, a skirt which is worn over the *almilla*, the main garment covering the woman's body which consists of two overlapping pieces of cloth fastened at the waist. The *axsu* is beautifully woven with geometric rows of animals, the design and colours of which depend on the fashion at the time.

The traditional instrument in Tarabuco, seen at carnivals, is the long pipe known as the *tuquru*. The omnipresent musicians and dancers wear the costume of the demon deity *tata phujllay*, galloping around on a white horse inspiring the carnival music. An altar, *tata pukara*, is constructed from the molle tree in the shape of a cross and erected in a field. Extra crosses are put up for people who have died in accidents. The *phujllay* is danced around the cross and offerings of corn, cheese, bottles and baskets are made to the altar. *Mallkus* or dancers, sing and dance around the *pukara*, playing an instrument made from the horns of a bull known as *erqes*.

people from the rural areas, but they are not happy about having their photos taken so be sensitive. You can buy beautiful local Candelaria weavings and many of the more common Bolivian handicrafts. To get an idea of prices and quality visit the shops on the plaza, and then bargain with the street sellers. From Sucre take micro B or C in Calle Ravelo to the Tarabuco bus stop at Av Las Americas and Manco Capac for the scenic 2 hour (60km) journey. There are also buses for tourists which leave from outside the front of the market on Calle Ravelo at 07.00. On the second Sunday in March each year more than 60 communities come to Tarabuco to participate in Pujllay, a colourful fiesta of music and dancing.

Only 7km from Sucre is **Castillo de la Glorieta**, the 19th-century mansion of Don Fransisco Argandona, built in a mixture of architectural styles including Moorish, gothic, Renaissance, baroque and neoclassical.

There are dozens of small villages around Sucre which are of interest for a variety of things such as textiles, ceramics, cave paintings and natural swimming pools. Further detailed information about how to get to the villages is available at the tourist office. If you are interested in textiles it is well worth making a visit to the village of Potolo, 60km from Sucre to the northwest and Candelaria to the southwest. For natural swimming pools and walking try Aritumayu (18km), San Juan (18km), Cachimayu (17km), Talula (45km), Charcoma (18km) and Las Seite Cascadas (8km). For cave paintings, archaeological remains and ceramics visit the villages of Presto (100km), Patataloyo (25km), Quila Quila (30km), Sotomayor (75km), Inca Pampa (120km), Tanga Tanga (55km) and Supay Wasi (20km).

TUPIZA

Telephone code 0694

Tupiza is a small, peaceful and friendly town set amid spectacular mineral-rich desert scenery. Tupiza (2,990m) is still not on the main tourist circuit and has relatively few backpackers. The surrounding countryside offers good walking and, for fans of Butch Cassidy and the Sundance Kid, the opportunity to travel in their footsteps through the area where they spent their last days.

Spending several days here will give you the time to visit some of the scenic spots around, on foot, on horseback or on one of the tours available. It is possible to hike out of Tupiza to visit some of the beauty spots. An easy half day walk is to the Valle de Los Machos, so called because of the phallic, eroded rock formations at the edge of the canyon called Quebrada de Palmira. The colours in the rocks, which are rich in minerals, are best appreciated at dawn and dusk. Another beauty spot is El Sillar, a saddle at 3,700m to the west of town, with superb views over the valley. Always take plenty of water on any walk out of town, and try to avoid the heat of the day. Don't forget a hat and sun protection and beware of flash floods if you are walking up narrow gullies.

Getting there and away

By road

You can reach Tupiza by bus from Villazón on the Argentinian border in 2–3 hours, from Potosí in 8 hours, Uyuni at least 10 hours. Buses leave Tupiza for Uyuni only on Mon and Thur at 12.00. The roads are rough and the journey, wherever you come from, or go to, is inevitably long and uncomfortable, but scenic. The many river beds to cross may make roads impassable in the worst of the rainy season.

By train

Check at the railway station for the latest information on times and prices. The times and even days are liable to change at short notice and there may not be any

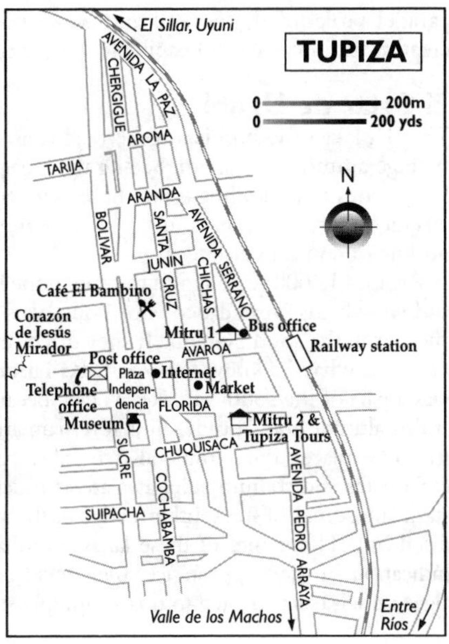

trains at all, as the economic situation of the now privatised train company is somewhat precarious.

From Oruro to Tupiza there is currently a very comfortable tourist train service, the Nuevo Expreso del Sur, from Oruro (dep 10.10) passing through Uyuni (16.25), Atocha (18.20) and Tupiza (21.15) on Mon and also running on Fri when it continues to Villazón on the Argentinian border (arrive Villazón at 00.30). The cost from Oruro to Tupiza is US$25. On Sun and Wed there is a local, much cheaper and slower train between Oruro and Villazón, leaving Oruro 19.00 passing through Tupiza at 08.05 and arriving Villazón 11.50 next morning, US$9. The return express train from Tupiza to Oruro leaves Tupiza on Tue 06.00, Atocha 09.05, Uyuni 11.15, arrives Oruro 18.50. On Sat the train from Villazón leaves at 15.30, Tupiza 18.20, Atocha 21.30, Uyuni 23.25, arrives Oruro 07.00.

Where to stay and eat

Both of the following are clean and friendly with hot water at times. There are several other places to stay in the town.

Hotel Mitru Calle Chichas 187 and Calle Avaroa (annexe). US$4 per person.
Residencia My Home Calle Avaroa 222. From US$3.50 per person.

You can get a good breakfast at the market from 07.00. **Los Helechos** café is recommended for reasonable food and friendly service.

Practical information

Internet Mihagui Centre, on Plaza Civica, and Consultario de Información, on Plaza Independencia, have Internet access, though phone lines aren't always working. US$4 per hour, 08.00–22.00.

Travel agencies Tupiza Tours Av Chichas 187, inside Hotel Mitru; tel: 3001. Provide tourist information for free, and organise very good horseback tours (US$4 per hour) through the Valley of Tupiza; I recommend going early morning or evening to avoid the heat of the day, and for better light. They also do jeep tours of 1 or 2 days in the surrounding countryside or following the Cassidy and Sundance Trail (US$18–25 per day, minimum 4 people).

UYUNI

Telephone code 0693

Uyuni lies in the middle of the Bolivian altiplano at 3,665m. It is a small, quiet town, popular with tourists as it is the gateway to the largest salt lake in the world El Salar de Uyuni, and to the spectacular lagunas and volcanoes of the southern part of the department of Potosí. In this part of the Bolivian central Andes the parallel peaks of the eastern and western cordilleras are at their furthest apart, creating an immense, inhospitable, high desert plain in between.

El Salar de Uyuni

The salt lake of Uyuni is huge, covering an area of approximately 11,000km^2 at an average altitude of 3,650m. Seeing the Salar for the first time is an amazing sight. It stretches in a blinding white haze, shimmering as far as the eye can see. In the distance there are islands in the salt, seemingly floating, and on the horizon, the outline of conical volcanoes.

Around 15,000 years ago, at the end of the last Ice Age, meltwater from the glaciers and snowfields created two enormous lakes in the altiplano, one in the north and another in the south. Gradually they dried out, leaving behind much smaller bodies of water, what we know today as Lake Titicaca and Lake Poopó. El Salar de Uyuni was a part of the southern lake. Today, because of the intense evaporation of water at this altitude and latitude, all that remain are the dried out layers of dissolved salts. In some places these mineral-rich salts, containing lithium, borium, potassium carbonates and sodium sulphates are as much as 20m thick on the Salar. Amid the stark landscapes of the southern edge of the altiplano there are salt-rich lakes not yet dried out. The names of these lakes, Laguna Verde and Laguna Colorada, give an indication of their appearance, their vivid colouring being caused by salt tolerant algae which have adapted to this seemingly sterile environment.

Getting there and away

By road

There are several companies operating buses out of Uyuni, to Potosí (daily at 10.00 and 19.00, US$4), Sucre (daily at 10.00 and 19.00, US$6) and Tupiza (Wed and Sun only, 10.00, US$5). The buses leave from the Av Arce area 3 blocks from Plaza Arce.

By train

There are trains to Oruro, Villazón and also to Camana in Chile. Check at the railway station for the latest times and prices. Currently the Nuevo Expreso del Sur passes through Uyuni at 16.25 going south to Tupiza on Mon and Fri (5 hrs). From Uyuni to Oruro there is a train at 23.25 on Sat and 11.15 on Tue (8 hrs). There is also a local train that runs between Oruro and Villazón (see page 327).

The local train to Camana leaves Uyuni at 05.00 on Sun and Wed (12 hrs). You may have to change trains at the border, and remember you can't take any fresh produce into Chile.

Where to stay and eat

There is often a water problem here. The whole town can be cut off at certain times throughout the day – ask in your hotel.

Hostal Marith Av Potosí 61; tel: 2174. US$3 for shared bathroom, private bath available. Clean and friendly, has good breakfast, clothes washing possible. Three blocks from the centre, a nice place with large central patio. Can organise jeep tours for you.
Hostal Avenida Av Ferroviaria; tel: 2078. US$4. Popular budget choice, central.
Hostal Europa next door to Avenida. Cheap, central.
Hostal Urkupiña on Plaza Arce. US$3 each, basic, friendly place.

If you want somewhere a little more luxurious try: **La Magia de Uyuni**, Calle Colon 432; tel: 0693 2541. US$10 per person with bathroom.

There are several reasonable restaurants around the main square, many of which serve pizzas and international style dishes. Try the market on Calle Potosí for local meals and fruit, water, bread etc.

Practical information

Tourist office There is supposedly a tourist office in the kiosk in the plaza, but it seems to be permanently unmanned. Travel agencies can provide you with information.
Post office on Av Arce.
Phone office ENTEL on Av Arce.
Money It is possible to change dollars at **Librería de la Juventud** on Calle Potosí.
Internet Office on Calle Bolívar corner of Calle Potosí. It has a rather erratic service with the mornings generally marginally better. Open 09.00–12.00, 14.00–19.00. US$4 per hour.

Travel agencies

There are several travel agencies that organise jeep tours, mostly based around the Plaza in Uyuni. It is easy to turn up in Uyuni and an hour later have your tour organised; even during low season there are three or four jeeps leaving Uyuni daily, usually at 10.00 in the morning. Recommended agencies are **Olivos**, **Tonita**, **Zamora**, **Pucara** and **Juliette**, but a lot depends on your jeep and driver. As for any tour you decide to join in Bolivia, check exactly what they offer you before you agree or pay. Each jeep is usually for 6 or 7 tourists plus a driver and a cook. This means that the amount of information you are given depends entirely on the knowledge and affability of your driver, as tours are not accompanied by local guides. Very few of the drivers speak any English and they generally don't know much beyond the basic about the area. It's particularly difficult to find anyone who knows about the archaeology and prehispanic people living here.

The cost of the trip (from US$65 per person for 4 days) should include all meals and accommodation, and some also include a limited amount of drinking water. Try to check out the quality of vehicle before committing yourself and paying for a tour. Most agencies can arrange for you to be dropped off at the Chilean border and picked up and taken to San Pedro de Atacama, usually for US$10 extra. If you are travelling in July and August night temperatures can be very cold, so it is wise to take a sleeping bag with you. Snacks and extra drinking water are also advisable. You can usually leave your main baggage at the agency, and take a smaller bag with you for the tour.

It is possible to hire a jeep in La Paz and explore the Salar de Uyuni yourself, but navigational aids such as GPS and maps are a must as there are no roads, just jeep tracks heading off in all directions. The Salar de Coipasa is not firm in all areas and is not driveable. If you try to drive across Coipasa you could easily get bogged down in a soft spot and have to hike out, leaving everything behind.

What to see

The Salar and volcanoes

The best way to see this remote part of Bolivia is on one of the many jeep tours leaving Uyuni daily; most companies follow pretty much the same route. The first

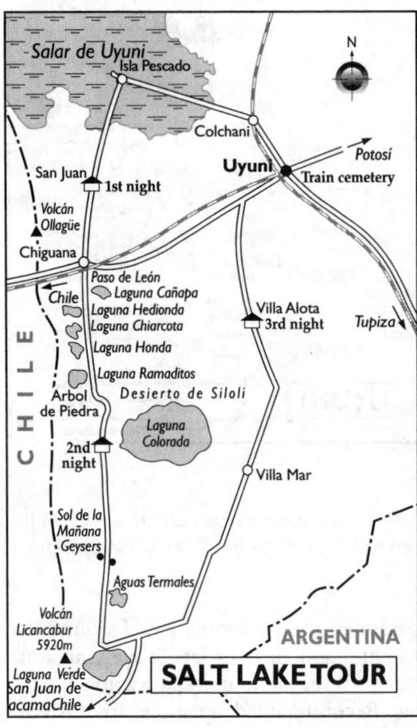

stop on the tour is at **Colchani**, where you see salt being processed. The whole town survives on this small industry. Out on the Salar itself you may see local people digging up the salt and packing it into large sacks to take back to be processed. You may stop at the Salt Hotel, where even the beds are made of salt! Nearby are the **Ojos de Sal** where rivers pass under the salt, and the **Isla de Pescado**, an island in the salt, covered in cactus trees with stunning views in all directions. In the afternoon you leave the Salar and won't see it again. The first night is spent in one of the local villages. Accommodation is usually in small local houses in bunk beds with basic facilities, such as running water and blankets, provided. The people are friendly and this is a great place to practise your Quechua.

The second day you drive on through the beautiful desert landscape, stopping to look at lakes full of flamingos, past the still active volcano of **Ollagua** to **Laguna Colorada**, situated inside the **Reserva Eduardo Avaroa** (see box on page 331). The contrast of the red-coloured laguna, filled with feeding birds, against the banks of sharp white salts around the water and hazy mountains behind is unique.

On the third day there is more dramatic scenery, with geysers and bubbling mud pools, and the welcome chance for a soak in hot pools, **Laguna Verde** and the **Chilean border**, where anyone wanting to continue to Chile can link up with a bus service. If you stay on the tour to return to Uyuni, the final day is mostly spent on the road, stopping off in several villages and at the old train yard just outside town.

Museo de Archaeología y Anthropología, Calle Arce, contains interesting information on the Salar and on the prehispanic cultures of the whole region. Worth a visit if you read Spanish.

ORURO

Telephone code 052

Oruro is a busy commercial city in the southern Bolivian altiplano at 3,706m. It is not particularly used to tourists, other than at carnival, and at first sight is not an attractive place. The climate is extreme and the city is surrounded by the cold, windswept desert of the altiplano. However, the local people are friendly and there are a few sites to see and things to do, making a visit well worthwhile. Very much in evidence is the mining industry, which has been at the hub of Oruro's economy since the early 16th century. Originally lead, antimony, silver and tin were mined from the hills around the city. Now gold is the principal metal mined here. The most important mines still in operation are Huanuni (tin) and Inti Raymi (gold). San José (silver, lead and tin), which was a working mine for over 400 years is now closed down but it is sometimes possible to visit.

Prehispanic Oruro was home to one of the most ancient civilisations of South America, the Urus, whose influence covered the whole of the Bolivian altiplano, as well as extending into Peru, northern Chile and Argentina, Venezuela, Ecuador and Colombia.

Getting there and away

By road

Oruro has a large modern bus terminal 15 minutes' walk from the centre of town on Av Bacovick to the north of the town centre. Take a bus (*micro norte*) or taxi (US$1.50) from the centre. There are hourly buses to La Paz (3½ hrs, US$3) and Cochabamba (4½ hrs, US$3), and early morning and evening services to Sucre (10

RESERVA NACIONAL DE FAUNA ANDINA 'EDUARDO AVAROA'

Located in the department of Potosí, with an area of over 700,000 hectares and at altitudes of between 4,000m and 6,000m above-sea level, this reserve was established to protect the endangered high-altitude forests of queñua (*Polylepsis tarapacana*) and the Andean wildlife found here, particularly flamingos, vicuña and ñandu. The climate is harsh with a daily range of between +25°C and –25°C; dry winter months are from May to August, summer (with a little rain) is from December to April, and there are particularly strong winds in July and August. Characteristic of the area are the extensive high-altitude cold desert landscapes, semi-desert areas, salt lakes, volcanoes such as Llicancabur behind Laguna Verde and the volcanic scenery of Sol de Mañana including geysers, mud pools and hot springs. The typical, though sparse, vegetation of the reserve is the very slow-growing *yareta* in distinctive bright green hard clumps, and the red-barked queñua tree. Both of these plants have been endangered because of overuse by miners of borax. The plants are burnt to dry out the borax. The local birdlife is also threatened by people stealing eggs and feathers to sell.

Fauna

There are three types of flamingo commonly seen in Laguna Colorada. With a decent pair of binoculars you should be able to distinguish one type from another. The **Andean flamingo** (*Phoenicoparrus andinus*) is white with a rosy tinge, a short black-tipped bill and pale yellow legs. The **Puna** or **James flamingo** (*Phoenicoparrus jamesi*) is pinkish white with a short mainly yellow bill, and red legs. The **Chilean flamingo** (*Phoenicopterus chilensis*) is longer legged than the other two, pinkish white, with a black and white bill and grey legs with noticeably red knees and toes. Other wildlife you could see include the shy llama family (**vicuñas**), an Andean **cat**, types of gallinule including **horned coot** (*Fulica cornuta*) and **giant coot** (*Fulica gigantea*) and the ostrich-like **ñandu** or **puna rhea** (*Pterocnemia tarapacensis*).

The reserve is 345km from Uyuni over rough roads only passable in four-wheel drive vehicles. You can also get to the reserve on roads from Tupiza, San Pedro de Atacames or Apacheta in Chile. The administration centre for the park is at **Laguna Colorada**, where there is a large hostel, with 50 beds. There are no shops, restaurants or petrol stations at all, so come with all supplies. To appreciate the reserve fully, allow at least three days.

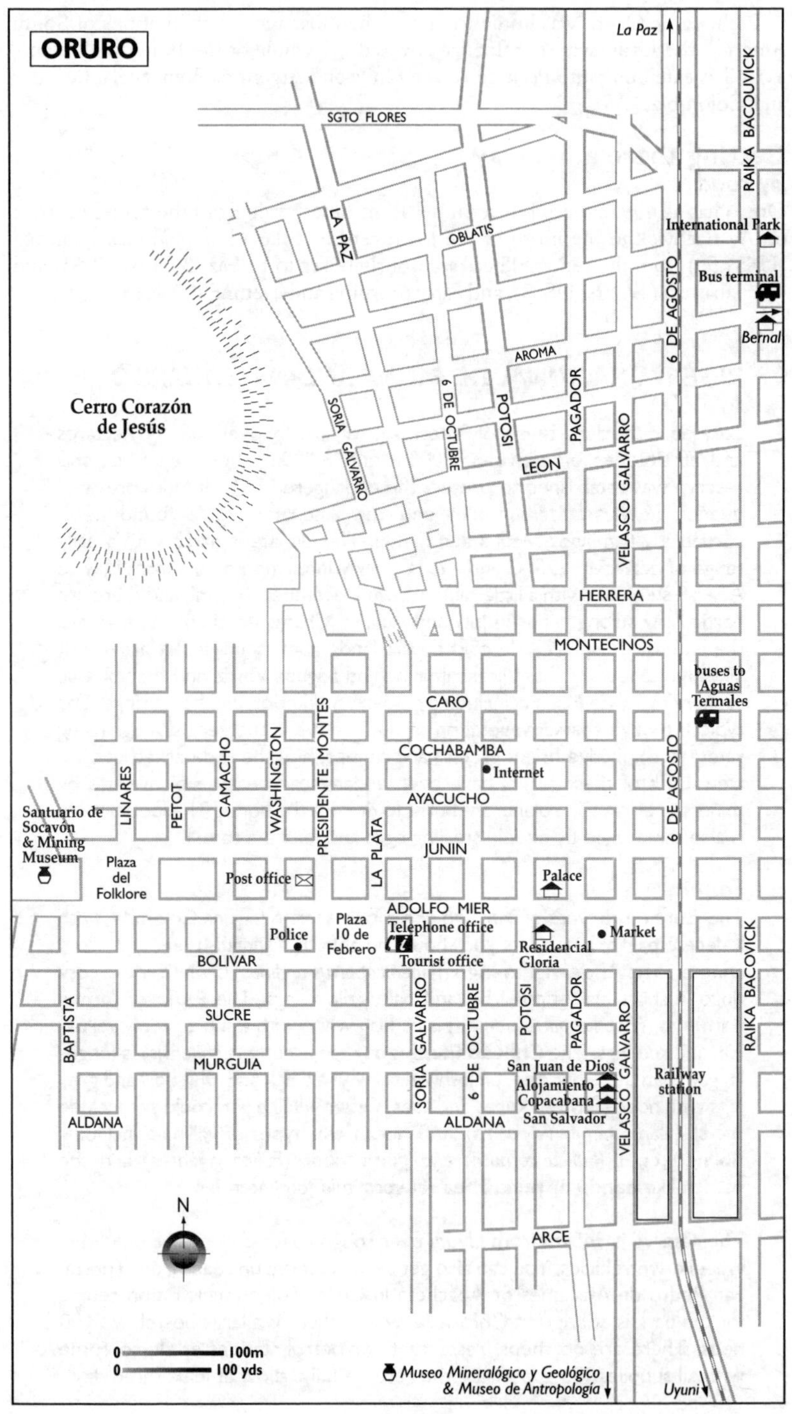
ORURO
La Paz
SGTO FLORES
RAIKA BACOUVICK
LA PAZ
OBLATIS
International Park
6 DE AGOSTO
Bus terminal
Bernal
AROMA
Cerro Corazón de Jesús
SORIA GALVARRO
6 DE OCTUBRE
POTOSI
PAGADOR
LEON
VELASCO GALVARRO
HERRERA
MONTECINOS
buses to Aguas Termales
CARO
COCHABAMBA
Internet
AYACUCHO
LINARES
PETOT
CAMACHO
WASHINGTON
PRESIDENTE MONTES
LA PLATA
JUNIN
Santuario de Socavón & Mining Museum
Plaza del Folklore
Post office
Palace
ADOLFO MIER
Plaza 10 de Febrero
Police
Telephone office
Tourist office
Residencial Gloria
Market
BOLIVAR
RAIKA BACOVICK
SUCRE
BAPTISTA
MURGUIA
San Juan de Dios
Alojamiento
Copacabana
San Salvador
Railway station
ALDANA
ARCE
N
0 100m
0 100 yds
Museo Mineralógico y Geológico & Museo de Antropología
Uyuni

hrs, US$7), Potosí (7 hrs, US$4), and Santa Cruz. There are also buses from Oruro to Villazón, Uyuni and Pisiga. For Tarija and Bermejo some bus companies have offices and departures on Av Ejercito block 800. There are buses to Chile, Arica and Iquique most days at 12.00 and 23.00, also from the terminal.

By train

Check at the station for the latest details. It is in the centre of town on Av 6 de Agosto. For current details of the Nuevo Expresso del Sur from Oruro to Tupiza, see page 328. The cost from Oruro to Villazón is US$28/22 for premier/salon class; Oruro to Tupiza US$25/20; Uyuni to Oruro US$11/9. The local, slower train to Villazón leaves Oruro on Wed and Sun 19.00, Uyuni 02.35, Atocha 04.55, Tupiza 08.05, Villazón 11.50. The return train leaves Villazón on Mon and Thurs 15.30, Tupiza 19.00, Atocha 23.00, Uyuni 02.00, arrives Oruro 08.35. Cost: Oruro to Villazón US$9, Oruro to Tupiza US$9, Uyuni to Oruro US$6.

Trans Copacabana sell tickets (US$4) in the bus station in La Paz for connecting bus services from La Paz to the Expreso del Sur train in Oruro.

Where to stay and eat

During carnival accommodation is difficult to find and costs are triple the quoted prices. If you can't find anywhere or don't want to pay the price, it is possible to make long day trips from La Paz.

Alojamiento Copacabana Calle V Galvarro 1856, opposite train station; tel: 54184. US$3 per person, shared bath, basic.
San Juan de Dios next door, similar.
San Salvador next door, opposite train station; tel: 76771. US$3 or US$7 per person with bath and TV. Modern building, reasonable rooms.
Hotel Bernal Right behind bus station. US$5–8 single/double shared bath, US$12–14 private bath. Clean, modern building, good value. Other cheap and basic hostels nearby, also plenty of restaurants near here.
International Park Hotel Above the bus station; tel: 76227; fax: 75187; email. iparkhot@nogal.oru.entelnet.bo This modern hotel has great views of Oruro. US$25–40. All mod cons.
Residencial Gloria Calle Potosí 6059 corner Bolívar; tel: 76250. US$4 per person shared bath. Central, big clean rooms, courtyard, quiet. Good budget choice.
Palace Hotel Calle Adolfo Mier 392; tel: 72121; fax: 55132. US$25–40 with bath, cable TV, heating, breakfast. Clean and very central.

The friendly markets (Calle Bolívar, near the station) are good for breakfast and lunch, and the area around the station has several good typical restaurants (Calle Pagador). Try Calle Bolívar and Junín for cafés and restaurants.

Practical information

Tourist office Calle Bolívar in a temporary kiosk. Very helpful with information and maps. Open Mon–Fri 10.00–12.00, 14.30–17.30, Sat 09.00–12.00.
Post office Calle Montes 1456.
Phone office ENTEL is on Calle Bolívar, next to tourist office.
Internet at University building, Calle 6 de Octubre between Ayacucho and Cochabamba. Open Mon to Fri 08.30–12.00, 14.00–20.00. US$2 per hour.

What to see

Santuario de Socavón, in the Plaza del Folklore, at the foot of the hills known as 'Pie de Gallo', is the reconstructed church of the Virgen de Candelaria. The site where the church stands today has always been of religious importance to the

BOLIVIAN DANCES

Without a doubt the best time to be in Oruro is during carnival when the city comes to life in a big way. Dance groups and musicians come from all over Bolivia to participate in what is considered to be the best carnival in the Andes. The most important of the dances are La Morenada and La Diablada.

La Morenada

One of Bolivia's typical dances, La Morenada originated in the time of independence and represents the inhuman treatment to which the black slaves were submitted by the Spanish conquistadors. The grotesque masks used in the dance, with protruding eyes and tongues, represent the suffering of the slaves, while richly decorated costumes represent the wealth of the mine owners. Slaves were brought to South America to work in the mines. They couldn't adapt to the conditions so those that survived were moved to the large Spanish-owned haciendas in tropical areas, particularly in the Yungas and the Luribay Valley, where they worked in agriculture in vineyards and coffee and coca plantations.

La Diablada

This is a dance that has been adopted in the mining communities of the Andes where miners make offerings to their deity *Dios Supay* or *Tío*, and dress up as devils in order to attract his favours or represent him in certain festivals. Dios Supay is the god of the underworld and as such is only venerated underground. The dance is a complex mixture of pagan and Catholic, worshipping not only the Christian God and Catholic saints introduced during colonial times, but also traditional native gods. In addition to Dios Supay, La Diablada has developed to be an offering to the Virgen de Socavón, patron saint of the miners. The participants of the dance are: the Archangel Michael; the devil, Lucifer or Satan; China Supay; the seven devils that represent the seven deadly sin; bears that lead the way for the dancers; a condor; and many little devils.

The costumes are amazing pieces of artwork, brightly coloured with tremendous masks and head-dresses. Lucifer wears beautifully embroidered

miners of Oruro because there is a particularly high concentration of mine entrances here. The building of a chapel there in the 16th century by the Catholic church was an attempt to replace the miners' pagan beliefs with Christianity. Inside the church you can see the beautifully painted fresco of the patron saint of miners, the Virgen de Candelaria, painted by an unknown artist in the 16th century directly onto the adobe wall. One of the tunnel entrances which led to a whole network of mines was called by the miners *Socavón de la Virgen* (*socavón* is Spanish for tunnel) and the painting of the virgin in the chapel became known as *Virgen del Socavón*, virgin of the tunnel. The current church was finished at the end of the last century, with the tower added in 1919. Since 1950 the religious order Siervas de María has taken over the running of the church, constructing a social centre consisting of a convent, school, clinic, sports centre and *comedor popular*.

Inside the church there is a small **mining museum**, where you can go down one of the original tunnels leading into the mine complex in the hills behind the town. There is a representation of Tío inside the tunnel, the god of the underworld believed by the miners to control their fortunes underground. Open Mon–Sat 09.00–12.00 and 15.00–18.00, Sun 08.00–12.00, 16.00–18.00.

and decorated clothes, together with a plaster mask with enormous horns and brightly painted representations of other animals moulded into the headpiece. Archangel Michael wears white silk trousers and shirt with a red cape and tunic, a characteristic mask and a military type helmet. The seven devils wear similar, slightly less elaborate costumes; they have masks of bats, serpents and dragons, while the goddess Supay has multi-layered skirts with a wig of wild blonde hair, a mask with grossly protruding eyes and long eyelashes. The bears wear a sheep's wool suit and animal mask, and the condor a black costume decorated with feathers, and a condor mask. The music is melodic and happy, the dancers leap and let out the occasional screech as they follow the musicians. Behind the Diablada there are dozens of other dance groups, smaller diabladas, Incas, jungle tribes, llama drivers and more. It's an impressive sight.

Preparations for carnival begin on the first Sunday after All Saints, in November, with a mass in honour of the Virgen del Socavón. From then on dance rehearsals are held each weekend with blessings to the Virgin until the week before carnival when there is a rehearsal of all the dance groups together on the street. On the Friday before carnival miners make a sacrifice of a white llama to Tío inside the mines. Outside the mines offerings to Pachamama are made and *Ch'alla* performed, which is the sprinkling of alcohol onto all objects to ask the gods to provide plenty. This is accompanied by music and dancing. In the evening there are celebrations in the streets with dancing and stalls selling *sucumbes*, a typical drink made from milk, *singani*, eggs and cinammon. The Saturday of carnival is the day of La Entrada, starting at 08.00 in the morning and going on past midnight as all the dancers dance their way to the Santuario de la Virgen del Socavón to be blessed by the priest and pass before the image of the Virgin. On Sunday and Monday there are dance processions throughout the day. Tuesday is another day for *Ch'alla*, this time a blessing of people's homes, and for the rest of the week there is plenty of partying with visits to the nearby sacred sites of *El Sapo* (the toad), *La Víbora* (the viper) and *El Condor* (the condor). During the following week some of the villages in the area will celebrate their own carnivals, and so the partying goes on and on.

Museo Mineralógico y Geológico, Ciudad Universitaria, is at the south end of the city. Take a minibus (*micro sud*) to the end. Great collection of minerals for the geologically minded. Open: Mon–Fri 08.00–12.00, 14.30–17.00.

The **Museo de Antropología**, Av España, houses an interesting collection of carnival costumes and masks, and pre-hispanic archaeological items, stone carvings, and the reconstructed *chullpas* (funerary towers) of Uru, Chipaya and Wankarani (800BC–AD400) people. Open Mon–Fri 0900–12.00, 14.00–18.00; Sat and Sun 10.00–12.00, 15.00–18.00.

There are **aguas termales** (hot pools) at Capachos 12km from the city centre, and at Obrajes (25km) which is nicer. For both take the micro from Calle Caro corner 6 de Agosto.

The stone and adobe funerary towers (*chullpas*) of Chusaqueri, a 2-hour walk (10km each way) from Oruro across the altiplano from Puente Español, are worth visiting if you are interested in prehispanic cultures.

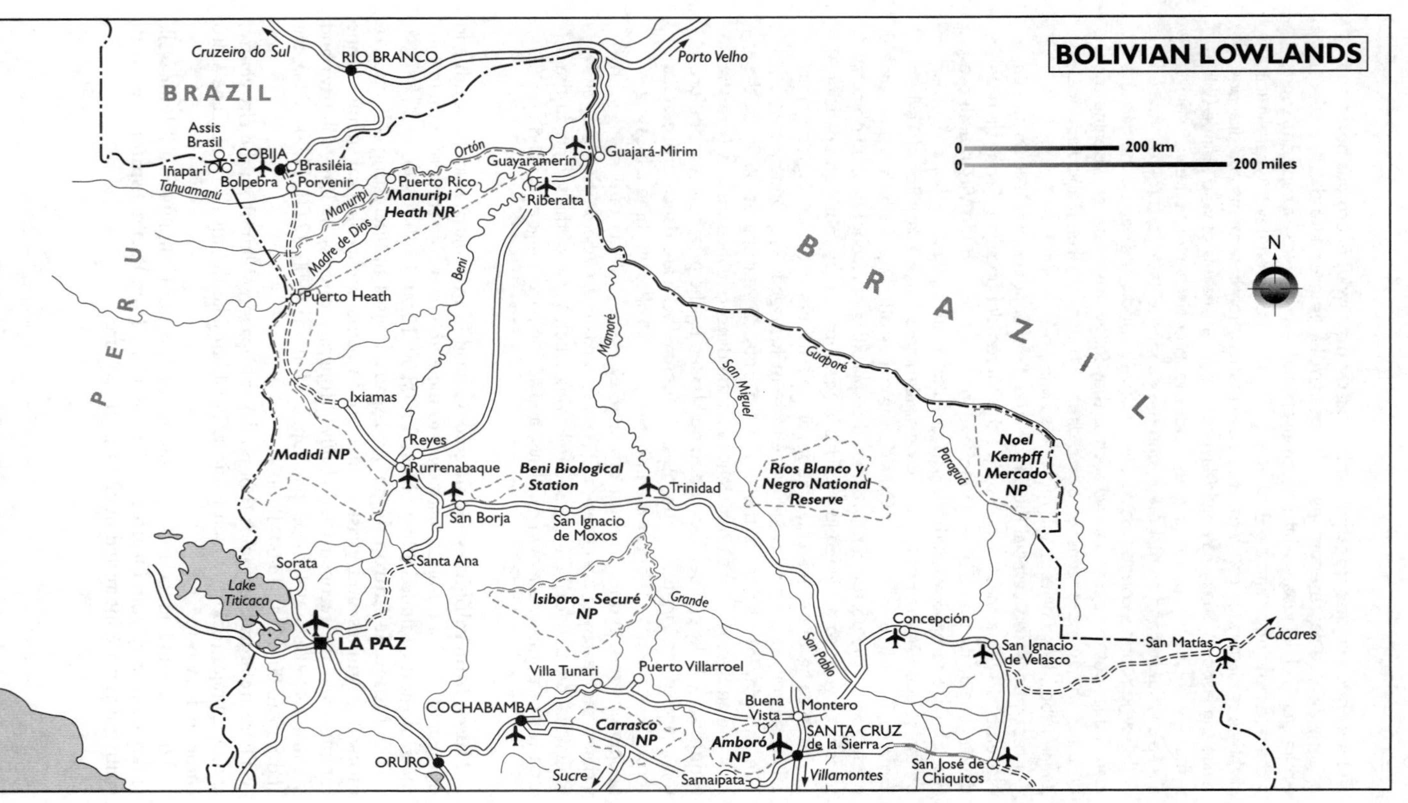

BOLIVIAN LOWLANDS
0 200 km
0 200 miles
N
BRAZIL
B R A Z I L
P E R U
Cruzeiro do Sul
RIO BRANCO
Porto Velho
Assis Brasil
Iñapari
COBIJA
Brasiléia
Bolpebra
Porvenir
Tahuamanú
Ortón
Guayaramerín
Guajará-Mirim
Puerto Rico
Manuripi
Manuripi Heath NR
Riberalta
Madre de Dios
Beni
Puerto Heath
Mamoré
San Miguel
Guaporé
Ixiamas
Reyes
Madidi NP
Rurrenabaque
Beni Biological Station
Trinidad
Ríos Blanco y Negro National Reserve
Paraguá
Noel Kempff Mercado NP
San Borja
San Ignacio de Moxos
Santa Ana
Sorata
Lake Titicaca
Isiboro - Securé NP
Grande
San Pablo
Concepción
LA PAZ
San Ignacio de Velasco
San Matías
Cáceres
Villa Tunari
Puerto Villarroel
Buena Vista
Montero
COCHABAMBA
Carrasco NP
Amboró NP
SANTA CRUZ de la Sierra
ORURO
Sucre
Samaipata
Villamontes
San José de Chiquitos

21

Central Bolivia and the Eastern Lowlands

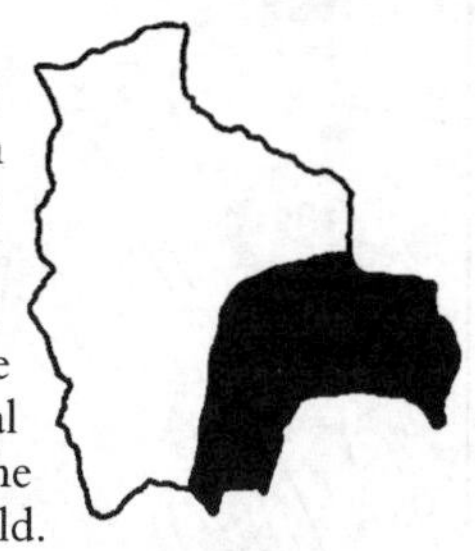

From the altiplano it can be a relief to head for the eastern lowlands after the harshness of the highlands. As you travel east, descending the steep slopes of the Andes, the vegetation becomes increasingly green and lush, and the climate increasingly tropical. Cochabamba, known as the bread-basket of Bolivia, because the surrounding fertile farmland produces high-quality crops, is a pleasant city. Some of the agricultural villages around it have interesting colonial buildings and colourful markets, where you can see the abundant agricultural produce being bought and sold.

Descending further, you enter the tropical heartland of Bolivia. You can visit Bolivia's fastest growing city which is Santa Cruz, and the remote Jesuit mission towns with their skilfully built churches; you can also access the wealth of natural resources of Bolivia's jungle and many lowland national parks.

COCHABAMBA

Telephone code 042

Cochabamba (2,570m) is a pleasant city to visit, with pretty squares and some of the best produce markets in Bolivia. The surrounding towns are possibly of more interest than the city itself, which although a thriving commercial and university town, doesn't have a great deal to offer the passing tourist. This is quite a popular place to stay for a couple of weeks to study Spanish, and there are several schools offering classes.

Getting there and away

The large, modern bus station is about 2km from the centre of town. It has cafés, toilets and a left-luggage office. Buses to Santa Cruz leave at 08.30 and 20.30 (10 hrs). To Oruro there are frequent buses from 05.30 (4 hrs), to Sucre buses at 19.00 and 19.30 (11 hrs), to Llallagua at 20.00 (8 hrs) and to Trinidad at 18.00. To La Paz buses leave throughout the day (7 hrs). You can take international buses to Iquique (16 hrs) and Arica, most days. Check at the bus station for details. Local buses to nearby villages and Villa Tunari go from Calle Oquendo at the corner of República.

Where to stay

There are many nice hostels, both near the bus station and in the centre of town. Prices in all hostels go up considerably in August.

Hostal Florida Calle 25 de Mayo S-0583; tel: 57911. Friendly and pleasant with central flower-filled patios. Can be noisy. Central, clean, good value.

Hostal Familiar Calle 25 de Mayo S-0234; tel: 27986. US$5 per person, US$7 with bath. Popular with Peace Corps, good value, spacious rooms, old colonial building with large patios. Also has a hostel at Calle Sucre E-0554.

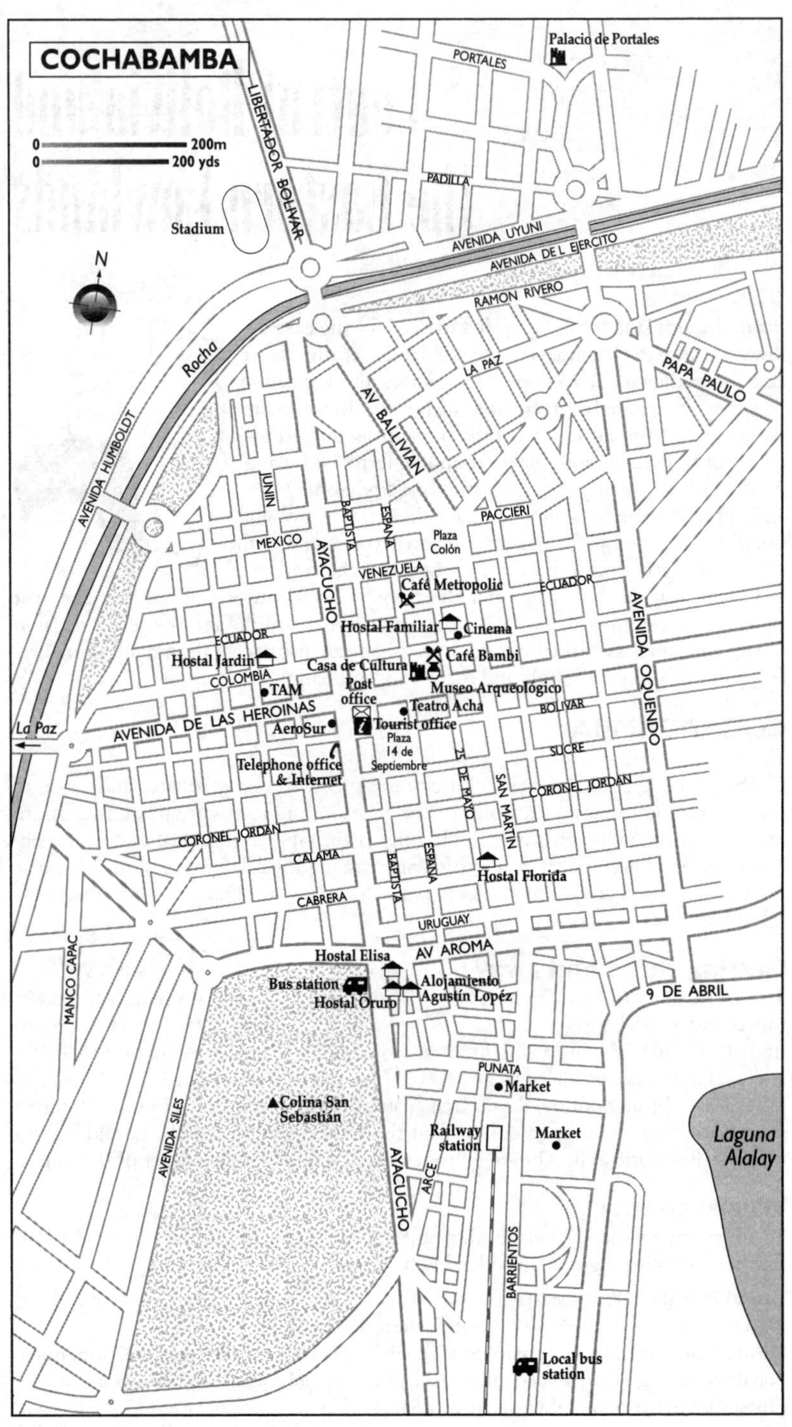

COCHABAMBA
0 200m
0 200 yds
N
Palacio de Portales
PORTALES
LIBERTADOR BOLIVAR
PADILLA
Stadium
AVENIDA UYUNI
AVENIDA DE L EJERCITO
RAMON RIVERO
Rocha
LA PAZ
PAPA PAULO
AV BALLIVIAN
AVENIDA HUMBOLDT
JUNIN
BAPTISTA
ESPAÑA
PACCIERI
Plaza Colón
MEXICO
AYACUCHO
VENEZUELA
Café Metropolic
ECUADOR
AVENIDA OQUENDO
Hostal Familiar
Cinema
ECUADOR
Hostal Jardin
Café Bambi
Casa de Cultura
COLOMBIA
TAM
Post office
Museo Arqueológico
Teatro Acha
BOLIVAR
AVENIDA DE LAS HEROINAS
La Paz
AeroSur
Tourist office
Plaza 14 de Septiembre
Telephone office & Internet
SUCRE
25 DE MAYO
SAN MARTIN
CORONEL JORDAN
CORONEL JORDAN
CALAMA
BAPTISTA
ESPAÑA
Hostal Florida
CABRERA
URUGUAY
AV AROMA
Hostal Elisa
Bus station
Alojamiento Agustín López
Hostal Oruro
9 DE ABRIL
MANCO CAPAC
PUNATA
Market
Colina San Sebastián
Railway station
Market
Laguna Alalay
AVENIDA SILES
AYACUCHO
ARCE
BARRIENTOS
Local bus station

Hostal Elisa Calle Agustín López S-0834; tel: 235102; email: helisa@comteco.entelnet.bo US$5 per person shared bath, US$10 each private bath and breakfast. Very popular with budget travellers, near the bus station. Spacious, nice garden, cable TV.
Hostal Oruro Calle Agustín López 0864; tel: 224345. US$5–8 shared bath, US$14 double with private bath. New in 1998, family run, good value, near the bus station.
Alojamiento Agustín Lopéz Calle Agustín López S-0853; tel: 257926. US$3 shared bath. Basic, but very cheap.
Hostal Jardín Calle Hamiraya N-0248; tel: 47844. US$7 shared bath, US$10–18 with bath. Modern building, clean and central.

Where to eat

There are several vegetarian restaurants including **Gopal**, Calle España 250, which does good value lunches, fresh fruit salads, yogurts etc. **Tulasi** on Av Heroínas N-0254 is also good.

Av Ballivián has numerous restaurants and bars with outdoor seating and typical dishes, *piqueos* (meat and potato dish), *lapi* (a beef dish), and local beer, Taquiña. Open daily until 01.30. There is a high concentration of student bars in the part of town between the plazas. **Bambi**, Calle Colombia and 25 de Mayo, is good for coffee and ice-cream.

The market in Calle 27 de Mayo has over 20 stalls serving a wide variety of typical food. From 05.00 the cooking begins, with soups such as *mani* (peanut), *lagua de choclo* (corn) and main courses such as *riñon en caldo* (kidneys in soup), *ranga asado* (potato soup with chopped liver), *cordero* (lamb), *ch'ajchu* (beef, potatoes, cheese, hard-boiled egg and chilli sauce), *witu* (beef stew with tomatoes) and *albóndigas* (meatballs and fish).

Entertainment

For nightlife try the thriving student bars on Calle Ecuador and Calle España, **Liverpool Rock Café**, **Café Metropolic**, and for live music at the weekend **El Boliche**. **Teatro Acha** in Calle España often has concerts and shows.

Practical information

Tourist office Calle General Acha. Sells maps and gives basic information.
Post office Av Ayacucho corner of Heroínas.
Tourist police Calle General Acha S-142.
Phone office ENTEL, Av Ayacucho. Open 07.00–23.00; Sunday 07.00–15.00. Also Internet US$2 per hour.
Money There are banks with ATM machines around the Plaza 14 de Septiembre. Change offices are also concentrated around this square.
Airlines Aero Sur, Edif América corner of General Acha; LAB, Av Ayacucho 0145.
Internet Offices are plentiful. The main ENTEL office has public internet access. Bolivia, Calle España 280, open 07.00–24.00 every day; US$1.50 per hour.
Travel agencies Fremen Tours, Calle Tumusla 0245; tel: 49885; web: www.andes-amazonia.com. Organise tours of the city and surrounding sites.

What to see

Cochabamba is centred in the streets around the Plaza 14 de Septiembre, which is where you will find the neoclassical **cathedral** (1571), and the churches of **San Francisco**, **Santo Domingo**, **La Compañía** and the beautiful **Convent of Santa Teresa**. **Plaza Colón**, a few blocks to the north, marks the beginning of Avenida Ballivían and the business centre of town. The excellent **Museo Arqueológico** (Mon-Fri 09.00-12.00 and 15.00-19.00; Sat 09.00-13.00) and the **Casa de Cultura** are next door to each other on 25 de Mayo and Heroínas.

Following Avenida Ballivían across the river is the wealthy residential area where you will also find the **Palacio de Portales** on Av Potosí 450. There are daily tours at 17.00 and 17.30 of this French Renaissance style mansion, built between 1915 and 1927 of European materials, for Simón Patiño, one of Bolivia's richest tin barons. You can walk here from the centre in 30 mins or take micro G. The Simón Patiño cultural centre is based here and consists of an art gallery and library.

The **Botanic Garden** at the foot of San Pedro hill has a collection of native species, open 07.30-12.00 and 14.00-17.00.

It's possible to climb **Cerro Pedro**, 235m above the city, where a 40m-high statue of Christ stands in commemoration of a visit to Cochabamba by Pope John Paul II.

Around Cochabamba

Just 13km from Cochabamba is the town of **Quillacolla**, well known throughout Bolivia for the celebration of the festival of the Virgen de Urkupiña. The main part of the festival is in August, usually the second week. More than a hundred dance groups, representing the whole of Bolivia, come together to celebrate with dancing, music and religious ceremonies. The festival has its origins in a legend. Many years ago, when Quillacolla was just a very small town, a young girl was out tending her sheep at the foot of Calvario hill when a beautiful woman with a young boy appeared beside her. They spent many happy hours talking to each other and the shepherdess played with the young boy. When she returned home she told her parents of the people she had met. Her parents did not know what to make of this so they informed the village priest, who asked them to let him know should the strangers appear again. One day the parents of the little girl went out to the fields with her and as they went their daughter suddenly pointed to something on the hilltop, and shouted 'Orqopiña ... orqopiña!', which in Quechua means 'There she is...!' It was the young girl's friend, a celestial being ascending towards the heavens. A chapel was built on the site and on August 17 each year, after the singing and dancing in Quillacolla, a pilgrimage is made to the chapel on Calvario hill to worship the Virgin of Urkupiña.

There is a weekly **Sunday market** in the town, which is worth visiting. It is mostly animals and local produce and is not at all touristy. Quillacolla is also well known for its *quintas*, or typical restaurants.

Near the village of Sipay Sipay, 27km from Cochabamba, is the Inca archaeological site of **Inkarraq'ay**. It is thought to have been a ceremonial centre, where the winter solstice was celebrated, as well as a military and administrative control point for the valley which was an important centre for maize production. Ask in Sipay for the trail to the site, about 6km away. You may also be able to hire a guide in the town. Take water, food and sun protection.

EAST FROM COCHABAMBA

The main route to Santa Cruz from Cochabamba goes through Villa Tunari. The drive from Cochabamba is dramatic, as you pass from fertile agricultural valleys, over high *puna* and down into verdant cloudforest. The road from Cochabamba to Santa Cruz is one of Bolivia's busiest and most of it is tarmac, although annual heavy rains and lack of maintenance mean that often great stretches are as pot-holed and slow as the majority of Bolivia's other roads. Villa Tunari is in the Chapare region, Bolivia's biggest coca producing area, so care should be taken and it's not a good idea to travel off the main routes, particularly in parts of Isiboro–Secure National Park. Check locally for details.

Villa Tunari

Telephone code 0411

At 166km from Cochabamba and 312km from Santa Cruz, this small semi-tropical town is a good stopping off point, and is near enough to Cochabamba to make an overnight visit worthwhile. There are several really nice relaxing places to stay, and though there isn't much to do, it's a quiet tranquil town with good walks, views of the jungle and a warm tropical climate.

Getting there and away

Most buses between Santa Cruz and Cochabamba pass Villa Tunari, so you can be dropped off or picked up here. The buses from Cochabamba usually go through late morning and the buses from Santa Cruz usually early in the afternoon. Wave them down on the road.

From Villa Tunari there are buses to Puerto San Francisco, Puerto Aurora and Puerto Villaroel. Puerto Villaroel is one of Bolivia's major river ports, from which boats go to Trinidad. Puerto San Francisco is on the river Chipiri, and from here there is access to the Isiboro–Secure National Park via the Chipiri and Isiboro rivers. From Puerto San Francisco it is possible to visit the small jungle village of Puerto Namatamojo, where a hostel is opening late 1999. Take a boat from San Francisco or ask there about transport.

Where to stay and eat

There is quite a variety of hotels, some with pools, some outside the town in the forest, which are quiet and relaxing, and some fairly basic hostels. The most basic are in town on Calle Panda, along by the River Espirito Santo.

Vallegrande Calle Panda, next to the River Espirito Santo US$3 double shared bath, US$8 double private bath, kitchen facilities.

Hotel San Martín Av Integración, main road; tel: 4115. US$15–25 with bath and breakfast, pool, garden and parking. Great views overlooking the river.

Sumuqué Overlooking the River San Mateo; tel: 4110. Cabins US$15 per person. Swimming pool, day use possible.

El Puente 3km from town, past town over the bridge and first right. US$27–38. Large, comfortable cabins, natural pools in the river and jungle trails, swimming pool, restaurant. Very comfortable, friendly staff, relaxing. Possible to see jungle wildlife including butterflies, tropical birds and snakes.

Local specialities include *surubí*, *pacú*, *doradillos*, *sábalo*, *blanquillo* and *bagre*. These are all local fish, well worth trying. The main street is lined with cheap stalls serving local dishes, but not particularly clean, and heading towards the plaza there are several better looking restaurants.

What to see

The **Parque Ecoturístico Machía** wildlife park is at the east end of town set in 36 hectares of tropical forest with marked trails. There are several semi-tame animals including puma, bears, parrots and monkeys. It is staffed by volunteers and helpers; donations or volunteers able to stay at least three months are always welcome.

Cavernas del Repechón, 20 mins by car (13km) into Carrasco National Park, are two caves inhabited by a nocturnal fruit-eating bird, the *guácharo* or oilbird (*Steatornis caripensis*), and one cave inhabited by bats. Resembling an owl and probably evolved from that group, the *guácharo* is a brown-coloured bird with white dots on the wing feathers. It feeds on fruit and palm fruit on the wing at night, and navigates by echo, emitting a high-pitched clicking sound. If *guácharo* are disturbed while roosting in the caves during the day they make a very noisy 'cree cree crrree' screech. Only open weekends and holidays.

The **Parque Nacional Carrasco** covers an area of over 6,000km^2, with altitudes between 300 and 4,700m above sea-level. It lies within the department of Cochabamba in the regions of Chapare and Carrasco. The diversity of landscapes and ecosystems within the park is remarkable, including mountainous area of high Andean *puna* with deep valleys, glacier lakes, cloudforest, semi-tropical and tropical forest. Most of the area receives over 5,000mm of rainfall each year. It is thought that a tribe of indigenous Yuracaré people lives in the park, but there has been very little contact with them. Access to the park is not easy and there is very little infrastructure. You can visit the Cavernas de Repechón, described above, or enter the park on the southern side near the town of Monte Puncu. There are several camping areas and a rough track into the park, but you must take all supplies. Monte Puncu is approximately 120km from Cochabamba on the old Santa Cruz road.

The **Parque Nacional Isiboro-Secure**, 12,000km^2, is also a protected area for the indigenous cultures Mojeña, Yuracaré and Chimane. It is estimated that there are 53 indigenous communities within the park boundary. The park is spread between the departments of Beni and Cochabamba and covers a wide range of altitude, from 180 to 3,000m, with a corresponding variety of habitats, from sub-Andean highlands to the Llanos of Moxos. The climate and rainfall vary considerably, the mountainous south receiving 5,000mm of rain each year while the Llanos receives around 1,600mm annually. The biodiversity within the park is high because of the range of ecosystems, but this unique area is threatened by advancing settlements on the southeast side, by the proliferation of coca plantations, drug trafficking, oil prospecting, timber exploitation and fish poaching. For tourists access to the park is difficult, and there are no facilities; because large parts of it are used for coca growing you should make careful enquiries about where is safe before setting off into remote areas.

SANTA CRUZ

Telephone code 03

The city of Santa Cruz de la Sierra was founded in 1561 by Don Ñuflo de Cháves, and is now Bolivia's most cosmopolitan and wealthy city with a population of over a million. The centre of the city is small and easy to find your way around, with many modern shops and facilities. For several blocks the central streets are of the original colonial architectural style so typical of lowland towns, the pavements shaded by red tiled roofs supported on wooden columns. This makes walking around, even in the heat of the day, much more comfortable. The modern city spreads outwards from the centre, with a series of concentric circular roads separating one neighbourhood from the next.

The wealth of the city is quite obvious when you see the variety of shops selling expensive goods, and the large numbers of smart cars. The drug trade has brought Santa Cruz a large part of its wealth. There are also many legitimate sources of income. The most important economic resources in Santa Cruz department are oil, gas, timber, precious stones, sugarcane, soya, gold and cattle farming. Santa Cruz's wealth has attracted floods of people from other parts of Bolivia, particularly from Potosí, Bolivia's poorest region. People come to seek work and easier living conditions.

Getting there and away

By road

Santa Cruz has a large chaotic bus station a few minutes by taxi, US$1, from the centre. There are buses to Cochabamba (8–10 hrs, 468km), La Paz (19–20 hrs,

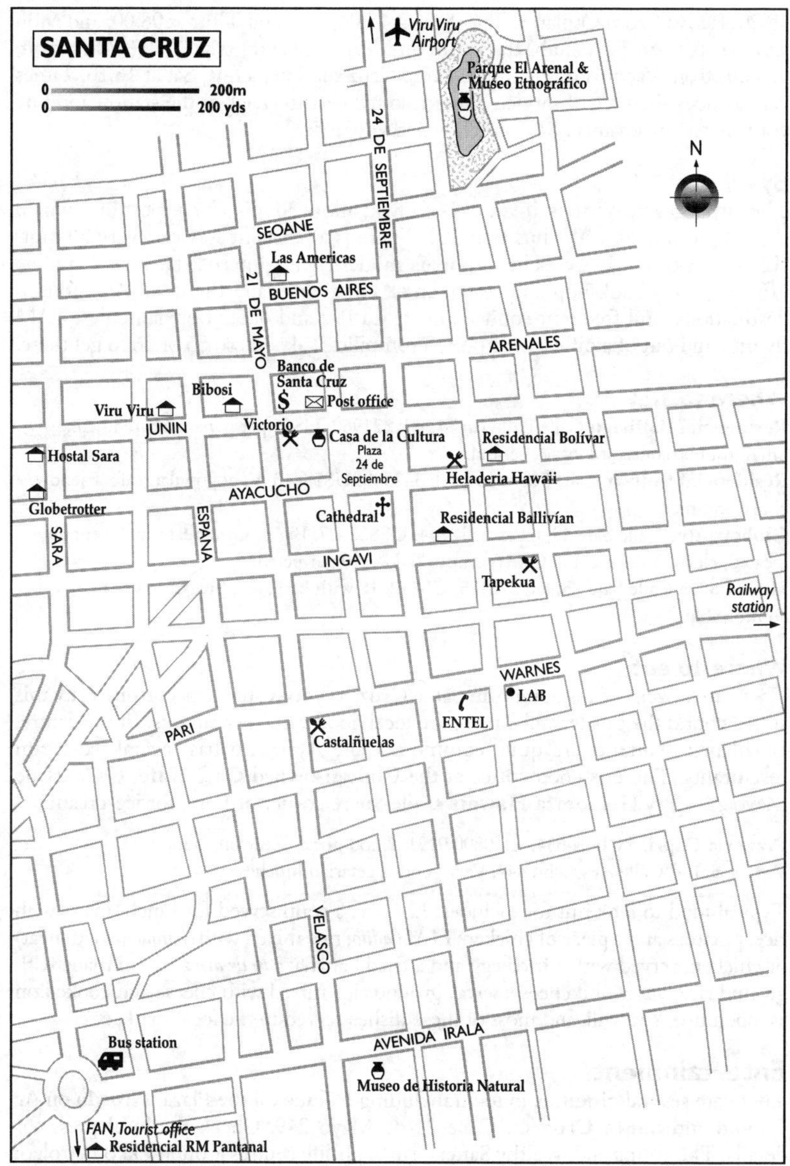

880km), Samaipata (2 hrs, 120km), Sucre (10–12 hrs, 610km), Trinidad (12 hrs, 556km), Villamontes (11 hrs, 462km) and Yacuiba (13 hrs, 562km).

By rail

Trains run daily from Santa Cruz to **Quijarro** on the Brazilian border (18–20 hours), Mon–Sat at 15.45 (US$6/8/17) with the option of deluxe super pullman class on Mon, Wed and Fri (*servicio bracha* from US$30). In addition there is a luxury *automotor* express train on Mon and Wed at 08.00 and Thur and Sun at

19.20. Return from Quijarro, Tue–Sun at 15.00, Tue and Thur at 08.00, and Mon and Fri at 19.20. To Yacuiba trains run on Mon, Wed and Fri at 17.00 (13 hrs, from US$6); from Yacuiba trains run to Santa Cruz on Tue, Thur, Sat at 16.20. Times vary as does the type of service offered, so it's best to check at the station and buy your tickets in advance. Station tel: 463388/463995.

By air

The airport, Viru Viru, is 16km out of town; allow 30 mins by airport bus, which departs from next to the bus terminal. There is a frequent service, every 20 mins (US$1). A taxi is US$8. The airport is modern with Internet facilities, a phone office, a good bookshop and restaurants. There are daily flights to Argentinean destinations, and frequent connections to La Paz and other Bolivian cities. TAM fly into and out of a different airport, Trompillo. Take micro 55 or 56 to get there.

Where to stay

Residencial Ballivían Calle Ballivían 71; tel: 321960. US$5 per person, shared bath. Small rooms, courtyard, basic, central.
Residencial Bolívar Calle Sucre 131; tel: 342500. US$8–13. Very popular, café, friendly, courtyard, nice.
Globetrotter Calle Sara 49; tel/fax: 372754. US$22–27. Big rooms, great value, centrally located, clean, TV, air cond. One room for 6, US$10 per person.
Hostal Sara Calle Sara 85; tel: 322425. US$12–18 with bath, fan, breakfast. Clean, comfortable.

Where to eat

There are dozens of restaurants in Santa Cruz, as you would expect from a city this size. Around the bus terminal there are local good value restaurants. In the centre, Brazilian restaurants are quite common. Calle Ayacucho has several ice-cream restaurants. There is good coffee at the Chilean-owned **Café Kafe**, Calle 21 de Mayo 225. Try **Heladería Hawaii**, Calle Sucre corner of Beni, for ice-cream.

Pizzería Capri, Av Irala 634; tel: 0800 9191. Good pizzas, near bus station.
Vida y Salud Calle Ayacucho 444. Very good vegetarian lunches.

Typical food to look out for includes: *El Locro*, a soup served for lunch, made with rice, potatoes and a piece of chicken; *El Majadito*, rice mixed with *charque* (dried meat) or chicken, served with a fried egg and a fried banana; *pan de arroz*, bread made with ground rice, yucca and cheese; *sonzo*, ground rice mixed with cheese and cooked on an open fire. You will find most of these dishes served in the local markets.

Entertainment

There are several **cinemas** in town including **Palace** on the Plaza, **Florida** on Av Cañoto and **Santa Cruz** on Calle 21 de Mayo 249. Check the local press for details. The young and wealthy Santa Cruz nightlife centres around Ekko Petroleo; take a bus 23 to Av San Martín for bars, fast food, discos etc.

Practical information

Tourist office Calle Omar Chaviz Ortiz (no number). Open 08.00–12.00 and 14.30–18.30 weekdays. Take micro 23, 58, 57 from the centre. Difficult to find but worth a visit. Remember your passport.
Money Banco de Santa Cruz, Calle Junín 154; Banco de Crédito, Calle 24 de Septiembre 158. Money changers include Cambio, Calle 24 de Septiembre 30 and on the plaza.
Shops Outdoor and camping gear, repellents etc: La Jara Calle Bolívar 458.

Internet Galería Los Angeles, Calle Florida. US$4 per hour 08.45–13.00 and 14.00–21.00 Several Internet cafés in this area.

Airlines

Aerolineas Argentinas Edificio Banco Nación; tel: 399776
Air France Calle Ingavi Comercial Paititi; tel: 347661
Aero Sur Calle Colón, corner Irala; tel: 364446
American Airlines Calle Beni 202; tel: 341341
LAPSA Calle 21 de Mayo, corner Florida; tel: 371999
Lan Chile Calle Libertad 144; tel: 335951
LAB Calle Warnes, corner Chuquisaca; tel: 344411
TAM Calle 21 de Mayo, corner Florida; tel: 371999
Varig Calle Junín 284; tel: 341144

Travel agents

Rosario Tours Calle Arenales 193; tel: 369656; email: aventura@tucan.cnb.net Organise city tours and trips to Cotoca, 1-day tours to Samaipata and 2-day tours to Amboró, the Jesuit mission towns and the Pantanal. They are expensive unless you can share the costs between several people.
Carlos Grandez Calle Lemoine 215; tel: 33 7719; fax: 36 8815. He has been recommended though is not known to me personally. He organises ecological tours to Amboró, Las Pampas de Beni, and Noel Kempff Mercado National Park.
Neblina Forest Casilla 683; tel/fax: 336831; email: neblinaforest@daitec.scz.com They organise trips into Amboró and Noel Kempff Mercado National Park.

What to see

The quiet, peaceful **Plaza de Armas** is at the centre of the political and social life of the city. It is a popular place for locals out for an evening stroll. Watch for the sloths that hang out here – there are two or three that are permanent residents in the plaza.

Museo Catedralico de Arte Sagrado Inside the cathedral. Open Tue, Thur and Sun 15.00–17.00.
Museo Etnográfico On the Island of Los Murales in the Parque Arenal. Often closed.
Museo de Historia Natural Av Irala. Open Mon–Fri 09.00-12.00 and 15.00-18.00. Interesting collection of fossils, rocks and minerals and natural history.

AROUND SANTA CRUZ

Santa Cruz department is the largest in Bolivia, covering about 30% of the total area of the country. It borders Brazil and Paraguay, and so lies on the route of many travellers in to and out of Bolivia, but as an area rich in natural resources it is worth making a detour to visit even if it isn't on your itinerary. If you use Santa Cruz as a base there are several good day trips out of the city. Within a few hours you can visit one of Bolivia's most important prehispanic archaeological sites, El Fuerte, just outside the subtropical town of Samaipata. With three or four days you can make the very worthwhile circuit of the Jesuit mission towns, visit the places where the legendary Che Guevara was shot and taken afterwards, or walk in one of Bolivia's more accessible national parks, Amboró.

Samaipata

Telephone code 0944

Only a two-hour drive from Santa Cruz on a good quality surfaced road, Samaipata is a quiet, pretty town. It is at an altitude of 1,650m on the border between west

and east Bolivia, with the huge Amazon basin to the north and the dry *Chaco* to the south. The town, which is beautifully situated with good views all around, was founded in 1612 on the orders of the Viceroy of Lima, Juan Mendoza, as one of a series of towns along the route to connect Lima with Santa Cruz. The idea was to protect travellers with merchandise from aggressive indigenous tribes.

Getting there and away

There are *colectivo* taxis from Av Cañoto next to the bus terminal in Santa Cruz. They run when they fill up, usually every half an hour.

Where to stay and eat

Samaipata is popular with people from Santa Cruz at weekends, but during the week is pretty quiet and hotel prices are negotiable. There are a couple of places in the town itself, but the best places are just outside.

Residencia Kim Just off the square; tel: 6161 US$4. A good budget choice, small, clean and friendly. Other central places are **Mi Casa**, tel: 6061 and **Mily**, tel: 6151.
La Víspera Guesthouse 1km from the square; tel: 6082. US$7 for backpackers. Dutch owned. Walking maps and information, excursions, hammocks, fireplaces, kitchen, garden. Quiet and peaceful.
Traudi Yessen Tel: 6094. Has cabins. Phone for directions.

SnackDany and restaurant **Paola** are both on the square and serve good local food.

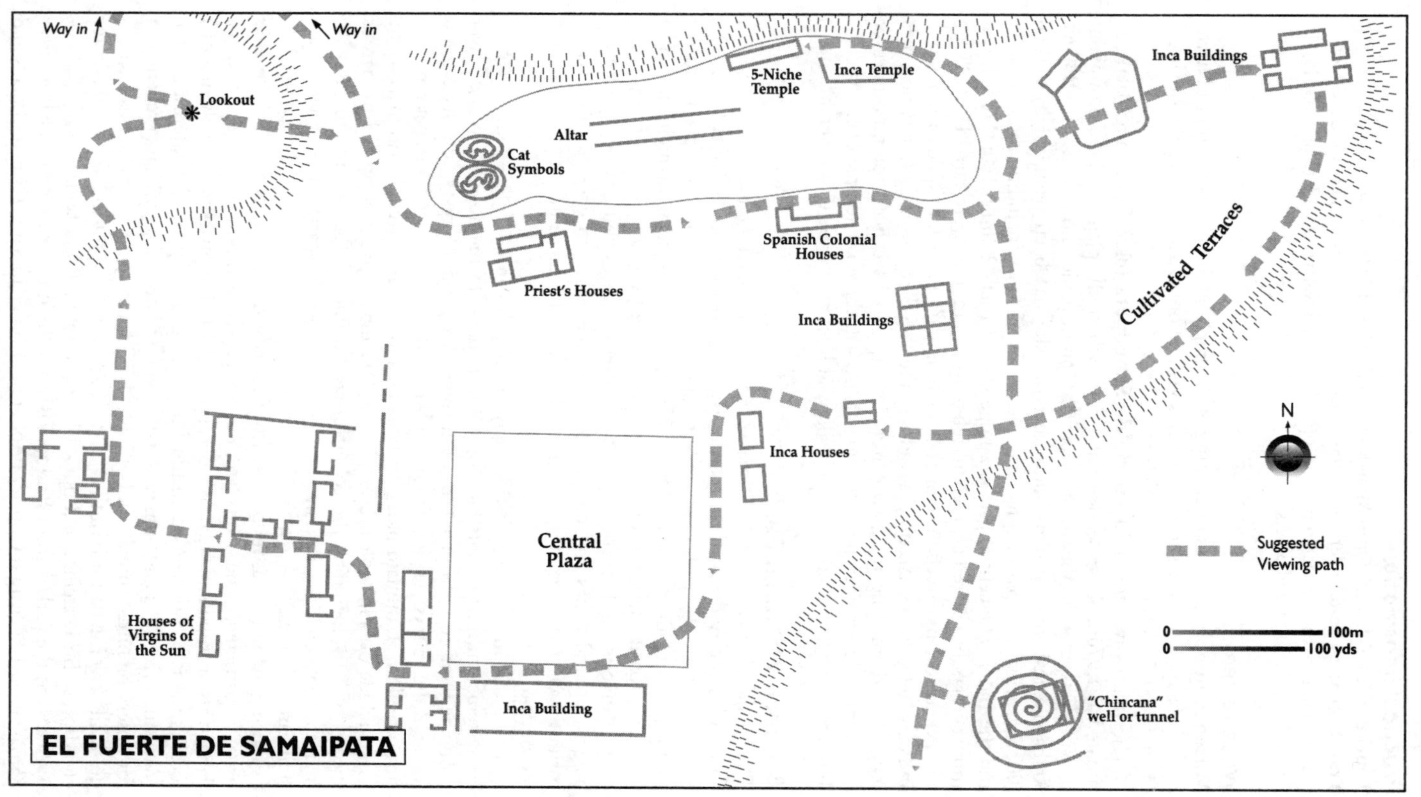
Way in
Way in
Lookout
Cat Symbols
Altar
5-Niche Temple
Inca Temple
Inca Buildings
Priest's Houses
Spanish Colonial Houses
Inca Buildings
Cultivated Terraces
Inca Houses
N
Central Plaza
Houses of Virgins of the Sun
Suggested Viewing path
0 100m
0 100 yds
Inca Building
"Chincana" well or tunnel
EL FUERTE DE SAMAIPATA

Practical information

Tourist office Tel: 6128. Open Mon–Fri 08.00–12.00 and 14.00–1800.

Travel agencies Roadrunners, tel: 6193. Organises guided tours to Amboró, US$50 for the day split between a maximum of 4 people. Caves and waterfalls walk (3 hrs, US$15); El Fuerte (3hrs, US$15), and others.

What to see

Museo Arqueológico has interesting photographs and information on El Fuerte, as well as a model of the site, so is worth a visit before or after visiting the site itself. Open 09.00–12.00 and 14.30–18.00.

The impressive site of **El Fuerte de Samaipata** (8km from Samaipata) site situated at 1,970m above sea-level at a point where the plains and the mountains converge, is one of the most important prehispanic monuments in Bolivia. Archaeological investigations show that the site has been occupied by several different tribal groups since its construction in 1500BC, including the Guaranies and the Incas. The central part is a huge slab of rock, 200m by 60m, which was almost certainly a sacred area where religious ceremonies were carried out. There are several designs carved into the rock including channels for liquid to run down, and cats and serpents. Around the sides of the slab there are niches, in typical Inca style, carved into the rock, which are thought to have been for mummies or ceremonial objects. On the north side of the slab there is a temple of five niches. The site is extensive and you should allow at least two hours to wander around.

Amboró National Park

This national park covers an area of 630,000 hectares straddling the eastern foothills of the Andes in the western part of the department of Santa Cruz. The area covered by the park is typically mountainous to the north and hilly to the south, with an altitude range of 300–3,300m, a cool climate in the highlands and a warmer tropical climate in the lower regions. The landscape is one of distinctive, deep canyons and picturesque table mountains. Four widely differing biogeographical zones converge in the park: the southern edge of the Amazon basin, the western edge of the Brazilian shield, the northern limit of the *chaco*, and the Andean foothills.

The flora in Amboró is extremely diverse because of the wide range of ecosystems within the four biogeographical zones, from sub-Andean and lower montane rainforest, through transition zones of semi-dry forest to the dry tropical forest of the valleys. Typical of the rainforest are the giant tree ferns, palm trees, a sort of walnut, mountain pines, mahogany, and endemic orchids. Animals of the park include otters, Andean bears, jaguar, anteaters, tapir, peccary and numerous species of bird, including the colourful and distinctive toucans and macaws. As many as 830 bird species have been recorded in the park, nine of which are Bolivian endemics.

During the rainy season, particularly February and March, access to the park is usually restricted. The roads are not in good condition and rivers may be dangerous or impossible to cross. Because of the lack of marked trails, the use of a local guide is recommended within the park. Areas of particular interest are the Macuñucú river bed and 40m waterfall, pools and caves; Saguay, an excellent area for observing birds, animals and orquids; La Chonta, good for birds; Los Cajones del Ichilo river delta for beautiful views; La Yunga for giant tree ferns; Siberia for cloudforest, birdwatching and flora; Mataracú waterfall and trail.

Access to the park is from **Buena Vista** for the northern section, or from near Samaipata at **La Yunga**. Contact FAN at their office in Santa Cruz for details and further information; the office is at kilometre 5 on the old road to Cochabamba; tel: 533389/333806. At La Yunga FAN have a guesthouse and guides who can take you into the park.

Buena Vista is readily accessible by bus from Santa Cruz. You can usually hire a guide here. The village has several places to stay including **Amboró eco-resort**, km 103 on the Cochabamba road; tel: 03 422372/428954; email: bloch@bibosi.scz.entelnet.bo.

Recommendations

- Take lightweight clothing with long sleeves, boots, rain protection, suncream, mosquito net and repellent, a torch and water bottle.
- Take a comprehensive first aid kit.
- Make sure you have a yellow fever vaccination, take precautions against chagas in the south and malaria and leishmaniasis in the north.

DO NOT:

- Hunt or in any way disturb the wildlife.
- Use soaps or shampoos in the water.
- Buy any animal or animal product.
- Leave litter. Carry everything out with you.
- Camp or light fires except in designated areas.

Noell Kempff Mercado National Park

Covering an area of over a million hectares of pristine wilderness at altitudes between 200 and 750m, this park lies in the northeast of the department of Santa Cruz, right on the border with Brazil. Characteristic of the park is the impressive scenery of the Caparú Plateau, a sandstone escarpment rising dramatically 600m above the rainforest, creating an elevated plain of grassland and cerrado forest. The scenery of steep, rocky red cliffs with cascading waterfalls is spectacular. The unique geographical location of the park means it is a convergence zone where Andean foothills, tropical Amazon rainforest, periodically inundated savannahs, subtropical dry Chaco and Brazilian *cerrado* (dry savannahs) merge creating a range of habitats rich in diversity. The average rainfall in the park is 2,000mm per year. The diversity of habitats provides for an equally diverse wildlife. There are probably over 700 species of bird in the park. There is also a variety of animal life, though harder to spot, including various species of monkey, tapir, jaguar and capybara.

The remote location of the park makes it impossible to visit unless you are prepared to spend at least four days and a fair bit of money. On a four-day trip based in Flor de Oro you have access to several habitat types and should be able to see plenty of wildlife, such as toco toucan, white woodpecker, the coatimundi and silvery marmoset, rufescent tiger heron, scarlet and blue-and-yellow macaws, white-faced whistling duck, sunbitterns, and possibly the endangered giant otters, jaguars, monkeys, tapir and peccaries.

There are two centres in the park with hotel accommodation, **Flor de Oro** (only accessible by plane or boat, 5–9 hrs from Cruce Piso Firme, 367km from Santa Cruz) and **Los Fierros**. There are also camping facilities at Los Fierros, Huanchaca 1 (only accessible by plane) and Paucerna (only accessible by boat from Flor de Oro, 5–9 hrs). To Los Fierros there is a bus from Santa Cruz on Fridays (18 hrs). Once in the park prices are high: US$15 to camp, and US$115 in the park hotel.

Fremen Tours Calle Pedro Salazar 537, PO Box 9682, La Paz; tel: 414069; fax: 417327; email: vtfremen@caoba.entelnet.bo. Organise 4-day trips from Santa Cruz to Noel Kempff.

Neblina Forest Casilla 683, Santa Cruz; tel/fax: 336831; email: neblinaforest@daitec.scz.com. They organise trips into Amboró and Noel Kempff Mercado National Park.

The park is administered by FAN (Fundación Amigos de la Naturaleza). Created in 1988, FAN is a private non-profit, non-governmental organisation dedicated to the conservation of biodiversity in Bolivia.

Vallegrande

Vallegrande and La Higuera have been put on the map by the legendary figure and national hero, **Che Guevara**. This is where he spent the last days of his life. He was buried near the airport in Vallegrande until being removed and taken back to Cuba in 1998. The school house where he was shot in 1967 in La Higuera is now a clinic, and the hospital laundry, *lavandería*, where he was brought after he was shot is still at the back of the hospital in Vallegrande, 15 minutes' walk from the centre of town. September 8 is the anniversary of Che's death and is a day on which many pilgrims, both Bolivian and tourists, come to commemorate their hero. *Bolivian Diaries* by Che Guevara reports on the campaigns he fought in Bolivia at the end of his life.

From the bus terminal in Santa Cruz there is a daily bus (departs 10.00, 5–6 hrs, US$4) to Vallegrande. There are several hostels including **Residencia Vallegrande** and **Hotel Vallegrande**, which is good value at US$3, new, clean and near the market. **Restaurant Julia**, just off the plaza, has good food, and the tourist office on the plaza is very helpful. The trip to Pucará (45km) is beautiful; take a minibus from the market and ask around for accommodation. From there to get to Higuera (15km) there is local transport but not much in the way of accommodation. The clinic will gratefully accept donations of medicines.

The Jesuit mission towns

If you have at least four days and feel like getting off the beaten track, a tour around the Jesuit mission towns is well worth while. The roads are rough, and it can be very hot, but the towns are friendly and the churches impressive, there are opportunities for seeing the lowland forest and some of its wildlife and for swimming and relaxing, and you will probably not meet many other tourists.

In 1691 the first Jesuits, led by Father Arce, arrived in Chiquitos to attempt to convert the native tribes, of which there were many, to Christianity. **San Javier** was the first mission town to be founded. The church, started in 1749 and finished three years later, has recently been restored to its former glory. Over a period of 80 years ten *reducciones* or settlements were established by the Jesuits, in close proximity to one another. With the help of accomplished Jesuit architects, craftsmen and musicians, these settlements of up to 5,000 native people developed into well-organised, highly cultured communities. The native Indians were able to protect themselves from slave hunters and aggressive tribes, and were taught the skills needed to establish a sedentary lifestyle and to build the Jesuit churches which were to become their own religious temples. Very little was left of their own cultures as they converted to Christianity and the Jesuit way of living.

Each settlement followed the same basic layout with the large church on the square, and mission buildings, schools and workshops alongside; around the square there were homes for orphans and widows, a mill, bread oven, communal kitchens, stores for grain, and weaving and other workshops. Father Martín Schmid was particularly influential in the building of the churches and teaching of the making and playing of musical instruments such as harps, wooden organs, violins and cellos to the indigenous people.

The Jesuits were expelled from Bolivia in 1767 despite the success of their settlements. The Spaniards disliked the level of autonomy and control the Jesuits had, so they were ordered to leave and were replaced by less sympathetic Catholic priests. Treatment of the indigenous people worsened and many communities fell apart. Fortunately most of the mission buildings survived and are still in use today, thanks to the restoration work, overseen by architect Hans Roth since 1972 and still going on in many of the Jesuit mission towns.

Misiones del Oriente run buses from Santa Cruz to San Ignacio at 08.00 and 20.00 (10 hrs, US$12). In Santa Cruz their office is on Calle Virgen de Cotoca 235, between 2nd and 3rd anillos; tel: 467878. The service is good, with drinks (served in plastic cups which are then thrown out of the window unless you stop the other passengers) and lunch stop at Concepción. **Trains** from Santa Cruz to Quijarro stop at San José. Watch for pickpockets at the station and boarding the train, where amid the bustle there is plenty of opportunity for the expert thief to sneak wallets and bags away from unwary travellers.

San José

Telephone code 0972

San José is a sleepy village with baked red-earth roads, a few streets and, at the centre, a well laid out and cared for plaza bordered by colonial covered pavements on three sides, and the Jesuit church complex on the other. If you have time on your hands it's worth a trip to the swimming pools 5km from town. Walk or take a taxi. These are beautifully located and great for a relaxing day, although popular at the weekend with locals and busy from midday with music, bar etc. Open 10.00–19.00.

The land around here is flat and largely hot, humid lowland forest, with some cattle farming. There are plenty of mosquitoes but if you take a walk out of town into the forests there is a good chance you will see interesting birds, like toucans, and even monkeys. There is very little traffic on the road, and just a few scattered native villages along the way, so take food and water with you on the bus and be prepared for hot and long journeys.

Getting there and away

From San José, Flota Universal run buses to San Ignacio Mon, Wed and Fri at 07.00 and Sat at 14.00 (6 hrs, US$7), from the station. These buses are used to bring Mennonites from their community, 45km away, into the market most mornings, arriving at 08.30, so if there is a breakdown and bus shortage you may have to wait a few days, or hitch out. The train to Santa Cruz takes 6 hours, the departure time depending on when it left Quijarro. See pages 343–4 for time of trains to San José.

Where to stay

There are a couple of hostels in the centre of the village, **Hostal Raquelle** and **Hostal Victoria**; tel: 2136. At US$5 these are friendly, basic and clean. You can visit the Aldea, the children's home run by Padre Alfredo. There is little in the way of restaurants or variety of things to eat – generally chicken and chips is all that's available.

San Rafael

The mission of San Rafael was founded in 1696 by Father Jaun Bautista de Zea and a group of Tabica and Tau indians. The church, built between 1740 and 1749 by Father Martín Schmid, has been completely restored. In the small village there are a couple of extremely basic hostels, and several uninspiring restaurants, but the people are friendly. There are minibuses from San Rafael to San Ignacio, the first at 06.00.

Santa Ana

Santa Ana is also very small with a couple of cheap and basic hostels. It was founded is 1755 and has one of the more simple churches. This church was finished by the indigenous people after the expulsion of the Jesuits and is testament to the high level of skill and order attained by these communities. Several *colectivos* a day run to San Ignacio from Santa Ana, the first at 06.00.

San Ignacio

Telephone code 0962

San Ignacio is one of the largest of the mission towns. It is hot and dusty, but set amid lush lowland forest. The town is on the main road to Brazil and has hotels, cafés and restaurants to provide for the large numbers of people passing through. The church, which was reputedly the most beautiful of all, was destroyed in 1948 as it was in a dangerous state of disrepair. It is currently undergoing reconstruction. In town there is little to do: you could visit the Swiss-run **Escuela Granja Hogar**, where local girls are taught weaving and other traditional crafts, swim in the lake or sit at one of the many pavement cafés around the plaza. The lake, about 20 minutes' walk, is great for swimming – ask the locals for the best spot, at the far end near the bridge.

The National Park office for Noell Kempff in the **Casa de Cultura**, Calle Comercio, sometimes has information about access, flights etc. The road to Los Fierros, where there is vehicular access to the park passes through here.

Getting there and away

There are buses to Santa Cruz at 08.00 and 20.00 run by Missiones del Oriente, with a lunch stop at Concepción. Several other companies also run at night to Santa Cruz from the market area.

Where to stay

A lovely place to stay is **Casa Suiza** (US$10 including all meals) the house of Horst and Cristina Schultz on Calle Sucre, four blocks from the plaza. They are extremely welcoming and provide delicious food, lovely clean rooms, a garden to sit in, and somewhere to wash clothes. **Guapamó**, Calle Sucre, is good value at US$8, with fans, hammocks, patio. **San Ignacio** is the most luxurious, though not cheap at US$15 per person; tel: 2157. It has air conditioning and a pool, and is pristine.

There are several good restaurants around the plaza and several hotels of remarkably good standard.

Concepción

This is one of the most beautiful of the Jesuit mission towns, with a restored church also built by Father Martín Schmid between 1752 and 1756, and a very attractive plaza bordered by colonial covered pavements and ornately painted buildings. There are several places to stay ranging from the basic to luxurious (Gran Hotel Concepción), and there are some excellent restaurants, mostly on the plaza itself.

SOUTH FROM SANTA CRUZ

South of Santa Cruz lie the southern highlands of Bolivia, a remote and little visited area. The main town is Tarija, the centre of Bolivia's wine producing area. This is a good area to travel through if you feel like getting away from the tourist trail. There is a strong Argentinian influence in this part of Bolivia.

Tarija

Telephone code 066

Tarija is a peaceful place, except during fiestas. The city was founded in 1574 and is named after Bernardo de Tarixa, the first Spanish explorer to visit the area. At 1,840m it has a spring-like climate all year round (the average temperature is 19°C), shady plazas and tree-lined streets. The centre has an interesting mixture of colonial and new buildings, an excellent palaeontology and archaeology museum, and a relaxed air about it. Around the city you can visit the vineyards which produce wine and *singani*, Bolivia's best-known spirit, swim in the Guadalquivir River, walk the river banks, or join in with local festivities if you happen to coincide with one of the colourful festivals. There are festivals most months in Tarija, the most important being carnival, February 22, 23 and 24; Corpus Cristi in June; Santiago in July; and San Roque, Festival de la Primavera and Festival de la Tradición Chaqueña in September.

Getting there and away

Tarija has a modern *terminal terrestre* on Av Las Américas, 20 minutes' walk or a few minutes by micro from the centre. There are frequent bus services to Yacuiba (10 hrs, 290km), Villamontes, Entre Rios and La Paz (24+ hrs).

Where to stay

There are several reasonable hostels right in the centre of town.

Alojamiento 8 Hermanos Calle Sucre 0782; tel: 42111. US$5–8 shared bath. Clean, very central, comfortable, around a courtyard.
Hostal Rosario Calle Ingavi 0777; tel: 42942 US$ 5–8 shared bath, US$8–14 private bath. Clean, basic, around a courtyard, clothes washing possible.
Hostal Carmen Calle Ingavi 0784; tel: 43372. US$10–17 private bath, cable TV, breakfast. Recommended. Organises tours and transport.
Hostal Libertador Calle Bolívar 0649; tel: 44231. US$14–26 with bath, TV, breakfast, new building. Family run.
Hostal Loma de San Juan behind the Mirador de San Juan. US$40–50. New, modern, clean, spacious rooms, cable TV, pool.
Gran Hotel Baldiviezo Calle Madrid 0443; tel: 37711. US$25–30 with bath, cable TV, telephone and Internet, breakfast. New, clean and central, also does tours of the area.

Where to eat

As Tarija lies so close to the Argentinian border, there is a considerable influence in the diet – meat, especially large steaks, is widely available and popular. There is great food, wine and coffee at **Gattopardo** on Plaza Luis de Fuentes, with some outside tables. The **market** on Calle Sucre does good local dishes for breakfast and lunch. Just off the square on General Trigo are the restaurants **Riconcito Andaluz** and **Mateos**, both recommended. For more upmarket places try **Milano**, Calle Bolívar and Victor Paz, **Cabaña de Don Pepe**, Campos 0136, **Cabaña Don Pedro**, Av Victor Paz near the bus station. Vegetarian **Restaurant El Solar**, Calle Campero corner V Lema, is only open 12.00-14.00.

Practical information

Tourist office Calle General Trigo on the Plaza. Open Mon–Fri 09.00-12.00 and 15.00–18.00.
Phone office ENTEL, Calle Lema corner Daniel Campos.
Airlines LAB, Calle General Trigo.
Internet Calle Ingavi 449; web: www.tarijanet.com; open Mon–Sat 09.00–12.30 and 15.00–22.00, Sun 15.30–20.00 US$2.5 per hour. Also there is Internet access in Hotel Buenos Aires, Calle Sucre. US$2.50 per hour, and Gran Hotel Baldiviezo (see above).

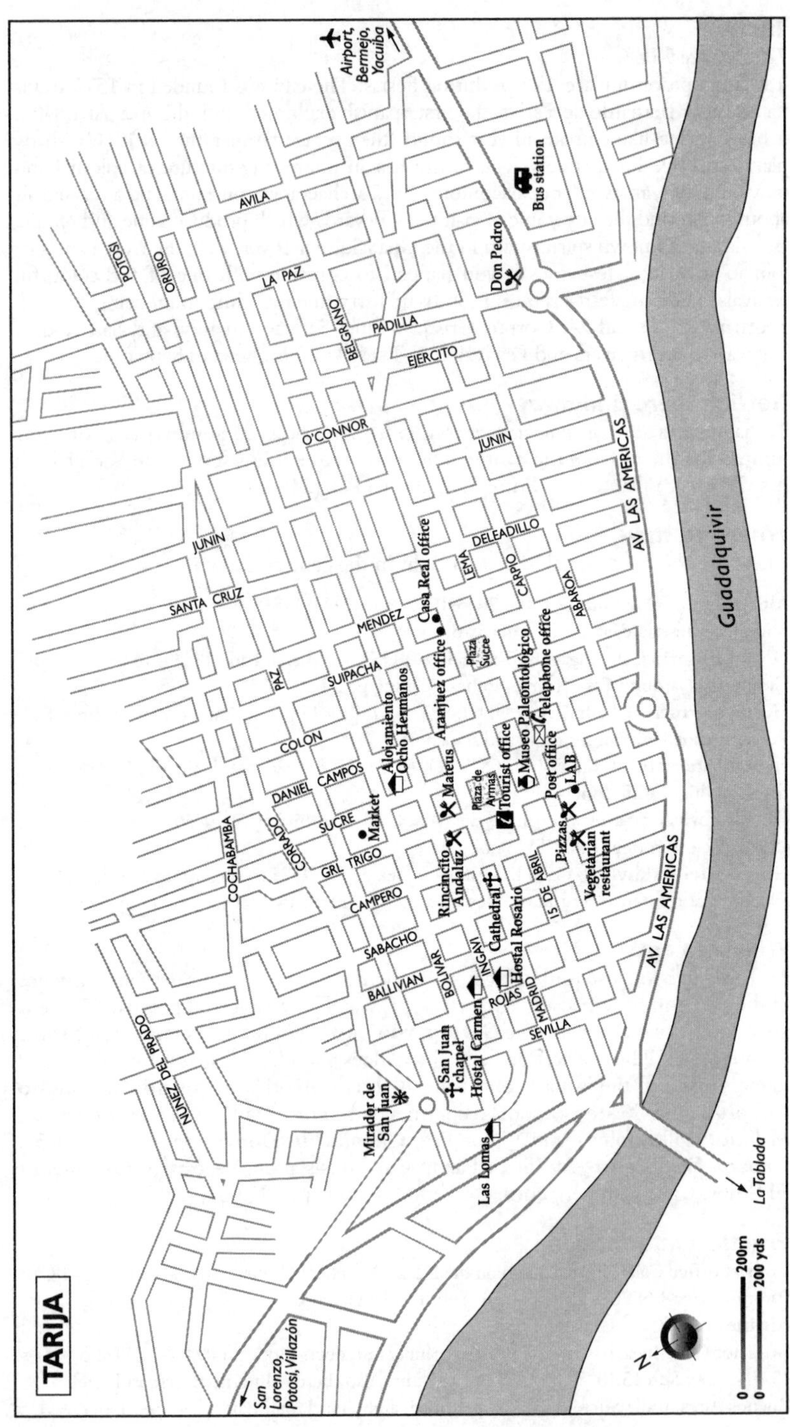
TARIJA
Airport, Bermejo, Yacuiba
San Lorenzo, Potosí, Villazón
La Tablada
Bus station
Don Pedro
AVILA
POTOSI
ORURO
LA PAZ
BELGRANO
PADILLA
EJERCITO
O'CONNOR
JUNIN
JUNIN
AV LAS AMERICAS
AV LAS AMERICAS
Guadalquivir
DELEADILLO
LEMA
CARPIO
ABAROA
Casa Real office
MENDEZ
SANTA CRUZ
Aranjuez office
Plaza Sucre
Telephone office
Museo Paleontológico
SUIPACHA
PAZ
Alojamiento Ocho Hermanos
COLON
DANIEL CAMPOS
Mateus
Plaza de Armas
Tourist office
Post office
LAB
SUCRE
Market
CORRADO
COCHABAMBA
GRL TRIGO
Rincincito Andaluz
Pizzas
Vegetarian restaurant
15 DE ABRIL
CAMPERO
Cathedral
Hostal Rosario
SABACHO
BOLIVAR
INGAVI
BALLIVIAN
ROJAS
MADRID
SEVILLA
Hostal Carmen
San Juan chapel
Mirador de San Juan
NUNEZ DEL PRADO
Las Lomas
N
0
200m
0
200 yds

What to see

The **Museo Paleontológico y Arqueológico** is on Calle General Trigo 0402 corner Calle Lema. Open Mon–Sat 09.00–12.00 and 15.00–18.00. The museum has an amazing collection of remarkably whole fossils from six different mammals found in the Tarija area and dating from the Quaternary period, 250,000 years ago. Some of the mammals were obviously related to present-day mammals, such as the horse, elephant, llama, bear and rodents, but others are from families long since extinct such as gyptodontes – distant relatives of the armadillo – and giant sloths. The museum also has an archaeological and mineral collection. It used to be possible to visit the fossil rich areas around Tarija, but because of irresponsible behaviour and the removal of fossils these places are now protected and entrance prohibited. Ask at the tourist office for details.

La Casa Dorada, Calle Ingavi corner General Trigo, is open Mon–Fri 09.00–12.00 and 15.00–18.00, Sat 09.00–12.00. Voluntary payment. Also the **Casa de Cultura**, which has exhibitions and concerts from time to time. The Casa Dorada is a fascinating house that was built at the end of the last century and lived in by a Tarijeño merchant and glassware producer Moises Navajas until his death, and by his wife until 1970. The house was then abandoned and many of its contents stolen until in the 1980s local authorities and the university started to renovate it. The contents of the house are mostly European art nouveau, with examples of the glassware Navajas manufactured and plenty of gold, giving a good insight into the relative wealth of Tarija's high society earlier in the century.

Tarija's interesting churches include **San Francisco** in Calle Madrid corner Av Daniel Campos. It is a beautiful church, founded in 1606, and has an impressive Franciscan library containing many important historical books. The **cathedral** on Calle Madrid was built in 1810 and contains the remains of the founder of the city. The church of **San Juan de la Loma** at the end of Calle Bolívar was built in 1632. It is historically important as it is where the Spanish signed their surrender after the battle of La Tablada. The church of **San Roque**, built between 1885 and 1887 is the church of the patron saint of Tarija.

The wine industry

The countryside around Tarija is used for grape growing and visiting one of the many **bodegas** is a good way to sample some of the wines and *singani*, Bolivia's national drink, a spirit made from distilled wine, very similar to the Peruvian and Chilean *pisco*. It is usually drunk very cold, alone or mixed with lemonade or lemon juice, or in a cocktail. The Jesuits who settled in Tarija in the 16th century first cultivated grapes here, finding the climate to be perfect. The combination of altitude, low rainfall and warm temperatures means a good level of production, a high level of sugar in the grapes and quality wine and *singani*. The bodegas are difficult to get to unless you have your own transport or take a taxi, but once you get there they are very happy to show you around. Ask at the tourist office for more details or visit the bodegas' offices in town to get directions. You can sometimes travel out on the workers' truck early in the morning.

Casa Real

The 20-year-old bodega of Casa Real, located 18km from the city in the valley of Santa Ana (town office: Calle 15 de Abril, near Plaza Sucre), produces 600 metric tonnes of grapes annually, which are used to produce red wines and 2 million bottles of *singani*. Several grape varieties are grown, including Merlot, Cabernet Sauvignon, Riesling, Franco Lombart and Moscatel Alejandría which is used for *singani*. Viticulture has been in the Ballivían family for three generations – Don

Julio Linares distilled the first wine in 1925. They are just beginning to export, principally to the United States.

Next to the Casa Real is the **Kholberg** bodega, and nearby are several others. Most have offices in town where you can get information about visiting.

Near Tarija

San Lorenzo is a small town 15km from Tarija, easily reached in 20 minutes by *micro* from the roundabout at the Mirador de San Juan. Worth a visit is the museum of **Moto Méndez**, where all the personal belongings of the hero of the battle of La Tablada, José Eustaquio Méndez, are displayed. Open Mon–Fri 09.00–12.30 and 15.00–17.00; Sat–Sun 09.00–12.00.

On the way to San Lorenzo you pass **Tomatitas**, a good place to stop for lunch and even swim in the river. Good value typical food is available at the many riverside restaurants.

Only 4km from the centre of Tarija is **La Tablada**, site of the battle of April 1817 which contributed to the liberation of Bolivia when the royalist forces were defeated by Méndez and his army.

CROSSING THE BORDER TO ARGENTINA

There are three possible border crossings from Bolivia to Argentina, at Villazón/La Quiaca, Bermejo/Aguas Blancas and Yacuiba/Pocitos. The crossing at Yacuiba is the busiest and probably the slowest as a result as it is on the main route to Santa Cruz. At the other two crossings the paperwork is straightforward and shouldn't take more than a few minutes. From the Bolivian side the three border posts are all remote and involve long journeys from the nearest city.

From **Tarija to Bermejo** the bus takes 7 hours (US$7). The journey to Bermejo is hot and dusty and the road is rough, but it's very scenic, passing through mountainous cloudforest. The border is a bridge 3km before the town of Bermejo, so you can get off the bus at 'El Puente' and go through Bolivian customs avoiding the town. Do not pay at the border – they sometimes try to charge, but you do not have to pay either to leave or enter Bolivia. You then walk 100m across the bridge into Argentina, where your luggage is searched and your passport stamped. It is 50km from here to Orun, US$12 for a shared taxi. There's no money exchange at the border, so you have to go into Bermejo for that. There are two more luggage checks between the border and Orun. From Orun there are buses to all Argentinian destinations. It is possible to buy through bus tickets in Bolivia, but this is not worthwhile as it limits you to one company, inevitably costs more and has no advantages as you still have to go through the same procedures.

From **Tarija to Yacuiba** the bus takes 10–12 hours (US$9). The Yacuiba/Pocitos border is busy, and it's slow to get out of Bolivia, although quick to get in. From the bus station in Pocitos, Argentina, it's just two blocks to the border. Go through customs, cross the bridge and from here it's a few kilometres to Yacuiba and the bus station. Taxis cost US$2 from the bus station to the border. Buses from Yacuiba to Santa Cruz take 14 hours (US$20), Tarija 10–12 hours, with departures 16.00-18.00. To Villamontes is 1½ hours. If you have to stay in Yacuiba there are several cheap, reasonable hostels. Next to the bus station is **Residencial Urkupiña**, tel: 0682 2320. US$6–8 shared bath, showers US$1. Nearby is **Residencial Tropical** of a similar standard.

From Yacuiba there are trains to Santa Cruz departing Tue, Thur and Sat at 16.20, 12 hours, US$7.

22 North of La Paz

Lake Titicaca and the small town of Copacabana lie to the northwest of La Paz, just a few hours away by local bus. From Copacabana the crossing into Peru is straightforward. The great chain of majestic peaks of the Cordillera Real also lies to the north of La Paz, dominating the landscape and providing excellent opportunities for trekking and mountaineering, or just scenery gazing. Sorata, a small and friendly village nestled at the foot of the peak of Illampu, is a good base for treks or just enjoying the surroundings, and is readily accessible from La Paz. To the northeast of La Paz on the steep eastern slopes of the Cordillera Real is the subtropical paradise of Coroico. A beautifully set small town a few hours from La Paz, this popular place in the Yungas region is also the gateway to the northeastern lowlands.

LA PAZ TO COPACABANA AND LAKE TITICACA

From La Paz to Copacabana is an interesting four-hour journey across the altiplano. You leave La Paz, climbing steep city streets out of the depths of the canyon, passing through the ever-spreading suburb of El Alto and then out onto the spacious but quite bleak high plains of the altiplano. The predominantly Aymara-speaking people who live around this side of the lake have a way of life that hasn't changed in centuries, farming sheep, llamas and alpaca, and growing a few varieties of grain but primarily dozens of varieties of potato. There is a short ferry crossing over the strait of Tiquina, where you need your passport and a few bolivianos. The bus is ferried across on a pontoon, and all passengers squeeze into small wooden boats for the crossing. The views of the lake and surrounding countryside are remarkable.

Lake Titicaca is a truly impressive sight, a huge body of water that changes colour throughout the day. It is one of the world's highest navigable lakes, at 3,800m above sea-level. You'll certainly notice the altitude if you arrive here from nearer sea-level. On the east side loom the majestic peaks of the Cordillera Real in Bolivia. Around the other sides of the lake is the dry, brown altiplano, farmed for centuries by Aymara and Quechua people. The lake level varies according to the season, but over the last few decades the overall trend is a fall in water level, and the size today is considerably less than in Inca times. However, the lake still stretches as far as you can see, almost 200km from end to end. There are many islands, some of which are densely populated. The easiest to visit are the islands of the Sun and the Moon on the Bolivian side, and the islands of Amantani and Taquile on the Peruvian side (see page 264). Around the shores of the lake and on some of the islands, there are ancient ruins which are testament to the sacred significance given to this enigmatic body of water by the prehispanic civilisations of this area. Inca legend states that the founders of their dynasty, Manco Inca and

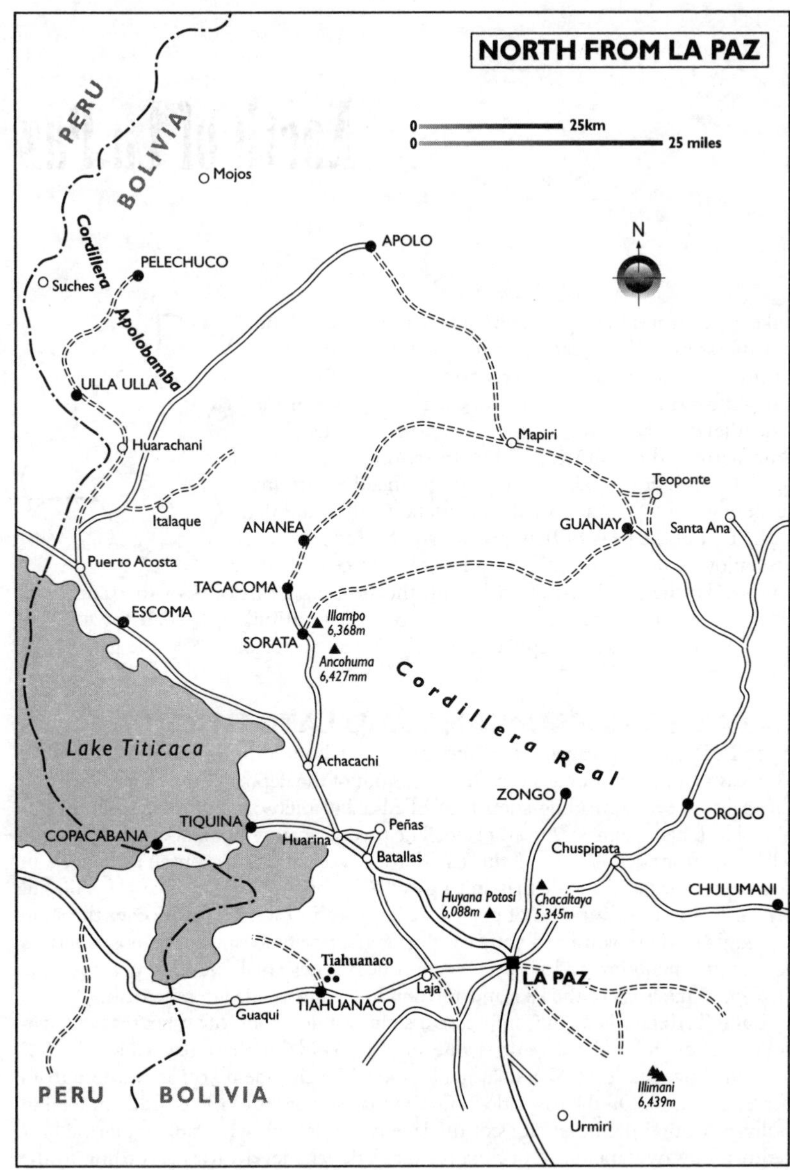

Mama Oclla, arose from the waters of the lake before heading off on their mission. The Tiahuanaco culture was centred near Lake Titicaca, and even today the people in the vicinity pay special homage to this sacred water.

COPACABANA

Telephone code 0862.

Copacabana is a really nice little town, situated right on the shores of Lake Titicaca. It is the jumping off point for boat trips out to the Isla del Sol (Island of the Sun) and the Isla de la Luna (Island of the Moon), and it also boasts a shimmering white 17th-century church dedicated to the Virgen de Candelaria. Copacabana's festival at the beginning of August (5–8) sees thousands of pilgrims from all over the altiplano come to Copacabana to pay homage to the Virgen de Candelaria. It is very difficult to get transport or accommodation during the festival.

Getting there and away

There are frequent buses to Copacabana from the cemetery in La Paz (4 hrs), or through one of the travel agents such as Diana Tours. You can make connections to Puno in Copacabana. Whichever company you travel with you will have to change buses in Copacabana before continuing to Peru. Buses are generally quite busy at the weekends and quiet during the week.

Crossing the border to Peru

The border between Peru and Bolivia is just a few kilometres from Copacabana. There are frequent minibuses and shared taxis. Crossing the border itself is very straightforward. You have to get your passport stamped on the Bolivian side, walk up the road 100m and get your passport stamped on the Peruvian side. The border is open daily from 08.00–17.00, except on national election days. If you buy a through ticket from La Paz to Puno, you will go through Copacabana, where you may have an hour's break before changing to another bus that will take you across the border. The whole crossing is quick and easy. There are money changers at the

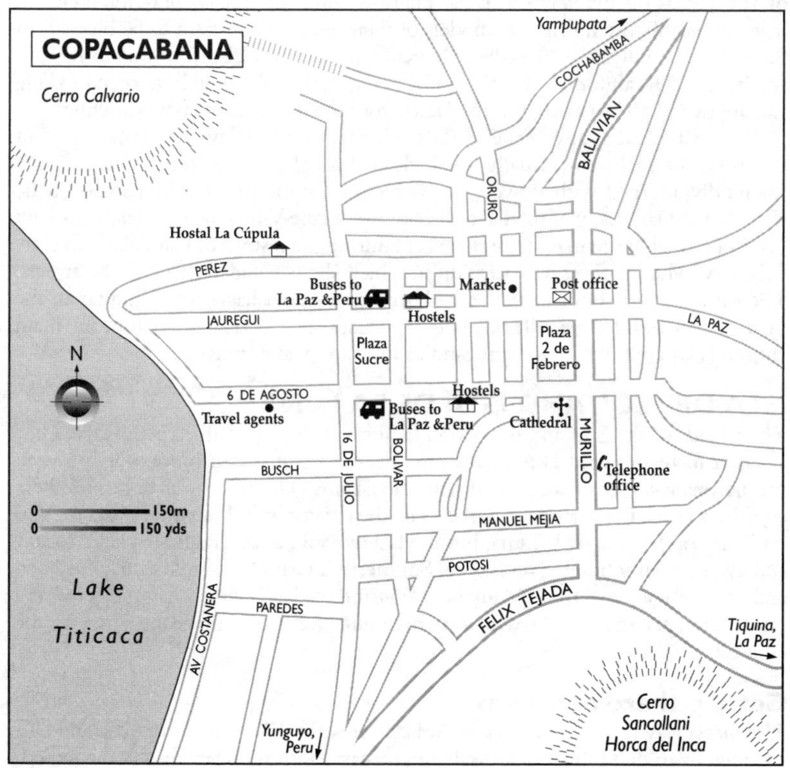

border who give a reasonable rate, or in the Peruvian town of Yunguyo, where most buses stop at the money change office.

Where to stay and eat

There are plenty of hotels in Copacabana ranging from the cheap and basic to quite luxurious. Most of the cheaper places are on Calle 6 de Agosto, Calle Murillo and Calle Jauregui. Most of the restaurants are concentrated in the same streets as the hotels. You can get good lake trout here, and set lunches are particularly good value.

Hostal Emperador Calle Murillo 235; tel: 2250. Popular with backpackers, cheap and basic.

La Cúpula Calle Amanda; tel: 2029. A little out of town, but worth finding, a couple of blocks above the port on the north side of town, 15 minutes' walk from Plaza Sucre. Videos, book exchange, TV, kitchen facilities, dorm rooms, restaurant.

Practical information

The bank, post office and phone office are in the centre of town. Opening hours are a bit erratic. Changing cash isn't a problem, although travellers' cheques could be more difficult. On 6 de Agosto there are a couple of travel agents who will arrange tours to the Isla del Sol and Isla de la Luna, from US$5 per person.

What to see

At the north edge of town there is a small hill, **Cerro Calvario**, with the **Stations of the Cross** on the way up. Local pilgrims climb the hill to pray for luck and material wealth, often bringing models of their desires with them to be blessed. At the top of the hill there are stalls selling all nature of models, from cars to money, and houses. The altitude makes the walk breathtaking, unless you have been trekking and are fit and acclimatised, but the views from the top make it all worthwhile.

The **cathedral** is also scene to these blessings on Sundays and holy days, but this time the real item, usually a vehicle, is brought to the front of the church splendidly adorned with flowers, to be blessed by the priest. The patron of the church, the Dark Lady of the Lake, also known as the Virgen de Candelaria, is kept inside a chapel in the main church, except during the festival of Candelaria in early February, when there is a procession in which she is paraded through the streets. The cathedral was built in the early 17th century, and has a fine gilt altar in the main chapel with four smaller chapels. The Capilla de Velas to the left of the main church is where the people light candles to support their prayers.

ISLA DEL SOL AND ISLA DE LA LUNA

The islands of the Sun and the Moon lie just off the Yampupata peninsula. They are rich in history and both have some pre-Inca ruins, which are worth a visit. Numerous legends are associated with the islands. The first Incas began life here after Viracocha, the deity considered to be the creator, put them on the island. You can't stay on the Isla de la Luna, but the Isla del Sol has several basic places to stay and even a luxury hotel. The Isla del Sol merits a visit of a couple of days at least, and more if you have time. Many people visit the islands which have suffered as a result. Respect the people who live here and don't encourage begging by the children.

Getting there and away

The nicest way to get to the Isla del Sol is to trek the 17km to Yampupata and take a launch from there. It's a great walk, pretty easy, with no steep climbs and superb

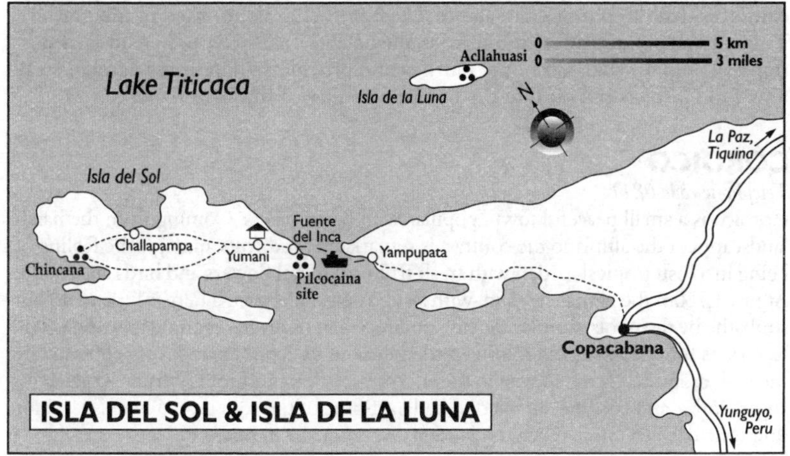

views of the lake. Follow the road leaving Copacabana along the lakeshore northwards. It costs US$3–8 for a boat across to Isla del Sol landing at Fuente del Inca at the southern end of the island. Boats from Copacabana leave morning and afternoon. There are day tours too, which often include the Island of the Moon.

What to see

Boats land at a jetty at the foot of an Inca stairway, at the top of which you will find a freshwater spring. Follow the path upwards to reach the village of Yumani, where there is basic accommodation in four hostels. There is a high quality hotel owned by Crillon Tours here, but you have to be on one of their tours to stay. You can walk northwest from here to Challa and Challapampa, the other villages on the island, both with basic accommodation. The villages are well connected by trails. It's a full day walk from one end of the island to the other, and it can be very dry and hot, so come prepared. There are other ruins near the Inca stairway at Pilkokaina in the south of the island; these are of fairly rudimentary stonework (2km from the jetty and the village of Yumani, accommodation available here too). The most interesting and beautifully located ruins are on the northwest side of the island at Chincana. Here, high above the water level, you will find a stone built labyrinth and a large sacred stone.

The Isla de la Luna is considerably smaller than the Isla del Sol, and less populated. There is nowhere to stay and no supplies here. There is an archaeological site you can wander around, although little is still standing.

THE ROAD TO COROICO

Coroico is located in the Yungas, which are the subtropical mountain valleys found between the highland Andean peaks and the eastern lowlands and tropical jungles. The road to Coroico is infamous, and with good reason, as it is scary. Setting off from the bus terminal in Villa Fatima, La Paz, you follow a good tarmac road up through typical *puna* scenery with lakes and ice-covered high peaks all around you, and grazing llamas, before beginning the tortuous descent. The road narrows, barely wide enough for one vehicle; frightening drops gape on one side and there are often waterfalls over, above and around you. All descending vehicles pass on the outside, seemingly overhanging the abyss below, where you catch the odd glimpse of crushed buses and trucks which have fallen over the edge. The scenery is dramatic if you can take your eyes off the road, with cloudforested steep mountain slopes. Most of the locals are used to the journey. They obviously don't feel the fear, as they sleep. In 1999 a new road is almost finished, which will shorten the journey and provide a safer, if less dramatic way to get to Coroico and on into the lowland jungles of the Beni region.

COROICO

Telephone code 0811

Coroico is a small peaceful town, popular with backpackers. Coming from the harsh landscapes of the altiplano the contrast is remarkable, and you can enjoy the feeling of being in a lush tropical garden with fresh fruit, colourful flowers and birds all around. At just 1,760m the climate is mild, with a subtropical feel to it. There is little to do but sunbathe by the pools, wander the hills and recover energy to continue travelling. The town was founded as a gold mining settlement but its economy today is supported by the cash crops that grow so well in the subtropical climate. Tropical fruits, vegetables, sugar, coffee and coca are supplied to La Paz. Some of the coca grown here is legal for domestic consumption. There is also a growing tourist industry.

Getting there and away

There are minibuses hourly between La Paz and Coroico (4 hrs, US$3), and mostly night buses to Rurrenabaque (15 hrs, US$11). They also transport to Caranavi, Guanay, San Borja, Santa Rosa, Tumupasa and Santiago de Guachi. Buses in La Paz leave from Villa Fatima. Minibuses are the best bet; they are narrower, which is a great advantage on the narrow winding road.

Where to stay and eat

There are several really nice places to stay here, to recharge yourself before continuing on your travels. The nicest places have swimming pools to laze around and lush gardens.

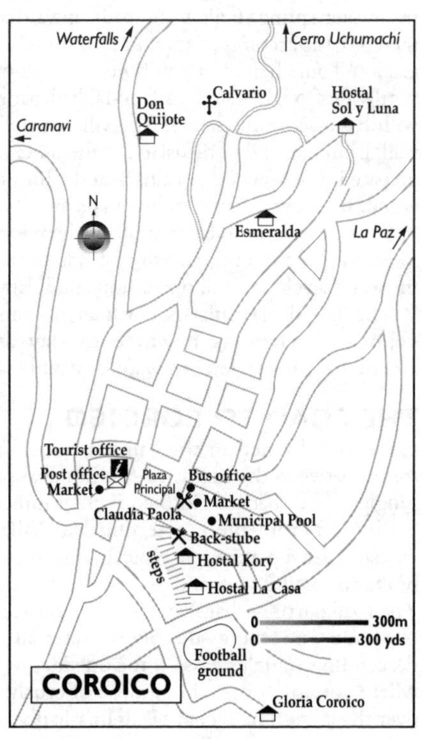

Hostal Uchumachi and **Las Penas** are the cheapest at US$3 approx. These are very basic hostels opposite the bus offices in the centre of the village.

La Casa Calle Antofagasta; tel: 6024; email: lacasa@mail.entelnet.bo From US$4 per person shared bath. This is a small, central German-owned hostel. It is also an excellent fondue restaurant. There is a small pool and good views across the valley.

Hostal Kory Tel: 2 431311. US$5 per person shared bath, US$8 private bath. The Kory has a big pool, restaurant, terrace, and spacious, nice rooms. This is a popular place and not the quietest.

Sol y Luna A 20 minute walk from the centre but well worth it. From US$6 per person. There's a choice of accommodation type here, cabins, camping, or rooms in a shared house.

There is a small pool in a beautiful garden, and this is the place for total tranquillity. There is a friendly restaurant and kitchen facilities in the cabins. Massages are also available.
Esmeralda Calle Julio Suazo; tel: 6017; email: esmeralda@latinwide.com From US$7 per person. Restaurant, email, book exchange, big clean pool. This place is lovely and is very popular so book ahead. To save you the walk they will pick you up in the centre of town.
Hotel Coroico Tel/fax: 6020. US$10 per person with bath and breakfast, US$8 shared bath. Large, at the bottom of town, with pool, videos, games room, café. Often empty, negotiable prices.

There are quite a few restaurants in Coroico. **Back Stube** on the plaza has vegetarian food, **Vicos** and **Claudia Paola** do fast food, also on the plaza, and the **Comedor Popular** does lunch 12.00–13.00 and dinner 18.00–19.00 for cheap local food. There are a few others in the streets around the square.

Practical information

Tourist office On the plaza. Tue–Sat 09.30–12.30, 15.30–21.00; Sun 10.00–14.00. Very helpful.
Municipal swimming pool Next to the market; open to all.
Money There are two banks (Banco Mercantil changes travellers' cheques).
There is also a **phone office** and a **laundry**.

What to see

A good walk with great views takes you to the hill of **Uchumachi** (2,500m). From Calavario church and cross you continue climbing the well worn path up behind Coroico. It takes two to three hours to reach the top, where there is native cloudforest with plenty of birds, orchids and beautiful mountains all around. A second walk is to the **waterfalls** on the far side of Uchumachi, around two hours each way. At Calavario take the trail to the left and follow it round the hillside.

SORATA

Telephone code 0811

Sorata is a small peaceful colonial town spectacularly located on the lower slopes of Illampu and Ancohuma, two of Bolivia's highest peaks (6,362m and 6,427m respectively). The town itself, at 2,678m, has a very comfortable subtropical climate, lush vegetation and spectacular views of the snow-capped peaks. It is perfect for sitting around, reading, lazing by the pool and catching up on yourself. If you feel like being energetic there are several possibilities for short walks and Sorata is a good starting point for some of the well-known Cordillera Real treks such as the Illampu Circuit or the Mapiri Trail. (See Bradt Guide to Peru and Bolivia: Backpacking and Trekking, 1999.)

Getting there and away

Buses run to and from La Paz every few hours throughout the day. In La Paz they leave from Calle Bustillos near the cemetery between 05.00 and 15.00 (4–5 hrs, US$2). Be very careful with your bags in this part of La Paz as it is notorious for pickpockets and bag snatchers. Coming from Copacabana, change buses at Huarina to pick up the Sorata bus.

Where to stay and eat

The two most popular backpacker hostels are owned by expats. They both have book exchanges and large libraries of videos. You can idle away the evenings catching up on missed movies.

Residencial Sorata On the plaza; tel: 5044; fax: 5218; email: resorata@mail.entelnet.bo From US$5 per person, hot water, restaurant, patio, videos, book exchange. Varying room and bed quality. Wonderful views from the top floor rooms over the valley.
Hotel Copacabana Av 9 de Abril; tel/fax: 5042; email: agsorata@wara.bolnet.bo From US$5. German-owned, videos, restaurant. 10 min walk from the centre. Clean, recommended. The **Club Sorata**, a good source of trekking information, is based here.

There are a couple of other hostels around and near the plaza, including **Hostal Panchita** and **El Mirador**, which are basic hostels, from US$3 per person.

Several restaurants in and around the square serve cheap local food. For something a bit more upmarket try **Restaurant El Ceibo** on the square. They serve delicious vegetarian and meat meals. **Pizzeria Italiana**, Calle Villamil de Roda, is good quality though relatively expensive. For evenings try the **Spider Bar**, at the lower end of town.

Practical information

You can change dollars in the shops on the square but not travellers' cheques. The market sells some fruit and vegetables and there are shops where you can buy everything you need in the way of food for trekking expeditions. You can't buy maps or rent equipment in Sorata – bring what you need from La Paz.

Around Sorata

San Pedro Caves

If you feel like doing a day walk from Sorata this large cave with a lake inside is three to four hours' hike down the valley. There is a trail along the valley or you can walk down the dirt road. You could walk down and try to hitch a ride back up this road, but there is not a lot of traffic. Take plenty of water on this trek. Rumour has it there is a large amount of treasure buried somewhere inside the cave, but numerous expeditions have failed to find it. There are electric lights in the cave now and you have to pay a few bolivianos entrance fee. The walk is as interesting as the cave itself, which is located above the village of San Pedro. Look for the small white building just below the main road, above the village.

Other walks

There are small tracks and trails leading out of Sorata in all directions. If you have a good map and compass you can set off on any of the trails and walk where you want to. The local farmers are not always helpful, so don't rely on them for directions. It's a good idea to hire a local guide from the guide's office just off the plaza for longer treks. The Residencial Sorata and Hotel Copacabana can also give you further ideas and assistance.

Beyond Sorata

It is possible to travel from Achacachi on northwards to the Cordillera Apolobamba, and across the border to Peru. Check with immigration in La Paz about getting your passport stamped. This part of Bolivia is very remote, the roads are in bad condition and there is very little public transport, mostly trucks going to markets. There is a weekly bus on a Wednesday morning from Calle Reyes Cardona near the cemetery in la Paz to Pelechuco, an 18–24 hour rough journey. There are several buses a week from the same street to Charazani, 10–12 hours.

The Bolivian Amazon

THE BENI AND PANDO

To the east of the Andes, in the north of Bolivia, lies the lowland area of the Amazon Basin (see map on page 336), comprising the two departments of the Beni and Pando. Together they cover over 50% of the total land area of Bolivia. This is a massive area of remote and relatively inaccessible land, which requires time and flexibility to visit and enjoy. The easiest and most popular place to visit is Rurrenabaque, from which you can easily pick up a tour into the jungle or the pampas. Further north you can visit the offbeat towns of Cobija, Riberalta and Guayaramerín. These towns were at the centre of the rubber boom at the beginning of the 20th century, the buildings still reflecting their former wealth.

RURRENABAQUE

Telephone code 0832

A short flight from La Paz or a long bus journey from Trinidad or Coroico brings you to this popular jumping off point for Bolivia's truly amazing Amazon basin. Twenty years ago very few tourists ventured to this part of the Amazon, preferring instead Peru, Ecuador or Brazil. Now Rurre, as it is locally known, is well engrained on the tourist map, thanks to the adventures in the 1980s of a young Israeli traveller, who spent several weeks wandering through deep jungle after having been thrown from a raft in the infamously deep and dangerous San Pedro Canyon. A book of the story (*Back From Tuichi* by Yossi Ghinsberg) brought travellers here in search of adventure. They sought out Tico Tudela, the man who eventually rescued the lost Israeli traveller, to verify the tale's authenticity. This was just the beginning of a boom, which has seen the opening of several hotels and agencies offering great value, unforgettable trips to the jungle or the pampas. On these tours you have a golden opportunity to see several species of monkey, toucan, parrot, macaw, water bird, snake, caiman and capybara, and learn of the traditional uses for some of the lowland jungle plants. In addition if you venture out into the pampas you may see many other species of water bird, river turtle, pink dolphin and even anaconda.

It is not a good idea to visit this part of Bolivia between January and March because of the heavy rains, which make the roads impassable and the insects unbearable. Keep your baggage to a minimum, pack light, drip-dry clothes with long sleeves, hiking boots, tennis shoes, waterproof jacket or poncho, insect repellent, malaria tablets, sunglasses and sun protection, hat, binoculars, camera and 200mm lens, and a torch. If you are not going on a tour but travelling independently, you will probably also need the following items: fishing gear, water sterilisation tablets, tent and plastic bags. Don't forget your passport. Wrap everything in plastic to keep it dry.

Getting there and away

By road

Several bus companies have services from La Paz to Rurre, leaving from Villa Fatima in La Paz usually at 08.00 in the morning and returning at around 12.00 daily (18–20 hrs, US$12). There are buses from Rurre to Trinidad, Riberalta and Guayaramerín.

By air

TAM fly four times a week to Rurrenabaque from La Paz. From US$45, each way. Currently Mon, Wed, Thur and Sat, returning only on Wed, Fri and Sat. It is a good idea to book these popular flights as much in advance as possible to ensure you get a seat. The TAM office in Rurre is on Av Santa Cruz.

Where to stay and eat

There are several hostels in Rurrenabaque, all within walking distance of the centre.

Hotel Tuichi Calle Eduardo Avaroa. From US$3, is a popular backpacker hostel. Good value and good for meeting others looking to form a tour group.
Hostal Beni Calle Comercio. From US$5 per person, on riverfront, with a great terrace.
Selva Tambo River lodge, ask at the Restaurant Tambo for details.

The **Club Social**, Calle Comercio, is good for large portions of local food including fresh fish. Other restaurants are found on Av Santa Cruz. **Camilla**, **El Tambo** and **Bambi** are recommended. There's no shortage.

Practical information

Post office Centre of town.
Phone office Centre of town.
Swimming pool Calle Santa Cruz. A good place to relax.

Travel agencies

The principal travel agents are the following listed ones, but there are others that offer much the same trip. Check carefully exactly what is included.

Amazonia Adventures Calle Santa Cruz has been recommended for jungle and pampas tours.
Fluvial Tours Based at the Hotel Tuichi, Calle Abaroa. One of the oldest agencies, offers jungle, pampas and fishing tours, group size 3–6 people per guide.
Nahama Tours Calle Abaroa or Hotel Santa Ana. Offers jungle and pampas tours.

What to see

Jungle tours

The tours into the jungle are usually four days, each agency offering pretty much the same package. The trips head up the rivers Beni and Tuichi into the area known as Alto Beni. A guide, and usually a cook, accompany the group and all equipment such as camping gear, mosquito nets, blankets, life jackets, food and drinking water is provided. Prices depend to some extent on the season and are generally the same with all agencies, approximately US$25–30 a day.

Pampas tours

Pampas tours are usually two to three days and visit the flatlands around the River Yacuma. They are jeep based and the route taken and length depends on the five or six people in the jeep. Prices are slightly more than for the jungle, at around US$30 per day.

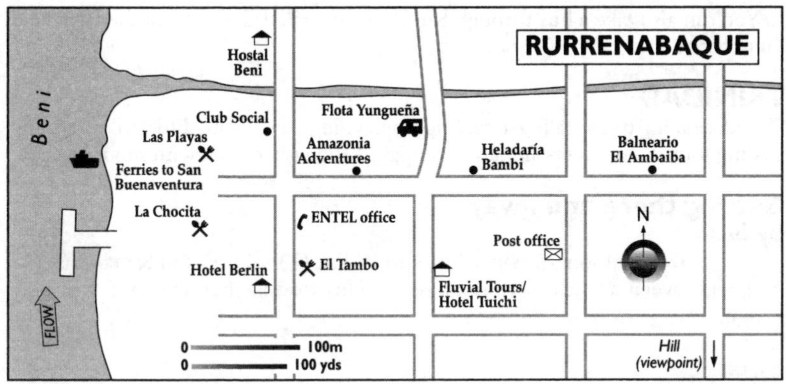

MADIDI NATIONAL PARK

Formed in 1995 to protect almost 2 million hectares of pristine land, Madidi National Park covers a wide range of habitats from the forested Andean foothills down into the lowland tropical forests and savannahs of the Amazon basin. It is home to over a thousand species of bird, more than half of all neotropical bird species, 44% of neotropical mammals and 38% of neotropical amphibians. The richness of the flora is equally astounding, with a large number of endemics and, in combination with the neighbouring Tambopata-Candamo Reserve in Peru, it is thought to be the most biodiverse of all the South American national parks. Probably because of the very low numbers of *mara*, mahogany (*Swietenia*) found here it has escaped the destruction by loggers which many other rich tropical forests have suffered. The community of 500 Quetchua-Tacana Indians living in San José form the only settlement within the park. They have lived here for over 200 years in harmony with the jungle around them, surviving from subsistence farming. The Chalalán project is designed to benefit the whole community creating an alternative sustainable economic activity while preserving the resources of the park.

Fremen Tours can organise 4-day excursions into Chalalán from La Paz. **EcoBolivia Foundation** also arranges tours to the national park (see page 311).

Chalalán Eco-Lodge

This solar-powered, community-run eco-lodge is located 5 hours by boat up the River Tuichi from Rurrenabaque within the Madidi National Park. It was financed by the Inter-American Development Bank, with the technical help of Conservation International. It has four wood and palm cabins with bathrooms, sleeping 16 in total. There is a dining room overlooking Laguna Chalalán and 20km of jungle trail. Guiding, cooking and all other services are provided by local Josesanos people. Contact Fremen Tours. It is also possible to trek to San José from Tumupasa (2 hrs from Rurre by vehicle) or hire a motorised canoe.

BEYOND RURRENABAQUE

It is perfectly possible, though not particularly comfortable, to travel on from Rurrenabaque northwards to Riberalta, Guayaramerín and Cobija. There are long distance buses to these jungle towns and flights with LAB and TAME. The great wealth achieved through rubber exploitation at the end of the 19th and beginning of the 20th century is still apparent in some of the old mansions, home to the rubber barons. Brazil nut factories are now an important industry in this whole area.

You can also take a bus through San Borja to Trinidad, capital of the Beni, and on to Santa Cruz.

TRINIDAD

Trinidad is an unappealing large, hot, sprawling town with little to attract the passing tourist. Its streets are largely unpaved and either thick with mud or dusty.

Getting there and away

By bus

There are frequent long-distance buses to La Paz (22–24 hrs) and Santa Cruz (12 hrs), and several a week to Rurrenabaque. This road is often closed in the rainy season.

By air

LAB and Aero Sur have daily flights to Santa Cruz and La Paz. TAM fly to the more remote jungle towns.

By boat

There are cargo boats between Villarroel and Trinidad (3–5 days), and on northwards to Guayaramerín (3–4 days). Be prepared for basic conditions, bring water purifiers, food and a hammock, mosquito repellent, binoculars and a good book. You could take this route all the way down the Amazon.

Where to stay and eat

There's a wide selection of hotels and restaurants around the centre of town if you decide to stay.

Squirrel monkey

Appendix 1

LANGUAGE

There isn't enough space to include more than the briefest of vocabulary here. I recommend you make the effort to learn some Spanish before travelling to South America, and take a good phrasebook and dictionary with you.

Spanish

Useful words and phrases

What?	*Qué?*	Thankyou	*Gracias*
When?	*Cuando?*	How are you?	*Como está?*
Where?	*Dónde?*	Good-bye	*Adiós*
Why?	*Porqué?*	Please	*Por favor*
How?	*Cómo?*	today/tomorrow	*hoy/mañana*
Hello	*Hola*	good/bad	*bueno/malo*
Good morning	*Buenos dias*	What's your name?	*Como se llama?*
Good afternoon	*Buenas tardes*	Do you speak English?	*Habla ingles?*
Goodnight	*Buenas noches*	I don't understand	*No entiendo*

What time does the bus/train to....leave?	*A qué hora sale el caro/tren para…?*
What time does it arrive?	*A qué hora llega?*
Where does it go?	*A dónde va?*
Where is…?	*Dónde está…?*
Where does the bus/lorry to… leave from?	*De dónde sale el caro/camion para…?*
How much is it?	*Cuanto es?*
Where are you from?	*De dónde es?*
Do you have a single/double room?	*Tiene una habitación simple/doble?*
Does it have a private bathroom?	*Tiene baño privado?*
Is there hot water?	*Hay agua caliente?*
Is there a safe?	*Hay caja de seguridad?*
Is breakfast included?	*Incluye desayuno?*
For one/two night(s)	*Para una/dos noche(s)*
Big/small	*Grande/pequeño*
Expensive/cheap	*Caro/barato*

Days of the week

Monday	*lunes*	Friday	*viernes*
Tuesday	*martes*	Saturday	*sábado*
Wednesday	*miercoles*	Sunday	*domingo*
Thursday	*jueves*		

Months

January	*enero*	July	*julio*
February	*febrero*	August	*agosto*
March	*marzo*	September	*septiembre*
April	*abril*	October	*octubre*
May	*mayo*	November	*noviembre*
June	*junio*	December	*diciembre*

Numbers

one	*uno*	seventeen	*diecisiete*
two	*dos*	eighteen	*dieciocho*
three	*tres*	nineteen	*diecinueve*
four	*cuatro*	twenty	*veinte*
five	*cinco*	twenty one	*veinte uno*
six	*seis*	thirty	*trienta*
seven	*siete*	forty	*cuarenta*
eight	*ocho*	fifty	*cinquenta*
nine	*nueve*	sixty	*sesenta*
ten	*diez*	seventy	*setenta*
eleven	*once*	eighty	*ochenta*
twelve	*doce*	ninety	*noventa*
thirteen	*trece*	a hundred	*cien*
fourteen	*catorce*	two hundred	*dos cientos*
fifteen	*quince*	five hundred	*quinientas*
sixteen	*dieciseis*	a thousand	*mil*

Food

Fish dishes

arroz con mariscos	rice with shellfish
ceviche	raw fish or shellfish marinated in lemon juice with onions and chilli peppers.
chupe de camamrones	prawn soup
conchas	scallops
corvina	Pacific sea bass
pejerrey	king fish
pescado a la chorillana	fish with a tomato and onion sauce
pescado a lo macho	fish covered in a shellfish sauce
pescado sudado	steamed fish
picante de mariscos	spicy shellfish

Meat dishes

aaguadito de pollo	chicken cooked in soup with rice, potato and herbs
ají de gallina	shredded chicken with cheese sauce
anticuchos	kebabs
arroz con pato a la chiclayana	rice with duck
cabrito a la norteña	roast goat kid
carapulcra	yellow potatos and pork
causa	steamed fish with mashed potato
chicharrones	deep fried pieces of meat
churrasco/lomo	steak
espesado	tender meat stew with corn
lomo saltado	stir fried beef
parrillada	grilled meat
sancochado	stew of meat with vegetables and garlic
pachamanca	an oven is dug in the ground and lined with hot stones beef, pork, lamb, potatoes, beans and corn are lowered in to the hole, herbs and spices are added

Snacks

humitas or *tamales*	corn pasties
papa rellena	stuffed potato
choclo	sweet corn

Vegetable dishes

chuño	freeze dried potato
palta	avocado
rocoto relleno	stuffed peppers
papa a la huancaina	potatoes covered in a sauce made from cheese, aji, oil, lemon and egg yolk blended and garnished with lemon and olives, lettuce.

Jungle dishes

caldo de sarapatera	river turtle soup
cebiche de charapa	turtle
chicharron de lagarto	fried chunks of caiman
inchi capi	chicken cooked in peanut and corn sauce
juane	rice wrapped in palm leaves
paiche	pango fish cooked in a clay pot with sliced banana
sajino	wild boar
tacacho	grilled bananas mixed with *chicharron* and onion

Quechua

Quechua is the most widely spoken Indian language of South America. It was the language of the Incas. In Peru there are an estimated 5 million Quechua speakers, in Bolivia 1.5 million, and in Ecuador half a million. If you are trekking into remote highland areas it is more than likely that you will come across local people who only speak Quechua. If you can ask their name and exchange a few greetings they will instantly become more friendly. The Lonely Planet publish a Quechua phrasebook or once in the Andes you can buy books on Quechua from any bookshop. Aymara is the second most widely spoken Indian language with around 1.25 million speakers, mainly in the Titicaca area of Bolivia. Check out the web site Andean Links (www2.best.com/~gibbons/bookmark.html) for links to Quechua and Aymara related sites.

English	**Quechua**	**Aymara**
Hello	*Maynalla*	*Kamisaki*
Where is?	*Maypi?*	*Kaukasa*
Yes	*Ari*	*Jisa*
No	*Manan*	*Janiwar*
good	*walej pacha*	*walikuskiu*
bad	*mana walej*	*janiwa walikiti*
food	*mikuna*	*manka*
water	*yaku*	*uma*
house	*huasi*	*uta*
river	*mayu*	*jawira*
bridge	*chaka*	*vhaka*
lake	*cocha*	*vota*
path	*chakinan*	*tupu*
help!	*yanapaway*	*yanaptita*

Useful Quechua phrases

What's your name?	*Iman sutiyki?*
Where do you live?	*Maypin tiyanki?*
See you tomorrow	*Paqarinkama*
There isn't any (for kids asking for sweets)	*Manan kanchu*

FURTHER READING

Travel narratives

Conroy, Chris *A Beggar in Paradise*. ColourBooks Ltd, 1997. The personal story of an Irish priest who spent 15 years living with Indian communities in the Peruvian highlands.

Darwin, Charles *Voyage of the Beagle*. London, 1989. Darwin's fascinating journeys, well worth a read.

Murphy, Dervla *Eight Feet in the Andes*. John Murray, 1983. An outdated but still interesting account of a personal journey through the Andes by the author with her young daughter.

Parris Mathew *Inca Cola*. Weidenfeld & Nicolson, 1990. Amusing and observant colourful tale of the author's trip through Peru with friends.

Simpson, Joe *Touching the Void*. Jonathan Cape, 1988. Well worth reading if you are going climbing or trekking in Peru. An amazing story of the author's fight for survival after a climbing accident in the Cordillera Huayhuash.

History and archaeology

Bingham, Hiram *Lost City of the Incas*. New York, 1972. The book to read about Machu Picchu and Bingham's explorations.

Hemming, John *Conquest of the Incas*. London, 1970. A very readable book full of information about the Incas.

Heyerdahl, Thor et al *Pyramids of Túcume*. Thames and Hudson, 1995. Fascinating account of the Moche sites of Peru's northern coast.

Mason, J *The Ancient Civilisations of Peru*. Penguin, 1991. Exhaustive information on the pre-hispanic cultures of Peru.

Stone-Miller, Rebecca *Art of the Andes*. Thames and Hudson, 1995. A readable reference book to the history of Andean art and architecture from the Chavin to the Inca cultures.

Climbing and trekking guides

Bartle, Jim *Trails of the Cordilleras Blanca and Huayhuash of Peru*. 1980. Out of print, but sometimes copies are available at the Casa de Guías in Huaraz. Great trekking guide (though a bit out of date) with detailed descriptions and maps.

Biggar, John *The High Andes: A Guide for Climbers*. BigR Publishing, 1999. This book covers the whole of the Andes and is the only available guidebook for the mountains in most of Peru.

Bradt, Hilary *Peru and Bolivia Backpacking and Trekking*. Bradt, 1999. Up-to-date detailed information and maps on a wide range of accessible treks in Peru and Bolivia.

Brain, Yossi *Trekking in Bolivia*. Cordee, 1997. Detailed maps, descriptions and background information.

Brain, Yossi *Bolivia – a Climber's Guide*. The Mountaineers, 1999. Bolivia's expert on mountaineering covers the country's main mountain ranges.

Harris, Roger and Hutchison, Peter *The Amazon*. Bradt, 1998. A comprehensive guide to travelling the length of the Amazon, with detailed natural history coverage.

Rachowiecki, Rob et al *Climbing and Hiking in Ecuador*. Bradt, 1997

Sharman, David *Climbs of the Cordillera Blanca*. Whizzo Climbs, 1995.

Health

Ellis, Dr Matthew and Wilson-Howarth, Dr Jane *Your Child's Health Abroad: A Manual for Travelling Parents*. Bradt, 1998. Indispensable companion to anyone travelling with children.

Wilson-Howarth, Jane *Healthy Travel: Bugs, Bites & Bowels*. Cadogan, 1995. Informative and entertaining.

Wildlife

Arzubialde, Abel *Qosqo en Flor*. Municipalidad de Cusco, 1991. Guide to the flowers of the Cusco and Inca Trail area, in Spanish.

Canaday, Chris *Common Birds of Amazonian Ecuador*. Libri Mundi, 1997. Clearly illlustrated book of 50 common birds, useful for the amateur in the Ecuadorian Amazon.

Emmons, Louise *Neotropical Rainforest Mammals*. University of Chicago Press, 1997. A field guide for the wildlife enthusiast.

Fjeldsa, Jon & Krabbe, Niels *Birds of the High Andes*. Zoological Museum, University of Copenhagen, 1990. Large, expensive, but the best bird book for the Andes.

Horwell, David and Oxford, Pete *Galápagos Wildlife: A Visitor's Guide.* Bradt 1999, covers the wildlife and natural history of the Galápagos in full colour, and has details of all the island trails.

Kolff, Helen & Kees *Wildflowers of the Cordillera Blanca*. Mountain Institute, 1997. The only useful pocket-sized field guide, also handy in the Cusco area. Well illustrated with colour photos.

Miscellaneous

Frost, Peter *Exploring Cusco*. Nuevas Imágenes, 1999. A very useful, newly revised and updated, pocket-sized guidebook with all the information you need for exploring the Cusco area.

Hancock, Graham *Fingerprints of the Gods*. Mandarin, 1996. Thought-provoking theories about the connections between various ancient civilisations.

McFarren, Peter *An Insider's Guide to Bolivia.* Fundación Cultural Quipus, 1992. Packed full of background information .

Meadows, Anne *Digging up Butch and Sundance*. St Martin's Press, 1994. The last days of Butch Cassidy and the Sundance Kid.

Smith, Randy *Crisis under the Canopy*. Rainforest Information Centre, 1996. This book is part of a report written about the future survival of the Huaorani, one of the last tribes of the Ecuadorian Amazon.

Vargas Llosa, Mario *Aunt Julia and the Scriptwriter*. Avon, 1982. A Peruvian writer and politician with a wealth of interesting books. This is one of his more accessible novels, clever, funny and a good insight into Peruvian life.

Latin America Bureau

The Latin America Bureau publish a number of specialist books on Peru, Bolivia and Ecuador. Contact them at 1 Amwell St, London EC1R 1UL; email: clee@lab.org.uk; web: www.lab.org.uk

Poole, D and Renique, G *Peru: Time of Fear.* Latin America Bureau, 1992. All about Sendero Luminoso and the time of violence and fear in Peru.

Magazines

The *National Geographic* over the years has published some fascinating articles on the Andean countries. See March 1992 'Sacred Peaks of the Andes', May 1996 'Peru Begins Again', June 1996 'Peruvian Mummies', January 1997 'Peruvian Mummies', March 1999 'El Niño', November 1999 'Inca Sacrifice'.

Index

Page references in* bold *indicate main entries; those in italics indicate maps or illustrations